Lecture Notes in Computer Science 3547

Commenced Publication in 1973
Founding and Former Series Editors:
Gerhard Goos, Juris Hartmanis, and Jan van Leeuwen

Editorial Board

Frank Bomarius   Seija Komi-Sirviö (Eds.)

Product Focused
Software Process
Improvement

6th International Conference, PROFES 2005
Oulu, Finland, June 13-15, 2005
Proceedings

Volume Editors

Frank Bomarius
Fraunhofer Institute for Experimental Software Engineering
Sauerwiesen 6, 67661 Kaiserslautern, Germany
E-mail: frank.bomarius@iese.fraunhofer.de

Seija Komi-Sirviö
VTT Electronics
P.O. Box 1100, 90571 Oulu, Finland
E-mail: seija.komi-sirvio@vtt.fi

Library of Congress Control Number: Applied for

CR Subject Classification (1998): D.2, K.6, K.4.2, J.1

ISSN   0302-9743
ISBN-10   3-540-26200-8 Springer Berlin Heidelberg New York
ISBN-13   978-3-540-26200-8 Springer Berlin Heidelberg New York

Springer is a part of Springer Science+Business Media

springeronline.com

© Springer-Verlag Berlin Heidelberg 2005
Printed in Germany

Typesetting: Camera-ready by author, data conversion by Scientific Publishing Services, Chennai, India
Printed on acid-free paper   SPIN: 11497455   06/3142   5 4 3 2 1 0

Preface

On behalf of the PROFES organizing committee we are proud to present to you the proceedings of the 6th International Conference on Product Focused Software Process Improvement (PROFES 2005), held in Oulu, Finland.

Since 1999, PROFES has established itself as one of the recognized international software process improvement conferences.

The purpose of the conference is to bring to light the most recent findings and results in the area and to stimulate discussion between researchers, experienced professionals, and technology providers. The large number of participants coming from industry confirms that the conference provides a variety of up-to-date topics and tackles industry problems. The main theme of PROFES is professional software process improvement (SPI) motivated by product and service quality needs. SPI is facilitated by software process assessment, software measurement, process modeling, and technology transfer. It has become a practical tool for quality software engineering and management. The conference addresses both the solutions found in practice and the relevant research results from academia. This is reflected in the 42 full papers, which are – as in the years before – a well-balanced mix of academic papers as well as industrial experience reports.

The business of developing new applications like mobile and Internet services or enhancing the functionality of a variety of products using embedded software is rapidly growing, maturing and meeting the harsh business realities. The accepted papers focusing on wireless and Internet are grouped into a special "mobile and wireless" session.

We wish to thank VTT Electronics, the University of Oulu including Infotech, and Fraunhofer IESE, for supporting the conference. We are also grateful to the authors for high-quality papers, the program committee for their hard work in reviewing the papers, the organizing committee for making the event possible, and all the numerous supporters who helped in organizing this conference.

Last, but not least, many thanks to Patrick Leibbrand at Fraunhofer IESE for copyediting this volume, Kari Liukkunen and his team at University of Oulu for developing PROFES 2005 web pages, and Gaby Klein at IESE, for helping in the organization of this conference.

April 2005

Frank Bomarius
Seija Komi-Sirviö
Markku Oivo

Conference Organization

General Chair

Markku Oivo, University of Oulu (Finland)

Organizing Chair

Kari Liukkunen, University of Oulu (Finland)

Program Co-chairs

Frank Bomarius, Fraunhofer IESE (Germany)
Seija Komi-Sirviö, VTT Electronics (Finland)

Tutorial Chair

Marek Leszak, Lucent Technologies Bell Labs (Germany)

Workshop and Panel Chair

Jyrki Kontio, University of Helsinki (Finland)

Industry Chair

Rini van Solingen, Logica CMG (The Netherlands)

Doctoral Symposium Co-chair

Juhani Iivari, University of Oulu (Finland)
Reidar Conradi, NTNU (Norway)

PR Chair

Pasi Kuvaja, University of Oulu (Finland)

Publicity Chairs

Europe: Petra Steffens, Fraunhofer IESE (Germany)
USA: Ioana Rus, Fraunhofer Center - Maryland (USA)
Japan: Kenichi Matumoto, NAIST (Japan)
Korea: Ho-Won Jung, Korea University (Korea)
Finland: Tua Huomo, VTT Electronics (Finland)
Scandinavia: Tore Dybå, Chief Scientist, SINTEF (Norway)

Table of Contents

Keynote Addresses

Systems and Software Process Improvement

Systems and Software Quality

Mobile and Wireless Applications

Requirements Engineering and Usability

Industrial Experiences

Process Analysis

Process Modeling

SPI Methods and Tools

Experimental Software Engineering

Validation and Verification

Agile Methods

Measurement

Keynote Address:
Competitive Product Engineering: 10 Powerful Principles for Winning Product Leadership, Through Advanced Systems Engineering, Compared to 10 Failure Paths Still Popular in Current Culture

Tom Gilb

www.gilb.com

Many companies have to outwit their competitors, in order to survive. The great Finnish company Nokia, one of our clients, is a good example. To engineer a product, especially one with software in it, that works well, and is delivered on time, is an usual feat in itself. Most all software developers fail miserably at this simple task, with 50% total project failure being the international norm, and another 40% partial failure reported.

So, to be the best, and to beat the quality and price levels of multinational competitors is even more difficult, than merely delivering a low bug product on time. But some of you have to do that. I will present 10 principles that will help you compete, and 10 failure paths that will destroy your competitiveness.

Here is a taste of those ideas:

10 Competitive Principles

- Stakeholder focus
- Stakeholder value focus
- Value delivery first
- Learn rapidly
- Delivery frequently
- Deliver early
- Hit the ground running
- Quantify valued qualities
- Control value to cost ratios
- Rapid reprioritization

10 Failure Paths

- Focus on feature and function
- Let marketing and sales decide
- Adopt a bureaucratic development process like CMMI or RUP
- Allow yourself to be design driven
- Allow 100 major defects per page on specs to development
- Assume a tool will help
- Fail to quantify critical quality requirements
- Assume that code can be reused in next generation
- Assume the solution is in the latest silver bullets (patterns anyone)
- Fail to specify risks, dependencies, constraints, issues

F. Bomarius and S. Komi-Sirviö (Eds.): PROFES 2005, LNCS 3547, p. 1, 2005.

Keynote Address:
From Products and Solutions to End-User Experiences

Ari Virtanen

NOKIA Corporation

The traditional way to meet a market demand is to develop a product and sell it to the customers. In some cases all the requirements cannot be addressed with a single product, but a larger system with multiple products is needed. Further, a lot of tailoring takes places to convert these products and systems into solutions that are supposed to meet customer requirements exactly. All of these approaches have been widely used for a long time in mobile communications, and as a result we are surrounded by large amount of products and solutions. But this technology explosion has not necessarily resulted in better customer satisfaction.

Thanks to the rapid spread of mobile devices and new services enabled by network technologies, it is increasingly difficult to differentiate just by improving products. The value for the end-user is more and more in personalized experiences that are created based on a customer's need, preferences and location. Rather than building generic solutions, companies need to think how to provide customers with unique value they are willing to pay for.

All this has many implications on how solutions and services are developed. Typically a good co-operation between many companies is needed to deliver a seamless end-user experience. These industry ecosystems and value networks are already established in many areas and their importance is growing as we speak. To play this game a company must have openness in product, system and solution architectures and capability for networked product creation. Delivering a superior end-user experience will be the differentiator between successful companies and the rest.

F. Bomarius and S. Komi-Sirviö (Eds.): PROFES 2005, LNCS 3547, p. 2, 2005.
© Springer-Verlag Berlin Heidelberg 2005

What Formal Models Cannot Show Us:
People Issues During the Prototyping Process

Steve Counsell[1], Keith Phalp[2], Emilia Mendes[3], and Stella Geddes[4]

[1] Department of Information Systems and Computing, Brunel University,
Uxbridge, Middlesex, UK
steve.counsell@brunel.ac.uk
[2] Empirical Software Engineering Group, University of Bournemouth, Dorset, UK
khalp@bournemouth.ac.uk
[3] Department of Computer Science, University of Auckland, New Zealand
emilia@cs.auckland.ac.nz
[4] School of Crystallography, Birkbeck, University of London
s.geddes@mail.cryst.bbk.ac.uk

Abstract. Modelling a process using techniques such as Role Activity Diagrams (RADs) [13] can illustrate a large amount of useful information about the process under study. What they cannot show as easily however, are the informal practices during that process. In this paper, we analyse the prototyping process as part of an IS development strategy across five companies. Interview text from project managers, prototypers and other development staff across the five companies was analysed. Interestingly, results point to several key recurring issues amongst staff. These include non-adherence to any prototyping guidelines or standards, sketchy change request procedures, concern over time and cost deadlines and the importance attached to developer experience during the overall process. The notion of prototyping as a simple and easily managed development strategy does not hold. Our analysis provides complementary qualitative data about the opinions of prototyping to inform business process re-engineering of those formal RADs.

1 Introduction

A commonly cited reason for systems being delivered late and over budget is inadequate requirements elicitation due to poor communication between developers and users. Prototyping, as an information systems discipline, provides an opportunity for free and unhindered interaction between developers and users in an attempt to overcome this problem [2, 4]. The prototyping process itself can be modelled formally using a technique such as Role Activity Diagrams (RADs) [13, 9] where actions and interactions between the different prototyping staff in the form of roles can be shown by lines joining, and internal to, the set of roles. What techniques such as RADs cannot show however, are the different concerns encountered during the process, some of which may influence the effectiveness of that very process.

In this paper, we focus on those issues found in the prototyping process of five companies, all of which used prototyping as part of their IS development strategy.

F. Bomarius and S. Komi-Sirviö (Eds.): PROFES 2005, LNCS 3547, pp. 3–15, 2005.

Interview text with twenty different members (in ten interviews) of the prototyping team across the five companies was analysed using principles of grounded theory [7] and the key issues extracted. A number of centrally recurring issues emerged from our analysis, in particular those related to change requests, standards and quality issues, developer experience and perception of the user by the prototoyper.

Our analysis provides an insight into the less tangible reasons why prototyping may not deliver the benefits it promises. It also allows reflection on the formal RADs with a view to the possibility of business process re-engineering; it may also inform the manner in which future prototyping projects can be viewed and finally, it highlights the importance of carrying out qualitative analysis of textual documents using theoretical techniques such as grounded theory. As part of our analysis, we refer back to the prototyping RADs of each of the five companies studied and assess whether the informal data we collected can inform the prototyping process in that company (expressed using RADs).

The paper is arranged as follows. In Section 2, we describe the motivation for the research and related work. In Section 3 we describe the format of the interview text, the companies studied and the grounded theory approach adopted for text analysis. In Section 4 we look at the extracted information and comment on the themes running through the text. We then discuss some of the issues that arise as a result of our analysis (Section 5) and finally draw some conclusions and point to future work (Section 6).

2 Motivation and Related Work

The motivation for the work described in this study stems from a number of sources. Firstly, the prototyping process is widely promoted for the benefits it may provide; capturing user requirements accurately and pro-actively involving the user is bound to provide advantages, in theory at least. Yet very little literature has been published on some of the key human issues (i.e., qualitative issues) that may arise during this process [1]. Such issues could have a profound effect on how prototyping is perceived and carried out.

Secondly, it is our belief that the majority of problems in the IS world stem from the *process* of IS development (we view the end product as merely a function of that process - getting the process right must be a priority). In particular, those problems related to the subtle influences during development. Using notation such as RADs does not allow for these subtle influences to be modelled. Extraction of the informal aspects during the prototyping process thus complements the knowledge already incorporated into RADs. We also believe that whatever the type of information system, whether web-based or more traditional in nature, problems of an informal nature will always occur and that they therefore need to be documented.

A third motivation arises from a previous study using the same data [6]. A personality test carried out on prototyping development staff (including some of the staff used herein) concluded that prototypers tended to be extrovert in nature, while project managers tended to be less extrovert. Analysis of some of the problems during the prototyping process may give us further insight into these personalities and an indication of the motivation of the different staff involved.

In terms of related work on RADs themselves, research by [15] used a coupling metric based on interaction and role behaviour to establish traits in prototyping roles. It was found that the level of coupling in a RAD was highly correlated to the size of the prototyping team and the number of participants. In [14], metrics were applied to the same set of roles used for the analysis herein. Results showed the project manager tended to exert control over the prototyper far more in large companies than in small. On the other hand, in small companies, the project manager tended to interact with the end-user far more frequently, perhaps reflecting the lack of formality found in small companies.

A number of other previous studies have investigated the prototyping process *per se*. Lichter et al. [11] describe a study of five industrial software projects. Results of the study emphasised the importance of involving the user in the development process. Finally, a point and counter-point argument about prototyping and a weighing up of its pros and cons was presented in [16]. Finally, we remark that to our knowledge, no literature on the informal problems arising during the prototyping process has been published so far.

3 Study Format

3.1 Interview Details

The interviews on which our analysis rests were carried out over a period of two years by a single investigator. Often, a return visit was made to the same interviewee/s to clarify and check certain points. A set of questions was prepared by the investigator prior to each meeting according to a meeting template containing details such as: interview date, duration of meeting, meeting agenda, location and a reference number for future analysis. On several occasions, more than one member of staff was interviewed at the same time (where appropriate, we make this clear). The questions asked were directed primarily towards establishing features of the prototyping process (for later analysis and modelling via RADs) and all interviews were made anonymous. The chief motivation of the interviews was to extract information for modelling RADs, rather than as we are doing in this paper namely, investigating the informal aspects of prototyping. An example RAD illustrating some of its common features (external interactions between roles and internal role actions) can be found in Appendix B. However, we feel an understanding of what a RAD is and what it represents, informs our understanding of the informal aspects of the prototyping process.

Table 1 gives a sample of some of the typical questions asked by the investigator during interviews. As would be expected, the majority of the questions were geared towards construction of the corresponding RAD of the prototyping process. On the other hand, a number of questions probed the informal aspects of the process and in the table these questions have been asterisked. For example, differences between prototyping and the traditional approach to development give useful insight into the prototyping process, but cannot be shown on a RAD. Equally, the final question in the table about standards cannot be represented on a RAD. It was responses to this type of question that were used as a basis for our analysis in this paper.

Table 1. Sample of questions asked during the ten interviews

What are the distinct roles involved in a typical prototyping project?	
What do you need to do before the prototyper can start to build the proto-types?	
How are initial requirements gathered?	
Do any change requests come to you from the prototyper, user group or end user?	
What and who is involved in the decision making process?	
Who is involved in the final sign off?	
Could you please briefly tell me more about your prototyping practice? And first of all, how your prototyping team is made up?	
What if any are the differences compared with traditional development?	*
Do you have any controls over quality?	
What are the sizes of project you're involved in and how much effort is de-voted to prototype building?	*
Do you think it's important to have some company wide methods and stan-dards?	*

We note that in all five companies, the focus of the prototyping process was to produce evolvable prototypes, i.e., prototypes that eventually become the end product. This is distinct from throwaway prototypes, where the prototype is discarded after the prototyping team have finished their work. Furthermore, for clarity we make no distinction between 'customer' and 'user' in this paper and view the two roles as identical. There are subtle differences in certain cases, but of minor relevance to this paper.

Table 2 shows the job title of the subjects interviewed, the company and department to which they belonged, together with the duration of the meeting and the number of participants. For later reference, and where appropriate, we have categorised interviews carried out in the same company by giving each a serial number, e.g., three interviews were carried out in Company A: A(1), A(2) and A(3).

In terms of company type, Company A was a company developing information systems for airlines, e.g., ticketing and reservation systems. Company B represented a team of in-house IT staff for a bank, developing typical banking applications; Company C was a small software house developing general information systems and Company D an IT group developing telecommunication systems; finally, Company E was a University Computer Centre developing in-house academic-based administrative applications.

In most cases, a project manager is also involved in the prototyping process and this has been indicated as such in the table. For example, in Company A, the Project Manager was also a prototyper, i.e., was involved in the development of the prototype. In our grounded theory analysis, it was sometimes the case that an interview provided no useful reflection on recurring themes; in later analysis (Tables 3 - 5), omission of a company from a table therefore reflects this fact. In the next section, we describe some of the principles of grounded theory.

Table 2. Interview details from the five companies

Id.	Job Title/s	Dur.	Part.
A(1)	Project Manager (was prototyper as well)	60 mins.	1
A(2)	Project Manager	90 mins.	1
A(3)	4 Project Managers, (3 of whom were proto-typers also)	120 mins.	4
B	Project Manager	60 mins.	1
C(1)	Design Manager	90 mins.	2
C(2)	Design Manager	45 mins.	1
D(1)	Project Manager	60 mins.	1
D(2)	Prototyper, Sales Manager	90 mins.	2
D(3)	Technical Director, Sales Manager, Project Manager (also a prototyper) and 3 protoypers	120 mins.	6
E	Project Manager	45 mins.	1

3.2   Grounded Theory

Grounded theory (GT) [7] was used as the mechanism for analysing the interview text because it offered a means by which a corpus of data (including interview data) could be analysed in a rigorous way and the inter-relationships in that data uncovered. According to [7], theories are developed through observation; scrutiny of text as we have done, falls into this category. The idea behind GT is to read and re-read text in order to reveal inter-relationships and categories. The motivation for analysing the prototyping interview text was to extract issues that prototyping staff identified as common to their prototyping experiences. GT itself has been used in a number of situations to analyse qualitative interview text. It has also been applied to the analysis of organisational behaviour [12] as well as the use of ICASE tools in organisations [10]. Analysis of the interview text in the case of our research followed a series of four steps in accordance with GT principles. These were as follows:

1. Coding: each sentence in the interview text was examined. The questions: 'What is going on here?' and 'What is the situation?' were repeatedly asked. For the purposes of the analysis herein, each sentence in the ten interviews would be either identification of an 'issue' or 'concern' and allocated to the relevant category. We are not interested in any other information, since it is embodied in the prototyping RADs for each company. Coding is thus a process of filtering the text. A question that was also asked during this step was: 'Is this information inappropriate for modelling using a RAD?' If true, then it was of use to us in our analysis.

2. Memoing: A memo is a note to yourself about an issue or concern that you are interested in. In other words, any point made by one of the interviewees which fell into one of the categories could be used to pursue the analysis. This step should be completed in parallel with the coding stage. The memoing stage thus

allows a certain amount of reflection and interpretation of the interview text as it is being read.

3. Sorting: a certain amount of analysis and arrangement of the collected data is then necessary.
4. Writing-up: the results of the analysis are written-up in a coherent way and conclusions drawn.

In the next section, we describe the results of our analysis of the interview text, pointing to specific recurring issues and areas of concern.

4 Text Analysis

Analysis of the text using GT principles identified seventy-two occasions where an issue reflecting a qualitative opinion was expressed by an interviewee/s. Analysis using GT principles revealed three key informal areas from the text:

1. Change request control: a key feature of prototyping (we would assume).
2. Quality and standards: since the prototypes are evolvable, we would expect some quality issues and standards to be in place.
3. Experience, skill and prototyper perception of the user. We would expect the user to be nurtured carefully by the prototyper and be involved significantly at the same time.

4.1 Patterns in Change Requests

Table 3 summarises the pattern in change requests and control therein across the five companies; it contrasts the formal responses to the interviewer's questions and the informal response to the same questions. The latter cannot be modelled on a RAD. The first column gives the interviewee Id. The data in the second column is the response to the following interviewer questions: 'Who handles change requests when they arise?' The information from this question can be modelled easily on a RAD.

On the other hand, Table 3 (third column) shows the informal responses received to the questions: 'How about change request control?' and 'Are there any procedures or guidelines for managers, developers and customer/user?' The responses in this column were extracted from the latter two questions.

Clearly, only company B had any sort of formal guidelines for change control, yet even in this company, large changes were resisted due to cost implications. In company E, no information was available on the second question and is marked as such. Interestingly, in company D the prototyping team were reluctant to make changes to the prototype whether those changes were small or large. In company D, interview D(2) revealed the view of users as constantly changing their mind, suggesting that prototyping staff dislike constant requests for changes. This would seem to contradict the argument that the whole point of prototyping is to allow frequent change and interaction with the user. One explanation may be that because the prototypes are evolvable and hence produced under time pressure, there is less willingness on behalf of the prototyper to accommodate constant requests for changes by the user.

Table 3. Patterns in change request controls across the five companies

Id.	RAD (formal)	Informal
A(1)	Change requests normally come from the user representative or the end-users.	No specific guidelines.
A(2)	Change decisions made by developers in consultation with the users.	No formal decision process. Quality of work produced unknown.
A(3)	Changes to the prototype made independently of user.	No specific guidelines.
B	Committee of systems manager, user manager and auditor make change decisions.	Committee decides on small changes. Large changes resisted because of cost implications.
C(2)	Change requests fed back to systems design group. Negotiation with user used for large changes.	No specific guidelines for the prototyping phase.
D(1)	Change requests come from the customer.	No specific guidelines
D(2)	Manager makes decision on functional changes. Costs agreed for any changes.	No specific guidelines. Customer's tend to change mind constantly. Fundamental changes are treated as a new project.
D(3)	Identical to D(2)	Identical to D(2)
E	Change requests come from design manager, group leader or customer.	No information provided.

In terms of change request patterns, the results thus support those found in an earlier study of RADs from the same companies [6], where it was noticeable how little in the way of iteration between the user and prototyper was found for any of the RADs studied. In other words, the change request process plays a minor role at best in four of the five companies studied.

The general result of sketchy change control again goes against the underlying principle of prototyping of facilitating quick and easy changes to the prototype through interaction with the user. On the other hand, an explanation for this trend may be that it merely reflects the informal nature of the prototyping process in those companies. A key motivation for the research in this paper is to show that some features of the process cannot be modelled, yet may be fundamental to its success. Inclusion of change control (or lack of it) is one case of a feature about which more information, other than that missing from the RAD, may inform future prototyping projects.

4.2 Patterns in Quality and Standards

Table 4 (see Appendix A) investigates the role that adherence to quality and standards play in the prototyping process. In common with the data in column 3 of Table 3, we summarise informal answers to the questions: 'Do you think it's important to have standards?', 'Any quality checks at all?' and finally, 'What about the method compared with conventional development'. We note that because the prototypes are evolvable prototypes and will be used by formal development teams later on, we would expect certain quality guidelines (in common with the broader development process overall) to be adhered to.

The general trend identified from Table 4 is that surprisingly, standards are rarely used except for perhaps in larger projects where they were identified as potentially useful, yet still unused. It is interesting that in many cases, just as for change control, there is a general lack of awareness of, and certain scepticism for, the value of standards. In a number of cases, the fact that prototyping is part of the overall development process was seen as an excuse to avoid using any standards or carrying out any quality checks. The 'quick and dirty' approach seems to be common for small projects at least. Only in Company E are any standards adopted in common with company wide procedures.

One theme which comes across strongly in the reason stated for not having standards is the role that experience of the prototypers plays and, connected to that, the time restrictions which prototypers are placed under. Standards and quality issues seem to be viewed as a time-consuming process which detract from the creative abilities of the developer and thus from the real purpose of prototyping (i.e., to be innovative without the burden of control). This is expressed well by interviewee A(2), who criticises the 'tick box' approach to prototyping as something which is not considered useful.

4.3   Patterns in Experience, Skills and User Perception

Table 5 examines the role that factors such as the skills and experience of the prototyper play in the overall process. It also gives some indication of how the user is perceived by the prototyping staff.

From Table 5, it would seem that firstly, users prefer to keep things simple during interaction with the prototyper; there is evidence that they (users) also change their mind frequently (supporting data from Table 3). While this is to be expected during prototyping, the general sense is that this causes irritation amongst the majority of prototypers. At least two references in the interview text suggest 'concealing' the prototype from the user so that they have no opportunity to change their mind or make change requests (Company A and Company C). The fact that prototyping staff find this feature of users annoying may well reflect the time constraints on the prototyper for production of a quick prototype. In the authors' opinion, this would be counterproductive and is contrary to the way that prototyping should be carried out. A reasonable amount of time should be allocated to building the prototype, free from extreme time burdens.

It is also interesting that from Table 5 we get the impression that intuition was identified as an important characteristic of a prototyper. In a previous study [5], a personality test revealed 7 out of 12 prototypers were found to rely heavily on their personal characteristics of intuition and extrovert nature.

Another feature evident from Table 5 is that the level of experience of the prototyper is of paramount importance when nurturing trust and communication with the user/customer, making sure user expectations are realistic and prioritising the features which users want to talk about and see. Experience also seems to be the key factor in

Table 5. Experience, skills and perceptions of the user by prototyping staff

Id.	Experience and skills	Perceptions of the user
A(1)	Prototyping staff are able to talk business language with the user, rather than just technical IT language. Prototyping staff have very good intuition, and generally know what they're doing.	What works for the customer is most important. Using formal models such as RADs with the user don't work.
A(2)	Building up a good user relationship and trust is important.	No information available.
A(3)	Effort invested is not always appreciated by the customer. Quick, visual effects are usually the most effective, while long-winded time-consuming features don't generally impress the user.	Customers get annoyed if requirements elicitation is too focused, but this can backfire if too laissez faire approach is adopted, leading to a system the user didn't ask for.
B	Junior members of the prototyping team need support from senior members of the team in terms of business knowledge, languages and tools used etc.	Getting the user requirements right is a question of talking to the users, not drawing formal models which only creates design conflicts.
C(2)	Prototyping staff have to use their judgement to tell users what is realistic and what isn't, whether functionally or due to time pressure. Trust in prototyper by project managers is important.	Users too often have unrealistic expectations.
D(2)	Experience of the prototyper dictates the allocation to projects of the prototypers.	Customers change their mind all the time and under restricted time and cost constraints, this makes life difficult.
D(3)	Experience is used to avoid having to employ standards.	No information available.

the choice of staff for a particular project, with the view that more experienced members of staff are allocated to the larger projects, but yet still have a duty to help less experienced members of the team. Again, there is a strong sense that pressure to produce prototypes channels the best prototypers to the largest projects. In the next section, we discuss some of the issues raised by our analysis.

5   Discussion

In terms of discussion points, we have to consider a number of threats to the validity of the study described. Firstly, the interview text has been assumed to reflect accurately the prototyping as it existed in each company. We have to accept that the interviewees may have lied and/or withheld information about the true situation in the company. In defence of this threat, the investigator did return to clarify points with interviewees which they had not been clear about and certain cross-checking would have been inevitable (especially with multiple interviews in the same company). A related threat is that in interviews where more than one member of prototyping staff were involved, junior members of staff may have felt under pressure to say what they felt was the 'appropriate' answer rather than the 'real' answer. In defence of this threat, the commonality of results (including the single person interviews) across the five companies suggests that this was not a widespread or common feature.

One threat which is not so easy to defend is the possibility that the lack of change control and standards may actually be more effective in terms of productivity of the prototyping team (than if they did exist). In other words, the prototyping process works because these features are absent. The impression gained is that for small projects this is true. For larger projects however, there is evidence that standards and controls are necessary.

A further but related threat to the validity of the conclusions is that for the data in this paper, we have no way of deciding whether or not use of stringent change control procedures and/or adoption of standards and quality checks would necessarily bring any benefits to the prototyping process. In defence of this threat, it was noted that in several instances, it was acknowledged that some form of standards would be useful. There was also an 'intention' by at least two companies (A and D) to introduce standards in the very near future.

Interestingly, the use of software tools does not figure prominently in the interview text which we have studied. Only on two occasions were the significance of development tools mentioned. A recent survey of tools used for web development showed relatively simple tools such as Visio and Dreamweaver to be the most commonly used tools [8] by developers. We suggest that one reason why this may be true (and supported by the interview text) is that tools are less of a concern during prototyping simply because the user wants to see something simple, yet effective; in addition, gathering requirements effectively may well be compromised by use of an overly complicated software tool. In the following section, we describe some conclusions and point to some future work.

6 Conclusions and Future Work

In this paper, we have described a study in which the informal aspects of the prototyping process have been investigated. Interview text from ten interviews with twenty members of staff was analysed and using Grounded Theory principles, three recurring themes emerged. Firstly, only one of the five companies studied had any formal change control mechanism in place. Secondly, adherence to standards and quality checks were also found to be largely missing across all companies. Finally, experience seemed to play a key part in allocation of staff to projects and in reducing time and cost pressures; finally, the perception of the user is of someone who constantly changes their mind and is not as positive as we would have expected. The results of the study are surprising for the lack of interest in a framework for prototyping and the strong belief that intuition, experience and enthusiasm are what really counts in prototyping – we accept that these features are important, but need to be supplemented with appropriate procedures. It may well be that prototyping is best done without any controls whatsoever and giving the prototyper complete freedom is the way to achieve proper prototyping, however. In terms of future work, we intend to investigate how the corresponding RADs could be modified in some way to accommodate the features we have uncovered herein. We also intend assessing the impact of making such changes, from a performance point of view, using appropriate metrics.

Acknowledgements

The authors gratefully acknowledge the help of Dr. Liguang Cheng for use of the interview material in this paper [3].

References

1. J. Brooks, People are our most important product, In E. Gibbs and R. Fairley, ed., Software Engineering Education. Springer-Verlag, 1987.
2. D. Card, The RAD fad: is timing really everything? IEEE Software, pages 19-22, Jan. 1995.
3. L. Chen, An Empirical Investigation into Management and Control of Software Prototyping, PhD. dissertation, Department of Computing, University of Bournemouth, 1997.
4. G. Coleman and R. Verbruggen. A quality software process for rapid application development, Software Quality Journal, 7(2):107-122, 1998.
5. S. Counsell, K. Phalp and E. Mendes. The 'P' in Prototyping is for Personality. Proceedings of International Conference on Software Systems Engineering and its Applications, Paris, France, December 2004.
6. S. Counsell, K. Phalp and E. Mendes. The vagaries of the prototyping process: an empirical study of the industrial prototyping process, submitted to: International Conference on Process Assessment and Improvement, SPICE 05, Klagenfurt, Austria, April 2005.
7. B. Glaser and A. Strauss. The Discovery of Grounded Theory. Strategies for Qualitative Research. Aldine Publishers, 1967.
8. GUUUI survey. Results from a survey of web prototyping tools usage. The Interaction Designer's Coffee Break. Issue 3, July 2002. available from: www.guuui.com/issues 01 03_02.
9. C. Handy, On roles and Interactions. Understanding Organisations, Penguin.
10. C. Knapp. An investigation into the organisational and technological factors that contribute to the successful implementation of CASE technology. Doctoral Dissertation, City University, New York, 1995.
11. H. Lichter, M. Schneider-Hufschmidt and H Zullighoven. Prototyping in industrial software projects: Bridging the gap between theory and practice. IEEE Transactions on Software Engineering, 20(11):825-832, 1994.
12. P. Martin and B. Turner. Grounded Theory and Organisational Research. Journal of applied Behavioural Science. 22(2), pages 141-157.
13. M. Ould. Business Processes: Modelling and Analysis for Re-engineering and Improvement, Wiley, 1995.
14. K. Phalp and S. Counsell, Coupling Trends in Industrial Prototyping Roles: an Empirical Investigation, The Software Quality Journal, Vol. 9, Issue 4, pages 223-240, 2002.
15. K. Phalp and M. Shepperd, Quantitative analysis of static models of processes, Journal of Systems and Software, 52 (2000), pages 105-112.
16. J. Reilly. Does RAD live up to the hype? IEEE Software, pages 24-26, Jan. 1995.

Appendix A

Table 4. Standards and relationship with conventional development

Id.	Standards and/or Quality	Conventional Development
A(1)	No point in 'ticking boxes'; would be counter-productive.	No information available
A(2)	Any standards would unduly affect ability to respond. Prototyping has to be an energising force rather than an imposition.	Conforming to in-house development and improvement programme seen as an imposition. Time and cost limitations much more stringent than in conventional development. Getting user requirements right is far more important than doing a nice design.
A(3)	No quality standards. Prototyping for small projects use 'quick and dirty' approach. Proper analysis and design for larger projects is probably more usual.	No information available.
B	Standards used according to the size of the project. No quality checks.	Converntional development much more rigorous. Users tend to blame prototypers for inadequacies in prototype. No excuse for missing functionality during conventional development.
C(2)	Standard procedures used, but not rigorously. A quality group guides and enforces standards, but prototyping staff broadly unaware of standards.	Prototyping seen as part of the conventional development process and fits in within that framework. This justifies lack of standards in prototyping.
D(2)	No standards or quality checks.	Prototyping seen as part of the overall development process. Justifies lack of standards in prototyping.
D(3)	No quality checks. Justified because projects tend to be quite small. Recognition of need when projects start becoming larger. Rely on experience for getting projects finished on time. Quality checks are also difficult to implement.	No information available.
E	Company wide standards used give flexibility and a practical system development framework to work within.	No information available.

Appendix B

Example Role Activity Diagram (RAD) – three roles

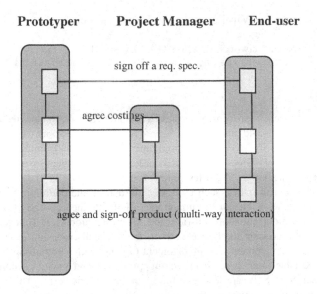

Prototyper   Project Manager   End-user

sign off a req. spec.

agree costings

agree and sign-off product (multi-way interaction)

Process Improvement Solution for Co-design in Radio Base Station DSP SW

Virpi Taipale and Jorma Taramaa

Nokia Networks, P.O.Box 319, FIN-90651 Oulu, Finland
{Virpi.Taipale, Jorma.Taramaa}@nokia.com

Abstract. Process improvement studies have tended to focus on one technology area at a time, and on process improvement frameworks, like CMMI (Capability Maturity Model Integration), and measurements from the top-down point of view. In addition, the management has been the trigger force of process improvement activities. Much less interest at process level has been shown in cross-technological issues, such as co-design, and on the bottom-up approach. In this paper, we point out the importance of the defined co-design activities and the synchronisation of software and hardware processes. Hardware and software designers are the best experts in this difficult co-design process area and thus the development staff involvement together with a bottom-up approach is a respectable alternative to improving processes and practices along with traditional SPI (Software Process Improvement) frameworks. The study is based on empirical studies carried out in Nokia Networks base station unit ASIC (Application-Specific Integrated Circuit) development and DSP (Digital Signal Processing) software development teams. The bottom-up approach was used to study the processes and the CMMI was used in analysing the findings and linking them to different process areas. We found that, despite the software and hardware, the processes themselves are quite well defined, the deficiencies are related to the invisibility of co-design activities. The technical experience and view was found to be relevant in improving the processes related to the interfaces between two technologies, like hardware and software. Traditional SPI and other process areas improvement work concern themselves typically with their own technology area only, and the process deficiencies close to other technology areas might be blurred. The paper also presents new process improvements for the software and hardware co-work area.

1 Introduction

Tough competition in the telecommunication business pressures companies to shorten their time-to-market, widen their product portfolio as well as improve their product quality and performance. These aspects force companies to critically study working practices and put effort into upgrading processes.

3G (third generation) standards require complex algorithmic calculations for voice and data channels. The major share of the required processing occurs in the baseband portion of the 3G-channel card, as well as the terminal as the radio base station part

F. Bomarius and S. Komi-Sirviö (Eds.): PROFES 2005, LNCS 3547, pp. 16–28, 2005.
© Springer-Verlag Berlin Heidelberg 2005

[2]. A baseband typically consists of HW accelerators, i.e. Application-Specific Integrated Circuits (ASIC), and DSP (Digital Signal Processing) software producing the signal processing capacity for a baseband. A radio base station, as an embedded system, provides a complex challenge for the product development process. Concurrent specification, design and verification work of hardware and software can be viewed as co-design. As signal-processing requirements grow, the role of hardware-software co-design becomes increasingly important in system design [12].

From the development process point of view, hardware and software development typically follows its own process flows and co-work in the interface area of two technologies strongly relies on personal contacts not supported by the processes. Several studies present software process improvement (SPI) frameworks and experiments using those in product development. [9], [6] Process improvement is then the elimination of differences between an existing process and a standard baseline. The top-down approach compares an organisation's process with some generally accepted standard process [19].

This paper reveals the experiences of processes in the co-design area in base station development of Nokia Networks and suggests improvements for these process areas. The study is based on empirical studies performed with DSP software and ASIC teams on the basis of their own needs to improve working practices. In the context of empirical software engineering, the study consists of a qualitative part and a literature part. [5] The selected starting point for the process improvement is a bottom-up approach. The bottom-up approach assumes that the organisation must first understand its process, products, characteristics and goals before it can improve its processes [19]. Collecting information is performed via interviews, questionnaires and projects' documentation reading, forming the qualitative part of the empirical study. The other aspect to the study is to compare the findings to the process literature. The focus in the literature survey is the CMMI (Capability Maturity Model Integration) literature, as CMMI is generally used in Nokia Networks process improvement projects [14].

The text of this study consists of five parts. In the following section, we introduce the factors influencing base station development and the profile of a base station product compared to other network elements. Section three focuses on the improvement frame, how the problem was studied. The findings of the studies and the suggested process improvements are presented in sections four and five. Section 6 contains the conclusion along with recommended tasks to be undertaken in future studies.

2 Base Station Development

Standardisation has a strong role in the mobile network business. In a 3GPP (3rd Generation Partnership Project) standardisation commission, competitors and customers, network suppliers together with operators, define the most useful, value-adding new features to be implemented into UMTS (Universal Mobile Telecommunications System) network. [20] Layer 1 fulfils the standard requirements via software (SW) and hardware (HW) partitioning thus comprising a fundamental part through the network in the development race. [2]

Different network elements have different profiles within a range of three attributes: life cycle, frequency of new product launches and product volume (Fig. 1). New mobile phones, mass volume consumer products, are launched very regularly for different user groups. The utilisation time of a phone has become quite short compared to other network elements due to the low price of new phone models and new fancy features, which appeal to phone customers. Network elements, like switches and network controllers, are small volume infrastructures, the functionality of which mostly grows in software releases. From the software point of view, the vertical axis represents the need for reusable software components. The horizontal axis on the other hand can be interpreted as growing software maintenance work. The profile of a base station can be regarded as an intermediate form of the mobile phones and other network elements, since base stations and mobile phones include the radio interface part of a wireless network and, on the other hand, the base station is a network element. Compared to the mobile terminal life cycle, the base station life cycle can be expected to be relatively long, from 5 years to as long as 20 years. Other network elements have typically even longer expected life cycle. Base station production volumes are not that massive as in the mobile phone business, but much bigger than in the case of other network elements, since the mobile network serving area is based on a covering area of base station cells. The new base station platforms

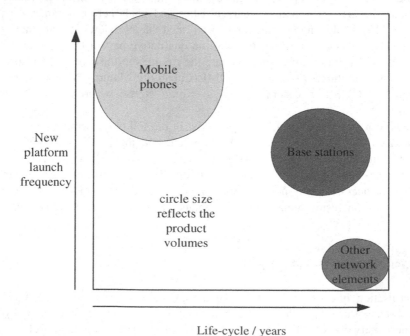

Fig. 1. Network element profiles in terms of product volumes, platform launch frequency, life-cycle

are launched fairly often as technology development enables new cost and size effective solutions. It is important to consider these different characteristics of network elements when new platforms and standardised Layer 1 features are developed and HW-SW partitioning is defined.

Base station layer 1, i.e. physical layer functionalities, are typically provided by the combination of DSP SW and HW accelerators implemented by baseband. [2] Contrary to many other embedded systems, in digital signal processing, the hardware components that are controlled by software are not simple or passive (such as fans or temperature gauges), but elements that perform complicated mathematical tasks [17]. An expectation and a requirement for a new base station development is that the platform should be a long-term solution, which can adjust to the new feature requirements defined by the standardisation commission. The long-lasting nature of products demand that companies put effort into evaluating and defining their practices and processes in order to succeed and stay in the network business. The HW-SW partition should be optimal in such a way that new functionalities can be added on top of the base station platform years after product launch in SW releases. Moreover, the partition should be such that the software is easy to adapt to a new platform.

The base station development practices at Nokia Networks are described in the base station product family process. The process has its own sub-process flows for software and hardware, as well as for system development. Each sub-process describes its work phases, deliverables and milestones. At Nokia Networks, organisational process improvement activities have mostly been based on assessment-based software process improvement (SPI) practices like SW-CMM (Capability Maturity Model for Software) and nowadays also CMMI and, on the other hand, on using measurements, like the GQM method (Goal/Question/Metric), in indicating and fine-tuning process improvement needs and activities [16], [18]. All of these approaches are so called top-down SPI practices. A management commitment is essential in all process improvement activities to succeed, but the management has so far also been the trigger to start assessment or measurement projects. Typically, the separate internal or external process team has surveyed the program or project practices via interviewing project personnel with defined questions or measuring the project's data. SPI activities have started based on the process team's statement of improvement areas.

3   Improvement Frame

Traditionally, software process improvement studies have largely concentrated on different frameworks, such as generic baseline models (e.g. CMM, CMMI, and ISO15504), SPI models (e.g. IDEAL, Initiating, Diagnosing, Establishing, Acting & Learning, and PDCA, Plan-Do-Check-Act), as well as the Quality Improvement Paradigm (QIP) [10], [15], [7], [1]. The organisation's process is compared to these generally accepted standard processes and the process improvement is then the elimination of the differences between an existing process and a standard one. Nokia Networks software process improvement work has widely been based on SW-CMM and recently on CMMI maturity models. [14] The newer bottom-up approach to process improvement is to utilise the experience of the organisation.

In this study, the bottom-up approach is used to study ASIC and DSP software processes and their interfaces, and the CMMI is the approach used to analyse and communicate the results.

3.1 Bottom-Up Approach

The bottom-up approach, as well as others, assumes that process change must be driven by an organisation's goals, characteristics, product attributes, and experiences. Moreover, the underlying principle is that all software is not the same. [19] Every product, project and software technology brings its own requirements to the software process. In this context, we highlight that the best knowledge of an organisation's characteristics is among the technical development staff. The involvement of the development teams or human factors is naturally taken into account, as the originators of the study were technical teams. Literature also emphasises the importance of developers' involvement in process improvement [4], [8], [11].

The bottom-up approach assumes that every development organisation must first completely understand its processes, products, software characteristics, and goals before it can select a set of changes meant to improve its processes. Thus, the best experience of base station baseband and its processes is by the designers who develop the base station DSP software and hardware accelerators, ASIC's. In the context of two technology areas interface, the bottom-up approach utilises the feedback from both software and ASIC designers, not limiting the scope into one process only and not ignoring the improvement needs in the challenging interface area.

3.2 CMMI Continuous Model

CMMI was developed to sort out the problem of using multiple CMMs. CMMI combines three capability maturity models: the SW-CMM, the Systems Engineering Capability Model (SECM) and the Integrated Product Development CMM (IPD-CMM). There are two different representations of CMMI: the staged model and the continuous model. This chapter introduces the main principles of the CMMI method from the continuous representation point of view. Continuous representation offers a more flexible approach to process improvement than the staged model, and thus it is also widely used in Nokia Networks process improvement projects.

The CMMI continuous model allows the organisation to focus on specific Process Areas (PA's) to improve the performance of those areas. The process areas are grouped into four main categories, namely Process Management, Project Management, Engineering and Support (Fig. 2.). [13]

Each process area can be evaluated separately and reach its own capability level. A capability level tells about the organisation's ability to perform, control and improve its performance in a process area. The six capability levels are: Level 0: Incomplete Level 1: Performed Level 2: Managed Level 3: Defined Level 4: Quantitatively Managed Level 5: Optimizing. The capability level for a process area consists of related specific and generic goals. Each goal, specific or generic, consists of practices

Process Management	Engineering
Organisational Process Focus (OPF) Organisational Process Definition (OPD) Organisational Training (OT) Organisational Process Performance (OPP) Organisational Innovation and Deployment (OID)	Requirements Management (REQM) Requirements Development (RD) Technical Solution (TS) Product Integration (PI) Verification (VER) Validation (VAL)
Project Management	Support
Project Planning (PP) Project Monitoring and Control (PMC) Supplier Agreement Management (SAM) Integrated Project Management (IPM) Risk Management (RSKM) Integrated Teaming (IT) Integrated Supplier Management (ISM) Quantitative Project Management (QPM)	Configuration Management (CM) Process and Product Quality Assurance (PPQA) Measurement and Analysis (MA) Decision Analysis and Resolution (DAR) Organistional Environment for Integration (OEI) Causal Analysis and Resolution (CAR)

Fig. 2. CMMI Process Areas

Requirements Management (REQM) SG1 - Manage Requirements	**Product Integration (PI)** SG1 - Prepare for Product Integration SG2 - Ensure Interface Compatibility SG3 - Assemble Product Components and Deliver the Product
Requirements Development (RD) SG1 - Develop Customer Requirements SG2 - Develop Product Requirements SG3 - Analyse and Validate Requirements	**Verification (VER)** SG1 - Prepare for Verification SG2 - Perform Peer Reviews SG3 - Verify Selected Work Products
Technical Solution (TS) SG1 - Select Product-Component solutions SG2 - Develop the Design SG3 - Implement the Product Design	**Validation (VAL)** SG1 - Prepare for Validation SG2 - Validate Product or Product Components

GG1 - Achieve Specific Goals GG2 - Institutionalize a Managed Process GG3 - Institutionalize a Defined Process GG4 - Institutionalize a Quantitatively Managed Process GG5 - Institutionalize an Optimizing Process

Fig. 3. Specific and generic goals of Engineering Process Areas

that give more detailed information on activities considered as important in achieving
the goal at different capability levels. By satisfying the specific and generic goals of a

process area at a particular capability level, the organisation benefits from process improvement. [3], [13]

The base station baseband development processes are related to CMMI engineering process areas, because engineering processes indicate the specialities of baseband development creating the basis of other main processes such as process management, project management and support. Engineering process areas cover the development and maintenance activities that are shared across engineering disciplines, (e.g. systems, software, hardware, mechanical engineering) (Fig. 2.). With this integration of different technical disciplines, the engineering process areas support the product-oriented process improvement strategy. The focus of this study is to improve the processes related to a baseband 'product'. The specific and generic goals related to engineering process areas are presented in Figure 3. The generic goals are generic to multiple process areas, and in the engineering category to all process areas. [3], [13]

4 Empirical Studies

This report is based on two empirical studies carried out during autumn 2003 in Nokia's base station development. In the context of Empirical Software Engineering, the study focuses on a qualitative part in the study phase and, on the other hand, on a literature survey part in analysing the results against the CMMI [5]. One study concentrated on ASIC design and another on DSP software development. Thereby ASIC design, in this study, represents the hardware design part and DSP SW development, the software design part in the HW-SW co-design concept. The goal was to discover the current status of both ASIC and DSP working practices and the process area limitations. Another goal was to capture the tacit knowledge about the processes that resides with co-workers. This chapter summarises the findings of the two studies from the HW-SW co-design point of view and links those findings to CMMI engineering process area goals.

4.1 DSP Questionnaire

The DSP software working practices were inspected via a free-form questionnaire study sent to base station DSP software designers at four different sites. Thirty questionnaire answers were received, mostly from experienced designers. The designers' experience in SW development varied from 2.5 to 20 years; the average being 7 years.

The questionnaire study concentrated on DSP SW special characteristics and commonalities with other base station software development and on possible holes and potential improvements in the software process from the designers' point of view. Roughly 20 questions related to the SW process area and only those fall within the scope of this study. The questions were open and there was room for new ideas. A few examples of the questions: "What drives your DSP SW implementation work?", "What DSP SW specific parts are there in your software process?", "What should be improved in your process descriptions?".

4.2 ASIC Study

The ASIC study was carried out for 27 ASIC projects that were active during 1998 to 2003; it was performed by Nokia's own personnel. The study consists of two phases – a project documentation study phase and a project key person interview phase. Only the SW-HW co-design and –verification related findings are discussed in this report. The documentation study phase was conducted by studying the projects' documentation. The interview part consisted of closed questions related to project schedules, etc., and open questions related to lessons learned from ASIC development phases. An example of interview questions: "Describe the co-operation with the SW team, good/bad experiences".

4.3 Findings

The literature survey focused on CMMI literature. The literature survey was conducted after the qualitative part in order to see whether the problems mentioned in the studies were also mentioned in CMMI literature and to map the findings into the CMMI concept. Using CMMI concepts, to communicate the results within Nokia Networks organisation, as it is strongly committed to CMMI in process improvement, was found to be relevant.

As a whole, the designers were quite satisfied with the current processes; this study highlights the limitations discovered. Both of the studies indicated similar limitations in processes, only from different viewpoints. The key findings from the studies and the concerning CMMI process area goals are listed in tables 1 and 2.

Table 1. Findings of the ASIC process and their links to the CMMI process areas specific and generic goals

ASIC Finding	PA & Goal
No software resources available in co-design phase, work is done by ASIC designers only.	TS-GG2
Software design has to be started earlier, parallel with ASIC design.	TS-GG2
ASIC-SW project schedules poorly aligned, synchronising of deliverables is important.	TS-GG2
Test software for sample testing comes late.	TS-GG2, VER-GG2

All of the findings of ASIC study are related to process area Technical Solution generic goal 2. The deficiencies in processes lie in planning the process, providing resources, assigning responsibility and identifying and involving relevant stakeholders. One finding can also be seen to belong to the Verification process area.

Correspondingly, the DSP software questionnaire enlightened the following limitations.

Table 2. Findings of the DSP SW process and their links to the CMMI process areas specific and generic goals

DSP Finding	PA & Goal
Software participation in HW-SW co-design phase needed.	TS-GG2
HW competence needed for product integration and bug fixing after the ASIC project ends.	TS-GG2
Informal requirements for HW test software.	RD-SG2, REQM-SG1
There's no process description for co-verification.	VER-GG2

A few findings from the DSP study also indicated limitations in Technical Solution process area generic goal 2. In fact, those findings are identical to those experienced by ASIC designers. The one finding proves weaknesses in requirement process areas. The lack of co-verification process refers directly to verification process area generic goal of institutionalising a managed process.

The characteristics of these findings are timing and responsibility. The results show that software and ASIC design process flows and their milestones and deliverables are not as well aligned as they could be. There are unaccounted discontinuities in the development work and software and ASIC designers are not aware of each other's working practices. Also, some confusion lies in the participation and responsibilities of co-work activities: co-design and co-verification. Some co-work tasks are invisible in other process flows and thus the work has not been planned properly, causing delays in a project. The current view to these HW-SW co-design processes is described in figure 4. The system design process supports the base station system level design work. After the base station system is specified, the detailed baseband system design work is started. The ASIC project development work starts earlier than software projects. Usually, software designers are still involved in the earlier project

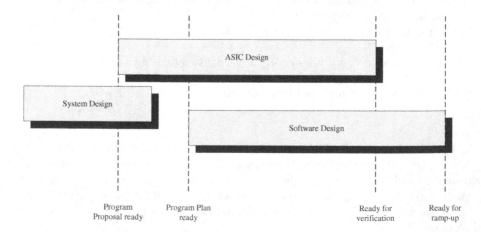

Fig. 4. Current process model

integration work. Thus, the baseband co-design activities fall into the ASIC project's responsibility. On the other hand, software designers raised in the study, the importance of hardware competence in the product integration phase, while ASIC designers have already moved on to a new project.

The co-work in projects seemed to be based on personal contacts, not enough support by the processes. Currently, the software and ASIC design processes are too separate from each other. Both processes define their own activities without enough connections (i.e. checkpoints, milestones, deliverables) to each other. Also, the activities where co-work would be beneficial, are not clearly stated in processes.

5 Improvement Solution

As a result of this empirical study, some changes were proposed for the software and ASIC design processes. The alignment of these processes were found to be essential both at the start and end phases. The baseband co-design activity was proposed separately from ASIC and software processes, to the system design process. The hardware-software co-design is a multi-technology task, and thus it requires several competences, meaning system, hardware and software competences. In the new process model, the actual ASIC and software work starts at the same time after both the base station and the baseband system level requirements and architectures have been defined (Fig. 5.). By aligning the work of these two technology areas, the availability of both competences is assured in the product integration phase.

To improve the co-work and visibility between ASIC design and software projects, some checkpoints and checklist items were added to the milestones. These items concern issues like checking resource availability in co-work activities described only in one process flow, the documents needed from another project as an input, and the documents delivered as an output to the other project.

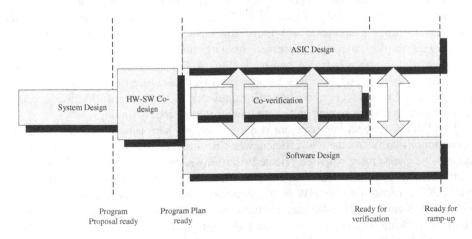

Fig. 5. The new process model

The findings related to co-verification were corrected with the new task of co-verification. The co-verification task is described in a new process flow as both the software and the ASIC design projects' responsibility. The task comprises requirement definitions for the test software, software implementation, the co-verification and the reporting sub-tasks. The software project provides the test software according to the requirements defined by the ASIC design project. The effective verification task is carried out as a co-operation between the two projects.

6 Conclusions

This study presents the experiences of Nokia Networks baseband development ASIC and software processes and introduces an improvement solution for these processes. The co-design processes were studied with a bottom-up approach and the results were analysed within the framework of the CMMI continuous model. The most essential findings of the co-design processes were related to time schedule synchronisation and co-work of hardware and software projects. The multi-technology competence and hardware-software projects' co-work was found to be essential in both early co-design and later co-verification activities, and the process flows must support this kind of co-operative activities. Moreover, to improve the projects efficiency and timing, tight connections between the ASIC design and hardware related software development should also be visible at the process level. These connections can be ensured with the added milestone checklists of needed input/output deliverables from/to other process flows. The result, a new, improved operations model of processes is a supporting tool for the management for better project planning, task alignment and easier follow-up, as well as for designers for planning their own work better. The new process also encourages software and hardware designers to co-work with each other and supports them to widen their work scope into new technology areas.

The bottom-up approach, together with CMMI, was considered as a respectable alternative for process improvement in a challenging hardware-software co-design area. The bottom-up approach was found to be successful in finding the concrete weaknesses of the co-design processes. In particular, in improving the processes related to the interface between two technologies, like hardware and software, the technical experience and view was found to be essential. Once the weak points were discovered, CMMI, as a commonly used framework in Nokia Networks, was a good tool for interpreting, analysing and communicating the process findings.

This kind of process improvement is not a one-time performance project, rather it is continuous work. As the cost efficiency has become a major factor in the wireless systems business, more software-oriented solutions need to be considered. Moreover, ASIC technology has faced serious competitors in the form of alternative technologies like FPGA, reconfigurable HW and customised IC. Not only are the changing technologies and new HW-SW architectures exerting pressure on processes, but new kinds of working methods are also adding pressure to continuous process work. Not all hardware and software development will be done internally in the future. The software development trend is towards integrating commercial software components into own systems. Furthermore, customised IC (integrated circuit) development is the joint development of a system developer and a vendor. The co-design and verification processes are playing increasingly bigger roles in the future as these new technologies and working methods are adopted.

Acknowledgements

The authors would like to thank Nokia Networks' experts for providing their input to this paper.

References

1. Basili, V., R., Caldiera, G., Rombach, H., D.: Experience Factory Encyclopaedia of Software Engineering. John Wiley & Sons. (1994) 469-476
2. Blyler, J.: Will Baseband Technology Slow Base-Station Evolution? Wireless Systems Design. Vol. 7, Issue 7, Jul./Aug. (2002) 19-21
3. Chrissis, M., B., Konrad, M., Shrum, S.: CMMI®: Guidelines for Process Integration and Product Improvement. Pearson Education, Inc. (2003)
4. Conradi, R., Fuggetta, A.: Improving Software Process Improvement. IEEE Software, Vol. 19, Issue 4, Jul./Aug. (2002) 92-99
5. Conradi, R., Wang, A., I.(eds.): "Empirical methods and Studies in Software Engineering - Experiences from ESERNET". Lecture Notes in Computer Science LNCS 2765, Springer Verlag, Berlin Germany (2003) 7-23
6. Debou, C., Kuntzmann-Combelles, A.: Linking Software Process Improvement to Business Strategies: Experiences from Industry. Software Process: improvement and practice, Vol. 5, Issue 1 (2000) 55-64
7. Deming W., E.: Out of Crises: Quality, Productivity and Competitive Position. MIT Center for Advanced Engineering Study, Cambridge, MA (1986)
8. Hall, T., Rainer, A., Baddoo, N.: Implementing Software Process Improvement: An Empirical Study. Software Process Improvement and Practice, Vol. 7, Issue 1 (2002) 3-15
9. Harter, D., Krishnan, M., S., Slaughter, S., A.: Effects of Process Maturity on Quality, Cycle Time, and Effort in Software Product Development. Management Science, Vol. 46, Issue 4, Apr. (2000) 451-466
10. ISO/IEC 15504-7: Information Technology – Software Process Assessment – Part 7: Guide for use in process improvement. (1998)
11. Jakobsen, A., B.: Bottom-up Process Improvement Tricks. IEEE Software, Vol. 15, Issue 1, Jan./Feb. (1998) 64-68
12. Kostic, Z., Seetharaman, S.: Digital Signal Processors in Cellular Radio Communications. IEEE Commiunications Magazine, Vol. 35, Issue 12, Dec. (1997) 22-35
13. Kulpa, M., K., Johnson, K., A.: Interpreting the CMMI®: A Process Improvement Approach. Auerbach Publications, A CRC Press Company (2003)
14. Leinonen, T-P.: SW Engineering under Tight Economic Constrains. Proceedings of 4th Int'l Conf., PROFES 2002, Springer-Verlag, Berlin Heidelberg New York (2002)
15. McFeeley, B.: IDEAL^SM: A User's Guide for Software Process Improvement. Pittsburgh, Pennsylvania 15213: CMU/SEI-96-HB-001 (1996)

16. Paulk, M., C., Weber, C., V., Curtis, B., Chrissis, M., B.: The Capability Maturity Model for Software, Guidelines for Improving the Software Process. Addison-Wesley Publishing Company (1994)
17. Ronkainen, J., Taramaa, J., Savuoja, A.: Characteristics of Process Improvement of Hardware-Related SW. Proceedings of 4th Int'l Conf., PROFES 2002, Springer-Verlag, Berlin Heidelberg New York (2002) 247-257
18. van Solingen, R., Berghout, E.: The Goal/Question/Metric Method: a practical guide for quality improvement of software development. McGraw-Hill International (UK) Limited (1999)
19. Thomas, M., McGarry, F.: Top-Down vs. Bottom-Up Process Improvement. IEEE Software, Vol. 11, Issue 4, Jul. (1994) 12-13
20. Toskala, A.: Background and Standardisation of WCDMA. In: Holma, H., Toskala, A. (eds.): WCDMA for UMTS, Radio Access For Third Generation Mobile Communication. John Wiley & Sons Ltd (2000) 41-52

A Framework for Classification of Change Approaches Based on a Comparison of Process Improvement Models

Otto Vinter

DELTA, IT Processes,
DK-2970 Hørsholm, Denmark
otv@delta.dk

Abstract. In this paper we describe a framework for classifying possible change approaches according to the stage(s) in the life-cycle where the approach is most applicable. The life-cycle model of the framework is based on an analysis of a number of existing life-cycle models for change from three different domains. The focus of this framework is on the individual improvement project and the palette of available approaches to its project manager.

1 Introduction

The Danish Talent@IT project (www.talent-it.dk) [18] studies change approaches used by companies in order to define a model for successful improvements. We want to find the applicability of these change approaches and how the applicability is related to a company's ability to perform successful changes.

Studies by Somers & Nelson [15] and Kinnula [8] have shown that different change approaches should be applied depending on where in the life-cycle the change project is. E.g. Somers & Nelson [15] have shown that "management commitment" is important in the beginning and conclusion of the life-cycle of the change project, and of less importance in the middle part. And that "dedicated resources" are only important during the actual development of the changes.

Consequently, when we should recommend a project manager which change approach to use, a classification according to the life-cycle stage of a change project seems both relevant and promising. It is also evident that there are change approaches, which extend across all of the life-cycle stages. Such issues are commonly referred to as life-cycle independent or continuous issues. These issues are currently not included in our framework for classification.

For a classification of change approaches by life-cycle stage we need a life-cycle model which extends over the entire life of a change from the original inception of the idea for the change until the stage where new ideas for change emerge based on the experiences and learning obtained from the project.

Selecting an existing life-cycle model for our classification framework would of course be the most natural. However, as we will show in this paper, some of the well-known models focus primarily on the earlier stages of a change project, while others put little emphasis on these and concentrate on the later stages. A combination of

F. Bomarius and S. Komi-Sirviö (Eds.): PROFES 2005, LNCS 3547, pp. 29–38, 2005.

existing life-cycle models into one comprehensive life-cycle model would seem to solve our problem.

Based on such a combined life-cycle model we will be able to classify all possible change approaches by the stage(s) where they will be most useful for a manager of a change project.

2   Life-Cycle Models for Change Projects

The life-cycle models we have studied and compared cover a number of change domains all characterized by having IT as an important enabler. For further analysis we have selected from each domain two life-cycle models which seem representative (e.g. extensively documented and referred to by others). The change domains we have selected life-cycle models from for our comparison are:

- Software Process Improvement (SPI)   – section 3
- New Technology Implementation   – section 4
- Business Process Reengineering (BPR)   – section 5

All change models divide the execution of the project into a number of phases or stages. The number of stages and the activities performed in each stage seem to vary quite a bit. However, a closer look at the models shows an agreement on what should take place during a change project. The differences are mainly in which stage it should take place and what emphasis the model places on the issue. Our comparison of the life-cycle stages of the models can be found in section 6.

Based on our comparison of life-cycles we have then constructed a combined model (section 7) by extracting the most representative stages and distribute the activities from the models on those stages.

We shall use this combined model as the framework for classification of change approaches on the Talent@IT project.

Finally, by means of a few examples we shall demonstrate how the framework can be applied (section 8). However, to fully populate this framework with known change approaches from industry and literature remains part of our future work on the Talent@IT project.

3   Life-Cycle Models in "Software Process Improvement (SPI)"

Systematic efforts to improve software processes originated in 1986 when the Software Engineering Institute at Carnegie Mellon University (SEI) was formed by the US military with the purpose of creating a model to assess potential software system suppliers.

The SPI domain contains many life-cycle models. A comprehensive study of life-cycle models in this domain can be found in Kinnula [7]. Two of the most well-known SPI models are closely connected to maturity assessment frameworks: CMM [12] and SPICE [4]. The work on the Talent@IT project is heavily influenced by these assessment frameworks. We have therefore decided to analyze the SPI models related to CMM and SPICE:

– IDEAL 1.0 [10]
– ISO 15504-7 (SPICE) [5]

IDEAL is the most well known model for SPI. The model originates from the Software Engineering Institute (SEI). The model is the proposed model for how to perform improvements of software processes in the CMM assessment framework. The model has been developed by SEI and later successfully applied on a number of actual industry cases.

IDEAL 1.0 [10] is the original and best documented version of the model. A number of not too detailed descriptions exist of an updated version 1.1 [13]. Apart from calling the last phase "Learning" in stead of "Leveraging" there doesn't seem to be much change in either phases or their content.

ISO 15504-7 [5] is part of the international standardization effort based on the SPICE assessment initiative [4] and is the proposed model for how to perform improvements of software processes in this framework. It builds on and extends the IDEAL model. However, as far as we know the model is a theoretical model and has not been tested in actual industry cases.

4   Life-Cycle Models in "New IT Technology Implementation"

Implementation of new IT technology is a domain which is normally seen as closely related to the SPI domain. However, the focus of change in this domain is not the improvement of processes *per* se but to improve the competitiveness of a company through implementation of new IT technology *and* accompanying processes.

There seems to be no common agreement on how to implement new IT technology. The domain is typically characterized by the use of *no* model for the implementation. However, two prominent models exist and were therefore selected for our analysis of models in this domain:

– INTRo [14]
– Cooper & Zmud [1]

INTRo [14] is the result of the continuing efforts of the Software Engineering Institute (SEI) in the SPI domain, which have lead to the definition of a model for implementation of new (IT) technology in a company. The model is directly focused on implementation of (customized) standard software products (COTS). The acronym INTRo stands for: IDEAL^{SM}-Based New Technology Rollout, which shows its close connection to the SEI model for software process improvement.

SEI has made the model generally available via their home page (www.sei.cmu.edu/intro/overview) and has created a "community of practice" around its use, where companies can exchange their experiences with the model. Until now the model has been tested by more than 50 organizations, primarily US-based.

Cooper & Zmud [1] have developed another well-known model for implementation of IT solutions in an organization. The model is descriptive, based on a study of how the implementation of (customized) standard IT solutions for the support of business processes should take place in practice.

They evaluated the model on the implementation of IT solutions for Material Requirements Planning (MRP). Other evaluations of the model have been performed by Somers & Nelson [15] [16] on the implementation of IT solutions for Enterprise Resource Planning (ERP).

5   Life-Cycle Models in "Business Process Reengineering (BPR)"

Business Process Reengineering (BPR) is the third change domain we have studied. BPR is designed for comprehensive organizational changes aimed at improving the competitiveness of a company, in which changed IT processes and technology implementations are a supporting element.

The concept of BPR was initially coined by Hammer [3]. To him, improving an organization's processes cannot take place as a series of adjustments, only through a complete redesign of the processes (revolution instead of evolution). He talks about establishing a "clean slate". This attitude has been adopted by subsequent authors in the field. Davenport [2] e.g. states that you should design completely new processes (process innovation) not only improve (reengineer) existing processes.

BPR has been successfully applied in a number of well-known cases. However, it is also reported that the rate of failure of BPR projects is even higher than for SPI projects (70% according to Malhotra [9]).

BPR is a domain characterized by an abundance of models. It seems as if every consulting company has developed its own proprietary model. Furthermore the life-cycles of the different models do not even seem to have a common basic structure. There seems, however, to be two strands among BPR models on the market: one which claims that BPR projects are only performed once in an organization, and one which believes in repetitive cycles of improvement. Stoica et al. [17] give an overview of a number of publicly available BPR models.

The Talent@IT project believes in continuous improvement. Therefore both of the models we have analyzed belong to the strand of BPR models which have life-cycles that include a stage for continuous improvement. The BPR models we have analyzed are two relatively recent ones, which according to the authors are based on a combination of earlier models:

- Muthu et al. [11]
- Kettinger & Teng [6]

Muthu et al. [11] have developed a BPR model combined from five well-known BPR models. They do not, however, explain how their model is related to these other models, and since the models have quite different focus it is unclear how they have arrived at their model. The model itself, however, is very well documented in a detailed set of IDEF diagrams. It is not clear whether the model has been evaluated in practice by companies.

Kettinger & Teng [6] have developed one of the most recent models in the BPR domain. The model is based on an analysis of 25 BPR models, both academic and commercial. From these they have developed a combined life-cycle model. They have subsequently checked the model through interviews in three companies that had completed BPR projects. It is not clear to which extent the model has been evaluated in practice by other companies.

6 Comparison of the Models' Life-Cycle Stages

We have based our comparison of the above models on the available detailed activity descriptions. We have aligned the different stages in order to achieve the best possible match of the activities across the models. The comparison of the models' life-cycle stages can be found in Fig. 1.

In Fig. 1 we have added our proposed combined life-cycle model as the rightmost column. This model will be described in more detail in section 7. The combined life-cycle model will be used for our classification of change approaches.

The comparison of activities prescribed by the models has shown that the content (e.g. activities) in some life-cycle stages seems to be very much the same, even though the models use a different name for these stages. In these cases we have aligned the stages of the models to the same row in Fig. 1.

We have also found that some models have reserved a separate stage for some activities, where other models have included these activities in another stage. This means that the models have a different number of stages even in cases where the overall content may be more or less the same.

We have marked with an "*" in Fig. 1 those cases where one model has included some of its activities in another stage, where another model has described these in a separate stage. Thus a blank cell in the figure indicates that a model does not mention the type of activity which one of the other models does.

The comparison of the models' life-cycle dependent activities clearly shows that improvements take place at two levels in an organization:

- strategic/organizational level
- execution/project level

The SPI models try to describe both of these levels in one common stage model, because they emphasize the importance of continuous improvements. The BPR and IT technology implementation models on the other hand are aimed at one specific improvement action e.g. focus specifically on the execution/project level, even though both of theses domains have great strategic and organizational implications.

Some models regard planning and staffing of the improvement project as so important that they have devoted a separate stage for these (ISO 15504-7, INTRo, and Kettinger & Teng), other models include this in another stage (IDEAL), and some models don't mention it specifically (Cooper & Zmud and Muthu et al.).

It is evident from Fig. 1 that the model by Cooper & Zmud is very detailed in the later stages of an improvement project where the improved process and product is deployed and used as part of the normal work of the organization. In this area the BPR models seem especially weak (in particular the models we have not selected for analysis). It seems as if BPR models are more interested in planning the implementation than executing the plans. The SPI models mention rollout and use, but do not make an effort in describing how. They assume that this happens as a natural consequence of the improvement project.

Software Process Improvement Models		New IT Technology Implementation Models		Business Process Reengineering Models		Combined Model
IDEAL 1.0	ISO 15504-7	INTRo	Cooper & Zmud	Muthu et al.	Kettinger & Teng	Talent@IT
Initiating	Examine	*	Initiation	Prepare for Reengineering	Strategy Linkage	Initiation
*	Initiate	Project Initiation & Planning			Change Planning	*
Diagnosing	Assess	Problem / Domain Analysis		Map & Analyze As-Is Process	Process Problems	Diagnosis
Establishing	Analyze	Technology / Based Solution Definition	Adoption	Design To-Be Processes	Social & Technical Re-Design	Analysis
Acting	Implement	Technology Customization & Testing	Adaptation	Implement Reengineered Processes	*	Development
		Whole-Product Design	*			*
*		Breakthrough		*		Evaluation
*	*	Rollout	Acceptance	*	Process Re-Generation	Rollout
Leveraging	Confirm	*		Improve Continuously	Continuous Improvement	*
*	Sustain		Routinization			Routinization
			Infusion			Infusion
*	Monitor	*		*	*	*

Fig. 1. Comparison of the Models' Life-cycle Stages . A "*" means that similar activities are included in another stage

Cooper & Zmud is the only model which devotes a separate stage (Infusion) for the exploitation of the new technology in new ways following its implementation and use. On the other hand, the Cooper & Zmud model seems very weak in the earlier stages of an improvement project. E.g. the Diagnosis/Assessment/Analysis of the organization's current state before a new IT solution is implemented is confined to the selection (Adoption) of the proper IT product and vendor. Similarly the Cooper & Zmud model sees no need for stages for evaluation or whether the goals have been achieved or not.

INTRo is the only model that defines a separate stage for those issues that are concerned with complementing the development and test activities of the IT technology, e.g. the design of a comprehensive solution (Whole-Product Design). The stage is executed in parallel with the adaptation of the technology, and it seems that the other models see these activities simply as part of the normal development activities. Cooper & Zmud, however, mention these activities as part of their model's Adaptation stage. Seemingly the model by Kettinger & Teng mentions such activities in their dual part stage: Social & Technical Re-Design. However, the activities here are aimed at designing new processes and technologies – not about creating holism in the design.

The ISO 15504-7 model defines as the only model a separate stage (Monitor) for measuring and monitoring an improvement project although the description clearly states that this is an on-going activity across the stages and therefore should have been described as a life-cycle independent (continuous) activity.

7 A Life-Cycle Model for Classification of Change Approaches

Based on the above comparison of the selected models, we propose the following combined model as our framework for classification of change approaches.

In the combined model we have extracted all essential activities from the above models and put them into a combined model. By essential we mean activities which should provoke and inspire us in our search for change approaches to populate the framework.

The life-cycle stages of this combined model can be found in Fig. 2, and also as the rightmost column in Fig. 1 for direct comparison with the other models. The detailed activities in each stage are too extensive to be included in this paper. They are described in an internal Talent@IT document, which can be received through personal contact with the author.

The combined model consists of eight stages. We have not described any repetitions (continuation cycles) in the model in Fig. 2, but it is evident that individual improvement initiatives should be part of a more extensive plan (strategy) for change in the organization. Some of the stages in our combined model are clearly executed by dedicated project teams, while the line organization clearly is responsible for other stages.

Currently, we have tried to limit our combined model to cover the execution/project level of a change initiative, because we see a clear need for helping and supporting project managers choosing the best change approaches for his/her project. A framework for classification of change approaches for the strategic/organizational level is of course also important, but we see this as following a quite different life-cycle more closely connected to the maturity of the organization. We have postponed the elaboration of this framework until later in the Talent@IT project.

Our experience with studying successful improvements at the execution/project level has shown us how important it is to secure that the new processes/products are adopted and used on a normal basis by the organization. We have therefore chosen to emphasize the activities in the later stages e.g. primarily adopting the later stages of the model by Cooper & Zmud. However, in the earlier stages of a general change initiative, where there is a need for more detailed diagnosis and development activities than for an implementation/customization initiative, we have chosen to follow the stages of the other models.

We have also chosen to follow the INTRo model and describe piloting activities and trial implementations in a separate stage (Evaluation). Other models (IDEAL and Muthu et al.) mention the importance of these but include them as part of their regular design and development activities. Our experience, however, is that these activities normally involve persons and organizational units outside the project team, and sometimes even a change in responsibility for the work. This clearly represents a source for problems in the execution of the change project. Consequently we see a need to define special change approaches for this part of the work to secure the success of the improvement project.

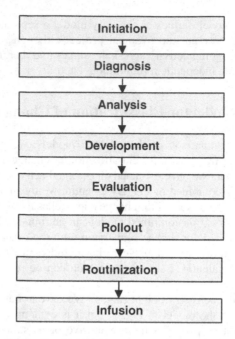

Fig. 2. The Combined Life-cycle Model in Talent@IT

Conversely we have chosen not to separate planning and staffing of the improvement project in a separate stage, which half of the models do (ISO 15504-7, INTRo, and Kettinger & Teng). We find, along with the IDEAL model, that this should take place in the same life-cycle stages where critical decisions about the future progress of the project takes place (Initiation and Analysis respectively).

In general our choice of number of life-cycle stages and their contents has been based on our wish to have as many distinct stages as possible, because it would make the classification of change approaches easier. However, we do not want more stages than actually needed for classification of change approaches. We have performed a pilot classification of changes approaches used in practice, where we wanted to be able to identify at least three different change approaches for each of our stages, before the stage was included in our model.

8   Application of the Framework for Classification of Change Approaches

In Fig. 3 we give a few examples of how the proposed framework can be used to classify change approaches according to the stage in the life-cycle where they are applicable to the manager of an improvement project. Currently we are in the process of expanding these examples into a comprehensive set of change approaches as one of the results of the Talent@IT project.

In the classification of change approaches so far, we have found it difficult to find names and descriptions for change approaches, which do not implicate that some approaches are right/better or wrong/poorer. Whether a change approach is right depends completely on the nature of the organization, its current practices, and change goals. There are no universally right or wrong change approaches.

9   Conclusion and Future Work

We have analyzed important life-cycle models from three different change domains and combined their activities into a comprehensive framework which we shall use for classification of change approaches. We have found that this framework should be based on eight life-cycle stages.

Our next step will be to populate our combined model with known change approaches taken from actual industrial cases both from our own experience, the experience of the Talent@IT industrial partners, and actual cases found in the literature.

Other modeling work on the Talent@IT project studies which factors are critical to the success of process improvement. This modeling work has lead to an assessment model, which measures the ability of an organization to perform successful changes. Based on this assessment of improvement abilities we hope to be able to use the populated classification framework to select which set of change approaches to recommend the organization.

Life-cycle Stage	Change Approach	Description
Initiation	"Top-down"	Dictated by management. Management scopes the project without further discussion: This is what we want.
	"Bottom-up"	The need for the change is identified by employees/users who want to drive the project: This is what we need.
Diagnosis	Formal assessment	BOOTSTRAP, CMM, CMMI, SPICE etc.
	Problem diagnosis	Study of problem reports, project records etc.
Analysis	"To-be" analysis	Definition of new processes
	Prevention analysis	Evaluation of preventive actions
Development	Tool-driven	The tool determines the processes/product
	User-driven	Solution developed by the users of the processes/product
Evaluation	Piloting	A pilot project uses the processes/product to evaluate the results
	Limited use	Part of the organization or processes are put in use to evaluate the results
Rollout	Start-up workshops	Workshops are held for selected persons/groups when they should start using the processes/product
	Hot-line	Expert assistance is provided during initial use
Routinization	Organizational maintenance	Support and updates handled by a designated organizational unit
	Outsourced maintenance	Support and updates handled by an external partner e.g. tool vendor
Infusion	Experience exchange	Learning new ways through use by others
	Organizational learning	Collection, consolidation, and dissemination of experience

Fig. 3. Examples of classification of change approaches

References

1. Cooper, R. B., Zmud, R. W.: Information Technology Implementation Research: A Technological Diffusion Approach. Management Science, Vol. 36 No. 2, (1990), 123-139
2. Davenport, T. H.: Process Innovation: Re-engineering Work through Information Technology. Harvard Business School Press (1993)
3. Hammer M.: Reengineering Work: Don't Automate, Obliterate. Harvard Business Review, July-August (1990), 104-112
4. International Organization for Standardization: Information Technology – Software process assessment – Part 1: Concepts and introductory guide. ISO/IEC TR 15504-1:1998(E) (1998)
5. International Organization for Standardization: Information Technology – Software process assessment – Part 7: Guide for use in process improvement. ISO/IEC TR 15504-7:1998(E) (1998)
6. Kettinger, W. J., Teng, J. T .C.: Conducting Business Process Change: Recommendations from a Study of 25 Leading Approaches. Process Think: Winning perspectives for Business Change in the Information Age, Grover & Kettinger (eds.), Idea Group Publishing, (2000)
7. Kinnula, A.: Software Process Engineering Systems: Models and Industry Cases. Oulu University Press, (2001). URL: http://herkules.oulu.fi/isbn9514265084/
8. Kinnula, A., Kinnula, M.: Comparing SPI Activity Cycles to SPI Program Models in Multisite Environment. Proceedings of the PROFES'04 Conference, (2004)
9. Malhotra, Y.: Business Process Redesign: An Overview. IEEE Engineering Management Review, Vol. 26 No. 3, (1998)
10. McFeely, R.: IDEAL: A User's Guide for Software Process Improvement. CMU/SEI-96-HB-001, (1996)
11. Muthu, S., Whitman, L., Cheragi, S. H.: Business Process Reengineering: A Consolidated Methodology. Proceedings of the 4th Annual International Conference on Industrial Engineering Theory, Applications and Practice (1999)
12. Paulk, M.C., Weber, C., Curtis, B., Chrissis, M.B.: The Capability Maturity Model: Guidelines for Improving the Software Process. Addison-Wesley, Reading, Mass (1995)
13. Software Engineering Institute: The IDEAL^{SM} Model: A Practical Guide for Improvement. (1997), URL: http://www.sei.cmu.edu/ideal/ideal.bridge.html
14. Software Engineering Institute: Improving Technology Adaptation Using INTRo. (2003), URL: http://www.sei.cmu.edu/intro/documents/users-guide.doc
15. Somers, T.M., Nelson, K.: The Impact of Critical Success Factors across the Stages of Enterprise Resource Planning Implementations. Proceedings of the 34th Hawaii International Conference on System Sciences, (2001)
16. Somers, T.M., Nelson, K.: A taxonomy of players and activities across the ERP project life cycle. Information & Management 41, Elsevier, (2004)
17. Stoica M., Chawat, N., Shin, N.: An Investigation of the Methodologies of Business Process Reengineering. Proceedings of the ISECON 2003 Conference, EDSIG (2003)
18. Vinter, O., Pries-Heje, J. (eds.): På vej mod at blive bedre til at blive bedre – Talent@IT projektet. DELTA Report D-266, Hørsholm, Denmark, (2004)

A Qualitative Methodology for Tailoring SPE Activities in Embedded Platform Development

Enrico Johansson[1], Josef Nedstam[1], Fredrik Wartenberg[2], and Martin Höst[1]

[1] Department of Communication Systems Lund University, Lund, Sweden
{enrico.johansson, josef.nedstam, martin.host}@telecom.lth.se
[2] Ericsson AB, Göteborg, Sweden
fredrik.wartenberg@ericsson.com

Abstract. For real time embedded systems software performance is one of the most important quality attributes. Controlling and predicting the software performance in software is associated with a number of challenges. One of the challenges is to tailor the established and rather general performance activities to the needs and available opportunities of a specific organization. This study presents a qualitative methodology for tailoring process activities to a specific organization. The proposed methodology is used in case study performed in a large company that develops embedded platforms. A number of suggestions for modification and addition of process activities has been brought forward as a result of the study. The result can further be summarized as SPE in embedded platform development holds more opportunities for reuse, but also requires more focus on external stakeholders, continual training and coordination between projects.

1 Introduction

Software performance (i.e. response times, latency, throughput and workload) is in focus during the development and evolution of a variety of product categories. Examples of products are websites, network nodes, handheld devices, transaction systems, etc [1, 5, 15, 17, 21].

A number of software process activities have been proposed to help an organization with software performance engineering (SPE). Typical performance issues can include identifying performance bottlenecks, giving guidelines for functional partitioning, and help selecting the best alternatives of a number of design proposals. A normal challenge in introducing such process activities is to tailor the established and rather general performance activities to the needs and opportunities of the specific organization.

A product platform is per definition the basis of a variety of product versions. Each product version should be constructed with a low effort, compared to developing the complete platform [4, 13]. An embedded [10] platform is a specific type of product platform where a computer is built into the product platform and is not seen by the user as being a computer. Most real-time systems [3] are embedded products.

F. Bomarius and S. Komi-Sirviö (Eds.): PROFES 2005, LNCS 3547, pp. 39–53, 2005.

For embedded platforms, specific possibilities and needs are present and should be considered in a process to support software performance work. Embedded platforms often have high-priority requirements on low cost. When this is the case, it is not possible to solve performance problems by, for example, increasing the hardware performance. A very long lead-time to change the hardware platform would be required, and it would also be expensive. During the development of an embedded platform, consideration of both the software design and hardware design must be taken. The design of the hardware architecture must be dimensioned based on the needs of the software applications that in many cases are yet to be implemented.

This study presents a qualitative methodology that can be used to tailor process activities to a specific organization. In the methodology, a conceptual framework containing software performance activities and software process activities is mapped to the needs and possibilities of the development within a case company. The case company develops real-time embedded platforms where software performance is one of the most important quality attributes of the product. The following research questions are investigated:

1. What restrictions or opportunities for a software performance engineering process are imposed by an embedded platform?
2. Does the presented methodology provide valuable input when tailoring an SPE process?

The paper is structured as follows. Section 2 introduces the qualitative methodology used, in Section 3 the methodology is applied to a specific company and in Section 4 the conclusions are presented.

2   Method

The research is carried out using a qualitative methodology [12, 20] designed to reveal which behaviors and perceptions that drive the studied organization towards a specific goal. This implies that the results of qualitative research are of a descriptive nature. Qualitative research is particularly useful for determining what is important to individuals and why it is important. In this context, qualitative research provides a process from which key research issues are identified and questions formulated by discovering what really matters to the organizations and why they matter.

The general method for qualitative studies [11, 14, 16] shown in Figure 1 is modified for tailoring software process activities to a particular area and company. One modification is the addition of the actual tailoring activity where new, changed and the deletion of activities can be proposed based on the pattern found. Also, a conceptual framework is introduced to set up the dimensions used during the pattern finding. The conceptual framework includes general process activities, development phases and stakeholders. These three different parts are initially populated by established and general knowledge of the particular process that is to be tailored. Performing an archive analysis in the studied

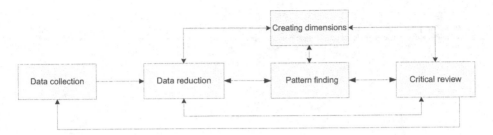

Fig. 1. A general model for qualitative research presented by [11]

company is done to find additional stakeholders and development phases which should be added to the initial conceptual framework.

2.1   Data Collection

Interviews were performed with 16 selected members of the personnel from the case organization. The duration of each interview was approximately one hour. During the interviews, open questions were asked, related to software performance engineering. The subject's own reflections on needed activities for software performance were also collected. The sampling of subjects was based on availability, knowledge and experience in a way that resulted in as broad a spectrum of knowledge as possible related to the work in the organization. The context of the interview was the upgrade of an existing platform, by addition of new functionality. The purpose of the interviews was two-fold: one purpose was to find general needs in the process related to software performance activities; another was to investigate the possibility of different activities to promote the software performance work. The interviews were carried out as open ended in order to catch the needs and possibilities of a software performance methodology, without excluding issues that the researcher did not foresee. Furthermore, since all participants are from the same company and project it is believed that the discourse in the interviews is equal for all interviews. The following open-ended questions have been used as a starting point for the interviews.

1. In what phases do development projects need performance information about the system, or part of the system?
2. For what part of the system is it most important to get performance estimates and how accurate do the estimates need to be?

2.2   Creating Dimension

There exist as described above an established process for software performance engineering [21]. The workflow and individual activities are not described in this paper due to limitations in space but an overview of the workflow is given in Figure 2. These SPE activities are included in the conceptual framework in order to capture knowledge about general SPE activities. The SPE process presented

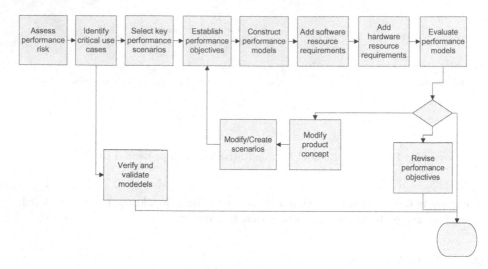

Fig. 2. The SPE workflow presented by [21]

by [21] is willingly made general, with no mapping of each activity in process phases and stakeholders. For the conceptual framework to be useful in the research context, it must be complemented with a list of potential stakeholders and applicable development phases. From [4, 7, 8, 18, 23, 25] a number of success factors for a process tailored for embedded platform development are given. Stakeholders in terms of development units must at least contain hardware development, software development, and product management. The phases performed during the development and evolution of a software platform is not believed to be specialized for that purpose. Therefore, rather general process phases related to the evolution of a platform are chosen to be part of the conceptual framework.

A conceptual framework that includes process activities, stakeholders and development phases involved is proposed as a starting point for the research. The initial framework includes the following parts:

1. **Process Activities:** Those included in the SPE workflow in Figure 2.
2. **Process Stakeholders:** Hardware Development, Software Development, Product Management.
3. **Development Phases:** System Feasibility Study, System Design, Module Design, System Integration.

The applicability and refinement of the conceptual framework is carried out by going through documentation produced for the development and upgrade of the platform, with the objective to search for data related to software performance. Such data is for example used to parameterize the performance models, compare design alternatives, and when setting the requirements of the platform. The intention is that the documentation should show the available information flow used in the process of upgrading a platform.

2.3   Data Reduction

The interview transcripts are reduced to a number keywords and comments as a result of the the data reduction activity. A further coding is done be grouping the keywords into process categories determined by SPICE [22]. The qualitative data is grouped into five process categories defined in part 2 of the standard; Customer-Supplier, Engineering, Project, Support and Organization.

2.4   Pattern Finding

The objective is to construct a visualization of the material from the data collections relations the conceptual framework. The visualization is carried out by relating the material collected in to a triplet consisting of an SPE activity, a project phase and a stakeholder. This activity is presented in two matrixes.

2.5   Critical Reviews

During all parts of the qualitative methodology (i.e. data collection, data reduction, creating dimensions and pattern finding) critical reviews are made by the researchers and employees at EMP. In the presented research the data collection was performed and reviewed by three researchers, and contained both a document analysis and open-ended interviews [11, 14, 16]. Data reduction and critical review was performed on the transcript from the document analysis and from the interviews. During the document analysis the researcher carried out the data reduction and the reviewing. The interviewees performed the critical review for the open-ended interviews; they read the transcripts in search for erroneous citations and omissions. Both the pattern finding and tailoring was done independently by two researchers and reviewed by a third researcher at the case company. It has been an iterative processes, where both the activities and the reviews where performed until all participants could agree upon the result.

3   Case Study

The case study was performed at Ericsson Mobile Platforms AB (EMP). EMP offers complete embedded platforms to manufacturers of mobile phones and other wireless devices. The technology covers 3G [9] and older mobile phone systems. Results from the different parts of the presented qualitative methodology is presented in the following subsections. In the last subsection proposals for new activities are presented.

3.1   Creating Dimensions

The activity resulted in an overview of currently available SPE data and a mapping of stakeholders and data to the different phases of the development process. Two stakeholders that were not listed in the initial conceptual framework were found to play a role in the SPE work. These two stakeholders, the project management and the customer or buyer of the platform, are in the further analysis added to the stakeholder list in the conceptual framework.

3.2   Data Collection and Reduction

The following keywords and comments are the result after the data collection and reduction of the interview material.

Customer-Supplier

1. Usage specification: Platform customers demand a performance specification of the system and its services early in the process in order to develop interfaces for the applications on top of the platform.
2. Prioritizing use-cases: Late requirement changes can be solved by a product management organization by prioritizing the use-cases that are the basis for the requirements specifications. Such use-case analysis gives information of which parallel use cases are possible, providing a more complete picture of the system requirements. In addition, room for performance flexibility must be included in the use-case analysis. The flexibility is set in terms of the maximum execution times and response times that can be tolerated by the use- cases. In addition, the different variation of the use case should be included; as for example, what different multimedia codecs are needed. In this way, developers can focus on prioritized requirements, and it is easier to remove functionality that overruns the performance budget.
3. Rough performance indications: Product management needs to get a feeling for what is possible or not, in terms of parallel use cases and new functionality. Indications are required to understand the scope of the performance requirements of a new product portfolio. Early performance estimations can be used as such indicators. There is in this case not a strong demand of accuracy on the performance estimations; even rough performance estimations are acceptable for this purpose. In addition, in critical changes regarding available processing power or memory there must be an immediate performance feedback to performance stakeholders. The feedback might initially be rough indications, which can be used for decisions on whether or not perform a more thorough impact analysis.

Engineering

4. Feedback: There is a need to give feedback on the estimation from the analysis phase. This can be done through performance measurements in the subsequent phases. Making updates to documents that contain such estimates risks taking significant lead-time, which to some degree hinders continuous updates of estimates and metrics. The solution is to see the estimates as changing over time and not "a fixed truth", and validation of the estimates is necessary to promote organizational learning.

5. Static worst-case estimations: Using static worst-case memory estimation can be satisfactory when analyzing sequential tasks. The demands of sequential tasks can often be considered linearly, which is however not true when several processes are running at the same time, where the worst-case scenario is rare and order of magnitudes more resource-consuming than ordinary operation. It might therefore be hard to interpret the result in parallel, non-deterministic processing environment.

6. Define performance metric: There is generally a need for common definition and understanding of software performance metrics, as in the case of instructions-per-second versus cycles-per-second metrics. Such metrics should be defined with the customers' and users' perception of performance in mind.

7. Hardware requirements: The hardware developing unit needs to know the performance requirements in terms of memory sizes and processing power early enough to be able to deliver hardware in time for internal integration of the platform. These prerequisites have intricate implications on estimates, metrics collection, and any performance prediction models that are to be introduced into an organization.

8. Hardware/software partitioning: The hardware project needs requirements on CPU and memory load and possible hardware accelerators. The requirements on hardware accelerators stems from the hardware and software trade-offs made. All these requirements are needed before the software project reaches the implementation part.

9. Measurements: When a project reaches the design and implementation phase, it becomes possible to make measurements on the actual performance and validate the performance model. In this phase the performance can be tracked on module level and be compared with the predictions of the model. The system performance due to interaction between functionality originating in different sub-projects will be validated in the integration phase.

10. Algorithms: The performance analysis of new functionality can be done on algorithm level with regards to CPU processing performance requirements, and static worst-case memory demands can be estimated. There is however, a big step from algorithm-level estimates of new functionality, to the system-level metrics collected from previous platforms. The interviewees therefore sought for models that could use performance estimates of the hardware and hardware related software, and produce estimates of the dynamic system behavior. The modules that are performance bottlenecks are often commonly known, and they should set the level of granularity in the model (i.e. the model should use the same granularity).

11. Interaction between software processes: It is difficult to intuitively make software performance estimates of software that interacts and is dependent of the scheduling and synchronization of other software real-time processes. One of the reasons is because of its many possible states and non-deterministic use-cases.

12. Validated: In order to make a model both useful and trustworthy, the result must be validated when the project reaches implementation.

13. Forecast and outcome: If the software needs in terms of memory size and CPU are greater than the estimates, the specified functionality will not fit into the platform. On the other hand, if the outcome is less than the estimates, the platform will be more expensive than necessary, in terms of hardware costs. The performance estimates therefore need to have a high level of accuracy since they are related to both the specifications and to the outcome.

14. Accuracy needed: There is not one value defining the needed accuracy of the estimates for each different phase. What can be stated is that the need for accuracy is increased for each phase the nearer the project is the system integration. However, when deciding the requirements of hardware, the software development units should reach an optimistic accuracy of 10-30% in their performance estimates in the pre-study phase.

15. Optimization: Most software in embedded platforms is optimized for the specific hardware it is running on, which means that even hardware enhancements might degrade performance if new optimizations are not done. To move functionality from one processor type to another requires further optimizations. It is also dangerous to take performance metrics from a previous product for granted, as these implementations can often be optimized further.

16. Software architecture: Technological solutions to performance issues do not only involve hardware improvements. The software architecture also has impact on performance. An architectural change to simplify performance estimation can for example be to limit the number of modules and simultaneous processes considered.

17. Ability to understand: In order to make a model both useful and trustworthy, the assumptions behind the model must be visible.

Project

18. Knowledge and education: Software developers need to know about the hardware they are running on, understand performance aspects, and understand the different types of memory that are available. They also need to know how the compilers and operating systems treat the code they write. There is also a difference between a simulated environment and the actual hardware; things that work in the simulator might not work on hardware. Apart from training, an organization should give credit to expert developers in order to promote performance-related development competency.

19. Iterative platform development: An iterative development process can be used to get hold of early systems performance estimates. After each iteration the implemented software system can be measured. On the other hand, there are also problems related to such a process, at least when it comes to iterative specifications. Sometimes not all of the specified functionality fits in the performance constraints, so the performance requirements on the

software often have to be renegotiated anyhow towards the later stages of projects.

20. Hardware/Software co-design: In a platform development scenario, hardware developers are typically ahead of software developers. A characteristic overlap is created between projects, where hardware developers start a new project before software developers have finalized theirs, making it not so obvious how to transfer resources and experiences from project to project. Software developers therefore can have a shortage of time to carry out performance estimate analysis in the beginning of projects, while the hardware developers do not have the complete set of prerequisites at hand, when starting their analysis and specification activities.

Support. None of the keywords could be grouped in this category.

Organization

21. Project focused organizations: In order to reuse metrics between two development projects coordination is needed from the management in charge of the overall product and development quality in the company. A characteristic scenario where this prerequisite is not fulfilled is in the project-focused organization (where the project controls all resources). In such cases, the return on investment of the methodology used must be visible in the actual project budget. Therefore, it is difficult to make improvements in methods and processes that overlap two projects. An example is the collection of data in previously developed projects to be used in future projects.

3.3   Pattern Finding

Each of the keywords (1-21) was during the pattering finding mapped to the conceptual framework. Table 1 visualizes the keywords in relation to SPE activities and project phases. Each row in the matrix represents SPE activities and for keywords that do not fit into an activity there is an activity depicted as "Other activity". In cases where the keywords only partially adheres to the activity the keyword is denoted with a star (*). The development phases have been coded as following: SFS (System Feasibility Study), SD (System Design), MDI (Module Design and Implementation, SI (System Integration). Table 2 visualizes the SPE activities relation to the stakeholders. In order to further clarify the stakeholder's role an additional coding is used, besides the one to keywords. Each stakeholder is coded as an initiator of an activity, executor of an activity or a receiver of the result from an activity. For each pair of SPE activity and stakeholder more than one of the codes I (Initiator), E (Executer) or R (Receiver) can be appropriate. The following codes has been used to denote the development phases: SwD (Software Development), HwD (Hardware Development), PrM (Product Management), ProjM (Project Management and UBPI (Users and Buyer of the Platform).

Table 1. Keywords mapped contra SPE process activities

	SFS	SD	MDI	SI
Assess performance risk	2, 3			
Identify critical use cases	2, 3			
Select key performance scenarios	2, 3			
Establish performance objectives	7			
Construct performance model(s)	1, 5, 6, 10, 11	1, 5, 6, 10, 11	1, 5, 6, 10, 11	
Add software resource requirements	6, 16			
Add computer resource requirements	1, 8, 7			
Evaluate performance model(s)	17	17	17	
Modify and Create scenarios	2	2	2	
Modify product concept	7, 8, 15*	7, 8, 15*	7 , 8, 13, 15*	
Revise performance objectives				
Verify and validate models	4, 9, 14	4, 9, 14	4, 9, 14	4, 9, 12, 14
Other activity	18, 19, 20, 21	18, 19, 20, 21	13, 18, 19, 20, 21	18, 19, 20, 21

3.4   Proposal for New Activities

From table 1 a number of observations can be made. For example, an observation is that there is a number of new activities that are mapped to keywords that cannot be related to any of the SPE activities set up by the conceptual framework, and are placed in the "Other activity" row. Another observation that can be made is which activities and project phases that are mapped to one or more keywords are candidates, in which phase most of the activities are performed.

1. The row 'Other activity' contains keywords 18, 19, 20, 21 for all phases and 13 for the 'Module Design and Implementation' phase. Since the keywords do not fit into the conceptual framework and are present in all phases, it implies that they should generate new SPE activities.
2. Most of the activities are involved in the early phases.
3. Keywords in the row 'Construct performance model(s)' and 'Evaluate performance model(s)' is in focus in three phases.
4. The row 'Verify and validate models' contains a number of keywords (4, 9, 14) that are present during all phases.

Table 2. SPE process activities contra stakeholders

	SwD	HwD	PrM	ProjM	UBPl
Assess performance risk	E	E	R	I	I
Identify critical use cases	E,R	E,R	I		I
Select key performance scenarios	E,R	E,R	I		I
Establish performance objectives	E	E		I	
Construct performance model(s)	I,E,R				
Add software resource requirements	E,R	R	I		
Add hardware resource requirements	R	E,R	I		
Evaluate performance model(s)	I,E,R				
Modify and Create scenarios	R	R	I,E		I
Modify product concept	E,R		I		I
Revise performance objectives	E,R	E,R	I		
Verify and validate models	I,E,R				

Similarly, a number of observations can be made from table 2. In this case, an observation that can be made is which role the stakeholders play in different activities. The activities proposed should be updated to conform to responsibility and mandate given to each stakeholder compared to what is needed to bring the activity into accomplishment.

5. In the column HwD (Hardware Development) there are nearly as much execution of activities (coded as Executor) as in the SwD (Software Development) column. This implies that the department that develops the hardware part of the platform is significantly involved in the SPE work.
6. In the column UBPI (User and Buyer) there are many initiations of activities (coded as Initiator). This implies that buyers and users of the platform initiate performance activities.

The general observation is that the collected data is in line with the general and established SPE literature. There are nevertheless a few observations that can be made for the specialized case of an SPE approach of the development and evolution of an embedded software platform. When using a platform development there is the possibility to learn through the maintenance and evolution of the different versions (observation 3). This is not too different from the objectives of the experience factory [2]. In the case presented, the motivation and the possibility are given by the nature of platform development, where new versions are constructed from the same platform. Therefore, the same performance model can be reused and further validated and evaluated through every version. However, when the platform itself is updated by changing hardware the reuse is less straightforward than when updates are made to build variations of the platforms (i.e. versions of the platform). Another observation is that the validation and evaluation of the model is done throughout the whole evolution and maintenance cycle (observation 4). There are two reasons motivating this observation, one is that an ongoing validation and verification will give the project staff enough confidence in the result of the models. The second reason is of course that the model itself can be improved. A further observation is that the evaluation and validation of the model is very much coupled to each other, because the same model is reused in the analysis phase of the next version of the product or platform. Observation 6 shows that the performance activities largely have external driving forces, from buyers (consumers) or project managers. The reason could be that when developing many versions there is a continuous discussion of the performance requirements of the platform. In addition, buyers of the platforms are concerned with the performance of the platform since they need to build applications on top of the platforms. They therefore need to set their own performance objectives, scenarios and requirements. They perform the same activities as mentioned in the conceptual framework, regarding the embedded platform as the hardware resource. In addition, project managers and buyers do not demand a high level of accuracy concerning the performance estimations. Even accuracy levels that are usable only as indications are valuable for the platform development. The value is present as long as the estimates can be used for strategic decisions about the project or the product.

4   Conclusions

The organization under study carries out several large and related projects, while the SPE workflow in Figure 2 is focused on single projects. Mapping the two together therefore implies that the first three activities of Figure 2 are carried out before the projects are initiated. They are carried out as a part of long-term product management, and in feasibility studies ahead of projects. The fourth activity, establish performance objectives, is then used to mediate long-term objectives with project objectives when a project is initiated. It is also used to concretize performance objectives defined in the previous phases, and therefore involves iterations where customers, product management and project management define specific performance criteria for a certain project.

The keywords that are not possible to map to the conceptual framework (observation 1) are candidates to elicit new activities needed for platform development. A number of observations can be made concerning these keywords (13, 18, 19, 20, 21). When dealing with embedded platforms and hardware/software co-design with tight real-time constraints it is important to continuously train the software personnel about the performance implication of new hardware and hardware related software. Competence in this field will also facilitate the performance modeling (keyword 18 and observation 2) when a change of hardware in the platform is performed.

Another observation is that in hardware/software co-design there is a need for performance estimates in practice before the general feasibility study phase is started within the software project (keywords, 19, 20, 21 and observation 2). Observation 5 further emphasizes this. The reason why all these activities fall out of the conceptual framework is that the SPE workflow used in the framework does not take into consideration aspects of the organization or the product development process used. An SPE workflow cannot be introduced and used with only the activities proposed. There are other activities found in this study that must be included in an overall SPE effort. Promoting knowledge and education about SPE aspects of the system developed is one of the activities that should be added. However, it is not enough to include a training course at the start of the project, the activity must be ongoing and bridge over different product lifecycles and projects. A solution could be, for this kind of product, to have a specific organization to carry out performance modeling and estimations that is not tied to the different projects. The final observation concerns the optimization (keyword 15), which is similar to modifying the product concept, however in this case the concept is not changed but optimized for the original concept. The initial conceptual framework seems to include many of the needs required from an organization that develops software for an embedded platform. However the analysis of the collected data shows that new activities must be added, together with new stakeholders compared to the ones present in the initial conceptual framework.

The goal of qualitative research is looking for principles and understanding behind actions performed under specific circumstances. The same goals appear when wanting to improve by tailoring it to the need and possibilities of a specific company. Therefore it was rather appealing to marry a qualitative methodology with a software process improvement initiative. Software performance is still a troublesome quality attribute to control and predict in the software industry despite of many suggested approaches. This is especially true for software products with limited hardware resources. An example of a software product with limited resource is an embedded product platform. Therefore the case study is performed on such a product.

The result of this paper presents an updated qualitative methodology for software process tailoring and contributes also to the understanding of software performance engineering during the maintenance and evolution of an embedded software platform. The company considered the results as both valuable and relevant, showing that the methodology presented gives highly valuable input for tailoring a SPE processes. A number of observation and suggestions related to an established and general SPE process has been brought forward. They can be summarized as that SPE in embedded platform development holds more opportunities for reuse, but also requires more focus on external stakeholders and a continual training and SPE effort rather than confined to individual projects, as suggested by current SPE models. These are believed to be some of the key success factors of and SPE process for the development and evolution of an embedded software platform. It is also believed that it is possible to compile a tailored workflow based in the explanations and information about the interaction between development phases, stakeholders and process activities.

To strengthen the generalizability of this the results, further studies on other companies have to be made. It is e.g. likely that different companies will have different roles responsible for performance issues.

Acknowledgment

The authors would like to thank all the participants from Ericsson Mobile Platform AB. This work was partly funded by the Swedish Agency for Innovation Systems, project number P23918-2A.

References

1. S. Balsamo, P. Inverardi, C. Mangano, "An approach to performance evaluation of software architectures", Proceedings of the 1st International Workshop on Software and performance (WOSP), Santa Fe, New Mexico, United States, 1998.
2. V. Basili, G. Caldiera, F. McGarry, R. Pajerski, G. Page, S. Waligora, "The Software Engineering Laboratory-an Operational Software Experience Factory", Proceedings of the 14th International Conference on Software Engineering, Melbourne, Australia, 1992.
3. A. Burns, A. Wellings, *Real-Time Systems and Programming Languages. Addison-Wesley*, 3rd edition, 2001.
4. P. Clements, L. Northrop, *Software Product Lines: Practices and Patterns*, Addison-Wesley, 2001.
5. G. De Micheli, R. Gupta, "Hardware/software co-design", *Proceeding of IEEE*, Vol. 85, No. 3, pp. 349-365, March 1997.
6. E. Gelenbe (editor), *System Performance Evaluation: Methodologies and Applications*, CRC Press, 1999.
7. M.Höst, E. Johansson, "Performance Prediction Based on Knowledge of Prior Product Versions", Accepted at 9th European Conference on Software Maintenance and Reengineering (CMSR), Manchester, UK, 2005.
8. E. Johansson, F.Wartenberg, "Proposal and Evaluation for Organising and Using Available Data for Software Performance Estimations in Embedded Platform Development", 10th IEEE Real-Time and Embedded Technology and Applications Symposium (RTAS), Toronto, Canada, 2004.
9. J. Korhonen, *Introduction to 3G Mobile Communications*, Artech House Mobile Communications Series, 2nd edition, 2003.
10. J. Labrosse, *MicroC/OS-II: the Real-Time Kernel*, CMP Books, 2nd edition, 2002.
11. A. Lantz, *Intervjuteknik* Interview method in Swedish, Studentlitteratur, Lund, 1993.
12. M. Polo, M. Piattini, F. Ruiz, Using a qualitative research method for building a software maintenance methodology, *Software: Practice and Experience*, Vol. 32, No. 13, pp. 1239-1260, 2002.
13. M.H. Meyer, A.P. Lehnerd, *The Power of Product Platforms: Building Value and Cost Leadership*, Free Press, New York, 1997.
14. M. Miles, A. Huberman, *Qualitative Data Analysis*, Sage, California, 1994.

15. P.J.B, King, *Computer and Communication System Performance Modelling*, Prentice-Hall, Hemel Hempstead, 1990.
16. C. Robson, *Real World Research: a resource for Social Scientists and Practitioner Researchers*, Blackwell, 1993.
17. J.A. Rolia, K.C. Sevcik, "The Method of Layers", *IEEE Transactions on Software Engineering*, Vol. 21, No. 8, pp. 689-700, 1995.
18. J.T. Russell, M.F. Jacome, "Architecture-level performance evaluation of component-based embedded systems", 40th conference on Design automation (DAC), Anaheim, CA, USA, 2003.
19. A. Schmietendorf, E. Dimitrov, R. R. Dumke, "An approach to performance evaluation of software architectures", Proceedings of the 1st International Workshop on Software and performance (WOSP), Santa Fe, New Mexico, United States, 1998.
20. C.B. Seaman, "Qualitative methods in empirical studies of software engineering", *IEEE Transactions on Software Engineering*, Vol. 25, No. 4, pp. 557-572, 1999.
21. C. Smith, L.G. Williams, *Performance Solutions*, Addison Wesley, 2002.
22. ISO/IEC TR 15504:1998(E), "Information Technology - Software Process Assessment", Parts 1-9, Type 2 Technical Report, 1998.
23. K. Suzuki, A. Sangiovanni-Vincentelli, "Efficient software performance estimation methods for hardware/software codesign", 33rd annual conference on Design automation (DAC), Las Vegas, Nevada, US, 1996.
24. E. Zimran, D. Butchart, "Performance Engineering Throughout the Product Life Cycle", Proceedings of Computers in Design, Manufacturing, and Production (CompEuro), pp. 344-349, 1993.
25. W.H. Wolf, Hardware-Software Co-Design of Embedded Systems, *Proceedings of the IEEE*, Vol. 82, No. 7, pp 967-989, July 1994.

An Empirical Study on Off-the-Shelf Component Usage in Industrial Projects

Jingyue Li[1], Reidar Conradi[1,2], Odd Petter N. Slyngstad[1], Christian Bunse[3], Umair Khan[3], Marco Torchiano[4], and Maurizio Morisio[4]

[1] Department of Computer and Information Science,
Norwegian University of Science and Technology (NTNU),
NO-7491 Trondheim, Norway
{jingyue, conradi, oslyngst}@idi.ntnu.no
[2] Simula Research Laboratory, P.O.BOX 134, NO-1325 Lysaker, Norway
[3] Fraunhofer IESE, Sauerwiesen 6, D- 67661 Kaiserslautern, Germany
{Christian.Bunse, khan}@iese.fraunhofer.de
[4] Dip. Automatica e Informatica, Politecnico di Torino,
Corso Duca degli Abruzzi, 24, I-10129 Torino, Italy
{maurizio.morisio, marco.torchiano}@polito.it

Abstract. Using OTS (Off-The-Shelf) components in software projects has become increasing popular in the IT industry. After project managers opt for OTS components, they can decide to use COTS (Commercial-Off-The-Shelf) components or OSS (Open Source Software) components instead of building these themselves. This paper describes an empirical study on why project decision-makers use COTS components instead of OSS components, or vice versa. The study was performed in form of an international survey on motivation and risks of using OTS components, conducted in Norway, Italy and Germany. We have currently gathered data on 71 projects using only COTS components and 39 projects using only OSS components, and 5 using both COTS and OSS components. Results show that both COTS and OSS components were used in small, medium and large software houses and IT consulting companies. The overall software system also covers several application domains. Both COTS and OSS were expected to contribute to shorter time-to-market, less development effort and the application of newest technology. However, COTS users believe that COTS component should have good quality, technical support, and will follow the market trend. OSS users care more about the free ownership and openness of the source code. Projects using COTS components had more difficulties in estimating selection effort, following customer requirement changes, and controlling the component's negative effect on system security. On the other hand, OSS user had more difficulties in getting the support reputation of OSS component providers.

1 Introduction

Due to market requirements concerning cost and time-to-market, software developers are searching for new technologies to improve their projects with respect to these qualities. Software components promise to have a positive impact on software reuse, resulting in time and cost efficient development. Therefore, software developers are

F. Bomarius and S. Komi-Sirviö (Eds.): PROFES 2005, LNCS 3547, pp. 54–68, 2005.

using an increasing amount of COTS (Commercial-Off-The-Shelf) and OSS (Open Source Software) components in their projects. Although both COTS and OSS component are claimed to save development effort, they are still very different. COTS components are owned by commercial vendors, and their users normally do not have access to the source code of these components. On the other hand, OSS components are provided by open source communities. Thus, they offer full control on the source code [15].

When planning a new software project, project decision makers need to decide whether they should buy a COTS component, or acquire an OSS component if it was decided to use OTS components. To make such a decision, it is important to investigate previous projects using such components and summarize the relevant decision-making processes and project results.

The study presented in this paper has investigated 71 finished software projects using only COTS components and 39 projects using only OSS components. It compared the COTS components with the OSS components in three dimensions: (1) Who is using OTS components, (2) Why project members decide to use them, and (3) What were the results of using them.

The remainder of this paper is organized as follows: Section two presents some previous studies on benefits and risks of using OTS components. Section three describes the research design applied. Section four presents the collected data, whereby the discussion of results is given in section five. Finally, conclusions and future research are presented in section six.

2   Previous Studies on OTS Component

COTS components promise faster time-to-market and increased productivity of software projects [1]. At the same time, COTS software introduces many risks, such as unknown quality of the COTS components, which can be harmful for the final product, or economic instability of the COTS vendor who may terminate maintenance support [2]. Furthermore, the use of OSS in industrial products is growing rapidly. The basic idea behind open source is very simple: When programmers can read, redistribute, and modify the source code for a piece of software, the software evolves. People improve it, people adapt it, and people fix bugs. And this can happen at a speed that, if one is used to the slow pace of conventional software development, seems astonishing [15].

OSS has many proposed advantages [3]: *OSS is usually freely available for public download. The collaborative, parallel efforts of globally distributed developers allow much OSS to be developed more quickly than conventional software. Many OSS products are recognized for high reliability, efficiency, and robustness.* Despite its wide appeal, OSS software faces a number of serious challenges and constraints. *The popularity of OSS increases the risk that so-called net-negative-producing programmers will become involved. Many software tasks, such as documentation, testing, and field support are lacking in OSS projects. If developers produce or sell a product, which integrates OSS as source code, they may need the licensor's permission. Otherwise, the licensor might claim for damages or force them to end the product's further development, delivery and sale [4].* Furthermore, many common perceptions about OSS need further empirical clarification. For example, there is still no empirical evidence that OSS fosters faster system growth [10]. There is also no strong evidence that OSS is more modular than closed source software [10].

Some previous studies have investigated the process of using COTS components in software development, such as COTS component selection [5] and COTS-based development processes [6]. Other studies have investigated how to use OSS software in product development [4], such as mission-critical development [11] and information system infrastructure development [12]. Although these studies present recommendations on how to integrate COTS or OSS component into the final product, few studies have investigated a higher level question: Why should I use COTS component instead of OSS components, or vice versa?

3 Research Design

This study is the second phase of a systematic study on process improvement and risk management in OTS based development. We started from a pre-study focused on COTS components, which was performed in the form of structured interviews of 16 COTS projects in Norwegian IT companies [9]. This study presented in this paper extended the pre-study in two dimensions. First, it included OSS components because they represent an alternative to COTS components. Second, this study included samples from Norway, Italy and Germany. In addition, the sample was selected randomly instead of on convenience as in the pre-study.

3.1 Research Questions

To investigate the motivation of using OTS components, we first want to know who is using OTS components. Therefore, the first research question is:

RQ1: *What are the commonalities and differences in profiles on projects using COTS components vs. those using OSS components?*

After we know who is using OTS components, we want to know why they decided to use OTS components. Thus, the second research question is:

RQ2: *What are the commonalities and differences in the motivation of projects using COTS components vs. those using OSS components?*

After we know who and why, we need to know the possible problems of using OTS components. We intended to investigate whether the current motivation and expectations of using OTS components are proper or not. Therefore, the third research question is:

RQ3: *What are the commonalities and differences in possible risks (problems) of projects using COTS components vs. those using OSS components?*

3.2 Research Method

In this study, we used a questionnaire to collect data, organized in six sections:

1. Background questions to collect information on the company, and respondents.
2. Background information concerning projects, such as development environment, application domain, and non-functional requirements emphasis.

3. The motivation of using OTS components.
4. The specific motivation of using COTS or OSS components.
5. Information relevant to process improvement and risk management in OTS component-based development.
6. Detailed information about one specific OTS component used in the actual project.

3.3 Concepts Used in This Study

Concepts used in this study are listed in the first page of the questionnaire, for example:

– **Component:** Software components are program units of independent production, acquisition, and deployment that can be composed into a functioning system. We limit ourselves to components that have been explicitly decided either to be built from scratch or to be acquired externally as an OTS-component. That is, to components that are not shipped with the operating system, not provided by the development environment, and not included in any pre-existing platform.
– **OTS component** is provided (by a so-called **provider**) from a COTS vendor or the OSS community. The components may come with certain obligations, e.g. payment or licensing terms. An OTS component is not controllable, in terms of provided features and their evolution and is mainly used as closed source, i.e. no source code is usually modified.

3.4 Data Collection

Sample Selection. The unit of this study is a completed software development project. The projects were selected based on two criteria:

– The project should use one or more OTS components
– The project should be a finished project, possibly with maintenance, and possibly with several releases.

We used random selection to gather representative samples in three European countries:

– In Norway, we gathered a company list from the Norwegian Census Bureau (SSB) [7]. We included mostly companies which were registered as IT companies. Based on the number of employees, we selected the 115 largest IT companies (100 biggest IT companies plus 15 IT departments in the largest 3 companies in 5 other sectors), 150 medium-sized software companies (20-99 employees), and 100 small-sized companies (5-19 employees) as the original contacting list.
– In Italy, we first got 43580 software companies from the yellow pages in the phone book. We then randomly selected companies from these. For these randomly selected companies, we read their web-site to ensure they are software companies or not. 196 companies were finally clarified as software companies, and were used as the original contact list.
– In Germany, we selected companies from a list coming from an organization comparing to the Norwegian Census Bureau. We then used the existing IESE customer database to get contact information of relevant IT/Software companies, in line with the Norwegian selection.

Data collection procedure. The final questionnaire was first designed and pre-tested in English. It was then translated into the native language of the actual country and published on the SESE web tool at Simula Research Lab [8]. Possible respondents were first contacted by telephone. If they had suitable OTS-based projects and would like to join our study, a username and password was sent to them, so that they could log into the web tool to fill in the questionnaire (they can also use a paper version). The average time to fill in the questionnaire is between 20 to 30 minutes.

3.5 Data Analysis

According to the focus of the different research questions, we used different data analysis methods:

- For **RQ1**, we analyzed the distribution of the variables.
- For **RQ2**, we want to see both the commonalities and differences of variables. To compare differences, we first used box-plots to show the median and distribution of the variable. We then compared the mean difference of variables. S.S. Stevens classified "permissible" statistical procedures [18] according to four main scales: nominal, ordinal, interval and ratio scale [19]. For the ordinal scales, the permissible statistics included median, percentiles, and ordinal correlations. Mean and standard deviations are allowed for interval and ratio scales. In our study, although the scale of our data is Likert scales, we also compared the mean value of different variable to see if they are significant different. A number of reasons account for this analysis: First, Spector [20] showed that people tend to treat categories in Likert scales as equidistant, regardless of the specific categories employed. Second, using parametric tests for scales that are not strictly interval does not lead, except in extreme cases, to wrong statistical decisions [21]. Third, D.J.Hand concluded that *restrictions on statistical operations arising from scale type are more important in model fitting and hypothesis testing contexts that in model generation or hypothesis generation contexts. In the latter, in principle, at least, anything is legitimate in the initial search for potentially interesting relationship* [22]. Although we used a t-test to compare the mean difference, the intention of this study is still model generation and hypothesis generation. We therefore believe that it is permissible to treat Likert-scales items as leading to interval scales measurements that can be analyzed with parametric statistics.
- For **RQ3**, we used the same analysis method as in RQ2.

4 Research Results

Although the data collection is still on-going in Germany and Italy, we have gathered results from 115 projects (47 from Norway, 25 from Italy, and 43 from Germany). In these 115 projects, 71 used only COTS components, 39 used only OSS components, and five used both COTS and OSS components. In this study, we discarded the projects using both COTS components and OSS component, because they will confound the results and cover only 4% of the total projects.

Most respondents of the 110 projects, which used either COTS components or OSS components, have a solid IT background. More than 89% of them are IT managers, project managers, or software architects. More than 88% of them have more than 2 year experiences with OTS-based development. All of them have at least a bachelor degree in informatics, computer science, or telematics.

4.1 Answers to RQ1 – Who Is Using OTS Components

To answer RQ1, we designed two sub-questions:

- **RQ1.1:** What are the commonalities and differences in profiles of the companies and projects using COTS components vs. using OSS components?
- **RQ1.2:** What are the commonalities and differences in emphasis in projects using COTS component vs. using OSS components?

Results are coming from projects in several domains, as showed in Figure 1. The distribution of company size and the companies' main business area are shown in Figure 2 and Figure 3.

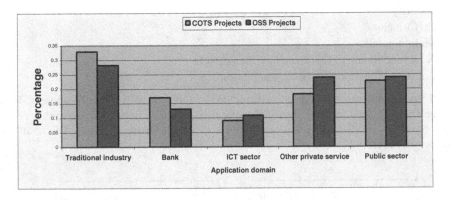

Fig. 1. Distribution of the application domain of the final system

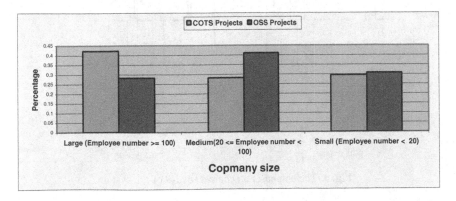

Fig. 2. Distribution of company size

For **RQ1.2**, we listed some possible characteristics of the actual system:

- Time-to-market
- Effort (cost)

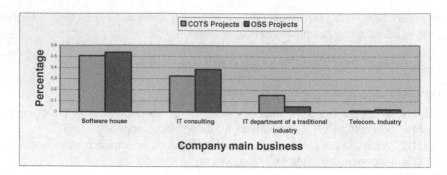

Fig. 3. Distribution of companies' main business areas

- Reliability
- Security
- Performance
- Maintainability
- New functionality (first launch in the market)
- Improved functionality (over competitors)

Respondents were asked to answer "don't agree at all", "hardly agree", "agree somewhat", "agree mostly", "strongly agree", or "don't know". We assign an ordinal number from 1 to 5 to the above alternatives (5 means strongly agree). The results are shown in Figure 4.

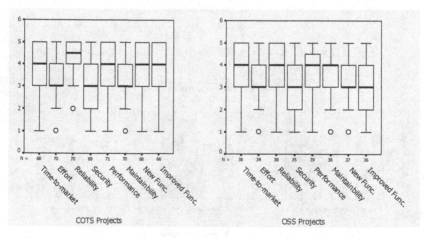

Fig. 4. The emphasis on characteristics of the system

To compare differences in the characteristics of the system, we compared the mean values of each characteristic in systems using COTS vs. systems using OSS. The results show that there is no significant difference. Answers to **RQ1** are summarized in Table 1.

Table 1. Answers to research question RQ1

Research question	Commonalities (COTS and OSS)	Differences (COTS vs. OSS)
RQ 1.1	Both are being used in systems of several application domains (see Figure 1).	No difference
RQ1.1	Both are being used in small, medium, and large IT companies (see Figure 2)	No difference
RQ 1.1	**Software house** and **IT consulting** companies are the main users (see Figure 3)	No difference
RQ 1.2	Both systems emphasis on **time-to-market**, **reliability**, and **performance** (see Figure 4)	No difference

4.2   Answers to RQ2 – Why Was It Decided to Use OTS Components?

To answer **RQ2**, we designed three sub-questions:

– **RQ2.1:** What were the differences of users' general expectations on COTS components vs. OSS components?
– **RQ2.2:** What were the specific motivations of using COTS components?
– **RQ2.3:** What were the specific motivations of using OSS components?

For **RQ2.1**, we gathered some common expectations of using OTS components from our pre-study [9] and from literature reviews [1][3]:

– Shorter time-to-market
– Less development effort/cost
– Less maintenance effort/cost
– Larger market share
– Compliance with industrial standards
– Keeping up with the newest technology
– Better system reliability
– Better system security
– Better system performance

We used the same format and measurement as **RQ1.2**. The results are shown in Figure 5.

We used SPSS 11.0 to compare the mean values of each motivation of using COTS vs. using OSS. The results show that there is no significant difference.

For **RQ2.2**, we gathered some specific motivations of using COTS components:

– Reduce risk of bad quality, because components were paid for
– Reduce risk of poor security, because source code was closed/unavailable
– Provider could give adequate technical support
– Provider may provide give components following market trends
– It was decided by customer
– Political reasons (company policy, licensing conditions)

The results of **RQ2.2** are shown in Figure 6.

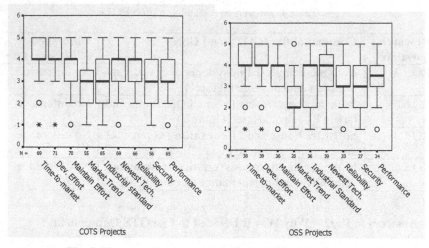

COTS Projects   OSS Projects

Fig. 5. The general expectations of using OTS components

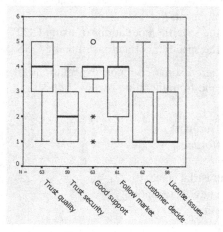

Fig. 6. Specific motivation of using COTS components

For **RQ2.3**, we gathered some specific motivations of using OSS components:

- Reduce risk of provider going out of business
- Reduce risk of provider changing market strategies
- Reduce risk of selected components evolving into an unwanted direction
- Component can be acquired for free
- Source code is available and can easily be changed
- It was decided by the customer
- Political reasons (company policy, licensing conditions)

The results of **RQ2.3** are shown in Figure 7.

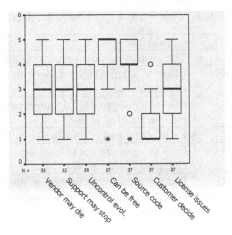

Fig. 7. Specific motivations of using OSS components

Answers to research question **RQ2** are summarized in Table 2.

Table 2. Answers to research question RQ2

Research question	Commonalities (COTS and OSS)	Differences (COTS vs. OSS)
RQ 2.1	Both COTS and OSS users expect that the components can contribute to shorter time-to-market, less development effort, less maintenance effort, and newest technology (see Figure 5)	No difference
RQ2.2	COTS users believe that paid software will give good quality and will follow market trends. They also believe that the COTS vendor will provide good technical support (see Figure 6).	
RQ 2.3	The main motivations of using OSS are that code could be acquired for free, source code is available, and to avoid the possible vendor support risk (see Figure 7).	

4.3 Answers to RQ3 – What Were the Results of Using OTS Components

To answer **RQ3**, we formulized 15 possible risks (as showed in Table 3) on OTS-based development.

We asked respondents to fill in whether these problems had actually happened in the investigated project or not. We used the same measurement as **RQ1.2**. The results are shown in Figure 8.

Table 3. Possible risks in OTS based development

Phase	ID	Possible risks
Project plan phase	R1	The project was delivered long after schedule [13].
	R2	Effort to select OTS components was not satisfactorily estimated [14].
	R3	Effort to integrate OTS components was not satisfactorily estimated [13].
Requirements Phase	R4	Requirement were changed a lot [14].
	R5	OTS components could not be sufficiently adapted to changing requirements [14].
	R6	It is not possible to (re)negotiate requirements with the customer, if OTS components could not satisfy all requirements [9].
Component integration phase	R7	OTS components negatively affected system reliability [4,16].
	R8	OTS components negatively affected system security [4, 15, 16].
	R9	OTS components negatively affected system performance [16].
	R10	OTS components were not satisfactorily compatible with the production environment when the system was deployed [16].
System maintenance and evolution	R11	It was difficult to identify whether defects were inside or outside the OTS components [14].
	R12	It was difficult to plan system maintenance, e.g. because different OTS components had asynchronous release cycles [13].
	R13	It was difficult to update the system with the last OTS component version [13].
Provider relationship management	R14	Provider did not provide enough technical support/ training [4, 13].
	R15	Information on the reputation and technical support ability of provider were inadequate [4, 13].

To compare differences, we compared the mean values of each risk in projects using COTS vs. projects using OSS. The significant results (P-value < 0.05) are shown in the following Table 4.

Answers to research question **RQ3** are summarized in Table 5.

Table 4. The mean differences of three risks between COTS projects and OSS projects (Independent Samples T-Test without considering equal variances)

Risk	Mean Difference(COTS - OSS)	Significance (2-tailed)
R2	0.54	0.033
R5	0.39	0.027
R8	0.50	0.014
R15	-0.56	0.033

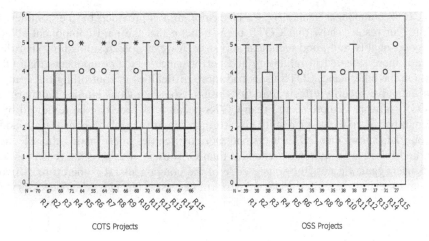

Fig. 8. Existing Problems in projects using COTS components vs. projects using OSS components

Table 5. Answers to research question RQ3

Research question	Commonalities (COTS and OSS)	Differences (COTS vs. OSS)
RQ 3	Common risk is that it is difficult to estimate the integration effort and to identify whether the defects are inside the component or outside.	COTS users had a higher risk on estimating the selection effort, following requirement changes, and controlling COTS components' negative effect on security. OSS users had a higher risk on getting the information of providers' support reputation.

5 Discussion

5.1 Comparison with Related Work

By analyzing all activities normally performed when integrating OTS components, Giacomo, P. D. concluded that the OSS component is not completely different from the COTS component [24]. Our results show that both COTS and OSS components were used in projects and companies with similar profiles. Software houses and IT consulting companies were their main users.

COTS and OSS components promise shorter time-to-market and increased productivity [1]. Some previous studies claim that OTS components are generally more reliable than in-house built components, because they have been used by different users in different environments. Our results confirm that both COTS and OSS components were used in projects with emphases on time-to-market, reliability, and performance. In addition, the key motivations of using OTS components were to save development time and effort, and to get newest technology.

A COTS component generally is a black-box and is provided by the commercial vendor. Our results show that COTS users believe that the paid component should have good quality and good technical support. However, our results show that they were not more satisfied in reliability and performance of the components than OSS users. On the other hand, COTS users had more difficulties in controlling the components' negative security effects than OSS users. Some previous studies have argued that OSS software is more secure than COTS because its code can be reviewed by a huge number of coders. Our results give further support on this conclusion. In addition, our data shows that COTS users had more difficulties in estimating the selection effort and following requirement changes than OSS users. The possible reason is that COTS users cannot access the source code of the components. It is therefore difficult for them to review the source code and perform necessary changes when necessary.

OSS components are generally provided by an open source community with source code. Our results show that the main motivation of using OSS components is the open and possible free code, which can be changed if necessary. Although OSS user did not have commercial support contract with OSS component providers, they were not less satisfied on the technical support than COTS users. However, we need to explain this fact carefully. The reason might be that OSS users would like to read and change the code themselves, instead of asking for help, as we found in the key motivations of using OSS.

Holck J. et al. concluded that a major barrier on using OSS in industrial project is the customer's uncertainty and unfamiliarity with OSS vendor relationship [23]. Our data showed that OSS users were less satisfied on knowing OSS provider's technical support reputation. How to establish credible and mutually acceptable combinations of OSS delivery and procurement models therefore needs future research.

5.2 Possible Treats to Validity

Construct validity. In this study, most variables and alternatives are taken directly, or with little modification, from existing literature. The questionnaire was pre-tested using a paper version by 10 internal experts and 8 industrial respondents. About 15% questions have been revised based on pre-test results.

Internal validity. We have promised respondents in this study a final report and a seminar to share experience. The respondents were persons who want to share their experience and want to learn from others. In general, we think that the respondents have answered truthfully.

Conclusion validity. This study is still on-going. More data will be collected from Germany and Italy. A slightly larger sample will be gathered to give more significant statistical support on the conclusions of this study.

External validity. We used different random selection strategies to select samples in different countries. It is because the limited availability of the necessary information. In Italy, the information of the official organization as a national "Census Bureau" in Norway and Germany is not available. The samples had to be selected from "yellow pages". The method problems by performing such a survey in three countries will be elaborated in a future paper. Another possible limitation is that our study focused on fine-grained OTS components. Conclusions may be different in projects using complex and large OTS products, such as ERP, Content management systems, and web service in general.

6 Conclusion and Future Work

This paper has presented preliminary results of a state-of-the practice survey on OTS-based development in industrial projects. The results of this study have answered three questions:

- **RQ1: Who is using OTS components?**
  Both COTS and OSS components were used in projects with similar profiles. There is also no difference on the profiles of companies using COTS or OSS components.

- **RQ2: Why was it decided to use OTS components?**
  The main motivation of using either COTS or OSS component was to get shorter time-to-market, less development effort, and to get newest technology. COTS users have bigger trust in the COTS quality and COTS vendor support ability. Possible free source code is the key motivation of OSS users. OSS users prefer to have access the source code so that they can revise it when necessary.

- **RQ3: What are the possible problems of using OTS components?**
  It was more difficult for COTS component users to follow requirement changes than OSS users. It is also more difficult for COTS users to estimate the selection effort and to control COTS components' negative effect on system security. OSS users were more uncertain on OSS provider support reputation than COTS users.

Results of this study have shown state-of-the-practice data. The next step is to do a follow up qualitative study to investigate the cause-effects of the conclusions of this study. We have held a seminar at OSLO in Feb. 2005 and preliminary investigated possible cause-effects of our results with participants of this study and other industrial colleagues. The next step is to do a larger qualitative study with personal interviews to further study these cause-effect assumptions.

Acknowledgements

This study was partially funded by the INCO (INcremental COmponent based development) project [17]. We thank the colleagues in these projects, and all the participants in the survey.

References

1. Voas, J.: COTS Software – the Economical Choice?. IEEE Software, 15(2):16-19, March/April 1998.
2. Voas, J.: The challenges of Using COTS Software in Component-Based Development. IEEE Computer, 31(6): 44-45, June 1998.
3. Fitzgerald, B.: A Critical Look at Open Source. IEEE Computer, 37(7):92-94, July 2004.

4. Ruffin, M. and Ebert, C.: Using Open Source Software in Product Development: A Primer. IEEE Software, 21(1):82-86, January/February 2004.
5. Brownsword, L., Oberndorf, T., and Sledge, C.: Developing New Processes for COTS-Based Systems. IEEE Software, 17(4):48-55, July/August 2000.
6. Lawlis, P. K., Mark, K. E., Thomas, D. A., and Courtheyn, T.: A Formal Process for Evaluating COTS Software Products. IEEE Computer, 34(5):58-63, May 2001.
7. SSB (Norwegian Census Bureau) (2004): http://www.ssb.no
8. SESE web tool (2004): http://sese.simula.no
9. Li, J., Bjørnson, F. O., Conradi, R., and Kampenes, V. B.: An Empirical Study of Variations in COTS-based Software Development Processes in Norwegian IT Industry. Proc. of the 10th IEEE International Metrics Symposium, Chicago, USA, September, 2004, IEEE CS Press (2004) 72-83.
10. Paulson, J.W., Succi, G. and Eberlein, A.: An empirical study of open-source and closed-source software products. IEEE Transactions on Software Engineering, 30(4):246-256, April 2004.
11. Norris, J. S.:Missioin-Critical Development with Open Source Software", IEEE Software, 21(1):42-49, January/February 2004.
12. Fitzgerald, B. and Kenny, T.: Developing an Information Systems Infrastructure with Open Source Software. IEEE Software, 21(1):50-55, January/February 2004.
13. Rose, L. C.: Risk Management of COTS based System development. Cechich, A., Piattini, M., Vallecillo, A. (Eds.): Component-Based Software Quality - Methods and Techniques. LNCS Vol. 2693. Springer-Verlag, Berlin Heidelberg New York (2003) 352-373.
14. Boehm, B. W., Port, D., Yang, Y., and Bhuta, J.: Not All CBS Are Created Equally COTS-intensive Project Types. Proc. of the 2nd International Conference on COTS-Based Software Systems. Ottawa, Canada, February, 2003, LNCS Vol. 2580. Springer-Verlag, Berlin Heidelberg New York (2003) 36-50.
15. Open Source Initiative (2004): http://www.opensource.org/index.php
16. Padmal Vitharana: Risks and Challenges of Component-Based Software Development. Communications of the ACM, 46(8):67-72, August 2003.
17. INCO project description, 2000, http://www.ifi.uio.no/~isu/INCO
18. Stevens, S.S: Mathematics, Measurement, and Psychophysics. In S.S.Stevens (Ed.) Handbook of Experimental Psychology (1951), New York: Wiley.
19. Stevens, S.S: On the Theory of Scales of Measurement, Vol. 103. Science (1946) 677-680.
20. Spector, P.: Ratings of Equal and Unequal Response Choice Intervals. Journal of Social Psychology (1980), Vol. 112:115-119.
21. Velleman, P. F. and Wilkinson L.: Nominal, Ordinal, Interval, and Ratio Typologies Are Misleading. Journal of the American Statistician, 47(1):65-72, February 1993.
22. Hand, D.J.: Statistics and Theory of Measurement. Journal of the Royal Statistical Society: Series A (Statistics in Society), 159(3): 445-492, 1996.
23. Holck J., Larsen, M. H., and Pedersen, M. K.: Managerial and Technical Barriers to the Adoption of Open Source Software. Proc. of the 4th International Conference on COTS-Based Software Systems. Bilbo, Spain, February, 2005, LNCS Vol. 3412. Springer-Verlag, Berlin Heidelberg New York (2005) 289-300.
24. Giacomo, P. D.: COTS and Open Source Software Components: Are They Really Different on the Battlefield? Proc. of the 4th International Conference on COTS-Based Software Systems. Bilbo, Spain, February, 2005, Vol. 3412. Springer-Verlag, Berlin Heidelberg New York (2005) 301-310.

A Rendezvous of Content Adaptable Service and Product Line Modeling[*]

Seo Jeong Lee[1] and Soo Dong Kim[2]

[1] Division of Information Technology Engineering, Korea Maritime University
1 Dongsam-Dong, Yeongdo-Gu, Busan, Korea 606-791
sjlee815@ssu.ac.kr
[2] Department of Computer Science, Soongsil University,
1-1 Sangdo-Dong, Dongjak-Ku, Seoul, Korea 156-743
sdkim@comp.ssu.ac.kr

Abstract. Content adaptable applications are often used in ubiquitous computing environment, and it aims to service the adaptable contents to users. In this environment, the services are dynamically selected and provided, the contexts are changed frequently. Then, the application services are to be modeled to derive the adaptable service effectively and to reuse the model. Modeling with software features and product line concepts may support for making service decision strategy. In this paper, we propose a service decision modeling technique for content adaptable applications in ubiquitous environment. It consists of defining variation points and their variants, finding out the dependencies between them, and then building the variant selection strategies. These can accomplish to define the decision model based on content adaptable service, and the definition templates help the reuse more effective.

1 Introduction

In the age of ubiquitous computing, computing devices and information are everywhere and user has multiple ways of accessing and exploiting them. So, the developers must consider relevant features which are for context awareness, location awareness, self adaptation and decision capability.

In such environments, a device can vary from a workstation, to a mobile phone, a PDA or any other limited terminal. Moreover these devices are likely to be heterogeneous, requiring special considerations in terms of their physical resources and computing power. The problem in these environments is to deliver a content understandable service by the end user.

To respond efficiently to the heterogeneity of the environment, multimedia systems must dispose of advantage mechanisms that allow adapting services according to users' interests and capabilities. These mechanisms must be capable to negotiate the best document variant if it exists but also to negotiate the best adaptation to apply on the original document in order to meet the client requirements. In this context, a good

[*] "This work was supported by Korea Research Foundation Grant. (KRF-2004-005-D00172)".

description of: the user (its preferences and the used device capabilities), the server (its content and adaptation capabilities) and the network play a major role to make the final delivered service well adapted to the end user.

The content adaptability is another important issue for this environment. This can serve an adaptable content on the fly so that the application has to the strategies to decide the appropriate service. These services have to be predefined and modeled. If well defined and modeled, they can be reused for another application which has same objective or same concern. And to support the reuse issue, it has to be modeled more systematic. The reuse of service means the reuse of service decision strategy. As a result, the service decision model is needed. The issue of how to specify the service is becoming interesting theme recently.

Michalis Anastasopoulos took his effort to illustrate how pervasive computing applications can benefit from a software product line approach and especially from the PuLSE™ (Product Line Software Engineering) method, which was developed at the Fraunhofer Institute for Experimental Software Engineering (IESE) [1].

Besides, by adopting an architecture-based approach, [2] provides reusable infrastructure together with mechanisms for specializing that infrastructure to the needs of specific systems. Some researchers suggest frameworks that facilitate the development and deployment of web services aware, respectively [3] [4]. So far, the attention of web service is now being directed as how to resolve the context awareness not how to define the strategy and reuse. They suggest reasonable concepts or architecture even though the modeling techniques or processes are not embodied yet.

The product line engineering concept is introduced to practice a dependable low-risk high-payoff practice that combines the necessary business and technical approaches to achieve success [5]. Variation point and variant are the core concept of product line. In [6], the authors took their effort for describing the taxonomy of variability dependencies and the types of variability dependencies. This concept can be useful for establish the decision process of web based application.

In this research, we suggest the process model of service decision for content adaptable application. This model is using product line concept such as variation points, variants and dependency.

Section 2 describes the related works, section 3 introduces our suggestion, section 4 shows the framework to support proposed model and section 5 assesses our challenges and contributions.

2   Related Works

2.1   Variability of Pervasive Computing with PuLSE

IESE(Institut Experimentelles Software Engineering) illustrates how pervasive computing applications can benefit from a software product line approach and especially from PuLSE (Product Line Software Engineering) method. It discusses the variability in pervasive computing [1].

This is based on that Human-centric character of pervasive software development requires dealing with ever-increasing variability at different stages of the software life cycle and ultimately at run-time [7]. And, then it works to customize a pervasive software application means customizing the other four fundamental forces of pervasive computing as envisioned by Michael Dertouzos [8]: Natural interaction, automation, individualized information access and collaboration. The variability in these areas is no doubt significant as shown exemplarily in the table 1.

Table 1. Pervasive Computing Variability

Capability	Variability
Natural Interaction	☐ Language ☐ Accessibility features
Automation	☐ Levels of automation ☐ Information Models ☐ Semantics ☐ Network quality
Individualized Information Access	☐ User Profile ☐ User Interest ☐ User Location ☐ User Device/Platform
Collaboration	☐ Synchronous collaboration ☐ Asynchronous collaboration ☐ People to People collaboration ☐ People to Machine collaboration ☐ Machine to Machine collaboration

This research illustrates merely the variability and how to use PuLSE^{TM}, not how to handle explicitly yet. When transformations occur between a Platform-Independent Model (PIM) and a Platform-Specific Model (PSM), the synchronization is performed for data mobility. This idea is to be valuable for resolving variability.

2.2 Dependency Decision Model

Binding a variation point involves establishing a relationship between the variation point and the selected variant. This relationship may imply certain dependencies (constraints), e.g., a system generally requires that specific variation points are bound to have a working, minimal system. There can be many different types of dependencies and pinpointing them requires a more formal way to describe variability [6].

The following nomenclature aims for describing variability in system-independent terms, i.e., independent from a particular system, method or organization:

- The set of all variation points: $VP = \{vp_a, vp_b, vp_c, \ldots\}$
- The set of variants for vpx: $vpx = \{vx_1, vx_2, vx_3, \ldots\}$
- The power set (the set of subsets) of all variants:
  $$V = \{\{va_1, va_2, va_3, \ldots\}, \{vb_1, vb_2, vb_3, \ldots\}, \{vc_1, vc_2, vc_3, \ldots\}, \ldots\}$$
- A relationship between vpx and vx_n, i.e., vpx binds vx_n: (vpx, vx_n)

The dependencies between variation points and variants can be expressed in the form of conditional expressions:

- if vp_x is bound then vp_y should be bound: **if** vp_x **then** vp_y
- if vp_x is bound then vp_y should bind v_{yn}: **if** vp_x **then** (vp_y, v_{yn})
- if vp_x binds v_{xn} then vp_y should be bound: **if** (vp_x, v_{xn}) **then** vp_y
- if vp_x binds v_{xn} then vp_y should bind vy_m: **if** (vp_x, v_{xn}) **then** (vp_y, v_{ym})
- if vp_x binds v_{xn} then vp_y should not bind v_{ym} : **if** (vp_x, v_{xn}) **then not** (vp_y, v_{ym}).

Then the taxonomy shows sixteen different subtypes of variability in table 2.

Table 2. The taxanomy of variability

Type	Description	Subtypes
I	Dependencies between variation points vp_x and vp_y	**if** vp_x **then** vp_y **if** vp_x **then** $\neg vp_y$ **if** $\neg vp_x$ **then** vp_y **if** $\neg vp_x$ **then** $\neg vp_y$
II	Dependencies between variation point vp_x and variant v_{yn}	**if** vp_x **then** (vp_y, v_{yn}) **if** vp_x **then** $\neg(vp_y, v_{yn})$ **if** $\neg vp_x$ **then** (vp_y, v_{yn}) **if** $\neg vp_x$ **then** $\neg(vp_y, v_{yn})$
III	Dependencies between variant v_{xn} and variation point vp_y	**if** (vp_x, v_{xn}) **then** vp_y **if** (vp_x, v_{xn}) **then** $\neg vp_y$ **if** $\neg(vp_x, v_{xn})$ **then** vp_y **if** $\neg(vp_x, v_{xn})$ **then** $\neg vp_y$
IV	Dependencies between variants v_{xn} and v_{ym}	**if** (vp_x, v_{xn}) **then** (vp_y, v_{ym}) **if** (vp_x, v_{xn}) **then** $\neg(vp_y, v_{ym})$ **if** $\neg(vp_x, v_{xn})$ **then** (vp_y, v_{ym}) **if** $\neg(vp_x, v_{xn})$ **then** $\neg(vp_y, v_{ym})$

These sixteen subtypes may explain why dependencies often exhibit different kinds of behavior while appearing similar in the first instance. The constraints imposed by each type have been explored in various areas of research, e.g., the configuration management community, however implicit specification may bother adopting to realize.

3   Content Adaptable Service Decision Modeling

This paper tries to the rendezvous of content adaptable service and product line modeling. To do so, we found the coincident point of them. Figure 1 shows them, where the bi-directional arrows mean the coincidence between two parts. If a service is to be the product of this system, the critical point for service, like 'bandwidth', is to be a variation point and its value is one of variants, and then the 'network' is to be a functional feature.

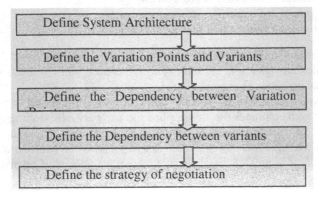

Fig. 1. The Content Adaptable Service Decision Process

This chapter suggests a process model for content adaptable service. As in figure 4, the process consists of 5 activities, and each activity is further defined in subsequent sections.

3.1 Define System Architecture

The first activity is 'Define System Architecture'. The content adaptable system architecture has useful handling mechanisms for efficient exchange of request and data between different mobile devices. Therefore, the architecture has to support the properties of web application, pervasive computing.

Web applications are most often used in a request/response interactive way. The message is service-oriented. So, web application architecture should identify who or which component is responsible for:

- providing service
- request service
- description where service providers publish their service descriptions
- description where service requestors find services and how to binding

Then, the web applications contain the following functions for their services [9].

- Service Registration
- Service Discovery
- Service Interface
- Definition Repository
- Publication
- Service Binding
- Authentication
- Authorization
- Functions
- Load balancing support
- Fault-tolerance support

For pervasive applications, the inadequacy of existing distributed systems raises the question of how to structure system support since the following requirements: [10]

- Requirement 1: Embrace contextual change
- Requirement 2: Encourage ad hoc composition
- Requirement 3: Recognize sharing as the default

The services which directly address the requirements are needed to design. So, the system designer has take into account relevant concerns [11] which are integrated functional considerations above mentioned.

Table 3 is the template to specify the concerns of content adaptable system architecture, which embraces the web application and pervasive computing.

If the architecture has the way to resolve the concern, *If exist, who resolve it* may be written down by the resolving component(s) such as behavioral elements or service. *If not, how to resolve* may be written down by the way of resolving.

Table 3. Architecture Definition Concerns

Concern	If exist, who resolves it?	If not, how to resolve?
Handling Request input authorization request verification		
Registration new Service		
Creating Service find strategy retrieve service		
Binding at run time		
Publishing Service		
Providing Application Specific functions		
Adapting Contextual change		
Conventional network architecture concerns load balancing fault tolerance authentication		

3.2 Define Variation Points and Variants

The context in ubiquitous computing consists of the profile of network, device, service, user and so on [12]. They are presenting current or changeable context and then used for service decision which is context aware and content adaptable. Let's get a scenario. "If the bandwidth is lower than 2.4GHz, service is not available." In this case, 'bandwidth' is the critical point for service and the value of bandwidth means the margin of service.

In this paper, we consider network status, device status, service commitment, avail data status and user bias as functional features, though there are potentially additional functional features. Network status contains the information of the physical transmission ability. Device status represents which device type, how much memory is remained, how fast the processor, and so on. Service commitment describes that any user can take any service in some location. Avail data status describes the hardware requirement and data properties. And, users can specify their own preference on user bias.

The functional feature is composed of some variation points, but not limited:

- Network status = (protocol, bandwidth, latency)
- Device status=(device_type,available_memory, processor_speed, color_depth)
- Service commitment=(user_id, location, device_type)
- Avail data status=(data_type, scaled_depth , memory_request, bandwidth_ request, latency_tolerance, speed_request, [language| color_depth])
- User bias=(language, response_time, text_bias, image_bias, video_bias, location)

Using set notation, these can be represented as:

N ={ni | 1<=i<=j}, n represents the variation point of network status
D ={di | 1<=i<=k}, m represents the variation point of device status
S ={si | 1<=i<=l}, s represents the variation point of service commitment
A ={ai | 1<=i<=m}, a represents the variation point of avail data status
U ={ui | 1<=i<=n}, u represents the variation point of user bias

The graphic notation is often used to set up or understand the model easier. Figure 2 represents the notations for dependency. Notations for feature, variation point and variant are from COVAMOF [13], and compose_of_vp, depends_on_vp and depends_on_variant are introduced in this paper newly. And then Figure 3 shows that the feature model is composed of several variation points and can be extended.

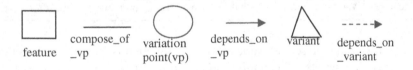

Fig. 2. Notations for Representing Dependency

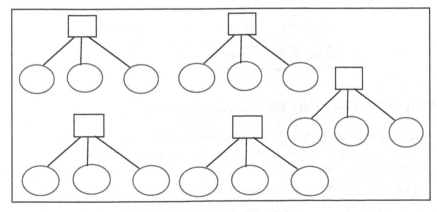

Fig. 3. Features and Variation Points

To present the variant, it has to be identified which type the variant is, such as character, string, integer, float, or user defined object type; and whether it is one element of a set or a value in some range. This paper differentiates them from each other.

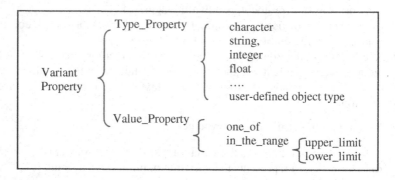

Table 4 is the template which can reveal the properties as mentioned. Each feature has several variation points and their variant type. Table 4 (a) has five columns of the *feature, variation point, data_type, value_property* and *depends_on_vp*. The *depends_on_vp* is written down with which variant affect to decide current variation point. This will be filled in section 3.3.

Table 4(a). Template for Variation Point and Variant

feature	variation point(vp)	data_type	value_property	depends_on_vp

Table 4 (b) can represent all variants of each variation point which is described in table 4 (a). It consists of *variation point, variant* and *depends_on_variant*. The *depends_on_variant* is written down with which variant affect to decide current variant. This will be filled in section 3.4.

Table 4(b). Template for Looking-up Variants

variation point	variant	depends_on_variant

3.3 Define the Dependency Between Variation Points

This section is to define the dependency between variation points. The dependency means a relation that a variation point effects to decide another variation points.

Figure 4 is an example of define the dependency between variation points. Here, "n_1 *depends_on_vp*($\rightarrow$) s_1" means that decision of n_1 is dependent to decision of s_1.

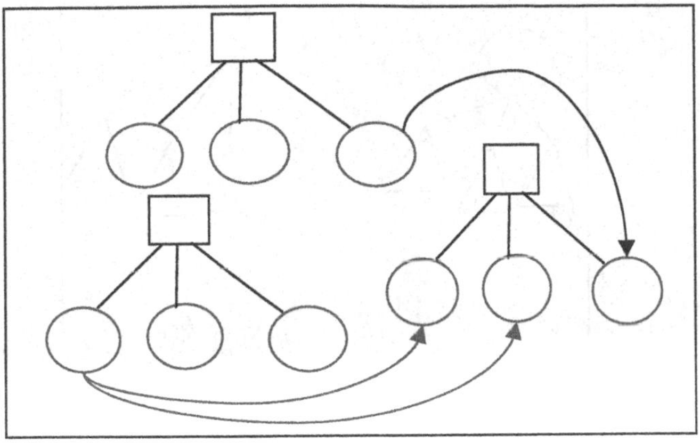

Fig. 4. Dependency between Variation Points

There are guidelines to define as following:

- A variation point can *depends on* (→) one or more variation point(s).
- $n_1 \rightarrow s_1$ and $n_1 \rightarrow s_2$ is possible.
- One or more variation point(s) can *depends on* (→) one variation point.
- $n_1 \rightarrow s_1$ and $n_2 \rightarrow s_1$ is possible.
- Some variation points may not *depends on* (→) any variation point.
- No dependency
- It is not allowed that a variation point *depends on* (→) itself.
- $n_1 \rightarrow n_1$ is not possible.

This dependency information can be used to fill up *depends_on_vp* of feature N in table 4 (a).

3.4 Define the Dependency Between Variants

In some cases, a specific variant may affect to decide another variant, so it can fix other variant's value or exclude other variant. It is called the dependency between variants [6]. This section introduces to define it.

The dependency between variants is a relation that a variation point effects to decide another variation points. Figure 5 is an example of define the dependency between variants. Here, "$n_{1.1}$ *depends_on_variant* (⇠) $s_{1.1}$" means that decision of $n_{1.1}$ is dependent to decision of $s_{1.1}$.

There are guidelines to define as following and table 6 shows the subpart of filling up *depends_on_variant* based on figure 5.

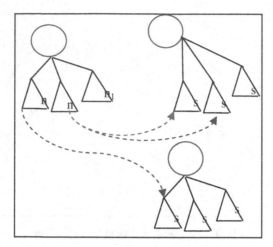

Fig. 5. The Dependency between Variants

- All variation points are composed of one more variants
- If no variant, it supports not variability.
- All variants have their own *data_type* and *value_properties*.
- Described in section 3.3
- If dependency between 2 variation points, at least one variant in a variation point should *depends_on_variant* (-- -▶) one variant in the other variation point.
- For example, if n_1 ⟶ s_1 then at least, $n_{1.x}$ -- ▶ $s_{1.y}$ should be.
- A variant can *depends_on_variant* (__▶) one more variation point(s).
- $n_{1.2}$ -- ▶ $s_{2.1}$ and $n_{1.2}$ -- ▶ $s_{2.2}$ is possible.
- Two more variant can *depends_on_variant* (-▶) one variant.
- $n_{1.1}$ -- ▶ $s_{1.1}$ and $n_{2.1}$ -- ▶ $s_{1.1}$ is possible.
- Some variants may not *depends_on_variant* (-▶) any variant.
- No dependency
- It is not allowed that a variant *depends on_variant* (-▶) itself.
- $n_{1.1}$ -- ▶ $n_{1.1}$ is not possible.

This dependency information can be used to fill up *depends_on_variant* of feature N in table 4 (b).

3.5 Define the Strategy of Negotiation

The dependency between variations represents just whether one variation point affects to another variation point. It is similar to variants. To service the content adaptable, the decision to select content has to be performed, called negotiation [12].

The strategy of negotiation is dependent on domain, service and application, so in this section, we introduce the basic guidelines for successful definition.

- Every *depends on* (➝) should be defined by one more strategies
- Every *depends on_variant* (--➤) should be defined by one more strategies
- The decision value of strategy should be *one_of* or *in_the_range_of* variants value

These can be potentially additional.

3.6 Select Adequate Algorithm and Module

The last activity is to select adequate algorithms, which is self adaptable. And then, adequate module for that algorithm is selected. It can be not merely imported existing, but also implement newly. In both cases, these modules may imply common properties such as:

- to freeze hardware environment in the moment
- to capture current context and required context
- to find out adequate content service
- to send the service to client device

For example, [14] suggests a QoS-based selection algorithm that find the best sequence of adaptation services which can maximize users' satisfaction with the delivered content. And, [15] describes a context modeling approach with context modeling language (CML) and suggests a programming library to support automatic development.

4 Case Study

In order to realize the proposed process in section 3, we propose a problem statement and follow activities.

Problem statement: Executive Information System (EIS) in motion

EIS in motion provides executives with a powerful, yet simple tool that allows them to view and analyze key factors and performance trends in the areas of sales, purchasing, production, and finance. It is developed for all main mobile platforms, such as Windows CE, J2ME, Symbian and Palm. The wireless communication plays with using both WLAN and Bluetooth.

Otherwise, *EIS in motion* has the properties to provide the content-adaptable service so that executives can be serviced continuously in spite of hardware context change from laptop to PDA.

Activity 1. Define System Architecture
To support the content adaptable service, system architecture may be composed of Presentation layer, Service layer, Data layer and Communication layer. Presentation layer consists of device adapter, network adapter and content publisher. Service layer

consists of strategy adopter, content finder and service binder. Communication layer is made up of protocol manager and platform manager.

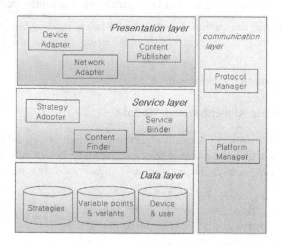

Fig. 6. System Architecture for *EIS in motion*

Composite elements of each layer can be tailored and customized.

Activity 2 and 3. Define variation points and their dependency
Table 8 shows an example of the variation points and their zero or more *depends_on_vp* s.

Table 8. Template for Variation Point and Variant

Feature	variation point(vp)	data_type	value_property	Depends_on_vp
Network (N)	Bandwidth(n_1) Network_type(n_2)	real string	in_the_range_of one_of	
Device (D)	resolution(d_1) Available_memory(d_2)	object_type real	one_of in_the_range_of	
User bias (U)	Vedeo_bias(u_1) Response_time(u_2)	object type real	one_of in_the_range_of	n_2, d_1, d_2 n_1, n_2

Activity 2 and 4. Define the dependency between variants
Table 9 is a part of an example of the *depends_on_variant* with which variant affect to decide current variant.

Activity 5. Define the strategy of negotiation
Define the strategies of negotiation for all dependency which is described in table8 and table 9. For example,

• S1. *Vedeo_bias*(u_1) of *User bias*(U) is to be less than *Available_memory*(d_2).

Activity 6. Select adequate algorithms and modules

Table 9. Template for Looking-up Variants

variation point	Variant(s)	Depends_on_variant
Bandwidth(n_1)	(real value)	- (none)
Network_type(n_2)	T1($n_{2.1}$)	-
	Bluetooth($n_{2.2}$)	-
	LAN($n_{2.3}$)	-
resolution(d_1)	Mobile1($d_{1.1}$)	-
	Laptop1($d_{1.2}$)	-
Available_memory(d_2)	(real value)	-
Image_bias(u_1)	Vbias1($u_{1.1}$)	$d_{1.1}$
	Vbias1($u_{1.2}$)	$d_{1.2}$
Response_time(u_2)	(real value)	-

As specified in section 3.6, it is the realization activity for finding or building algorithms to make the service realizable.

5 Assessment

Recently, the ubiquitous and pervasive computing is becoming comprehensive. On various devices and network circumstance, the content adaptable service is to be a critical issue.

Perceiving context, adopting appropriate strategy and initiating contents are key processes to make that service. To do these, we have to consider which context factor affects to select content or decide a strategy and whether any relation is found between the factors. If a model can describe them systemically, it would be able to reuse not only model itself but also framework and their components.

This model is to resolve it with product line concepts such as variation point, variant and dependency. This section assesses the contributions of our research.

5.1 Adapting Product Line Concept to Ubiquitous Environment

The product line engineering and dependency is useful for adjusting variability of a product family. The content adaptable service is deciding appropriate one among all available services. This model inoculates these two concepts.

And the templates are useful for represent the dependencies between variation points or variants, instead of describing just with XML or graph. The more complicated the dependency, the more effective the templates in this paper as a tool of expression

5.2 Systematic Decision Strategy

As a result of inoculating product line concept and content adaptable service modeling, we can define factors and properties for deciding service with product line concepts, such as variation points, variant and the dependencies between them. As using them, defining decision strategy would be more complete. And, the guidelines to define them help this model more systematic.

5.3 Reuse Decision Model

This decision model specifies the process from defining architecture concern to defining strategies in detail. So, it can be reused when working upon different requirement in terms of system concern, variation points, variants, dependencies or even though deciding strategies.

6 Conclusion

Context awareness is an important issue in ubiquitous computing. We proposed a service decision modeling method for content adaptable service. It is based on product line concepts such as variation point, variant and dependency. The process consists of defining system architecture, defining variation points and variants, defining the dependency between variation points, defining the dependency between variants, and defining the strategy of negotiation.

We also introduced a specific modeling method for content adaptable service and it can bring about defining decision strategy systematically. The concept of product line helps to specify the model systematically. Otherwise, it can be reused when working upon different requirements. And the more complicated the dependency, the more effective the templates in this paper as a tool of expression.

References

1. Michalis Anastasopoulos, "Software Product Lines for Pervasive Computing," *IESE-Report No. 044.04/E version 1.0*, IESE, April 2004.
2. Robert Grimm, Tom Anderson, Brian Bershad, and David Wetherall, "A System Architecture for Pervasive Computing," *Proceedings of the 9th ACM SIGOPS European Workshop*, pages 177-182, September 2000.
3. Tayeb Lemlouma and Nabil Layaïda, "Context-Aware Adaptation for Mobile Devices," *Proceedings of International Conference on Mobile Data Management (MDM)*, IEEE, January 2004.
4. Markus Keidl and Alfons Kemper, "Towards Context-Aware Adaptable Web Services," *Proceedings of World Wide Web (WWW'04)*, ACM, pages 55-65, 2004.
5. Paul Clements and Linda Northrop, Software Product Lines, Practices and Patterns, Addison-Wesley, 2002.
6. Michel Jaring and Jan Bosch, "Variability Dependencies in Product Family Engineering," *Product Family Engineering(PFE) 2003*, pages 81-97, 2003.
7. http://oxygen.lcs.mit.edu/Overview.html, Homepage of the MIT Project Oxygen
8. Dertouzos, Michael L. The Unfinished Revolution: How to Make Technology Work for Us-Instead of the Other Way Around, HarperCollins Publishers, October 2002.
9. G. Di Caprio, C. Moiso, "Parlay Web Services Architecture Comparison," *EXP online*, Vol. 3, Num. 4, December 2003.
10. Robert Grimm et. al, "System Support for Pervasive Applications," *ACM transactions on Computer Systems*, Vol.22, No.4, pages 421-486, November 2004.

11. David Garlan, Shang-Wen Cheng, An-Cheng Huang, Bradley Schmerl and Peter Steenkiste, "Rainbow: Architecture-based Self-Adaptation with Reusable Infrastructure," *Computer*, IEEE, pages 46-54, April 2004.
12. Girma Berhe, Lionel Brunie and Jean-Marc Pierson, "Modeling Service-Based Multimedia Content Adaptation in Pervasive Computing," *Proceedings of ACM International Conference on Computing Frontiers (CF'04)*, ACM, April 2004.
13. Marco Sinnema, Sybren Deelstra, Jos Nijhuis and Jan Bosch, "COVAMOF: A Framework for Modeling Variability in Software Product Families," *The Third Software Product Line Conference (SPLC)*, LNCS 3154, pages 197-213, 2004.
14. 14.K. El-Khatib, G. v. Bochmann, and A. El Saddik, "A QoS-Based Framework for Distributed Content Adaptation", *First IEEE International Conference on Quality of Service in Heterogeneous Wired/Wireless Networks*, Oct. 2004.
15. Ted McFadden and Karen Henricksen, "Automating Contextaware Application Development," *2004 International Conference on Cyberworlds*, Nov. 2004

A Framework for Linking Projects and Project Management Methods

Tony Dale, Neville Churcher, and Warwick Irwin

Software Engineering and Visualisation Group,
Computer Science and Software Engineering Department,
University of Canterbury
{Tony.Dale, Neville.Churcher, Warwick.Irwin}@canterbury.ac.nz
http://www.cosc.canterbury.ac.nz/research/RG/svg/index.html

Abstract. Software development processes such as the Waterfall process and Extreme Programming are project management methods (PMMs) which are well known and widely used. However, conventional project management (PM) lacks the process concepts expressed in PMMs, and the connection between PMMs and PM is not much explored in the literature.

We present data models for PM and PMM, in a framework that can articulate the PM–to–PMM relationship, illustrating with simple examples. A java/XML implementation of this framework can create and then revise a "PMM–aware" project, conforming to a specified PMM. In terms of the framework, we describe a simple project data visualization and associated method that can be used to synthesize a PMM for a project instance that was initially created without reference to any PMM.

Keywords: Project management, software engineering, project management methods, project processes, data modelling, XML, visualization.

1 Introduction

Conventional PM attempts to manage tasks and resources as closely as possible to a predefined, static plan.

However, a project plan doesn't indicate how its particular tasks or resources were created, except perhaps for a textual description. This is because the PM domain has no concept of why a task or resource appears in the plan. PMMs have this descriptive power because they use process concepts to formalise the specialist knowledge which any real project requires; when creating or changing. a project plan. Applying PMMs and process concepts to conventional PM creates a fundamental problem: PMMs dynamically change projects, but conventional PM is static, and has difficulty tolerating change.

It is possible to create data models for both PM and PMMs, and to link these models together in a unified framework. This framework has the power to express complicated PMM ideas but is simple and logical to apply to PM data: project tasks and resources have PMM concepts added to them as simple

F. Bomarius and S. Komi-Sirviö (Eds.): PROFES 2005, LNCS 3547, pp. 84–97, 2005.

attributes, for example. This strategy makes it possible to move backwards and forwards between the PM and PMM domains, so that a project can be created and changed according to a PMM, yet viewed with existing PM software tools.

The motivation for creating this framework is to provide a bridge between the process–dominated world of PMMs and the plan–dominated world of PM. We hope to encourage the more widespread use of process concepts and PMMs in conventional PM, and to augment PMMs with the project history and context available using conventional PM tools.

The rest of the paper is set out as follows: Section 2 introduces concepts of conventional project management (PM) as it is widely practised, and introduces a data model for PM software tools. We show in Sect. 3 how the specialist knowledge that all projects make use of can be formalized as a Project Management Method (PMM), and create a data model for describing PMMs in Sect. 4. In Sect. 5 we create a framework for linking the PM and PMM data models, and using this framework Sect. 6 illustrates how a PMM is applied to produce a project instance. Section 7 uses the framework to create a simple visualization and a heuristic method to derive a PMM from raw project data, and illustrates a scenario for applying process improvement to the derived PMM. Section 8 concludes our discussion.

2   Background

Large–scale project management has been practised for centuries, to the extent that Burbridge [1] says

> one hallmark of civilization is the ability to engage in group activities for the execution of major projects, be they tombs and temples or manned flights into space.

A crucial change has been, from the 19th century onwards, the increasing importance of time and cost in project management. Projects must be completed on time and within budget, according to comprehensive project plans, for reasons such as increasing company profitability or reducing expenditure of public funds. Unfortunately, the failure rate of projects in certain fields such as Software Engineering is very high, with the Standish Group reporting in 2001 that only 28% of IT projects completed on time and within budget [2], although this is an increase from the 16% of 1994 [3]. There is thus a motivation to provide more powerful tools for project management.

Conventional project management is encapsulated in the following five steps, as exemplified by Lewis [4]:

1. define the problem
2. plan the project
3. execute the plan
4. monitor and control progress against the plan
5. close the project.

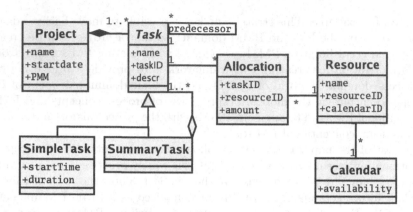

Fig. 1. A conceptual data model of conventional PM data: a project is made up of Tasks, Resources and Allocations of tasks to resources

These steps provide a simple framework for creating and executing projects using a static, unchanging plan. Such a plan can be produced from a template that has been predefined for a particular goal. For example: Microsoft Project [5] provides a template for software development. Carefully filling in this template will result in a project plan for developing software that looks quite plausible. However, there is no indication whether the project is a sure–fire success or doomed from the start, and nothing to tell us what to do if the actual progress begins to deviate from the plan. This is not a problem specific to Microsoft Project: the problem is with the domain of conventional PM in which this software tool works. Conventional PM lacks the capability to say why the tasks and resources in the Microsoft Project templates are there, except with textual descriptions. We cannot say what created the templates, or compare them. This lack of descriptive ability is one of several reasons that change in a project plan is regarded as a bad thing by conventional PM, and uncontrolled change in a project is identified as a major cause of many software project disasters [6][7][8].

Once a project is started, conventional Project Management is concerned with monitoring the progress of a project using various well–known methods to measure and report on the project, such as the Critical Path method, Gantt charts, Network charts and Earned Value Analysis. These are all methods aimed at keeping the progress of a project as close as possible to a static, pre–defined plan.

Project Management software such as Microsoft Project and Planner [9] support the management and measurement of conventional PM, and provide templates for project plans. PM software tends to be variations on a theme, so that Gray [10] writes of PM software tools: "Differences among [PM] software in the last decade have centered on improving 'friendliness' and output that is clear and easy to understand."

Each tool has its own data format, but there are common features so that, for example: Microsoft Project and Planner can exchange data using XML. Analysis

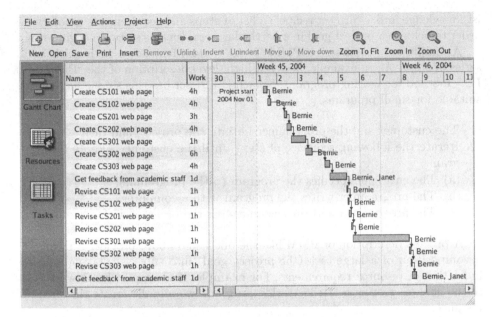

Fig. 2. A conventional PM view of a project: the free software tool Planner is illustrating project data, as modelled in Fig. 1, with a Gantt [13] chart

of the facilities and data models used for a number of project tools, including Microsoft Project, the freeware tools Planner and PyGantt [11] and the public XML schema PMXML [12] shows that their data models reflect and record tasks, resources and allocations of resources to tasks. This data model is summarized in a conceptual way in Fig. 1. Figure 2 instantiates this data model, and shows a typical view of a project presented by conventional PM tools.

3 Project Management Methods (PMMs)

Any real project occurs in a specialist domain of some kind, whether it is bridge construction, software engineering or a company restructuring. A real project therefore requires specialist knowledge to inform the planning and implementation process. For example: estimating the time a particular task will take requires specialist knowledge of the work involved in the task.

Conventional PM has little to say about how to use this specialist knowledge in a project: conventional PM methods for representing and applying specialist project knowledge stop at the the use of predefined project templates, and the advice Lewis offers for task estimating is that you will get better at it as you do more of it. Often, specialist knowledge is applied to a project in an informal way, using whatever skills a project manager may bring to bear.

Specialist project knowledge can be formally described and applied using a Project Management Method (PMM). A PMM is a notation for turning specialist knowledge into a "project recipe": a list of steps and requirements to follow in order to achieve a project goal in a particular area, such as software engineering.

A simple way to describe PMMs is to write them down in English as a series of steps. As an example, here is a high–level description of the "Build and Fix" method for writing programs. Schach [14] describes this simple method as suitable for small programs.

1. The customer and the programmer initiate the project, and then
2. Iterate the following sequence of steps until the customer accepts the program:
   (a) The customer specifies the program to the programmer
   (b) The programmer writes the program with a computer
   (c) The programmer and the customer test the program with a computer

A process description or PMM like the one listed above provides a means of decomposition of a large task (the project goal) into sub–tasks, along and an indication of resource requirements. For example: if we apply the above PMM to the goal of creating a "Hello World" program, we initially create this project instance:

Step 1: Initiate the "Hello World" project. *Requires a Customer*
Step 2(a): Specify the "Hello World" program. *Requires a Customer and a Programmer*
Step 2(b): Write the "Hello World" program. *Requires a Programmer and a computer*
Step 2(c): Test the "Hello World" program. *Requires a Customer, a Programmer and a computer*

At this point, we have reached the task of testing the program,Step 2(c), and we use the result of this test to decide whether to repeat step 2: suppose that the customer is dissatisfied with the program. We then have to start step 2 again, so that the project instance might become:

Step 1: Initiate the "Hello World" project. *Requires a Customer*
Step 2(a): Specify the "Hello World" program. *Requires a Customer and a Programmer*
Step 2(b): Write the "Hello World" program. *Requires a Programmer and a computer*
Step 2(c): Test the "Hello World" program. *Requires a Customer, a Programmer and a computer*
Step 2(a): Specify the "Hello World" program. *Requires a Customer and a Programmer*
Step 2(b): Write the "Hello World" program. *Requires a Programmer and a computer*
Step 2(c): Test the "Hello World" program. *Requires a Customer, a Programmer and a computer*

If, after the second iteration of the PMM, our customer is satisfied with the program, the loop terminates, the PMM finishes and we are left with the above project instance.

We can see that a PMM specifies the production of a project instance or, conversely, a project instance may represent the "footprints" produced by the operation of a PMM when it is applied to a particular goal. When a PMM is applied, PMM steps are translated to project tasks and resource requirements are translated into project resources and allocations of resources to tasks.

If we were to apply conventional PM to the production of the "Hello World" program then we would produce a project plan which lacks any PMM information:

Project start: May 11, 2004, 10am.
Task 1: Initiate the "Hello World" project. *Requires a Customer*
Task 2: Specify the "Hello World" program. *Requires a Customer and a Programmer*
Task 3: Implement the "Hello World" program. *Requires a Programmer and a computer*
Task 4: Test the "Hello World" program. *Requires a Customer, a Programmer and a computer*

In this case, we are in a quandary if the acceptance test of task 4 fails: the plan does not admit this possibility. Perhaps a "Change the program as needed" task could have been included in the original plan after task 4, but that might not be enough—a complete reimplementation might be required, for instance. Changes like this are a problem characteristic of conventional PM: extra tasks, resources and allocations are almost always inserted into a real project, but the only coping strategy of conventional PM is to try to minimize change.

Because conventional PM lacks the formal concepts to deal with project change, software tools for conventional PM don't support change very well: reports can be produced to indicate the degree of variance from the original plan, but the plan is not supposed to change. The result is that changes to a conventional project often happen in an uncontrolled way. The PMM–driven project at least specifies what changes should be made to the project instance, and why. The disadvantage of the PMM–driven project is that the lack of a static plan precludes a fixed–cost quote for a project, for instance. Iterative PMMs such as XP [15] can work around this limitation, by guaranteeing to deliver a working system no matter when the project is halted (eg: by budget limitations). However, in this case the project deliverables are not fixed in advance.

4   Modelling PMMs

We examined a number of Software Engineering PMMs including the Waterfall process [16] and Extreme Programming, and workflow languages such as BPML [17]. Although some PMMs were essentially sequential and others essentially iterative, we found that the three constructs identified by Boehm and

Jacopini [18]: sequence, selection and repetition, could describe the flow of control in all PMMs. We also used a container step, the `UnSequencedStep`, for parallel activities, to synchronizes parallel flows of control. We can see in our example PMM of Sect. 3 that these constructs are sufficient to describe the flow of control of the Build–and–Fix PMM: The main control structure of this PMM is repetition (step 2) that generates a series of implement/test sequences (steps 2(a)–2(c)) in the resulting project instance.

The control structures of a PMM constitute the fundamental difference with conventional PM: the result is that PMM steps may be repeated, or not used at all, whereas every task in a conventional PM project plan is expected to be actioned exactly once. The concepts of control flow, that create and change project instances, are not represented in conventional project management techniques, as supported by common PM software tools.

To describe PMMs and allow their programmatic representation, we have used the concepts above to design the conceptual data model in the upper left quadrant of Fig. 3 (a). By describing PMMs in this way, a number of advantages accrue: we can describe PMMs, and compare them. We can apply PMMs in a repeatable way, and we can describe the relationship between PMMs and project instances. This model relates in a straightforward way to existing process modelling architectures. For example, the development process architecture of SUKITS [19] consists of a process instance level that is described by a process definition level, similar to Fig. 3 (a). We can instantiate the PMM data model in many different ways; using XML [20], Java classes, etc. For example, we can create an XML representation of the "Build and Fix" method of Sect. 3, shown abbreviated in the lower left quadrant of Fig. 3 (a). More complicated PMMs such as Extreme Programming can also be represented with this PMM data model.

5   The PM/PMM Framework

We have formulated conceptual data models for PM (Fig. 1) and PMM (Fig. 3 (a)). The example of Fig. 2 illustrates how the PM data model is instantiated: `Tasks`, `Resources` and `Allocations` are recorded to create a `Project`. The lower left quadrant of Fig. 3 (a) instantiates the PMM data model to record the "Build and Fix" PMM description.

We now tie these two data models together to form a unified framework, as shown in Fig. 3: The PMM data model (a) is related to the conventional Project data model (b) by the mappings `applied--to--goal`, `describes` and `role`. To record these mappings to relate as "PMM–aware" project data, we have added the following attributes to the PM model of Fig. 1, to create an augmented PM model, shown in Fig. 3 (b): The `Task` class gains a `stepID` attribute, the `Project` class gains a `PMM` attribute and the `Resource` class gains a `resourceTypeID` attribute.

Because our framework relates PMMs to PM, we can make use of the complementary strengths of both areas. Conventional PM can provide a useful "big

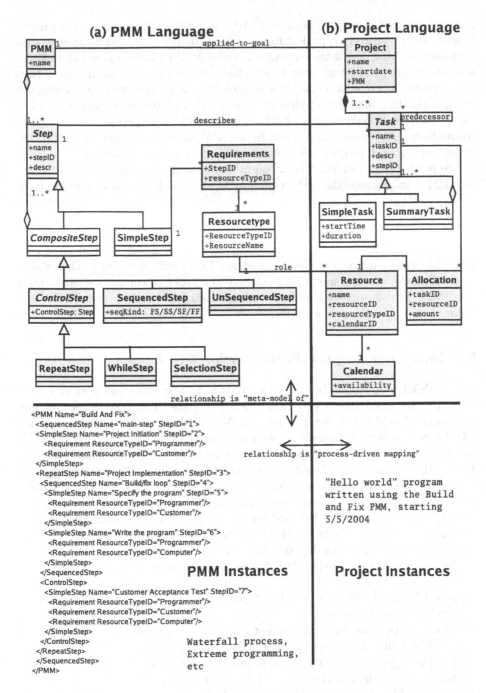

Fig. 3. UML diagram showing the PMM/PM framework, with instances. A feature of the PMM and PM data models is the Composite design pattern [21], that provides a tree–structured decomposition of objects, useful for XML representation

picture" view of a project, because PM tools provide the context of a project history, and a (projected) project future. PMMs do not intrinsically provide such a project context, but if the current state of a PMM can be viewed in the context of the project history, as a Gantt chart makes possible, for instance, then much more context is available than in a solely process–oriented view. Using our framework, this "big picture" view of a project is available with conventional PM tools, whilst still making use of PMM concepts. The connection from PMMs to conventional PM makes it possible to use PMMs for attempts to predict the future course of a project, and for scenario comparisons. Since predicting the future is what conventional PM attempts to do when planning a project, the use of a PMM to produce the project plan at least provides some systematic basis for the predictions. For example: the use of different PMMs could be compared, when applied to the same goal.

The framework also provides new methods for improving project processes: if we change a PMM project instance, say: by reversing the order of two tasks, then the project instance no longer fits the PMM that produced it. One way of reconciling the changes might be to change the order of the associated steps in the PMM. In this way we could use conventional PM tools to alter PMMs and tailor them for more specific applications.

6   Implementing the Framework

A Java/XML implementation [22] was written to test the framework of Fig. 3. The program manipulates two Java DOM [23] trees: The first DOM tree represents the PMM being instantiated. The XML Schema [24] that describes this DOM tree is a straightforward implementation of Fig. 3 (a). The second DOM tree records the tasks, resources and allocations produced by the PMM instance. The XML schema for this DOM tree is that of the freeware Planner [9] program. Similar to other PM software tools, the planner schema allows for custom properties to be added to projects, tasks and resources, and so these were used to record, for example: the PMM used for the project (the `PMM` attribute added to the `Project` class) and which PMM step was associated with each project task (the `stepID` attribute added to the `Task` class).

The mappings described in Sect. 5 were implemented in Java code as follows:

applied-to-goal. When a PMM is applied to a goal, these attributes are set in the `Project` instance:
  `start date` defaults to the current time, but may be changed with ordinary PM tools without impacting on the PMM process.
  `project goal` is set to the goal required to be accomplished.
  `PMM` is set to the PMM name used for the project.
describes. The steps of a PMM describe the tasks produced in the project instance. The kind of task produced depends on the kind of PMM step that describes it: a PMM `SimpleStep` produces a `SimpleTask` in the project instance: they contain a task name, start time and duration. Any kind of

`CompositeStep`, such as a `RepeatStep`, produces a `SummaryTask` in the project. Summary tasks, are tasks aggregated from other tasks or summary tasks, and are a common notation in projects. Summary tasks can be "rolled up" to hide the tasks they contain, so only the summary task is displayed by a software tool, for instance. Summary tasks derive their temporal information (eg: start time and duration) from the tasks they contain. In our framework, we make use of these features of summary tasks, so that PMM control step instantiation can be recorded in the project instance in such a way that no spurious temporal information is added to the project, and the hierarchical structure of the project data recorded reflects the structure of the PMM that produced the instance.

Attributes in the `SimpleTask` and `SummaryTask` instances are set as follows:

`task name` is set from the PMM `Step` name.

`start date` is set to the start time of the project, plus the the sum of the task durations up to this point.

`duration` defaults to one day, but may be changed with ordinary PM tools without impacting on the PMM process.

`stepID` is set from the PMM `StepID`.

Our PMM model uses five kinds of `CompositeSteps` which are mapped to `SummaryTasks` in the following ways:

`RepeatStep` The PMM steps contained in a `RepeatStep` are instantiated as project tasks contained in a summary step, which is a predecessor of a `ControlStep`, also mapped to a project task. Continuation of the loop depends on whether the `ControlStep` task succeeded or failed: if the task succeeded, no further actions are taken. If the task failed then another group of project tasks and associated control step is created, and so on.

`WhileStep` This step works similarly to the `RepeatStep`, except that the `ControlStep` is instantiated first, and success or failure of that task determines whether to instantiate the steps contained in the `WhileStep`.

`SelectionStep` The `ControlStep` in a `SelectionStep` is instantiated as a project task that determines one and only one of the steps contained in the `SelectionStep` to be instantiated.

`SequencedStep` The PMM `SequencedStep` has the `seqKind` attribute to describe the kind of step sequence it contains: finish–to–start, finish–to–finish, start–to–finish, start–to–start (FS/FF/SF/SS). When a `SequencedStep` is instantiated, the steps it contains will be instantiated as a corresponding sequence of tasks with a `predecessor` relation, set to specify the kind of sequence (FS/FF/SF/SS).

`UnSequencedStep` The PMM steps contained in an `UnSequencedStep` are instantiated in the project instance within a summary step, with no predecessor information set.

role. The PMM describes what kind of resources are required with the `ResourceType` instance. When a new resource is created in the project instance, the `resourceName` attribute of this instance is mapped to the `name` attribute of the resource. When a PMM `Step` has a particular `requirement`, the project instance is searched for resources having the same name (ie: the resource name is used as it's classification). If such a resource does not already exist then it is created in the project instance. The association of task to resource is then recorded in the `taskID` and `resourceID` attributes of an `Allocation` instance in the project.

At any time, the Java program can serialize the project DOM tree and write it out to a file, so that the "big picture" view of a PMM–driven project, described in Sect. 5, is available when the project instance is viewed with the Planner software tool. For viewing the project state in this way, it is convenient to serialize and then later re–instantiate an active PMM process, ie; to "pick up where you left off" with the PMM. To do this, a custom property, `Step-Nesting`, is used at serialization time to record in the project instance the state of the PMM process, along with the project data.

7 Synthesizing a PMM Using a Visualization and Heuristic

The java program of Sect. 6 allows us to instantiate a PMM to produce a project instance. However, examining a project instance that has been created without reference to a PMM in an attempt to synthesize a PMM which "fits" the project is difficult, because a potentially infinite number of PMMs might have created a particular project instance. A visualization may assist a human to deduce a PMM by examining project data, and using some heuristic method. Using the framework, we can create such a visualization, as follows:

1. Classify and group (using summary tasks) the project tasks and resources according to some scheme, so that we decorate the project instance with PMM "Kind of step" and "Kind of resource" data.
2. Decide whether particular groups of tasks are the result of sequence, selection or repetition control constructs.
3. Construct a PMM with steps reflecting these control constructs.
4. Add resource roles to the PMM steps that reflect the resource use in the project instance.

A simple visualization is to use the custom fields of the Planner program to record the "Kind of step" data mentioned above. Not only do the fields record the data, but the arrangement of the data in the Planner task and resource views makes patterns in the data obvious.

As an example: consider the project of Fig. 2. If we classify and group the tasks and resources of the project according to made–up classifications of "create page", "revise page" and "get feedback" for project tasks, then Planner will present the task view of Fig. 4.

There are obvious patterns in the task classifications of Fig. 4: the "create page" and "revise page" tasks are grouped together, and each group is followed by a "get feedback" task. From this, we could guess control structures such as:

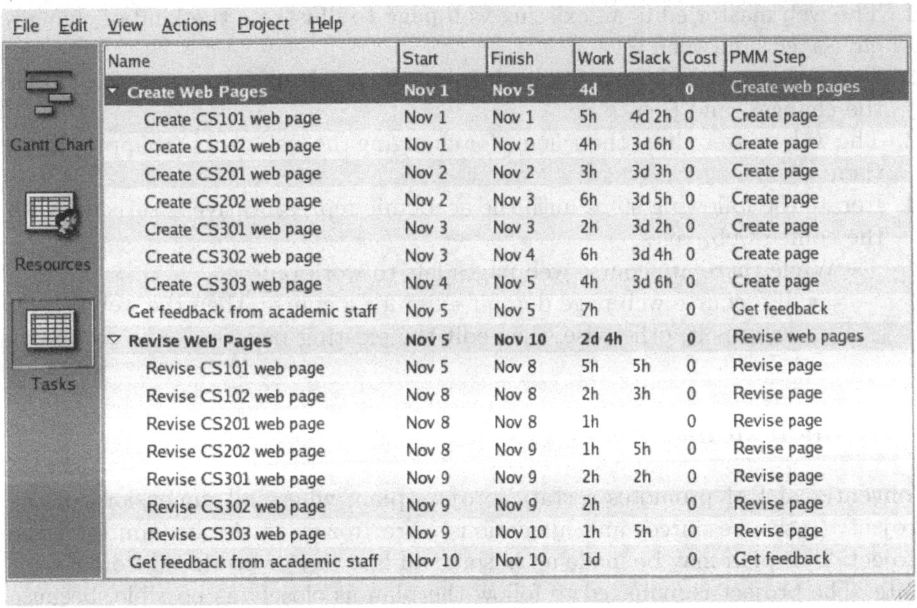

Name	Start	Finish	Work	Slack	Cost	PMM Step
▾ **Create Web Pages**	**Nov 1**	**Nov 5**	**4d**		**0**	Create web pages
Create CS101 web page	Nov 1	Nov 1	5h	4d 2h	0	Create page
Create CS102 web page	Nov 1	Nov 2	4h	3d 6h	0	Create page
Create CS201 web page	Nov 2	Nov 2	3h	3d 3h	0	Create page
Create CS202 web page	Nov 2	Nov 3	6h	3d 5h	0	Create page
Create CS301 web page	Nov 3	Nov 3	2h	3d 2h	0	Create page
Create CS302 web page	Nov 3	Nov 4	6h	3d 4h	0	Create page
Create CS303 web page	Nov 4	Nov 5	4h	3d 6h	0	Create page
Get feedback from academic staff	Nov 5	Nov 5	7h		0	Get feedback
▽ **Revise Web Pages**	**Nov 5**	**Nov 10**	**2d 4h**		**0**	Revise web pages
Revise CS101 web page	Nov 5	Nov 8	5h	5h	0	Revise page
Revise CS102 web page	Nov 8	Nov 8	2h	3h	0	Revise page
Revise CS201 web page	Nov 8	Nov 8	1h		0	Revise page
Revise CS202 web page	Nov 8	Nov 9	1h	5h	0	Revise page
Revise CS301 web page	Nov 9	Nov 9	2h	2h	0	Revise page
Revise CS302 web page	Nov 9	Nov 9	2h		0	Revise page
Revise CS303 web page	Nov 9	Nov 10	1h	5h	0	Revise page
Get feedback from academic staff	Nov 10	Nov 10	1d		0	Get feedback

Fig. 4. The task view of Planner, showing the task groupings and classifications with which we decorated the project instance

- While there are course web pages left to work on, work on the web pages.
- Change the course web pages until the academic representative is satisfied.
- If a course web page doesn't exist for a course, then create it, otherwise, edit the existing page.

Finally, we could synthesise the control structures into a "Change Course Web Pages" PMM like this:

- Iterate the following steps until the academic representative is satisfied with the course web pages:
  - While there are course web pages left to work on:
    - If a course web page doesn't exist for a course, then the web master creates it, otherwise, they edit the existing page.

Having created a PMM, we can compare it to other PMMs and attempt to improve it. For example: a well-known strategy in IT projects is to run a pilot phase to elicit early feedback from the client. If we were to assume that the changes to the course web pages were all of a similar nature, then changing just one page and obtaining feedback for that page might reduce or remove the second round of web page changes we can see in the project instance of Fig. 2. The resultant PMM would be as follows:

1. The web master edits an existing web page to illustrate the kind of changes envisaged, and then
2. The web master obtains feedback from the academic representative about the changes, and then
3. The web master alters the scheme for changing the web pages, as appropriate, then
4. Iterate the following steps until the academic representative is satisfied with the course web pages:
   - While there are course web pages left to work on:
     - If a course web page doesn't exist for a course, then the web master creates it, otherwise, they edit the existing page.

8   Conclusions

Conventional PM promotes a static project plan, where all dimensions of the project; (tasks, resources and allocations), are frozen at the beginning of the project. This plan may be made up in some ad hoc way or produced from a template. The project is managed to follow the plan as closely as possible, because conventional PM has difficulty in coping with change in a project. However, both the formulation and management of a real project need specialist knowledge from the domain in which the project operates, to describe what tasks and resources are required to accomplish a goal and also to control the progress of the project.

PMMs formalize this specialist knowledge and form a reactive system that constrains the course of a project, according to the current state of the project. This is a more powerful and expressive concept than conventional PM, however, it results in a project that constantly changes it's composition. For example: the operation of *selection* construct in a PMM results in one task being selected from several possibilities, and this is something that does not normally happen in conventional PM. PMMs such as XP have workarounds for this characteristic.

We have used data modelling to create a framework that relates PMMs to conventional PM. A simple Java program was described which implemented the framework and could create a "PMM–aware" project, given a PMM description and project goal.

The framework can also assist with producing visualizations of project data that could be used to synthesise PMMs to fit "non–PMM–aware" project instances. A simple visualization and PMM-creation heuristic was given as an example, and examination of the PMM so created revealed possible improvements to it.

Future work will centre around implementations of the framework with a variety of process description languages, the investigation of larger and more realistic applications of the PMM–based project generator, and the production of more visualizations of project data to, for example: compare and evaluate PMMs.

References

1. Burbridge, R.N.G.: Introduction. In Burbridge, R.N.G., ed.: Perspectives on Project Management. IEE Management of Technology Series 7. IEE, London (1988) xv–xxv
2. Standish: Extreme Chaos. In: http://www.standishgroup.com, The Standish Group (2001)
3. Standish: The Chaos Chronicles. In: http://www.standishgroup.com, The Standish Group (1994)
4. Lewis, J.: Fundamentals of Project Management. AMACOM, New York (1995)
5. Microsoft: Microsoft Project 2003. In: http://www.microsoft.com/, Microsoft Corporation (2003)
6. Flowers, S.: Software Failure, Management Failure: Amazing Stories and Cautionary Tales. Wiley, Chichester; New York (1996)
7. Collins, T., Bicknell, D.: Crash, Ten Easy Ways to Avoid a Computer Disaster. Simon and Schuster (1997)
8. Small, D.F.: Ministerial Inquiry into INCIS. In: http://www.justice.govt.nz/pubs/reports/2000/incis_rpt/index.html, Wellington, NZ Justice Department (2000)
9. Hult, R., Hallendal, M., del Castillo, A.: Planner, a Project Management Application for the Gnome Desktop. http://www.imendio.org/projects/planner/ (2004)
10. Gray, C.F., Larson, E.W., eds.: Project Management, The Managerial Process. McGraw–Hill, New York (2000)
11. Fayolle, A., Scheller, M., Roberts, J.: PyGantt, a Gantt Chart Generation Tool. In: http://www.logilab.org/pygantt, Logiclab http://www.logilab.org/ (2000–3)
12. PMXML: Project Management XML Schema. In: http://www.projectoffice.com/xml/, Pacific Edge Software (2000)
13. Gantt, H.L.: Organizing for Work. George Allen & Unwin Ltd, London, UK (1919)
14. Schach, S.R., ed.: Object–Oriented and Classical Software Engineering. McGraw–Hill, New York (2002)
15. Beck, K.: Extreme Programming Explained: Embrace Change. 6th edn. XP series. Addison-Wesley (2000)
16. Royce, W.W.: Managing the Development of Large Software Systems: Concepts and Techniques. In: IEEE WESTCON, Los Angeles (1970) 1–9
17. BPML: Business Process Markup Language. In: http://www.bpmi.org/, BPMI Initiative (2000)
18. Boehm, C., Jacopini, G.: Flow Diagrams, Turing Machines and Languages with only Two Formation Rules. Communications of the ACM (1966) 366–371
19. Westfechtel, B.: Models and Tools for Managing Development Processes. Volume 1646 of Lecture Notes in Computer Science. Springer, Berlin, London (1999)
20. XML: Extensible Markup Language: XML. In: http://www.w3.org/xml. (1998)
21. Gamma, E., Helm, R., Johnson, R., Vlissides, J.: Design Patterns: Elements of Reusable Object–Oriented Software. Addison–Wesley, Reading, Massachusetts (1995)
22. Dale, T.: TPMM and PM/PMM framework. In: http://www.cosc.canterbury.ac.nz/tony.dale/msc/index.html. (2005)
23. DOM: Document Object Model Level 3 Core Specification. In: http://www.w3.org/TR/2004/REC-DOM-Level-3-Core-20040407/, The W3C Consortium (2004)
24. XSD: XML Schema Definition. In: http://www.w3.org/2001/XMLSchema/, The W3C Consortium (2001)

Software Defect Analysis of a Multi-release Telecommunications System

Marek Leszak

Lucent Technologies Bell Labs
Lucent Technologies Network Systems GmbH, Optical Networking Group,
Thurn-und-Taxis-Str. 10, 90411 Nuernberg, Germany
Phone: +49 (0) 911 5263382
mleszak@lucent.com

Abstract. This paper provides a study of several process metrics of an industrial large-scale embedded software system, the Lucent product Lambda-Unite™ MSS. This product is an evolutionary hardware/software system for the metropolitan and wide-area transmission and switching market. An analysis of defect data is performed, including and comparing all major (i.e. feature) releases till end of 2004. Several defect metrics on file-level are defined and analyzed, as basis for a defect prediction model. Main analysis results include the following. Faults and code size per file show only a weak correlation. Portion of faulty files per release tend to decrease across releases. Size and error-proneness in previous release alone is not a good predictor of a file's faults per release. Customer-found defects are strongly correlated with pre-delivery defects found per subsystem. These results are being compared to a recent similar study of fault distributions; the differences are significant.

Keywords: Case study, software process metrics, defect prediction, error-proneness, defect density.

1 Introduction

Measurement and evaluation of product and process characteristics is a critical activity throughout the entire software development, evolution, and maintenance lifecycle. It is fundamental to determine whether the software products we develop have the desired functional and non-functional properties; it is fundamental to determine whether we have achieved the desired quality, cost, and schedule attributes in our development projects.

The subject of our empirical study is LambdaUnite™ MSS [1] -a multi-release, large embedded hardware/software system which is still in evolution. For further details of this product see the related previous study [2]. Lifespan of this product reaches from its first commercial release in 2001, and subsequent feature release approx. every 6 month. Up to now (end of 2004) 11 releases have been or are being

F. Bomarius and S. Komi-Sirviö (Eds.): PROFES 2005, LNCS 3547, pp. 98–114, 2005.

delivered to various telecom service providers worldwide. As basis for our case study, we take the change evolution over these 11 releases.

Our development approach can be shortly characterized as follows. R&D processes applied for the LambdaUnite product are defined, applied in all releases, and quality con trolled. The product lifecycle is divided into several phases, reaching from system requirements & architecture, (software and hardware) design & development, software (and hardware) integration, system test, general availability (GA), to maintenance. The software part consists of software source and build files, and of architccture and design documentation - the latter being out-of-scope for this study. Roughly 85% of the sources are written in C++ and C; a smaller portion using shell script, tcl/tk, and perl. Source files mostly represent C++ classes and associated header files. Some principles from which we could profit for our study, to obtain consistent and complete raw data:

- all changes to software files are guarded by identified and managed Modification Requests (MRs) in the central change management database, adapted from ClearDDTS™ (from IBM-Rational)
- all software files are version controlled in ClearCase™ (from IBM-Rational)
- links between MRs and touched files are stored automatically during check-out and check-in
- various descriptive attributes per file and per MR are kept and integrity-controlled by a dedicated change management team, the change control board
- all this data is consistently available, in one environment, for all product releases

Goals of This Study

The underlying objective for the investigation in this paper is to obtain insight into software changes, esp. into error-proneness, to get quantitative decision input for better focusing quality improvement activities. Decision making input is provided mainly for

- prioritization of software and system testing, and assigning resources to corrective maintenance
- hints for re-design and refactoring of error-prone software parts

To support these objectives, our investigation is driven by following goals:

G1. Predict number of defect MRs (observed defects), overall and distribution per software subsystem

G2. Predict error-proneness, by studying defect distributions both on file level and on subsystem level

In order to achieve stronger focus on the defect model and analysis of concrete measurements, several correlations between defects and other metrics are studied.

G3. Predict number of post-release defects per product release, by studying correlation with e.g. pre-release defects

G4. Complexity of file changes associated with an MR, experimenting with source file size, file age, defect density per file and release, as performed by Ostrand and Weyuker for some systems at AT&T [12,13,14].

Can the goodness of their estimation model be confirmed in our case study? In our trial to replicate their study, we succeeded to extract all the raw data their studies are based upon. Looking on the evaluation results, we could confirm some of their results; other results differ significantly. We intend to continue with subsequent studies, see outlook in *chapter 6*:

- utilize AT&T's defect prediction model
- we have at our disposal more attributes of MRs, faults, and files available that we could evaluate with this single case study

2 Related Work and a Taxonomy of Defect Prediction Models

We attempt to provide a taxonomy of typical industrial goals for measuring and analyzing defect metrics, by surveying some recent case studies [3,4,5,10,11,12,13,14,18]. The taxonomy in [18] is classifying various models more generally to assess software quality. Our taxonomy is based on a software defect model, both with respect to a classification of the defect metric goals (e.g. analyze error-proneness; estimate amount of defect Modification Requests (MRs) found) and with respect to concrete properties / attributes in the MR model of complex industrial software systems.

The class of software systems to which our survey should be applicable, encompasses *evolutionary, multi-release systems* that incorporate incremental changes - both for new features and fixes to defects detected in previous releases. In addition, we would like to restrict our survey on software systems. Their complexity leads to a decomposition into several *subsystems*, so that one dedicated software team is in charge of developing a certain subsystem. However, except of our own work [2,6,7,8,9,20], we have not found any other case studies studying *defect distribution over subsystems*. We like to encourage other companies and researchers to consider this topic in their future work. A recent motivation for subsystem-based evaluations is the need for higher software productivity, by exploring deployment of agile development methods to large-scale development in a team-based, subsystem-based, and evolutionary product development.

We claim the mentioned case studies can be classified into (at least[1]) the following three categories C1, C2, C3, based on the industrial business goals they support. We describe the typical analysis techniques applied for each category, and some practical constraints (i.e. occurring in real, large-scale projects) that often preclude a straightforward replication of the associated published case studies.

C1: Predict error-proneness, to optimize test management, e.g. to better prioritize test case execution.

---

[1] Compare to [18] for another taxonomy with a wider scope.

Technique: study distribution of defects in (software source) files. Provide prediction for future releases, based on historic data of previous releases.

Typical defect metrics: defect distribution by lifecycle phase detected, by severity; defect density (using code-based size measurements per file); file size, and file age. There are numerous studies published in the last 20 years. However, only a few of those have studied defect histories across multiple releases. Some recent work includes [3,12,13,14] using defect distribution across files. Our own previous work on error-proneness has been using complexity measures (esp. cyclomatic number) and compliance to the organizational software process [8,9].

Constraints on case study replication: Other studies have not used file clusters into subsystems, thus precluding insights on software team level. (This issue may be irrelevant for organizations that follow a completely unconstrained file ownership model.) Further, the relationship of observed defects (called MRs in our organization) to affected (i.e. changed) files may differ. Another issue which may prevent replicability of case studies: how is generated code and test code handled, should it be ignored for the study? Looking on the various parameters of a code size counting model [19] still no agreed and consistently applied parameter setting seem to exists. See *chapter 3* for a description of our size measurement and change model.

C2: Predict defect rates, i.e. their distribution over time, to achieve better resource planning for subsequent releases. See e.g. [4,10,11].

Technique: Find a 'best-fit' distribution function for the shape of defects found; calibrate the function's parameters, extrapolate defect amount from release histories. Constraints on case study replication: Although the studies mentioned provide very valuable results, they restrict their scope to post-release defects, and to the distribution of defects related to their creation date. Following extensions would be beneficial in an industrial setting: study distribution of pre-release defects in addition, and explore also the defect fix (i.e. correction) rate. We are not aware of any published studies which would cover such extensions.

C3: Propose which defect prevention technique is most effective, based on defect data and their relation to other process metrics.

Technique: Study change behavior in software files and relate it to defects found; study root-causes for defects observed, etc. Studies and typical defect metrics: [16] predicts rework effort, [6,8] analyzes root-caus-es for defects, based on an extended Orthogonal Defect Classification scheme, and proposes effective defect prevention techniques.

Overall, our impression of the amount of published studies for defect analysis and prediction of large, multi-release industrial software systems is that rather few such studies has been performed (or, at least, published). We assume that some other projects may not have the data needed for such studies, or their process may not be that much consistent or detailed. An experience we made during our empirical research: Even if all raw data is available, it is not trivial and very time consuming, to extract and analyze the data, esp. over several large product releases.

3 Model of Software Changes

3.1 Terminology and Basic Data Attributes

MR
Modification Request, the basic change unit for software and other work products throughout the R&D lifecycle

defect MR
MR used to correct any fault in specification, design, or implementation. For each problem detected, a new MR is issued, called *eMR* in this study. (Other kinds of MRs for e.g. feature enhancements are not considered in our study.)

software MR
MR used to update any software *files*. (Other kindsof MRs, for changes of documents, hardware, and tools are not considered in our study.)

eMR
'error related' MR, an observed defect on *system* level. In our study, we consider software eMRs only.

sMR
a sub-MR ('spawn') of an eMR, as basic change request for an affected *subsystem*. An eMR can have one or more sMRs associated. Only if all associated sMRs of a eMR are solved correctly, the associated error is considered as being fixed

working sMR
an sMR which is actually used to change files

fixed-by sMR
an sMR which is not used for file changes directly, but is linked to a working sMR

defect
general term, used for any fault or error

fault
a single change (i.e. version update) of a *file*, caused by one or more *sMRs*. If an observed defect (as eMR) affects n subsystems and for each subsystem S_i $(i=1,2...,n)$ m_i files need to be modified then this is counted as $sum(m_i)$ $(i=1,2...,n)$ faults. (Similar counting conventions have also been applied in the related case studies [3,13].)

system
for this study, corresponds to a LambdaUnite 'network element'. Consists of one or more (software and hardware) *subsystems*

(software) subsystem
a unit of team planning and tracking, configuration and change management, unit testing, and feature integration. Consists of a collection of functionally related components, which altogether form an architectural unit. Components consists of one or more *files*.

file	software source or build file, belonging to exactly one *subsystem*. Source files are usually related to C++ classes. For the goals of counting files related to product-effort only, we exclude 1) non-C/C++ code 2) all generated software files, 3) files which do not appear in any official load build of a product release,, i.e. 'dead code', 4) test code, and 5) COTS software included in our product[2]. There is a tight link between source files in the Configuration Management environment and the MR system: a new version can only be produced using an MR; the link to the associated assigned MR is kept as file attribute.
NCSL	Non-Commentary Source Lines (empty lines and comment lines are not counted)
CNCSL	changed/added NCSL (used as relative code size measure between product releases. Deleted lines are not considered)

File Data Attributes

For each 'product effort related' software file (i.e. excluding files in any of the 5 categories in the file definition above), following data are extracted for our study:

- *path* (incl. filename), used as primary key for the file records analyzed. Note that the path determines the unique *subsystem* the file is part of
- *first release* the file has been created
- if the file was changed in any release, then for each release:
- *no. of software-found faults* (i.e. the amount of defect sMRs which changed this file in release R, such that the *phase-detected* attribute of these sMR is set to 'software found')
- no. of systemtest-found faults
- no. of customer-found faults
- *absolute code size*, counted in [NCSL]
- *relative code size*, i.e. added and changed lines during development of a release R, counted in [CNCSL]

MR Data Attributes

We consider software defect sMRs which have been accepted for changing software files. Following MR attributes have been extracted for this study; those not yet used for analysis are marked with an asterisk '*':

- * *severity*, ranging from 1 (highest) to 4 (lowest), is a measure of the potential customer impact of the change. Severity 1 and 2 MRs are ,customer visible' i.e. indicate a potential system failure. (Our previous study [2] indicated that most MR related measurements are quite insensitive to MR severity.)

---

[2] See [19] for numerous other possibilities to count lines of code.

- * *creation date*. This is the basis to study MR evolution over time. (To study defect correction, attributes like *resolution date* and *approval date* would be needed in addition.)
- *target release*. This is the release of the product in which the corresponding software change is intended to, or already has been included
- *subsystem*. This is the part of the software which has really been changed
- *phase detected*, ranging from 'software-found' over 'systemtest-found' to 'customer-found'. The first value is an abstraction for any lifecycle phase prior to system test, the third value includes MRs observed by the customer service organization during e.g. field testing and acceptance testing
- * *number of check-in events*. This indicates the number of faults, one in each distinct file touched, during carrying out bug fixes with this sMR. I.e. each sMR adds at most one fault per affected file. Note that faults caused 'indirectly' by fixed-by sMRs are counted as well. (See [2] for our previous evaluation of what could be considered as measure of change complexity.)

3.2 The MR Workflow Model

As outlined in *figure 1*, the workflow of defect related changes is at follows. There are three sources of defects observed for a software load of a certain product release R. Defects found in deployed communication networks or field tests are forwarded to the responsible development organization, in case the defect is systematic, i.e. caused by erroneous implementation. Pre-delivery defects, be it found by system testing or earlier stages, together with post-delivery defects, are assessed by a product's change control board. Each such defect is represented as MR in our change management system, called eMR which indicates that we are in the problem domain. An MR wrongly reported as defect gets 'killed' (false positive). MRs not caused by the system's software part (e.g. caused by hardware or by interfacing other systems) are excluded from our consideration. Suppose for an eMR created for release R, the change control board checks if this eMR shall be fixed in the currently active release R' in development, $R' \geq R$. If an eMR is decided not to be solved in R', it is also not counted for R', but appears then as MR for a subsequent *target release*, $R'' > R'$. If the software eMR is decided to be fixed in R' then it is assigned to the team owning the affected subsystem to be changed. In case of several affected subsystems, one sMR is created for each such subsystem. An engineer within the subsystem team can update (only) existing files of S, or can create new files. He can also bundle several assigned defect MRs into one, use one 'working' MR for file check-outs / check-ins, and link his other related MRs to the 'working' MR as so-called 'fixed-by' MRs. For each file, both working and fixed-by MRs are counted as separate faults.

Looking backward, each fault is traceable to a unique set of sMR's (one working MR plus zero or more fixed-by MRs, leading to an n:m mapping between sMRs and files). Each sMR is traceable back to a unique eMR.

4   Basic Measurements

INPUT Metrics

For each product release of the LambdaUnite™ MSS product line:

- software defect MRs, related to subsystems
- files per release, plus associated faults and overall, new and changed NCSL
- features, related to subsystems contributing to implementation of the feature (Feature data has not been evaluated in this study, see [2] for some results.)

Basic Quantities

- 11 feature releases
- 10,100 software defects (sMRs) and 32,400 faults over all releases
- mean ratio eMRs : sMRs is 1.4, fairly stable over all releases
- ratio of sMRs found in lifecycle stage 'software development' (early pre-release)', 'system test' (late pre-release), 'post-release' (customer found) is 55.3% : 43.0% : 1.7%, measured over all releases

Fig. 1. MR workflow model for Release R and subsequent releases R', R''

- ratio of faults for the same three lifecycle stages is 65.0% : 34.3% : 0.6%
- 11,500 software source files, 4,500 of which have been faulty, distributed over 31 subsystems
- size of 1.2 Million non-commentary source lines, written mostly in C++. This excludes COTS software parts, test code, and generated code. In the previous study [20] we have included these parts, yielding 4.5 M-NCSL
- 700 features, over all releases

Table 1 depicts the basic feature, defect, fault, and size quantities.

Features are identified and specified by Product Management for each new planned product release. Note that features can have very different complexity, i.e. are not very useful as effort and size estimation units. Nevertheless, a strong correlation of features vs. defect MRs per subsystem has been observed for our product [2].

Files are counted acc. the conventions in *section 3.1*. The portion of faulty files in a release R (i.e. number of files with at least one fault in the respective release) tends to decline if the product matures, a good prerequisite for defect prediction. 61.0% of all files overall are never changed (zero faults in all releases) - a remarkable and surprising observation. (Not shown in *table 1*: the portion of accumulated faulty files for R, i.e. occurring in any release <= R, is fairly constant from 39.5% to 42.8%.)

Table 1. Quantities of features, files, sMRs, faults, code sizes

Release	# new features	# files	# sMRs	# faults	% earlyfaults	% faulty files	size abs.[K-NCSL]	size rel.[K-CNCSL]	DD [sMRs / K-NCSL]
1	241	6125	2541	7501	80.2	25.3	512	n/a	4.96
2	61	6436	882	3666	63.2	13.1	557	34	1.58
3	115	7122	1371	4901	54.9	18.0	679	63	2.02
4	51	7891	1255	3139	53.1	1.2	790	75	1.59
5	7	7908	127	178	43.3	1.1	659	15	0.19
6	57	8413	1017	3069	58.6	13.3	860	97	1.18
7	23	9656	592	1593	62.0	7.2	947	29	0.63
8	94	10144	519	1758	59.4	7.7	1122	52	0.46
9	11	10235	405	865	47.9	4.0	1044	89	0.39
10	27	10825	751	3324	64.4	6.9	1313	63	0.57
11	65	11466	629	2379	79.7	5.4	1262	29	0.50

sMRs and *code sizes* vary largely across releases, due to the still very actively ongoing feature development. "Early" sMRs indicate those which are software-found. The percentage is an indication of effectiveness since it is much cheaper to fix faults early. Note that this portion cannot be increased arbitrarily, just by adding resources, due to the nature of embedded systems, i.e. certain features require a complete system and its interaction with its environment to be tested adequately; often not achievable during software unit and integration testing.

Measurement of *defect density* (denoted 'DD' in *table 1*) is discussed in *section 5.1*.

5 The Analysis - Towards a Defect Prediction Model

A file-level prediction of number of faults per file for a release R, just by considering fault distribution and other file characteristics from previous releases $1,2,...,R-1$ has been achieved in the recent AT&T study, based on multivariate analysis [13] of several file attributes. Before we try to replicate their study, we have analyzed some aspects of fault distribution between subsequent releases $(R,R-1)$ for $R=2,...,11$. This analysis intends to gain confidence whether it is worthwhile to undertake the more sophisticated and time-consuming multi-factor analysis.

A simple correlation analysis of $R-1$ faults vs. R faults does not reveal such a simple relationship, as can be seen in the last two columns of *table 2*. Correlation tend to decrease for more mature releases. Therefore, we focus onto another hypothesis:

Fault-proneness is inherited across releases, i.e. a file which has been faulty in a previous release R-1, will also be faulty in release R.

For the sake of investigating in this hypothesis, we partition the number of files of each release $R=2,...,11$ into four parts:

P1(R) portion of files in R which are faulty AND have been faulty in R-1
P2(R) portion of files in R which are not faulty AND have not been faulty in R-1
P3(R) portion of files in R which are faulty AND have not been faulty in R-1
P4(R) portion of files in R which are not faulty AND have been faulty in R-1

Obviously, the higher the portion of P1(R)+P2(R) of all files of a release R, the better the hypothesis is fulfilled. On the other hand, files belonging to P3(R) and P4(R) correspond to the somehow negative case for which the inheritance hypothesis is not supported. Columns 2-5 of *table 2* depict the results for releases R=2,..,11. The negative cases per release range from 37% to 18%, with a trend to decrease in mature releases. Still we consider this a very encouraging result - taking into account that only files being faulty at all (i.e. in at least one release) are analyzed here, and that around 60% of all files have never been faulty up to now.

Fortunately, our data is not detracted by a high amount of new files per release which would be some 'noise' to derive a good defect prediction model from historic file data: For new files, such a model is not applicable, reducing the model's predictive power. Looking e.g. on the last 3 releases in *table 2*, there has been less than 5% of new files a quantity which probably contributed to the '0, >0' case to a

Table 2. Relation of fault quantities per *faulty* file, for release R=2,3,..,11 vs. predecessor release R-1

Release R	P1 (R)	P2 (R)	P3 (R)	P4 (R)	% new files in R	Pearman correlation	
						#faults in release R vs. R-1	#faults in release R vs. all cumulated faults until R-1
2	12.2	58.8	6.5	22.4	7.6	0.64	0.93
3	9.9	62.5	18.7	8.9	15.2	0.50	0.84
4	10.9	57.3	14.1	17.6	11.1	0.44	0.76
5	1.4	74.4	0.6	23.7	0.3	0.24	0.64
6	1.4	74.4	23.7	0.6	7.0	0.23	0.24
7	7.0	66.3	8.6	18.0	7.8	0.43	0.57
8	5.6	72.6	11.8	10.0	6.1	0.40	0.40
9	3.9	77.3	5.2	13.5	1.6	0.35	0.37
10	3.8	77.9	12.9	5.3	4.4	0.18	0.39
11	4.6	74.1	9.1	12.2	2.6	0.20	0.42

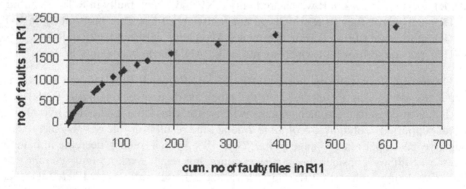

Fig. 2. Distribution of no. of faulty files fixed in R11 vs. faults in release R11

large extent. Also in the AT&T studies [12,13], the amount of new files decreased in mature releases, making it more feasible as basis for a prediction model.

Figure 2 demonstrates a rather skewed distribution of faults vs. faulty files for release R11. 90% of all faults fixed in R11 (2153 out of 2379 faults) reside in 63% of all faulty files in R11 (388 out of 614 files) and in 5.4% of all files overall (614 of 11466 files). The characteristic of this distribution cannot be explained by the related code size of the faulty files, since we did not find any significant correlation here, see next section. So reasons for this phenomenon still need to be explored.

5.1 Analysis of Defect Density

Numerous authors has studied defect density (DD) measures and their correlation with other metrics. There are well-known problems with this metric in general

- based on measurement theory, Zuse observed several issues with using DD, the most obvious for industrial practice being the paradox of 'non-scaleability' [17] if certain properties of the relation of defects vs. code size do not hold
- usage of DD for comparison of different projects or even organizations is questionable since this metric is highly process-dependent
  - number of defects depends e.g. on in which lifecycle phase defect recording starts, if defects are distinguished from enhancements, etc.
  - amount of lines on code depends on the algorithm to count lines, and there is no unique standard and agreement on the counting rules

As probably new issue, our impression is that the impact of using a multi-release project history adds a third category of issues related to DD.

Most authors who have studied DD in industrial projects, see e.g. [3] and [12], have defined DD for a release R, as ratio of defect MRs over the *absolute* number of lines of code. Since this size contains also all the code written in releases 1, 2, ..., R-1 this definition assumes an equal distribution of defects over code - a hypothesis which seems to contradict 'common sense' in industry. We would rather assume a skewed distribution acc. the Pareto rule, i.e. defects in release R affect 80% new code in R vs. 20% changed code of R-1. Rationale: before delivery, old code is very likely much better tested than new code.

We have considered to take the ratio of defects found in R over the amount of new/ changed code in R, as 'relative' DD metric. In the right-most three columns of *table 1*, the values for absolute/relative code size and defect densities per release are depicted. Absolute DD tend to decrease over releases - assuming a skewed defect distribution in old vs. new code this is expected and has also been observed in the related AT&T studies [12,13]. But this measure cannot be seen as adequate to be interpreted as a quality metric for a certain release -one cannot infer that a more mature product has higher quality simply because the DD measurements are decreasing. Rather, the relative DD measure seems to be adequate for this intuitive interpretation.

However, we have found no evidence at all for the following hypothesis which is based on the two components of any DD metric, i.e. on size and on faults:

Absolute and relative code size are a good predictor of faults in a release R

For both kinds of code sizes, this hypothesis can be rejected: Correlations for most LambdaUnite releases are in the order of [0.05,0.20][3], whereas in the AT&T studies this was a very good predictor. See *table 3* for possible interpretations of these differences.

---

[3] The correlation of 0.2 can be slightly improved if we partition all files into groups of similar sizes, but is still not higher than 0.4.

5.2 Analysis of Post-release Defects

Acc. *figure 1*, a certain portion of defects after delivery, be it found by customers or our field service, are 'design relevant' and appear then as defects for R&D to fix. The portion of these defects is 1.7% per release, compared to the sum of software-found and systemtest-found defects. For the LambdaUnite system, we have falsified in previous studies on subsystem level that post-release defects are a good predictor for pre-release defects of the same subsystem. In the current study, we observed that pre-release faults and post-release sMRs are well correlated with coefficient 0.74, see also *figure 3*. This is surprising since most other studies did not observe such a strong relationship. As with other similar measurements, still causal models are missing which could explain those differences. Some interpretation has been provided by our software architects: Subsystems with high amount of customer-found sMRs (>=9) are either 'platform subsystems' (i.e. are more frequently affected by defects found) or contain rather new features - this would explain the higher number of customer complaints. Subsystems with high amount of faults (>= 3000 over all releases) are all part of the software platform - most likely , the same argument on defect propagation applies as well.

As reported in the previous study [20] with 10 releases only, the hypothesis:

The amount of systems delivered to customers for a release R is a good predictor for the amount of post-release defects reported for R

has been only weakly supported by a Pearman correlation coefficient of 0.58. See [20] for a detailed discussion.

As an essential conclusion, we apparently found some driving factors for the amount of post-release defects, in order to drive improvements towards higher quality perceived in the field. Further analyses are necessary to validate our results and achieve causal models.

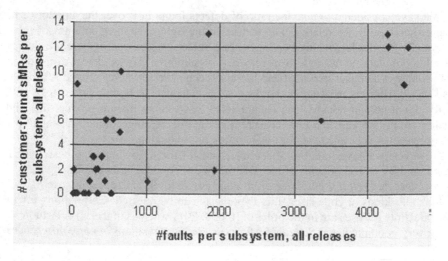

Fig. 3. Customer-found sMRs vs.faults per subsystem, cumulated over all releases

6 Summary and Outlook

Our file-level defect analysis provides important input towards

1) predicting error-proneness of files,
2) re-designing error-prone files or components,
3) deciding how to prioritize testcases on software level and system level, and
4) better planning of maintenance efforts.

Meanwhile our software organization decided to include our analysis inputs into their project management activities.

The analysis of our data shows several similarities, as well as substantial differences, tothe studies performed at AT&T. *Table 3* outlines details and provides interpretations.Although the root causes (i.e. main driving factors) for such differences are unknown,we assume that the differing application domains encounter for part of the differences which are discussed in *table 3*. Further, many of the new features in our system affects existing files to some extent, while in an information system new functionality can often be added largely decoupled from existing files, as observed in [13] "new files frequently represent new features". We assume that in our application domain, the degree of cohe- sion between files in different subsystems is higher than in other domains. (For the current study, no architectural information about file and inter-subsystem dependencies has been used - this could be the starting point for another interesting study.)

Looking on *table 1*, the ratio sMRs to faults ranges up to 5.5 per release, indicating a high 'change complexity' since this can be interpreted as mean number of files affected by an sMR, i.e. a defect on subsystem level.

One lesson we have learned during our study is that no single factor alone, like file age, absolute/relative code size, or defects in previous releases can be taken as adequate predictor for error-proneness. As next step, we therefore intend to pursue a multivariate statistical analysis like reported in [13].

Several refinements of the current study are in discussion:

- Analysis refined onto subsystem-level would support test prioritization and refactoring for each software development team.
- Analysis of MRs and faults by development stage would lead to improvements in finding more defects earlier, leading to higher productivity.
- The amount of features as possible predictor for the number of pre-release de- fects, per product release and subsystem. In the previous analysis [2], there was a very high correlation (0.7- 0.8) observed between features affecting a certain subsystem, and the number of defects found for this subsystem. It is interesting to explore whether this very useful evidence can be (re-)validated for subsequent releases of our product.
- Enhancing our defect analysis by architectural information, e.g. by the amount of import/export relationships per file and between subsystems, could possibly be valuable in explaining skewed defect distributions, towards a causal model for defect distribution in large software systems.

Table 3. Comparison of our study to AT&T's study [12,13]

Criterion	AT&T study	Our study
Application domain	information system (software only)	embedded system
Project characteristics	multi-release evolutionary development	
System size	medium - 500 K-LOC	high - 1.2 M-NCSL
Size of our system ranges up to 4.5 M-NCSL, depending on metric definition		
Software change identification, if caused by a defect	needs empirical estimation or interview	reliable data, based on consistent process
In our study, each MR is clearly classified as being a defect or an enhancement. The classification is built into our MR model, and its correctness is ensured by the project's change control board. Thus, we could easily sort out all changes related to new functionality or enhancements. In other related publications, we saw additional effort to derive this classification in context of the study, while it has been missing in the MR and file data.		
Fault distribution of files per (mature) release	skewed - 90% faults in 6% of all files	skewed - 90% faults in 3.6% of all files
Faulty file portion decreases per release	yes	yes
In our study, portion of files containing any faults in a certain release tend to decrease (25% to 5%), although accumulated portion of files of all previous releases and the current one remains roughly constant (40%) across releases		
Fault-proneness depends highly on file size	yes	no
In our study, file size in LOC or NCSL has not been an appropriate predictor for defects. We observed correlations, between defects and absolute/relative code sizes, not higher than 0.2. A similar result has been reported by Fenton's and Ohlson's case study [3]. Our previous study [2] on the first three releases of the same product showed high correlation for release 1 (0.80) and low correlation for releases 2, 3 (0.16), but this has been performed on subsystem level, whereas our current study is on file-level and therefore not comparable directly.		
Portion of defects found prior to system test	80%	55% defects 65% associated faults

Criterion	AT&T study	Our study
In our embedded system, such a high portion may be very hard to achieve. AT&T has analyzed an accounting system where no hardware/software integration is needed - a step which makes earlier defect detection very costly: the amount of early found MRs (prior to system test) cannot be raised arbitrarily in an embedded domain for which host and target environment differs.		
Amount of post-release defects	1%	1.7%

Acknowledgments. This work has been carried out with the excellent assistance of Gerd Moessler who provided the basic non-trivial measurements on files, faults, and MRs out of our change management and configuration management system.

References

[1] Lucent Technologies: LambdaUnite™ MultiService Switch (MSS) product description. Online at http://www.lucent.com/solutions/core_optical.html

[2] M. Leszak, W. Brunck, and G. Moessler: Analysis of Software Defects in a Large Evolutionary Telecommunication System. 12th Int. Workshop on Software Measurement (IWSM), Magdeburg, Germany. Shaker Publ. (2002)

[3] N.E. Fenton and N. Ohlson: Quantitative Analysis of Faults and Failures in a Complex Software System. IEEE Trans. on SW Engineering, 26 8(Aug. 2000), 797-814

[4] P. Hartman: Utility of Popular Software Defect Models. Proc. IEEE Reliability and Maintainability Symposium (2002)

[5] A. Gana, S.T. Huang: Statistical Modeling Applied to Managing Global 5ESS-2000 Switch Software Development. Bell Labs Techn. Journal (Winter 1997) 144-153

[6] M. Leszak, D.E. Perry and D. Stoll. A Case Study in Root Cause Defect Analysis. IEEE International Conference on Software Engineering (ICSE-22), Limerick/Ireland (June 2000)

[7] M. Leszak: Practical Product and Process Measurement - Lessons Learned from 6 Years of Experience. DASMA Software Metrik Kongress (MetriKon 2001), Dortmund, Germany (Oct. 2001)

[8] M. Leszak, D.E. Perry, and D. Stoll. Classification and Evaluation of Defects in a Project Retrospective. Journal of Systems and Software 61/3, Elsevier Publ. Company (June 2002) 173-187

[9] D. Stoll, M. Leszak and T. Heck: Measuring Process and Product Characteristics of Software Components - A Case Study. 3rd Conf. on Quality Engineering in Software Technology (Conquest), Nuernberg, Germany (Sept. 1999)

[10] Li, P.L., Shaw, M., and Herbsleb, J.D.: Selecting a Defect Prediction Model for Maintenance Resource Planning and Software Insurance. Position paper for the Fifth Workshop on Economics-Driven Software Research (EDSER-5), affiliated with the 25th International Conference on Software Engineering (2003). Online at http://www-2.cs.cmu.edu/%7ECompose/li%2Bedser5.pdf

[11] Li, P., Shaw, M., Herbsleb J., Ray, B., & Santhanam, P. Empirical Evaluation of Defect Projection Models for Widely-deployed Production Software Systems. ACM Symposium on the Foundations of Software Engineering (2004)

[12] T.J. Ostrand and E.J Weyuker: The distribution of faults in a large industrial software system. ACM SIGSOFT Int. Symp. on Software Testing and Analysis (2002)

[13] T.J. Ostrand, E.J. Weyuker and R.M. Bell: Where the bugs are. ACM SIGSOFT Int. Symp. on Software Testing and Analysis (2004)

[14] T.J. Ostrand and E.J Weyuker: A Tool for Mining Defect-Tracking Systems to Predict Fault-Prone Files. Proc. MSR 2004: International Workshop on Mining Software Repositories, affiliated with the 26th International Conference on Software Engineering (2004) Online at http://msr.uwaterloo.ca/papers/Ostrand.pdf

[15] G. Denaro, M. Pezzè: Software evaluation: An empirical evaluation of fault-proneness models. IEEE 24th Int. Conference On Software Engineering (2002)

[16] A. Mockus, D.M. Weiss, P. Zhang: Understanding and predicting effort in software projects. IEEE 25th Int. Conference on Software Engineering. Portland, Oregon (May 2003)

[17] H. Zuse: Lecture on Defect-Density. Online at http://irb.cs.tu-berlin.de/~zuse/metrics/lecture02.html

[18] J. Tian: Quality-Evaluation Models and Measurements. IEEE Software 21(3) (May/June 2004) 84-91

[19] R.E. Park: Software Size Measurement: A Framework for Counting Source Statements. Tech. Report CMU/SEI-92-TR- 20. SEI, Carnegie Mellon Univ., Pittsburgh (1992)

[20] M. Leszak: The Versatility of Software Defect Prediction Models (or why it's so hard to replicate related Case Studies). 14th Int. Workshop on SW Measurement (IWSM/ Metrikon). Berlin, Shaker Publ. (Nov. 2004)

Performance Rather than Capability Problems. Insights from Assessments of Usability Engineering Processes

Timo Jokela

P.O. Box 3000, 90014 Oulu University, Finland
timo.jokela@oulu.fi

Abstract. Improving the performance and effectiveness of usability engineering in software and product development in companies is perceived as a true challenge by many usability professionals. Findings from interviews and observations in eleven assessments of usability engineering processes indicate that usability engineering include typically problems such as poor impact of usability activities in product designs; limited skills and knowledge on usability among the designers and management; unawareness on various activities of usability engineering life-cycle; inappropriately used usability methods; even political games around usability. On the other hand, issues such as project and configuration management, and process performance measures are not the key problems of usability. It is concluded other kinds of methods but standard process assessment should be considered for revealing the problems of usability engineering. The problems identified in the assessment should be clearly communicated to the management, but for developers an assessment should aim for a constructive training occasion on usability.

1 Introduction

Usability has been recognized as one of the important quality characteristics of software systems and products. Usable systems are easy to learn, efficient to use, not error-prone, and satisfactory in use [1]. Usability brings many benefits such as "increased productivity, enhanced quality of work, improved user satisfaction, reductions in support and training costs and improved user satisfaction" [2].

Usability is defined in ISO 9241-11 [3] as follows: "The extent to which a product can be used by specified users to achieve specified goals with effectiveness, efficiency and satisfaction in a specified context of use". This definition emphasizes how the usability of a product relates to its context of use. The definition is largely used in the HCI community. For example, it is used as a reference for usability in the Common Industry Format (CIF) for usability testing [4].

To guide the development of usable products and software systems, *usability engineering* approaches and methodologies have been proposed. The standard ISO 13407 [2] is a widely used general reference of usability engineering, and is an important reference also in this study. ISO 13407 identifies four principles of usability engineering: user involvement, iterative design, multi-disciplinary teamwork, and appropriate

F. Bomarius and S. Komi-Sirviö (Eds.): PROFES 2005, LNCS 3547, pp. 115–127, 2005.

allocation of functions between users and the system. The standard further identifies four main activities of usability engineering, illustrated in **Fig. 1**. These activities represent a general overview of a user-centered development process: analyzing users and the context of use, determining user-driven requirements, producing designs and evaluating the usability of the designs.

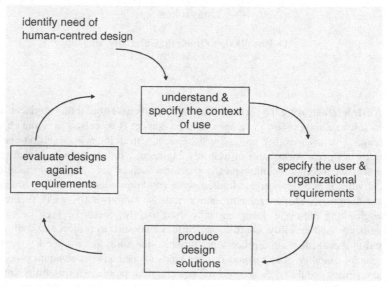

Fig. 1. The four usability engineering processes of ISO 13407

Many products or systems with usability problems reveal that the position of usability engineering is not effective in many organizations. Thus the improvement of the position of usability engineering has been widely recognized as a challenge in practice and in the literature: [5], [6], [7], [8], [9], and [10]. The integration of usability engineering and software engineering has also been a topic of a number of recent workshops, e.g. [11] and [12]. The problem has been persistent over the years. Even the recent issue of ACM Interactions – the 'flagship' magazine of the HCI community - addresses the topic [13].

A logical first step in the process of making organizational improvements is to carry out a current state analysis of the development practices of a company. Following the capability maturity model trend in software engineering, several *usability capability maturity (UCM)* models[1] have been presented from the early 1990s. The first UCM models are Trillium [14] by Bell Canada (a general assessment model including a specific part for usability engineering), Usability Leadership Maturity Model, UMML, [15] by IBM, HumanWare Process Assessment, HPA, [16] by Philips, and User Centred Design Maturity, UCDM, [17] by the Loughborough University. In the late 1990s, Usability Maturity Model: Processes, UMM-P, [18] - which follows the format of software process assessment (ISO 15504) - and Usability Maturity Model: Human-Centredness Scale; UMM-HCS [19] were developed in a Euro-

---

[1] Other terms, such as usability maturity model, UMM, are also used in literature.

pean research project INUSE. Later, a technical report ISO TR 18529 [20] was produced from the basis of UMM-P. The latest developments are ISO 18152 [21] – a more detailed version of ISO TR 18529 -, DATech [22] in Germany, SDOS [23] in Japan, and KESSU [24] in Finland. A more detailed overview of the various UCM models will be shortly published [25].

The literature on assessments of usability engineering mainly focuses on presenting the different individual assessment models [26]. Empirical research results on assessments are not widely reported. IBM reports that they conducted a large number of assessments [27] but they do not report any experiences or other research findings from the assessments. Bevan and Earthy [28] report the experiences from a European TRUMP project where they used the ISO TR 18529 model in two organizations. They carried out an assessment in the beginning and in the end of the project, and found that improvements in usability engineering had taken place in both organizations. They conclude that ISO TR 18529-based assessments are generally useful ("the results were judged to be highly beneficial") but they also identified some challenges (the customer had an "initial difficulty in understanding the assessment model").

The purpose of this paper is to report about organizational problems of usability engineering, based on findings from eleven assessments of usability engineering. Although process assessment was our basic procedure, we interviewed and observed more widely various organizational issues related to the position of usability. A general finding from the interviews and observations was that many of the true problems in usability engineering were not in the scope of process assessment. We also report the implications of these findings to the practice and research on UCM models.

There is a recent and growing interest in UCM models. The recent developments in Germany [22] and Japan [23] and the initiative of the Usability Roundtable [29] in the USA indicate and support this interest and popularity. In this article, empirical experience of conducting assessments is presented, about which there is very little literature to date. This is of relevance for practitioners and researchers alike. The lessons learnt and the implications from the assessment should be useful for practitioners who either wish to conduct an assessment themselves, or wish to have an assessment conducted. From the research perspective, developments in UCM models can take place only when one has a good understanding of the relevant issues around practical assessments. Thus, this research provides a platform for further research into UCM models.

2 Research Method

The main context of the assessments was two national research projects[2] in Finland between 1997 and 2003. The main objective of the assessments was to provide a basis for improvement actions in usability engineering in the companies – i.e. the assessments were not performed primarily for the reason of conducting research into UCM assessments. All the eleven assessments – apart from the last one - were conducted in companies on real development projects; and even the last one – where an experimental project of a research organization was examined [30] – had aims for improvement action in the long run.

---

[2] Called *KÄYPRO, KESSU*.

The main source of data arose from the assessment interviews and observations of the assessors gathered in the different assessment cases, and in different situations within the assessments. We also gathered feedback: how other stakeholders – i.e. the development staff, management, and usability specialists of the organizations – perceived the assessments during and after the different types of interventions (briefings, interviews, workshops and result reporting sessions). Feedback from the companies was gathered by questionnaires, interviews and email. The details of how the data was gathered varied from case to case.

In all cases, we used theme interviews; i.e. we let the interviewees quite freely tell about what they found important from their projects. The number of researchers varied from seven to one. After various assessment sessions, the assessment team gathered together to explore and discuss their findings. We took additional feedback from our contact persons (usability specialists) in the companies by email and in project meetings.

3 Overview of the Case Studies

Eleven usability capability assessments in different development organizations were carried out. The first two assessments took place in 1997. The third assessment took place two and a half years later, in spring 2000, when a new national research project was set up in Finland. Further assessments followed so that the eleventh one was conducted in autumn 2003. In the first assessments (#1 - #4), we used very much the same UCM model as Bevan & Earthy, i.e. the different versions of the UMM-P model. Later (assessments #5 - #11), we used the KESSU[3] model developed by ourselves; in order to overcome some interpretation problems that we met with UMM-P and to fit better our specific assessment contexts.

The companies involved in the assessments were different sizes: they included R&D or project groups in Nokia, SME companies and VTT. Although the companies were very different in size (Nokia vs. SMEs), the sizes of the organizational units assessed were not so different. The size of the groups or projects assessed varied between 10 and approximately 100 people. All the companies operate in international markets. The applications were different, and included mobile consumer products, transportation management devices and software, web based software, customer documentation, electro-mechanics and software of telecommunication network elements and mobile wireless services. In some organizations, the assessment was carried out twice.

The background in usability engineering in the organizations varied. One organization had had a usability lab from the late 80s, while in another organization the first usability person had joined the company not long before the assessment was carried out. There was some variation in the usability engineering methodologies the companies used. Contextual Design [32] was used in two organizations, while the usability engineering book by Hackos & Redish [33] was used as the main reference in another organization. Some of the organizations did not refer to any specific main usability engineering methodology.

---

[3] For details: see [31], [25].

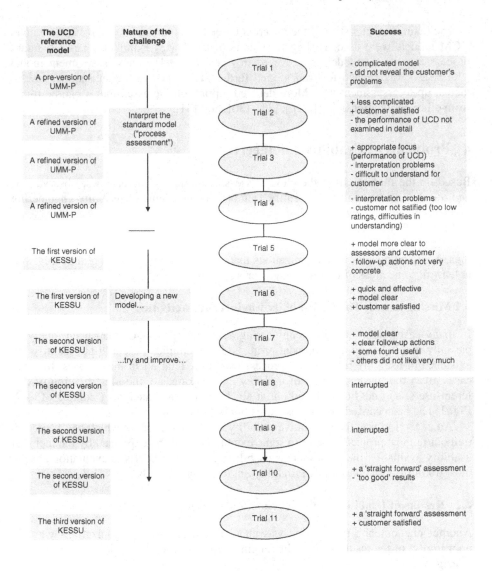

Fig. 2. Overview of the trials

The author - with usability experience from the early 90s and with formal training in process assessment - was the lead assessor or member in the assessment team in all assessments. There were several researchers as assistant assessors. Some assessors participated in most of these assessments, while some people attended only one assessment. All of the researchers had at least the basic knowledge of usability and usability engineering, and received training on process assessment. The members of the assessment teams came from the Oulu University (at least one representative in all cases), Helsinki University of Technology (cases #2, #4), Lloyds Register (case #1), TeamWare (case #1), and Nokia Research Center (case #2).

The main characteristics of the different cases are summarized in **Fig. 2**. Two main UCM models were used. Different versions of the UMM-P model – i.e. a standard process assessment model - were used in trials #1 - #4. A new assessment model ('KESSU') was created for trial #5 and further developed in the subsequent assessments, up to assessment #11. More detailed reports on the assessments can be found from other publications: [34], [26], [35], [30], and [31].

4   Problems of Usability Engineering

Based on the findings from the eleven assessments through interviews, observations and questionnaires, we could identify a number of problems of usability engineering in development organizations.

In the following, we discuss such problems. One should, however, understand that even if we focus on the problems in this paper, there were also many positive findings. Many companies and organizations that we assessed performed remarkably well at least in some areas of usability engineering.

4.1 Missing or only Partial Usability Engineering Activities

In many cases, some usability engineering activities (processes) had been totally or partially missing from development projects. For example, we could not identify the existence of usability requirement process (ref. **Fig. 1**) at all in many cases. In some cases, even the 'basic' process of usability engineering, i.e. the identification of different users, had not been carried out at all. User and task analysis ('context of use', **Fig. 1**) had been carried out in most cases but only partially.

An exception was the qualitative usability evaluation process which had been carried out in most projects at least to some extent. This can be explained by the fact that usability evaluation methods such as usability testing and heuristic evaluation are the most traditional and best known usability engineering methods.

4.2   Results of Usability Activities Not Considered

Another phenomenon that clearly was characteristic in some organizations was the poor impact of the results of usability engineering activities in the product – or system - designs.

In one case, for example, usability evaluations had shown clear, even severe usability problems in a new user interface concept. Still, this user interface concept had been chosen in the final product, even if usability evaluations had shown that there had been better alternatives available.

4.3   Quality Problems

In some cases, the usability activities had clearly been carried out in an unprofessional way. There had been, for example, problems in the procedures of usability tests. The basic procedure of usability tests is observing users when they carry out predefined, realistic tasks. In some cases, however, users had been shown user interface designs, and asked opinions of the designs. In another case, the user tasks for usability tests had not been realistic and did not form a coherent story.

An extreme case had been one where usability evaluations had been carried out in an ad-hoc manner by persons without any training on usability - the only basis was seemingly that these persons had interest on usability and had earlier seen usability test conducted.

4.4 Knowledge and Skills Problems

Knowledge and skills problems appeared in two levels: among persons involved n practical usability work and among other staff, including designers, marketing and management.

Some of the persons working on usability issues had not had any training and had no theoretical knowledge on usability. They had started their usability career from other background, such as marketing software engineering, and taken their position as a usability practitioner based on their interest rather than education. Some of them had really missed a sound theoretical basis.

The knowledge problems had been, not surprisingly, even more severe among other staff: designers and management. In one case, 'usability' had earlier been regarded as a competitive factor of the company even if there had been no usability professionals in the company at all. Usability had been used as a term by many, without any understanding of its essential contents. For example, to some persons usability was a synonym for a big display or visually appealing designs.

The misconceptions on the principles and activities of usability engineering had been remarkable as well. 'Friendly user tests' had been regarded as sufficient for assuring usability. In an extreme case, the opinion of a manager - a person without usability background – had been regarded as the truth of usability.

4.5 Efficiency Problems

In one case, a lot of resources had been invested into a large comparative usability testing tour carried out internationally. The purpose of the tests had been to select the best one from several user interface concepts for future products. However, the results of the tests had produced only marginally useful results. The reason had been that the tests had been carried out with early prototypes of the user interface concepts. The results of the tests, comparative evaluations, had not been useful at all, due to the qualitative problems of the prototypes. – A positive aspect had been that the tests had revealed the qualitative problems. However, it had been possible to identify these kinds of problems with remarkable fewer efforts.

4.6 Low Organizational Positions

Typically, the usability practitioners had been young people, recently recruited. In practice, their organizational position in the projects was often similar with the role of 'normal' designers. If a company does not have prior experience on usability engineering, this kind of setting is quite demanding for a usability practitioner While successful usability engineering requires new activities in a development process as well as new awareness and attitudes among designers and other staff, the task of a usability practitioner is often just too demanding.

4.7 Organizational Conflicts

In some cases, project management had had a fear that usability activities had delayed the project schedule. In other cases, the user interface software designers had perceived the usability practitioners as being in the role of 'police' (usability evaluations are about finding problems in user interface designs). In some cases, the marketing people had perceived that usability practitioners had stepped on their toes: they had not seen a difference between users and customers.

In a number of cases, these kinds of frictions had led to personal level conflicts between usability practitioners and other individuals of a development project. In one case, for example, a usability practitioner reported that she 'hated' the software development manager.

4.8 Ethical Misconducts

This was not a common phenomenon but an interesting one. In one case, a person without any education or experience in usability had taken the role of 'the usability guru' of the company. For example, the senior management of the company had later advised the usability professionals of the company to ask this person's advice in 'complicated usability matters'.

In the case discussed earlier, usability evaluations had shown clear, even severe usability problems in a new user interface design but still design had been chosen in the final product. Later, it was revealed that this design had been justified by this person to the senior management through claiming that the design is 'usability driven'. In other words, the term 'usability' – which had a positive image in the company - had been purposefully used to justify unusable solutions.

4.9 Frustration

As a consequence of the things mentioned above, many usability practitioners were frustrated in their position. This phenomenon is naturally related to the problems mentioned above: poor impact and ethical misconducts. A clear indication of this is the fact that in some cases the usability practitioners hoped that the assessments would give bad results.

5   Implications to the Assessments of Usability Engineering

We have identified several types of problems that may be true problems of usability engineering. But what do these findings imply to the assessments of usability engineering?

In the following, we discuss the implications first from the viewpoint of the assessment model, and then from the viewpoint of conducting assessments.

5.1 Implications to the Assessment Model

One natural implication of the findings is that one should use an assessment model such that reveals the specific problems of usability engineering. A clear conclusion from the assessments is that examination of process management issues – the scope of standard process assessment - is not interesting and relevant for the usability practitioners, at least in the types of cases that we had. Instead, an assessment should focus on the *performance* rather than capability of usability engineering activities. With performance we do not only mean the extent to which usability engineering activities are carried out but also the quality of the activities and the impact of the results of the activities to the design decisions.

To meet these objectives, we modified the traditional process assessment model for the last assessment cases, and ended up with the KESSU model. The key difference of the KESSU model compared with ISO 15504 is in the style of process definitions, and a set of *performance attributes* for rating the assessment results. The processes are defined through outcomes (vs. base practices) - the outcomes define what a process should produce. The performance of processes is determined based on three performance attributes: the *extent*, *quality*, and *integration* of the outcomes. A four-grade scale[4] (none, partially, largely, fully) is used to rate the extent to which an outcome is produced, as well as the quality and integration of the outcome (for details, see [24]).

This kind of assessment model made possible for us to examine not only whether processes are carried out (*extent*) but also reveal potential *quality* and impact (*integration*) problems of usability engineering, Thereby the KESSU model could be used to reveal many of the organizational problems discussed above, although the basic focus of the assessment is processes.

5.2 Implications to Carrying out Assessments

An assessment is always an organizational intervention with organizational consequences. Ideally, assessments could just be a neutral way of determining the status of usability engineering in a development organization. However, during an assessment, the assessors are in touch with the organization in several ways. Assessors discuss with staff, interview them and present briefings and the results. In other words, an assessment is always an organizational intervention. In our cases, we clearly could see that assessments had some impact on the people and the organization – positive or negative (or both).

An assessment should be carried out so that it truly supports the improvement of the position and performance of usability engineering. We found that in our cases, the usability practitioners had different purposes the assessment (reported more detailed in [31]).

(1) In some cases the aim of the usability practitioners was to use the assessment as *an asset to communicate towards management* about the organizational problems of usability engineering. This setting is appropriate when the purpose of the assessment is to open the eyes of the management to the organizational problems of usability engineering. This is typically the situation when there are organizational or ethical

---

[4] The scale is adopted from process assessment (used in rating the achievement of base practices).

misconducts or misunderstandings about usability. In this kind of setting, the assessment results should clearly point out the organizational problems of usability. If the KESSU model is used, the specifically the performance attributes quality and integration can be used to pinpoint the organizational problems.

(2) In other cases, *the target customer of the assessment was the development staff*. The aim should be to make the developers understand the essentials of usability and usability engineering. When an assessment of this kind of situation is considered, the goal should be that the overall perception of the assessment is positive among people. The goal is to improve the position of usability through increasing buy-in for usability and understanding what exactly is needed for designing usability.

In these kinds of cases, it is not very important to find out the exact status of usability engineering in the organization. Rather, an assessment is a success when it can be a constructive training occasion on usability and usability engineering. Our finding was that the exact assessment results - the ratings of the current status of usability engineering - are not that critical.

6 Discussion

Improving the performance and effectiveness of usability engineering in software and product development in companies is perceived as a true challenge by many usability professionals. Findings from interviews and observations in eleven assessments of usability engineering processes show that typical problems of usability engineering include poor impact of usability activities in product designs; limited skills and knowledge on usability among the designers and management; unawareness on various activities of usability engineering life-cycle; inappropriately used usability methods; even political games around usability. On the other hand, issues such as project and configuration management, and process performance measures are not the key problems of usability. It is concluded other kinds of methods but standard process assessment should be considered for revealing the problems of usability engineering. Further, the target customer of the assessment has an impact on how an assessment should be conducted. The problems identified in the assessment should be clearly communicated to the management, but for developers an assessment should aim for a constructive training occasion on usability

6.1 Limitations of the Research

Our findings are based on eleven cases in Finland. This is naturally only a limited set of companies. However, presentations by other usability practitioners in conferences, articles in magazines and journals, professional email discussion groups and personal communication with other usability practitioners indicate that the kinds of problems found in this study are not that rare – even if there surely are differences in the details of the problems in different organizations.

A specific feature in the assessments – and in our research generally – is the viewpoint of a usability person (vs. e.g. one of management). The background and driver of this research are the problems perceived by the usability practitioners, as discussed in the beginning of the paper. Most of our assessments were initiated by usability practitioners rather that management. Thereby, the setting is different from the one of typical software process assessments.

Our assessment approach, the KESSU model, should not be understood as 'the' model for assessing usability engineering processes. It has evolved case by case. Overall, it is probable that it will be further developed, even remarkably.

Our research does not provide a solid answer whether 'awakening the management' type of assessments would really be useful. Clearly, usability practitioners wanted to make 'management to understand' but we do not have any empirical evidence of a successful assessment in this category. The effectiveness of an assessment is probably dependent on the specific situation in the organization. The organizational problems may be so entrenched that even pinpointing the organizational problems might lead to no significant changes.

One limitation of this research is that we were not able to systematically follow up whether training designers through assessments really had impacts. On the other hand, it is not easy to isolate the role of assessment in the success or failure of the improvement actions that follow. The success of improvement depends on many factors: the resources that the organization can assign to improvement efforts; the ability and interest of the usability specialists to change, etc; how the staff generally feels towards usability; the support of management; etc.

6.2 Further Research Topics

A follow-up study could be a survey research on the problems of usability in the companies. The study reported in this paper is of qualitative nature. As said, many sources of information indicate that these problems would be quite general. However, quantitative research is required to validate this.

The usability assessment model has a very critical role in assessments. It represents more or less the truth of usability engineering in the organization to be assessed. This raises a question: what exactly is the ideal usability engineering reference model? The existing UCM models have differences in how they define 'ideal usability engineering'. The assessment cases of our research led to the development of another model (KESSU). Research into understanding the fundamental contents of usability engineering would be most relevant.

Overall, any assessment should be approached as a research action. The assessment model should be challenged. It should be understood that no assessment model represents an absolute truth. One should be critical of any assessment approach and learn from the experience.

References

1. Nielsen, J., Usability Engineering. 1993, San Diego: Academic Press, Inc. 358.
2. ISO/IEC, 13407 Human-Centred Design Processes for Interactive Systems. 1999: ISO/IEC 13407: 1999 (E).
3. ISO/IEC, 9241-11 Ergonomic requirements for office work with visual display terminals (VDT)s - Part 11 Guidance on usability. 1998: ISO/IEC 9241-11: 1998 (E).
4. ANSI, Common Industry Format for Usability Test Reports.. 2001: NCITS 354-2001.

5. Axtell, C.M., P.E. Waterson, and C.W. Clegg, Problems integrating user participation into software development. International Journal of Human-Computer Studies, 1997(47).
6. Wilson, S., M. Bekker, P. Johnson, and H. Johnson. Helping and Hindering User Involvement. InInvolvement - A Tale of Everyday Design. in Proceedings of CHI '97. 1997: ACM Press.
7. Bloomer, S. and S. Wolf. Successful Strategies for Selling Usability into Organizations. in CHI 99. 1999. Pittsburgh, USA.
8. Rosenbaum, S., J. Rohn, J. Humburg, S. Bloomer, K. Dye, J. Nielsen, D. Rinehart, and D. Wixon. What Makes Strategic Usability Fail? Lessons Learned from the Field. A panel. in CHI 99 Extended Abstracts. 1999. Pittsburgh, USA: ACM, New York.
9. Anderson, R., Organisational Limits to HCI. Conversations with Don Norman and Janice Rohn. Interactions, 2000. 7(2): p. 36-60.
10. Rosenbaum, S., J.A. Rohn, and J. Humburg. A Toolkit for Strategic Usability: Results from Workshops, Panels, and Surveys. in CHI 2000 Conference Proceedings. 2000. The Hague: ACM, New York.
11. John, B.E., L. Bass, R. Kazman, and E. Chen. Identifying Gaps between HCI, Software Engi-neering and Design, and Boundary Objects to Bridge Them. in CHI 2004. 2004.
12. Harning, M.B. and J. Vanderdonckt. Closing the Gaps: Software Engineering and Human-Computer Interaction. Workshop. in Ninth IFIP TC13 International Conference on Human-Computer Interaction (INTERACT 2003). 2003. Zürich, Switzerland.
13. Henderson, A., The Innovation Pipeline. Design Collaborations between Research and Devel-opment. ACM interactions, 2005. 12(1).
14. Coallier, F., R. McKenzie, J. Wilson, and J. Hatz, Trillium Model for Telecom Product Devel-opment & Support Process Capability, Release 3.0. Internet edition. 1994, Bell Canada.
15. Flanagan, G.A., Usability Leadership Maturity Model (Self-assessment Version). Delivered in a Special Interest Group session, in CHI '95: Human Factors in Computing Systems, I. Katz, et al., Editors. 1995: Denver, USA.
16. Taylor, B., A. Gupta, W. Hefley, I. McLelland, and T. Van Gelderen. HumanWare Process Improvement - institutionalising the principles of user-centred design. In Tutorial PM14 H Hu-man-centred processes and their impact. in Human-Computer Interaction Conference on People and Computers XIII. 1998. Sheffield Hallam University.
17. Eason, K. and S.D. Harker, User Centred Design Maturity. Internal working document. 1997, Department of Human Sciences, Loughborough University: Loughborough.
18. Earthy, J., Usability Maturity Model: Processes. INUSE/D5.1.4(p), EC INUSE (IE 2016) final deliverable (version 0.2). 1997, Lloyd's Register: London.
19. Earthy, J., Usability Maturity Model: Human Centredness Scale. INUSE Project deliverable D5.1.4(s). Version 1.2.. 1998, Lloyd's Register of Shipping: London.
20. ISO/IEC, 18529 Human-centred Lifecycle Process Descriptions. 2000: ISO/IEC TR 18529: 2000 (E).
21. ISO/IEC, 18152 A specification for the process assessment of human-system issues. 2003: ISO/PAS 18152: 2003.
22. DATech, DATech-Prüfbaustein. Usability-Engineering-Prozess, Version 1.2. 2002, Deutsche Akkreditierungsstelle Technik e.V.: Frankfurt/Main. p. 70.
23. Kurosu, M., M. Ito, Y. Horibe, and N. Hirasawa. Diagnosis of Human-Centeredness of the Design Process by the SDOS. in Proceedings of UPA 2000, Usability Professionals Association. 2000. Asheville, North Carolina.
24. Jokela, T., The KESSU Usability Design Process Model. Version 2.1. 2004, Oulu University. p. 22.

25. Jokela, T., M. Siponen, N. Hirasawa, and J. Earthy, A Survey of Usability Capability Maturity Models: Implications for Practice and Research. Behaviour & Information Technology. Ac-cepted, 2005.
26. Jokela, T., Assessment of user-centred design processes as a basis for improvement action. An experimental study in industrial settings. Acta Universitatis Ouluensis, ed. J. Jokisaari. 2001, Oulu: Oulu University Press. 168.
27. Flanaghan, G.A., Usability Management Maturity, Part 1 Self Assessment - How Do You Stack Up? SIGCHI Bulletin, 1996(28 (4), October 1996).
28. Bevan, N. and J. Earthy. Usability process improvement and maturity assessment. in IHM-HCI 2001. 2001. Lille, France: Cépaduès-Editions, Toulouse.
29. Ease. of Use Roundtable, Why the PC Industry Must Improve New Technology's Quality and Ease of Use, http://www.eouroundtable.com/. 2004.
30. Jokela, T. and P. Abrahamsson. Usability Assessment of an Extreme Programming Project: Close Co-Operation with the Customer Does Not Equal to Good Usability. in Profes 2004. 2004. Kansai Science City, Japan: Springer.
31. Jokela, T., Evaluating the user-centredness of development organisations: conclusions and implications from empirical usability capability maturity assessments. Interacting with Com-puters, 2004. 16(6): p. 1095-1132.
32. Beyer, H. and K. Holtzblatt, Contextual Design: Defining Customer-Centered Systems. 1998, San Francisco: Morgan Kaufmann Publishers. 472.
33. Hackos, J.T. and J.C. Redish, User and Task Analysis for Interface Design. 1998: Wiley Com-puter Publishing.
34. Kuutti, K., T. Jokela, M. Nieminen, and P. Jokela. Assessing human-centred design processes in product development by using the INUSE maturity model. in Proceedings of the 7th IFAC/IFIP/IFORS/IEA Symposium on Analysis, Design and Evaluation of Man-Machine Sys-tems -- MMS'98. 1998. Kyoto, Japan: IFAC.
35. Jokela, T., N. Iivari, M. Nieminen, and K. Nevakivi. Developing A Usability Capability Assess-ment Approach through Experiments in Industrial Settings. in Joint Proceedings of HCI 2001 and IHM 2001. 2001: Springer, London.

Using the MOWAHS Characterisation Framework for Development of Mobile Work Applications

Alf Inge Wang, Carl-Fredrik Sørensen, Heri Ramampiaro,
Hien Nam Le, Reidar Conradi, and Mads Nygård

Dept. of Computer and Information Science, Norwegian University of Science
and Technology (NTNU), NO-7491 Trondheim, Norway
{alfw, carlfrs, heri, hiennam, conradi, mads}@idi.ntnu.no

Abstract. This paper describes an evaluation of a characterisation framework to analyse mobile work scenarios in order to make corresponding software systems. The framework identifies complexity issues to be taken into account when implementing a system. The framework can also be used to elicit requirements from a scenario. Three research questions are investigated in this evaluation: 1) Can the framework be used to identify relevant challenges in the final system? 2) Can the framework be used to identify functional requirements for the final system? and 3) Can the framework be used to identify non-functional requirements for the final system? The evaluation was performed using the framework to analyse and implement an IT-support scenario. The paper also describes a web-tool for this framework that makes the characterisation process simpler. The tool introduces consistency rules to ensure stricter characterisation of the scenarios.

1 Introduction

The explosive development the last decade in mobile computing has changed the way we communicate, learn, entertain and work. Mobile phones and PDAs have become necessary tools to make life easier through functionality such as SMS, calendars, WAP-browsers etc. As mobile devices have become more powerful, it is now possible to create software systems for mobile workers that can improve the work processes. Such systems typically consist of various mobile clients connected to a server. They provide the mobile worker with necessary information and opportunity for filling in forms and reports on various locations. Development of mobile systems is different from development of distributed systems. When designing a mobile system, we have to overcome challenges in wireless communication, physical mobility, and portability [1]. Thus, it is important that these issues are examined carefully when considering the system requirements. In this paper, we review a framework that is used to identify challenges and possible requirements related to system development for mobile work. By mobile work, we consider work where the worker must move physically to some location to carry out his task. The goal of this framework is to identify the parts that are most complex and probably would be hardest to implement in a mobile support system. The framework has previously been used successfully to analyse mobile scenarios (like mobile journalist, mobile

F. Bomarius and S. Komi-Sirviö (Eds.): PROFES 2005, LNCS 3547, pp. 128–142, 2005.

researcher, mLearning [6]) to compare their characteristics. Although we found this analysis useful, it did not imply that the framework is adequate for developing software to support mobile work. The framework it self has been published before, and the contribution of this paper is the m tool used to apply the framework on scenarios, consistency rules to improve the quality of the characterisation, and most important an evaluation of the framework. In this evaluation, we want to investigate three research questions:

- RQ1: Can the framework identify *relevant challenges* related to the development of mobile support systems for mobile work?
- RQ2: Can the framework introduce *new functional requirements* related to the development of mobile support systems for mobile work?
- RQ3: Can the framework introduce *new non-functional requirements* related to the development of mobile support systems for mobile work?

The first question investigates whether the framework does what it is supposed to do i.e. to identify complexity in a system. The next two questions investigate whether new functional and/or non-functional requirements can be derived from using the framework. To answer the questions, we used the framework to analyse mobile scenarios when developing a system for mobile work.

The rest of the paper is organised as follows: Section 2 describes the characterisation framework, Section 3 describes how the framework was applied on the IT-support scenario. Section 4 describes the results of the evaluation, Section 5 relates this paper to similar work, and Section 6 concludes the paper.

2 The Characterisation Framework

The MOWAHS characterisation framework is a tool for analysing mobile work scenarios to create a mobile computing system supporting these scenarios. Such a system will typically be a process support system tailored for supporting mobile professions, and consists of one or more servers and some mobile clients (laptops, PDAs, mobile phones etc.). The framework can be used in at least two ways: *Firstly*, it can be used as a check-list of issues you should consider when making computer support for mobile work. *Secondly*, the framework can be used to perform a more careful examination of the requirements for making a system to support mobile scenarios. This examination will produce requirement indicators to identify complex parts of the system, type of client device, type of network, services needed etc. To use our framework, a mobile scenario must be described as a set of tasks. A task is here similar to a use case in design of software systems. To apply our framework to a mobile scenario, we use the following steps:

1. Select the mobile scenario and identify the different roles/actors
2. For each role identify tasks
3. For each task:
   a) Write a task description using a task description template
   b) Assign task priority (1-5, where 5 is most important)

c) Characterise the task using the framework (see Table 1).

d) Calculate the requirement indicators for the task

4. Derive system requirements and priorities from the characteristics and indicators.

Table 1. The MOWAHS Characterisation Framework for Mobile Work

Characteristics	Possible values	Description
General		
G1. Decomposable	(1 No, 3 Uncertain, 5 Yes)	Composed of sub-tasks?
G2. Part of sequence	(1 No, 3 Uncertain, 5 Yes)	Order dependencies with other tasks?
G3. Pre-planned	(1 Planned, 3 Partial, 5 Ad-hoc)	To what degree planned in beforehand?
G4. Data synchronisation	(1 Never, 3 After end, 5 Duration)	When update data with other tasks?
G5. Data exchange rate	(1 Never, 3 Once, 5 Many)	How often will the task exchange data with other tasks within its lifetime?
Information		
I1. Information contents	(1 Text, 3 Graphics, 5 Multimedia)	Complexity of info required/produced?
I2. Information streaming	(1 NA, 3 Discrete, 5 Continuous)	Does the task require streaming of data?
I3. Freshness of data required	(1 NA, 2 Day, 3 Hour, 4 Min, 5 Real-time)	How fresh must data received from a server be to execute the task?
I4. Freshness of data produced	(1 NA, 2 Day, 3 Hour, 4 Min, 5 Real-time)	How fresh must data received by a server and produced by the task be?
I5. Data transmission	(1 NA, 2 Slow, 3 Medium, 4 Fast, 5 Very fast)	What is the expected transmission speed required to execute the task?
Location		
L1. Location dependent	(1 No, 3 Partial, 5 Yes)	Must be executed at a specific location?
L2. Require services at location	(1 No, 3 Partial, 5 Yes)	Require electronic services at the location?
L3. Produce services at location	(1 No, 3 Partial, 5 Yes)	Produce electronic services at the location?
L4. Location report	(1 No, 3 Partial, 5 Yes)	Must report its current location to a server?
L5. Route constraints	(1 No, 3 Partial, 5 Yes)	Must follow a specific route when moving?
Time		
T1. Event-triggered	(1 No, 3 Partial, 5 Yes)	Is the task triggered by an event?
T2. Time constraint	(1 No, 3 Partial, 5 Yes)	Must it be executed at a specific time?
T3. Temporal coordination	(1 No, 3 Partial, 5 Yes)	Must it be timed with other tasks?
T4. Task resumption	(1 No, 3 Partial, 5 Yes)	Can it be halted for later to be resumed from where it left off without a restart?
T5. Task lifetime	(1 Sec, 2 Min, 3 Hours, 4 Days, 5 Weeks)	What is the expected lifetime?

To measure the different characteristics in the framework, we use an ordinal (Lichert) scale (1-5). High values indicate more complexity in terms of system requirements, while low values indicate lower complexity. Many of the characteristics do not use the full scale, but use the values 1, 3 and 5 to get a uniform representation of extreme values. We are aware that it is mathematically incorrect to calculate average value of the ordinal scale, but we have found it useful to do so. We define the importance of a task by assigning a weight on a scale 1-5 (from very low to very high).

2.1 Requirement Indicators

From the scores on the twenty characteristics in our framework (see G1-G5, I1-I5, L1-L5 and T1-T5 in Table 1), we can compute indicators that can help us analyse the mobile scenario and help us prioritise and extract non-functional and functional requirements. The requirement indicators we have identified for our framework are (the first four are simple aggregates and the six following are combined aggregates):

General Task Indicator (GTI) is an average of G1-G5. A high GTI score indicates that the underlying process and transaction infrastructure (e.g. workflow system) must be advanced.

Information Complexity Indicator (ICI) is an average of I1-I5. A high ICI score indicates that the end-system must cope with complex information presentation, management and transmission. The ICI can also be used to select the appropriate hardware and software to be used as a mobile client and server.

Location Complexity Indicator (LCI) is an average of L1-L5. A high LCI score can indicate that the end-system must be location-aware, include Geographic Information System (GIS) functionality, and use a mobile client suitable for mobility in terms of weight, size, battery power etc.

Time Complexity Indicator (TCI) is an average of T1-T5. A high TCI score indicates that time management and coordination of tasks, and advanced transaction support might be necessary. In addition, the TCI also indicates the level of performance and availability required.

Network Connectivity Indicator (NCI) is an average of G3, G4, G5, L4, and T1 and indicates the level of connectivity between the mobile client and the server. It determines the required networking capabilities of the mobile client. Further, it indicates non-functional requirements for the system such as reliability and latency.

Network Speed Indicator (NSI) is an average of I3-I5. A high NSI score means that the transmission speed and quality of service must be high between the mobile client and supporting servers. The NSI also indicates what wireless network technology can be used for the end-system.

Energy Consumption Indicator (ECI) is an average of I5, L1, L2, L3, and T5. A high ECI score means that it is likely that the mobile client device can complete the task will consume much energy.

Transaction Support Indicator (TSI) is an average of G3, G4, G5, T1, T4, and T5. TSI describes the need for flexible/advanced transactional support. A high TSI score indicates that the transactional support must go beyond ACID transactions.

Mobility Indicator (MI) is an average L4 and L5, and indicates how much mobility is involved. The MI is useful for determining the complexity of the environment the mobile client will operate in, e.g. variation in wireless networks. A high MI will affect the choice of equipment (device) and tools necessary to accomplish the task.

Task Complexity (TC) is an average of all characteristics of a task and indicates the complexity of one task. The TC is useful for finding the most complex task that should have the most attention in a further examination.

3   The Framework Applied to Develop a Mobile Application

In this section, we describe how we applied the framework to implement a system for supporting mobile IT-support.

3.1   The Mobile IT-Support Scenario

In 2002, we investigated ways of improving the software used by our IT-support department to manage incoming requests from users, assigning these requests to appropriate personnel and following up these requests. The IT-support department used a system called the Request, Users, and Sys-admin To-do Ticket System (RUST) [7]. RUST is web-based, mainly used to manage requests from users by putting the requests in queues, assigning user requests to IT-personnel, tracking status of requests etc. A big problem with this system was that the IT-support staff did not update the status of tasks in the system when completing the task. This caused the number of user requests in RUST to grow uncontrolled, and it was impossible to know the actual status of user requests. We therefore proposed to extend the RUST system with mobility support, to make it possible for the IT-support staff to use mobile clients at work. This would make it possible to bring important information about the tasks to the labs or offices of concern, write a short report of how the task was solved, and change the state of the task as "resolved" when completed. To extend the RUST system, we started to create a scenario that described the mobile tasks. We first identified the roles involved: Support manager, Support desk and Support engineers. We found that only the support engineers *had* to move around to do their job. We then identified the mobile tasks for the support engineer role:

Task 1. Install new PCs (Support engineers): Install new hardware and software. Priority: High (4).

Task 2. Upgrade such PCs (Support engineers): Upgrade existing computers with new hardware and/or software. Priority: Low (2).

Task 3. Assist users (Support engineers): Help users to solve computer problems (like malfunctioning mouse, keyboard, software etc.). Priority: Very high (5).

3.2 Characterisation of the Scenario

The scenario was characterised using a web-based tool called **m**. Initially, we started to use a simple spreadsheet to characterise mobile scenarios using our framework. However, inexperienced users of the framework found it difficult to know what numbers to choose for the different characteristics. To make this easier, we decided to make a web-based system that could guide the user through the framework by providing useful information for every step of the process, and warn the user when he tried to enter inconsistent values for related characteristics. We created seven consistency rules used by the tool:

Rule 1: $I3 \geq 4$ ($I4 \geq 4 \Rightarrow I5 \geq 4$ If the freshness of data required or produced by a task is within seconds, the data transmission must be fast.

Rule 2: $L4 = 5$ ($L5 = 5 \Rightarrow L1 = 5$ If the task must follow a specific route or if it must report its location, the task is location dependent.

Rule 3: $T3 = 5 \Rightarrow G2 = 5$ If a task must be coordinated with other tasks in respect to time, the task is then part of a sequence.

Rule 4: $I2 = 5 \Rightarrow G5 = 5$ If a task requires streaming, it will require exchanging data many times with another task (the server).

Rule 5: $G3 = 5 \Rightarrow T1 = 5$ If a task is ad-hoc, then it is event-triggered.

Rule 6: $G2=5$ ($L5=5$ ($T2 = 5 \Rightarrow G3 = 1$ If a task has time constraints or is part of a sequence, or has route constraints, it must be planned in advance.

Rule 7: $T4 = 5 \Rightarrow T5 \geq 2$ If a task can halt and later resume from where it left off, it must have a lifetime that can at least be measured in minutes.

The **m** tool can be used to analyse any scenario as long as the process described in Section 2 is followed. The tool allows redefining our existing framework by adding, changing and removing characteristics, but also by creating new frameworks for analysing other properties than mobility. In addition, the consistency rules can be added, changed or removed. We found it necessary for the tool to support evolution, since we have revised the framework three times up till now. These changes have been both editing characteristics and editing consistency rules.

When using the tool, the user is guided through all the necessary steps to carry out a proper characterisation. The process can be divided into two main parts:

Part 1: Defining the Scenario. First, the user is asked to create a scenario by giving it a name and a short description. The scenario description is then extended by adding all the roles that are involved in the scenario (see Fig. 1a).

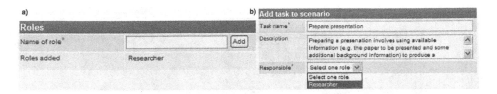

Fig. 1. Defining a scenario in the **m** tool

The next step is then to describe all the tasks that should be a part of the scenario along with selecting the responsible roles for each task (see Fig. 1b). A task is described by a name, description, responsible role, and pre- and post condition related to location, resources and other tasks. It is up to the user to decide the level of detail in task descriptions, but name and responsible role are mandatory.

Part 2: Characterising the Scenario. The characterisation is performed by giving scores to the twenty characteristics in the framework as shown in Fig. 2. The user interface for the characterisation consists of three main parts: The upper left area, where the user applies drop-down menus to select score for every characteristic; the right area, where the current task is described with is attributes; and the down left area, where the user is warned about violations of consistency rules.

The user can choose to ignore these rules or change his/her characteristics to comply with the rules. In the following section, we present the results of applying the **m** tool on the IT-support scenario.

3.3 Results of the Characterisation

The results from applying the MOWAHS characterisation framework to the IT-support scenario are shown in Table 2. To improve the quality of the characterisation, the scenario was characterised independently by three people before the results were compared. The three results were consistent only with small variations. Compared with previous characterisation, we see that the consistency rules and the tool have improved the precision of the framework.

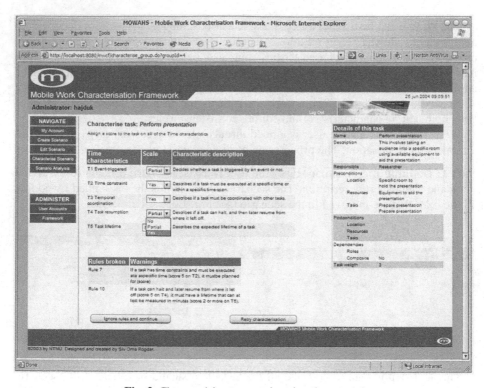

Fig. 2. Characterising a scenario using the **m** tool

Table 2. Scores from the IT-support scenario

Requirement Indicator	T1: Install PCs	T2: Upgrade PCs	T3: Assist users
General Task Indicator (GTI)	2,2	2,6	3,4
Information Complexity Indicator (ICI)	2,4	3,4	3,4
Location Complexity Indicator (LCI)	2,6	2,6	3,4
Time Complexity Indicator (TCI)	3,0	3,0	4,0
Network Connectivity Indicator (NCI)	2,2	2,2	5,0
Network Speed Indicator (NSI)	2,0	3,7	3,7
Energy Consumption Indicator (ECI)	2,5	2,5	3,3
Transaction Support Indicator (TSI)	2,3	2,3	4,5
Mobility Indicator (MI)	3,0	3,0	3,0
Task Complexity (TC)	2,6	2,9	3,6

We can see from task complexity (TC) scores in the table that Task 3 is the most complex of the three tasks. We can also see that Task 3 has the same or higher values on all indicators than the other two tasks. Task 3 has also the highest priority and we will concentrate the analysis on this task, as it will most likely cause the main challenges in the system. If we first consider the GTI, ICI, and LCI, we can see that they all have the value *3,4*. This means that they are all above average complexity. A more thorough analysis shows that Task 3 requires workflow/process support enabling dynamic and unpredicted behaviour, like defining new activities on the spot and redefining parts of the process during enactment. Further, it is necessary to enable synchronisation of data between enacted activities.

An analysis of ICI shows that the mobile client should be updated frequently to notify changes to others using the system. Also the mobile device should be able to display graphics, but a full-fledged multimedia device is not necessary.

A further analysis of the LCI shows that Task 3 is location-dependent, as it might utilise and produce services at the location, and that the location should be reported. This indicates that the system should provide some kind of location-awareness.

The TCI score is *4,0* which indicates that system should allow scheduling of tasks and that the process model should have a time attribute as a part of the task description.

The NCI indicator is *5,0*, and indicates that the mobile client must be continuously available (online) to support the system engineer. This means also that the system can only be used effectively within the actual range of a wireless network. If we consider the NSI with the value *3,7*, the network speed should be between medium (UMTS) and high (IEEE 802.11b). This will also put limitations on the kind of hardware we can use in the final system.

The ECI for Task 3 is *3,3*. It indicates that the mobile client to support the task will consume about half of maximum power. If the ECI has been very high, it could have indicated that the mobile client might need to recharge between every task and could not perform several tasks without access to electric power.

The TSI for Task 3 is *4,5*. It indicates that such a system is likely to require a transaction support beyond standard ACID and that strict locking cannot be used. This also means that we need some mechanism/infrastructure to warn users and enable negotiation between users that try to access and modify the same data.

Finally, the MI has a value of *3,0*. It shows that Task 3 has average mobility, and this indicates that the mobile client device should be rather small and light. In addition, since mobility is involved, the mobile client device should also survive a fall down on the floor or likewise. Further, this will also mean that the user interface of the system has to adapt to a small screen, and a full-size keyboard cannot be used.

3.4 Requirements Found by the Framework

The following requirements were found by using the framework (the indicator the requirement is extracted from is given in parenthesis):

Functional requirements for the system:
- RS1: Must provide a workflow infrastructure to enable management of updates/changes of tasks during enactment (GTI).
- RS2: Must enable data exchange between tasks during enactment, e.g. between two mobile clients (GTI).
- RS3: Should provide location-aware services to the user (LCI).

- RS4: Must enable tasks to be related to time and support for executing tasks at a specific time (TCI).
- RS5: Must offer a transaction support beyond standard ACID-properties (more flexible) (TSI).
- RS6: Must provide infrastructure for handling conflicts between users accessing the same data (TSI).
- RS7: Must provide user interfaces adjusted for the small mobile device that only show the necessary information and widgets (ICI, LCI and MI).
- RS8: Must allow buffering of necessary information on the client in case of network disconnection (ICI, LCI and MI).

Non-functional requirements for the mobile client device:
- RM1: Must be able to display some graphics, but full multi-media capability is not necessary (ICI).
- RM2: Should have a built-in network interface for IEEE 802.11b or better (NCI and NSI).
- RM3: Must have a battery that can last several hours even if the wireless network is used continuously
- (LCI, MI, NCI, and ECI).
- RM4: Must be small, light, and endure falling down to the floor (LCI and MI).

Non-functional requirements for the infrastructure:
- RI1: Must have full coverage of a wireless network in the areas the system will be used in (NCI and NSI).
- RI2: Must have a wireless network capacity of IEEE 802,11b or faster (NCI and NSI).
- RI3: Must provide a way of detecting the position of mobile clients to enable location-aware services (LCI).

3.5 Development of a Mobile IT-Support System

Our first idea of developing a system for mobile IT-support was to extend the existing RUST system [7]. However, we found that the architecture of RUST was not easy to extend and also had poor performance because all data was stored in various text files and not in a database. Since our IT-department was familiar with the RUST system, we wanted to provide roughly the same user interface and functionality as the existing system. In addition, we wanted to expand the system with mobility functionality based on the requirements found in Section 3.4.

3.5.1 The Mobile IT-Support System
From the requirements given in Section 3.3, we started to investigate how these could be integrated in the design of the system.

Firstly, we found that the original process model of RUST had to be extended to relate location and time to a task. In addition, we had to add a location model that could relate rooms, buildings and campuses to a location. We ended up with a hierarchical location model that can identify object position based on room, section, floor, building, and campus. The model describes every level in a distance matrix, enabling us to determine the distance between two locations.

Secondly, we started to look at what kind of location-aware services we should provide to the user. For the support manager role, we found it useful to be able to ``sort'' tasks according to their location. Thus, we could assign all tasks that are geographically close to the same support engineer to improve work efficiency. We wanted to track the locations of the engineers using the system, to automatically assign new incoming tasks in the same area. For a support engineer, we wanted to provide a service for sorting the assigned tasks according to proximity. The mobile client should automatically show relevant tasks for an engineer in a specific area. This would, e.g., make it possible for a support engineer to go to a PC-lab and get a list of all the tasks related to this lab on the mobile client.

Thirdly, we found that an advanced transaction model was required for the system. Support engineers share information on pre-assigned, on-going and completed tasks. In addition, they share data concerning their experiences and knowledge about previously performed tasks. To be able to do this, a knowledge base storing such information had to be provided. Maintaining consistency and durability is important ensuring that all involved parts can have access to the correct information at any time. However, since sharing is emphasised, an engineer should be allowed to see what another engineer is doing. To enable this, transaction isolation could be relaxed. Further, as a task may last a long period of time, it is important to allow engineers to save parts of their on-going tasks. It could happen that tasks must be terminated due to some failures or other situations. When tasks are aborted we also have to be able to allow them undo only parts of their tasks rather than aborting all. This calls for a relaxed atomicity. To summarise, ACID transactional support would be too rigid for this kind of application; instead, we have to allow relaxed atomicity and isolation, but at the same time preserve consistency and durability. A transactional framework proposed in [5] can be used to achieve this. Unfortunately, we did not have a finished implementation of a transactional framework that could be used, so we had to leave out this part in the final system.

3.5.2 The Mobile Client and the Infrastructure

From our characterisation, we found that the mobile device used as a client in the system should be small and have an interface to a wireless network with high bandwidth. All the buildings the IT-support is responsible for have full coverage of an IEEE 802,11b wireless network (WLAN). This means that the mobile clients used in the system can either be laptop PCs or PDAs with WLAN capabilities. In addition, the whole campus has full coverage of a GSM wireless network allowing the use of mobile phones as client devices. The main problem of using mobile phones is the slow GSM network and the cumbersome input device. We found that the PDA would fit best as a mobile client, because of network capabilities and size. However, as most of the staff of the IT-department owns a mobile phone we wanted to provide a client for such devices as well. Our system ended up with support for three kinds of devices: Portable and stationary PCs using standard web-browsers; WLAN-enabled PDAs using limited web-browsers; and mobile phones using WAP browsers.

As these devices have very different characteristics, we did not offer all the system's services to all devices. For instance, the assignment and management of tasks is only possible in the client for PCs. On mobile phones, it is only possible to look through the relevant tasks and change status of these tasks. The functionality of the system is not tailored for each type of client, but the PDA and mobile phone provides a subset of the available functionality. The user interface, however, is tailored for the three kinds of clients. The mobile phone is supported through a WAP/WML interface, while a HTML interface is provided for the PDA and the PC. The HTML for the PDA is adjusted for small screens and does not include frames. Fig. 3 shows how the system looks at a portable PC (a), a mobile phone (b), and a PDA (c).

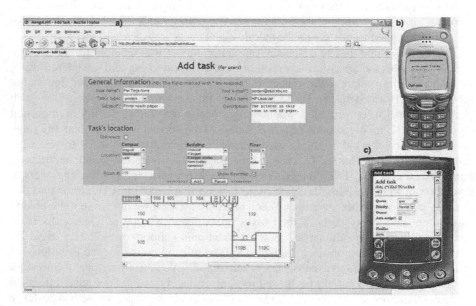

Fig. 3. Screenshots from the system for Mobile IT-support

One problem of our system was to localise the mobile clients. We planned to use the base-stations in the WLAN network for positioning, but could not it was not supported in the network. We solved this problem by letting the user explicitly report his position through a user-interface.

4   Results of the Evaluation

In the spring of 2003, we completed the implementation of the prototype we called MObile Nagging Geek Organiser (MONGO) [9]. The MONGO system had all the functionality of RUST, had support for mobile clients and had mobility support through location-awareness. Two students working for about one year carried out the work. From the early beginning of the project until the project was finished, we made a note about how the usage of the framework affected the development of the system. This was done to be able to answer the research questions we wanted to investigate.

The first research question (RQ1) **asked whether the framework could identify relevant challenges**. From the findings in Section 3.3, the main challenges (requirement indicators with highest value) identified were an unpredictable and dynamic process, complex timing of tasks, users updating/accessing the same data, high level of required network connectivity, and high-speed network. The three first challenges are functional challenges, while the two last are infrastructure challenges. For the latter, we discovered that this was not really a challenge for deploying the system as we had the infrastructure in place. It is perhaps wrong to say that high scores on network connectivity and network speed introduce complexity in the system. However, if the infrastructure in our campus area had not been in place, it would be quite expensive and time consuming to install such networks. For the former three functional challenges, we found these problems too complex to implement ourselves. One solution would be to acquire an advanced workflow system that handles dynamic processes, scheduling, and advanced transactions. The conclusion is that the framework indeed identified relevant challenges from the scenario, even if we did not overcome the challenges in the final implementation.

The second research question (RQ2) **asked whether the framework could be used to identify new functional requirements**. In Section 3.4, eight functional requirements (RS1-RS8) identified by using the framework are listed. Some of these requirements are related to the main challenges described in the previous paragraph (RS1, RS4, RS5, and RS6) and was not implemented in the final system. The rest of the functional requirements were implemented in the system. When designing and implementing the system, all the functional requirements were relevant and important to the system. However, could we have come up with this list without using the framework? The requirements that we already had identified before using the framework were RS1, RS2, RS4 and RS7. Analysing the scenario using the framework discovered the rest of the requirements. It is not only the computed numbers of indicators that lead to the new requirements, but the characterisation itself forced the designers of the system to consider various aspects. To conclude, we found that the framework is a useful tool for identifying new functional requirements.

The third research question (RQ3) **asked whether the framework could be used to identify new non-functional requirements**. In Section 3.4, seven non-functional requirements are listed (RM1-RM4 and (RI1-RI3). The non-functional requirements that we identified were relevant to the final system, but were not very useful. Most of these requirements must be tested with respect to response times and system performance before knowing for sure that the correct equipment and infrastructure is used. However, when we tested the system on a GSM phone and a WLAN PDA, we discovered that the network speed indicated by the framework was correct. To conclude, we found the framework only partly useful for identifying new non-functional requirement. This was mainly because the framework could not give any quantifiable non-functional requirements that could formally be checked.

5 Related Work

We are not aware of any other similar characterisation framework for mobile work. We will therefore in this section outline research that is related to characterisation of mobile scenarios.

Maccari [2] presents an example of requirement engineering challenges in the mobile telephones industry due to the complexity of mobile phone architecture and performance. In addition, requirement engineering for mobile telephones has to cope with many issues such as protocols and technology standards. Also, the limitation of wireless devices, such as network connectivity and network speed, implies important challenges that developers have to deal with. The author argues that requirement engineering is a collaborative task.

Zimmerman [10] suggests the "MOBILE" framework to determine when mobile computing technology should be used to solve challenges related to mobility. This framework focuses on the current technology and software development trends in mobile computing. Further, common related scenarios are discussed, including news reporting and hotel operations. The framework provides a useful overview of necessary support needed for specific mobile environments. However, the framework does not provide any guidelines for how to develop or design systems for mobile support.

Satyanarayanan [8] identifies four constraints of mobile computing concerned with limited resources, physical security (e.g. theft), and communication and durability issues. Another approach is proposed by Forman and Zahorjan [1] who examine three basic features of mobile computing including wireless communication, mobility and portability. These two approaches provide different ways of addressing mobility issues. The former focuses on connectivity issues, while the latter deals with Quality of Service (QoS), such as network bandwidth and device durability.

Rakotonirainy [4] discusses current and future technologies (e.g. CORBA and mobile IP), adaptable to mobile computing environments. For this, he presents a scenario revealing the limitations of the current technology. Although characteristics of mobile work can be derived from this approach, he does not provide a comprehensive framework for characterising mobile work environments.

The related work above mainly focuses on the technical aspects of mobile computing. Our framework investigates mobile computing from another point of view by focusing on the mobile scenario to be supported and identification of the various system complexities introduced by the scenarios. In addition, our framework focuses on software support for mobile work and identifies issues that are not directly related to mobility like process and transaction infrastructure.

6 Conclusions

In this paper we have presented an evaluation of a characterisation framework that can be applied to mobile work scenarios in order to create a software system to support such scenarios. The evaluation shows that the framework is useful for identifying challenges and functional requirements when developing systems that should provide support for mobile work. We discovered that the framework was not so useful for identifying non-functional requirements. The framework was found useful for analysing the mobility aspects of a scenario to be implemented as a system. The characterisation process is useful in itself by systematically focusing on the various aspects of mobile scenarios. Further, the computed requirement indicators will produce a profile of the characteristics of the scenario. The indicators help the designer of a system to identify the complex parts of the mobile system that could lead to decisions on buying COTS components that must be integrated in the system. The framework can also help improve the planning and resource usage in later phases of the project by outlining the hard parts.

From our experiences of using the MOWAHS characterisation framework as a tool to develop systems to support mobile work, we have found the framework useful. The system that was developed using the framework (MONGO) has been tested in actual usage with people from our IT-support department. From these tests, the users have given positive feedback on the mobile features of the system. The main complaints from the users were related to the lacking support for a more flexible process enactment (refining the process on-the-fly) and more advanced management of data updates (transaction management). Both these issues were identified by the framework, but were not implemented in the final system. The support engineers testing the system said that the most useful feature of the MONGO system was that they could bring the system along when working away from the office. This would make it easier to update the state of tasks in the system at the spot and write resolutions at problems at hand that could be reused later. The future will bring many possibilities in providing computer support for mobile work, and believe that our framework can help in developing such systems.

Acknowledgement

This paper is a result of work in a project called MObile Work Across Heterogeneous Systems (MOWAHS) [3]. The MOWAHS project is sponsored by the Norwegian Research Council's IT2010 program. We would like to thank Øystein Hoftun and Per Terje Aune for their contribution in implementing the MONGO system.

References

1. G.H. Forman and J. Zahorjan. The Challenges of Mobile Computing. *Computer*, 27(4):38-47, April 1994.
2. A. Maccari. The Challenges of Requirements Engineering in Mobile Telephones Industry. In *10th International Conference and Workshop on Database and Expert Systems Applications (DEXA '99)*. Springer Verlag, 1999. LNCS 1677.
3. MOWAHS. MObile Work Across Heterogeneous Systems. Web: http://www.mowahs.com, 2004.
4. A. Rakotonirainy. Trends and Future of Mobile Computing. In *Proc. of the 10th IEEE International Workshop on Database and Expert Systems Applications*, pages 136-140, Florence, Italy, 1-3 September 1999. IEEE CS.
5. H. Ramampiaro and M. Nygård. CAGISTrans: Providing adaptable transactional support for cooperative work - An Extended Treatment. *Information Technology & Management (ITM) Journal*, 5(1-2):23-64, 2004.
6. H. Ramampiaro, A. I. Wang, C.-F. Sørensen, H.N. Le, and M. Nygård. Requirement Indicators Derived from a Mobile Characterisation Framework. In *Proc. of the IASTED International Conference on Applied Informatics (AI'2003)*, Innsbruck, Austria, 10-13 February 2003. 8 pp.

7. C. Ruefenacht. The RUST Mail System. In *The 10th annual LISA Conference*, Chicago, Illinois, USA, September 29 - October 5 1996.
8. M. Satyanarayanan. Fundamental Challenges in Mobile Computing. In *Fifteenth Annual ACM Symposium on Principles of Distributed Computing*, pages 1-7, Philadelphia, Pennsylvania, United States, May 23-26 1996. ACM Press.
9. C.-F. Sørensen, A.I. Wang, and Ø. Hoftun. Experience Paper: Migration of a Web-based System to a Mobile Work Environment. In *IASTED International Conference on Applied Informatics (AI'2003)*, pages 1033-1038, Innsbruck, Austria, February 10-13 2003.
10. J.B. Zimmerman. Mobile Computing: Characteristics, Business Benefits, and the Mobile Framework. Technical Report INSS 690 CC, University of Maryland European Division, April 2nd 1999.

Design Patterns and Organisational Memory in Mobile Application Development

Riikka Ahlgren and Jouni Markkula

University of Jyväskylä,
Information Technology Research Institute
P.O. Box 35, FIN-40014 University of Jyväskylä, Finland
{ahlgren, markkula}@titu.jyu.fi

Abstract. Mobile application development is a challenging task for the software companies due to complicated technological and business environments. Patterns have been recognised to be a valuable tool in software development, for they allow design experiences and solutions to be documented systematically and facilitate the communication of design issues. Patterns can be seen as a part of organisational memory, a means to preserve the design knowledge and enable its reuse in later products and projects. In this paper we study how the design patterns can support organisational memory in mobile application design. We present the utilisation of patterns as a dynamic process and analyse their relationship and suitability to the process of organisational memory. As a result, we present a framework, which can be used for supporting and evaluation of patterns as a means for storing organisational memory in software companies.

1 Introduction

Mobile application development is rather new business area that presents a challenging environment for the software companies. Applications need to be developed rapidly and flexible adaptation to new technologies is required. Plans and design solutions need to be changed frequently. New technologies emerge constantly and they are inherently complex. Adaptation to the changes of technology and to the evolvement of business requires innovativeness from the software designers. Since innovation is based on creation of new knowledge, but also on efficient use of existing knowledge [1], the skills of the designers and their experience about past design solutions are highly valuable.

If design expertise is not shared, the work process is both ineffective and inefficient, as the needed knowledge is not available for all and the communication takes a lot of time. Loss of key personnel makes the process also fragile [2]. To enable the knowledge sharing, it is essential to make the knowledge explicit [1]. Explicit knowledge facilitates individual learning, which in turn is a prerequisite of organisational learning [1]. Organisational learning is needed to allow the organisational memory to accumulate, and further, organisational memory is needed to support the retention, maintenance and retrieval of learned knowledge [3].

F. Bomarius and S. Komi-Sirviö (Eds.): PROFES 2005, LNCS 3547, pp. 143–156, 2005.

Design patterns are recognised to be a tool to learn, document and to share experimental design knowledge [4, 5], that is an essential part of software company's organisational knowledge. Although the pattern origins lay in building architecture, they are successfully applied in software development [5]. Patterns enable reuse of good design solutions in an effective manner, facilitate communication and are a tool to document the software code [5]. Patterns are essential development aid particularly in mobile application development, as the business and the technologies evolve rapidly, and this requires the tools to evolve as well.

In our study we develop a framework, where design patterns' use is seen as a dynamic process, which includes design pattern acquisition, retention, maintenance and retrieval. Our research is focused on how this dynamic process fits to the processes of organisational memory in the context of mobile application design. We analyse pattern features and attributes and the support they provide to pattern users in different processes of organisational memory. As a result we form a framework, which brings the theories of organisational memory and design patterns closer to each other, thus enabling the organisational memory research to be applied in later pattern studies.

Our focus lies in mobile application development, where the need of rapid development, together with high quality requirements, is combined. However, the idea of using organisational memory theories in applying design patterns can be applied in other software development as well, when the need of agile tools and high quality are both emphasized.

This paper is organised as follows. We start by describing the environment where the design patterns are needed, namely the mobile application development. Next, the concept of organisational memory is defined and the four processes of it are presented in more detail. The fourth section concentrates on describing the contents of design knowledge in the context of mobile application development. After that, design patterns are presented as a way to communicate the design information. Fifth section concentrates on analysing and comparing the dynamics of design patterns' use to the processes of organisational memory. As a result we present the developed framework. Sixth section draws conclusions of the paper.

2 Mobile Application Development Environment

Mobile application development takes place in development projects, where experts of different domains form an effective team. The fields of expertise may vary even greatly inside one team and communication problems may occur [6]. Typically, one project may last from few months to several years. The team members may change from one project to another, and even during a project.

The application development is affected by the constantly changing mobile business environment, which is formed by a number of players, who together form a value network [7]. Players' effective cooperation requires that the companies have a common view to the mobile business, even though they all have their own business strategies and visions to follow [8]. Typical in this environment is multi-site development, where one product feature is added to several products. The products can be developed in different projects and by different partners, which are situated in different locations. [9]

In addition to the complicated business environment, also the technological environment can be characterized as highly complex. The following factors contribute to this technological complexity:

- The *heterogeneity of mobile devices*. An application is often required to operate on a variety of mobile devices, which are built on different platforms and have heterogeneous capabilities. [10]
- The *heterogeneity of connectivity modes*. Different mobile devices may use distinct network access methods (e.g. GSM, CDMA, WLAN), as well as different network protocols [11].
- Constant *evolution of the technological environment*. In addition to the heterogeneity, the technological environment is also evolving rapidly [12].
- *Constraints of mobile devices*. The contemporary mobile devices have a number of limitations including small displays, small and multifunctional keypads, limited computational power, limited memory, short battery life, etc. [11].

Taken together, multi-sited development environment, rapidly developing technologies and the complicated business environment make mobile software companies' operating environment extremely challenging. Remaining competent in the business requires first of all skilled employees and efficient and agile software development. To be adaptive and productive in any business field requires knowledge how to avoid the costly errors. Since there are no years old tradition or experience on mobile application development, learning from ongoing development projects and creation and exploitation of organisational memory is truly essential.

3 Organisational Memory

The mobile industry is a challenging, busy and complex working environment where agility and rapid software development are necessities. However, in order to survive in the competition, the software companies cannot rely on ad-hoc solutions. The companies need to systematically monitor and collect information about their successes and failures, and develop their processes, methods and expertises, which support their long term efficiency. The companies should learn from the past and constantly improve as an effective organisation.

The concept and theories of organisational memory are closely associated to organisational learning. For organisational learning to occur, learning agent's discoveries, inventions and evaluations must be imbedded in organisational memory [13].

Organisational memory is a form of collective memory, which can be seen as composed of individual minds that share their information through the exchange of symbols [3]. Organisational memory can be defined as stored information from organisation's history that can be brought to bear on present decisions [14]. The contents of the organisational memory include artefacts, relationships, rules and procedures that carry the organisational knowledge [3]. Planned management of organisational memory can have significant effects on company operations.

In organisational memory the human component is essential, for much of the memories are carried by people in their minds. Knowledge and experience accumulate over time and developing expertise can take many years. Social networks and interactions are major means to collect and distribute the knowledge. When the experts leave the company or reorganisations are carried out, organisational memory is often strongly affected. Understanding the forms and processes of organisational memory can significantly support retention and utilisation of organisational knowledge in the company. Efficient utilisation of that knowledge can lead to higher level of organisational effectiveness, which can result in competitive advantages. [3]

The development of organisational memory can be seen as a continuing dynamic process involving the different aspects of the organisational knowledge. Organisational knowledge is mostly carried by individual people and it is not necessarily explicit. Making organisational knowledge explicit, communicable and integrated can increase organisational effectiveness. Turning implicit, tacit knowledge into explicit knowledge is essential for allowing the organisational memory to develop and accumulate. Nonaka [1] has presented a theory of this dynamic organisational knowledge creation. He sees it as continuous dialogue between tacit and explicit knowledge. Explicit knowledge refers to knowledge that is transmittable in a formal, systematic language. Tacit knowledge in turn, has a personal quality, which makes it difficult to formalize and communicate. It often includes individual mental models, know-how and skills that apply only in certain context.

In order to ensure the development of organisational memory, the processes of organisational memory are needed to facilitate acquisition, collection and storing of the organisational knowledge, as well as making the knowledge available for other people at other times and other places. Furthermore, the other individuals need to acquire the organisational knowledge and expertise through learning. Organisational learning is built on individual learning; learning individuals are a necessary requirement for learning organisation. [13]

3.1 Organisational Memory Process

As mentioned earlier, the overall development of organisational memory and learning of organisation can be seen as an evolving dynamic process. In that process, certain phases, or sub-processes, can be specified. In the review on concepts of organisational memory, Stein [3] identifies the following processes, which define the organisational memory: acquisition, retention, maintenance and retrieval. These processes are illustrated in figure 1 below.

Fig. 1. The processes of organisational memory

The first process is acquisition of knowledge. It includes all the ways with which a new knowledge can be introduced to the organisation. In the studies of organisational memory, the focus has mostly been on learning. However, the knowledge can be acquired for example as a human capital through recruiting or acquisition of different types of records. [3]

Second process of organisational memory is knowledge retention, which is often seen as most important part of organisational memory. The major categories of knowledge retention means, which can work on individual and organisational level, are schemas, scripts and systems. Schemas are individual cognitive structures that help to organise and process information and they are hierarchically arranged. Common, shared schemas are called cognitive maps and they include for example norms and efficient working habits. Scripts describe the sequencing of events in familiar situations. Scripts include for example roles and their typical tasks, routines and rituals. Systems, in turn, are a set of inter-related elements which are interconnected either directly or indirectly. These are for example formal organisational structures, such as reporting channels, or informal networks between organisational actors. Also different kinds of records (files, databases etc.), distributed information systems and artificial intelligence systems can be used to facilitate retention of organisational memory related to the organisational activities. [3]

Third process, knowledge maintenance, ensures that the knowledge and expertise of an organisation are accessible to organisation's members, even after a longer time period [3]. Knowledge gaps may be caused by destruction of files or databases or by personnel turnover. Reorganising of teams or breaking down other social structures may as well lead to holes in the expertise.

Last process, knowledge retrieval, is needed to support decision making and problem solving. To make the retrieval successful, the ability to search, locate and decode the information is needed. An important factor is also the costs of locating the information compared to re-inventing the solution from scratch. [3]

The processes are used as a means to exploit the various contents of the organisational memory. In mobile software company, information on past solutions is a central content of organisational memory.

3.2 Design Information as a Part of the Organisational Memory of Mobile Software Company

In general, organisational memory can include all the various aspects related and relevant to the operation of an organisation. The richness of these different aspects becomes evident when studying the organisational memory theories. However, we concentrate here to design information. Design information is the most significant business asset for a mobile software company, and it has a specific role when seen from the organisational memory point of view.

In a mobile software company, business knowledge, technical skills and design knowledge are central knowledge to have and to exploit [9, 2]. Design knowledge combines the business visions and the technical solutions into a purposeful entity, adding value to a single solution by giving it a context and purpose. Failure to manage design knowledge can result in low-quality designs, late and costly error detection, late deliveries and personnel frustration [2]. Design information as such is information about different design solutions and their applications. It becomes design knowledge, when an individual learns the information and understands the intentions and aims of the information as well (see for example [1]).

The significance of design information and good design solutions of software architecture can be enlightened from the perspective of software quality. In any soft-

ware development, a number of quality goals need to be achieved [15], which is especially important in the highly complex mobile application development. Among the
qualities to be achieved, the groups of business qualities, development-oriented qualities, and customer-related qualities can be identified.

The business quality goals encompass qualities related to costs and schedules, as
well as qualities dealing with marketing considerations. The attributes are for example
time to market, costs of development and targeted market. The group of development-
related qualities includes such qualities of the system being designed, which are not
discernable at runtime. These qualities reflect how flexible and maintainable the designed software is. Modifiability, portability and testability among others, belong to
this group. Business and development-related qualities are to be achieved simultaneously with customer-related qualities. These qualities are discernable at runtime and
include, for example, performance, security, reliability and functionality [15].

Many of the quality attributes depend on the architectural design. For example,
availability is achieved by replicating critical processing elements and connections in
the architecture. In turn, business qualities often affect the architecture; when given
development time is limited, the architecture should more intensively reuse existing
components. During design, the quality requirements appear in design trade-offs,
where designers need to decide upon particular structural or behavioural aspects of
the system [16].

The significance of collection and storing of the design information in mobile
software company's organisational memory becomes evident considering the challenging business environment. Extensive need of design re-use is typical for mobile
software development [9]. Since the development time is limited and technologies
are complicated, it is faster and more reliable to use known and tested solutions,
rather than trying to solve similar problems every time in a different way. In addition
to transferring design information in time, from past to present, also spatial transfer is
often needed. Multi-site development is common in mobile software development [9]
and there might be going on parallel development of the same application for different
platforms.

4   Patterns as a Way to Present Design Information

Learning from past designs corresponds to the theories of organisational memory, as
the core of organisational memory evolves over time from decisions that has been
made and from problems that has been solved [14]. During the last decade, the software community has adopted patterns as a means to collect, store and distribute design information and knowledge about successful, tested solutions.

The origins of patterns lay in building architecture, when in 1970's Christopher
Alexander with his colleagues introduced architectural patterns as a tool for designing
houses and other architectural entities [17]. In 1995 the concept of patterns was
brought to software development and the term "Design Pattern" was introduced [5].
After that, the interest to patterns has grown and patterns have been extended to new
application areas, for example to distributed systems, resource management and enterprise architectures [18, 19, 20].

Patterns are common, and typically well known, solutions to recurring problems. Experts have solutions to many recurring design problems and patterns build on the collective experience of skilled designers and software engineers. Patterns capture proven solutions in an easily-available structured form and build a common vocabulary for communication. Programmers, designers, and software architects can use patterns to improve their understanding of architectural issues and their communication about them. Thus, patterns can serve as a software analysis and description tool, as well as means for learning, teaching, communication and complexity handling. [4].

An advantage of patterns, compared to general design guidelines, which are mainly descriptive in nature, is their structural composition [21]. In this structure, the lessons learned during the design are stored in a usable way. The structure of patterns, that reveals pattern consequences and implementation trade-offs, can also be used to keep track of design alternatives, including the ones that were not approved for implementing [22]. This data can be exploited when strategic decisions are made in future iterations, for example in the maintenance phase, or in future projects.

Interrelated patterns are organised into pattern catalogues, which further forms pattern systems and pattern languages. A pattern language covers all aspects of certain context and the patterns build on each other and generate a system [22]. Pattern languages will not remain static, but evolve [22]. As also knowledge evolves due to introduction of new technologies and dying of old ones, new patterns emerge and existing patterns die. The descriptions of patterns evolve as well, in order to remain useful. The nature of patterns as a developing system supports also modification of the patterns and pattern systems. They can be adapted and adjusted to specific needs and for particular community or organisation.

4.1 Mobile Patterns

The specific interests of a mobile software company are related to mobile patterns. Mobile patterns are patterns that cover problem areas that are commonly present in mobile application designs. The mobile patterns are not only applicable for mobile designs, but for other software designs as well. However, they are good candidates for new mobile application designs, since they often occur particularly in mobile application context.

Some mobile design patterns are presented in [19], including Synchronisation pattern and Remote Proxy pattern. Synchronisation pattern presented in figure 2 solves the problem of identical data stored in different locations going out of sync. The solution is a sync engine, which is implemented in both mobile terminal and stationary host. The sync engines communicate through sync interfaces and keep track of modifications applied to local data, exchange modifications with corresponding databases and detect conflicts and realise a conflict resolution strategy.

Remote Proxy pattern illustrated in figure 3 provides a solution to the limited computational resources and network bandwidth by using a proxy between the terminal and the network. The proxy connects to the actual service provider and performs the requested tasks, processes the results and sends them back to the mobile device. [19].

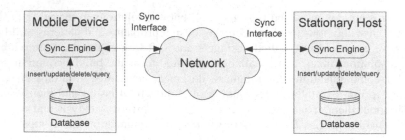

Fig.2. The communication in the synchronisation pattern [19]

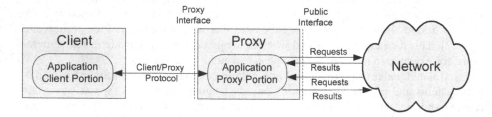

Fig. 3. Remote proxy pattern (Adopted from [19])

Also other mobile design patterns for various problem areas exist. The problem areas are for example portability [23], interactive content development [24], distribution [19, 25], resource management [20] and point-to-point communications [26]. Some patterns are platform dependent (e.g. J2ME), and some patterns are specific to certain mobile programming language (e.g. Symbian patterns) [27, 24].

The drawbacks of domain specific patterns are revealed when using the patterns as a means of communication. If a pattern is treated as a specific to one domain only, the experts of other domains are not familiar with it and the idea of patterns as abstractions of specific problems and solutions is lost. Agerbo and Corncils describe similar case in programming language context. The advantage of common vocabulary is lost in communication between programmers, if the patterns are held as language specific [28]. Similar problem can be confronted when using domain specific patterns.

In project environment people change rather often, and if the company does projects for several domains, also the domain area may change. This poses a new challenge for the design patterns' use, for if the patterns are strictly domain specific, the developers need to learn a new set of patterns every time they are assigned to new tasks on a new domain. Thus, the advantages and disadvantages of domain specific patterns vary according to the definition of domain, and a decent level of abstractness needs to be preserved to maintain the pattern generality that is needed for example in learning the patterns.

5 Patterns and Organisational Memory

As discussed earlier, the knowledge about design solutions used and developed within a software company is a form of organisational knowledge, which has a high value for the company. This knowledge should be collected and stored in an explicit form. Patterns provide a means for this; to capture and express the knowledge of proven solutions. In that respect, patterns and pattern systems can be used as a means to collect and store the essential information as a part of the software company's organisational memory.

Traditionally patterns are seen as collective property. Pattern systems are developed and shared within the software community openly and publicly. Following this scope, companies can utilise general knowledge pool and adopt it to their own purposes. However, pattern approach can be adjusted also to company scope, and this is the view applied here. Narrowing the scope to the specific company's interests enables the theories of organisational memory to become closer and thus applicable.

Use of patterns can make the tacit knowledge explicit, communicative and integrated into everyday design tasks. Particularly in-house patterns can store a great deal of the experimental design knowledge. Patterns provide a template for the experts to express their design expertise in the terms that others can understand. Without any template, it is hard to decide which particular detail or entity in the skills is essential, and which sides of the issue should be described and in what way.

Particularly in the context of mobile application development, aid in communication and in learning is needed, for the project based organisation makes learning extremely difficult. Projects may last several years and experts whom to ask or to learn from may not be present in all project phases. The long time scale is problematic also when thinking about learning by doing, for there is no support for learning, if the tasks are repeated only once or twice in every few years. Also, limits of time and weaknesses in organisational support prevent the organisational routines to conserve [29], making the hectic mobile application development rather challenging environment to create and exploit organisational knowledge.

Patterns have several characteristics and features which support patterns' use as a dynamic part of organisational memory. Pattern acquisition is facilitated by the template that the patterns provide for expressing the design information. When solving new design problems, abstract conceptualization is supported by the design pattern structure, thus enabling the designer to become aware of the different sides of the problem. This further encourages writing down the design knowledge and thus enables it to be preserved. Written format of patterns and explicit pattern name enable the learner to get hold on the contents of a pattern, thus facilitating the knowledge acquisition.

In pattern retention the names of patterns may act as scripts providing a memory rule or reference, which helps the designers to remember the previously used solutions. The structure of patterns facilitates the user to grasp the core of the design solution and the forces that lie behind it.

Akgün, Lynn and Reilly have studied the learning of new product development team and suggest that ordering the new information as clusters may facilitate the internalizing and sense making [30]. Concerning the design information, the structure of patterns, and especially their explicit made relations with each other, can be used when forming these knowledge clusters.

Pattern chunks provide an interconnected structure of patterns, which may act as schemas offering mental categorisation of design problems and their solutions. Often the correct design solution uses several patterns and their combinations, for the problems, for which the help is looked, are most likely rather complicated ones and more than one pattern is needed to solve them [22].

Categorising of patterns and pattern chunks, together with making their relations explicit, is essential to enable the patterns to be used in later times, for use situation of a particular pattern is best interpreted if there are enough cues to the context. Thus, pattern classifications are essential in facilitating the choice of a correct pattern.

Maintenance of design knowledge is supported by having the patterns in written, explicit form. Particularly pattern catalogues facilitate the access to design knowledge, by providing an organised collection of proven solutions. Though, keeping the pattern catalogues up to date may be problematic, particularly in fast evolving mobile application development. Other problems related to pattern repositories are merely political, thus training and other support from management is essential [31].

In pattern retrieval the patterns' explicit relations, decently organised pattern catalogue and the formal structure of a single pattern may facilitate the design knowledge retrieval. Since some parts of the organisational memory are more available for the retrieval than others, the accessibility that the patterns offer is highly valuable in making the strategic design decisions.

The interpretation of the knowledge is also essential [3]. Relevant information can only be interpreted in the context of the background information. Patterns include the context in their structure and presentation format, and this further facilitates the interpretations needed in knowledge retrieval.

Organisational memory processes affect the magnitude, distribution, location and form of the organisational knowledge [3], which implicates that the organisational structures, practices and tools are shaped as well. Also design patterns' use can be seen as a dynamic process illustrated in figure 4, which have phases of acquisition, retention, maintenance and retrieval of design patterns.

The dynamics of design patterns' use affects the organisational structures, practices and tools, and vice versa the organisation has effects on the use of design patterns. The structure of the organisation is essential for allowing the design knowledge to accumulate and further to enable effective organisational learning [32]. In mobile application development projects, where people change rather often, this learning is endangered. Also the long time-scale of projects hinders the learning, as presented above.

Organisational practices include the formal and informal habits of work and communication. Regular meetings of organisations veterans for example, is a practice that can either promote or complicate the design pattern adoption, for often these veterans act as a opinion leaders [31]. Tools, such as information systems, can also greatly affect and be affected by the processes of design patterns' use, as any technical solution to usage of any new technology (e.g. [2, 31]).

Design pattern acquisition is affected mostly by the organisational practices. Organisations values are reflected in the working habits and the informal behaviour of employers. For example, the practical organisation of employers into teams and

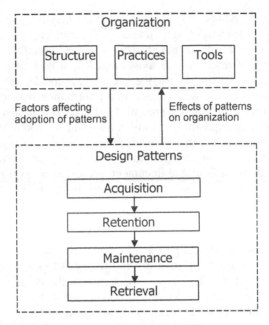

Fig. 4. The framework on the dynamics of design patterns

working groups, as well as whether knowledge sharing and teaching others is appreciated in the organisational culture, makes a difference on how the design patterns can be acquired. Also quality requirements and general working atmosphere, for example, if productivity and efficiency means being constantly in the hurry, can hinder the design pattern acquisition, and also their retention.

Design pattern retention must be supported also by the tools that are used. Grasping the complicated patterns requires a possibility to modify the presentation format in an understandable format, and tools can be either facilitators or aggravators of this task.

In addition to the pattern retention, tools are central also in design pattern maintenance and retrieval. Making sure that patterns are accessible requires some kind of database or other arrangement that enables the knowledge to be saved and mined when needed. How the different features of the tools support these activities is a key issue in putting the design patterns in the ballpark.

Organisational structures are as well needed to support the design pattern maintenance. As discussed in section 3, social structures are essential in maintaining the organisational knowledge, but also in allowing it to be retrieved.

6   Conclusions

In this paper we presented the problem of successful use of previous design knowledge in mobile application design. The challenges in the rapidly evolving mobile business are plenty, thus making it important to restore and use good and tested design solutions and successful organisational memories. Patterns are an important tool particularly in mobile application development, for the rapidly evolving technological and business environment requires the development tools to evolve as well.

To avoid collecting and restoring knowledge which may become obsolete too soon and to ensure the knowledge relevancy in later design projects, the abstraction level of re-used knowledge should be high enough. Thus, the more specific the patterns are, the narrower is their area of reuse and the sooner they might become old-fashioned. This highlights the need of understanding also the forces and rationale behind the solutions.

Organisational memory was defined as stored information from organisation's history that can be brought to bear on present decisions. The means used in memory processes are knowledge acquisition, retention, maintenance and retrieval.

The suitability of design patterns in the different processes of organisational memory was evaluated to show the benefits and drawbacks of our approach. We concentrate in using the patterns as a tool to document, preserve and exploit particularly design knowledge in mobile application development. In addition to the formality and the structure, also the pattern catalogues and continuous evolvement of design patterns was seen as key features that most facilitate the different processes of organisational memory. Our view of patterns as a continuously evolving process is consistent with the previous study of [31] and presentation of [33].

In our study we developed a framework illustrated in figure 4, where design patterns' use is seen as a dynamic process, which affects the organisational structures, practices and tools, and vice versa the organisation has effects on the design patterns' use. The phases are similar to the processes of organisational memory, namely design pattern acquisition, retention, maintenance and retrieval. Particular pattern features supporting these processes were discussed in section 5.

The aim of the framework is to bring the theories of organisational memory closer to the design patterns' theory, and thus enable the design pattern studies and usage to exploit the findings of organisational memory literature. Seeing design patterns' use as an evolving process enables the pattern usage to become closer to everyday work in software companies and thus facilitates the pattern adoption in small steps.

In future the framework can be used as a tool in empirical evaluations of design patterns and their suitability as organisational memories. Another open research issue is the technological solutions and their features that support design patterns in becoming a part of organisational memory.

Acknowledgments

The research work presented in this paper was done in MODPA research project [http://www.titu.jyu.fi/modpa] at the Information Technology Research Institute, University of Jyväskylä. MODPA project was financially supported by the National Technology Agency of Finland (TEKES) and industrial partners Nokia, Yomi Software, SESCA Technologies and Tieturi.

References

1. Nonaka, I., A Dynamic Theory of Organizational Knowledge Creation, Organization science, 5 (1994).
2. Terveen, L. G., Selfridge, P. G.,Long, M. D., From "Folklore" to "Living Design Memory", SIGCHI conference on Human factors in computing systems, ACM Press, Amsterdam, Netherlands, (1993).

3. Stein, E. W., Organizational Memory: Review of Concepts and Recommendations for Management, International Journal of Information Management, 15 (1995), pp. 17-32.
4. Buschmann, F., Meunier, R., Rohnert, H., Sommerlad, P.,Stal, M., Pattern-oriented software architecture - A system of patterns, John Wiley & Sons ltd., Chicester, West Sussex, England, (1996).
5. Gamma, E., Helm, R., Johnson, R.,Vlissides, J., Design Patterns: Elements of reusable object oriented software, Addison-Wesley, Boston, USA, (1995).
6. Galbraith, J. R., Competing with Flexible Lateral Organisations, Addison-Wesley, USA, (1994).
7. Chen, G., Wireless Location based Services, Technologies, Applications and Management, (2002).
8. Kar, E. v. d., Maitland, C. F., Montalvo, U. W. d.,Bouwman, H., Design guidelines for mobile information and entertainment services: based on the Radio538 ringtunes i-mode service case study, 5th international conference on Electronic commerce, Pittsburgh, Pennsylvania, USA., (2003).
9. Ketola, P., Integrating Usability with Concurrent Engineering in Mobile Phone Development, Department of Computer and Information Sciences, University of Tampere, Tampere, (2002).
10. Rupnik, R.,Krisper, M., The Role of Mobile Applications in Information Systems, The Second International Conference on Mobile Business, Austrian Computer Society, Vienna, Austria, (2003).
11. Siau, K.,Shen, Z., Mobile communications and mobile services, International Journal of Mobile Communications, 1 (2003), pp. 3-14.
12. Nokia, Mobile Internet Technical Architecture - Visions and Implementations, Edita Publishing Inc. IT Press, (2002).
13. Argyris, C.,Schön, D., Organizational Learning: A Theory of Action Perspective, Addison-Wesley, (1978).
14. Walsh, J. P.,Ungson, G. R., Organizational memory, Academy of management review, 16 (1991).
15. Bass, L., Clements, P.,Kazman, R., Software Architecture in Practice, Addison-Wesley, United States, (1999).
16. Gross, D.,Yu, E., From Non-Functional Requirements to Design through Patterns, Requirements Engineering, 6 (2001).
17. Alexander, C., Ishikawa, S., Silverstein, M., Jakobson, M., Fiksdahl-King, I.,Angel, S., A Pattern Language. (Volume 2). Oxford University press, New York, (1977).
18. Fowler, M., Patterns of enterprise application architecture, Addison-Wesley, Boston, Mass.; London, (2003).
19. Roth, J., Patterns of mobile interaction, Personal and Ubiquitous Computing, 6 (2002).
20. Noble, J.,Weir, C., Small Memory Software: Patterns for Systems with Limited Memory, Addison-Wesley Professional, (2000).
21. Granlund, Å., Lafrenière, D.,Carr, D. A., A Pattern supported approach to the user interface design process, 9th International Conference on Human Computer Interaction, New Orleans, (2001).
22. Coplien, J., Software Patterns, SIGS Books & Multimedia, New York, (2000).
23. Tasker, M., Professional Symbian programming: Mobile solutions on the EPOC platform, Wrox Press, Inc., (2000).
24. Hui, B., Big designs for small devices, http://www.javaworld.com/javaworld/jw-12-2002/jw-1213-j2medesign.html, (2002).

25. Yuan, M., Developing Web-service-driven, smart mobile applications, O'Reilly Media, Inc. Available from www.ondotnet.com/pub/a/dotnet/ 2004/02/23/ mobilewebserviceapps. html, (2004).
26. Guidi-Polanco, F., Cubillos F., C., Menga, G.,Penha, S., Patterns for point-to-point communications, Dip. Automatica e Inormatica, Politecnico di Torino, Italy, VikingPLoP 2003, http://plop.dk/vikingplop/2003/Patterns/guidi.pdf, (2003).
27. Allin, J., Dixon, J., Forrest, J., Heath, M., Richardson, T.,Shackman, M., Professional Symbian Programming. Mobile Solutions on the EPOC platform., Wrox Press Ltd., USA, (2000).
28. Agerbo, E.,Cornils, A., How to preserve the benefits of Design Patterns, 13th ACM SIGPLAN conference on Object-oriented programming, systems, languages, and applications, Portland, Oregon, USA, (1998).
29. Lewitt, B.,March, J. G., Organizational learning, Annual Review of Sociology, 3 (1988).
30. Akgün, A. E., Lynn, G. S.,Reilly, R., Multi-dimensionality of learning in new product development teams, European Journal of Innovation Management, 5 (2002).
31. Manns, M. L., An investigation into factors affecting the adoption and diffusion of software patterns in industry, De Montfort University, United Kingdom, Leicester, (2002).
32. Galbraith, J. R., Designing the innovating organization, in K. Starkey, ed., How organizations learn, International Thomson Business Press, London, UK, (1996), pp. 156-181.
33. Alexander, C., The Timeless Way of Building, Oxford University Press, New York, (1979).

Specifying Patterns for Mobile Application Domain Using General Architectural Components

Oleksiy Mazhelis[1], Jouni Markkula[1], and Markus Jakobsson[2]

[1] University of Jyväskylä,
Information Technology Research Institute,
P.O. Box35, FIN-40014 University of Jyväskylä, Finland
{mazhelis, markkula}@titu.jyu.fi
[2] Ab SESCA Technologies Oy,
P.O. Box77, FIN-68601, Jakobstad, Finland
markus.jakobsson@sesca.com

Abstract. Software companies adopt patterns as a means to improve architecture and design practices. During recent years, the application of patterns has extended from general software applications to specific problem domains. In a new domain, suitable patterns fitting to the essential design problems in the new context need to be identified. In this paper, we introduce a general architectural model of mobile applications, which can be used to identify and organise essential patterns in mobile-application design process. This model is employed to construct a high-level architecture of a particular application. For each component of the architecture, the model may suggest candidate patterns that can be used for elaborating the component. Subsequently, the results of the design process are used iteratively to further develop the architectural model. The presented model is verified and tested by employing it to address the design problem of supporting multiple user interfaces in a real mobile application product.

1 Introduction

Mobile technology domain is a challenging environment for software design. The complexity and peculiarities of the environment as well as fast development of the technologies beget design problems which are not present in traditional application environments. This, in turn, often necessitates design solutions differing from those commonly applied in other conditions. These solutions should take into account the specifics of mobile terminals, such as limited battery power and small screen size, and the limitations of wireless networks, such as restricted bandwidth and availability. Furthermore, the applications should be future-proof, i.e. remain up-to-date in the quickly evolving technology, and they need to be implemented and ported quickly to new technologies and platforms. Thus, mobile applications need to possess specific qualities including, in addition to required functionality, the qualities of modifiability, reliability, efficiency, etc. These qualities are largely achieved by architectural means [1], and therefore, careful architectural design is important.

Patterns have been introduced and adopted by the software community to support systematic design of architectural solutions with the desired qualities. A number of

F. Bomarius and S. Komi-Sirviö (Eds.): PROFES 2005, LNCS 3547, pp. 157–172, 2005.

design patterns and pattern systems have been elicited during last decade. A pattern in software engineering has been defined by [2] as a description of communicating objects and classes that are customized to solve a general design problem in a particular context. Patterns should present a solution to a problem in a context, and their essential elements include [2]: the pattern name; the description of the design problem and its context; the solution describing elements, their responsibilities and collaborations; and the consequences of applying the patterns, e.g. the benefits and trade-offs. Patterns range in their abstraction level, varying from abstract architectural styles to design patterns and low-level programming idioms [3]. They can be divided into general (or domain-independent) patterns [2, 3] and domain-oriented patterns tailored to specific areas of applications and/or to specific development tools or platforms [4, 5].

Patterns are typically collected in pattern catalogues. The patterns in catalogues are organised according to certain characteristics, and relationships between them are described. To be useful, the catalogues should contain only a *restricted* number of patterns which reflect the most commonly encountered design problems, in general or in a specific domain[1]. Among domain-independent pattern catalogues, one of most well-known is the famous GoF catalogue presented in [2]. An example of a domain-specific catalogue is the Core J2EE Pattern Catalog[2] [4], where many of the patterns useful in designing enterprise applications with J2EE are collected.

As noted above, the mobile environment represents a technology domain which has its peculiarities strongly affecting the design solutions. In solving a design problem with patterns, these peculiarities should be taken into account in order to identify suitable patterns. Namely, the patterns fitting to the current design problem and *matching the context* of current application need to be selected [2]. While rich collections of patterns are already available through different sources, their applicability in mobile domain needs to be evaluated by the designer, as the consequences of patterns (and possibly, other characteristics as well) may have different significance in the context of mobile applications. Some domain-independent and domain-specific patterns available in pattern catalogues might appear inappropriate in this context or require modification. On the other hand, some patterns address the problems often encountered in designing mobile applications, and, hence, are highly valuable in the mobile domain.

The patterns applicable in the mobile domain can be divided into i) the patterns specific to (or particularly useful in) the mobile domain, and ii) the patterns from other domains or domain-independent patterns that can be also used in the mobile domain. Examples of *mobile-domain specific patterns* are the Synchronization and the Remote Proxy patterns [6] as well as the Symbian two-phase construction and the cleanup stack idioms [7]. The patterns from other domains *directly applicable* in the mobile domain can be exemplified by Model-View-Controller (MVC) [7] or by the Remote façade pattern [8, 5].

Thus, the use of patterns promoting the development of flexible and reusable architectural and design solutions is vital for mobile software companies, and identifying essential and appropriate patterns for mobile technology domain is an important issue for mobile software architects. These patterns could be seen as forming a catalogue of

[1] By domain, we refer to a particular set of constraints applied to the platforms, problems, etc.
[2] Available e.g. at http://corej2eepatterns.com/Patterns2ndEd/index.htm

core patterns for mobile domain, by analogy with core J2EE patterns mentioned above. In this paper, we present an approach, which is applied in the MODPA research project, and which is aimed at organising and identifying suitable collection of patterns.

To facilitate the pattern identification process, we propose the use of a general architectural model providing a hierarchically organized collection of base components, whereon a mobile application or service may be built. In the process of designing a particular application, these components are employed to construct a high-level architecture of this application. The components of this high-level architecture are then refined using design patterns. For each of its components, the proposed model may suggest the related patterns, out of which the most appropriate patterns may be selected by the designer and used in the refinement process. Subsequently, the results of the design process are used to update the model (both the components and the relationships between them and related patterns), i.e. the model evolves with each iteration of its use in the design. The model aims to be of practical use for both industrial and academic environments. In mobile software companies, the model may be employed as a skeleton for selecting and cataloguing appropriate patterns and refining a core architecture for their software products. From an academic viewpoint, the model may be seen as a tool assisting in pattern evaluation in the context of mobile domain.

Within the MODPA project, we are planning to implement a mapping between the model's components and the patterns most useful in the mobile domain. The mapping may be further refined within a developing organization by prioritising the design problems which the organization encounters, and by mapping these problems to the patterns (either publicly-available patterns or proprietary patterns elicited within organization) being applied in the design.

In the following section, we describe the place and the role the proposed model plays in the design process. A more detailed description of the model is provided in Section 4. In Section 5, using a case application, the model and its use in the development process is empirically tested. Finally, conclusions to the paper are given in Section 6.

2 Using General Architectural Model to Support Utilisation of Patterns

Below, we consider how the development of good architectural solutions and identification of appropriate patterns can be supported by using a general architectural model.

When following a top-down approach in the process of system design, we proceed from requirements analysis through high-level design to detailed design and implementation. According to [9], the design process in this case includes five activities: partitioning requirements, identification of subsystems, assignment of requirements to subsystems, specification of subsystems' functionality, and definition of subsystems' interfaces. This process can be seen as consisting of two stages [10]. At the first stage (conceptual architecture design phase), the components of the system, which are needed to satisfy the stated requirements, are identified (this corresponds to three first activities above). At the second stage (concrete architecture design phase), these components are refined and interactions between the components are specified using design patterns.

Both stages may be supported by a general architectural model, which provides a hierarchically organized collection of base components and suggests candidate patterns to refine them (Figure 1). In particular, at the first stage, where the conceptual architecture is designed in terms of high-level components, the general model may support the design process by suggesting the potential high-level system components. Ideally, if the general model is comprehensive and well designed, the conceptual architecture of a particular system may be produced from the general model by excluding irrelevant components and relationships. Following the pattern approach, the components in the general model are organized according to one or several architectural patterns, which present known good solutions for the structure of an architecture [3]. As a result, these architectural patterns are likely to be preserved in the design of architectures based on this model. At the second stage, the general model may suggest the design patterns relevant in the refinement of high-level components.

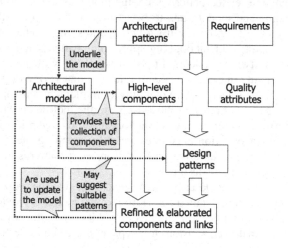

Fig. 1. Supporting design process with a general architectural model

Afterwards, the knowledge obtained during the design can be used to refine (update) the model, both the model components and the mapping between components and patterns. This can be seen as an iterative process: as a product is being designed and developed within an organization, the obtained knowledge and experience can be used to update the components and their relationships (e.g. replace outdated components with new ones or add new ones) and to update the mapping (e.g. by modifying the descriptions of patterns, or by modifying the links between patterns and problems).

In the following section, the description of the general architectural model is provided.

3 General Model of Mobile System Architecture

As described above, a general model may be used to facilitate the identification of relevant design patterns. A tentative general architectural model, wherein the generic elements of mobile applications or mobile systems are united, was developed for the present purpose. The model was built based on the Nokia's MITA layered element model [11], OMA's OSE architecture [12], and Parley's OSA architecture [13]. In Figure 2, the general structure and components of the produced model are shown.

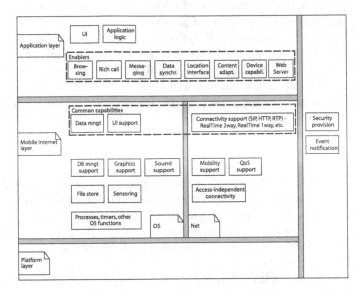

Fig. 2. An outline of the tentative general architecture model and its components

The model follows the layered approach described in the Layers architectural pattern [3]. Each layer is comprised of a number of components with approximately the same level of abstraction. A component represents a software or hardware unit that performs some functions at runtime. In general, the components of a layer use the functionality provided by the lower level as well as the functionality provided within the same layer. A component may as well serve as a re-transmitter of the lower-level functionality to higher levels.

The model includes the Application, the Mobile Internet, and the Platform layers introduced in Mobile Internet Technical Architecture (MITA) layered element model [11]. The Platform layer contains core OS components, hardware components along with related drivers, and network drivers corresponding to various access technologies. At the Mobile Internet layer, three groups of components are designated according to [11]. The first group consists of the SDK libraries enabling e.g. the use of OS functionality for the applications. The second group of components provides the application and user interface (UI) support; it includes supporting components for the user interface, for application inter-working, and the components allowing applications to manage their data sources. The third group of components, in turn, is responsible for satisfying the connectivity requirements of an application; it implements a set of the Internet protocols.

The Application layer includes a User Interface part, an Application Logic part, and a number of enablers. The User Interface implements the presentation logic of the application such as displaying the information and the handling of user requests, and Application Logic, also referred to as domain logic [5], represents the set of operations, which, in aggregate, form the core of the service provided by the application.

Enablers can be defined as technology building blocks intended for use in the development, deployment or operation of a Service [14]. Various enablers are described in MITA [15] and a number of enablers are being standardised by Open Mobile Alliance[3] (OMA). Examples of enablers are browsing, messaging, or location interface. Implementation of enablers may involve the cooperation of multiple distributed sub-components, and hence may require network connection. Messaging, for example, involves the use of a specific server responsible for storing and retransmitting a message between the sender and the recipient. The use of an enabler as a single component in an architecture increases the abstraction level of this architecture, and, by encapsulating underlying complexity, makes the architecture more understandable.

The components of the Mobile Internet layer, in turn, represent building blocks for the enablers. From the viewpoint of enablers, many of these components implement functions that can be reused by multiple enablers, providing common capabilities upon which other capabilities are built, and are therefore called as common capabilities [14]. In the model, the common capabilities are the higher-level components within the Mobile Internet layer.

According to the principles of layered architecture introduced above, a component may request the functionality of the lower-level components, or the components within the same layer. However, some components invalidate this principle as they are requested by (and may request) the components of different layers. Such components correspond to basic mechanisms enabling the use of other components, and are referred to in the model as common functions [13]. Security services could be considered as an example of common functions. Different layers may require data encryption for confidentiality provision.

Due to space constraints, the description of the components illustrated in Figure 2 is omitted in the paper. The collection of components in the model is not considered as complete; instead, it is to be extended and refined by analysing the feedback obtained during the application of the model in the design of mobile applications or services.

As mentioned above, wherever possible, the model should suggest the relevant design patterns for refinement of its components. For this, a mapping needs to be established between the model's components and a collection of patterns applicable in the mobile domain. In addition to suggesting potentially suitable patterns, the model should provide additional information, which would help the designer to evaluate the pattern applicability to a particular problem in hand. This additional information may include examples of successful or unsuccessful use, consequences, platform or programming-language related constraints, and other information reflecting the credibility that could be assigned to the patterns as well as their relevance to the design problems encountered in the organisation.

---

[3] http://www.openmobilealliance.org

4 Developing Mobile Applications Using General Architectural Model and Design Patterns

The model (Section 3) and its use in software development process (Section 2) have been tested with a case of a real software product. The case application was SESCA Reservation system (SE-RE) developed by SESCA Technologies [16] and the work was carried out in co-operation with the company. The testing involved two objectives. First, the sufficiency of the model's components was tested by using the model to create the high-level architecture for the case product. Second, with the aid of the case, the use of the model in the course of the system design process was tested. This case reflects a single iteration of the use of the model, wherein the model is applied to produce a high-level architectural design, to refine the components and wherein the results of the design are used to update the model's components and the mapping between the components and patterns.

In the development of the case system, the attention was paid only to one part of the system, which is related to the generation and support of Multiple User Interfaces (MUI). The problem of supporting MUI is frequently encountered in the design of applications and services in mobile, and multi-channel, environment [17, 18, 19], and therefore related patterns are of high importance within the mobile technology domain.

4.1 SE-RE System and Its Development

SESCA Reservation system SE-RE represents an online resource-reservation system. Using SE-RE, company resources such as persons, laptops or meeting rooms can be reserved for a specific period of time [16]. SE-RE is accessible through multiple web UIs, e.g., XHTML UI for desktop browsers as well as smaller XHTML or HTML based UIs for mobile browsers. Screenshots of these UIs are presented in Figure 3. SE-RE is provided as an ASP service; therefore, the system must be able to serve hundreds of users simultaneously.

The main functionality in SE-RE consists of creating, viewing, updating, and deleting reservations. SE-RE also includes other desktop UI related features, such as help pages and administration of users, resources and companies. This additional functionality is not considered in this paper.

The main page in SE-RE is the calendar page, where the user is presented with the reservation table for the requested resource and week. In the desktop UI, empty slots in the calendar are links to a reservation page for that slot. The filled slots are reservations and contain links to further information about the reservation. The reservation page includes fields for entering subject, requestor name, date, starting and ending time for the reservation, and also allows modification or deletion of existing reservations. The mobile UI has no links in the empty spots, instead the reservation form is included at the bottom of the page. This is to minimize page size and count and to minimize the number of links in the UI.

In the earlier version of SE-RE, separate UIs had been designed for each type of platform. Furthermore, specific versions of the UI had to be maintained even for some devices, because of the device-dependent browsers versions affecting, for example, the interpretation of HTML format.

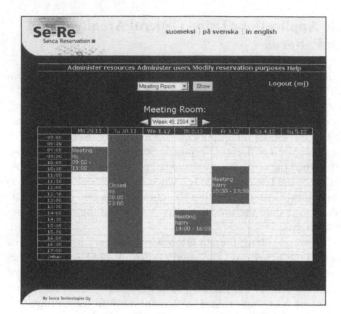

Fig. 3. Screenshot of the desktop UI and a mobile UI in SE-RE

This limitation needed to be addressed during the development of a new version of the system aimed at improving the system maintainability. In it, a single-source presentation architecture was aimed at reducing the maintenance overhead of the SE-RE application. The description of the UI should not be dependent on the end device; instead, a general UI should be able to adapt to the end devices at run-time. At the same time, efficiency should not suffer on the expense of better maintainability. For the new version of the system, the following requirements and quality attributes were stipulated [16]:

- Adaptability. The user interface should adapt to the capabilities of the mobile terminals and to the roles of the users. Different platforms require different sets of content and different style. Before the adaptation, terminal capabilities have to be recognised.
- Efficiency. The efficiency is characterised by the response time and by the resource utilisation. The response time consists of the server request-processing time and the data transmission time. For desktop browsers, where the data transmission time is short, long delays are not tolerated, and therefore the required processing time is shorter. Meanwhile, on mobile-terminals, where the transmission time is inevitably longer due to relatively slow GSM or GRPS transfer rates, a longer processing time is not so noticeable. The server-side processing time was required to be < 200ms for desktop UIs and < 1000ms for mobile UIs. In order to be efficient, the system should have good performance quality [1].
- Changeability. The multiple interfaces supported by the system should be easy to change. For this, the specification of the content, the specification of user interface, and the specification of the presentation (defining the outlook of the UI and the content) should be done independently. Also, the content and UI must be described in one place for all platforms. This requirement corresponds to the modifiability

quality attribute [1]; specifically, the system architecture should support easy modification of the user interfaces.

- Design robustness. This feature encompasses the need for the stability of the presentation and the need for the analyzability of the architecture. The stability of presentation implies the absence of the unexpected effects in the representation due to changes in the UI or content specifications and is closely related to the modifiability quality attribute [1]. The analyzability refers to the easiness of identifying the architecture parts that require modification. To achieve the stability and analyzability requirements, the architecture should be modular and not over-complicated.
- Ease of development. This feature could be mapped to the buildability quality attribute [1]. In order to avoid long development time, the development should not be overly complex. Because of this quality attribute, the length of the UI descriptions must be restricted, while enabling sufficient control over the resulting UI.

4.2 Application of the General Architectural Model

Following the approach introduced in Section 2, we applied the general architectural model, presented in Section 3, to the SE-RE system. The SE-RE system was decomposed into the high-level components based on the general architectural model. The decomposition was carried out by adapting and specialising the model through the exclusion of irrelevant components. The remaining high-level components included in SE-RE are shown in Figure 4 below.

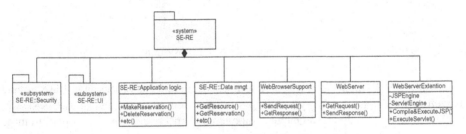

Fig. 4. High-level components of SE-RE system

The UI subsystem implements user-system interaction. It is responsible for sensing the user input, for reacting to the user input information by requesting specific system services, and for displaying the system response information to the user.

The Application logic component implements the core services of the SE-RE system, i.e. access to and modification of the reservations-related information. The Application logic component requires the use of one or several databases; access to and management of these databases is facilitated by the data management (Data mngt) component.

The SE-RE system is distributed between a server and a terminal. The user interacts with the system through a Web-page interface on the terminal. The processing of user requests is performed on the server side. The WebBrowserSupport component and the WebServer component enable the communication between the terminal and the server parts. The WebServer delegates part of the processing to the extension (WebServerExtention) component, whose responsibilities include, for example, the compilation of JSP files and execution of servlets.

The security subsystem is aimed at preventing unauthorized access to the resources of SE-RE. For this, authentication and access control services are implemented.

For the purposes of the case study, we focus our attention only on the UI subsystem. The decomposition of this subsystem into lower-level components is presented in Figure 5.

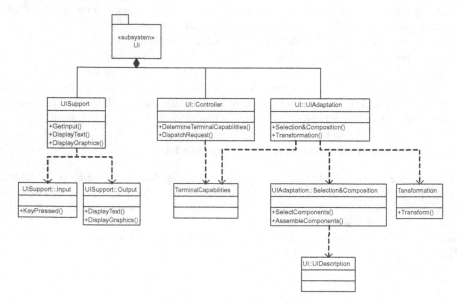

Fig. 5. Components of UI subsystem

The low-level functionality responsible for sensing and pre-processing of user input, as well as for displaying the system output information on the screen of user device is implemented by the Input and Output components, respectively. The UISupport, in turn, represents a façade that provides an interface to the lower-level functionality.

The Controller handles the user input information. It determines the service requested by the user, and dispatches the request to an appropriate Application logic component (method). Dispatching may take into account user roles and the capabilities of the user terminal.

After the system completes the processing needed for the provision of the requested service, the result of the processing are presented to the user. The process of generating the presentation can be divided into the selection and combination of the presentation elements and their subsequent transformation according to the capabilities of particular terminal. The selection and transformation are performed by the Selection&Composition and Transformation components, respectively. The UIAdaptation component serves as a façade for them.

The TerminalCapabilities enabler is included in the model. Using the description of the device capabilities provided by the TerminalCapabilities component, the UIAdaptation component adjusts the content to be rendered to the user. The adjustment may involve the modification of UI elements (e.g., for mobile terminals, a table may be substituted with a list element), as well as the modification of the information presented (e.g., long names may be cut, or the resolution of images may be reduced).

4.3   Identification of Design Problems and Specifying Solutions Using Patterns

The lower-level model of the UI subsystem, presented in Figure 5, was used to locate the design problems requiring appropriate solutions. In this case, three design problems, discussed below, were identified. Available design patterns were applied, in order to specify the solutions satisfying the system requirements described in Section 4.1. The components which are inspected in detail are the components in the UIAdaptation subsystem: UIDescription, Selection&Composition and Transformation.

Platform-Independent UI Description

The UIDescription component in Figure 5 is responsible for offering a description of the UI. For easy modifiability, the description of the UI needs to be made platform-independent. In order to improve maintainability, the repetition of code should be minimal in such description.

XHTML was chosen as the UI description language for SE-RE. The pages generated by the server can be sent to desktop clients for Cascade Style Sheets (CSS) adaptation without any transformations, thereby decreasing response times for desktop users and, more importantly, drastically decreasing the server load. As XHTML MP has been adopted by the mobile industry, XHTML content description is becoming the standard in all web browsers, both desktop and mobile, which eliminates the need to produce content in different formats for different devices [11].

Improving code maintainability through the avoidance of code duplication and the reuse of modular UI components is described in the Composite View pattern [4]. The Composite View pattern, in turn, is based on the Composite design pattern [2], which suggests decomposing a complex object into a hierarchy of components, in which all the constituting components would be treated in a similar manner.

In Figure 6, a class diagram of Composite View design pattern is shown. In Composite View, components of different hierarchy levels are treated equally, and therefore, a component does not need to know whether it is a root component (root CompositeView), a middle-level component (non-root CompositeView), or a leaf-level component (SimpleView). The layout of UI components is defined in a separate module (Template). The uniformity of components in the hierarchy allows a component to be reused a number of times in different places in the composition. In the context of SE-RE, this reusability is employed for component reuse in several compositions rather than within a same composition. For SE-RE, the Composite View offers better maintainability through the elimination of duplication and the separation of layout definitions, and it offers better efficiency by limiting transformations.

In order to make the identification of the Composite View pattern easier for the designer, a reference to this pattern needs to be included in the UIDescription component (Figure 5) of the model.

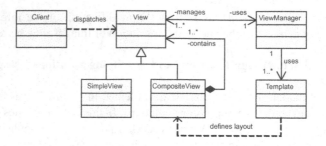

Fig. 6. Composite View design pattern

Platform-Dependent Selection of UI Components

Different platforms require different UI elements due to different formats, types and sizes of terminals. For instance, the control elements for managing the resources should be available for a user with administrative rights at a desktop interface, while they should be hidden in the UI at a mobile terminal. Transformations can be used to remove information from the general UI, but this has performance drawbacks. Therefore, in the SE-RE system, the UI components are selected separately for each platform; the components being selected are described in the UI definitions [16]. For each platform, a separate root definition is created, wherein the specific UI components of this platform are specified.

The mechanism for choosing an appropriate root definition (Composite View) for a particular platform is implemented using Abstract Factory design pattern [16] illustrated in Figure 7. The selection of this pattern is justified by its usefulness for configuring a system with one of multiple families of products [2]. In case of SE-RE, the role of products is played by the definitions of UI in the form of Composite Views, one of which is to be selected.

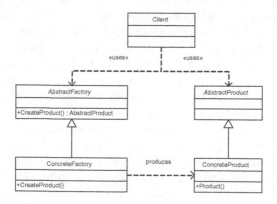

Fig. 7. Abstract Factory design pattern

The Abstract Factory pattern "provides an interface for creating families of related or dependent objects without specifying their concrete classes" [2]. In the context of the SE-RE system, the role of AbstractFactory is to provide an abstract interface to retrieve a composite UI definition by its name, independently of the factory implementation. As a result, the fact that there exist multiple UIs is hidden from the rest of the application. This is especially useful for the UIController component, as it can dispatch requests from different user agent in the exact same way and leave the responsibility of producing platform dependent responses to the Selection&Composition component. Therefore, a reference to this pattern needs to be included in the Selection&Composition and UIController components of the model.

Adaptation of the UI Components
The UI elements should be adjusted to the peculiarities of a particular terminal. As the Selection&Composition component composes the appropriate UI data, the adjustments deal only with formatting issues. The Transformation component in Figure 5 implements this functionality.

A straightforward solution would be to implement separate transformations for each web-page used in the application and for each supported type of terminal/browser. Such transformation can be implemented e.g. using Transform View pattern [5]. This, however, would result in a large repetition of code, as the same transformations would need to be specified for multiple pages, and similar transformations may be needed for different terminals/browsers. In order to avoid code repetition, the process of transformation may be decomposed into several operations applied consequently, so that the same transformational operations could be applied/reused for different pages or for different terminals/browsers.

In order to be reusable and easy to add and remove, the components implementing transformational operations should be i) independent of each other and ii) loosely coupled with the other components of the system. The Intercepting Filter pattern introduced in [4] addresses these issues by implementing pluggable self-contained pre- and post-processing filters.

The FilterManager intercepts the requests and/or responses, which are sent between the Client and the Target, and invokes the chain of filters to perform their tasks. In fact, the FilterManager wraps the functionality of the target with additional functionality (implemented by Filters), and thus follows the Decorator pattern [2].

In the SE-RE system, a chain of four filters are employed to implement the necessary transformations; the last two filters are application-independent and therefore may be reused in other applications:

1. The first filter is transforming the components according to the constraints of a particular group of terminals.
2. The second filter is responsible for adding predefined style (in a form of style tags) to the UI components.
3. The role of the third filter is to implement workarounds required for adapting the UI components to the limitations or misbehaviour of particular versions of browsers and/or other software components at the terminal.
4. The final fourth filter implements the transformations, which adapt the UI to the markup language understood by the browser.

With the aim to improve the efficiency (performance) of the system, the definition of the interface is implemented in the design of SE-RE so that no transformations would be required for the desktop UI. This is motivated by the observation that requests from desktop clients constitute the vast majority of issued request, and skipping the transformation phase saves a lot of resources on the server. Thus, the UI in the SE-RE system follows the graceful degradation approach [19], where the UI is designed for the platform with the richest capabilities, and is subsequently simplified (degraded) to meet the constraints of platforms with inferior capabilities.

4.4 Results and Discussion

Owing to the use of patterns, the development of SE-RE has resulted in a system that meets the specified requirements. The wanted qualities of the system, as described in section 4.1, have been achieved mainly by architectural means. The high *performance* (efficiency) measured as system response time was improved due to i) the UI component selection and ii) the adoption of the graceful degradation approach, allowing the response time for desktop PCs to be minimised at the expense of longer response times for mobile terminals. The *modifiability* (changeability, design robustness) of user interface was achieved by i) splitting the responsibilities among the architectural components (separation between content and presentation and the use of separate transformation filters), and ii) by avoiding the repetition of the UI code, thanks to the use of a hierarchy of UI component definitions, and to the inclusion of reusable transformation filters. Separation of responsibilities/concerns also reduces the risk of unexpected effects caused by modifications.

Patterns played a significant role in specifying the architectural solutions with desired qualities. The Composite View design pattern (based on the Composite) was used in the specification of UI components in order to reduce code repetition. The selection of the appropriate UI components was implemented using Abstract Factory design pattern. In turn, the Intercepting Filter pattern (based on Pipes and Filters architectural pattern and Decorator design pattern) was used to implement platform-tailored transformations of UI components.

The SE-RE case showed that by applying the patterns to a particular design solution, the general architectural model can be refined and updated iteratively. Namely, it was shown that the mapping between model's components and suitable patterns can be enriched with new links. For instance, assuming that the UIDescription and Selection&Composition components do not contain the links to the Composite View and Abstract Factory patterns, the appropriate links should be added to these components. In a similar vein, the Transformation component of the model should be supplemented with the link to the Intercepting Filter pattern. If these links are already present in the model, the description of the patterns may still need to be modified. For example, the frequency of use characteristics may be updated, the code examples section may be enriched with new examples, etc. Similarly, the collection of components included in the model may need to be updated taking into account the results of the design process.

With iterations, the content of the model should be gradually tailored to the needs of the particular developing organization using it, i.e. the components and patterns used in the organisation will be reflected in the model. Such a tailored model can be seen as a form of organisational memory, whereby the knowledge can be transferred from past to present, and retention of which is important for sustaining the competitiveness and competence of the organisation [20].

5 Conclusions

In order to enable fast development and efficient maintenance of high-quality applications and services, crucial in the rapidly evolving mobile domain, carefully thought and tested architectural designs are important. The knowledge of past successful solutions in the forms of architectural and design patterns can be employed in order to accelerate the emergence of architectural solutions meeting the stated requirements.

The tentative general architectural model has been proposed in the paper as a means to support the identification of patterns suitable in a particular context. The aim of this model is to suggest the high-level architectural components and the patterns that can be used to refine these components. The general model can be, for example, applied within a company developing certain types of mobile applications. When it is used generatively, the model can be updated and/or extended iteratively by analyzing and incorporating the feedback obtained in the process of designing applications. This process refines and further develops the general architecture and the incorporated design solutions, which can be used as a reliable basis for building new applications or services. On the example of online reservation system, it was illustrated how the model can be employed in the architectural design, and how the results of the design activities can be utilized to refine the model.

Further work will include the evaluation of available patterns and pattern systems with respect to their suitability in the context of mobile applications and services. For this, the relevance of the problems addressed by patterns for the mobile domain need to be evaluated. For example, problems can be ranked according to their importance using the opinions of experts involved in the development of mobile applications and services. Then, for the patterns addressing important problems, the consequences of their use need to be analyzed taking into account the specificity and limitations of the mobile domain. The results of the evaluation will be employed to refine mapping between patterns and components in the proposed general model.

Acknowledgement

This research work presented in this paper was done in MODPA research project [http://www.titu.jyu.fi/modpa] at the Information Technology Research Institute, University of Jyväskylä. MODPA project was financially supported by the National Technology Agency of Finland (TEKES) and industrial partners Nokia, Yomi Software, SESCA Technologies and Tieturi.

References

[1] Bass, L., Clements, P. and Kazman, R., *Software Architecture in Practice*, Addison-Wesley, United States, (1999).
[2] Gamma, E., Helm, R., Johnson, R. and Vlissides, J., *Design patterns: elements of reusable object-oriented software*, Addison-Wesley, Boston, Mass., (1995).
[3] Buschmann, F., Meunier, R., Rohnert, H., Sommerland, P. and Stal, M., *Pattern-oriented Software Architecture. A System of Patterns*, John Wiley & Sons, (1996).

[4] Alur, D., Crupi, J. and Malks, D., *Core J2EE Patterns: Best Practices and Design Strate-gies*, Prentice Hall / Sun Microsystems Press, (2001).

[5] Fowler, M., *Patterns of enterprise application architecture*, Addison-Wesley, Boston, Mass.; London, (2003).

[6] Roth, J., *Patterns of Mobile Interaction*, Personal and Ubiquitous Computing, 2002 (2002), pp. 282-289.

[7] Tasker, M., *Professional Symbian programming: Mobile solutions on the EPOC plat-form*, Wrox Press, Inc., (2000).

[8] Yuan, M., *Developing Web-service-driven, smart mobile applications*, O'Reilly Media, Inc.   Available   from   http://www.ondotnet.com/pub/a/dotnet/2004/02/23/ mobilewebserviceapps.html, (2004).

[9] Sommerville, I., *Software engineering*, Harlow: Addison-Wesley, (1998).

[10] Matinlassi, M., Niemelä, E. and Dobrica, L., *Quality-driven architecture design and quality analysis method. A revolutionary initiation approach to a product line architec-ture*, VTT Publications, Finland, (2002).

[11] Nokia, *Mobile Internet Technical Architecture - Visions and Implementations*, Edita Pub-lishing Inc. IT Press, (2002).

[12] OMA, *OMA Service Environment, Draft Version 1.0*, Open Mobile Alliance, (2004).

[13] OMA, *Inventory of Architectures and Services V1.0, Draft Version 1.0*, Open Mobile Al-liance, (2004).

[14] OMA, *Dictionary for OMA Specifications V1.0.1*, Open Mobile Alliance, (2004).

[15] Nokia, *Mobile Internet Technical Architecture - Solutions and Tools*, Edita Publishing Inc. IT Press, (2002).

[16] Jakobsson, M., *User interface adaptation in dynamic web applications for mobile de-vices*, Helsinki University of Technology, Department of Computer Science and Engi-neering, (2004).

[17] Vandervelpen, C. and Coninx, K., *Towards model-based design support for distributed user interfaces*, NordiCHI '04: Proceedings of the third Nordic conference on Human-computer interaction, ACM Press, Tampere, Finland, (2004).

[18] Eisenstein, J., Vanderdonckt, J. and Puerta, A., *Applying model-based techniques to the development of UIs for mobile computers*, IUI '01: Proceedings of the 6th international conference on Intelligent user interfaces, ACM Press, Santa Fe, New Mexico, United States, (2001).

[19] Florins, M. and Vanderdonckt, J., *Graceful degradation of user interfaces as a design method for multiplatform systems*, in J. Vanderdonckt, N. J. Nunes and C. Rich, eds., *Proceedings of the 9th international conference on Intelligent user interface*, ACM Press, Funchal, Madeira, Portugal, (2004), pp. 140--147.

[20] Stein, E. W., *Organizational Memory: Review of Concepts and Recommendations for Management*, International Journal of Information Management, 15 (1995), pp. 17-32.

A Meta-model for Requirements Engineering in System Family Context for Software Process Improvement Using CMMI

Rodrigo Cerón[1,*], Juan C. Dueñas[1,*], Enrique Serrano[1], and Rafael Capilla[2]

[1] Department of Engineering of Telematic Systems,
Universidad Politécnica de Madrid,
ETSI Telecomunicación, Ciudad Universitaria, s/n, E-28040 Madrid, Spain
{ceron, serrano, jcduenas}@dit.upm.es
http://www.dit.upm.es/
[2] Department of Informatics and Telematics,
Universidad Rey Juan Carlos, Madrid, Spain
Rafael.Capilla@urjc.es

Abstract. Software industries are pursuing the development of software intensive systems with a greater degree of re-use, reduction of costs, and shorter time to market. One of the successful approaches taken is based on the development of sets of similar systems where development efforts are shared. This approach is known as System Families. This article discusses an important issue in system family engineering activities: requirements modelling in system family context. The requirements must contain both the common and variable parts. Also, functional and non-functional aspects have to be considered in system family approach. Besides, an organization framework must be taken into account for requirements management. Some meta-models for these issues in system family are proposed and discussed. Based on the proposed model, a process for requirements management and development according to CMMI practices has been created.

1 Introduction

For many years, software industries have been trying to achieve the development of software intensive systems with a greater degree of re-use, cost reduction, and shorter of time to market. System Families (SF) are considered to be one of the most successful approaches to carrying it out. It focuses on the reduction in the time to market and development costs through the provision of a set of elements that are common to a number of systems. An SF is therefore a set of systems that share a significant part of the development effort; since they share many elements. It is

* Rodrigo Cerón is a visiting professor from Universidad del Cauca, Colombia. Rodrigo Cerón is sponsored by COLCIENCIAS - Colombia. The work carried out by Juan C. Dueñas has been partially undertaken as part of the CAFE and FAMILIES projects (Eureka 2023, ITEA ip00004, ip02009), partially supported by the Spanish company Telvent and by the Spanish Ministry of Science and Technology, under reference TIC2002-10373-E, TIC2002-12426-E

F. Bomarius and S. Komi-Sirviö (Eds.): PROFES 2005, LNCS 3547, pp. 173–188, 2005.
© Springer-Verlag Berlin Heidelberg 2005

sensible to think that the concepts behind them are also common[1]. The main goal of this article is to present one approach to the requirements modelling and management in system families. In addition, Capability Maturity Model Integration (CMMI^{SM}) is taken as a base for improvement of software process.

The basic work behind the results presented here has been carried out within the CAFÉ [1] and FAMILIES projects. The CAFÉ reference framework (CRF) provides a guide to classifying the activities and models related to SF development. It is based on the model used in the ESAPS project; in addition, it is enhanced [1]. In summary, CRF can be divided into two main parts CAFÉ Process Reference Model (CAFÉ – PRM) and CAFÉ Assets Reference Model (CAFÉ - ARM). In Fig. 1 CAFÉ-PRM is shown. The objective of this model is to represent major activities and methods operating on the core assets, to allow the mapping of the contribution/tools against a common reference. In the upper part we found Application Engineering, its main purpose is to obtain products based on assets. In the lower part we found Domain Engineering, its main purpose is to develop the assets of the SF. And, in the middle part, we found those elements that support both Application and Domain Engineering. Our research work is aimed at solving problems in the transition from Domain Analysis to Application Analysis and the reverse.

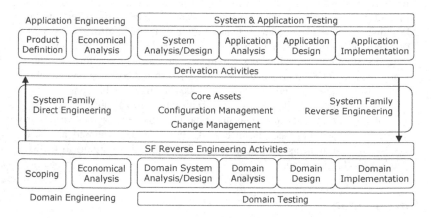

Fig. 1. CAFÉ Process Reference Model

The rest of the paper is organized as follows. In the next section, we present a general review of the most important related work. In addition, we outline the current issues that we found throughout all the most important work in this arena. In section 3, we present the paper of the requirements with respect to SF engineering organizations. In section 4, we show the present our requirements meta-model and its connection with CMMI. In section 5, we present our requirements development and management process, its support by means of our developed tool and a short outline of a project assessed by it. Finally, in section 6, we conclude with some remarks and future research.

---

[1] Some authors do distinguish between "product line", "product family" and "system family". We will use them interchangeably.

2   Related Work

One of the main activities in our research work is conceptual modelling for system families. There are several unrelated works in this area for example: [2-7], in consequence, we have identified the need of a shared set of common concepts. Even more, in our analysis of the requirements management models, we have found that no single model covers in full extent the current needs of system family engineering (SFE). Thus, the work presented in this document takes as inputs the published meta-models provided, among others, by:

- ALCATEL-SPLIT (Alcatel Software Product Line Integrated Technology) [8]; whose key issue in the management of product line requirements is the capability to distinguish if a certain requirement is optional, alternative or parameterized for a certain product [4].
- The Helsinki University of Technology HUT model [9] provides a different view of goals, features and constraints. Its meta-model also focuses on the creation of hierarchies and ordering requirements for priority.
- Siemens model for requirements modelling and traceability [10] allows the division of the set of requirements into shared, discriminated (optional, single-adapter, multiple-adapter, required-adapter and excluding-adapter).
- Telelogic DOORS® model for requirements engineering [11] allows marking requirements as common to the whole product family, specific of a single product or parameterised (which would define a different product for each parameter value chosen).

Our attempt is to cover the specific needs in SFE regarding requirements management and development. A view of these needs has been provided by SEI [2], referring to the number of requirements in a system family (higher than for a single product), the number of stakeholders involved, also higher; the risks imposed by wrong requisites affecting the whole family; and the differentiation between common and specific requirements.

In our work, we also try to explore the relationships between requirements engineering activities and the BAPO (Business, Architecture, Process and Organization) model [12]. It is currently being developed in the FAMILIES project and it proposes a conceptual framework for the analysis of complex technology phenomena, where those four dimensions are explicitly addressed. In the rest of the article, we describe a meta-model that supports requirements management, and where some of the concepts appearing in the Business and Organization are included.

Thus, the management of the SF reference requirements is supported by the capability to represent the information into a single model, containing both the common and variable requirements in it. The same can be said about system family architecture (that common to the set of systems in the same system family [2]), and system family implementation (both vertical and horizontal components and component infrastructure [2]); thus, providing the capability to get a single model of the requirements of the system family is a primary focus to handle the full process efficiently. In addition, CMMI guidelines helped us with the definition of what the requirements meta-model have to contain.

From the revision of the actual tools and research papers, we found several key specific issues that must be considered when performing requirements development and management in a system family. These problems can be seen as follows.

– Traceability: the system family approach extends the complexity of the development by adding the variable-common dimension in each of the assets in the system family. In this way, we need an automatic support. We will use it to obtain special information, i.e.: navigation, traceability and calculation of coverage matrixes. Therefore, this support is more complex than in traditional system engineering.
– The separation of common and specific requirements can be further elaborated into several aspects: the explicit representation of the variability in requirements, including the basic relations [13], as well as other more detailed variability options.
– Binding, variability derivation or selection of the system specific requirements is the other side of the requirements management for system families. When a system or application engineering cycle is executed, requirements from the system family repository must be selected, adapted or modified.
– Decisions and conflicts management: keeping the set of requirements that are common for the system family is not enough for its efficient management; also, the requirements that are specific of a certain system must be kept in the common base. Thus, contradictory requirements (for different systems in the family) may coexist and the decision making process must reflect the conflicts that can appear while in the development. In any case, the decisions that lead to the requirements for a system must be recorded and justified.
– Reuse and evolution of requirements: keeping a central database with the requirements for the system family is desirable. Obtaining the system specific requirements is a must. However, the system family cannot be maintained alive if there is no capability for a requirement that appears in several systems to become a common requirement for the system family.

To improve the quality of the whole software development process involving system family development we have also taken into account the guidelines related to requirement engineering practices, exposed in the CMMI [14]. A detailed full requirements development and management process covering SFE has been elaborated according to those CMMI practices. It could be seen as a step by step guide and it is based on our requirements meta-model. This process has been defined according to the Software Process Engineering Metamodel (SPEM) specification [15]. We have also developed a tool that fully supports such requirements development and management process.

In general, we found that the requirements development and management processes heavily rely on a set of conceptual models for all the entities and relationships that are handled in them. For this reason, we define a set of well defined meta-model. In this way the process definition are eased. In conclusion, the quality and completeness of the meta-models limit the set of potential activities that can be done; moreover, the tool implementation is eased by the definition of it.

3   The Context for Requirements in SFE

The system family can be described by several models and relations between them (See Fig. 2). Models give a way of communication for the people into the organization. SF environment contains requirement, architectural, design and test models. Basically, the requirement models deal with the functional and non-functional definitions for the systems in the family. The architectural models describe high-level design definitions of the systems in the family. The design models show the different components that the architectural models describe. Moreover, the test models contain the tests the system family must satisfy. In fact, there are two different kinds of test: common to the whole system family and specific of a single system. This test reutilisation shortens the test creation phase.

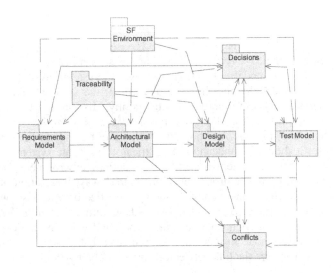

Fig. 2. System Family and some of its assets

In addition to the traditional models, we can see traceability, decisions and conflicts packages in Fig. 2. As CMMI states, full traceability relationships among models are mandatory. This is shown by the traceability package in Fig. 2. In fact, trace mechanisms are important to perform change management activities and to understand the overall system. Higher abstraction level requirements can be traced to the detailed requirements that refine them and even to the artefacts that implement them. Decisions and conflicts among elements are part of the system family, being related to the models too. Using traceability relationships it is possible to find out which conflicts affect a specific requirement and which decisions were proposed to solve such conflicts. Decisions and conflicts must be solved in order to obtain systems. Decisions will solve some of the variability issues [16]. The later the variability issues are solved the more flexible the system family is. In this way, we can state that there are requirements, architectural, design and test decisions. Conflicts must be solved in order to obtain coherent systems, and they depend on the multiple possibilities of solution inside a system family; different alternatives would lead to different conflicts, but there should be at least one solution for each conflict.

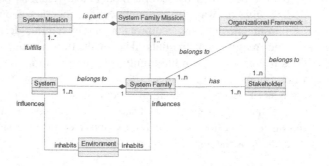

Fig. 3. System Family Environment package

A detailed view of the SF environment package is shown in Fig. 3. This package is related to the different models as shown in Fig. 2. System, System Mission and Environment are related following the general ideas of the standard IEEE 1471-2000 [17], in a similar way System Family, System Family Mission and Environment too. The system family must fulfil at least one mission, and in a similar way, the system must fulfil at least one mission. Additionally, the system belongs to the system family and in this sense; it should be understood as a mean to facilitate system development. The System Family and its systems inhabits in its defined environment. However, the first one is influenced by the environment in an indirect way. In addition, it belongs to an organizational framework and its development is justified only in this context. In this way, the organizational framework is related with the O dimension of the BAPO model. Stakeholders belongs to an organizational framework, and work in the development of the system family as a whole. In this way, we can state that system family has one or more stakeholders. They are the link between B and O of the BAPO model.

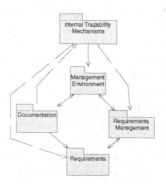

Fig. 4. Requirement models

A detailed view of "Requirements Model" package is shown in Fig. 4. As can be seen in the figure, this is itself composed of five packages. First, "Documentation" package contains the classes used to generate glossaries. Additionally, they help us in requirements management and development practices as is in CMMI. Second, the "Management Environment" package contains elements needed to organize SF. In fact, they help us in requirements management practices as is in CMMI. Third, "Internal Traceability Mechanism" package contains elements related with horizontal traceability. Therefore, they help us in maintain bidirectional traceability between requirements as is in CMMI. Fourth, "Requirement Management" package is responsible for managing and controlling requirements and their links with systems and SF. Therefore, it helps us in configuration management practices for requirements as is in CMMI. Finally, the "Requirement" package provides the means to define requirements, their types and their relationships; therefore, it contains all those necessary characteristics that requirements must fulfil. The partition of the requirements model in these packages is based in the CMMI and all the related work studied.

In section 4, a detailed view of these five packages will be provided in order to clarify the proposed meta-model.

4   Requirements Meta-model

One of the aims desirable in SFE is having a common vocabulary that eases communication among the different members of an organization. This is the main reason for the existence of the "Documentation" package as shown in Fig. 5(a). Stakeholders involved in the SF will create entries in a glossary, in order to have a common vocabulary to unify the language used to define the requirements [18]. This will also establish and share common non-ambiguous domain knowledge. The elements in this package help us in obtain understanding to Requirements as stated in CMMI specific practices.

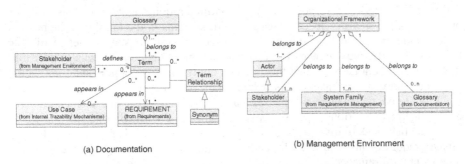

(a) Documentation   (b) Management Environment

Fig. 5. Documentation and Management Environment Packages

Obviously, the glossaries will lie under the umbrella of an organizational framework, described in the "Management Environment" package. An organization will possibly be in charge of several system families, among which these glossaries can be shared (see Fig. 5(b)). The elements in this package help us in obtain commitment to Requirements as stated in CMMI specific practices.

A traceability mechanism will be necessary to manage the complexity associated to the development process inside a system family. This is the main purpose of the

"Internal traceability mechanism" package (see Fig. 6). High abstraction level goals (related to functional aspects) and "softgoals" (related to quality aspects) will be the first approach to elicit the requirements, in direct relationship with CMMI. This is how business level objectives are expressed. Then, functional requirements will be defined by means of use cases. Such use cases will help discovering new features. Decisions in the development process will possibly derive in conflicts. These conflicts will have an impact on the use cases previously built. Relationships among conflicts, decisions and use cases will be kept in this package (see Fig. 6). Requirements can also be traced to the artefacts, which describe or implement them. The elements in this package also help us in maintain bidirectional traceability of Requirements as stated in CMMI specific practices. Additionally Decision and Conflict help in identifying inconsistencies between Project Work and Requirements as is in CMMI practices.

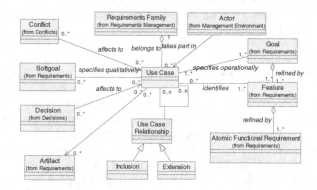

Fig. 6. Internal traceability mechanism package

The stakeholders are responsible for providing requirements, and these can be common to all systems or specific to a subset of systems in the family. In the process of derivation from the SF domain to the specific system, stakeholders will take decisions. Specific requirements for a system will be obtained by means of decisions taken by the stakeholders. Within this process, conflicts might appear and they should be solved again by the stakeholders before going on. These relationships are kept in the "Requirement management" package as shown in Fig. 7. The elements in this package help us in various aspects in relation with the CMMI. By one side, they help us in establish a Definition of Required Functionality. By other side, they help in manage requirements changes. In addition, they help us in allocating product-component requirements.

SF manages a huge amount of requirements. Taxonomy will be indispensable in order to organise and effectively manage them [19]. Taking as resources [20], [21] and [22], we have built a classification of the requirements. As a first criterion, requirements can be classified as functional or non-functional (see Fig. 8). Functional requirements can be classified again into other three categories: goal, feature and atomic. The elements of the more abstract categories are composed of elements from the more specific categories. Goals help defining new use cases while such use cases identify new features. Those features are user visible functional requirements that refine goals. A feature is later refined by atomic functional requirements. Non-functional requirements are initially discovered according to the defined softgoals. Then the discovered non-functional requirements have to be specified in terms of ISO-9126 (its definition can be found there [22]). Non-functional requirements can have parameterised quantitative values. This is another SFE variability mechanism as each parameter value could lead to a different final system.

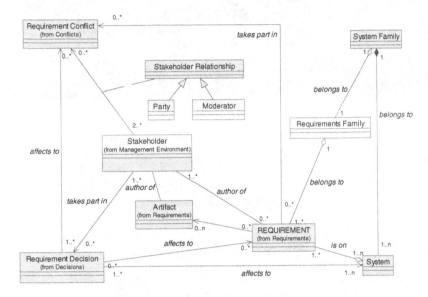

Fig. 7. Requirement management package

Requirements reuse in SFE is another objective of our requirements meta-model. Only requirement groups can be reused if there is enough domain knowledge available as to assure that higher-level requirements will be satisfied. Consequently, features may be reused while atomic requirements cannot be reused. When creating a new system, the selected reusable features have to be checked to confirm that the chosen feature set is valid. This is known as a constraint satisfaction problem [23].

Relationships among requirements have to be taken into account for reusing and maintainability purposes in SFE (see Fig. 9). Several kinds of relationships considered in the meta-model are the following: generalization, coexistence, refining and revision. Requirements can also be defined as common to the whole system family or specific of a particular system, in order to provide other requirements reuse and SFE variability mechanisms.

Each requirement should be characterised by a set of features: priority, cost, importance, state and future stability. In addition, requirement related risks are considered along the full development process (see Fig. 9). This information is a first approach to support project management practices as shown in the CMMI. In addition, such information would be useful to automate conflict resolution, decision process and evolution of the system family. The elements in this package help us in develop customer and product requirements as stated in CMMI specific practices. In addition, they help us in analyze requirements.

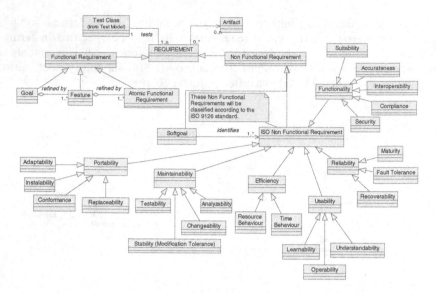

Fig. 8. Requirement package (1)

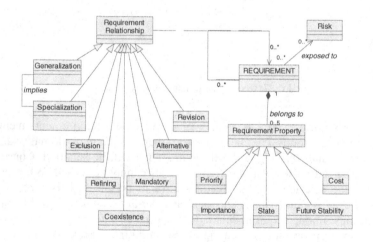

Fig. 9. Requirement package (2)

5   Requirements Development and Management Process

The CMMI guidelines for software process improvement are declared as being neither processes nor process descriptions see [14] page 1. Our aim was to develop a step by step requirements development and management process based on CMMI. This new process would serve as a complete guide for requirements engineering based on our requirements meta-model. To express our process model in a normalised non-ambiguous way the SPEM specification [15] was used. Therefore, our process model is more specific than the principles exposed in CMMI. However, it still has enough generality as to be useful for different organisations, and environments.

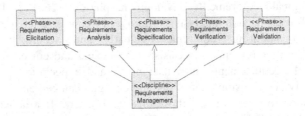

Fig. 10. Phases of the requirements development process

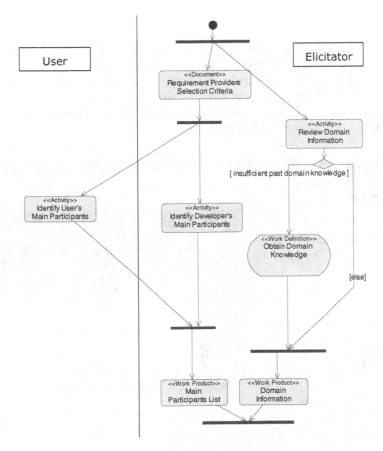

Fig. 11. A partial view of the requirements elicitation phase

Our process covers the requirements discipline of the full software development process. It can also be applied to system engineering projects. Moreover, it takes into account the relationship between requirements definition, architectural implementation and some detailed design aspects.

The defined process is a sequence of activities that distinguish the roles and responsibilities of the customer and the requirements engineer. We specified the following traditional requirements development phases (see Fig. 10): elicitation (discovering of user needs), analysis (refining of requirements and constraints), specification (documenting requirements clearly and accurately), verification (checking that the requirements are consistent, complete and correct) and validation (checking that the requirements meet user needs and expectations). Requirements management activities (version controlling and change management) are defined as a discipline common to every one of those phases. The CMMI practices follows the same phases described. For example, in Fig. 11 we can see a partial view of the sequence of activities for the requirements elicitation phase.

We have also considered the sequential evolution through CMMI levels. At CMMI maturity level 3 the requirements development activities have reached their maximum evolution. Our model covers the evolution from level 1 to 3, clearly distinguishing which activities belong to each level. This way allows progressive and feasible evolution, and avoids level skipping.

Other generic process management practices that are beyond the scope of requirements engineering are only partially taken into account. Nevertheless, the requirements conceptual model covers some basic project management aspects such as cost and time estimation and risk management.

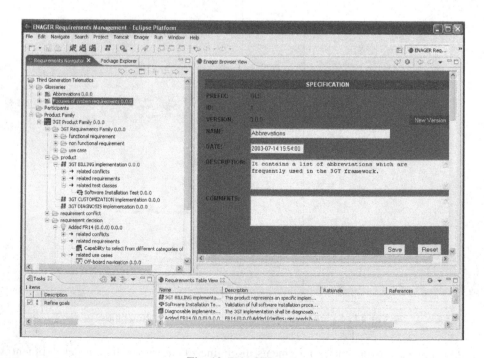

Fig. 12. ENAGER tool

CMMI does not provide any system family specific practices [24]. In spite of this, our process takes into account some proven system family practices also considered on our requirements meta-model. Some of these practices are determining possible variation points and identifying requirements and test classes common to the whole system family.

We have also developed an integrated requirements tool based on our SFE requirements meta-model that fully supports this requirements process. This tool, called Environment for Requirements Analysis and Management (ENAGER), provides functionality to define every requirements meta-model element, such as glossaries, participants, systems, requirements, use cases, conflicts, decisions, test classes, artefacts, etc. A screen caption is shown in Fig. 12. This window is divided into four areas. In the upper left window, we can see a tree for the framework containing the system family. In the upper right window, we can see a specification for a selected element in the tree. In the bottom left window, we can see some task for the requirements. Finally, in the bottom right window, we can see a table view of the requirements. Our meta-model is very complete and in consequence, the construction of the tool was not very difficult.

Using this tool, traceability relationships can be established between meta-model elements. Among other supported traceability relationships, ENAGER allows tracing requirements to their containing systems, implementing artefacts, original use cases, test classes, refining requirements and other related requirements. ENAGER supports automated traceability matrix generation too. The tool also provides other requirements management functionalities, such as version controlling.

ENAGER uses a central data repository, which can be accessed remotely via web. As mentioned in [25], these web based tools ease communication among different stakeholders and increase the overall process performance.

Using ENAGER, we identify the common and variable requirements of an open project. The project is in the field of customer applications related with home systems and automotive. By means of ENAGER, we can study traceability characteristics, relation between common and variable requirements, glossaries, decisions and conflicts in the system family of this project.

6   Conclusions and Future Work

We have performed this work trying to cope with the industrial requirements for methods, tools and mechanisms for SFE. In this domain, models are organized accordingly to organizational needs. The paper gives a partial answer for the requirements modelling context. Further research must be done to solve it completely. In any case, the meta-model presented here covers several of the specific needs of the system family engineering as regards requirements management and the traceability to other systems-models (we have used UML [26] for the meta-model and for the experiments performed so far and the SPEM profile [15] for the proposed process) in the development.

While CMMI best practices are an abstract guideline, our CMMI based requirements management and development process proposed is a step by step procedure. In addition, besides CMMI does not define specific practices for system family engineering, our process takes into account some system family related activities [24].

Back to the specific issues in requirements management for system families, the meta-model allows:

- The full navigation and traceability matrixes generation for internal traces, despite the complexity of requirements in the system family. Experiments performed with tool support for more than forty kinds of traceability matrixes (for example, with Functional Requirement, matrixes for Use case, Requirement decision, Stakeholder, Requirement conflict, Requirement family, System, Non functional requirement, Term). The usage of a web navigation schema helps in keeping the complexity under control.
- The basic relations between requirements are covered (exclusion, coexistence, mandatory, alternative), as well as relations during evolution (revision), hierarchies (generalisation, specialization) of requirements are also supported.
- The concept of system in the system family appears in this model as a set of requirements. Being these requirements related, the meta-model allows for the calculation of "coherent" systems, containing sets of non-conflicting requirements. As well, the progress in development of a certain system can be represented by the growing set of requirements covered.
- Decisions are represented explicitly. It is possible to navigate from each requirement to the decisions related, and the decisions related to each system. Conflicts are also expressed, so its reasons and stakeholders related can be identified and solved.
- The differentiation between common and specific requirements is not statically wired (although it appears as an attribute); instead, as there is navigational capability from-to systems and each requirement, it is possible to know in a certain point in time how many of the systems in the system family are related with one requirement.

A tool implementing the meta-model presented in the paper has been developed. The models give the primary foundations to build the tool. The approach presented here is very promising because requirement reuse could be used in System Family context. In addition, a SPEM [15] model for using that tool following our CMMI based process has been defined.

With respect to the meta-model described in the paper and their application in the development cycle, let us remind that we are focusing on the system family engineering activities described by the CAFÉ reference framework, and very especially in the derivation of system requirements from system family requirements.

Support for traceability among common parts in domain analysis, architecture and implementation is still a problem, which is still more acute for the variable elements. Variable attributes in each of these fields should be identified, and links among variants at these three levels would allow for a higher reuse degree in the family.

References

1. van der Linden, F.: Software Product Families in Europe: The Esaps & Café Projects. IEEE Software, Vol. 10 No. 4. IEEE Computer Society, Los Alamitos, CA (2002) 41-49
2. Clements, P., Northrop, L.: Software Product Lines: Practices and Patterns. Addison Wesley, Boston (2002)
3. El Kaim, W.: Managing Variability in the LCAT SPLIT/Daisy Model. In: Gacek C., Jourdan J., Coriat M. (eds.): Product Line Architecture Workshop, First Software Product Line Conference (2000) 21-31
4. Salicki, S., Farcet, N.: Expression and Usage of the Variability in the Software Product Lines. In: van der Linden (ed.): Proceedings of 4th international workshop on Software Product-Family Engineering PFE-4, LNCS 2290. Springer, Berlin (2001) 304-318
5. Griss, M.: Implementing Product-Line features by Composing Component Aspects. In: Donohoe P. (ed.): Software Product Lines: Experience and Research Directions: Proceedings of First International Software Product Line Conference. The Kluwer International Series in Engineering and Computer Science, Volume 576. Kluwer Academic Publishers (2000) 271-288
6. Jacobson, I., Griss, M., Jonsson, P.: Software Reuse, Architecture, Process and Organization for Business Success. ACM Press, Addison-Wesley, New York (1997)
7. van der Linden, F. (ed.): Development and Evolution of Software Architectures for Product Families. Proceedings International Workshop IW-SAPF-3, Las Palmas de Gran Canaria, Spain. Lecture Notes in Computer Science, 1951. Springer, Berlin (2000)
8. El Kaim, W., Cherki, S., Josset, P., Paris, F., Ollagon, J. C.: Applied technology for designing a PL architecture of a pilot training system. In: Knauber, P., Succi, G. (eds.): Software Product Lines: Economics, Architectures, and Implications, Workshop #15 at 22nd International Conference on Software Engineering, Limerick, Ireland. IESE-Report No. 070.00/E. Fraunhofer IESE, Sauerwiesen (2000) 55-64
9. Kuusela, J., Savolainen J.: Requirements Engineering for Product Lines. In: Proceeding of the 2000 International Conference on Software Engineering, ACM-IEEE, New York, NY (2000) 60-68
10. Luttikhuizen P. (ed.): Requirements Modelling and Traceability. ESAPS, WP3, Derivation of Products and Evolution of System Families WP3-0106-01 Technical Report, (2001)
11. Dueñas, J., Monzón, A: Experience-based Approach to Requirements Reuse in Product Families with DOORS®. In: Dueñas, J., Schimd, K. (eds): Proceedings of International Workshop on Requirements Reuse in System Family Engineering, Eight International Conference on Software Reuse, Universidad Politécnica de Madrid, Madrid, Spain (2004) 38-43.
12. van der Linden, F., Bosch, J., Kamsties, E., Känsälä, K., Obbink, H.: Software Product Family Evaluation. In: Nord, R.: Software Product Lines. Proceedings Third International Conference SPLC 2004, Boston, MA. Lecture Notes in Computer Science, 3154. Springer, Berlin Heidelberg (2004) 110-129
13. Keepence, B., Mannion, M.: Using Patterns to Model Variability in Product Families. IEEE Software, Vol. 16 No. 4. IEEE Computer Society, Los Alamitos, CA (1999) 102-108
14. CMMI Product Team: Capability Maturity Model Integration (CMMI^SM) Version 1.1: CMMI^SM for Systems Engineering and Software Engineering (CMMI-SE/SW, V1.1), Staged Representation Technical Report CMU/SEI-2002-TR-002. Carnegie Mellon University, Software Engineering Institute, Pittsburgh, PA (2002)
15. OMG: Software Process Engineering Metamodel Specification. Version 1.0. Object Management Group, Needham, MA (2002)

16. Alonso, A., León, G., Dueñas, J.C., de la Puente, J.A.: Framework for Documenting Design Decisions in Product Families Development. In: Proceedings of the Third IEEE International Conference on Engineering of Complex Computer Systems. IEEE Computer Society, Los Alamitos, CA (1997) 206-211
17. IEEE-SA Standards Board: IEEE Recommended Practice for Architectural Description of Software-Intensive Systems. IEEE std 1471, 2000. Institute of Electrical and Electronics Engineers, New York, NY (2000)
18. IEEE Standards Board: IEEE Recommended Practice for Software Requirements Specifications. IEEE std 830, 1993. Institute of Electrical and Electronics Engineers, New York, NY (1993)
19. Thayer, R., Dorfman, M.: Software Requirements Engineering. 2nd edn. IEEE Computer Society Press, Washington (1997)
20. IEEE-SA Standards Board: IEEE Guide for Developing System Requirements Specifications. IEEE std 1233, 1998. Institute of Electrical and Electronics Engineers, New York, NY (1998)
21. González-Baixauli, B. Laguna, M., Crespo, Y: Product Line Requirements based on Goals, Features and Use cases. In: Dueñas, J., Schimd, K. (eds): Proceedings of International Workshop on Requirements Reuse in System Family Engineering, Eight International Conference on Software Reuse, Universidad Politécnica de Madrid, Madrid, Spain (2004) 4-7
22. ISO/IEC: Software engineering -- Product quality -- Part 1: Quality model. ISO/IEC 9126-1:2001. International Organization for Standardization, Geneve, (2001)
23. Benavidez, D., Ruiz-Cortés, A., Corchuelo, R., and Martín-Díaz, O: SPL Needs an Automatic Holistic Model for Software Reasoning with feature models. In: Dueñas, J., Schimd, K. (eds): Proceedings of International Workshop on Requirements Reuse in System Family Engineering, Eight International Conference on Software Reuse, Universidad Politécnica de Madrid, Madrid, Spain (2004) 27-32
24. Jones, L., Soule, A.: Software Process Improvement and Product Line Practice: CMMI and the Framework for Software Product Line Practice, Technical Note CMU/SEI-2002-TN-012. Carnegie Mellon University, Software Engineering Institute, Pittsburgh, PA (2002)
25. Day, L.: Requirements Re-Use in the IT Business Process WEB Implementation Product Family. In: Dueñas, J., Schimd, K. (eds): Proceedings of International Workshop on Requirements Reuse in System Family Engineering, Eight International Conference on Software Reuse, Universidad Politécnica de Madrid, Madrid, Spain (2004) 44-48
26. OMG: OMG Unified Modeling Language Specification. Version 1.5. Object Management Group, Needham, MA (2003)

Functional and Non-functional Requirements Specification for Enterprise Applications

Renuka Sindhgatta and Srinivas Thonse

Infosys Technologies Limited,
Bangalore, India, Phone 91- 80-5117 3908
{renuka_sr, srinit}@infosys.com
http://www.infosys.com

Abstract. Comprehensive and accurate software requirements capture is essential for successful development of software systems. Enterprise applications have an additional challenge of eliciting requirements that need to be well understood by i) the business users of the system having extensive domain knowledge ii) application developers having extensive system implementation and development knowledge. Current tools vary from providing textual descriptions to formal semantic languages for specifying requirements. The business users are unable to actively participate in the analysis, as formal and textual specifications represent two extreme ends of requirements elicitation. Ambiguity or lack of understanding often poses a challenge on validation and verification of system requirements specification. The paper presents a Use case Specification Framework that brings structure to requirements specification while retaining its simplicity. The framework enables business users to understand and verify functional requirements and two critical non functional requirements – performance and usability.

1   Introduction

Use cases form a standard mechanism of capturing software system requirements. Use cases of an enterprise application are documented using UML Use case diagrams. Use case diagrams are further detailed to include scenarios of system user interaction, and conditions for execution. Documenting use cases has been detailed in [1, 2]. Narrative Text has been recommended in [3] to ensure simplicity and active participation of all the stakeholders. However, in practice simplicity and natural language causes ambiguity and multiple interpretations. Verification of use cases by the stakeholders is a challenge leading to several change requests raised through the later stages of system development. This results in additional development effort and causes deployment delays.

Enterprises comprise of applications that automate a set of business processes. Hence, use of business process models to derive use cases for these applications is recommended and practiced. Business processes are elicited using process maps or workflows. BPMN (Business Process Modeling Notation) [4], an outcome of the standards body - Business Process Management Initiative (BPMI), is one such work-

F. Bomarius and S. Komi-Sirviö (Eds.): PROFES 2005, LNCS 3547, pp. 189–201, 2005.

flow language used by enterprises for documenting their processes. BPMN is the graphical notation for representing business process and most of its notations cater to the business users who are comfortable with flow charts representing process flows. The paper proposes a Use case Specification Framework that uses of BPMN to represent details of the system requirements or to document use cases. The framework aims at enabling business users to understand and verify the functionality of the system in a specification they are most familiar with.

UML [5] proposes use of sequence or activity diagrams to document use cases. However, activity diagrams provide an illustration of what happens in a workflow and have notations that are a subset of business process workflow notations. Hence, the paper proposes a framework which helps in eliciting use cases by incorporating Business Process Modeling to document the scenarios of use cases. The major contribution of this framework is

- Detail use case scenarios using process flow notations that enables business users to understand and verify the application functionality
- Capture additional inputs along with the process flow to enable capture of non functional requirements vis-à-vis usability and performance requirements.

The rest of the paper is organized as follows: Section 2 briefly reviews the existing techniques. Section 3 details the principles used for specifying functional and non-functional requirements using Use case Specification Framework. Section 4 concludes the paper with contributions and future research possible.

2   Related Work

Researchers and practitioners have spent significant effort to improve the clarity of use cases. Use case specification using formal semantics like Abstract State Machine Language (AsML) [6] enables verification and analysis of the use case scenarios or flow of events. Similar is the advantage of representing the use case using Finite state machines and State Charts as described in [7, 8]. Finite state machines (FSM) are helpful in detecting missing events and integration issues. Use case maps [9] are used in describing the use case scenarios using abstract application components. They are used to realize the use cases during the analysis and design phase of the application development where the application components are identified.

All the above techniques are useful to the software development team during analysis, after use cases that have been documented, verified and commonly understood by business users and the development team. UML proposes use of activity diagrams or sequence diagrams to details the use cases. While these diagrams handle most of the scenario representations, it has been observed that BPMN is more suitable of representing complex scenarios like Inclusive OR of two parallel operations, looping of operations. Hence, we propose the use of business workflow and BPMN to detail the use case. The advantage of using BPMN is

- Business users are familiar with business process and workflow models.
- BPMN has notations to describe complex scenarios – Parallel splits and joins Loops and events.

With the Use of BPMN, Use case Specification Framework aims at strengthening description of use case scenarios to provide a common understanding to all the stakeholders.

3   Use Case Specification Framework

Experience shows that eliciting use cases of any application that is fairly complex poses the challenge of describing and verifying large number of use cases. In addition, focused application centric view causes oversight of some of the critical application scenarios and integration scenarios with external application. Description of identified use cases results in voluminous documents. When given to the application stakeholders for verification, it rarely results in any critical changes due to the difficulty involved in reviewing and understanding the textual descriptions. However, application requirements, typically, undergo several changes after the initial application release. This observation has led us to believe the need to bring structure and simplicity in identifying and specifying use cases. The following sections describe the steps involved in specifying the use cases and the related non-functional requirements using the Use Case Specification Framework. The framework consists of three steps.

3.1   Identify Use Cases from Business Process Models

Classical use-case identification techniques require analysts to enquire business users about the needs of the proposed system. These needs form candidate use-cases. Describing business processes and analyzing how the processes should be automated has been found to be a good approach for identifying use-cases. This approach has been recommended by Martin Fowler [10] for applications where workflow dominates the functional execution. Business processes are defined as sequences of activities undertaken by roles and systems to realize business goals. Activities in business process models that need to be performed by the system are identified as candidates for use-cases. The mechanism of arriving at use cases from the activities in the business process workflow has been described in [11].

Many notations are available to represent business process models. Business users and management consultants have conventionally used Process Maps [12]. UML specification recommends use of activity diagrams to define a business process. The framework uses BPMN for depicting business process flows as these notations have been derived from flow chart and workflows conventionally used by business users. Table 1 shows some of the most common notations used to describe business process flows.

The paper uses a sample process flow to describe the framework. The application to be realized is a Lab management system of a pharmaceutical enterprise that conducts medical tests on samples for various customers and provides reports on the samples. A snapshot of business process described using BPMN is shown in figure 1.

Table 1. Notations use for use case scenario description

Description	Notation	Description	Notation
Event – is a trigger or an impact that effects the flow	Start ◯ End ◯ Exception ◉	**AND split** or join where it is required to divide or join to parallel paths.	
Task is an atomic activity done by the user or system	▭	**Exclusive OR** is used when the flow is to be restricted to one of the two alternatives	
Normal flow is the sequence flow that originates from the start event and continues through the tasks	⟶	**Inclusive OR** is used when one or more paths can be taken simultaneously	
Group is a grouping of activities for documentation purpose only	⌐ - - - ¬	**Task Looping** indicates if a task in performed more than once	

The sample business process describes the initiation of a project after a proposal is won by the Marketing Team. The Marketing team updates the Marketing System (MAR Proposal system). The Marketing System interfaces with the Lab Management System and Creates a Project. The Project Manager is notified about the new project. The Project Manager then activates the projects, assigns team members, verifies availability of assets, and configures a study (referring to a set of tests that need to be done in the lab) in parallel. The process continues further.

There are two types of activities in the given business process. First, activity performed by other systems on Lab Management System – Create Project and Notify Project Manager. Second, activity performed by users on the Lab Management System – Activate Project, Defined Project Mile Stones, etc. While the Business Process consists of activities done on all systems that automated the process, the use cases for the system to be developed can be obtained by identifying all activities where the system under consideration is used. For example, the Project Manager checks the availability of assets in the Asset Management System. However, this activity would not form the part of use cases identified for Lab Management System.

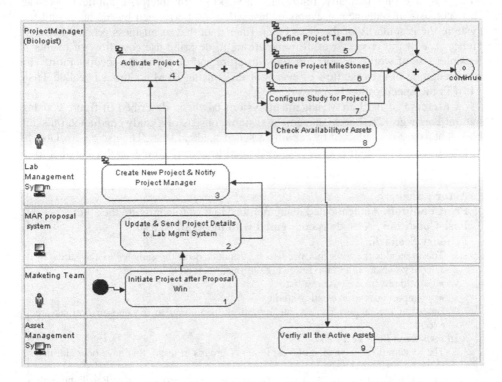

Fig. 1. A snap shot of Business Process Model for Project Initiation

For the given business process, the identified use cases of the Lab Management System are shown in figure 2.

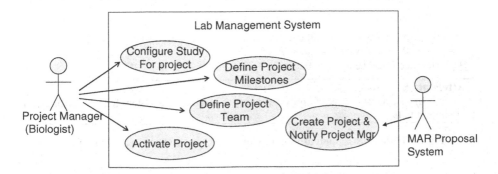

Fig. 2. Use cases derived from Business Process Model for Project Initiation

3.2   Describe Use Case Flow of Events with Task-Flow Models

After the use cases are identified, the use case flow of events has to be documented. The flow of events typically, represents a workflow in enterprise applications. The flow consists of sequence of events or tasks that are performed by the actor and the system, the granularity of the tasks being finer than that of business process activity. Hence, use of the process workflow notations to describe use case flow of events is feasible. Use of workflow notation adds structure and clarity to the specification. The representation of use case flow of events or tasks using BPM notations is called **Task Flow** in the Specification Framework.

A use case of the Lab Management system has been described in figure 3 using natural language. The Lab Management system consists of a study conducted on samples. The study is conducted by running a set of medical tests. The use case relates to a biologist configuring the set of tests that need to be carried out on the samples for a given study.

Actor : Biologist
Pre-Condition: Authenticated team member logs in to configure the study
Post-Condition : A Study is configured with the required tests
Primary Scenario
1.   The user adds the tests that need to be conducted on the samples of the study by selecting one or both of the following options provided to him
   • Add test from a base test list
   • Import tests from existing studies
2.   Based on the options chosen, all operations pertaining to the chosen options are executed.
Add tests from Base Test List
3.   The System displays the list of Test Panels (groups of tests) that have been defined in the base set previously
4.   The User selects a complete Test Panel or a single test from the Test Panel and adds to the study. (Go to Step 8)
Add Tests from the Existing Studies
5.   The system displays the list of studies
6.   The user selects the study and a Test Panel or Test that needs to be imported to the current study.
7.   The user modifies the imported tests to make it relevant for the existing study. (Go to Step 8)

8.   The user may specify an alias to the test that is relevant to the lab or the client for whom the study is conducted.
9.   The user saves the tests for the study.

Alternate Scenario
   6.1   In case a test existing in previous study is inactive, the system flags an error and the import fails.

Fig. 3. Textual description of Use flow of events for Use Case - Configure Study

As the use case flow of events depicts the user and system interaction, there is a constant transfer of the control between the user and the system. For example, entering a form with user details is a task performed by the user and can be classified as an

interactive task. The system validating user details can be classified as a **system task**. The inputs aspects that need to be captured for understanding these tasks vary. Hence, the task notation of BPMN is extended to classify and depict interactive and system task as shown in Table 2

Table 2. Extended notation to classify system and interactive tasks

Task Type	Notation
Interactive Task - A task where the user is involved in interacting with the system	
System Task - A task where the system performs the task without any human intervention	

Task classification enables identification of system and user responsibilities for executing a scenario. Figure 4 shows the use case flow of events for the Configure Study use case using a task flow. The use BPMN helps in depicting the Inclusive OR scenario where one or both paths can be followed. The exception can be easily identified using the exception event notation. This graphical representation using task flow provides for a standard interpretation of use case flow of events.

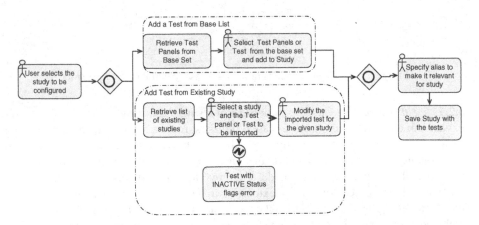

Fig. 4. Task flow for the Use case Configure Study

Classification of actions into user and system actions has been discussed in [13] for use case analysis. The use of this approach however has not been described in detail. The Use case Specification framework uses task classification for capturing different specifications that also help in eliciting the non-function requirements.

The meta-model of the framework and their relationship is shown in figure 5. A use case comprises of one or more task flows. Each of the multiple task flow depicts main flow of events, alternate flow of events or exception flow of events. A task flow consists of one of more tasks performed in a sequential or parallel manner. An Interactive task is associated with a screen or set of screens through which the user interacts. It contains screen validation rules that specify validity of inputs entered by a user. A system task is associated with domain entities being created, updated, validated, processed, etc by the system task. Business rules relevant for processing or validating the entities are associated to the system task. The rule description is framework independent and hence the rules can be defined in plain English or in formal rule language.

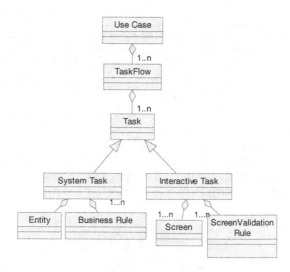

Fig. 5. Concepts and relations in the Use Case Specification Framework

3.2.1   Advanced Use Case Documentation Using Task Flows

Advanced documentation of use cases requires representing extend and include relationship. An extend relationship shows the augmentation of additional functionality of added use case to the base use case for certain conditions. The attributes that a use case metamodel captures for the extends relationship are i) Extension Point ii) Condition for extension to take place. An include relationship shows the use cases that is added to the base use case. The point where the use case is included is captured. These basic attributes are captured in the textual flow of events while describing a use case. Activity diagrams do not typically depict extension points when used for describing use cases.

Documenting include and an extend relationship using a task flow is shown in figure 6. The extention point is the task at which the decision is made. The condition for extension is shown using a condition gateway. For an incude use case, the task when the use case is included is depicted in a task flow. Advanced documentation using a task flow provides clarity by depicting tasks where a use cases are included or extended.

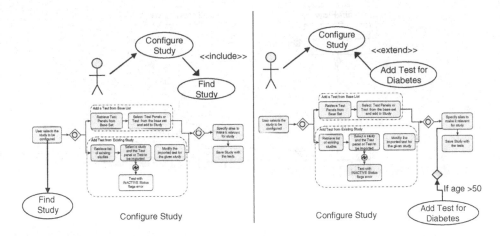

Fig. 6. Task Flow to depicting <<include>> and <<extend>>

3.3   Describe Non-functional Requirements with Task-Flow Model

In practice, the requirements phase of enterprise application development includes understanding the functional and non-functional requirements. IEEE-Std 830 defines 13 non functional requirements. For enterprise application the critical non functional requirements are Reliability, Performance, Security, and Usability. Usability and Performance are one of most evident non-functional parameters of the system. A user is immediately able to decide if the system is causing functional inefficiencies due to bad design of the user interface. Similar is the impact of poor performance on the users' efficiency or productivity in using the application. The Use Case Specification Framework enhances the Task flows for capturing performance and usability requirements and maps these non-functional requirements along with the use cases.

Usability in an application is primarily decided by the ease information exchange to or from the user and application. The framework enables capture of system usability by associating screens with each interactive task in the task flow. Hence, each interactive task is associated with a screen. A screen comprises of the layout of the information that would be entered by or displayed to the user. For each actor of the use case, user personas are captured. User persona consists of the preferences of the user. The persona descriptions can cover role details and demographic profile information: general description including things such as preferred working hours, location, age, and so on. The details capture here helps in designing the screens.

The usability of a use case can be verified by navigating through all the screens associated to the interactive tasks in the task flow. A set of navigated screens is called a screen flow. A task flow can further have multiple screen flows due to decisions gateways involved. For example a login screen could lead to the home page or an error display page depending on the validity of the details entered. Figure 7 shows the details of the concepts that enable usability requirements capture.

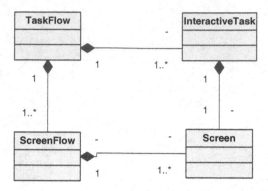

Fig. 7. Concepts used for capturing usability

A task flow has one or more screen flows. A screen is associated to a task. A central repository of screens would enable re-use of screen across multiple use cases and task flows. Figure 8 shows the tool that allows for designing and linking screens to form a screen flow. In the tool, the StudySelect screen is associated to the interactive task "User Selects the Study to be configured". To create a screen flow, the StudySelect screen is linked to any one of the screens associated to the interactive tasks in the task flow. Linking the screens of the task flow facilitates usability verification by simulating the screen flow.

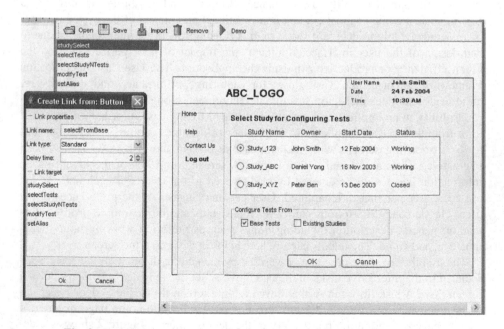

Fig. 8. Defining Screens for Interactive tasks and Linking with other screens

The ease of elicitation and verification provides for active participation from the operational users in the use case elicitation.

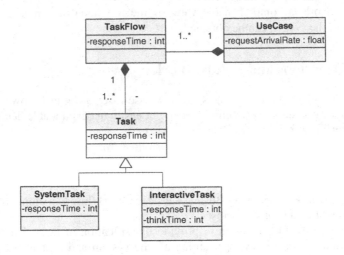

Fig. 9. Attributes for capturing the performance requirements

Performance requirements include the workload of the application in terms of rate of requests of service, number of users of the application and the response time expected from the system. . The attributes captured for performance is shown in figure 9.

The expected response time or service time is captured for each task in the task flow. The rate at which a use case is requested is captured for each use case. The sum of response times of all the tasks in the task flow provides for the response time of a use case executing a certain task flow. The think time represents the minimum amount of time the user spends in entering or reading information on the screen. The think time is captured for each interactive task.

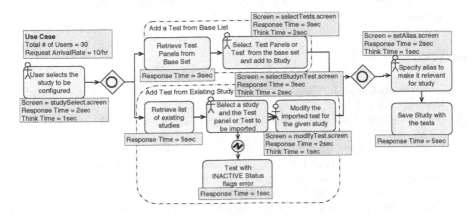

Fig. 10. Use case task flow capturing usability and performance attributes

Figure 10 illustrates the example use case depicting the functional flow of events using the task flow along with the usability and performance attributes captured for the tasks. By capturing the requirements for every use case with the Use case Specification Framework, a comprehensive view of the functional and non-functional requirements of the system can be obtained.

4   Contributions and Future Works

This paper gives an overview of the specifying use cases using task flows. The specification framework aims at providing formal yet easily understandable descriptions by adopting workflow notation to document use cases. Use of notations and concepts which the stakeholders are most familiar provides for accurate requirements. The framework enhances use case elicitation by bringing in new concepts. These are as follows.

1. Provides task flows using Business Process Workflow Notations to define use case flow of events or scenarios.
2. Enhances the task notation to provide classification of tasks. The interactive and system tasks help in representing all the system and user interactions for a given scenario.
3. Provides for extensions that facilitates capture of non-functional requirements.

It has been observed that active participation from the business or end users is very important during requirements capture. In practice, there are situations where the users fail to comprehend the final application functionality and usage during the requirements capturing stage and complain of several missing aspects of the domain during testing phase of the development life cycle. The framework aims at solving these issues by providing a structure while retaining the involvement and understanding of the application users. However, the current framework does not incorporate verification of the use cases for soundness which formal representations provide. By providing a mechanism of translating the task flow diagrams to formal representations like Finite State Machine, the verification of use case for soundness and completeness can be achieved. This will be the future direction of the Use case Specification Framework.

References

1. Geri Schneider, Jason P. Winters, Applying Use Cases, 2nd Edition, Addison-Wesley, New Jersey (2001)
2. Alistair Cockburn, Writing Effective Use cases, 1st Edition, Addison-Wesley, New Jersey, (2000)
3. I. Jacobson, The Use Case Construct in Object-Oriented Software Engineering, In John M. Carroll (ed.), 'Scenario-Based Design: Envisioning Work and Technology in System Development', John Wiley and Sons, pp 309-336. 1995.
4. Business Process Modeling Notation (BPMN) Version 1.0. BPMI.org. May 2004.
5. OMG Unified Modeling Language Specification Version 1.5, Object Management Group Inc. March 2003

6. Mike Barnett, Wolfgang Grieskamp, Wolfram Schulte, Nikolai Tillmann, *Margus Veanes*.: Validating Use Cases using AsmL Third International Conference on Quality Software, Dallas 2003 238–246
7. P. Hsia, J. Samuel, J. Gao, D. Kung, Y. Toyoshima, and C. Chen, Formal Approach to Scenario Analysis, *IEEE Software*, pp. 33-41, Mar. 1994
8. Woo Jin Lee et.al , Integration and Analysis of Use Cases Using Modular Petri Nets in Requirements Engineering, IEEE Transactions on Software Engineering , Vol 24, December 1998.
9. D. Amyot and G. Mussbacher, On the Extension of UML with Use Case Maps Concepts. <<UML>>2000, 3rd Int. Conf. on the Unified Modeling Language, UK, Oct 2000.
10. Martin Fowler, Kendall Scott. UML Distilled Applying the Standard Object Modeling Language, Addison Wesley, 1997.
11. R.M. Dijkman, and S.M.M. Joosten. An Algorithm to Derive Use Cases from Business Processes. Proceedings of the 6th IASTED International Conference on Software Engineering and Applications (SEA), ACTA Press, Anaheim, CA, USA, pp. 679-684, 2002.
12. Geary A Rummler, Alan P Brache. How to manage the White Space on the Organization Chart.2nd Edition, Jossey-Bass Inc, 1995.
13. Bjorn Rengell, Kristofer Kimbler, Anders Wesslen. Improving the Use Case Driven Approach to Requirements Engineering. Proceedings of the Second IEEE International Symposium on Requirements Engineering. pp 40-47, Mar 1995.

Framework for Integrating Usability Practices into the Software Process

Xavier Ferre, Natalia Juristo, and Ana M. Moreno

Universidad Politecnica de Madrid
Campus de Montegancedo
28660 - Boadilla del Monte (Madrid), Spain
{xavier, natalia, ammoreno}@fi.upm.es
http://www.ls.fi.upm.es/udis/

Abstract. Software development organizations wanting to introduce usability practices into their defined software process have to undertake laborious efforts for that purpose, since, for the time being, there exists a lack of reference model or framework which indicates where and how in the software process usability needs to be considered. They also have to overcome the important differences between HCI (Human-Computer Interaction) and SE (Software Engineering) in terminology and approach to process definition. We offer developers who have the objective of integrating usability practices into their software process, a framework that characterizes 35 selected HCI techniques in relation to six relevant criteria from a SE viewpoint, and organizes them according to the kind of activities in the development process where they may be applied, and to the best moment of application in an iterative life cycle. The only requirement for the existing software process is to be based on an iterative approach.

1   Introduction

Usability has been present in software quality attribute decompositions since the late 70s [1], but it has been recently that it has begun to appear as a highly relevant attribute for customer-perceived software quality. For managers, for example, usability is a major decision factor, particularly for selecting a product [2]. Emerging fields like web development have contributed to this increased impact of usability into software development. According to Donahue, having a competitive edge in usability is crucial for e-commerce sites [3]. But not only web development is concerned by usability, it is relevant for any interactive software system with human users.

The HCI field has been pursuing the development of usable software products for a long time. HCI offers a large number of techniques which may be applied for the aim of producing usable software. They are widely applied in development projects where usability is the main (or only) quality attribute taken care of. But the application of HCI techniques is decoupled from the overall software development process.

This state of things is changing. Recently, software developers are becoming aware of the importance of usability issues [4]. A clear sign of the importance that usability issues and their integration with the rest of development activities is gaining, lies in the newly created Usability Process in the first amendment to the ISO/IEC Standard

F. Bomarius and S. Komi-Sirviö (Eds.): PROFES 2005, LNCS 3547, pp. 202–215, 2005.

12207 for Software Life Cycle Processes [5]. The first activity in the Usability Process deals with specifying how user-centered activities fit into the whole system lifecycle process, and to select usability methods and techniques. In this way, usability practices integration into software the process is no more an area of interest for some specialists, but an endeavor that matters for the SE software process area.

In despite of that, software development organizations wanting to properly manage the usability level of their software products, still face a real challenge when dealing with the integration of HCI techniques into their defined software development process [6]. Current SE practice does not correctly address usability issues throughout development. Developers sometimes wrongly consider usability as being just related to the design of the visual elements of the GUI, and therefore it is dealt with late in the development. On the contrary, a proper user-centered development (the HCI approach to software construction) deals with usability issues all over development. In particular, observing users and checking that their needs and likings are considered early in the process is crucial for the production of usable software. On top of that, usability integration into the process is hindered by the differences in terminology and development philosophies between HCI and SE [2] [7]. HCI literature does not offer to organizations that follow a strong SE approach a ready-to-use manual for HCI technique application in a SE development process. Some HCI techniques are not allocated to particular activities in the process, and the activities terminology varies between HCI authors [8]. As a result, the effort of interpreting HCI literature from a SE perspective presents an added difficulty to the task of usability practices integration.

Our approach is to offer software developers a selection of HCI techniques which are more appropriate to be incorporated into a defined software process. The HCI techniques are integrated into a framework organized according to the kind of SE activities and to the moment in an iterative development where their application yields a higher usability improvement. The characterization of HCI techniques is based on a SE perspective, in order to use a terminology which is familiar to developers. The framework aims to be a flexible enough tool so that a particular process model is not required for its application. The only requirement for the existing development process is to be based on iterative refinement, since it is necessary characteristic of any user-centered development effort. Our general approach to HCI integration into SE development processes is discussed in [9], along with a review of other existing proposals to the integration issue.

The framework is aimed to software development organizations with a strong SE background, which have identified the importance of usability and want to enhance their software process with HCI techniques and activities. The selection of HCI techniques for inclusion in the framework responds to these organizations needs. For example, it favors techniques which require less training for a software engineer, and techniques that yield a higher improvement in the usability of the product compared to the application effort.

The research presented in this work has been carried out as part of the project STATUS, financed by the European Commission (IST - 2001 - 32298). Two software development companies were partners in the project consortium, and they participated in the definition and refinement of the framework presented here. They provided us with input about real industrial needs regarding usability practices integration into the software process.

For the definition of the framework it has been necessary to perform a study on HCI activities and techniques in the first place, and to carry out a selection of techniques for the framework. This study is summarized in section 2. Once selected, techniques have been assigned to SE activities in section 3, so that developers know which kind of existing activities some techniques correspond to, and which additional activities need to be added to the process for properly handling usability. We have also performed a study on the conditions to be met by a software process to be considered for usability practices integration. Additionally, as there are some indications in the HCI literature about the best moment of application for a certain number of techniques, as detailed in section 4, we have considered as well the moment of application of the selected HCI techniques in an iterative development. The results are packaged for developers in a framework that offers three views, and section 5 details the usage of the framework. Section 6 describes the conclusions reached. Finally, the framework in its view by development activities is included as an appendix.

2   Selection of HCI Techniques

Whereas one of the goals of SE has been to formalize the process to make software development systematic and disciplined, HCI does not take a similar formalized view of the development. HCI concerns include, on top of software systems, their interaction with the user and with the social environment where system-user interaction takes place. The complexity of these issues has led HCI to focus on certain development issues, and to consider some issues with less detail than SE. That is the case with process issues. Each author in the HCI field has a particular view of the development in terms of what activities should be undertaken to produce a usable software product, and techniques for this purpose are not always described associated to a particular activity. Therefore, it has been necessary for our purpose of usability practices integration into the software process, not only to survey HCI literature for proposed activities and techniques, but also an effort to clarify some activities with different names, different activities with similar names and an assignment of techniques to activities. In this way, we have been able to get well-established practices redefined into concepts closer to SE that allow relating them with the software process. The survey on HCI activities and the classification of the identified 95 HCI techniques into such activities is detailed in [7].

The number of techniques identified in HCI literature (95) is too large for a developer to consider when aiming usability practices integration into the development process, so we have performed a selection of the techniques that, for one reason or another, seem to be more appropriate for the integration purpose. In order to evaluate the appropriateness, we have characterized the HCI techniques according to the following criteria:

- **User Participation:** One of the basic points of a user-centered approach is the active involvement of the future system users. Some usability techniques are specifically designed to encourage this involvement. Since the goal of this work is to facilitate the use of usability practices during development, and user involvement is one of the main and critic of these practices, techniques that specially support user involvement in development will be preferred for integration into the software process.
- **Training Needs:** This criterion refers to how much training average software engineers would need to be able to apply the technique with any chance of success. Techniques which require less training will be less costly to adopt for organizations with little previous HCI experience.
- **General Applicability:** This criterion reflects the scope of the technique, that is, how applicable it is to a wide range of software development projects. Some HCI techniques, for example, are aimed to studying expert user performance in optimal conditions of usage, which only a fraction of software systems may consider the most relevant usability attribute (for instance, a pilot cockpit system). Since we are aiming to cover a big variety of development projects, we will select first wide-ranging techniques.
- **Proximity to SE:** This criterion reflects whether the principles on which the technique is based match the principles and approaches usually present in SE. Techniques with a high value in this criterion will be less difficult to introduce in an organization with a strong SE background.
- **Usability Improvement/Effort Ratio:** This criterion refers to how much the use of the technique can improve the usability of the final product compared to the effort involved in its application. As resources are usually scarce in many software development projects, we believe that cost/benefit information can be very useful for technique selection.
- **Representativeness:** This criterion reflects how commonly the technique is applied in the field of HCI. As an indicator of this criterion, we are going to use the number of consulted authors who recommend the technique. We will favor in technique selection the ones that reach a higher consensus.

The values for these six criteria have been assigned to each HCI technique based on a SE perspective, aiming to ease the integration by reducing the number of techniques for consideration. The complete characterization is detailed in [10].

As the goal is to select techniques, we have summarized the combined value of each criterion in an additional summary criterion called **Total Rating**. This criterion can adopt the following values:

- **Very useful:** Techniques that are especially useful for our purpose because their usability improvement/effort ratio is high, they do not require a lot of training, they are within the medium to high applicability range, and they are either very close to SE or are techniques that are commonly applied in the HCI field.
- **Useful:** Whereas the techniques that meet the above conditions are the best for the aim we pursue, other techniques may also be useful because they either have a high usability improvement/effort ratio (which is considered useful just by itself), or it is medium but they have besides either a medium to high applicability or they encourage user participation.

- **Not very useful:** Techniques that do not meet the requirements for belonging to either of the above categories have been labeled as not very useful in the total rating. Although they may be useful for some development projects, we do not think that this is enough to merit the effort of integrating them into the software process. Notice that the goal of this work is not the inclusion of the whole HCI field into the development, so not all the existent techniques should be selected.

The proposed framework is not designed as a solution that has to be adopted as a whole, because it will include a range of techniques that could be useful in some cases. Additionally, one goal we aim to is to keep the complexity of the framework within reason, in order to enhance comprehensibility and applicability from the viewpoint of SE. Accordingly, we have decided to select both techniques whose total rating is "very useful" and techniques for which the total rating is "useful", as the resulting set of techniques (35) achieves the above goals. The characterization of the selected techniques is detailed in the framework view presented in the appendix.

3 Mapping of HCI Techniques to Software Process Activities

The main purpose of this work, apart from offering a set of selected HCI techniques, is to characterize them according to software process terminology from the SE field, so they can be naturally integrated into the software process. With this aim, we have first studied the correspondence between HCI activities and SE activities, to identify which kind of activities in the software process will include HCI techniques, and then we have mapped the individual selected techniques to such kind of activities in the software process.

3.1 Software Process Activities Affected by Usability

When approaching HCI activities we identify that there are two types of activities with regard to SE: The ones that share objectives and, therefore, should be integrated, and the ones that deal with issues that are not commonly dealt with in SE processes. When mapping HCI activities to their respective SE ones, IEEE Standard 1074-1997 [11] activity group names have been used for describing high-level process activities grouping. Nevertheless, this work aims to be useful for any organization with a defined software process, regardless of the particular approach taken for developing software life cycle processes. Therefore, we have not adhered to a particular software process standard, because our recommendations regarding usability practices integration into the software process do not require the organization compliance with any standard. For this reason, we have used generally accepted SE terminology for the classification of software process activities, instead of using activity names from a specific software process standard. The mapping between HCI and SE activities is represented in Figure 1.

The greatest degree of similarity in objectives lies in requirements activities, since they overlap with the concerns in HCI about specifying the context of use, analyzing users and their tasks, specifying usability requirements, developing a product concept, producing low-fidelity prototypes, and validating them with representative users. As a result, existing requirements-related activities of the software process may be enhanced by the introduction of HCI techniques and approach.

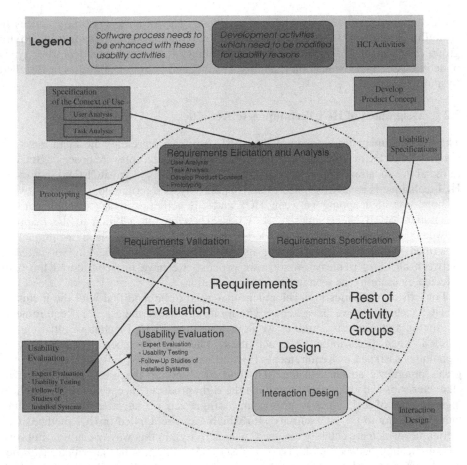

Fig. 1. Mapping of HCI Activities to SE Activities in the Software Process

Other HCI activities, not related to SE requirements activities, do not have a direct coincidence of objectives with existing SE activities, so they have to be added to the existing development process for it to produce usable software. These new kinds of activities are Interaction Design and Usability Evaluation.

Interaction Design is concerned with the definition of the interaction environments and their behavior, including the coordination of the user-system interaction. It also includes the design of the visual elements making up the GUI (Graphical User Interface) and their behavior, when the user interface is graphical. Interaction Design gathers a kind of activities with a certain degree of independence from activities in the Design activity group, but it is related to the sort of tasks carried out in such activities. Therefore, we have considered that Interaction Design belongs to the Design activity group, but with its own place inside it.

Usability Evaluation includes all the activities that aim to evaluate the usability of the product being developed. Consequently, they can fit in the Evaluation activity group. Nevertheless, they are quite independent from other activities in the group because usability practices for evaluation differ to a great extent from SE evaluation practices. Therefore, we have gathered all kinds of usability evaluation practices in Usability Evaluation, and placed this kind of activities inside the Evaluation activity group. The typical HCI decomposition of Usability Evaluation considers three types of activities: Expert Evaluation, Usability Testing, and Follow-Up Studies of Installed Systems.

3.2   Assignment of HCI Techniques to Activities

The previous mapping between HCI and SE activities represents the main basis for assignment of HCI techniques to kinds of activities into the software process. But, due to the above mentioned lack of formality in process issues in the HCI field, not every HCI technique is clearly assigned to an HCI activity, and terminology varies between authors, so the mapping between HCI and SE activities is not enough for the assignment of HCI techniques to activities. Therefore, in addition to the mapping between activities, we have considered the particularities of each technique, as described in the HCI literature, for its assignment to a specific kind of activity. Between all the activities in a software process, we have just considered the ones affected by usability, as seen in the previous section.

For existing activities in development that need to be modified with the inclusion of HCI techniques, we have kept SE terminology. Nevertheless, for Requirements Elicitation and Analysis activities we have identified 15 HCI techniques that can be applied when performing such activities. The large number of HCI selected techniques assigned to Requirements Elicitation and Analysis activities is due to the great importance attached in the HCI field to observing the users, analyzing their characteristics and tasks, and developing the right product concept. Since 15 is quite a high number of techniques to present in a single set, we have decided to structure them according to the HCI activity into which they are applied in HCI methods (for techniques which are actually assigned to an activity). In this way, we aim to improve communication between usability specialists and developers in the critical activities of Requirements Elicitation and Analysis. They are the kind of activities which require a greater degree of integration of current SE practices with HCI ones, and, therefore, they present a greater need of communication inside joint SE-HCI teams.

The final results of the framework detailed in the appendix show the resulting organization of techniques according to the kind of development activities where they apply. A more thorough discussion of the reasons for assigning each technique to a particular kind of activity, along with a more detailed description of the mapping between HCI and SE activities, can be found in [10].

4   Embedding HCI Techniques in an Iterative Life Cycle

We have studied the HCI literature to identify the characteristics that software development should have for it to be considered user-centered. [12], [13], [14], [15], and [16] agree on considering iterative development as a must for a user-centered development approach. The complexity of the human side in human-computer interaction makes it almost impossible to create a correct design at the first go. Cognitive, sociological, educational, physical and emotional issues may play an important role in any user-system interaction, and an iterative approach is the most sensible way to deal with these issues.

The other three characteristics that are mentioned by several sources are: active user involvement; a proper understanding of user and task requirements; and multidisciplinary knowledge. The three conditions can be met by introducing HCI practices into the software process. They may contribute with knowledge from other disciplines, they may also offer participatory ways for software developers to integrate users into the design process, and they may enhance requirements activities with specific usability aspects as well. On the contrary, the first condition (that is, to be based on an iterative approach), is an intrinsic characteristic of the process, and it will be the only requirement for a defined software process to be a candidate for usability practices integration through the proposed framework.

There are indications in the HCI literature on when in development time each technique yields the most useful results for improving the usability of the final product. In particular, HCI literature favors an early application of certain HCI techniques, while others yield useful when a working system is installed in the user organization.

An iterative life cycle is made up of cycles, but not all the cycles are the same. Each cycle implies working in different kinds of activities, and the relative effort and emphasis change over time [17]. During the first development cycles, a greater effort is dedicated to activities related to problem delimitation and to establishing the solution outline, while, as development advances, design and implementation activities gain more weight. Therefore, different stages can be defined in an iterative life cycle.

On top of the assignment of HCI techniques to activities, we consider necessary to offer developers a guide about the more appropriate moments in development time for the application of each HCI technique. We aim to transmit this kind of information present in HCI literature to developers. Since each organization has its own terminology for phases and milestones, we have established a generic representation of moments in iterative development time, which condenses the most important stages for HCI technique characterization. We have considered the following three stages: Initial Cycles, Central Cycles and Evolution Cycles. Development time is roughly divided into these three stages by the following two milestones:

- **Product Concept Established:** In any iterative process, the early cycles are given over to the points identified as being the riskiest, and one of the biggest risks as far as usability is concerned is not having in mind the right product concept, the one that fits the user experience and expectations. Some HCI techniques focus on the production and/or evaluation of early tentative designs and, therefore, they are especially well suited for application in the Initial Cycles, which account for the cycles before the product concept has been established. Central Cycles begin once this milestone has been reached.

- **Some Part of the System Installed and Working:** Some usability evaluation techniques cannot be applied unless a version of the software system under development has been installed at the end user's workplace. Evolution cycles begin once this milestone has been reached.

Figure 2 shows this division of development time in stages. Developers need to match this generic representation to the terminology used in their organization, in order to interpret our proposed framework. We have graded every selected HCI technique according to their suitability for each stage described in the consulted literature, with one of the following values: **Especially well-matched** (meaning that the technique will be of utmost usefulness when applied in the development stage in question); **Neutral** (the technique is applicable in this stage, although this stage does not stand out as being any better matched than other development times); and **Not usual** (it is not the more appropriate stage for this technique application and there are other more appropriate techniques).

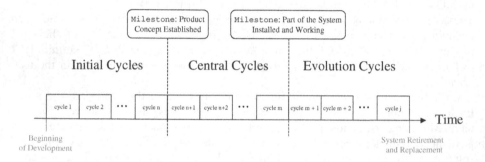

Fig. 2. Division of Iterative Cycles into Stages

The framework view detailed in the appendix includes the characterization of selected HCI techniques according to moments in an iterative life cycle. A detailed discussion of the reasons for grading each HCI technique with respect to their suitability to each development stage can be found in [10].

5 Integrating Usability Practices into the Software Process: A Framework

We have packed into a framework the characterization of HCI techniques detailed in previous sections. The framework allows developers to take decisions about the specific HCI techniques to include into their software process in order to improve the usability of the developed software product. It condenses all the information developers need to apply the solution we are proposing.

In order to ease the usage of the framework by its potential users, we offer developers three views:

- **View by HCI Techniques:** This view is organized by the name of the selected HCI techniques. It yields useful when developers already know about a particular HCI technique they have heard about, or whose usability benefits they have been convinced of. Accessing the framework through this view offers the possibility of knowing the characterization of a particular HCI technique.

- **View by Development Activities:** When developers are trying to find appropriate HCI techniques for activities in their process they access the framework through this view. In order to use the framework with this purpose, developers need to translate the generic activities in the framework to the specific activity names considered in their organization. Then, between the set of techniques suggested for each kind of activity, they may select those ones that better fit their particular objectives.
- **View by Moments of Application:** An organization of the selected HCI techniques according to stages in the development life cycle is offered to developers through this framework view. For example, an organization may have identified that they need to pay more attention to usability in the earlier stages of development, and wants to know which HCI techniques are more suitable for application at this stage. In order to use the framework through this view, developers need to fit the generic representation of stages in an iterative cycle used in the framework to the phases or stages considered in their organization.

The three views offered in the framework are not exclusive. They may be used independently, but the expected usage of the framework is by means of an information search that combines several views. For the task of integrating usability practices into the software process, developers may switch between views for reaching the kind of information they are dealing with at each moment. For example, when dealing with the introduction of HCI practices into a particular activity, the developer will make use of the view by activities, by matching his or her organization activity name with the corresponding kind of activity in the framework. Between the techniques proposed for such kind of activity, the developer will choose one or more techniques, considering both the criteria characterization and the information about the better moment of application of each technique. Then, the developer may change to the view by moments of application, to know about the techniques which are bound to be applied at the same moment in development time as the techniques selected. Finally, the developer may switch to the view by HCI techniques to look up a technique which he has already placed in the process, because he or she wants to remember the training needs of the technique, in order to know if some members of the development team will need to attend a lengthy usability training course.

We consider that these different views of the framework offer a flexible tool for easing the usability integration endeavor. In order to provide some more guidance to the user of the framework, techniques labeled as "Very useful" are highlighted in every view by presenting them as the first ones in each category. These techniques are suggested to the user as the best generic choice. Nevertheless, the developer may take into account the specific constraints of the organization or the project at hand, and, considering the characterization criteria for the techniques, he or she may choose a set of techniques which fit better his or her needs. The framework is not conceived as a tool for automatic generation of a custom process add-in, but as a tool for supporting the developer in the difficult task of integrating HCI practices into the software process. For this purpose, it condenses some knowledge about the HCI field in a way understandable by developers with a SE background.

Knowing where to plug HCI techniques and activities into the existing process does not automatically make software engineers capable of integrating HCI practices into their day-to-day work. We offer in the framework a basic reference for each HCI technique where developers may turn to if they need more detailed information on the application of the technique, but the application of the framework needs to be supplemented by appropriate usability training for developers. A basic catalogue of HCI techniques, with their main references and a training plan, can be found in [18].

The Appendix details the framework in its view by development activities.

6   Conclusions and Future Directions

Usability practices integration into the software process is a difficult issue due to the existing breach between SE and HCI. Both fields have a different approach to development, different terminology, and different view of process issues. HCI literature is not very helpful for the integration aim, since the information about techniques is not presented in terms a software engineer can easily understand.

We have presented a framework for usability practices integration into the software process that defines which kind of development activities are affected by usability, and characterizes HCI techniques according to such activities and according to the moments in an iterative cycle where their application yields more useful. Additionally, it characterizes each HCI technique according to six criteria which may be of interest to developers in the usability integration endeavor.

The framework has been applied by STATUS partners after a 24 hours (one week) usability course, with good results: Integration of usability has improved requirements understanding, and the usability level of software products developed has increased substantially (including user satisfaction). As a global valuation, developers consider that the effort employed in the application of HCI techniques pays off, considering the results obtained. They were previously unaware of the possible relationship of usability with their development practices, and they do know now where to look for HCI techniques to apply. They are also more aware of the criticality of usability in software development.

We have released a prototype of a web-based tool for easing the application of the framework [19]. With the release of the framework in the web, we expect to refine it with the feedback received from developers and usability specialists who may use it for their particular needs.

References

1. McCall, J.A., Richards, P.K., and Walters, G.F.: Factors in Software Quality. vol. 1, 2, and 3, AD/A-049-014/015/055, National Tech. Information Service (1977)
2. Seffah, A., Metzker, E.: The Obstacles and Myths of Usability and Software Engineering. Communications of the ACM, Vol. 47, no. 12 (December 2004) 71-76
3. Donahue, G.M..: Usability and the Bottom Line. IEEE Software, Vol. 18, no. 1 (January/February 2001) 31-37

4. Juristo, N., Windl, H., Constantine, L.: Introducing Usability. Guest Editor's Introduction. IEEE Software Special Issue on Usability Engineering, Vol. 18, no. 1 (January/February 2001) 20-21
5. ISO/IEC. International Standard: Information Technology. Software Life Cycle Processes. Amendment 1. ISO/IEC Standard 12207:1995/Amd.1:2002. ISO, Geneva, Switzerland (2002)
6. Ferre, X., Juristo, N., Windl, H., Constantine, L.: Usability Basics for Software Developers. IEEE Software, Vol. 18, no. 1 (January/February 2001) 20-29
7. Ferre, X., Juristo, N., Moreno, A.M.: Improving Software Engineering Practice with HCI Aspects. Software Engineering Research and Applications - Lecture Notes in Computer Science. Vol 3026, Springer (2004) 349-363
8. Ferre X., Juristo, N., Moreno. A.M.: Deliverable D.5.1. Selection of the Software Process and the Usability Techniques for Consideration. STATUS Project (2002) http://www.ls.fi.upm.es/status/results/deliverables.html
9. Ferre, X., Juristo, N., Moreno, A.M.: Integration of HCI Practices into Software Engineering Development Processes: Pending Issues. In: Ghaoui, C. (ed.): Encyclopedia of Human Computer Interaction. Idea Group Reference (2005)
10. Ferre, X., Juristo, N., Moreno, A.M.: Deliverable D.6.6 Final Results on the Integrated Software Process. STATUS Project (2004) http://www.ls.fi.upm.es/status/results/deliverables.html
11. IEEE: IEEE Std 1074-1997. IEEE Standard 1074 for Developing Software Life Cycle Processes. IEEE, New York (NY), USA (1998)
12. ISO: International Standard: Human-Centered Design Processes for Interactive Systems, ISO Standard 13407: 1999. ISO, Geneva, Switzerland (1999)
13. Constantine, L. L., and Lockwood, L. A. D.: Software for Use: A Practical Guide to the Models and Methods of Usage-Centered Design. Addison-Wesley, New York (NY), USA (1999)
14. Shneiderman. B.: Designing the User Interface: Strategies for Effective Human-Computer Interaction. Addison-Wesley, Reading (MA), USA (1998)
15. Preece, J., Rogers, Y., Sharp, H., Benyon, D., Holland, S., Carey. T.: Human-Computer Interaction. Addison Wesley, Harlow, England (1994)
16. Hix, D., and Hartson, H.R.: Developing User Interfaces: Ensuring Usability Through Product and Process. John Wiley and Sons, New York (NY), USA (1993)
17. Larman, C.: Agile and Iterative Development. A Manager's Guide. Addison-Wesley, Boston (MA), USA (2004)
18. Ferre, X,. Juristo, N. and Moreno A..M.: Deliverable D.5.2. Specification of the Software Process with Integrated Usability Techniques. STATUS Project (2002) http://www.ls.fi.upm.es/status/results/deliverables.html
19. Ferre, X. Web-Based Framework for Integrating Usability Practices into the Software Process (2005) http://www.ls.fi.upm.es/udis/miembros/xavier/usabilityframework/

Appendix: Framework View by Development Activities

Table 1 shows the development activities view of the proposed framework.

Table 1. Framework for Usability Integration into the Software Process: View by Activity

Kind of Activity	Technique	UP	TN	GA	PSE	UIE	Rep	Stages			Basic Reference
								IC	CC	EC	
Requirements Elicitation and Analysis (Reqs.)	Card Sorting	Y	L	H	M	H	3	N	N	N	Robertson, 01
	Competitive Analysis	N	M	H	M	H	1	SW	N	N	Nielsen, 93
	Affinity Diagrams	Y	L	H	M	H	1	SW	NU	NU	Beyer, 98
	Contextual Inquiry	Y	H	M	M	H	3	SW	NU	NU	Beyer, 98
	JEM (Joint Essential Modeling)	Y	M	M	H	M	1	N	N	N	Constantine, 99
	Ethnographical Observation	N	H	M	M	M	2	SW	NU	NU	Preece, 94
User Analysis [1]	Personas	N	M	M	M	H	3	SW	NU	NU	Cooper, 03
	Structured User Role Model	N	L	M	H	M	1	SW	N	N	Constantine, 99
	User Profiles	N	H	H	H	H	5	SW	N	N	Mayhew, 99
Task Analysis [1]	Essential Use Cases	N	M	H	H	H	1	N	N	N	Constantine, 99
	Task Scenarios	Y	M	M	M	H	1	N	N	N	Mayhew, 99
	HTA (Hierarchical Task Analysis)	N	M	M	H	M	1	SW	NU	NU	Preece, 94
Develop Product Concept [1]	Scenarios and storyboards	Y	M	M	L	H	3	SW	NU	NU	Carroll, 97a
	Visual Brainstorming	Y	L	H	L	H	1	SW	NU	NU	Preece, 94
Prototyping [1]	Paper Prototyping	Y	L	H	H	H	3	SW	N	N	Mayhew, 99
Requirements Specification (Reqs.)	Usability Specifications	N	M	M	M	H	4	N	N	N	Hix, 93
Requirements Validation (Reqs.)	Inspections	N	M	H	M	H	4	N	N	N	Nielsen, 94
	Heuristic Evaluation	N	H	H	L	H	6	N	N	N	Nielsen, 93
	Collaborative Inspections	Y	M	M	M	M	1	SW	N	N	Constantine, 99
	Cognitive Walkthrough	N	H	M	M	M	4	N	N	N	Carroll, 97b
	Pluralistic Walkthrough	Y	L	M	M	M	4	SW	N	N	Bias, 94
Interaction Design (Design)	Menu-Selection Trees	N	L	M	H	H	1	N	N	N	Shneiderman, 98
	Interface State Transition Diagrams	N	L	H	H	M	2	N	N	N	Hix, 93

---

[1] These are not kinds of SE activities, but HCI activities included in this view to offer the framework user a structured vision of the 15 HCI techniques which may be applied in Requirements Elicitation and Analysis activities

Kind of Activity		Technique	UP	TN	GA	PSE	UIE	Rep	Stages			Basic Reference
									IC	CC	EC	
Design		Product Style Guide	N	H	M	M	M	1	NU	SW	N	Mayhew, 99
		Navigation Maps	N	M	H	H	M	1	N	N	N	Constantine, 99
		Interface Content Model	N	M	H	M	M	1	N	SW	N	Constantine, 99
		Impact Analysis	N	M	M	H	M	3	NU	N	N	Hix, 93
		Organizing Help by Use Cases	N	M	M	II	M	1	N	N	N	Constantine, 99
Usability Evaluation (Evaluation)	Expert Evaluation	Inspections	N	M	H	M	H	4	N	N	N	Nielsen, 94
		Heuristic Evaluation	N	H	H	L	H	6	N	N	N	Nielsen, 93
		Collaborative Inspections	Y	M	M	M	M	1	SW	N	N	Constantine, 99
		Cognitive Walkthrough	N	H	M	M	M	4	N	N	N	Carroll, 97b
		Pluralistic Walkthrough	Y	L	M	M	M	4	SW	N	N	Bias, 94
	Usability Testing	Thinking Aloud	Y	M	H	L	H	5	NU	N	N	Nielsen, 93
		Post-Test Information	Y	M	H	M	H	1	NU	N	N	Constantine, 99
		Performance Measurement	Y	M	M	M	M	3	NU	N	N	Dumas, 99
		Laboratory Usability Testing	Y	M	M	M	M	4	NU	N	N	Hix, 93
	Follow-Up Studies of Installed Systems	User Feedback	Y	L	H	H	H	3	NU	NU	SW	Nielsen, 93
		Questionnaires, Interviews and Surveys	Y	M	H	M	M	3	NU	N	SW	Mayhew, 99
		Logging Actual Use	N	H	M	H	M	5	NU	N	SW	Shneiderman, 98

In order to use this view of the framework, a developer must look for the kind of activity he or she is interested in, and choose one or more of the proposed HCI techniques, according to the characteristics the organization values most (UP: User Participation, TN: Training Needs, GA: General Applicability, PSE: Proximity to SE, UIE: Usability Improvement/Effort Ratio, Rep: Representativeness), and to the stage where their application in intended (IC: Initial Cycles, CC: Central Cycles, EC: Evolution Cycles). Techniques labeled as "Very useful" are represented on a white background, while techniques labeled as "Useful" are represented on a gray background. The values for technique characterization are represented as follows: Y: Yes, N: No, H: High, M: Medium, L: Low. The values for development stage suitability are as follows: SW: Specially Well-matched, N: Neutral, NU: Not Usual.

Using Evolutionary Project Management (Evo) to Create Faster, More Userfriendly and More Productive Software. Experience Report from FIRM AS, a Norwegian Software Company

Trond Johansen

Head of Project Management, FIRM AS
Grindbakken 40, 0764 Oslo
Trond.Johansen@firmglobal.com

1   About the Company

FIRM was established in 1996, and has 70 employees in 4 offices (Oslo, London, New York and San Francisco). FIRM   delivers one software product: Confirmit. Confirmit is a web-based application which enables organizations to gather, analyze and report key business information across a broad range of commercial applications. Confirmit can be applied to any information-gathering scenario, but its three main data sources are: Customer Feedback, Market Feedback and Employee Feedback.

The FIRM R&D department consist of about 20 people, including a Quality Assurance department of 3 people. These people are mainly involved in product development of Confirmit, but we also do custom development for clients who fund new modules of the software.

2   Development Background and History

In the very beginning, when FIRM only had a couple of clients, our development was very ad-hoc and customer driven. We didn't follow a formal development process. The software was updated nearly on a daily basis based on client feedback. You can say that we had one of the important elements in Evo: Deliver stakeholder value fast.

This ad-hoc development resulted in nice features for the few dedicated clients we had, but it also resulted in a lot of defects, long stressful nights, and little control.

As our client base grew, we felt a need to introduce more-formal processes in order to increase our quality standards. Larger clients started to ask questions regarding our development processes.

We formalised the development process according to a waterfall model, and started climbing the CMM ladder. The reason for choosing the waterfall model was that it was the only development process we knew about.

After a few years with the waterfall model, we experienced aspects of the model that we didn't like:

− Risk mitigation was postponed until late stages.
− Document-based verification postponed until late stages.

F. Bomarius and S. Komi-Sirviö (Eds.): PROFES 2005, LNCS 3547, pp. 216–223, 2005.
© Springer-Verlag Berlin Heidelberg 2005

- Attempts to stipulate unstable requirements too early: change of requirements is perceived as a bad thing in waterfall.
- Operational problems discovered too late in the process (Acceptance testing)
- Lengthy modification cycles, and much rework.
- Most important; the requirements were nearly purely focused on functionality, not on quality attributes.
- Our experiences is backed up by statistics
  - In a study of failure factors on 1027 IT projects in the UK, scope management related to waterfall practices was cited to be the largest problems in 82% of the projects. Only 13 % of the projects didn't fail. (Thomas, M.2001. "IT project Sink or Swim," British Computer Society Review)
  - A large study showed that 45 % of requirements in early specifications were never used (Johnson, J. 2002. Keynote speech, XP 2002, Sardinia, Italy).

3 The Shift of Focus: From Waterfall to Evolutionary Development

Peter Myklebust, FIRM CTO, and I heard Tom Gilb speak about evolutionary project management (Evo) at a software conference autumn 2003. We had just released a new version of our software that contained a lot of new nice features, but it had limitations with respect to usability, productivity and performance (e.g. throughput and response time). We found the ideas very interesting, and Tom and Kai Gilb offered to give a more detailed introduction to the concept. They spent one day in our offices, giving a very compressed introduction to Evo. We saw that Evo attacked many of the flaws in our wa-terfall process; most importantly the high focus on quality attributes that we felt could have been better in our latest release.

We decided to do an Evo pilot with a development phase of 3 months. We decided to do a literature study ourselves and then use Evo as best as we could for the next release (Confirmit 8.5), without further Evo courses.

3.1 FIRM's Interpretation of Evo: Basis for the 3 Month Trial Period

Evo is in short: Quickly evolving towards stakeholder values & product qualities, while learning through early feedback. The beauty lies with the simplicity of the method, combined with advanced methods of measurement and control.

After the one day crash course with Tom and Kai Gilb and a literature study ("Competitive Engineer-ing" by Tom Gilb and other material on the subject), our overall understanding of Evo was this:

- Find stakeholders (End users, super-users, support, sales, IT Operations etc)
- Define the stakeholders' real needs, and the related product qualities
- Identify past/status of product qualities and your required goal level (how much you want to im-prove).
- Identify possible solutions for meeting your goals
- Develop a step-by-step plan for delivering improvements via the identified solutions, with respect to Stakeholder Values & product quality goals:

- And most importantly:
- Deliveries of measurable stakeholder-valued results every week (every Evo cycle)
- Measure weekly: are we measurably moving towards our goals?

3.2   Working with Requirements the Evo Way

With Evo, our requirements process changed. Previously we focused mostly on function requirements, and not on quality requirements. It is the quality requirements that really separate us from our competi-tors. E.g. spell checker in MS Word, why was this a killer application? There was no new functionality; authors of documents have been able to spell check with paper dictionaries for ages. The real differ-ence was superior product qualities: speed of spell checking and usability.

We tried to define our requirements according to a basic standard [1]

- Clear & Unambiguous
- Testable
- Measurable
- No Solutions (Designs)
- Stakeholder Focus

Example taken from our requirements in Confirmit 8.5:

Usability.Productivity
Scale: Time in minutes to set up a typical specified Market Research-report (MR)
Past: 65 min, Tolerable: 35 min, Goal: 25 min (end result was 20 min)
Meter: (how to measure if we are moving towards our goal): Candidates with knowledge of MR-specific reporting features performed a set of predefined steps to produce a standard MR Report. (The standard MR report was designed by Mark Phillips, an MR specialist at our London office).

The focus is here on the day-to-day operations of our MR users, not a list of features that they might or might not like. We know that increased efficiency, which leads to more profit, will please them.

After one week we had defined nearly all the top level quality and performance requirements for the next version of Confirmit; and we were ready to start on our first Evo step. We decided that one Evo step should last one week; because of practical reasons, even though we violate the general Evo pol-icy of not spending more than about 2 % of project schedule in each step. The rationale behind the 2% rule is not to spend more time than you can afford to loose. After one week, you'll find out whether you are on the right track (by getting feedback from stakeholders).

3.3   Find Solutions That Takes You Closer to Your Goals

For every quality requirement we looked for possible Solutions (Design Ideas).

E.g. for Quality Requirement: Usability.Productivity we identified the following Solutions: (identified by their name, not their description here as they are very domain-specific for market research)

	Development Team	Users (PMT, Pros, Doc writer, other)	CTO (Sys Arch, Process Mgr)	QA (Configuration Manager & Test Manager)
Friday	✓ PM: Send Version N detail plan to CTO + prior to Project Mgmt meeting ✓ PM: Attend Project Mgmt meeting: 12.00-15.00 ✓ Developers: Focus on genereal maintenance work, documentation.		✓ Approve/reject design & Step N ✓ Attend Project Mgmt meeting: 12-15	✓ Run final build and create setup for Version N-1. ✓ Install setup on test servers (external and internal) ✓ Perform initial crash test and then release Version N-1
Monday	✓ Develop test code & code for Version N	✓ Use Version N-1		✓ Follow up CI ✓ Review test plans, tests
Tuesday	✓ Develop Test Code & Code for Version N ✓ Meet with users to Discuss Action Taken Regarding Feedback From Version N-1	✓ Meet with developers to give Feedback and Discuss Action Taken from previous actions	✓ System Architect to review code and test code	✓ Follow up CI ✓ Review test plans, tests
Wednesday	✓ Develop test code & code for Version N			✓ Review test plans, tests ✓ Follow up CI
Thursday	✓ Complete Test Code & Code for Version N ✓ Complete GUI tests for Version N-2			✓ Review test plans, tests ✓ Follow up CI

Fig. 1. FIRM Evo week

- Solution.Recoding
- Solution.MRTotals
- Solution.Categorizations

– Solution.TripleS
– ..and many more

We evaluated all these, and specified in more detail those we believed would add the most value for the least effort. (take us closer to the goal level). This evaluation was based on 2-3 senior developers' "gut-feeling".

3.4   Working Evolutionary, the FIRM Evo Week

We organized the week in a special way.

On Friday we plan deliverables for version N, at the same time as we build and deploy version N-1 on the test server. Monday to Thursday is dedicated to design, code and test. During the week, the pro-ject collects feedback from stakeholders, based on the previous Evo step/week.

3.5   Evolutionary Project Planning

We collected the most promising Solutions and included them in an Evo plan (expressed by using an Impact Estimation Table: IET. See example below). The solutions were evaluated with respect to value for clients versus cost of implementation: choosing the ones with the highest value first. Note that value can sometimes be defined as removing risks by implementing technically challenging Solu-tions early.

The IET is our tool for controlling the qualities, and delivering improvements to real stakeholders: or as close as we can get to them. (E.g. support people, using the system daily, acting as clients).

Example: IET for MR Project – Confirmit 8.5, Solution: Recoding

Description: Make it possible to recode variable on the fly from Reportal. Estimated effort: 4 days

	B Current Status	Improvements		Goals			Step9 Recoding Estimated impact		Actual impact	
	Units	Units	%	Past	Tolerable	Goal	Units	%	Units	%
				Usability.Replacability (feature count)						
7	1.00	1.0	50.0	2	1	0				
				Usability.Speed.NewFeaturesImpact (%)						
9	5.00	5.0	100.0	0	15	5				
10	10.00	10.0	200.0	0	15	5				
11	0.00	0.0	0.0	0	30	10				
				Usability.Intuitiveness (%)						
13	0.00	0.0	0.0	0	60	80				
				Usability.Productivity (minutes)						
15	20.00	45.0	112.5	65	35	25	20.00	50.00	38.00	95.00
				Development resources						
21		101.0	91.8	0		110	4.00	3.64	4.00	3.64

Fig. 2. Example of Impact Estimation Table, MR project in Confirmit 8.5 development

4   Impacts on Our Product, Experiences and Conclusions

4.1   The Method's Impact on Confirmit Product Qualities

Firm is one of eleven industry partners in a Norwegian Software Process Improvement program – SPIKE (http://www.abelia-innovasjon.no/spike/). The program is a joint effort involving Norwegian software industry and academia investigating software engineering topics trough empirical studies of industrial practices. Researchers from SINTEF are evaluating the introduction and effects of Evo at Firm. This work is still in progress but preliminary results indicates that the introduction of Evo at Firm has a positive influence on product quality and process control. The impact described in this paper is based on internal usability test, productivity tests, performance tests carried out at Microsoft Windows ISV laboratory in Redmond USA, and direct customer feedback. Only highlights of the im-pacts are listed here. No negative impacts are hidden.

Table 1. Improvements to product qualities

Description of requirement/work task	Past	Goal	Status
Usability.Productivity: Time for the system to generate a survey	7200 sec	94 sec	15 sec
Usability.Productivity: Time to set up a typical specified Market Research-report (MR)	65 min	25 min	20 min
Usability.Productivity: Time to grant a set of End-users access to a Report set and distribute report login info.	80 min	2 min	5 min
Usability.Intuitiveness: The time in minutes it takes a medium experienced programmer to define a complete and correct data transfer definition with Confirmit Web Services without any user documentation or any other aid	15 min	4,5 min	5 min
Performance.Runtime.Concurrency: Maximum number of simultaneous respondents executing a survey with a click rate of 20 sec and an response time<500 ms, given a defined [Survey-Complexity] and a defined [Server Configuration, Typical]	250 users	1000	6000

These leaps in product qualities would not have been achieved without Evo. We have received many pleasant emails regarding these quality improvements from our customers:
"I just wanted to let you know how appreciative we are of the new "entire report" export functionality you recently incorporated into the Reportal. It produces a fantastic looking report, and the table of contents is a wonderful feature. It is also a HUGE time saver."

4.2   Feedback from Developers and Project Managers Within FIRM R&D

Evo has resulted in increased motivation and enthusiasm amongst developers because it opens up for empowered creativity. EVO and Continuous Integration is a vehicle for innovation and inspiration. The developers get their work out on test servers, and receive feedback. Every week.

Even though they embraced the method there are parts of Evo they found difficult to understand and execute at first:

- Defining good requirements can be hard.
- It was hard to find meters (ways of measuring numeric qualities) which were practical to use, and at the same time measure real product qualities.
- Sometimes it takes more than a week to deliver something of value to the client.
- Testing was sometimes postponed in order to start next step, some of these test deferments were not then in fact done in later testing.

4.3   Lessons Learned with Respect to the Method

Some of the lessons we learned after the trial period are:

- We will have increased focus on feedback from clients. We will select the ones that are willing to dedicate time to us. Internal stakeholders can give valuable feedback, but some customer interac-tion is necessary.
- Demonstrate new functionality with screen recording software or early test plans. This makes it easier for internal and external stakeholders to do early testing
- Tighter integration between Evo and the test process is necessary
- "Be humble in your promises, but overwhelming in your delivery

4.4   Conclusions

The method's positive impact on Confirmit product qualities has convinced us that Evo is a better suited development process than our former waterfall process, and we will continue to use Evo in the future.

What surprised us the most was the method's power of focusing on delivering value for clients versus cost of implementation. Evo enables you to re-prioritize the next development-steps based on the weekly feedback, what seemed important at the start of the project may be replaced by other solutions based on gained knowledge from previous steps.

The method has high focus on measurable product qualities, and defining these clearly and testable requires training and maturity. It is important to believe that everything can be measured and to seek guidance if it seems impossible.

One pre-requisite related to the method for using Evo is an open architecture.

Another pre-requisite is management support for changing the work process, and this is important in any software process improvement initiative.

The concept of Continuous Integration (CI)/daily builds was valuable with respect to deliver new ver-sion of the software every week.

Overall, the whole organization has embraced Evo. The release of Confirmit 8.5 showed some of Evo's great potential, and we will work hard to utilize it to the full in the future.

Literature

[1] Tom Gilb, "Competitive Engineering: A Handbook for Systems and Software Engineering Management Using Planguage", Elsevier, to be published End 2004- Beginning 2005. Manuscript, until publication, at www.gilb.com (free).

[2] Kai Gilb, "Evolutionary Project Management & Product Development, Evo, how successful people manage projects". Unfinished book manuscript for project planning to be found on www.gilb.com)

[3] Craig Larman, "Agile and Iterative Development, a Manager's Guide"

Comprehensive Documentation Made
Agile – Experiments with RaPiD7 in Philips

Ko Dooms[1] and Roope Kylmäkoski[2]

[1] Philips, Building SFJ-3, Glaslaan 2, 5616 LW Eindhoven, The Netherlands
ko.dooms@philips.com
[2] Nokia, Hatanpäänvaltatie 30, 33101 Tampere, Finland
roope.kylmakoski@nokia.com

Abstract. This paper addresses the almost never-ending headache the role of documentation has given for software projects. *Working software* has been given recently a focus over *comprehensive documentation*, yet the required documents should be authored. This paper "revisits" the approach developed by Nokia improving the documentation work without scarifying the quantity or quality of documentation. The method is called RaPiD7. The cases presented are from Philips Digital Systems Laboratory. This paper elaborates the method by providing insights to applying RaPiD7 in practice, explains the encouraging results of the experiments and gives tips for practitioners of the method by explaining the lessons learned in Philips.

1   Introduction

In recent years agile methods (see for example [3]) have been the focus of discussion in the area of software engineering. Agile methods seem to be a response to the heavily prescriptive processes (see for example [5]) that dominated the field in the early 1990s. Agile methods focus more on the human aspects of software engineering than these so-called prescriptive processes, and place human interaction over tools and processes [1]. Agile methods also state that documentation is often a heavy and unneeded form of communication.

In [4] another method for documentation work is presented that combines to a certain extent the good sides of both directions, in other words, from prescriptive processes and from agile methodologies. The method addresses the challenge of creating understanding, sharing understanding and storing the created understanding in software projects. These challenges are addressed by a stronger focus on planned human interaction and early joint decision-making by the project development team. In practice, this method is about planning the needed human interaction and decision-making as part of project planning in the form of facilitated workshops, and then subsequently carrying out this plan. The method is called RaPiD7 (Rapid production of documentation – 7 steps), and it has been developed by Nokia during 2000-2001.

Similar methods to RaPiD7 exist (see for example [2], [7], [6] and [8]), therefore the intention of this paper is not to provide a totally new or unique approach for

F. Bomarius and S. Komi-Sirviö (Eds.): PROFES 2005, LNCS 3547, pp. 224–233, 2005.

software engineering. Consequently, this paper is not comparing the different methods, but is rather a lessons-learned paper providing insights on a particular case with a selected collaborative method for software related documentation and design. A similar method to RaPiD7 called JAD [6] has existed since the 1970s and recently agile methods have been addressing the same field especially by a method called Agile Modeling [2]. However, it does not appear that any of these methods, be it JAD, AM or RaPiD7, have gained the industry de-facto status they should have. We believe that methods like RaPiD7 should be an integral part of almost any software process. Thus we also see publishing the usage results as paramount. There have been too few concrete steps taken on ensuring effective human interaction in the field of software engineering. Teamwork has often been encouraged, but the real support has been missing.

Early results from the use of RaPiD7 have already been presented in [4]. Work is still continuing inside Nokia, with more results to be published. RaPiD7 use has now spread outside Nokia too. First trials of the method outside Nokia were carried out in Philips during April 2004. This paper explains this case in detail, giving concrete suggestions how the method can be applied (something that was not presented in [4]) with some encouraging results similar to what has been published by Nokia before. Furthermore, the analysis of the applicability of the method in another environment besides Nokia is briefly discussed, too.

This paper first briefly explains RaPiD7 and the baseline status in Philips. Then the actual cases from Philips are presented with details about the planning and implementation phase. The results from the cases are presented and analyzed. Finally conclusions are drawn from the cases and from the whole paper.

2 RaPiD7 in Philips – A Case Study

2.1 Brief Introduction to RaPiD7

In RaPiD7, creating understanding for the specifications is mostly done jointly, information sharing is done continuously early on and document writing is done as far as possible jointly, too. Furthermore, the quality assurance is built into the way of working. In practice, all this is carried out in the form of facilitated workshops. The approach is presented briefly in Fig. 1.

Furthermore, RaPiD7 provides a three-layer structure. First the *project layer* describes how human interaction and joint decision-making is planned for software projects. In practice this means identifying the cases for applying RaPiD7. The *case layer* describes how the selected cases such as documents are to be created in consecutive workshops, and the *workshop layer* describes how the actual work is carried out in form of facilitated workshops.

RaPiD7 workshops comprise from seven steps. The steps aim at providing information on how to organize efficient workshops in software projects. The steps of RaPiD7 are shown in Fig. 2.

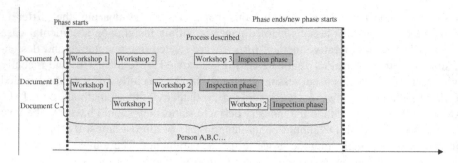

Fig. 1. RaPiD7 approach in brief

Fig. 2. Steps of RaPiD7 [4]

The workshops are planned in detail (1. *preparation*), then initiated properly (2. *kick-off*) and different ideas are gathered (*3. idea gathering*). Problem solving (*4. analysis*) and decision-making (*6. decisions making*) techniques are used in the workshops. The decisions are written down to a desired level (*5. detailed design*) and workshop results are verified and next steps are agreed on (*7. closing*). RaPiD7 workshops typically produce documents that can be finalized after the workshops in a few hours. Although the workshops play the role of an inspection as well, a short inspection is typical for the documents produced with RaPiD7.

2.2 Background

We, at Philips Applied Technologies, translate innovative product ideas from research into real product implementations, such as flat TV's and DVD recorders. During the creation of these products we have to write an extensive amount of project documentation. This documentation is required to create a common understanding of what has to be developed, what the proper system architectures are, and provide details on the design for development. Furthermore when a product reaches the maintenance phase the maintainers of the product have to use the documentation to solve problems in the product or extend the products with new features. Philips Applied Technologies is a CMM level 3 organization, which means projects should be created in a repeatable and defined way. To achieve this, an efficient documentation process should be in place.

To achieve this we first looked into challenges and common mistakes in the writing of project documentation. These are listed in Table 1.

Table 1. Challenges and common mistakes in writing project documentation

Challenges	Common mistakes
Readability by the customer (for example product management and business owners)	Unnecessary documentation produced by inexperienced project people
Being able to cover everything that is required in the document e.g.: What is essential and what isn't Are the captured items actually describing what the stakeholders of the documentation need Where do we get the right input	Too little documentation written by experienced project people Experienced people can either be too busy with other tasks or see some aspects as too obvious to be written down
How to keep/make it consistent with other documents or project deliverables, for example code or test scripts	
Achieving common understanding of the decisions written down	

We, at Philips Applied Technologies, have been looking for ways to improve our way of working and to address the mentioned challenges. When we first heard of RaPiD7, the method developed by Nokia, we were attracted by its structured workshop approach used in the creation of project documentation. Including workshops as part of the way of working was not new to us, but using a structured approach where the document at hand is really written inside the workshop was. We decided to get more out of the workshops by integrating them better into our daily way of working and add more structure to the workshops. In addition, we were intrigued by the possibility of finalizing the required documentation almost completely in the workshops. Furthermore, we also see inside Philips Applied Technologies an increasing number of requests from our customers to "do more with less". There are high pressures especially in:

- Shortening the time to market
- Reacting faster to changes of the product specification during development
- Spend less Non Recurring Engineering money

Due to these requirements, the introduction of a more agile approach for our software process is needed and we see that RaPiD7 can play a role in this. At the same time we need to maintain our CMM level. However, this should not be an issue with RaPiD7, as Nokia is also using RaPiD7 in parts of their organization that are concerned with CMM level too. No negative consequences on the achieved CMM level have been noticed; on the contrary an improved effect on the KPA review process was the case, due the intensive collaboration and reviews in the RaPiD7 workshops.

The most important expected benefits from working in a more agile way and from RaPiD7 in specific are:

- More interaction expected between the project stakeholders: Philips Applied Technologies project members, customer representatives and third parties if involved
- Focus on writing only the essential documentation
- Create a common understanding, share knowledge better
- Create more focus, which should result in quicker results
- Respond better to changes

As these were exactly the benefits we were looking for we started to prepare ourselves for the trials with RaPiD7.

2.3 Preparing for the Case

In preparation for the introduction of RaPiD7 in Philips Applied Technologies, we (two Philips Applied Technologies employees) first followed a two-day in-house training course at Nokia. During the training we used this method in the creation of several documents such as:

- Requirements for a mobile application
- Most important "use cases" for this application
- High level architecture
- Interface description of the building blocks
- Estimates for the development of the application

The eight trainees all played a specific role such as project manager, product manager, architect and so on. In addition, we were confronted with practicing the facilitator role, which was seen as very important for the success of the workshop. We were surprised that in only a two-day workshop (where most people were not familiar with each other and were still learning the method) we got both usable output and quality of the deliverables as mentioned above.

After the training our thoughts about the usability of the method in Philips Applied Technologies were positive. However, to avoid initial high costs we experimented in one of the software groups within Philips Applied Technologies. The following describes the first trial case in more detail.

2.4 The Case

2.4.1 The Baseline Status
Most of the employees in Philips Applied Technologies have a personal objective each year to write one or more so called "white cards". White cards are the starting point for intellectual property patents. Before RaPiD7 was used, a year ago, a group of 10 people had the idea to brainstorm together to generate new ideas for white cards. The group used one afternoon and first visited *the room of the future* in our Philips research laboratory to stimulate the flow of ideas for brainstorming. After this visit they did a brainstorm session and discussed the generated ideas. The end result of the afternoon was an Excel-sheet with around 20 ideas written down. A single line described the idea. Furthermore each member of the group was assigned one idea to expand it into a white card after further investigation about the usefulness of the idea. After one year a few (3-4) ideas were converted into white cards and the Excel-file was passed as "a hot potato" between the 10 people until the process came to completion.

The promise of RaPiD7 to really finish some documentation work inside the workshop by collective decision and communication was the reason we wanted to try out a similar session with the help of this agile method.

2.4.2 The Planning Phase
As a first step we planned a one-hour **preparation** meeting (step 1) together with the project leader and the team leader of the project team (in total 11 people) selected to generate white cards on the specific technology they were working on. During this preparation we went through the whole process (steps 2 to 7) and estimated time for the steps and assigned roles. Furthermore we decided upon techniques to be used and the materials we needed.

The most important outputs of the preparation were:

- The goal set by the manager of the group was: "Generation of a number of white cards related to the technology that the group was working on".
- The target set was:"3 to 4 detailed and submitted white cards, plus several ideas ready for next workshop".
- The project leader should present a short presentation to set the scene: known technology and trends of the subject.
- The team leader should present one patent (granted) in this field as an example (5 minutes needed).
- A detailed agenda (describing 4 hours of work) with all the steps and methods to be used was made.
- The list of needed material was as follows:
  - Enough laptops connected to the network
  - Post-it notes
  - A room
  - Invitations for the workshop and copies of the agenda

We found that the preparation of the above-mentioned subjects and the following of the process resulted in high and promising expectations for the workshop itself.

2.4.3 The Workshop

The workshop attendees were the manager of the department (who played the facilitator role), the project leader (who played the secretary role), the team leader and the team itself containing an architect and 7 software developers.

During the **kick-off** (step 2) the manager explained the goals and target of the workshop. A one-slide introduction was then given about RaPiD7 (explaining the steps). This was followed by two other short presentations about stimulating creativity (as already described above in the planning phase).

We then continued with **gathering ideas** (step 3). During this step, each person received a pen, an empty A3 sheet of paper and some post-it notes. The task was to think quietly, write a new idea on the note and then place the sticker on the A3 sheet. The sheet would then be passed to your neighbor and the process repeated. The idea was to stimulate further ideas on the same theme. This process continued for 25 minutes and after that each of the 76 stickers was placed on the white board. We then continued by clustering the ideas on the white board. After a further 10 minutes the facilitator took the lead and asked the contributors to clarify their ideas if necessary. We finished with 7 clusters of related ideas. The group was divided into three sub teams and each team picked a cluster that they liked to work on further. The remaining four clusters were saved by the scribe for later investigation (possible input for next workshop). After these two steps the team took a well-deserved break.

Each of the three sub-teams began with **analysing ideas** (step 4) of the cluster they picked. They asked for clarification when necessary and removed duplicates; they also wrote a one-line description of the ideas that were left. The final result was that two teams ended up with two ideas and one team with nine. Although the teams had different numbers of ideas to work on, the work seemed equally divided because the nine ideas were more easily to refine then the others.

Next step was **detailing** (step 5) the one–liners into a full description (text plus drawings). In this step, laptops were used so that the text was immediately written down in the right format. During this writing process an automatic review process took place. The fact that a single PC was used meant that review comments could immediately be taken into account. The team finished with a **decision** (step 6) on each produced white card and the result was submitted online. Each team member's personal opinion was taken into account. This way the work was completed in 4 hours, and the workshop finished on time. During the **closing** session (step 7) the team with nine ideas made an appointment (next day) to finish and submit the last white cards.

Looking back on the workshop the most important team remarks were:

- Surprised at the number of generated white cards. The target was to have 3-4 white cards, but the workshop finished with 13.
- The focus of the team and energy used was high during the whole workshop
- Good help with the structure (agenda) of the meeting
- Clear what was expected
- Very satisfied feeling at the end result

This was our first exposure to using RaPiD7 in the authoring of documentation within Philips Applied Technologies. We saw that the workshop provided a productive and very interactive way of working.

2.4.4 The Results

Although in the above case we did not produce any project documentation such as an architectural document or a design document, we could still draw important conclusions from this experiment. We could assume that if the method was successful in the creation of white cards it might also be successful in the creation of more technical project documentation later. This could be proven in another case.

Conclusions of this first RaPiD7 trial within Philips Applied Technologies:

- Compared to the white card generation workshop of one year ago, we accomplished much more output using the RaPiD7 method. In the initial trial only one-liners were described and no white cards were submitted. In the RaPiD7 case most of the work was done inside the workshop
- Almost no "homework" was required after the workshop, which gave people a satisfied feeling
- Proper preparation is essential to success
- RaPiD7 seems usable for generating documents needed in Philips Applied Technologies
- The decision was made to deploy the method further

Successes often flourish, and the same happened in this case. The team members talked to other software people in the department that liked to copy the workshop approach for white cards. The manager networked with a manager from another Philips division and explained to him the results and method used. So far we have heard of 4 successful copies of the white card creation workshop with similar results.

2.4.5 A Step Further – Another Case

The next step was to invite the project team to develop a part of their technical documentation using the RaPiD7 method. A training/workshop session of two days was organized.

The workshop was held at Philips Applied Technologies premises with support from Nokia. The goal was to write an architectural document (describing the functionality of the system to be build, the major subsystems and their interfaces) and two detailed design documents of important components of the system. A template for both types of documentation was available. Normally this kind of documentation takes 40-100 hours to finish (write, review and rework). During this workshop we managed to come up with the most important parts of the documents, but not the full document. Finalizing the documents can be done in follow-up workshops or by the author himself. The most important conclusions of this workshop are listed in Table 2.

If we study the pros in the table above we can conclude that using the RaPiD7 method we see some pretty results on the documentation process. Namely: Documents will be small, consist of the essential information, are reviewed and delivered quickly.

Table 2. Pros and challenges of RaPiD7 as seen by the workshop attendees

Pros of the method	Challenges of the method
Resulting documents are small in size, only the essential documentation is recorded and therefore easier to maintain	Trained and capable facilitators are needed
Results are written down in reviewed documentation	Risks if planning of workshop is not done properly are: Decisions are made too quickly Conclusions are drawn too quickly resulting in sloppy documents
Lots of collaboration and interaction took place, which stimulates discussions, common understanding and knowledge sharing of the problem at hand	Problem how to handle different knowledge levels of participants
Detecting of important issues (any kind) early in the process	Mismatch with quality system templates, these are not workshop friendly
Fast results when writing documents	Workshop teams should be formed carefully, only real stakeholders should be selected

2.4.6 Suggestions, Conclusions and the Future

After the above-described workshops were completed we at Philips Applied Technologies drew up some tips for the further introduction and deployment in our lab. These are listed in Table 3.

Table 3. General workshop and deployment tips for RaPiD7

General tips from the team	Deployment Tips from the team
Clearly define the goals of the workshop	1 hour RaPiD7 training for every employee should be enough, then practice in projects
Consider to have longer (30 minutes) breaks for: Looking up things Thinking silently Check things with others	Select cases carefully To maximize success of deployment choose a case which is not too difficult
Use the seven steps liberal (combine were needed)	Setup/organize training/coaching for facilitators at department level
The use of templates is helpful	Consider how to create a balanced workshop team?
Try to use (parts of) the method in all types of meeting	Consider how to arrange facilitator assignment

In conclusion, Philips Applied Technologies in conjunction with the SPI steering group decided to proceed with the introduction of the RaPiD7 method. A further deployment plan will be made. We expect to introduce it using a bottom-up approach by selecting newly created project-teams and then deploying the method within these teams. As with the white card examples success should spread itself. At the same time we will support from top-down, an action to make the design templates more workshop-friendly.

3 Conclusions

The results found were only from a few cases of using RaPiD7 in Philips. Nevertheless, the presented workshops have been mostly successful and detailed descriptions of the way the workshops have been organized are presented. Furthermore, the results are a step forward from the baseline situation in Philips for the mentioned cases. We have created more interaction between the project stakeholders within the few cases and we have been able to focus on writing only the essential documentation. Common understanding has improved and reaching the results has been faster. However, there are definitely more steps we can take within Philips with RaPiD7. This approach needs to be integrated into the general way of working rather than just having ad-hoc workshops occasionally. The work towards this approach is in progress. This is the way to systematically reach the expected benefits we set for the improved way of working.

On the other hand, when the results are compared to the results Nokia has published, we can present similar results from our individual cases already now. In addition, this paper provides a concrete and pragmatic view on organizing RaPiD7 workshops and thus provides part of the missing guidance on using RaPiD7. The results give us the confident feeling that, in fact, RaPiD7 can be applied in other environments not typical to Nokia. Naturally, the results cannot be generalized either by providing a single example outside Nokia. Nevertheless, the results emphasize the need for methods like RaPiD7 in overall.

References

1. Agile manifesto in web, http://agilemanifesto.org/, last visited in December 2004
2. Ambler Scott, Agile Modeling, John Wiley & Sons, Inc., 2002
3. Cockburn Alistair, Agile Software Development, Addison-Wesley, 2002
4. Kylmäkoski Roope, Efficient Authoring of Software Documentation Using RaPiD7, 25th International Conference on Software Engineering - Proceedings, IEEE, 2003
5. Sommerville Ian, Software Engineering, Addison-Wesley, 1996
6. Wood Jane, Silver Denise, Joint Application Development, John Wiley & Sons Inc., 1999
7. Coughlan Jane, Macredie Robert D., Effective Communication in Requirements Elicitation: A comparison of Methodologies, Springer-Verlag London Limited, 2002
8. Gottesdiener Ellen, Requirements by Collaboration: Workshops for Defining Needs, Addison-Wesley, 2002

A Case Study: Coordination Practices in Global Software Development

Darja Šmite

Riga Information Technology Institute,
Kuldigas iela 45b, LV-1083, Riga, Latvia
Darja.Smite@riti.lv

Abstract. Global Software Development (GSD) is a new challenge for software developers to reach mobility in resources, obtain extra knowledge, speed time-to-market and increase operational efficiency. However, the new trend is followed by specific risks and needs a deeper analysis for successful risk overcoming. This paper gives an insight into a research on GSD project performance improvement in one of the biggest software development companies in Latvia. Project management and coordination in distributed environment is a great challenge, though being not very widely explored. In this paper the author emphasizes the necessity of research in this area and provides an overview of coordination practices used in the organization chosen for the case study.

1 Introduction

The question explored in this paper is related to global software development (GSD) project coordination. To start with the term GSD has to be explained.

GSD is also known as a type of outsourcing relations. Campbell R. Harvey's Hypertextual Finance Glossary defines outsourcing as purchasing a significant percentage of intermediate components from outside suppliers [6]. There are various forms of outsourcing, e.g. business process outsourcing (BPO), application outsourcing or application service provider (ASP) outsourcing, hardware outsourcing, data centre outsourcing, selective or full software development outsourcing.

The area of author's research is devoted to selective and full software development outsourcing also known as global software development. In particular, the author examines relations between geographically distributed End Customer, a Mediating Partner and the Developer aiming to produce software (See Fig. 1).

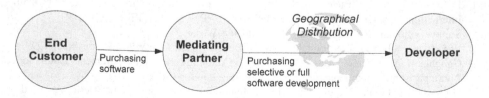

Fig. 1. The Model of Global Software Development Explored by the Author

F. Bomarius and S. Komi-Sirviö (Eds.): PROFES 2005, LNCS 3547, pp. 234–244, 2005.
© Springer-Verlag Berlin Heidelberg 2005

A review of related literature on the field of global software development shows that the topic of performance is poorly explored, especially from the supplier's point of view. Most of the related research is devoted to questions as decision making – whether to outsource or not ([9], [18], [21]), relationship risk management ([1], [3], [4], [8], [17]), contractual problems and advices ([2], [5], [9]), success factors, that will help to survive starting outsourcing relationship ([10], [12], [13], [15], [17]), and case studies from the field ([7], [13], [14], [16]).

Working on the research, the author explores an organization chosen as a case study. This organization competes in the global market as a software development supplier, in other words – developer. The lack of research that would answer the question "How to perform software development in distributed environment?" makes practitioners act intuitively and precludes the prognosticated success of global projects. Therefore, the main objectives for the research are as follows: *To build a framework for global projects, which would contain guidelines, practices and tools for effective performance in distributed environment.*

The paper is organized as follows. The following section describes the research structure and methodology, and gives an insight to the case study. Then GSD coordination practices are presented. The practices are followed by a discussion section. And the paper is concluded by a brief summary and an overview of further work.

2 Research Overview

2.1 Research Structure

The analysis of GSD coordination practices described in this paper is a part of a larger research, which aims to develop a framework for GSD projects, containing guidelines for global project management, software engineering methods adapted for global specifics, best practice knowledge base and project management tools for better performance in distributed environment [19].

The current results of the research, in particular GSD project coordination practices, are the output from the previous steps of the research – global project questionnaire and experienced project manager interviewing. These practices are further used as an input for GSD knowledge base and examination in ongoing projects.

2.2 Research Methodology

The overall research approach for the research is active methodology – "learning by doing", which aims to deepen the understanding of GSD projects and learn how to improve them [11]. According to this methodology the author performs cycles: Observe → Plan → Implement → Evaluate → Improve → Observe →.... In this case, the author is Observing global projects → Indicating risks → Planning preventive actions and developing guidelines → Implementing the guidelines in the ongoing projects → Evaluating the results, identifying areas for further improvement [20].

The author examines GSD projects by means of a case study. The GSD risks and practices have been explored carrying out global project questionnaire and the interviews with experienced project managers from the organization used for the case study. The questionnaire served as a preliminary step of the research aiming to deepen the understanding of GSD project performance and risks; and gathered information on 19 global projects [17]. The interviews with experienced project managers used the output of the questionnaire and addressed issues on GSD practices for performance improvement. The author conducted 13 interviews with 9 project managers. The interviews were held by means of semi-structured interviewing and open questions.

The interviewing uncovered a set of defined practices, which can be divided into two main groups – communication practices and coordination practices. Unfortunately, due to shortness of this paper the author addresses only coordination practices here. The practices related to communication issues are described in a related paper [20].

2.2 Case Description

The author performs her research in a company used for the case study, given a pseudonym XYZ. XYZ is one of the biggest software development company in Latvia. It is an ISO certified company with approximately 350 employees in total. The company is participating in global software development projects with partners from Western and Eastern Europe, and Scandinavia since early 90s [20].

Recently, XYZ became a part of a large international software development enterprise. Accordingly, the necessity to improve GSD project performance has increased. Even though XYZ follows a certified quality system, it doesn't provide particular regulations and practices taking into account global specifics. Following the results of audit observations and project measurements, the author concludes that the global risks make difference in project performance and have to be addressed notably.

2.3 GSD Project Knowledge Base

The interviews with experienced GSD project managers from XYZ resulted in a set of practices for further examination in ongoing projects. For efficient GSD practice implementation the author developed a Knowledge Base. XYZ project managers repeatedly pointed out a lack of knowledge share between project managers in the same organization. Therefore, implementing the GSD Knowledge Base, the author prescribes it will serve as a framework for accumulating XYZ best practices, tools and templates for better performance.

The Knowledge Base provides the users several functions as follows:

- Experience generalization;
- New issue proposal;
- Quality document templates addressing global specifics;
- Discussions;
- Notifications;
- Wide searching opportunities.

All the practices in the Knowledge Base are recorded using risk based analysis, describing threats, vulnerabilities, resulting risks, frequency and impact [20]. So far, the practices address such issues as communication between the remote participants, the role of trust, project starting guidelines, advisable organizational structures, GSD risk management issues and checklists, process distribution and personnel allocation practices.

Currently, the Knowledge Base is accessible by experienced GSD project managers who participated at the preliminary survey and interviewing. The further steps of the research prescribe gathering feedback from project managers; enlarge the content of the Knowledge Base and assess the current practices considering the following factors:

- Threat frequency of occurrence;
- Possible impact on project results;
- Additional preventive actions for risk mitigation.

Considering the risk that knowledge bases are rarely used by the practitioners, author plans to integrate it into the Risk Management process. The further steps of the research will aim to use GSD Knowledge Base practices and related information in the process of risk management in global projects as shown in Fig. 2.

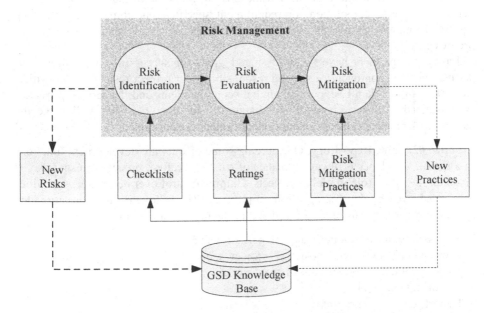

Fig. 2. GSD Knowledge Base information usage in the process of Risk Management

Using Knowledge Base practices during the Risk Management process will provide practice sharing and continues information accumulation at first hand.

3 Coordination Practices Addressing Global Project Specifics

In this chapter you will find an overview of the key practices and risks which deal with coordination of global projects.

Practice #1: Organizational Changes. Engagement in cooperation between the remote partners brings changes in both organizations. The processes which were held in-house before need different level of management by the partner's organization. Nevertheless, four of nine project managers independently reported that customer organizations are never willing to change. This causes risks related to both communication and coordination issues.

First of all, complex organizational structures and many problem escalation levels cause time delays in problem solution (Project Organizational Structures are discussed in the author's related paper [20]).

Secondly, remote supplier involvement in software development needs a new approach in software engineering. This means that distance brings differences in relations between the partners developing software. Questions which have been discussed next door now require powerful infrastructure for intercommunication. Besides, risk factors as language skills, cultural differences, terminology differences, etc. need to be taken into account. All these risks influence various processes as the degree of detailed elaboration for requirement specification, complicated planning and work amount evaluation, the level of management and control over project progress, etc.

Lastly, the partners have to build shared goals for successful cooperation. The partners need an approach for sharing responsibility for project results and activities. According to Jae-Nam Lee, partnership between the clients and the service providers is considered as a key predictor of outsourcing success [14]. This will make the parties work more effectively on improving mutual relationship.

Practice #2: Joint Repository. Outsourcing some of software development functions to a remote developer is always a matter of trust. Therefore, process transparency is given an important role in global projects. Gaining control over developer's activities can be achieved by developing a joint repository. The following functions provided by a joint repository can be used for global project management improvement:

- Access from the developer's and the partner's sides;
- Project documentation repository (project scope, calendar plans, risk overview, meeting minutes and carried decisions, etc.);
- Document approval;
- Reports on project progress;
- Work tasks and time recording;
- Problem tracking.

Joint repository provides effective configuration management, reducing misunderstandings related to different document version usage by the parties. It also provides a tool for better progress control for the remote partner. Reporting on work task completion provides timely risk identification.

Practice #3: Work Breakdown. A very important issue addressing software development in global projects is work breakdown. The smaller steps you make, the better you can control them. It is also important to gain an agreement between the developer and the partner on each requirement and each divided task. The work breakdown will further provide an opportunity to manage progress and risks related to task completion on time.

Practice #4: Process Breakdown. Process breakdown between the remote participants defines responsibility share and the way of further collaboration. The common process breakdown reported by XYZ project managers is shown on Fig. 3.

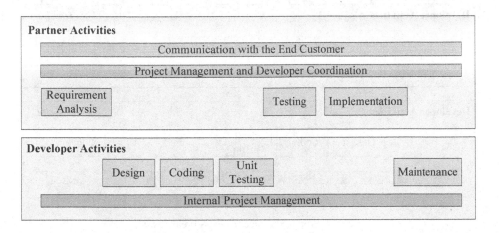

Fig. 3. Usual project process breakdown by XYZ and its partners

The interviews with project managers have shown that there are several approaches used by different partners in process breakdown. There are variations in planning activities allocation. Some partners strictly establish the deadlines and person-day evaluation. In other projects the developer is responsible for work amount evaluations and planning activities. In some cases projects are held under partner's management. In other cases the developer is responsible for overall project management.

Considering the gathered practices and experienced risks, the author proposes the following model of cooperation (See Fig.4).

The proposed process breakdown for global projects emphasizes the necessity of shared planning and coordination activities and regular on-site project meetings. Personal contact during the meetings and joint work on project coordination provides effective resource utilization and minimizes risks related to complications in project management brought by distance between the partner and the developer. It will also provide the distributed teams with the feeling of togetherness and deepen trust between the participants.

An XYZ project manager reported, *"Since we established joined meetings once in 2-3 months, we got rid of many misunderstandings related to task prioritization and goal achievement. Besides, we gained a deeper trust from the partner"*.

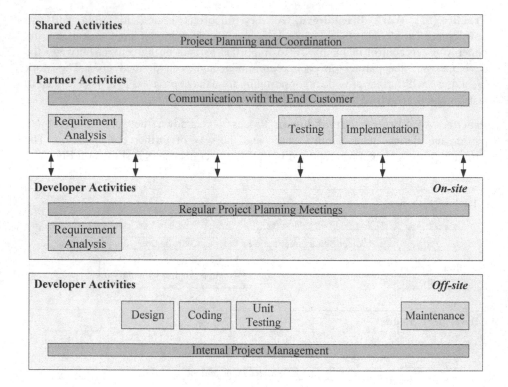

Fig. 4. Proposed project process breakdown

Another recommendation from the proposed project breakdown addresses Requirement Analysis process share (described in Practice #5 below).

Practice #5: System Requirement Analysis. Project managers point out that remote partners from different countries have different traditions for requirement analysis. Latvian software industry is used to detailed system requirement specifications which are clear and complete. Nevertheless XYZ partners from different countries offer low degree of detailed elaboration. Unfortunately, the distance brings difficulties in solving the problems and misunderstandings.

Therefore, project managers advise to perform joint on-site requirement analysis involving both the customer and developer parties. XYZ project managers' report that there it is useful to send at least one or two systems analysts to the remote partner's side in order to participate in requirement analysis. Usually, the developer analysts are given a second role in this process without a chance to meet and communicate with the end customer. Nevertheless, it provides a opportunity to prepare the specification according to developer's needs. After the analysts come back one of them usually leads the development project. The development team receives the knowledge about the project scope and tasks from first hand, reducing the risk of misunderstandings.

Practice #6: Terminology. Project managers from XYZ reported on frequent misunderstandings interpreting the requirements in the beginning of the project. These problems are sometimes caused by local language peculiarities, sometimes by lack of language skills in particular business field by the developer organization. As a result this causes delays in time for task confirmation.

Therefore, it is useful to create a special terminology dictionary aiming to agree upon the used terms for the entire project. This dictionary can be used by different developer representatives (analysis, developers, testers, documentation writers, etc.) in different project activities (designing, coding, testing, documenting, etc.). This also precludes the risk of loosing knowledge in case of loosing the analysts involved in the project.

Practice #7: Product Quality. Low personnel costs are not the only uppermost factor for developing countries to compete in software development market. Low productivity or product quality is often the reasons for searching another software development service provider.

Answering this risk, the process of software testing has to be adequately addressed by the developer. Although, system testing is usually performed by the partner, the developer is responsible for proper debugging, unit testing and integration tests before any delivery.

Practice #8: Process Quality. Process quality is as important as product quality. In many causes, project and process management is as mature as it is required by the partner's side. Although XYZ quality guidelines prescribe following quality procedures, process quality is often viewed as an issue for cutting costs. But how does it influence cooperation between the partner and the remote developer?

If the partner's quality processes are not defined and managed according to quality procedures, then by providing a minimum the developer can receive partner's appreciation and satisfaction – what is asked is done. But if the partner has a quality system, they wish to count on an appropriate service level. In this case, the developer can adopt the partner's procedures or use its own.

However, despite partner's maturity level, providing high quality configuration management, systems analysis, design and testing documentation, problem tracking, requirement traceability, planning and reporting on project results increases trust in the developer activities and competence.

One project manager reported, *"Our partner doesn't follow defined quality processes. Therefore, many activities as e.g. requirement specification and problem tracking are complicated. We came with our initiative to participate in systems analysis by drawing process diagrams and established a problem tracking database. This resulted partner's respect and trust in our competence and desire to cooperate as a unified team".*

4 Discussion

The major question which seeks for the answer is "If the GSD projects can be coordinated as in-house software development projects?" To start with, the author offers to look though different risks which are brought by the global appearance.

Such issues as distance, cultural and organizational differences between the partners involved in software development mark out the factors that make the global and in-house projects different (see Table 1) and additional risks, that are not relevant for in-house projects (see Table 2).

Table 1. The differences between global and in-house projects brought by global appearance

Global Projects	In-house Projects
Lack of personal contact	Next door closeness
Communication via electronic means or phone	Personal communication, as well as electronic and phone communication
N remote teams need N local managers	One team = one manager
Possible time zone differences	No time zone differences

The list of differences could be extended with such factors as lack of common goals, lack of trust, different contractual relations, project documentation kept in different places at each participant's side, misunderstandings on cultural ground, different approaches in software development methodology, low language skills and other factors. Nevertheless, all these risks can be possibly minimized. There are practices for better global project sourcing, infrastructure improvement, language skills problem overcoming, agreement on software development methodology and sharing goals for mutual cooperation, etc.

In its turn the factors given in the Table 1 are brought by distance and can't be avoided. These factors influence coordination and communication throughout the project and make global projects distinctive from the in-house projects. So, how practitioners will address these factors?

The author emphasizes the necessity of guidelines addressing the following areas:

- New practices for work amount evaluation, taking into account differences brought by the distance and several team management;
- High level infrastructure establishment for better communication between the participants;
- New coordination practices taking into account lack of personal contact, several team involvement, time zone differences and other risks, which are brought by global appearance.

5 Conclusions and Further Research

Summarizing the discussion the following conclusions can me made:

- The factors brought by global appearance make GSD projects different from in-house software development projects. Addressing these factors the new approaches for project coordination should be established.
- Global projects vary depending on the situation. XYZ is participating in many projects with different customers/partners from various countries. In some cases

the practices used for project coordination can be shared between the projects. But there are also practices which are applicable only for particular situations (e.g. there are projects with and without time zone differences). Therefore, there is a necessity in classifying the global projects and characterizing the situations for practice usage.

- Analyzing the information gathered from the interviews the author concludes that experience is not being shared in the organization. Practices put in the Knowledge Base forms the ground for knowledge share between the projects. This will also help to accumulate more practices according to the appropriate situations for their usage.
- As the current quality regulations are not extended for managing global specifics, the guidelines for better performance in GSD projects have to be developed and implemented.

The practices presented in this paper are only a part of possible solutions to the problems faced in global project coordination. The author plans to continue her research by interviewing more project managers, accumulating the practices in GSD Knowledge Base, participating as a consultant in new global projects in order to test the practices and receive a feedback for further improvement.

Acknowledgement

The author appreciates many valuable discussions with professor Juris Borzovs and professor Uldis Sukovskis, as well as the research input received from the experienced project managers.

This research is partly supported by the Latvian Council of Science project Nr. 02.2002 "Latvian Informatics Production Unit Support Program in the Area of Engineering, Computer Networks and Signal Processing" and European Social Foundation.

References

1. Aubert, B.A.; Dussault, S.; Patry, H.; Rivard, S. Managing the Risk of IT Outsourcing. CIRANO Working Papers, Montreal, June 1998
2. Aubert, B.A.; Houde, J.F.; Patry, H. and Rivard, S. Characteristics of IT Outsourcing Contracts. Proceedings of the 36th Hawaii International Conference on System Sciences, HICSS'03
3. Aubert, B.A.; Patry, H.; Rivard, S. and Smith, H. IT Outsourcing Risk Management at British Petroleum. Proceedings of the 34th Hawaii International Conference on System Sciences, 2001
4. Bahli, B.; Rivard, S. A Validation of Measures Associated with the Risk Factors in Information Technology Outsourcing. Proceedings of the 36th Hawaii International Conference on System Sciences, HICSS'03
5. Bodker, K., Is Development in an Outsourcing Context – Revisiting the IS Outsourcing Bandwagon.

6. Campbell R. Harvey's Hypertextual Finance Glossary, 2004, http://www.duke.edu/ ~charvey/Classes/wpg/bfgloso.htm (03.01.2005)
7. Carmel, E.; Agarwal, R. Tactical Approaches for Alleviating Distance in Global Software Development. IEEE Software, March/April 2001
8. Clemons, E.K.; Hitt, L.M. and Snir, E.M. A Risk Analysis Framework for IT Outsourcing. Draft, 2000
9. Department of Information Resources, Austin, Texas. Outsourcing Strategies: Guidelines for Evaluating Internal and External Resources for Major Information Technology Projects. June, 1998
10. Grover, V.; Cheon, M.J.; and Teng, J.T.C. The Effect of Service Quality and Partnership on the Outsourcing of Information Systems Functions. Journal of Management Information System, 12 (4), 1996, pp.89-116
11. Jarvinen P; On Research Methods. Opinpajan Kirja, Tampere, Finland, 2001
12. Lacity, M. Lessons in Global Information Technology Sourcing. IEEE Computer, August 2002, pp.26-33
13. Lacity, M.C.; Willcocks, L.O.; and Feeny, D.F. IT Outsourcing: Maximize Flexibility and Control. Harvard Business Review, May-June 1995, pp.84-93
14. Lee, J.N.; Huynh, M.Q.; Kwok, C.W. and Pi S.M. The Evolution of Outsourcing Research: What is the Next Issue?. Proceeding of the 33rd Hawaii International Conference on Systems Sciences, Maui in Hawaii, January 2000, pp.1-10.
15. Light, M. Matlus, R. Berg, T. Strategic Analysis Report Application Development Contracting: Lifeline or Noose? R-14-38791, 28 September 2001
16. Loh, L. and Venkatraman, N. An Empirical Study of Information Technology Outsourcing: Benefits, Risks, and Performance Implications. Proceeding of the 16th International Conference on Information Systems, Amsterdam, the Netherlands, December 10-13, 1995, pp. 277-288.
17. Report of Latvian Ministry of Economics, June 2002
18. Roy, V.; Aubert, B.A. A Resource Based View of the Information Systems Sourcing Mode. CIRANO Working Papers, Montreal, October 1999
19. Smite, D.; Global Software Development Project Management – Distance Overcoming. Software Process Improvement, The Proceedings of the 11th European Conference, EuroSPI, Trondheim, Norway, 2004
20. Smite D.; Sukovskis U. A Case Study: Coordination Practices in Global Software Development. Submitted to SPICE Conference, 2004.
21. Willcocks, L.; Fitzgerald, G. Guide to Outsourcing Information Technology. Business Intelligence, 1994

A Study of a Mentoring Program for Knowledge Transfer in a Small Software Consultancy Company

Finn Olav Bjørnson[1] and Torgeir Dingsøyr[2]

[1] Department of Computer and Information Science,
Norwegian University of Science and Technology,
NO-7491 Trondheim, Norway
bjornson@idi.ntnu.no
[2] SINTEF Information and Communication Technology,
NO-7465 Trondheim, Norway
Torgeir.Dingsoyr@sintef.no

Abstract. Mentor programs are important mechanisms that serve functions such as career development as well as knowledge transfer. Many see mentor programs as an efficient, inexpensive, flexible and tailored way of transferring technical knowledge from experts to less experienced employees. We have investigated how a mentor program works in a small software consultancy company, and propose that the learning effect of the program could be improved by introducing methods to increase the employees level of reflection.

1 Introduction

Small software consultancy companies have to leverage their position in the market to stay ahead of their competitors. In order to survive, the solutions provided by their consultants have to be of such quality that makes their customers return to the company when they need assistance with a new project, and the solutions should ensure a good reputation for the company that attracts new customers.

To ensure high quality in the systems developed, companies are dependent on a good software development process. The main parts of this process can be planned out in advance and used collectively in a firm in order to ensure quality, but in every project you will probably run into situations where it is important to be able to improvise in order to keep the project on tracks. This is especially true for small software intensive companies in turbulent environments [1]. In these situations experience play a major role in coping with the different challenges.

Experienced developers recognize many different problems and often know the appropriate solutions straight away. For new developers however, this is often not the case. Also if the company is dependent on remaining agile and changing their process in accordance with the demands of their customers, the experienced developers may loose their ability to see the best solution. In these circumstances a company has to have a good strategy to manage their collective knowledge.

Wickert and Herschel [2] examine various challenges that small businesses face when implementing knowledge management [3] efforts. Small businesses often do

F. Bomarius and S. Komi-Sirviö (Eds.): PROFES 2005, LNCS 3547, pp. 245–256, 2005.

not have the time and resources that larger companies have to implement large knowledge management efforts, yet they are more vulnerable to knowledge erosion through leaving of key employees. In such an environment it becomes vital to share knowledge to prevent knowledge erosion and staying up-to-date. One suggested solution is mentoring programs which can have an effect in leveraging personal knowledge and sharing knowledge between projects. Such programs can often be more effective than training and written documentation [4].

In this paper we describe an ongoing research project to improve the mentor program in a small consultancy company. The main purpose of the mentor program in this company is knowledge transfer, particularly concerning the software development process and project management. We have focused on how the mentor program supports learning, and changes that could increase the learning effect of the program.

The organization of the paper is as follows: First, we present theory on mentor programs and learning as a part of mentoring. Then, we present the research approach used in this work. We present a small software company where we have conducted a study on a mentoring program, present findings and results from initial interviews, and our work with improving the program. Finally, we conclude and present future work.

2   Mentoring Programs and Learning

In this section, we present work from management theory on what a mentor program is, how mentor programs can be designed, and how learning can take place in mentor programs.

Kram [5] suggests that existing theory predicts that effective mentoring should be associated with positive career and job attitudes. In a literature review, Ragins et.al [6] show that empirical studies supports this proposition. They also present results from a survey that indicate that persons in dissatisfying or marginally satisfying mentor relationship express the same or worse attitudes than people not involved in a mentor relationship at all. One of their conclusions is that it is clear that good mentoring may lead to positive outcomes, but bad mentoring may be destructive and in some cases worse than no mentoring at all.

2.1   What Is a Mentor and Protégé?

According to Kram [5], mentors are generally defined as "individuals with advanced experience and knowledge who are committed to providing upwards mobility and career support to their protégé". A protégé literally means "a person under the patronage, protection, or care of someone interested in his career or welfare" [7]. This is usually a younger employee who lacks experience in one or more fields.

2.2   Formal and Informal Mentoring Programs

According to a literature review of mentoring by Ragins et.al. [6], comparisons of non-mentored and mentored individuals yield the consistent result that individuals with informal mentors report greater career satisfaction, career commitment and career mobility than individuals without mentors. Many organizations have attempted to replicate the benefits of informal mentoring by developing formal mentor programs. Yet formal and informal mentoring relationships vary on a number of dimensions:

Informal mentor relationships often arise through a mutual developmental need, and often spring from mutual identification. The mentor may view the protégé as a younger version of themselves and the protégé may view the mentor as a role model. This mutual identification contributes to a closeness and intimacy of the mentor program which is often cited in mentoring literature [5]. An informal mentor program is often unstructured and the participants meet as often and as long as is desired. Such an informal mentor relationship usually lasts between three and six years. The purpose of informal mentoring relationships is often the achievement of long term career goals for the protégé.

In contrast, formal mentoring relationships usually springs from a third party assigning the mentor and protégé to the relationship. This may lead to people entering into these relationships not because of mutual need but to meet organizational standards. Meetings in a formal mentoring relationship is often sporadic or specified in a contract at the start of the program, and their duration is often from six months to one year, much shorter than informal relationships. Because of this short time span, the purpose of formal mentoring is often the achievement of short term career goals.

2.3 Mentoring as a Mechanism for Learning

We adopt the definition of learning from [7] "to gain knowledge or understanding of or skill in by study, instruction, or experience."
Kram and Hall claim that mentor activities are "prime and untapped resources in creating the learning organization" [8]. Allen and Eby [9] claim that mentors as well as protégés should benefit from a mentoring program including learning about "new technologies" and receiving updates on issues at other levels of the organization. But they also report that there is still a need to empirically examine these issues.

If we look into the literature on work-based learning, we find much work on the use of public reflection for learning [10]. Reflective practice can briefly be described as thinking about thinking, which is something that should happen in a mentor relationship during discussions.

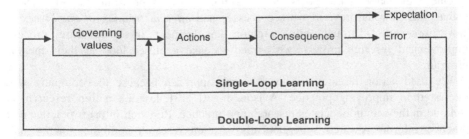

Fig. 1. Single and double loop learning

In theory on learning, Argyris and Schön distinguish between what they call single and double-loop learning in organizations [11]. Single-loop learning implies a better understanding of how to change (or "tune", say a process, to remove an error from a product. It is a (single) feedback-loop from observed effects to making some changes (refinements) that influence the effects, see figure 1.

Double loop learning, on the other hand, is when you understand the factors that influence the effects, and the nature of this influence, which is called the "governing values". This could be to understand why a process is usable, that is: Which premises must be satisfied for it to be worthwhile. To make changes based on this type of understanding will be more thorough.

In work-based learning, a mentor program is called a "developmental relationship" [12] where participants typically create learning agendas and action plans. The protégé receives feedback from the mentor, and it is likely easier for the protégé to be confident with the mentor than people representing formal line authority. Raelin [12] report that monthly or twice-monthly meetings between mentors and protégés are common. It is typical to start with an assessment of current practice for example through a 360 degree assessment. During the mentor program, good mentors "emphasizes the need for ongoing reflection and inquiry". When the protégé uses new knowledge in practice they will reflect on the application introspectively and with their mentor. An advice in mentor meetings is that the mentor asks open-ended questions, which might begin with "tell me a little more about your thinking behind that" [12]. This type of discussion can lead to discussion about governing values that lead to decisions, and thus move the learning from single-loop to double-loop.

3   Research Approach: Studying a Mentor Program in a Small Software Company

This research was carried out in a small software consultancy company, which currently employs 50 people, 30 at their main office and 20 at a branch office, located in a different city. Their main source of income comes from three different activities: hiring out developers for pure software development, developing complete solutions for customers and renting out senior personnel as strategic advisors in project management. They have concentrated their customer profile to the domains of healthcare, energy, trade and industry.

One of the main internal goals for this company is to "improve internal knowledge management through revised work processes and *internal training of employees in new processes*". Through our common involvement in a software process improvement research project, we agreed to take a closer look at their mentor program.

We used action research as our research approach because the company was interested in improving practice. Avison et. Al [13] describe action research as "unique in the way it associates research and practice. Research informs practice and practice informs research synergistically. Action research combines theory and practice (and researchers and practitioners) through change and reflection in an immediate problematic situation within a mutually acceptable ethical framework."

We have used an approach in five phases, which are iterated [14]: diagnosing, action planning, action taking, evaluating and specifying learning. This report sums up our work from the initial diagnosing-phase to the action-taking-phase, and details the findings and experiences we have made so far.

For the initial diagnosing phase, we used semi structured interviews. We interviewed six employees, two had acted as mentors, two had been protégés and two had never been involved in the mentor program. The interviews were carried out using an interview guide. All of the interviews were taped using a dictaphone and were subsequently transcribed and sent back to the interviewees for approval and clarification. The material was coded and analyzed using the constant comparison method [15] and the NVivo tool[1].

For the action-planning phase we started with a literature survey of research and management literature concerning mentoring. This was summarized in an internal note to the company. We then held a meeting to discuss the findings from the literature and how they compared to the findings in our interviews.

We are currently in the action-taking phase. We have conducted a workshop with several employees where the goal was to arrive at a new and improved mentoring approach based on the interviews and the research literature. The document detailing the official mentor program has been rewritten to reflect the findings in our research and the outcome of the workshop.

We are currently awaiting projects where the new mentor program can be tried out in practice. When new projects are launched, the researchers will have regular contact with the mentor and protégé and based on interviews with the participants we will evaluate the new approach, and discuss common learning points.

4 Mentoring in a Small Software Company

When we started our research on the mentor program, we got access to documentation that described the existing program. Two 1,5 page internal company memos described the mentoring program, one for the competency area of Rational Unified Process and the Unified Modeling Language, and one for Project management.

When interviewing employees about the mentor program, we discovered several adopted mentor schemes, we were able to gauge the employees' attitude towards the program, and got several suggestions for improvement.

4.1 The Existing Official Mentor Program

The purpose of the mentor program was to "spread knowledge and experience to everybody in the company", by "providing knowledge to projects and persons", "offer resources and champions [to projects]", and "offer practical experience in addition to theoretical knowledge". The mentor program should:

- Make RUP/UML and project management knowledge available for both projects and individuals
- Offer resource persons and initiators

---

[1] A tool from QSR International: http://www.qsrinternational.com.

- Offer practical experience in addition to theoretical knowledge
- Offer "controllers" who ensures correct use of RUP/UML/project frameworks in projects
- Offer the consultants "expert support"
- Increase the motivation of employees to use RUP/UML/project frameworks

The mentors were supported by project funds, and it was the project manager's responsibility to decide on the type and degree of effort of mentoring. The line management then assigned a mentor based on the requirements from the project manager. For large projects, it was written that "a mentor typically should use 1-2 days a week" to solve problems in the design phase. In smaller projects, the effort could typically be two days in the start-up phase, and then 2-4 hours a week thereafter.

4.2 Different Mentor Schemes

Even though we had been sent to investigate how the current official mentor program worked, we quickly discovered that the program was not that well known: "*I know very little about the formal mentoring program*", "*I do not know of it and do not know what it entails. So if we have this program we have not gotten any information about it*".

In addition to the official mentor program, we discovered several unofficial mentoring schemes that had been adopted. The one that most people mentioned was that the entire company functioned as a large network where there was no problem dropping by your colleagues for help: "*We have this kind of informal [mentoring] - the company functions as a large network. If you are working with a project and run into problems, there are always people who have worked with this problem before, and you can use them for support!*" This unofficial mentor scheme seemed to be mostly related to technical problems, but there was some degree of design and analysis problems being passed around too. In contrast, the official mentor program was mostly related to the software development process and project management.

The most important factor to keeping the informal mentoring scheme alive seemed to be various social initiatives in the company: "*I think the most important thing, what works best, is gatherings and such. Where you get away from the office. You talk, and get to know people and what they are doing. A lot of our colleagues are out [at customer sites] and you do not have much contact with them. So it's a good place to catch up on what they are doing. So after these gatherings its more easy to know where to go to get information that is important to you.*"

Another scheme adopted, was that when they staffed new projects, they always tried to put at least one experienced employee on the project who could act as a kind of mentor to the others. "*Whenever we get a new project and have to staff it - Then it is important that we put someone with experience there, one who has done similar projects before – that way it becomes a kind of mentoring.*"

In addition we discovered a program designed for new employees where they got a "sponsor" the first month after they were employed. The sponsor was responsible for showing them around and introducing them to the company. In that way it was kind of an introduction to the unofficial mentor scheme. "*It is mostly routines. How things are done here. Practical info to get you started – but we do have a greeting round, where you meet everyone and they tell you about what they are doing. In that regards it could be seen as an introduction to it [informal mentoring]"*

We also discovered that they already had a formal approach to mentoring, which they used when they hired out consultants as mentors, but this degree of formalism was seldom used in-house. *"When we are in the market and hire out consultants. Then it is clear that, ok this is mentoring, and that makes it a lot more formal. We try to do it in-house too, but it is much more formalized when we offer it in the market!"*

4.3 Attitudes to the Mentor Program

Even though the official mentoring scheme was little known in the company everyone we interviewed was invariably positive to having such a program. However the comments varied with the degree of involvement in the program.

The people who had not used the mentoring program commented that it would be nice to have access to such a program: *"I see it as a great advantage if we could do it that way"*, *"concerning process, we have a lot of knowledge in the company about that, it should be easy to create programs where the experts can help out in different situations."*

The people who had used the mentor program also commented on the importance of having the mentor program and on the positive effect of having a mentor to talk to about different solutions to a problem: *"It was quite nice to have someone you could turn to and consult about different approaches to a problem."*, *"mentoring is absolutely positive. It is important that we have this program."*

The people who had functioned as mentors were also positive to the program but their comments were more concerned with the benefits of the program: *"It improves our level of competence … we get to discuss our profession, because it is a lonely role [project manager], especially when we are hired out and are at the site of a customer. … The internal communication improves"*, *"It acts as a kind of quality control … it helps us deliver a better product to our customers"*, *"I think it makes people feel safe, safe in that they are not alone in their jobs. You create a transfer of competence and you create a relation between the two that can be used later on."*

4.4 Possible Improvements to the Mentor Program

During the interviews, the employees were also asked for suggestions on what could be done to improve the mentor program. Again the response varied according to level of involvement.

Those who had not been involved in the mentor program so far saw the need for more formalization on the routines of getting a mentor. *"We should have a checkpoint in the start-up routines of a project. You do not necessarily have to use a mentor, but you should at least make a conscious choice!"* That being said they were also concerned that it should not be too formalized. Another concern was how protégés were viewed in the organization, that it should not be considered a sign of weakness to ask for a mentor. They were also concerned for the people acting as mentors. They felt that a mentor should be prepared to accept the job voluntarily.

The employees who had used the mentor program were also concerned with the degree of formalization surrounding the program. *"I do not think the program is formalized enough. It is up to the individual to ask for it. And then – it becomes a limitation on who asks for it and who does not."* Among the other things they mentioned was that the program was not marketed enough and they felt the need for a more concrete framework and guidelines concerning the program.

One employee who had acted as mentor saw the need for more formalization in that a lot of potential interesting information and experience was lost in the current program *"It has potential for improvement in that we could try to make it more formalized. Then it would be easier to collect the experience resulting from the different instances ... So it can benefit more than just the two..."*

Another mentor mentioned that the interest in a mentor was greatest at the start-up of a project, and then the contact gradually dwindled as the project progressed. He felt that this could be explained by the fact that those who received the mentors help felt more and more confident as time went by, but on the other hand it could also be a bad thing since he felt that it was usually once the projects were well under way that the real problems emerged that experience could help a lot to relieve.

During the interviews we also got the impression that the learning in the mentor program consisted mostly of practical help, or as we saw it single looped learning. There was not a lot of discussion and reflection taking place in the program. *"It was mostly assistance with practical things, to get us started. To get started with the right procedures. Get the accounting going, how to keep track of income and so on."*

4.5 Main Conclusion from the Interviews

After analyzing the interviews, we presented the results for the company to get feedback and to see if they had any comments. Our main conclusion was that most of the learning in the mentoring program that took place seemed to be single looped, and that the company could benefit from trying a double looped approach. There seemed to be confusion about what the mentoring role should contain. What was the difference between mentoring, sponsoring and quality assurance work? There was also disagreement on how formalized the mentoring program should be and what areas it should cover.

5 Improving the Mentor Program

To improve the mentor program, we held a workshop with the people responsible for the program in which we revised the program based on input from the interviews and research literature. The workshop had the following agenda: short presentation of the results from the interviews, a brainstorm on what the main elements of the mentoring program should be, discussion concerning what separated the mentoring program from quality assurance and the sponsor program, and finally how the mentoring program should be facilitated in order to maximize learning. Before the workshop all participants got a copy of the main findings from the interviews and a short memo on mentoring based on findings in the research literature.

5.1 Important Elements of the New Mentor Program

The first brainstorm session consisted of the company's representatives writing down what they thought important about the mentoring program on yellow stickers and then grouping them together on a whiteboard. This resulted in eight groups of elements that should be considered important in the new mentor program:

- Mutual trust and confidence was stressed as important in order for the program to work, no one should feel threatened by the new program.
- The communication between the participants should be discussion-based in order to better facilitate learning. The mentor should act as a discussion partner and ease learning, not provide direct answers.
- There should be a certain amount of time set aside for mentoring and regular meetings should be scheduled in order to keep regular contact
- Mentoring should be available both on project management and on more technical subjects.
- There should be mutual feedback between mentor and protégé and the mentor should be proactive and not just wait for questions from the protégé.
- The mentor should be funded by project budgets if the projects were large, otherwise he could be supported by the company directly. Not all projects should necessarily have a mentor, but all projects should have the option of using one.
- Mentoring should be initiated both from project management and by whoever felt the need, it should not necessarily be narrowed to one on one consultations.
- Finally the need for all participants to be constructive was stressed.

5.2 A Clear Separation of Roles

The second part of the workshop was to determine where the separation between mentoring, quality assurance and the sponsor program was. They decided on the following separation of concepts:

A quality assurance employee makes sure that all the formal bits are done right. He usually appears later in the project. In small projects the project manager is responsible for this role, in larger projects they can create their own quality assurance role. The quality assurance is a check that the individual has done a good job. This was consistent with their old view on the quality assurance role, the news here was that a mentor should not have the responsibility of this role even though a lot of mentors had done so in the past.

A sponsor is responsible to introducing new employees to the company's routines and provides a social contact point. They do not have regular meetings and are not responsible for questions concerning the profession. A sponsor is only provided for new employees for the first month in the company. This was also consistent with their old definition. From our findings in the interviews we also suggested that this role should be conscious on helping the new employee get familiar with the unofficial mentoring scheme.

A mentor makes sure that the project is carried out professionally by providing expertise and advice. The need for mentors was usually greater in the start of a project. The mentor provides the individual with the help to perform a good job.

Furthermore it was decided that the official mentor program should be split into three parts:

- Non-formal mentoring: As we discovered in the interviews, this was already taking place and the environment was supportive of such a scheme. It functioned in an ad-hoc manner and it was decided that this should continue to function since it was obvious that it was working well. To further support this kind of mentoring it was suggested to invest in social initiatives to keep and improve this environment.
- Formal mentoring should continue more or less as it had functioned, but with few modifications. Basically the important elements defined above were taken into consideration. It should be project based, could potentially be one mentor who would work with several protégés, and be more discussion based.
- They also introduced a new type of mentoring, the trainee program. This was a new role in the company, and much more practical oriented than the previous mentor program. The idea was to introduce employees to new domains (business, technical or management) by allowing employee to follow seniors out to customers and letting them participating in customer meetings and project activities. In practice everyone could go into a trainee role to learn a new domain or a new role like project manager or learning how to handle customer relationships.

5.3   How to Improve Learning in the Mentor Program

The final discussion in the workshop was around the problem: How can we improve learning in the mentoring program. This resulted in seven main elements that could be considered by the mentors in the company:

- The mentors should to a large degree post open questions in order to make the protégés think for themselves.
- Confidence and trust between the participants was considered important in order to facilitate learning, this would to some degree be dependent on personal chemistry, but could also be facilitated by patience on both accounts, the ability to pick up signals, the ability of protégés to dare to ask "stupid questions".
- A mentor leading a group of protégés could also be considered; the more people the more discussions.
- The mentor should mainly explain and advise by giving examples of how thing had previously been done.
- A good mentor should allocate time, discuss their expectations and provide good feedback.
- A good protégé should realize their needs; this could be facilitated by better information from the company.
- It was also considered important to learning to have a clear definition of roles.

The main discussion points of the workshop was written into the memo describing mentoring in the company, which was extended from one and a half pages to three pages.

6 Conclusion and Future Work

We have investigated a mentor program in a small software consulting company in order to identify issues that could be improved. We found many different mentor schemes to be in place in the company, found arguments in favor and against a more formal approach to mentoring in the company. We found most of the learning that took place to be single looped. In order to increase the learning effect, we discussed how we could introduce more reflective practice into the mentoring program, and identified some efforts that were taken into a revised mentoring program. We also made a clearer separation of roles, and suggested that mentoring should have a greater availability in the company.

We believe that the new mentoring program will provide better support for double loop learning through increased reflection. The amount of reflection should increase when the mentors pose more open questions during meetings. Also, organizing mentoring in a group of protégés should lead to more discussion, which should also lead to more reflection on current work practices.

The new mentoring program has been introduced through a meeting with all employees, and now that the work of restructuring the mentor program is done, we switch to an observer role. We will follow mentor and protégé pairs in new projects and evaluate the changes brought on by redefining the mentor program. By performing the same interviews again on people using the new mentor program, and by observing how the new program runs over time, we hope to be able to ascertain how successful the knowledge initiative have been for the company, and how it influences their software development process.

Acknowledgement

This work was conducted as a part of the Software Process Improvement through Knowledge and Experience (SPIKE) research project, supported by the Research Council of Norway through grant 156701/220. We are very grateful to our contact persons in the software consulting company for providing stimulating discussions and help with organizing the work.

References

1. T. Dybå, "Improvisation in Small Software Organizations", IEEE Software, no. 5, vol. 17, pp.82-87, 2000.
2. A. Wickert and R. Herschel, "Knowledge management issues for smaller businesses", Journal of Knowledge Management, no. 4, vol. 5, pp. 329-337, 2001.
3. M. Lindvall and I. Rus, "Knowledge Management in Software Engineering", IEEE Software, no. 3, vol. 19, pp. 26-38, 2002.
4. F. J. Armour and M. Gupta, "Mentoring for Success", IEEE IT Pro, no. May - June, pp. 64-66, 1999.
5. K. E. Kram, Mentoring at work: Developmental relationships in organizational life. Glenview, IL: Scott Foresman, 1985, ISBN: 081916755X.

6. B. R. Ragins, J. L. Cotton, and J. S. Miller, "Marginal Mentoring: The Effects of Type of Mentor, Quality of Relationship, and Program Design on Work and Career Attitudes", Academy of Management Journal, no. 6, vol. 43, pp. 1177-1194, 2000.
7. Webster's, Encyclopedic Unabridged Dictionary of the English Language. New York: Gramercy Books, 1989.
8. K. E. Kram and D. T. Hall, "Mentoring as an antidote to stress during corporate trauma", Human Resource Management, vol. 28, pp. 493-510, 1989.
9. T. D. Allen and L. T. Eby, "Relationship Effectiveness for Mentors: Factors Associated with Learning and Quality", Journal of Management, no. 4, vol. 29, pp. 469-486, 2003.
10. J. A. Raelin, "Public Reflection as the Basis of Learning", Management Learning, no. 1, vol. 32, pp. 11-30, 2001.
11. C. Argyris and D. A. Schön, Organizational Learning II: Theory, Method and Practise: Addison Wesley, 1996.
12. J. A. Raelin, Work-based learning. Upper Saddle River, NJ: Prentice Hall, 2000.
13. D. Avison, F. Lau, M. Myers, and P. A. Nielsen, "Action Research", Communications of the ACM, no. 1, vol. 42, pp. 94-97, 1999.
14. G. Susman and R. Evered, "An assessment of the scientific merits of action research", Administrative Science Quarterly, no. 4, vol. 23, pp. 582-603, 1978.
15. M.B. Miles and A.M. Huberman, Qualitative Data Analysis: An expanded sourcebook, second ed. SAGE publications, 1994.

Impacts of Software Deployment in the Coffee Agribusiness of Brazil

Claudio T. Bornstein[1], Lucia Silva Kubrusly[2],
André Luiz Zambalde[3], and Ana Regina Rocha[1]

[1] COPPE/Sistemas, Federal University of Rio de Janeiro,
Caixa Postal 68511 – CEP 21941-972 - Rio de Janeiro – Brazil
Phone: +55-21-25628699 Fax: +55-21-25628676
{ctbornst, darocha}@cos.ufrj.br
[2] Instituto de Economia,
Federal University of Rio de Janeiro,
Rio de Janeiro - Brazil
luciak@alternex.com.br
[3] Federal University of Lavras,
Lavras, MG - Brazil
zamba@ufla.br

Abstract. The process of software deployment into an organization is a complex process that encompasses various aspects. Studies on the impact of software systems deployment in the customer's environment in the medium and long terms are hardly found, specially when the deployment of the software product and the introduction of data processing into the organization happen at the same time. Nevertheless the client's perception goes beyond the specific moment at which the software was installed. User's and customer's satisfaction can only be evaluated in the long term taking into account the satisfaction with the product use and with its impact on business. This paper describes an empirical study of the introduction of data processing into the coffee agribusiness in Brazil. The paper uses cluster analysis to group 0-1 variables. Theses variables describe the impacts of data processing on the coffee agribusiness in the state of Minas Gerais, one of the main Brazilian coffee producers. Influences on employment, employee and enterprise structure are examined. Some commonly used procedures as well as main changes at corporation and individual level are detected.

1 Introduction

The introduction of data processing into an organization together with software deployment is a complex process that encompasses various aspects. In the latest years an interest has arisen for research related to the software deployment in organizations. However, the interest is many times restricted to technical aspects or aspects related to infrastructure as we can see in [1] [2] [3]. Few papers cover the evaluation of customer's satisfaction like [4] [5] [6] [7]. Studies on the impacts of the introduction of data processing and software deployment in the medium and long terms are hardly found. However, customer's perception of a software, following [4], goes beyond the

F. Bomarius and S. Komi-Sirviö (Eds.): PROFES 2005, LNCS 3547, pp. 257–271, 2005.

specific moment at which the software was installed and the problems occurred. Customer's satisfaction which is one of the main elements of software validation and a important measure of success when introducing data processing in a organization, can only be evaluated in the long term. User's and customer's satisfaction with the product has to be evaluated and its impact on business has to be considered [8] [6] [9].

Nowadays, the use of information technology is compelling. However, in general, the introduction of data processing into organizations is a long, hard and not much studied process [10]. In this paper we study the impacts of the introduction of data processing into the coffee agribusiness in Brazil, examining the results of the first software deployments in a group of companies in this area..

The coffee worldwide agribusiness chain moves various billions of dollars every year. According to Love [11] world coffee exports in 1998/1999 reached US$11 billion, off 10% from 1997/1998, after rising to US$ 14 billion in 1996/1997. Brazil is the world's largest coffee producer [11]. In accordance with the results mentioned in [11], Brazil accounted for 33%, 24% and 27% of the world's coffee crop corresponding respectively to the three periods above. More recent data confirms this figures. Brazil's contribution in the world global production from 1999/2000 to 2001/2002 rises from 23% to 28% [12].

Coffee production is, therefore, responsible for a significant amount of Brazilian exports, for the creation of millions of jobs and for setting down labor in the rural zones. It occupies an important position in the Brazilian economy. Estimates indicate that the coffee industry is responsible for the employment of 4 million people in production and 10 million people, if we take other segments into account [13].

After 1990, with the discontinuance of the International Coffee Agreement, which regulated the prices all over the world, the Brazilian Government called off the subsidy to the coffee agribusiness, submitting the organizations to market rules. As a consequence, investments in data processing slowly begun. According to the Science and Technology Ministry [14], today 9% of Brazilian software companies develop products for the agribusiness sector.

This paper examines the social and economic consequences of software deployment and the use of data processing in the Brazilian coffee industry. The state of Minas Gerais was chosen because it concentrates 50% of the Brazilian coffee production. The research began in 1990 based on information obtained from a questionnaire answered by 10 coffee producers, 21 cooperatives, 34 roasting and grinding companies and 2 producers of soluble coffee.

Section 2 considers some general aspects of software engineering and the impacts of software development on organizations. Section 3 describes the methodology used in the research, mentioning the main points covered by the questionnaire and giving details of the use of cluster analysis. Section 4 mentions the main variables and the results obtained using this technique and section 5 presents the conclusions.

2 Impacts of Software Deployment at Organizational Level

Software Engineering describes processes, methods, techniques and procedures that lead to the development of high quality software. Much has been written and said about what is necessary to achieve these results [15][16][17]. However, there is little literature that considers and discusses the level of success obtained by introducing software products and data processing in general into organizations engaged in specific domains like agribusiness [5][6]. As mentioned by these authors, it is even hard to define the exact meaning of the term success.

Software products have supported advances in various areas, including agribusiness. However, basic questions do not always receive the necessary attention. The evaluation of customer's satisfaction is many times dealt without the necessary care. The quality of the product is often focused from the developers' perspective, without considering the customer's or user's point of view properly [9]. The ISO 9001:2000 international standard recognizes this necessity and emphasizes the existence of formal procedures to evaluate customer's satisfaction [18].

Another important aspect to be considered is the evaluation of the product's impact within the business environment for which it has been developed. We usually evaluate products and services taking into account only their technical quality. Rarely the scope is wide enough to include also a business perspective [19]. Although it is important to evaluate features like functionality, trustworthiness and usability [20], it is also necessary to evaluate if the results increased competitiveness and working capacity, leading to higher profits.

Hillam, Edwards & Young [6] present different definitions of success and failure for software applications. They point out two case studies: In the first case study success was associated to the return on investment and in the second to the user's satisfaction.

The relation between technology and organization happens both at the structural and human level. The structural level includes: impacts on the formal and the power structure, impacts on the competitiveness and the company's image as well as economic and financial impacts [21].

Main impacts of software deployment and data processing on the formal structure are fusion, creation or elimination of departments and reduction in the hierarchical levels. Many of these impacts lead to new forms of management [22]. Technology can impact the power structure by affecting the distribution of responsibilities. It can destabilize the hierarchy and the current power configuration of the enterprise. Impacts on competitiveness are related, basically, to two aspects: productivity and profitability [23][24]. Data processing may also improve the image of the company. It is frequently associated with the ideas of innovation and modernity. This is especially true for developing countries.

However, all this is only possible if the staff gains control of the whole process learning to master software systems and data processing properly. Impacts can be negative if there is no easy way of accessing the services, if people do not trust the results, if there is no competence in its execution or if the experts who develop the software are not conscious of the customer's needs. Finally, a cost-benefit analysis is necessary to check if there will or not be an adequate return on the investment. Of course, it is not always easy to measure the benefits of data processing accurately [25][21][18].

The only human impacts which will be considered here are those related to the individual and his job, i.e., to the employment and the employee [26][27]. As for the individual, the main impacts which will be examined are: changes in the content and the nature of tasks, increase or decrease in the levels of qualification, changes in the working pressures and working rhythm, increase or decrease in the levels of participation and changes in the level of individual interaction and control [28]. The impact of software systems on the content and nature of tasks can be viewed from two sides. On the one side, it generates positive impacts, reducing the routine and the number of monotonous tasks and making it possible to the users to spend their time on more complex and more challenging tasks, demanding greater responsibility. However, it can also have negative impacts disregarding accumulated skills and depriving jobs of some of its richness [29]. With respect to the users' qualification, the introduction of software systems on the one side stimulates the process of apprehension of new knowledge and creativity so as to face unexpected problems [30]. However, on the other side, it may decrease the level of qualification because activities may be performed automatically [31]. Data processing can trivialize work, lead to a decrease of the value of experience, reduce motivation, status and self-esteem. As for working pressure and rhythm, some authors point out to an increase in the quantity and quality of work while others state that data processing leads to more stress and higher levels of pressure [32] [33]. Finally, some authors consider that the working environment can loose some of its attractiveness due to the decrease of the importance of personal relations [34] [35] [36].

Finally, it is necessary to consider the impacts on employment and jobs. Without any doubt software systems saves manpower. Organizations which do not follow the trend towards automation tend to loose competitiveness and go out of business [31][37][38]. On the other side, new jobs (systems analysts, software and hardware engineers or technicians, computer maintenance specialists, etc) may also be generated in the computer sector.

3 Methodology

3.1 Data Analysis

Interviews were made with the staff using a questionnaire as a basis. The complete questionnaire used in interviews with the staff covers six basic areas. The areas were subdivided into several sub-areas.

(i) Company's basic profile: kind of administration (family-run, entrepreneurial or professional management or cooperative) and size (volume of coffee processed by the company); number of employees and level of education, percentage of the employees working with data processing; number of associates in the case of cooperatives; number of branches in the case of bigger companies.

(ii) Use of data processing (general): number of years data processing is been used; history and reasons for the introduction of data processing in the company; connection modes between equipment and data bases and main communication services used (connections to branches, stock market and internet, bank access).

(iii) Description of the hardware used by the company; adopted strategies for hardware maintenance.

(iv) Description of the main software used by the company; adopted strategies for software development/purchase (off-the-shelf vs. custom software for example); computer languages and data bases used; adopted strategies for software maintenance.

(v) Impacts of data processing on the organizational level of the enterprise: impacts on the formal and the power structure (centralization tendencies/power concentration; conflicts and disputes), impacts on competitiveness (productivity and profitability), impacts on the company's image; economic and financial impacts.

(vi) Impacts on the individual and jobs: changes in the content and nature of tasks; increase and decrease in the levels of qualification; changes in the working pressure and working rhythm; increase or decrease in the levels of participation; changes in the level of individual interaction and control; impacts on employment policies (hiring, firing or reallocating staff).

Data collection was performed through interviews. As a criterion to select coffee bean producers, we used the export activity. All coffee bean exporters of the state of Minas Gerais were included in the study. There was no need to select cooperatives and soluble coffee producers because, by their nature, these are big enterprises and there were only few establishments of this kind. They were all included in the study. With respect to the roasting and grinding companies, 34 out of 114 establishments of the state were selected through a proportional stratified sample. Interviews were made with at least two members of the staff in charge of the data processing activities. Often members of the board and the higher management were also included in the interviews.

This paper covers only aspects related to (v) and (vi). All the issues related to these two areas were included in the present analysis. Corresponding questions were redefined as 0-1 (binary) variables (yes = 1 and no = 0). Aspects related to (iii), (iv) and some points covered by (ii) are very specific and of more technical nature. In addition, questions related to (i) and (ii) have been excluded because no convincing link could be made of these questions to the impacts of data processing on the structural and social level of the company. Some of these issues are covered in [39]. Tables 1 and 2 give a brief idea of the more important aspects related to (i), more specifically, the kind of management and the size of the firms.

Table 1 gives an account of the kind of administration of the companies. One can see that the roasting and grinding (roast.& grind.) companies are mostly family-run enterprises and that the soluble coffee producers have a predominantly professional management. In the middle are the coffee bean producers with a quite balanced situation between family/entrepreneurial and professional administration. Cooperatives are enterprises with a special kind of management.

Table 2 describes the companies according to their size. Establishments were classified, according to the annual turnover measured in number of 60kg coffee bags, in big (more than 90000 bags), medium (5000 to 90000 bags) and small (less than 5000 bags). This criterion seems better than monetary values or number of employees

Table 1. Kind of administration of the companies

ORGANIZATION	ADMINISTRATION			Total
	Professional	Cooperative	Family/entrepren.	
Cooperatives	5 (25%)	15 (75%)	0 (0%)	20 (100%)
Coffee producers	4 (40%)	0 (0%)	6 (60%)	10 (100%)
Sol. coffee prod.	2 (100%)	0 (0%)	0 (0%)	2 (100%)
Roast.& grind.	1 (3,2%)	0 (0%)	30 (96,8%)	31 (100%)
Total	12 (19%)	15 (23,8%)	36 (57,2%)	63 (100%)

due to the fact that the classification applies to companies of very different technological levels and very distinct cost structures.

Cooperatives are predominantly big companies, soluble coffee producers are medium/big firms, the coffee bean producers are generally medium size organizations and the roasting and grinding companies are mostly small enterprises.

Table 2. Distribution of companies according to their size

ORGANIZATION	Size			Total
	Small	Medium	Big	
Cooperatives	0 (0%)	3 (15%)	17 (85%)	20 (100%)
Coffee producer	2 (20%)	6 (60%)	2 (20%)	10 (100%)
Sol. coffee prod.	0 (0%)	1 (50%)	1 (50%)	2 (100%)
Roast. & grind.	16 (52%)	13 (42%)	2 (6%)	31 (100%)
Total	18 (28%)	23 (36,5%)	22 (35%)	63 (100%)

In the next section, association between variables concerning areas (v) and (vi) will be examined using cluster analysis of binary variables.

3.2 Cluster Analysis of Binary Variables

Cluster analysis is an exploratory technique of data analysis that tries to identify similarities between objects or between variables. Lucas [40] defines cluster analysis in the following way:

Let X be the available data matrix with variables $x_{i1}, x_{i2}, x_{i3}, ...$ for each object i. Let $E = \{E_1, ... E_n\}$ be the set of elements we wish to group. If we group variables, E is the set of columns of X. If we group objects, E is the set of lines of X. Cluster analysis attempts to partition E in subsets so that:

$$\text{if } E_r \in g_i \quad \text{and} \quad E_s \in g_i, \quad r \neq s \quad \Rightarrow \quad E_r \text{ and } E_s \text{ are similar.} \tag{1}$$

$$\text{if } E_r \in g_i \quad \text{and} \quad E_s \in g_j, \quad r \neq s, i \neq j \quad \Rightarrow \quad E_r \text{ and } E_s \text{ are distinct.} \tag{2}$$

In order to measure similarities and differences between the elements, a metric, like, for example, the Euclidean distance, is usually applied. There are several metrics defined for binary variables. Most of them try to identify the simultaneous occurrence of zeros or ones (see [41]). Table 3 gives an example where variables $V1$, $V2$ and $V3$ are observed for 6 objects. Looking at these values, one can say that $V1$ and $V2$ are similar and that $V3$ differs both from $V1$ and $V2$. As already mentioned, a metric which is able to measure differences and similarities between the variables is the Euclidean distance, which may be calculated in the following way:

$$d(V1, V2) = \sqrt{(0-0)^2 + (0-1)^2 + (1-1)^2 + ... + (0-0)^2} = 1 . \tag{3}$$

$$d(V1, V3) = \sqrt{(0-1)^2 + (0-0)^2 + (1-0)^2 + ... + (0-1)^2} = 2 . \tag{4}$$

$$d(V2, V3) = \sqrt{(0-1)^2 + (1-0)^2 + (1-0)^2 + ... + (0-1)^2} = \sqrt{5} \cong 2,236 . \tag{5}$$

Table 3. Variables $V1$, $V2$ and $V3$

$V1$	$V2$	$V3$
0	0	1
0	1	0
1	1	0
1	1	1
0	0	1
0	0	1

The smaller distance between $V1$ and $V2$ indicates that this is the pair of variables with greater similarity. Another way to evaluate similarities is by calculating and comparing the number of equal or different answers. Table 4 gives the results for the example above.

Table 4. Number of equal/different answers

	$V1= 0$	$V1= 1$		$V1 = 0$	$V1 = 1$		$V2 = 0$	$V2 = 1$
$V2 = 0$	$a = 3$	$b = 0$	$V3 = 0$	$a = 1$	$b = 1$	$V3 = 0$	$a = 0$	$b = 2$
$V2 = 1$	$c = 1$	$d = 2$	$V3 = 1$	$c = 3$	$d = 1$	$V3 = 1$	$c = 3$	$d = 1$

In table 4 the variables a and d give the number of equal while b and c give the number of different answers. Some metrics based upon these values consider only similar answers (diagonal a and d). Other metrics take into account only different answers (diagonal b and c). A discussion about these metrics can be found in [42]. It is interesting to remark that $(b + c)$ is the square of the Euclidean distance.

Cluster analysis groups elements in sets so as to get a partition. Different ways of getting this partition define different methods of cluster analysis. The method that will be used here belongs to the class of the hierarchical agglomerative methods. These are iterative procedures that start from a partition of n groups or sets, where n is the number of elements. i.e., each set or group contains only one element. At every step the two groups which are closest are joined forming a new group. The clustering is ended with one single group containing all elements. Thus, starting from n groups and ending with one group, different partitions or clusters are generated. By carefully examining the results and looking for the partition which provides the best interpretation, it is often possible to decide for the best clustering. In this paper the method of Ward was used. The square of the Euclidian distance was used as a metric. A presentation of several clustering methods can be found in [43].

4 Definition of Variables and Results from Cluster Analysis

The impacts of data processing on the organizational level of the enterprise were evaluated by seven variables and the impacts on individuals and jobs were measured by thirteen variables.   The description of the variables follows:

Impacts on the organizational level of the enterprise:
estrfor   – impacts on the formal structure.
estrpd 1 – impacts on the power structure: power concentration.
estrpd 2 – impacts on the power structure: conflicts and disputes.
compt 1 – impacts on competitiveness: productivity.
compt 2 – impacts on competitiveness: profitability.
percep – impacts on the company's image.
cstben – cost-benefit analysis

For the first five variables, the yes answer means impacts of data processing on the formal structure (hierarchical levels and management), power structure and on the competitiveness of the enterprise. The no answer means that no such impacts were perceived. The yes/no answers to the *percep* variable means that data processing either had or did not have a clear impact on the company's image. And finally, the yes/no answer to the *cstben* variable means that a cost-benefit analysis was carried out to evaluate the effects of data processing.

Impacts on individuals and jobs:
motiva   –   impacts on employee's motivation.
satisf   –   employee's satisfaction with software and hardware.
educa   –   increase in the educational level.
treina   –   investments in personnel training.
valor   –   increase in the valuation of the experience and capacity of the employee.
participa –   increase in the level of participation of the employee in decisions.
integra   –   increase in the level of integration between individuals and departments.
controle –   increase in the level of control.
aument   –   increase in working rhythm and pace.
apreen   –   increase in employee's apprehension due to the use of new technologies.

demiss – employee's dismissal.
remane – employee's reallocation.
contrat – employee's recruitment.

The answer yes to the variable *motiva* means that with the introduction of data processing there was an increase in motivation, i.e., tasks became more motivating. The answer yes to *satisf* means that employees and management were content with programs and equipment, i.e. they worked properly. As for the *educa* variable the same answer means that with the introduction of data processing there was an increase in the required educational level. For *treina*, *valor* and *participa* the answer yes means respectively the occurrence of investments in personnel training, a better valuation of the employee's capacity and experience and that the employees participated in the decisions concerning the adoption and use of data processing. The same answer to the *integra*, *controle*, *aument* and *apreen* variables means respectively that data processing provided greater integration between employees and departments, increased the level of control over the employees, increased the working rhythm and pace, i.e. increased the working intensity and resulted in a higher level of apprehension among the employees. Finally, the answer yes to *demiss*, *remane* and *contrat* means respectively that, due to the introduction of data processing, employees were sacked, reallocated to other jobs and/or new personnel had to be recruited.

The next sections present the results of the cluster analysis. Section 4.1 presents the results concerning the impacts on the organizational level of the enterprise. Section 4.2 presents the results concerning the impacts on individuals and jobs. Finally, section 4.3 presents a general analysis where variables were selected from each of the two sets mentioned above in an attempt of associating questions addressed in both sets. The results were obtained with the SPSS version 11.0.

4.1 Impacts on the Organizational Level of the Enterprise

Table 5 gives the number of yes among a total amount of 58 answers for each variable of this group. This is an additional information which should help in a better understanding of the results.

Table 5. Number of positive answers from a total amount of 58 answers

Variable	Positive answers	Variable	Positive answers
Estrfor	13	*compt2*	27
Estrpd1	51	*percep*	25
Estrpd2	13	*cstben*	3
Compt1	28		

Figure 1 gives the results of the cluster analysis for the first set of variables. We can see that the clustering of *compt1* and *compt2* shows that productivity and profitability are strongly connected. Power concentration (estrpd1) is an almost consensus variable (see table 5) that is not much related to the other variables. The connection of *percep* with the competitiveness variables is weak. It is better to consider it apart. The association between *cstben, estrpd2* and *estrfor* is probably due to the fact that all three variables represent rare events, i.e., they received few positive answers. As a matter of fact, few companies carried out a cost-benefit analysis and determining the impacts of data processing on the formal structure of the enterprise as well as on conflicts and disputes is a complex and sensitive matter which people are often reluctant to comment.

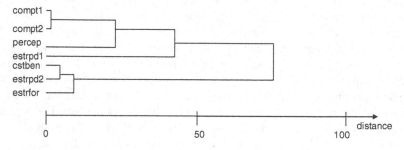

Fig. 1. Results of the cluster analysis for the first set of variables

4.2 Impacts on Individuals and Jobs

Again, first we present (table 6) the number of positive answers among a total of 58 answers for each variable.

Table 6. Number of positive answers from a total amount of 58 answers

Variable	Positive answers	Variable	Positive answers
Motiva	32	*controle*	54
Satisf	36	*aument*	21
Educa	20	*apreen*	46
Treina	13	*demiss*	9
Valor	42	*remane*	19
Participa	6	*contrat*	10
Integra	25		

Figure 2 discloses two major groups. The first comprises the *controle, apreen, motiva, valor, satisf* variables with predominately positive answers (see Table 6). The second major group contains the *participa, demiss, contrat* variables where negative answers strongly predominate and the *aument, treina, remane, educa, integra* variables with a more balanced number of positive and negative answers.

The increase in the level of control as well as the increase in the employee's apprehension, both variables belonging to the first group, are almost consensus variables. From the employee's point of view they may perhaps represent the negative side of the adoption of new technologies. On the other hand, the higher employee's motivation (*motiva*) and satisfaction (*satisf*) is associated with a higher rating of the experience and the capacity of the employee (*valor*). These variables may represent the positive side of the adoption of new technologies showing that if experience and capacity are prized, the result is an increase in motivation and satisfaction.

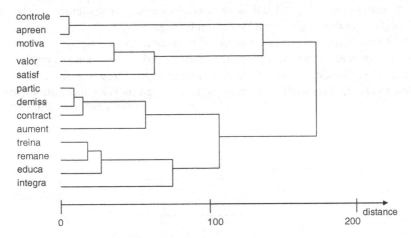

Fig. 2. Results of the cluster analysis for the second set of variables

Looking at the second major group we can disclose a very homogeneous subgroup composed of *participa*, *demiss* and *contrat*. With the help of table 6, we can conclude that neither there was much participation of the employees in the decision process concerning data processing nor did new technologies lead to much firing and hiring of employees. With respect to the last two variables one has to consider that the research was done in a predominantly rural environment. Due to lack of skilled labor, the reallocation of human resources is more frequent than the dismissal or recruitment of employees. The cluster of the *treina*, *remane* and *educa* variables may be better understood if we consider that establishments that have a policy of training and reallocating of personnel tend to give a higher value to the educational level of the employees. The integration between individuals and departments does not present strong association with the other variables. However, it is interesting to notice that the connection between integration and reallocation variables seems to indicate that companies that practice reallocation of personnel achieve a higher level of integration between individuals and departments. On the other hand, the (rather weak) association between the *aument*, *demiss* and *contrat* variables may point to a certain connection of the working rhythm and a hiring/firing policy. Both may be perceived as an increase in tension and stress.

4.3 General Analysis: Selected Variables

As already mentioned, this section presents results of the cluster analysis for a set of variables selected from the first two groups. The purpose here is to examine issues that may affect both 4.1 and 4.2., i.e., cover both sets of variables. Several runs with different variables chosen from each group were done. The best result, i.e. the best interpretation, was obtained choosing one variable for each of the main clusters disclosed in the previous analysis. We assume that this variable represents the group. Almost consensus variables, i.e., variables with a great majority of affirmative or negative answers, were excluded from the study because no relevant interpretation for the association of this kind of variables could be found.

For the first two sets of variables detected in section 4.1 (see figure 1) the variables *compt2* (impacts on competitiveness: profitability) and *estrfor* (impacts on the formal structure) were chosen. In order to represent each of the three main groups set up in 4.2 (see figure 2) the variables *motiva* (impacts on employee's motivation), *aument* (increase in working rhythm) and *educa* (increase in the educational level) were selected respectively. The results of the cluster analysis are shown in figure 3.

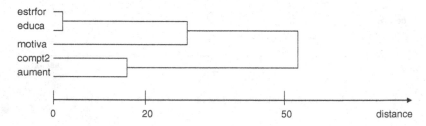

Fig. 3. Results of the cluster for a selected set of variables

The first set consisting of variables *estfor* and *educa* admits the following explanation. Companies where data processing affected the formal structure are generally companies concerned with the educational level of staff, carrying out, as seen in 4.2, a training program and a reallocation policy. The second set consisting of variables *compt2* and *aument* leads to an almost obvious association between competitiveness/profitability and an increase in the working rhythm. In this analysis the employee's motivation could not be strongly associated to any of the other variables.

5   Conclusion

There is not much literature discussing broadly the successes obtained by introducing data processing into organizations and sectors through software products deployment. In this paper we study the impacts of the introduction of data processing in the coffee agribusiness in Brazil.

The results may admit the conclusion that although the power concentration is an almost general result of data processing, only part of the companies increased competitiveness. It is interesting to notice that a cost-benefit analysis, which could have delivered a more precise measure for the increase of competitiveness, is generally not done. With respect to the impacts on the individuals and jobs there is an increase in the level of control and apprehension.

Finally, the attempt to associate the impacts on the organizational level of the enterprise with the impacts on individuals and jobs pointed to two important aspects. First, companies where data processing affected the formal structure are generally concerned with the educational level of staff, carrying out a training and a reallocation program. These are companies with some level of internal flexibility and internal dynamics and they achieve a higher level of integration among their employees. The second important aspect was to show that higher competitiveness is associated with an increase in the working rhythm and this, in its turn, is associated with a recruitment/dismissal policy as seen in section 4.2.

With respect to the statistical methodology, the cluster analysis of binary variables was able to associate variables pointing out to important relations between them. The utilization of frequency tables played an important role in the interpretation of results.

Although the focus was on the coffee agribusiness in Brazil we believe that some of its conclusions may be extended to other areas and other contexts with similar characteristics. The results may indicate possible impacts of software deployment and data processing on areas of the agribusiness sector where information technology is still in its coming.

References

1. Coupaye,T., Estublier,J.: Foundations of Enterprise Software Deployment, Fourth European Software Maintenance and Reengineering Conference, 2000
2. Turcan,E.; Shahumehri,N.; Graham,R.L.: Intelligent Software Delivery Using P2P, Second International Conference on Peer-to-Peer Computing (P2P'02), 1-8, 2002
3. Hall,R.S.; Heimbigner,D.; Wolf, A.L.: A Cooperative Approach to Support Software Deployment Using the Software Dock, International Conference on Software Engineering, 174-183, 1999
4. Pratt,W.M. Experiences in the Application of Customer-Based Metrics in Improving Software Service Quality, International Conference on Communications, 1991
5. Hellens, L.A.V.: Application Software Packages for Small Companies: Implementation Success and Supplier Strategy, Twenty-Fourth Annual Hawaii International Conference on Systems Sciences, volume iv, 446-457, 1991
6. Hillam,C.E.; Edwards,H.M.,; Young,C.L.: Successful Software Applications: Can They Be Evaluated?, The 24th Annual International Computer Software and Applications Conference, COMPSAC 2000, 528-534, 2000
7. Russel,B. Delivery Excellence: a Practical Program for Continuous Improvement, IT Pro, 2003
8. Dean,J.; Haynes,S.; Hersh,G.; Schmidt,G.; Stoffeth,T.: Transition Engineering, IEEE Industry Application Conference, IAS 96, volume 4, 2557-2562, 1996
9. Kan, S.H. Metrics and Models in Software Quality Engineering, 2nd Edition, Addison-Wesley, 2003
10. Boag, C.: Affordable IT, Manufacturing Engineer, 280-281, 2002
11. Love, J.: Coffee Exporters Counting on Improved Earnings in 1999/2000, Agricultural Outlook, Economic Research Service,USDA 6-8, 1999

270   C.T. Bornstein et al.

12. Lewin,B.; Giovannucci,D.; Varangis,P.: Coffee Markets-New Paradigms in Global Supply and Demand, Agriculture and Rural Development Paper 3, ARD, The World Bank, 2004
13. Farina, M.M.Q.; Saes, M. S. M.: Agribusiness do Café no Brasil. São Paulo: Editora Milkbizz, 1999.
14. MCT/SEPIN, Qualidade e Produtividade no Setor de Software Brasileiro, Ministério de Ciência e Tecnologia/Secretaria de Política de Informática, 2002
15. ISO/IEC – Information Technology - Software Lifecycle Processes, ISO/IEC 12207, Geneva, Switzerland, 1995
16. Mutafelija,B.; Stromberg,H.: Systematic Process Improvement Using ISO 9001:2000 and CMMI, Artech House, Norwood, MA, USA, 2003
17. Chrissis,M; Konrad,M.; Shrum,S.: CMMI – Guidelines for Process Integration and Product Improvement, Addison-Wesley, USA, 2003
18. ISO/IEC – Quality Management Systems – Requirements, ISO 9001:2000, Geneva, Switzerland, 2000
19. Pfleeger, S.L. Software Engineering: theory and practice, Prentice-Hall, , NJ, 2nd Edition, 2001
20. ISO/IEC – Software Engineering – Product Quality – Part 1: Quality model, ISO/IEC 9126-1, Geneva, Switzerland, 2001
21. Remenyi, D.; Money, A.; Sherwood-Smith, M.; Irani, Z.: Effective measurement and management of IT costs and benefits. 2nd edition. Butterworth-Heinemann, 2000.
22. Crowston, K.; Malone, T. W.: Information technology and work organization. In: Allen, T. J.; Morton, M. S. S.; Information technology and the corporation of the 1990s, Chapter 11. Oxford: Oxford University Press, 1994.
23. Brynjolfsson, E.; Hitt, L.: Beyond the productivity paradox: computers are the catalyst for bigger changes. Communications of the ACM., 41(8), 49-55, 1998.
24. Streeter,D.H.; Sonka,S.T.; Hudson,M.A.: Information technology, coordination, and competitiveness in the food and agribusiness sector. American Journal of Agricultural Economics, v. 73, no. 5, 1465-1471, 1991
25. Strassmann, P.: Information Productivity: assessing information management costs of U.S. Corporations. Information Economics Press, 1999
26. OCDE - Is there a new economy? Paris: OCDE, 2000.
27. Shapiro, R.: Digital economy. Washington, DC: Departament of Commerce, 2000.
28. Nardi, B.; O'Day, V.: Information ecologies: using technology with heart. Cambridge, MIT Press, 1999
29. Meirelles,F.S.: Informática nas empresas: perfil, indicadores, gastos e investimentos. In: Ruben, G.; Wainer, J.; Dwyer, T.; Informática, organizações e sociedade no Brasil. São Paulo: Editora Cortez, 2003.
30. Coriat,B.; Zarifian,P.: Automatization: filieres d'emploi et recomposition des categories de main-d'oeuvre, Paris, Travel, 1985
31. Soete, L.; Weel, B. T;. Computers and employment: the truth about e-skills. EIB Papers, V. 6, No. 1, 133-150, 2001 http://www.eib.org/efs/papers.htm acesso em 21/11/2003.
32. Iachan,R.: O impacto da automação de escritórios nas empresas brasileiras: um estudo prático, M.Sc. Dissertation, Puc-Rio, 1990
33. Rebecchi, E. : O sujeito frente à inovação tecnológica, IBASE - Automação e Trabalho, 1990
34. Shostak,A.B.; Mitchell,D.J.B. (editors): The Cyberunion Handbook: Transforming Labor Through Computer Technology (Issues in Work and Human Resources). New York: M.E.Sharpe, 2002.

35. Giuliano,V.: The mechanization of office work. Scientific American, v 247, n 3, 33-52, 1982
36. Mawshowitz, R. : The conquest of will: information processing in human affairs, Massachusetts, Addison-Wesley, 1976
37. Heap, N.; Thomas, G. E.; Mason, R.; Mackay, H.: Information technology and society. London: Sage Publications Ltd., Open University, 1995.
38. Fehlaber, A.: Impactos da Informatização nas relações de trabalho: o caso de Pernambuco, ENANPAD XVIII, v4, 257-271, Salvador, Bahia, 1994
39. Bornstein, C.T.; Kubrusly, L.S. and Zambalde, A.L.; "Análise de Algumas Variáveis Qualitativas na Agroindústria do Café" (Analysis of some qualitative variables in the coffee agribusiness), Annals of the XXXIII Brasilian Symposium on Operations Research, Campos de Jordão, SP, BR, p.5-11, november 2001.
40. Lucas, L.C.S.: Análise de Grupamento, Separata da Revista Brasileira de Estatística, n. 172, 1982
41. Johnson, R.A.; Wichern, D.W. – Applied Multivariate Statistical Analysis – Prentice-Hall, Inc., New Jersey, 1992
42. Anderberg, M.R.: Cluster Analysis for Application - Academic Press, New York, 1973
43. Everitt, B.: Cluster Analysis – Social Science Research Council, London, UK., 1974

Case Study: Software Product Integration Practices

Stig Larsson[1] and Ivica Crnkovic[2]

[1] ABB AB, Corporate Research, Västerås, Sweden
[2] Mälardalen University, Department of Computer Engineering, Västerås, Sweden
{stig.larsson, ivica.crnkovic}@mdh.se

Abstract. Organizations often encounter problems in the Product Integration process. The difficulties include finding errors at integration related to mismatch between the different components and problems in other parts of the system than the one that was changed. The question is if these problems can be decreased if the awareness of the integration process is increased in other activities. To get better understanding of this problem we have analyzed the integration process in two product development organizations. One of the organizations has two different groups with slightly different integration routines while the other is basing the development on well defined components. The obstacles found in product integration are highlighted and related to best practices as described in the interim standard EIA-731.1. Our conclusion from this study is that the current descriptions for best practices in product integration are available in standards and models, but are insufficiently used and can be supported by technology to be accepted and utilized by the product developers.

1 Introduction

Through investigations of many development organizations developing products with software as an important part, we have seen that the product integration is one of the processes where many of the problems in product development become visible. The origin of the problems is often in other processes performed early in the development cycle. These problems can be reduced through an increased understanding of the needs from an integration standpoint. Today, not enough care is taken to ensure that the system requirements are considered when components and parts developed. Proper preparation, understanding and performance of the product integration are believed to resolve part of this problem.

Integration of products that include software is described in several standards and collections of best practices. These best practices are collected from different companies and organization and include areas that are considered to be of good use for the development organizations in different application areas. There is however a lack of independent research which shows whether the practices described in these collections give the intended result when implemented in different organizations; a systematic validation of the practices is needed.

F. Bomarius and S. Komi-Sirviö (Eds.): PROFES 2005, LNCS 3547, pp. 272–285, 2005.

There are different perspectives from which the use of descriptions found in standards and models can be investigated and different questions to be answered. The first question is how it can be determined that the processes described in the standards and models are suitable for different types of development and the use of different life cycle models; are the generic principles of the descriptions valid for all types of product development? Another question is if an organization may run into problems even if the principles and descriptions are followed in a proper way. Are there ways to fulfill the principles described but not achieve the intended results? A third question is how to determine if the reason for an organization having problems is the fact that the principles are described as the prescribed working method, but are still not followed. Our approach to these different perspectives is to look at the *performance* of the process in the investigated organizations and compare the activities with the ones prescribed in the standards and models regardless of the development model used. We also look at the problems in the organizations and analyze these with respect to the practices that are *not* followed by the organization.

We claim that we by investigating a number of organizations and the practices in use can obtain support for the practices described in standards and models *or* determine a need for revisions of the standards and models. This leads to the following research questions for this paper: (i) How well can the practices described in a specific standard be expected to reduce problems encountered in the integration of products? and (ii) What deficiencies or incompleteness can we observe in the proposed practice?

We have in this paper selected to use the interim standard EIA-731.1 [1] as the reference model. The rational for this is that the interim standard model has been used as one of the inputs to CMMI [2], and is specifically intended to be used for internal process improvement, not for qualification of suppliers. In addition to this, the development of this interim standard has been carried out in cooperation between a number of national and international organizations such as EIA[3] and INCOSE [4] involving a large number of organizations and companies with substantial experience in software and system product development.

Our proposition in this paper is that the problems encountered in the investigated units relate to the lack of execution of practices that are described in the interim standard. We also propose that successful execution of the product integration can be mapped to specific implementation of practices described in the interim standard.

This case study is a continuation of the work described in [5], where a different case has been compared to CMMI. The purpose of this paper is to investigate one additional source for best practices, compare it to current industrial problems and to establish if there are connections between the problems and the lack of execution of proposed activities.

The remainder of the paper is organized as follows. Section two describes general structure of the interim standard EIA-731.1 as well as the main characteristics of the integration processes of a development process. In section three, the case study design is described with explanations about the data collection method, the analysis method and the threats of validity of the study. Section four includes a description of the findings from the case study. Section five analyzes how the findings relate to best practices. Finally section six contains the conclusion and proposed future work and is followed by the references list.

2 Product Integration in EIA-731.1

The interim standard EIA-731.1 describes a number of focus areas useful for organizations developing products and systems. The focus areas described are organized in three categories; technical, management and environment. For each focus area, a number of themes describe the suggested activities. All themes include a description, typical work products and specific practices for the focus area. For some of the focus areas there are comments that normally contain clarifications or suggested implementation details. In addition to the specific practices, there are a number of generic practices applicable for all specific practices with the different focus areas. The generic practices include tasks such as planning of the activities to perform the process, monitoring and checking that the activities performed are according to plan and the execution of corrective measures when these are identified and needed.

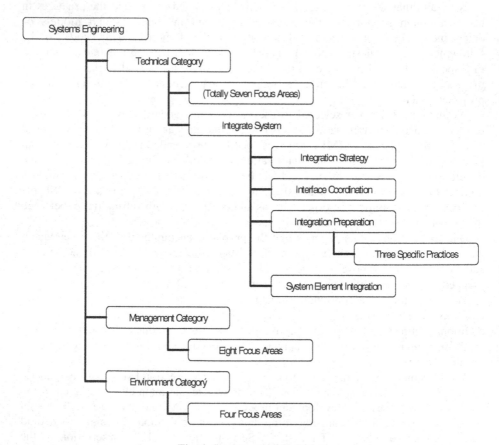

Fig. 1. Structure of EIA-731.1

The interim standard includes a possibility to determine the capability level of an organization in a specific area. This is based on the observation that organizations typically take observable distinct steps in the effort to improve the performance. In EIA-731.1 these levels are intended to be used as means to help the organization in the planning and implementation of the improvement efforts. Six different capability levels have been defined. Level 0 indicates that the specific practices are not performed. Level 1 indicates that the specific practices on level one are performed. For level 2 to 5 both the specific and generic practices on these levels are performed. Note that no effort has in this study been made to determine the capability level of the organizations investigated as the target is to understand if the specific practices for product integration give the intended result.

The rest of this section summarizes the product integration process as it is described in EIA-731.1. The standard prescribes a set of specific practices that are considered to be essential for accomplishing the purpose of the focus area designated Integrate System (Focus Area 1.5).

The purpose of the Integrate System focus area is to ensure that the product and system works as a whole based on the components that have been integrated. Interfaces between components and functions that extend over many components in the system are in the center of attention. It is also noted that the integration activities should start early and are typically iteratively performed.

Four themes have been identified for the focus area. An *Integration Strategy* (1) is considered to be the basis for the integration process. This theme includes the development of a strategy that contains an integration sequence and a plan for the integration tests to be performed. The *Interface Coordination* (2) is the second theme and includes handling of the requirements on the interfaces as well as specifications and detailed descriptions. As a third theme, the *Integration Preparation* (3) describes how components are received for integration and the checking that the components are in accordance with the strategy and interface documentation. The final theme is the actual integration: *System Element Integration* (4). The components are integrated according to the plan and the inter-operations between the components are checked. It should be noted that the actual verification is described in a different focus area in the interim standard EIA-731.1, FA 1.6 – Verify System.

The different specific practices on capability level 1, 2 and 3 for all themes can be found in Table 4. The descriptions in the interim standard are short and need to be interpreted with the description of the theme as a basis. Some guidance can be found in EIA-731.2 [6] that describes an appraisal method for EAI-731.1. However, the sample questions in this guide are also on a high level and require substantial expertise to be used.

3 Case Study Design

The case study was performed on three different product development groups in two different organizations. As the development methods are different in all three groups, the case study has been designed as a multiple-case holistic study as described by

Yin [7]. The units of analysis are the processes for integration as perceived by members of the development groups in the three different cases. The focus of the study was on processes used at the time for the investigation, not described in quality systems or handbooks and not on processes that were under development.

3.1 Research Method

The interviews made with members of the development groups are the main sources of data in this investigation. Additional information was obtained from descriptions and examples of how the integration was planned and performed. For each case at least two persons were interviewed. The selection of subjects for the interview was based on two criteria. The first was that for each organization, both a manager and a developer should be interviewed. The second criterion was that the subjects should have extensive experience spanning over several years from the development in the investigated group.

The interviews were performed as open-ended discussions and all interviews were made by the same researcher. The researcher was guided by a discussion guide to ensure that different aspects of product integration were covered in the discussion. The guide was developed by two researchers and included questions related to three different areas; organization, implementation, and effectiveness of the product integration. The questions included in the discussion guide were not taken from the standard, but were designed to give an understanding of the used processes independent from descriptions in standards and models. During the interviews, the guide was used to ensure that the interesting topics were covered, and the specific questions asked were depending on how much information was obtained through the explanations from the interviewees. The use of open-ended questions allowed the researcher to follow up interesting statements that lead to more information and a deeper understanding of the used process. Each interview was between one and two hours. The documentation from the data collection consists of notes taken during the interviews complemented with information from the written documentation.

The data collected can be divided into two types. The first type was descriptions of how the integration process was performed for each case and what activities were carried out. The second was descriptions of the problems that the units perceived in the integration process.

3.2 Analysis Method

After the interview sessions, the data collected was analyzed in several ways. This was done as a separate activity and without the involvement of the development organizations. For each case in the case study, the *activities* captured during the data collection were compared and mapped to the practices described in EIA-731.1. The result from the mapping showed if the development in the different cases were performed in accordance with the interim standard. As a second step, the *problems identified* were mapped to the specific practices in EIA-731.1 that are intended to ensure that the problems should not occur. Finally, the relations between activities performed and the problems were investigated. This resulted in Table 4 that indicates the relation between practices from EIA-731.1, activities performed and identified problems. A second phase of the analysis was to propose how the practices in EIA-731.1 should possibly solve the encountered problems. The results from this analysis in found in Table 5. The analysis was made by one researcher and reviewed by two other researchers.

3.3 Validity

Four types of validity threats are of interest for case studies [7]. In this section, we discuss these and the preventive measures to reduce them. *Construct validity* relates to the data collected and how this data represent the investigated phenomenon. *Internal validity* concerns the connection between the observed behavior and the proposed explanation for this behavior. The possibilities to generalize the results from a study are dealt with through looking at the *external validity*. Finally, the *reliability* covers the possibilities to reach the same conclusions if the study was repeated by another researcher.

The *construct validity* is dealt with through multiple sources for the data through more than one interview for each case. Additional interviews with other stakeholders as well as additional document investigations would have increased the construct validity. However, this would have required more intrusive investigations and would limit the availability to the organizations. The design of the discussion guide was based on available standards and methods and involved more than one researcher to ensure that the questions to be discussed were relevant. The researchers experience in software product development provided a basis for relevant discussions under the interview sessions.

The *internal validity* was secured in three ways. First, the connection between the behavior and the interim standard was done in several steps to avoid predetermined connections. Secondly, rival explanations have been listed and examined to exclude other causes to the findings. Finally, the analysis of the data and the connection to the interim standard has been reviewed by two additional researchers to avoid personal bias.

The *external validity* is dealt with through the use and description of three cases in two different application domains and through the use of several different standards and methods when defining the investigation area.

The *reliability* of the study has been secured through the description of the procedure used in the study and the documentation of the discussion guide.

4   Case Descriptions

Two product development organizations have been investigated, both developing systems for monitoring and control of different types of networks, but in different application domains. The systems operate in industrial settings with real-time requirements as well as high demands on availability and reliability. One of the units is developing products for two different environments. This has lead to the use of different processes and in this study they are treated as two cases resulting in a total of three cases. For each case the following sections contain a brief description of the product and the product development process. The descriptions also include the problems that were identified and described in the interviews. The problems are presented in tables where each problem is labeled with a P, the case number and a reference character.

4.1   Case One

The product in case one is a stand-alone product that is connected to a real-time data collection system. The development is done in one group with less than 20 developers and follows a clearly defined process. The product development of a specific release is based on a definition of the product that contains what should be included in each release. The first step in the development is the implementation of requirements on the functions for the release. Based on this, the unit and system verifications to be performed are defined. Development of the functions is done in units called components. The Rational Unified Process is used, and a document list defines the development process. The planning is made so the development is done in increments. The unit verification is performed by software developers. The strategy is that tests should not be done by the developer producing the software. The unit tests are often done through automatic testing. Specifications and protocols from the tests are reviewed by peers and system integrators. The tests are performed in the developer's environment and consist of basic tests. Functional tests are performed before the system tests.

The product integration is not defined as a separate process, but the product is integrated by the developers before the system verification. Before a component is checked in, it should be included in a system build to ensure proper quality. Delivery to the system test is done of the whole system. The test protocols and error reports from the unit verifications are reviewed with the system integrator before the system test. The system tests are performed by a core of system testers and temporary additional personnel. This strategy builds on well defined and detailed tests. The tests are focusing on functions and performance and are performed on different hardware combinations. This includes different variants of the product and different versions of the operating system. The test period takes approximately 12 weeks, with new versions of the assembled components received to system test every week. Although the development builds on increments, no integration plan is used for the product. The integration plan used is one for the whole system where this product is included. Typical time for the development of a release is less than one year.

The three most serious problems were captured for case one as described in Table 1. The routines are mainly followed, but due to tight deadlines, shortcuts may be taken. Sometimes uncontrolled changes are introduced in the software. This is typically done when a part of the system is changed due to an existing error that is uncritical and not planned to be corrected. Due to the dependencies in the system, new errors may appear in parts that have not been changed. Also other connections between components that are not explicit generate this problem.

Table 1. Problems captured for case one

Label	Problem description
P1-A	Functions are not always fully tested when delivered for integration. This leads to problems in the build process or in integration and system tests
P1-B	Errors are corrected that should not be. This results in new errors with higher influence on functionality and performance
P1-C	Errors appear in other components which have not been changed

4.2 Case Two

The second case is a product that includes software close to the hardware. The development group is small and follows a common development process. This process includes rules for what should be checked and tested before a component is integrated. The tests include running the application in simulators and target systems before the integration. A specification for what should be ready before start of functional and system test are available. The architect is responsible for implementation decisions. The target system includes a complex hardware solution with the application divided on two target systems. Typical time for the development of a release is 1.5 year. This includes the full development cycle from defining the requirements to system testing.

Most of the problems appear because of the incapability and version mismatch of the test system, the final product and the test and final hardware platform (Table 2). Efforts are now made to go towards incremental development, and to increase the formalism in the testing. The tests will be made in three stages with basic tests performed by the designer, functional tests performed by a specific functional tester and system tests with delivery protocol.

Table 2. Problem captured for case two

Label	Problem description
P2-A	Problems appear as a consequence that tests for the components are not run in the same environment as the test system. Different versions of hardware and test platform are used.

4.3 Case Three

The development organization in this case is responsible for the design of a user interface that acts as a client to a database server. The organization is small, around 15 developers.

The current architecture has been recently improved. The old version of the system suffered from problems with many common include files. Through global variables and similar solutions permitted by the selected technology, unintended side-effects made debugging and error correction tedious. Different attempts to reduce the problems within the available technology lead to the insight that a design that was built on isolation of interfaces should be beneficial. The solution was to start building a new system. Included in this decision was a strategy to design interfaces carefully and to use technologies that permitted isolated components to be used.

The system is built up of components that primarily implements different parts of the user interface. Each component handles the communication with the server. This design was used to allow the development of services that are independent and dedicated for each component. The component framework defines the required interface for each component and provides a number of services, such as capturing of key strokes. The technology used permits the developers to easily isolate problems and to minimize the uncontrolled interference and dependencies between the components.

The development is organized with frequent builds and continuous integration of new functions. The integration is handled by the integration responsible. However, the checks before the inclusion of new functions are done by the developers. There are no specific routines in place for handling the interfaces. Changes are in practice always checked by the system architect.

The new system design has reduced the implementation time for a function with 2/3. The turn-around time for a system release has been reduced from six months to between one and three months. At the same time, a need for maintaining the base platform has emerged. Also, some of the technical solutions have been questioned and may increase the need for maintenance (Table 3).

Table 3. Problem captured for case three

Label	Problem description
P3-A	Scattered architecture on the server side as a result of the decision to handle communication in each component

5 Collected Data and Analysis Results

In these three cases we found may similarities: size of the development groups, similar concerns, requirements of the products, similar product life cycle. What we have seen are the differences in the development processes and in used technologies and approaches. Our intention is to analyze what are the sources of the main problems and if they could have cause in deviation or absence of the activities pointed out in the best practices.

This section contains two parts. The first includes a table containing the analyzed data from the case study, while the second lists the problems found in the cases with a suggested implementation of the practices that could improve the performance.

5.1 Analyzed Case Study Data

The three steps of the analysis have been summarized and presented in Table 4. The table includes two parts for each practice. The first two columns show the description from EIA-731.1 for the specific practices for the focus area *Integrate System*. The first number in column one shows what theme the practice belongs to, and the second number is the capability level (i.e., 1-2 shows that the practice belongs to theme one

Table 4. Specific practices for Integrate System compared to data from case 1, 2 and 3

Specific Practice	Description	Case 1	Case 2	Case 3
1-1	Develop an integration strategy	+ *	+	+
1-2	Document the integration strategy as part of an integration plan	-	+	-
1-3a	Develop the integration plan early in the program	-	+	-
1-3b	When multiple teams are involved with system development, establish and follow a formal procedure for coordinating integration activities	-	-	-
2-1a	Coordinate interface definition, design, and changes between affected groups and individuals throughout the life cycle	- *	-	+
2-1b	Identify interface requirement baselines	- *	+	+
2-2a	Review interface data	-	-	-
2-2b	Ensure complete coverage of all interfaces	-	-	-
2-3a	Capture all interface designs in a common interface control format	-	-	-
2-3b	Capture interface design rationale	-	-	- *
2-3c	Store interface data in a commonly accessible repository	-	-	-
3-1a	Verify the receipt of each system element (component) required to assemble the system in accordance with the physical architecture	- *	- *	+
3-1b	Verify that the system element interfaces comply with the interface documentation prior to assembly	- *	+	+
3-2	Coordinate the receipt of system elements for system integration according to the planned integration strategy	-	+	-
4-1a	Assemble aggregates of system elements in accordance with the integration plan	+	+	+
4-1b	Checkout assembled aggregates of system elements	+	+	+

Table 5. Cross-reference between observed problems and relevant specific practices

Label	Problem description	Relevant specific practices and Proposed actions
P1-A	Functions are not always fully tested when delivered for integration. This leads to problems in the build process or in integration and system tests	3-1a Ensure a handover to a dedicated integration responsible
P1-B	Errors are corrected that should not be. This results that new errors are introduced, with higher influence on functionality and performance	1-1 Ensure that the strategy and decision are followed through a handover procedure
P1-C	Errors appear in other components than the changed	2-1a, 2-1b, 3-1b Specify and enforce interface descriptions for all dependencies between the components
P2-A	Problems appear as a consequence that tests for the components are not run in the same environment as the test system. Different versions of hardware and test platform are used.	3-1a Ensure that the proper test equipment as described in the integration strategy is made available to the developers. Check that proper tests are performed through a clear handover to an integration responsible
P3-A	Scattered architecture on the server side as a result of the decision to handle communication in each component	2-3b Ensure that the rationale for design decisions are documented and communicated

and is placed on capability level 2). Finally, if two or more practices exist on a capability level for a theme, these are distinguished by a character. The following three columns include data from each of the cases. These columns include two things: (i) an indication for each case if the practice has been observed as performed (+) or not observed (-), and (ii) if there are indications of problems connected to the practice (*). The indicated problems are further described and analyzed in section 5.2.

5.2 Analysis of Observed Problems

In each of the cases, problems encountered in the performed product integration process were captured and discussed. The problems are in Table 5 cross-referenced by the researcher to the specific practices for the Integrate System focus area of EIA-731.1. Each problem has a label composed of a P, the case number and a reference character as in the tables in section 4. In addition to the description and the reference, a proposed action based on the specific practice has been included in the table.

Based on the data, we have made two observations regarding the perceived problem situation. The first is that all the problems for case one and two are related to capability level 1 specific practices. This may indicate that additional problems may be observed once all capability level one practices are performed, or it may indicate that higher capability level practices have less influence on the actual product integration results. The second observation is that case three had a similar culture for process adherence as case one, but the developers were forced by the technology to perform the specific practices.

5.3 Analysis of Propositions

As a summary of the analysis, we conclude that case two is performing the product integration most in line with the specific practices described in EIA-731.1 It is also clear that case two and three follow almost all the recommendations from capability level 1 specific practices. We see that case one has the most problems, and that all these problems are related to capability level 1 specific practices and we have noticed that in case three, the technology may help the development team in following the capability level 1 practices. The results are displayed in Table 6.

Table 6. Summary of analysis

	# of specific practices performed of total number # of problems found		
	Capability level 1	Capability level 2	Capability level 3
Case 1	3 /7	0/4	0/5
	5 problems	No problem	No problem
Case 2	5/7	2/4	15
	1 problem	No problem	No problem
Case 3	7/7	0/4	0/5
	No problem	No problem	1 problem

The first of our two propositions was that *the problems encountered in the investigated units relate to the lack of execution of practices that are described in the interim standard* EIA-731.1. In the analysis of the data and the comparison, we conclude that the problems found can be mapped to specific practices which support our proposition. We have also observed that it is primarily the inability to perform capability level 1 specific practices that have lead to observable problems.

The second proposition was that *successful execution of the product integration can be mapped to specific implementation of practices described in the interim standard.* For many of the practices on capability level 2 and 3, no observations have been made that they were performed, but only one problem has been reported that could be related to level 2 or 3 practices. Based on this and the observations regarding capability level 1 practices, an additional proposition has evolved and should be tested in future studies. This can be formulated as follows: *A successful execution of the product integration can be mapped to specific implementation of practices described in the interim standard for capability level 1.*

5.4 Rival Explanations

The conclusion regarding the propositions above can be challenged and in this section we examine rival explanations and analyze the possibility that these give better reasons to the data found in the study.

The first explanation examined is that there is no real connection between the performance and the specific practices described and that the data match only is coincidental. We consider this explanation to be unlikely due to two facts. The first is that the interim standard build on long industrial experience from companies and organizations from a wide set of areas and applications. The second fact is that the pattern shown in this study is clear and builds on three cases from two different organizations.

The second alternative explanation could be that the organizations due to other factors succeed in the product integration process. However, if there are other factors involved, these may also help in following the proposed practices. This is also the situation in case three where the selected technology has imposed a way of working on the product developers.

6 Conclusions and Future Work

Data regarding the product integration process from two development organizations have been collected and compared to the requirements described in a standard description of the product integration process. The problems observed in the case study have been compared to practices that describe activities that should improve the performance in the product integration.

We can from the observations conclude that the basic level of practices described in the interim standard EIA-731.1 includes activities that can help the organizations to avoid problems which can appear when integrating components to systems. Basic activities include (i) development and a clear specification of the strategy for the integration, (ii) keeping well defined interface descriptions up to date throughout the life cycle, (iii) that the integration of components follow the strategy and (iv) that the assembly is verified as planned.

We have also observed that there are indications that skilled use of component technologies as described in [8] facilitates the integration process. The factors contributing to this support are well described interfaces, the need to test components before integration and the explicit definition of the environment required by the components.

Through this investigation, partial answers have been found to our research questions, but additional research is needed. Future work should include steps to strengthen and further investigate the propositions made in this paper. They are (i) improvement of validation of the results by providing the feedback to the case participants in a form of discussions of accuracy of collected data and the results at a common workshop, and (ii) additional case studies in industry. Additional descriptions of practices in standards and models need to be investigated in relation to industry practices. There is also a need to analyze the similarities and differences in the different standards and models. One additional research direction has been indicated with the purpose to confirm or refute the indications in this paper and in [5] that component technologies assist in the implementation of successful software product integration. Of specific interest may the integration problems related to COTS be.

References

1. EIA/IS-731.1, Systems Engineering Capability Model, Electronic Industries Alliance (Interim Standard), (01 Aug 2002)
2. Chrissis, M.B., M. Konrad, S. Shrum, CMMI, Addison-Wesley, Boston, MA, (2003).
3. http://www.eia.org/
4. http://www.incose.org/
5. Larsson, S., I. Crnkovic, F. Ekdahl, "On the Expected Synergies between Component Based Software Engineering and Best Practices in Product Integration", Euromicro Conference, France, August 2004, IEEE
6. EIA/IS 731.2, Systems Engineering Capability Model Appraisal Method, Electronic Industries Alliance (Interim Standard), (01 Aug 2002)
7. Yin R. K., Case Study Research: Design and Methods (3rd edition), ISBN 0-7619-2553-8, Sage Publications, 2003
8. Szyperski, C. et al, Component Software -- Beyond Object-Oriented Programming, (2nd edition), ISBN 0-201-74572-0, ACM Press, New York, (2002)

Improving the Express Process Appraisal Method

F. McCaffery, D. McFall, and F.G. Wilkie

Centre for Software Process Technologies,
Faculty of Engineering, University of Ulster, Newtownabbey
Co-Antrim BT37 0QB, Northern Ireland
{f.mccaffery, d.mcfall, fg.wilkie}@ulster.ac.uk

Abstract. In this paper we firstly describe the appraisal method that was developed by the Centre for Software Process Technologies (CSPT) to assess software processes within small to medium sized (SMEs) organisations that have little or no experience of software process improvement programmes. We then discuss our experience of developing and using our appraisal method within six SMEs organisations within Northern Ireland. Next we compare our assessment method with existing lightweight assessment methods that have also been used to assess software processes within SMEs software development organisations. We then describe new features that we are currently introducing to improve our software process appraisal method.

1 Introduction

The Centre for Software Process Technologies [1, 2] is a research and knowledge transfer group funded jointly by the University of Ulster and Invest Northern Ireland, a Northern Ireland governmental organisation responsible for the economic development of this geographical region. The CSPT is tasked with motivating and developing a culture of software process improvement within the Northern Ireland software industry.

Within the Northern Ireland software industry the majority of companies are SMEs organizations. The key characteristics of these SMEs organizations are that they have little or no experience of adopting Software Process Improvement (SPI) frameworks and assessment methods. The majority of these companies stated that they considered SPI frameworks and assessment to be too expensive, too time-consuming, too heavyweight and really only applicable to larger organizations [3]. In an attempt to make SPI more attractive to these SMEs the CSPT decided to adopt the continuous representation of the Capability Maturity Model Integrated (CMMI® [1]) [4] and to develop a more light-weight assessment model to assist with SPI within the Northern Ireland software industry. The continuous representation of the CMMI® provides a more attractive proposition for SMEs companies than the staged version of the model. Par-

---

[1] ®CMMI is registered in the U.S. Patent and Trademark Office by Carnegie Mellon University.

F. Bomarius and S. Komi-Sirviö (Eds.): PROFES 2005, LNCS 3547, pp. 286–298, 2005.

ticularly as most of the software development SMEs organisations within Northern Ireland have no compelling reason to achieve any particular maturity level rating, but would rather see the benefits from a software process improvement programme in a more gradual, progressive manner. Such an approach also enables process areas to be selected for appraisal that are deemed to be more critical in terms of the company's business goals.

As part of the product suite for CMMI®, the Software Engineering Institute has published the requirements for three categories of method which employ the CMMI® [5]. Methods developed to comply with these requirements are known as ARC (Appraisal Requirements for CMMI®) class-C, class-B and class-A. The Software Engineering Institute has developed its own class-A compliant method which is called SCAMPI^{SM}. The requirements of class-A methods tend to result in large methods which require a sizable effort from the appraised organisation both in terms of preparation for such an appraisal as well as considerable external effort from an appraisal team. This stems in part from the need to thoroughly investigate and support any evidence gathered during the appraisal. For much of the Northern Ireland software industry, class-A methods would not currently be appropriate because the scope of the appraisal would lead to increased and unsustainable costs. The CSPT approach is to build up awareness and understanding in the aims and objectives of software process improvement in a gradual manner by trying to keep the costs associated with such measures small to begin with, through an approach of limiting the scope of any appraisal. For this reason the CSPT has developed its own appraisal method which complies with the ARC 1.1 requirements for a class-C method. Our method is called Express Process Appraisal (EPA). As an ARC class-C method, the EPA method does not provide any form of rating.

In a pilot appraisal programme, the EPA method has been used to appraise six software development companies in Northern Ireland. The results of all six appraisals indicate that for most of the process areas, most appraised companies perform at either capability level 0 or 1. Details of the results of the six appraisals and the effectiveness of the performance of the EPA method are detailed in another publication [6]. The EPA method has been developed for assessing software processes with SMEs organisations however it could also be used for performing initial process assessments within larger organizations that have not previously embarked upon process assessments, as it will provide such companies with recommendations as to how they may improve their practices, as well as providing them with a starting point and a pathway to improvement.

The intention of this paper is to describe the method, our experiences using it, comparisons with other lightweight process appraisal methods, as well as our plans and efforts to improve the EPA method.

Section 2 describes the EPA method, while section 3 discusses our experiences with the method. Section 4 compares the EPA method against other lightweight process assessment methods. Section 5 focuses upon our current work to improve the EPA model and section 6 provides our concluding remarks.

---

^{SM} SCAMPI is a service mark of Carnegie Mellon University.

2 Express Process Appraisal

The development of the EPA method began in March 2003. Two members of the CSPT staff initially attended the official 'Introduction to CMMI®' course and subsequently the 'Intermediate Concepts of CMMI®' course, both at the Software Engineering Institute. One of the CSPT staff also had team member experience on both CMM and CMMI® appraisal teams led by fully (SEI) qualified Lead Assessors. A team of five CSPT staff then started developing sets of stock questions from the CMMI®. These stock questions enable us to ensure adequate coverage of the model during questioning sessions. Many additional questions are asked as an interview proceeds, based upon the answers provided to the stock questions.

2.1 Selecting Process Areas

After consulting local software companies one of the main objectives of the EPA method was to confine the interview session to one working day. Therefore, when developing the EPA method we decided to include six process areas as this was the maximum number of process areas that could reasonably be covered within one working day. We then decided to select the six most appropriate process areas (to software companies within Northern Ireland) at CMMI® maturity level 2 as the justification for starting a process improvement exercise with them is already well established in that they are present at the first level in the model. The following process areas were selected: Requirements Management, Configuration Management, Project Planning, Project Monitoring & Control, Measurement & Analysis, and Process & Product Quality Assurance.

2.2 The EPA Appraisal Plan

The EPA method is divided into eight stages and the appraisal team consists of two CSPT staff members who conduct the appraisal between them.

Stage 1 (Develop Appraisal Schedule) is the preliminary meeting to establish logistics and determine the schedule. This meeting involves 2 CSPT staff and at least one representative from the company. This meeting lasts approximately one hour. Therefore 2 person-hours of CSPT time and at least 1 person-hour of company time are normally required for this stage.

During stage 2 (Conduct Overview Briefing) the lead appraiser provides an overview of the method for all those from the appraised organisation who will be involved in subsequent stages. This session is used to remove any concerns that individuals may have and to establish codes of conduct and confidentiality. This overview session involves 2 CSPT staff and on average 7 company staff (the number of company staff involved depends upon the size of the company). The overview normally lasts 2 hours. Therefore 4 person-hours of CSPT time and 14 person-hours of company time (based upon an average of 7 staff attending) are normally required for this stage.

Stage 3 (Site Briefing) is used by the appraised organisation to explain elements of the company structures to the appraisal team. During this stage, the appraisal team learn a little about the company's history, the company's business objectives and about the types of ongoing projects, along with the lifecycle stage that each project has reached. This briefing involves 2 CSPT staff and on average 2 company staff (once again the number of company personnel involved depends upon the size of the company). The briefing normally lasts 2 hours. Therefore 4 person-hours of CSPT time and 4 person-hours of company time (based upon an average of 2 company staff attending) are normally required for this stage.

Stage 4 (Analyse Key Documents) provides a brief look at some samples of project and organisational documentation. Five samples of documents are requested: a typical project plan, a typical project progress report, a typical approved requirements statement, company quality assurance guidelines/manual and finally any documentation relating to the company policy on configuration management. The ARC class-C guidelines do not require the EPA method to consider documentation. The EPA method is required to consider "at least one source of data". The primary source of data for the EPA method is through a series of interviews conducted during stage 5. The brief consideration of some sample documents during stage 4 is additional and used mainly to craft further questions for stage 5. This stage involves 2 CSPT staff and usually 1 member of company staff. This stage normally involves the company member dedicating 1 hour to retrieving the requested documents. The 2 CSPT staff performing the appraisal then each analyse this data for approximately 3 hours. Therefore 6 person-hours of CSPT time and 1 person-hour of company time are normally required for this stage.

The main part of the EPA method is stage 5 (Examine and Document Objective Evidence). In this stage key staff members from the appraised organisation are interviewed. There are 6 interviews. Each interview is scheduled to last approximately 1 hour. Each interview focuses on one of the 6 process areas. The interviews involve an appraisal team consisting of 2 CSPT staff and at least one representative from the company (on average 3 staff are involved) are present for each process area interview. Therefore 12 person-hours of CSPT time and on average 18 person-hours (based on 3 company personnel being involved) of company time are normally required for this stage.

Stage 6 (Generate Appraisal Results) and stage 7 (Create Final Report) are very much a collaborative exercise between the appraisal team members. The final report consists of a list of strengths, issues and suggested actions for each of the process areas evaluated. Global observations covering all process areas are also covered. Stages 6 and stage 7 each involve 2 CSPT appraisal team members collaborating together for three hours. Therefore a total 12 person-hours of CSPT time is required for both these stages.

Stage 8 (Presentation of the Findings Report) involves presenting the findings report to the group of people in the appraised organisation who participated in the interviews. This presentation involves 2 CSPT staff and on average 7 company staff (this depends upon the number of the company staff that participated in the appraisal). The briefing normally lasts 1 hour. Therefore 2 person-hours of CSPT time and 7 person-hours of company time (based upon an average of 7 staff attending) are normally required for this stage.

Overall, the EPA method requires approximately 45 person-hours of the appraised organisation's time and 42 person-hours of the CSPT appraisal team's time. We normally try to complete the entire appraisal process over two elapsed weeks.

3 Experiences Using EPA

To date the EPA method has been used to appraise 6 separate organisations. Two of these organisations fall into the 'medium' category of SMEs, employing between 60-120 engineers. The other four organisations represent the 'small' category, having between 10-45 software engineering staff.

The six process areas, mentioned earlier were confirmed as applicable to all companies in our sample, prior to the appraisals taking place. On average one hour was sufficient time to cover each of the process areas and all companies liked the fact that the on-site assessment could be completed within one day.

The method involved two appraisal team members. During each of the interview sessions, one of the team led the questioning while the other recorded notes. The person leading the session had a PC based tool which enabled them to make snap judgments about the interviewee responses to the questions by judging them on a discrete set of values – Red (not practiced), Amber (partially practiced), Yellow (largely practiced) and Green (fully practiced). In this way, the opinions of the questioner could also be recorded for subsequent review. A screen-shot from the tool is presented in figure 1.

During stages 6 and 7, both appraisers discussed the findings and the spreadsheets (within the tool) used to record snap judgments were revised. When both appraisers were satisfied that the scores corresponding to each of the questions within the tool were accurate, the tool produced histograms which proved very useful in judging performance against CMMI® process area goals. The tool also produced histograms for practices within goals, but these proved less useful as some CMMI® practices resulted in more questions than others and therefore some practices were subject to smoothing effects from multiple answers to a greater extent than others. This issue was not present in the histograms that were produced for the goals as at the goal level, there were always many answers to be consolidated.

The EPA method is designed as a lightweight assessment model to be used within organisations that have very little experience of software process improvement. The method relies heavily on information obtained from interviewing company personnel and performs limited cross-referencing checks (due to the limited time available for data collection and analysis). As a result, this approach depends on the willingness of the company to engage in software process improvement. It is important that the company encourages it's employees to answer interview questions in a truthful and helpful manner so that the resultant findings report will provide an accurate reflection of the company's strengths and weaknesses within each of the appraised process areas. The findings report contains a list of recommendations which each company must prioritise into an action plan based upon their goals and aspirations.

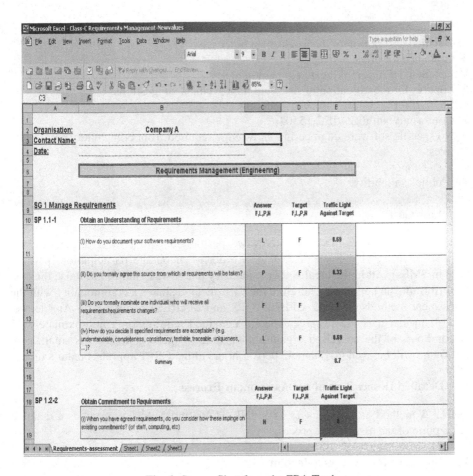

Fig. 1. Screen-Shot from the EPA Tool

4 Comparison with Other Lightweight Software Process Assessment Methods

Process assessment methods generally draw upon one of two process models: (i) ISO/IEC 15504 [7] and (ii) CMMI® [4]. Using each of these models there have been many attempts to develop lightweight process assessment methods. For example, RAPID [8], SPINI [9], FAME [10], TOPS [11], and MARES [12] are all lightweight models that are based on the ISO/15504/5 reference model. With regard to the CMMI®, the EPA method is an example of an ARC class-C compliant method.

Anacleto et al. [13] have considered lightweight process assessment methods for small software companies. In their paper they provide criteria for comparing assessment methods and have compared most of the methods mentioned above. The next part of this paper will compare the EPA method against the other assessment methods using criteria from the Anacleto et al. [13] comparison framework. The criteria they use to compare assessment models are as follows:

1. Low cost;
2. Detailed description of the assessment process;
3. Guidance for process selection;
4. Detailed definition of the assessment model;
5. Support for identification of risks and improvement suggestions;
6. Support for high-level process modeling;
7. Conformity with ISO/IEC 15504;
8. No specific software engineering knowledge required from companies' representatives;
9. Tool support;
10. Public availability.

4.1 Low Cost

After analysing the results of a survey we performed within the Northern Ireland software industry [13] we realised that in order to encourage participation (particularly in SMEs) within the local software industry that it was vital to minimise the cost of performing an appraisal. Therefore the EPA method shares a commonality with the assessment methods (RAPID, SPINI, TOPS and MARES) compared in Anacleto et al. [13] in that it is inexpensive. The EPA method requires only approximately 45 person-hours of the appraised organisation's time (if the organization is small, then this figure will be even less) and 42 person-hours of the CSPT appraisal team's time.

4.2 Detailed Description of the Assessment Process

The EPA method as in the cases of SPINI, TOPS and MARES provides a detailed description of the assessment process.

4.3 Guidance for Process Selection

From the assessment methods compared within Anacleto et al. [13] no evidence was available to suggest that any of them provide guidance for process selection. Likewise, the EPA method does not provide guidance as to what process areas should be assessed as only six process areas have been defined and all are assessed within the appraisal. This is similar to the RAPID assessment method as it also pre-defines eight process areas. However as in the case of the MARES project the EPA method is being enhanced to provide guidance for process selection. The EPA method will in the future still provide a one day on-site assessment within six process areas however any company wishing to engage in the appraisal will now be provided with twelve defined process areas from which they may select the six process areas that will form the basis of the assessment (this will be described further in section 5.2).

4.4 Detailed Definition of the Assessment Model

The EPA method like other assessment methods (RAPID, SPINI, TOPS & MARES) compared in Anacleto et al. [13] provides a detailed definition of the assessment model.

4.5 Support for Identification of Risks and Improvement Suggestions

Most of the assessment methods (SPINI, FAME & TOPS) compared in Anacleto et al. [13] provide support for the identification of risks and improvement suggestions, with this feature also being currently developed in the MARES method. The EPA method also fulfils this criteria. In stage 6 of the EPA method results are generated with focus being placed on the risk present within each process area to achieving a particular business goal. In stage 7 the findings report is developed to focus upon strengths, risks and improvement opportunities within each of the assessed process areas.

4.6 Support for High-Level Process Modeling

Most of the assessment methods compared in Anacleto et al. [13] are similar to the EPA method in that they do not provide support for high-level process modeling. In fact only one of the assessment methods (FAME) provide this feature with another (MARES) currently developing this feature.

4.7 Conformity with ISO/IEC 15504

All of the assessment methods (RAPID, SPINI, FAME, TOPS & MARES) compared in Anacleto et al. [13] are conformant with ISO/IEC 15504 whereas the EPA method is compliant with the ARC 1.1 requirements for a CMMI® class-C method.

4.8 No Specific Software Engineering Knowledge Required from Companies' Representatives

After performing a survey within the Northern Ireland software industry [3] we realised that in order to encourage participation (particularly in SMEs) within the local software industry that it was vital to minimise the overhead on the company engaging in the appraisal. It was therefore important to design an appraisal method that could be performed within an organisation without the assessment participants from the company having to firstly undergo a training programme in relation to the assessment model. Three of the assessment methods (RAPID, SPINI & MARES) compared in Anacleto et al. [13] also do not require the assessment participants to have specific knowledge of the assessment model. However the FAME and TOPS assessment methods require the assessment participants to have specific knowledge of the assessment model.

4.9 Tool Support

Tool support for the assessment methods compared in Anacleto et al. [13] appears to vary with the SPINI and FAME assessment methods having tools to assist with data collection, analysis and rating. Tool support is currently being developed for the MARES method. However, the RAPID and TOPS assessment methods do not include tool support and therefore depend upon paper forms. The EPA method provides tool support but also relies upon paper forms so that both assessors may compare data when preparing the findings report (one assessor uses the tool and the other assessor captures the interview responses using pen and paper).

4.10 Public Availability

Only two of the assessment methods (TOPS & MARES) compared in Anacleto et al. [13] are publicly available. The EPA assessment method is not publicly available.

In general the EPA method fulfils most of the criteria outlined by Anacleto et al. [13] and only failed to satisfy the categories of supporting high-level process modeling and making the method available publicly (at present we have no plans to add either of these features to the EPA method). In terms of comparison with the other assessment methods the EPA method appears to satisfy as many of the categories outlined by Anacleto as any of the other assessment methods. However we feel that the EPA method could be improved and the next section describes improvements that we are currently implementing.

5 Improving Existing Lightweight Assessment Models

From our initial work with the EPA method and comparing it with other lightweight assessment methods we have made a number of observations in terms of how to improve these methods. These are as follows:

1. Provide more sophisticated tools
2. Provide greater choice in terms of process areas

This section describes how we are currently incorporating these new features into the EPA method.

5.1 Provide More Sophisticated Tools

5.1.1 Introducing Speech Recognition Technology
We are currently trying to improve the effectiveness of the EPA method by automating some of the tasks that are performed by assessment teams through introducing a speech recognition and parsing system into process assessments. Although the assessment procedure was found to be generally satisfactory, the CSPT assessment team had some reservations in that the mechanics of the EPA method itself are very basic and suffer from a number of potential weaknesses:

The assessment team consists of two members. One member leads the interview within each of the process areas and makes an initial judgment as to whether a question relating to a specific CMMI® practice for that process area has been fulfilled: "Fully", "Largely", "Partially" or "Not at all". The other team member is then responsible for making notes based on the responses to the questions posed within the interview. This presents a number of issues in that some questions invoke lengthy responses and this creates a problem for the note-taker. Do they try to write-down every response verbatim, or try to understand a series of responses and then summarise based upon their understanding. The following issues may arise:

1. It is difficult for the note-taker to record in full detail the responses given to interview questions during the assessment. The volume of notes is often prohibitive and with the necessity to use qualified staff during the assessment, the option of using a person with short-hand skills is impractical.
2. Where the note-taker summarises their understanding of the responses made, it is possible that some important details go unrecorded. Further, the assessment then becomes dependent on the note-taker's proper understanding of the responses made. Simply taping the responses for later review is not practical given the time constraints on the assessment deliverables.

To create the findings report the assessment team review the handwritten notes obtained from the process area interviews and search for evidence that can be mapped against appropriate parts of the CMMI® model. This can be quite a time-consuming process that involves serially going through each specific practice within the CMMI® model and scanning the documentation for evidence. As the CMMI® contains a large number of practices this can be quite a long and tedious task. In an attempt to resolve these issues, the CSPT is currently engaged in a project to introduce speech recognition technology into software process assessment interviews. The project is composed of two phases.

Phase 1: This phase captures speech during the EPA interviews and produces answers to assessment questions in the form of text. This will help resolve the problems highlighted in issue 1, by removing the need for a note-taker. We are currently investigating the most appropriate hardware configuration and we are hoping to resolve the difficulties of distinguishing between speakers where more than one person attempts to speak at the same time.

Phase 2: This phase enables the output from the previous phase (i.e. the text captured at EPA interviews) to be parsed for keywords. Then evidence may be categorised and mapped to appropriate sections of the CMMI® model. This phase will help resolve the problems highlighted in issue 2, by automatically mapping the responses to the model based framework.

As no official benchmark is provided, these class C assessments provide an appropriate vehicle to use for trialing this technology. Also until we are satisfied with the performance of the project we will operate a dual system, with speech recognition technology plus note-taking both being present. Despite the initial overhead of having to use both capture techniques it is hoped that this will serve three purposes. Firstly, it will de-risk the assessment in case of technology failure due to the prototype nature of the system. Secondly, it will enable more thorough information to be captured as the note-taker's comments will be re-enforced by the text produced from phase 1 and the mappings from phase 2, so no evidence should be omitted or misinterpreted. Thirdly, the dual capture mechanism will enable us to assess how effective the speech recognition system is in comparison to note-taking. Results and feedback received from this exercise will also enable us to fine-tune the performance of the project. Finally, whenever we are satisfied with the performance of the speech recognition and parsing system, assessment may then be performed without the need for a note-taker. This would then mean that such assessments could be performed by one person and therefore reduce the expense of the assessment.

This speech recognition and parsing system project could reduce the error-prone and tedious aspects of the EPA method and therefore improve the effectiveness of such assessments, whilst reducing some of effort required by the assessment team.

5.1.2 Providing On-line Re-assessment Support

This section describes an on-line tool that is currently being developed within the CSPT to enable software development organisations to perform a self-assessment of selected process areas. As a result of an EPA the software development organisation receives a findings report. The findings report consists of a list of strengths, issues and suggested actions for each of the assessed process areas. The suggested actions detail how the company may improve their processes in line with their business goals. It would then be desirable if periodic appraisals could be performed within selected process areas to help determine if the capability for each process area has increased over time by following the improvement suggestions provided by the CSPT assessment team. However, as the Northern Ireland software industry is mainly composed of SMEs software development companies, it would be costly, both in terms of financial expense and time for such companies to engage in regular EPAs with the CSPT assessment team. Therefore as the main purpose of the CSPT is to instill a software process improvement culture into the Northern Ireland software industry an alternative solution had to be devised. After considering a number of alternatives it was decided that the most favourable approach was to develop an assessment tool that would enable companies to perform periodic "self re-assessment" of their software processes. We have developed a prototype of the tool that fulfils the following requirements:

1. Companies are assigned unique passwords and are able to access the tool upon demand;
2. Little preparation is required prior to performing an assessment;
3. The assessment may be performed in an informal manner;
4. The tool is web-based so that it may be easily distributed to many companies;
5. The tool provides full coverage of each process area;
6. A company may only access process areas that they have previously been appraised in by the CSPT assessment team;
7. The questions within each process area are multiple choice and the possible answers are expressed in a manner that does not require an understanding of the CMMI® model. However, a facility is also provided that enables users to enter a natural language answer if they feel that none of the options fully equate to their response. A member of the CSPT assessment team then receives this response and makes a judgment;
8. It is possible to complete a process area assessment in isolation from other process areas;
9. Records of each assessment are stored and used to monitor process improvement over time. This information is also accessible to the CSPT so that empirical software process improvement information may be compiled.

5.2 Provide Greater Choice in Terms of Process Areas

The lightweight assessment models mentioned in this paper provide a very limited set of process areas from which a company may select process areas that will be assessed. In fact for most of the assessment methods the process areas are pre-defined and choice is therefore not provided. From performing the pilot of the EPA method with six local SMEs we noted that for some companies additional process areas would have been applicable given the business goals of those companies. We are therefore currently expanding the EPA method from containing the six process areas of Requirements Management, Configuration Management, Project Planning, Project Monitoring & Control, Measurement & Analysis and Product & Process Quality Assurance to provide twelve process areas. The six additional process areas are Risk Management, Technical Solution, Verification, Validation, Requirements Development and Product Integration. A team of 5 CSPT staff have developed sets of stock questions from the CMMI® for these additional six process areas that may be used within future EPAs.

In addition to the development of the additional six process areas stage 1 of EPA method will now also involve advising the company representatives as to how each of the process areas will assist them in meeting their business goals. Additionally, stages 1 and 3 are being enhanced to assist the company in selecting which of the available process areas should be assessed in order to provide the most benefit to the company. If the company decides that it wishes for more than the standard six process areas to be assessed then the assessment schedule will have to be extended, however our preferred option is to limit the assessment to six process areas as this enables the interviews to be completed within 1 day.

6 Conclusion

In this paper, we described the EPA method for the lightweight assessment of software processes within small software development companies in conformance with the ARC 1.1 guidelines for a CMMI® class-C method. We then compared the EPA method with similar lightweight process assessment methods. Next we highlighted how such lightweight process assessment methods may be enhanced. Finally, we described how we are implementing our improvement suggestions into the EPA method. Future research will be required to assess to what extent adopting more sophisticated tools and a greater choice of process areas improves the EPA method.

Acknowledgements

The Centre for Software Process Technologies at the University of Ulster is supported by the EU Programme For Peace And Reconciliation in Northern Ireland and The Border Region Of Ireland (PEACE II).

References

1. The Centre for Software Process Technologies, University of Ulster, www.cspt.ulster. ac.uk.
2. Wilkie, F.G., McFall, D. and McCaffery, F. "The Centre for Software Process Technologies: A model for process improvement in geographical regions with small software industries", in proceedings of 16th Software Engineering Process Group Conference (2004), 8-11 March, Orlando, Florida, 5 pages.
3. McFall, D., Wilkie, F.G. McCaffery, F. Lester, N.G. and Sterritt, R. "Software Processes and Process Improvement in Northern Ireland", 16th International Conference on Software & Systems Engineering and their Applications, Paris, France, December 2003, ISSN: 1637-5033, p1-10.
4. "The Capability Maturity Model: Guidelines for Improving the Software Process", by Carnegie Mellon University Software Engineering Institute, Addison Wesley Longman, (1994), ISBN 0-201-54664-7.
5. "Appraisal Requirements for CMMI, Version 1.1 (ARC, V1.1)" by the CMMI Product Team, Software Engineering Institute, Carnegie Mellon University, Pittsburgh, PA. Technical Report CMU/SEI-2001-TR-034, ESC-TR-2001-034, pp1-49, (2001).
6. F.G. Wilkie, D. McFall & F. Mc Caffery, *An Evaluation of CMMI Process Areas for Small to Medium Sized Software Development Organisations* accepted for publication in Software Process Improvement and Practice Journal: Issue 10: 2, 2005. Wiley Publishers.
7. ISO/IEC 15504-3:2004 - Information technology - Process assessment - Part 3: Guidance on performing an assessment
8. Rout, T.P, Tuffley, A, Cahill, B, Hodgen, B. "The RAPID Assessment of Software Process Capability", in Software Process Improvement, ed. R.B. Hunter and R. Thayer, IEEE Computer Society Press, Los Alamitos, California, 2001.
9. Makinen, T, Varkoi, T, Lepasaar, M. "A Detailed Process Assessment Method for SMEs'", EuroSPI 2000.
10. FAME (Fraunhofer Assessment MEthod) -"A Business-Focused Method for Process Assessment", Fraunhofer Institute Experimentelles Software Engineering. http://www.iese.fraunhofer.de/fame
11. Cignoni, GA. "Rapid software process assessment to promote innovation in SME's.", Proceedings of Euromicro 99, Italy, 1999.
12. Anacleto, A, von Wangenheim, CG, Salviano, CF, Savi, R. "A method for Process Assessment in small software companies", 4th International SPICE Conference on Process Assessment and Improvement, Lisbon, Portugal, pp.69-76 (April 2004).
13. Anacleto, A, von Wangenheim, CG, Salviano, CF, Savi, R. "Experiences gained from applying ISO/IEC 15504 to small software companies in Brazil", 4th International SPICE Conference on Process Assessment and Improvement, Lisbon, Portugal, pp.33-37 (April 2004).

Relation Analysis Among Patterns on Software Development Process

Hironori Washizaki[1], Atsuto Kubo[2], Atsuhiro Takasu[1],
and Yoshiaki Fukazawa[2]

[1] National Institute of Informatics,
2-1-2 Hitotsubashi, Chiyoda-ku, Tokyo 101-8430, Japan
{washizaki, takasu}@nii.ac.jp
[2] Department of Computer Science, Waseda University,
3-4-1 Okubo, Shinjuku-ku, Tokyo 169-8555, Japan
a.kubo@fuka.info.waseda.ac.jp
fukazawa@waseda.jp

Abstract. The activity of the software process improvement can be supported by reusing various kinds of knowledge on existing successful software processes in the form of process patterns. There are several catalogs of process patterns available on WWW; however, all of relations among patterns are closed in each pattern catalog. To acquire the cross-cutting relations over the different process pattern catalogs, we have applied the technique for the automatic relation analysis among the patterns. Our technique utilizes existing text processing techniques to extract patterns from documents and to calculate the strength of pattern relations. As a result of experimental evaluations, it is found that the system implementing our technique has extracted appropriate cross-cutting relations over the different process pattern catalogs without information on relations described in original pattern documents. These cross-cutting relations will be useful for dealing with larger problems than those dealt with by individual process patterns.

1 Introduction

In the activity on software process improvement, we use various types of knowledge such as well-known successful organizational structures, successful existing development processes, and successful techniques for project management. If we can share and reuse such existing experience-based proven knowledge (i.e. know-how), we will be able to achieve more efficient software process improvement. One of sharing and reusing methods to express such knowledge is to describe the knowledge used in defining software processes as a software pattern.

A process pattern is a software pattern that describes a proven and successful approach for developing software[1]. Several catalogs of patterns regarding

F. Bomarius and S. Komi-Sirviö (Eds.): PROFES 2005, LNCS 3547, pp. 299–313, 2005.

software process are available in public on the World Wide Web (WWW) and in other resources, such as the business process reengineering pattern language[2], the development process generative pattern language[3, 4], and the process improvement patterns[5]. However, all of relations among provided process patterns are closed in each pattern catalog. Therefore, users of available process patterns can just reuse each process pattern in the context defined in each catalog. In other words, users cannot seamlessly reuse two or more process patterns that belong to the different catalogs. Some researchers have claimed that cross-cutting pattern relations over the different catalogs are not useful because the context that each of catalogs assumes might be different[6]; however, there is no experimental evidence for that claim. Therefore, there might be a useful cross-cutting relation, which is not explicitly described in original pattern documents.

The relation analysis among process patterns involves determining the relation among two or more patterns, and obtaining the set of patterns that relates mutually. The purpose of the analysis is to obtain a combination of patterns. A combination of patterns can deal with larger problems than individual patterns can. Moreover, two or more solutions with different constraints might exist for the same problem. Therefore, a variety of patterns giving a solution to a certain problem can exist. In this case, the user/developer should select the best pattern according to the constraints. At this time, the user wants to obtain many patterns that can be applied to the target problem. Therefore, it is important to analyze the relations among patterns.

There are several approaches for analyzing relations among patterns by hand, such as [7] [8] [9]. However, conventional approaches have only used the small number of patterns. There are difficulties in the following activities associated with the manual analysis (i.e. analyzing by hand).

- Analyzing the relations among a large number of patterns.
- Directly comparing patterns in different pattern forms with each other.
- Directly comparing patterns published in different catalogs with each other.

The relation analysis among a large number of patterns by hand is not realistic. An automatic approach that can be applied to a large number of patterns is required; however, to the best of our knowledge, there is no approach for automatic relation analysis. Moreover, none of the conventional manual approaches has been applied to process patterns.

In this paper, we have applied our technique for the automatic pattern relation analysis[10] to several process patterns that are collected manually from WWW, in order to acquire the cross-cutting relations over the different process pattern catalogs. Our analysis technique can treat major pattern forms and various process patterns belonging to different catalogs, by using a common pattern model and several text processing techniques (such as stop-word removal[11], stemming[12], the TF-IDF term weighting method[13], and vector space model[11]).

2 Pattern Documents and Process Patterns

In this section, we introduce several terminologies regarding software patterns, and explain process patterns.

2.1 Pattern Documents and Their Structures

One software pattern consists of the *context, forces*, and *solution*[14]. *Context* refers to the situation and problem that appear repeatedly in each phase of the software development. *Forces* describe constraints that should be considered when the pattern is applied. *Solution* refers to a concrete procedure to solve the corresponding problem.

The *pattern document* is the document in which a pattern is described. The *pattern form* specifies the kind of information described in the pattern document and the structure of the pattern document. Table 1 shows two different pattern forms. The *pattern catalog* is a set of pattern documents which concerns the same area and written in the same format. The *pattern application* is solving the problem in according to the solution.

Table 1. Well known pattern forms

Pattern form	Set of headings
GoF Form [7]	f_{GoF} = { Pattern Name, Classification, Also Known As, Motivation, Applicability, Structure, Particants, Collaborations, Consequences, Implementation, Sample Code, Known Uses, Related Pattern }
PoSA Form [14]	f_{PoSA} = { Name, Also Known As, Examples, Context, Problem, Solution, Structure, Dynamics, Consequences, Implementation, Sample Code, Known Uses, Related Pattern }

In the pattern document, according to the examples of a number of well known pattern forms, the headings and bodies appear alternately. A section is a combination of a heading and a body that appears next to the heading. We denote H as a set of headings, and B as a set of bodies. Then, Section s is defined as follows:

$$s = (h, b), h \in H, b \in B.$$

For a set S of sections, a pattern document d is defined as follows:

$$d = \{s_1, s_2, \ldots, s_n\}, s_1, s_2, \ldots, s_n \in S.$$

For example, Figure 1 is a pattern document which describes the *Command* pattern of the Gang of Four (GoF) 's design patterns[7]. Figure 2 shows the same pattern document in HTML. This pattern document contains six sections, such as *Name, Motivation, Applicability, Collaborations, Consequences,* and *Related Patterns*. The section *Related Patterns* specifies the related patterns, which usually belong to the same catalog as that of the target pattern.

```
Name
    Command
Motivation
    Encapsulate a request as a parameterized object; …
Applicability
    More flexibility on managing an execution sequence, …
Collaborations
    1. Client creates commands as needed, specifying …
Consequences
    Decouples an object from the operations performed …
Related Patterns
    Commands may be assembled using Composite or …
```

Fig. 1. Example of a software pattern document

```
 1:<html><head>
 2:  <title>Command Pattern [GoF]</title>
 3:  </head><body>
 4:    <h1>Command Pattern [GoF]</h1>
 5:    <h2>Name</h2>
 6:    <p>Command</p>
 7:    <h2>Motivation</h2>
 8:    <p>Encapsulate a request as a parameterized …</p>
 9:    <h2>Applicability</h2>
10:    <p>More flexibility on managing an execution…</p>
11:    <h2>Collaborations</h2>
12:    <ol>
13:       <li>Client creates commands as needed, …</li>
14:    </ol>
15:    <h2>Consequences</h2>
16:    <p>Decouples an object from the …</p>
17:    <h2>Related Patterns</h2>
18:    <p>Commands may be assembled using …</p>
19: </body></html>
```

Fig. 2. Example of a software pattern in HTML format

This pattern document follows the GoF form. In the pattern document of Figure 1, the context is described in the section *"Intent"*, the force is described in the section *"Force"*, and the solution is described in the section *"Solution"*. Thus, the kind of information described in a given pattern form is determined by the particular set of headings of that pattern form. Therefore, a pattern form f containing m headings is defined as follows:

$$f = \{h_1, h_2, \ldots, h_m\}, h_1, h_2, \ldots, h_m \in H.$$

2.2   Process Patterns

A process pattern is a software pattern which describes a proven, successful approach and/or series of actions for developing software[1]. Several catalogs of process patterns are available in public on WWW and in other resources, such as the Ambler's process patterns[1, 15], the business process reengineering pattern language[2] and the development process generative pattern language[3, 4].

In [3, 4], 43 process and organization structure patterns underlying successful and highly productive projects describe proven and successful approaches for organizing and managing people involved with the software process. Organizational structure patterns and process patterns go hand in hand and should be used together[1]. These patterns can be used to establish organizational structures and practices that will improve the prospects for success in a new software development organization[4].

In [2], 31 business process patterns captured in hyper-productive and adaptable companies have been described. These patterns can be used to design a new order of organization that relies on the infiltration of software applications and other technologies as an enablers of the core business processes of the organization[2].

For example, Figure 3 is one of process patterns described in [4]. This pattern, named *Size the Schedule*, provide a proven know-how regarding the decision of schedules. Figure 4 is one of organization structure patterns described in [4]. This pattern, named *Conway's Law*, provide a proven know-how regarding the decision of organization structures.

Regarding the available process pattern catalogs, such as [3, 4, 5, 2, 1, 15], all of relations among provided process patterns are closed in each catalog. There-

```
Name
     Size the Schedule
Problem
     How long should the project take?
Context
     The product is understood and the project size has
     been estimated.
Forces
     If you make the schedule too generous, developers
     become complacent, and you miss market windows. ...
Solution
     Reward developers for meeting the schedule, with
     financial bonuses, or with extra time off.
     Keep two sets of schedules: one for the market,
     and one for the developers. ...
```

Fig. 3. Example of a process pattern in [4]

```
Name
    Conway's Law
Problem
    Aligning organization and architecture
Context
    An Architect and development team are in place.
    The architecture is fairly well-established.
Forces
    Architecture shapes the communication paths
    in an organization. ...
Solution
    Make sure the organization is compatible with
    the product architecture. ...
Resulting Context
    The organization and product architecture will
    be aligned.
```

Fig. 4. Example of an organization pattern in [4]

fore, users cannot seamlessly reuse two or more process patterns that belong to the different catalogs. Moreover, users cannot easily compare process patterns provided by different catalogs with each other.

3   Automatic Relation Analysis

In this section, we will briefly explain our technique for the automatic relation analysis among the pattern documents[10].

3.1   Pattern Model

The context obtained by applying a pattern sometimes includes a problem supported by another pattern[14]. Here, we call the context before the pattern application "starting context". Similarly, we also call the context after the pattern application "resulting context". Therefore, we assume that a pattern application is a context transition from a starting context to a resulting context.

In addition, we include a force in the model because two patterns that differ only in terms of forces are considered different patterns. For example, the *Adapter Class* pattern[7] (shown in Figure 5) and the *Adapter Object* pattern[7] (shown in Figure 5) are similar in terms of starting context and resulting context. The starting contexts are similar in terms of mismatched interfaces (mismatch between `Target.request()` and `Adaptee.specificReq()`), and the resulting contexts are similar in terms of adaptation of the interface by interface conversion. However, there are the following differences in terms of force.

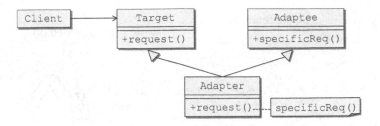

Fig. 5. Structure of *Adapter Class* pattern

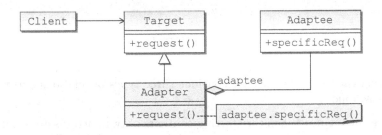

Fig. 6. Structure of *Adapter Object* pattern

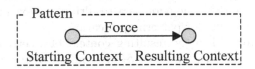

Fig. 7. Our pattern model

- In the *Adapter Class* pattern, combination among classes and reusability of the code increases.
- In the *Adapter Object* pattern, combination among classes and reusability of the code decreases.

We model the pattern with a labeled directed graph that illustrates a flow of the pattern application (Figure 7). The starting node is the starting context, the terminal node is the resulting context, and the label at the edge indicates force.

Formally, for a context set $C = \{c_1, c_2, \ldots, c_n\}$, pattern p is defined as follows:

$$p = (c_i, c_j, \lambda_k), c_i, c_j \in C, i \neq j, \lambda_k \in \Lambda.$$

The graph shown in Figure 8 illustrates a context transition system. We call this graph "Pattern Relation Graph" (PRG). A PRG visualizes the related pattern set. For a context set C, a pattern set P, and a force set Λ, PRG is defined as follows:

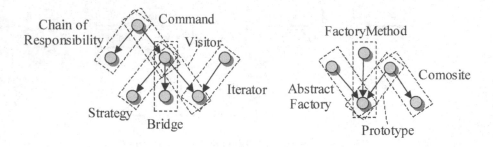

Fig. 8. Example of PRG extracted from Design Patterns[7]

$$PRG = (C, P, \Lambda).$$

If a node in a PRG is shared in multiple edges, it means that multiple patterns are sharing the same context. We consider three types of relations between two patterns as follows:

Starting–Starting: When the starting contexts of two patterns are similar, the two patterns share the same node as a starting context in the PRG. Thus, they provide different solutions to the same problem.
Resulting–Resulting: When the resulting contexts of two patterns are similar, the two patterns share the same node as a resulting context in the PRG. Thus, they provide similar results for pattern application.
Resulting–Starting: When the resulting context of a certain pattern p_1 and the starting context of another pattern p_2 are similar, we can apply p_2 after p_1. The node that is the resulting context of p_1 and the node that is the starting context of p_2 are mapped to the same node in the PRG.

3.2   Analysis Procedure

Figure 9 shows an overview of the analysis procedure in our technique. Many pattern documents that exist on the World Wide Web (WWW) are described using HTML. Therefore, our technique targets pattern documents described with HTML.

The outline of the proposed analysis procedure is as follows. First, the input pattern document is analyzed, and sections are extracted from the document in the *HTML Analysis* block. Next, the form of the input pattern document is judged in the *Pattern Form Judgment* block. Third, the pattern is obtained from the sections according to the judged pattern form in the *Pattern Extraction* block. Finally, the relations between patterns are analyzed in the *Relation Analysis* block.

HTML Document Analysis. In the HTML analysis, an HTML analyzer is used to analyze the structure of the pattern document, and it obtains sections. In the pattern document described with HTML, headings and bodies are often

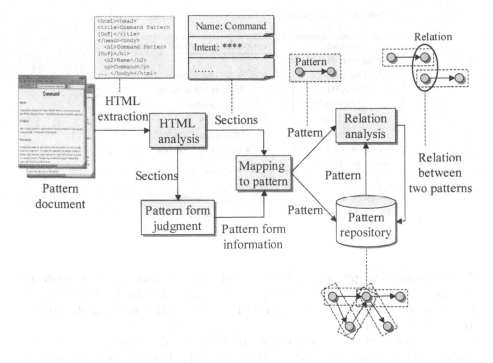

Fig. 9. Overview of analysis procedure

clearly marked up. Then, the document is automatically analyzed by defining the tag set corresponding to the markup policy for the document.

- Tags that mark headings up (for example: <font size="+1">,<h2>)
- Tags that mark bodies up (for example:<p>, <li>, <dt>, and <dd>, etc.)

The HTML analyzer is a finite state machine that has three states: **empty**, **heading**, and **body**. The initial state of the analyzer is *empty* state. The appearance of a specified HTML tag changes the state of the analyzer. In the *heading* state, the analyzer treats an appeared partial document as a heading. Similarly, in the *body* state, the analyzer treats an appeared partial document as a body. In the *empty* state, the analyzer discards an appeared partial document. By the above-mentioned procedures, sections (pairs of a heading and a body) can be extracted from the HTML document.

For example, we specify the <h2> tag for headings and the <li> and <p> tag for bodies, and input the pattern document of Figure 2. First, the analyzer discards from the first to the fourth line. Next, the analyzer goes into the heading state, in the <h2> tag of the fifth line. When the partial document *"Name"* appears, the analyzer treats that as a heading. Then, because the <p> tag appears in the sixth line, the analyzer goes into the *body* state. The analyzer treats the partial document *"Command"* as a body, at the <h2> tag in the sixth line. The analyzer again goes into the *heading* state, and treats the appeared

Table 2. Correspondence between sections and patterns

Section	Corresponding element of pattern
Pattern Name	-
Intention	Starting Context
Motivation	Starting Context
Applicability	Force
Solution	-
Consequences	Resulting Context
Resulting Context	Resulting Context
Related Patterns	-

partial document *"Motivation"* as a heading. The analyzer goes into the body state at the <p> tag in the eighth line. The analyzer treats the partial document of *"Encapsulate a ..."* as a body. Finally, the analyzer obtains six sections.

Pattern form Judgment. Because the extracted sections follow an uncertain pattern form, it is necessary to judge the pattern form. In our technique, we design the measurement that expresses the adaptability between the pattern document and pattern forms.

The pattern form is defined as a set of headings. We define $h(d)$ as a set of headings of the pattern document d. We define $ad(d, f)$ as the form adaptability of d for the pattern form f.

$$ad(f, d) = \frac{|f \cap h(d)|}{|f \cup h(d)|}.$$

To equate the inflected words such as *"Intent"* and *"Intention"*, we perform stemming previously, using the algorithm proposed by Paice [12].

For example, we calculated form adaptability between the Command Pattern document (Figure 2) and each pattern form of Table 1. We obtained the following results: $ad(d_c, f_{PoSA}) = 0.105$ and $ad(d_c, f_{GoF}) = 0.538$. Therefore, this pattern document is most likely to be GoF Form.

Pattern Extraction. The extracted sections are converted into a pattern.

The pattern form specifies the kind of information described in the pattern document. Therefore, each section is mapped to the element of pattern, or discarded. If the correspondences are defined in each pattern form, the pattern can be obtained from the sections.

For example, the section *"Consequences"* in the GoF form corresponds to the resulting context, and the section *"Motivation"* corresponds to the starting context. Correspondence is defined in Table 2.

Analysis of the Relation Between Patterns. To analyze the relations among patterns, we obtain the relations among the partial documents in the pattern. The technique for document similarity analysis is matured. Therefore, we obtain the relation among patterns using the similarity among the partial documents of the patterns.

First, partial documents are taken out of two patterns being analyzed according to the type of relation. Next, the similarity between two partial documents is calculated. We consider that similarity indicates the strength of the relation between two patterns. All of those relations are sorted by the strength of the relations. We consider that the relations higher than a certain specific rank are realistic. We call this rank *threshold*.

The degree of similarity between two partial documents is calculated by using the vector space model of the weighting by the TF-IDF method [13]. We suppose P is a set of patterns which contains N patterns. Then, stemming [12] and stop word removal [11] are applied to the words included in the pattern of P. The list of the words T is obtained because of processing. Because the pattern is a combination of three partial documents, the total number of partial documents is $3N$. Let $ts(s,t)$ denote the frequency of the word $t \in T$ in a partial document s, and $df(t)$ denote the number of partial documents that contain the word t. At this time, the weighting of the word t in the partial document s is defined as follows.

$$w(s,t) = tf(s,t)(\log_2 \frac{3N}{df(t)} + 1).$$

Using the word weight, the document vector is designed as

$$\boldsymbol{tv}(s,T) = (w(s,t_1), w(s,t_2), ..., w(s,t_m)),$$

where $t_1, t_2, \ldots, t_n$ are words in T. Then, we define the similarity between the partial documents s_1 and s_2 as follows.

$$sim(s_1, s_2) = \frac{\boldsymbol{tv}(s_1,T) \cdot \boldsymbol{tv}(s_2,T)}{|\boldsymbol{tv}(s_1,T)||\boldsymbol{tv}(s_2,T)|}.$$

We calculate the similarity of any pair of patterns, and extract the pairs whose similarity is more than pre-designed threshold as related patterns. Then, we let the corresponding nodes share the same node. Finally, we obtain a PRG like that shown in Figure 8.

4   Experiments in Process Patterns

We implemented a system that automatically executes this analysis process, and performed an experimental evaluation for a number of process pattern documents belonging to two catalogs.

As evaluation examples, we used 43 process and organization pattern documents in [16] (same documents in HTML as those in [4]) and 31 business process pattern documents in [17] (same documents in HTML as those in [2]). By calculating the strength of the relation among all of combinations of 74 example documents, we tried to extract cross-cutting relations over the two process pattern catalogs. The strongest relation of three types (Starting–Starting, Resulting–Resulting, and Resulting–Starting) per combination has been assumed as the representative relation.

For the relations extracted in the experiment, Table 3 shows the strength of relation and type of the relation for extracted cross-cutting relations. Described cross-cutting relations are sorted in order from the largest of each relation strength. Regarding the relation type, $S - S$ denotes the pattern p_1's starting context and the pattern p_2's starting context are similar, $R - R$ denotes p_1's resulting context and p_2's resulting context are similar, and, $R - S$ denotes p_1's resulting context and p_2's starting context are similar.

In Table 3, all of cross-cutting relations are not explicitly described in original pattern documents; however, we think many of these relations are valid since both of [16] and [17] deal with enterprise-level organization structures. For example, the obtained result suggests that the context after *Conway's Law*[16] has been applied is similar to that after *Encourage Productive Values* has been applied, although these patterns are different regarding problems that these patterns deal with. This cross-cutting relation is valid because of the following reasons:

– The application of *Encourage Productive Values* will change the values of the target organization from protective to productive. The organizational productive values include the productivity.

Table 3. Extracted crosscutting relations among process patterns (Top 20)

Rank	Pattern p_1	Pattern p_2	Strength	Type
1	Conway's Law	Encourage Productive Values	0.385	$R - R$
2	Conway's Law	Process Team	0.368	$R - S$
3	Model Office	Aesthetic Pattern	0.317	$R - R$
4	Promote On Ability	Domain Expertise in Roles	0.311	$R - R$
5	Case Application	Application Design is Bounded By Test Design	0.295	$R - S$
6	Learning Organization	Organization Follows Market	0.292	$R - S$
7	Compensate Results	Organization Follows Market	0.292	$R - S$
8	Enterprise Architecture	Mercenary Analyst	0.292	$S - S$
9	Learning Organization	Self Selecting Team	0.291	$R - S$
10	Compensate Results	Self Selecting Team	0.291	$R - S$
11	Enterprise Architecture	Application Design is Bounded By Test Design	0.281	$S - S$
12	Aesthetic Pattern	Encourage Productive Values	0.281	$R - R$
13	Enterprise Architecture	Architect Also Implements	0.255	$R - S$
14	Conway's Law	Enterprise Architecture	0.239	$R - S$
15	Business Architect	Conway's Law	0.229	$R - S$
16	Organization Follows Location	Learning Organization	0.227	$R - R$
17	Organization Follows Location	Compensate Results	0.227	$R - R$
18	Divide and Conquer	Vision Statement	0.227	$S - S$
19	Aesthetic Pattern	Promote On Ability	0.227	$R - S$
20	Minimal Reconciliation	Mercenary Analyst	0.227	$S - S$

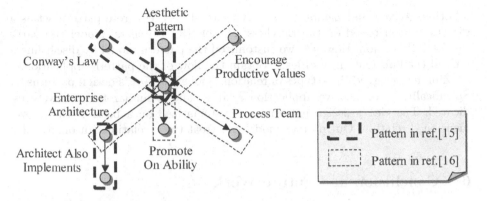

Fig. 10. PRG extracted from process/organization structure patterns belonging to different catalogs

- The application of *Conway's Law* will improve the target organization's productivity according to architectures of developing products.

Figure 10 shows the obtained PRG, which visualizes a part of results shown in Table 3. The obtained PRG suggests several useful cross-cutting relations, which are not explicitly noticed in original pattern documents. For example:

- After *Conway's Law* has been applied, each of three patterns (*Enterprise Architecture*, *Promote On Ability*, or *Process Team*) can be applied continuously. Users of our system can easily compare these three patterns by seeing forces described in each pattern document, and select one of these patterns. Such pattern combination deals with larger problems than those dealt with by individual process patterns.
- *Conway's Law*, *Aesthetic Pattern*, and *Encourage Productive Value* derive similar application results.

These cross-cutting relations will be useful for dealing with larger problems than those dealt with by individual process patterns by reusing two or more process patterns that belong to the different catalogs. Moreover, users of our system can easily compare process patterns belonging to different catalogs by observing the obtained PRG such as Figure 10.

5   Related Work

Ong et al. designed the relations among forces, such as *"Helps"*, *"Hurts"*[8]. They attempted to systematize patterns based on the relations between forces. Our technique can treat those relations automatically.

Borchers modeled a pattern as a list of sections[18]. This is common with our technique in that we design the pattern as a combination of sections. In addition, Acosta and Zambrano are trying to show a concrete pattern set as a directed graph based on the Borchers' model [19]. Borchers' model can carry precise information. However, we customized the pattern model by discarding a part of the information in order to obtain the flow of the pattern application.

Zimmer designed three types of relation among the GoF's design patterns[9]. Specifically, a consecutive application relation and a similar relation were indicated. The GoF's design patterns are systematized on a basis of the above-mentioned relation. Our pattern model can treat these relations automatically.

6 Conclusion and Future Work

We have applied the automatic pattern relation analysis to several process patterns to acquire the cross-cutting relations over the different process pattern catalogs. As a result of experiments, we succeeded in the analysis of the appropriate cross-cutting relations among process patterns without using explicit information in the pattern document. The system that implements our technique can suggest the relations that original pattern authors have not noticed. Using our system, users can seamlessly reuse two or more process patterns that belong to the different catalogs. Moreover, users can easily compare process patterns provided by different catalogs with each other. Our technique is expected to contribute the activity of retrieving process patterns. By using the results of analysis as a process pattern repository, a system of highly accurate retrieval for process patterns can be developed.

In the future, we have a plan to improve the precision of our system by applying natural-language processing technology in the future. Moreover, we will conduct large-scale experiments for evaluating usability of our relation analysis technique under a real process improvement activity.

References

1. Scott W. Ambler. Process Patterns: Building Large-Scale Systems Using Object Technology. Cambridge University Press, 1998.
2. Michael Beedle. Pattern Based Reengineering. Object Magazine, January 1997.
3. James O. Coplien. A Development Process Generative Pattern Language. Pattern Languages of Program Design, Vol. 1, pp. 183–237, Addison-Wesley, 1995.
4. James O. Coplien. A Generative Development Process Pattern Language. In Linda Rising. The Patterns Handbook: Techniques, Strategies, and Applications, pp. 243-300, Cambridge University Press, 1998.
5. Brad Appleton. Patterns for Conducting Process Improvement. Proc. 4th Conference on Pattern Languages of Programs (PLoP'97), 1997.
6. Tiffany Winn and Paul Calder: Is This a Pattern?, IEEE Software, Vol. 19, No. 1, pp. 59–66, 2002.
7. Erich Gamma, Richard Helm, Ralph Johnson, and John Vlissides. Design Patterns: Elements of Reusable Object-Oriented Software. Addison-Wesley, 1994.

8. Han-Yuen Ong, Michael Weiss, and Ivan Araujo. Rewriting a Pattern Language to Make it More Expressive. Proc. 6th Southwestern Conference on Pattern Languages of Programs (ChiliPLoP2003), 2003.
9. Walter Zimmer. Relationships between Design Patterns. In Pattern Languages of Program Design, Vol.1, Addison-Wesley, pp. 345–364, 1995.
10. Atsuto Kubo, Hironori Washizaki, Atsuhiro Takasu, and Yoshiaki Fukazawa. Analyzing Relations among Software Patterns based on Document Similarity, Proc. IEEE International Conference on Information Technology: Coding and Computing (ITCC2005), 2005 (to appear).
11. Gerard Salton, and Michael J. McGill. Introduction to Modern Information Retrival. McGraw-Hill, Inc., 1983.
12. Chris D. Paice. Another Stemmer, SIGIR Forum, Vol. 24, No. 3, pp. 56–61, 1990.
13. G. Salton, and C. S. Yang. On the Specification of Term Values in Automatic Indexing. Journal of Documenatation, Vol. 29, pp. 351–372, 1973.
14. Frank Buschmann, Regine Meunier, Hans Rohnert, Peter Sommerlad, and Michael Stal. Pattern Oriented Software Architecture: A System of Patterns. Wiley, 1998.
15. Scott W. Ambler. More Process Patterns: Delivering Large-Scale Systems Using Object Technology. Cambridge University Press, 1999.
16. http://www.bell-labs.com/user/cope/Patterns/Process/
17. http://www.easycomp.org/cgi-bin/OrgPatterns?BPRPatternLanguage
18. Jan O. Borchers. A Pattern Approach to Interaction Design. AI & Society Journal of Human-Centred Systems and Machine Intelligence, Vol. 15, No. 4, pp. 359–376, 2001.
19. Alecia E. Acosta, and Nancy Zambrano. Patterns and Objects for User Interface Construction. Journal of Object Technology, Vol. 3, No. 3, pp. 75–90, 2004.

Tailoring RUP to a Defined Project Type: A Case Study

Geir K. Hanssen[1], Hans Westerheim[1], and Finn Olav Bjørnson[2]

[1] SINTEF ICT, N-7465 Trondheim, Norway
{geir.k.hanssen, hans.westerheim}@sintef.no
[2] NTNU, N-7491 Trondheim, Norway
finn.olav.bjornson@idi.ntnu.no

Abstract. The Unified Process is a widely used process framework for software development. The framework is covering many of the roles, activities and artifacts needed in a software development project. However, a tailoring of the framework is necessary to fit specific needs. This tailoring may be accomplished in various ways. In this paper we describe a concrete attempt to tailor the Rational Unified Process to a defined project type; a Mainstream Software Development Project Type. The paper has focus on the process of creating the tailored Rational Unified Process as well as the resulting Rational Unified Process. The paper makes some conclusions and has a proposition for further research.

1 Introduction

The Unified Process [1] and the commercial variant, the Rational Unified Process, RUP [2] are comprehensive process frameworks for software development projects. RUP defines a software development project as a set of disciplines, e.g. requirements handling, implementation etc., running from start to end trough a set of project phases. A project is performed by a group of actors, each having one or more well defined roles. Each role participates in one or more activities producing one or more artifacts. A discipline can run in iterations, that is, repetitions within a phase. Activities, roles and artifacts are the basic process elements of RUP.

However, RUP is a comprehensive framework, meaning that it is a more or less complete set of process elements that has to be tailored to each case as no project needs the complete set of elements.

Jacobson, Booch and Rumbaugh says in [1] p.416:

"It [RUP] is a framework. It has to be tailored to a number of variables: the size of the system in work, the domain in which that system is to function, the complexity of the system and the experience, skill or process level of the project organization and its people." Further on they say: *"Actually, to apply it, you need considerable further information."*

So, it is clear that RUP needs to be tailored, downscaled and specialized to the context of use. Looking at literature there are not many guidelines on doing this [3], [4], [5] although the need for good practical guidelines and advice definitively is present.

F. Bomarius and S. Komi-Sirviö (Eds.): PROFES 2005, LNCS 3547, pp. 314–327, 2005.

While discussing adaptation of RUP, it is important to have in mind that RUP is a methodology suited for some software development projects, not all. Before you consider using RUP as a basis for your processes you should think of what you really need and what you really do not need. RUP is designed to support four basic properties of software projects: use-case based customer dialogue and documentation, an architecture focus, iterative processes and incremental product development. The idea of adapting RUP is to make it fit each specific project not loosing these properties. It is important to keep the integrity of RUP as a framework. So, an adapted or downscaled variant still defines a project in terms of phases and still describes the work as a complimentary set of disciplines. However, some disciplines may be omitted or even added.

The goal of this paper is to provide others considering remodeling and adapting a process framework in general, and RUP particularly, an insight in how this has been done in a small software company. Some aspects of the specialization process seems to have been working well, others not. This paper presents the adaptation process and also gives an analysis of this process and its result.

The work detailed in this article was carried out as part of a national research project in process improvement and software quality called SPIKE. SPIKE is short for Software Process Improvement through Knowledge and Experience. The participants are SINTEF, NTNU, the University of Oslo and several partners (companies) in the Norwegian ICT-industry. The industrial partners are interested in improving their development process, and are seeking concrete processes and methods to help them deliver high quality software with shorter time to market.

The paper starts with a **Theoretical context**, giving a brief introduction to methodologies and frameworks and various strategies of making these fit specific project needs of process support. It then describes the action research as the **Research method** of choice. The rest of the paper is arranged according to the research method phases; **Diagnosing**, **Action planning**, **Action taking**, **Evaluating** and **Learning**. Finally a **Conclusion** is given and **Further research** suggested.

2 Theoretical Context

2.1 Software Development Methodology and Frameworks

The term methodology is defined as "A body of methods, rules, and postulates employed by a discipline: a particular procedure or set of procedures" by the Merriam-Webster dictionary [6]. Basically, a methodology describes how someone, e.g. an organization performs a task, e.g. software development. In a broad sense, a software development methodology describes aspects such as how to communicate with customers, sales strategy, how to describe requirements, use of tools, test practices, documentation, planning, reporting and so on. In our context we talk about methodologies for running projects with a defined customer having more or less defined goals initially. Besides describing techniques, roles etc. most methodologies are based on a set of basic values. Examples are *User centric, Architecture centric, Agile, Risk driven* and many more. RUP has four basic values: *Use-Case Driven,*

Architecture-Centric, Iterative and *Incremental.* These values should be retained regardless of how RUP as a framework is adapted. A methodology framework is a comprehensive description of a methodology describing approximately all possible details of almost all possible processes within the scope of the framework. This means that a framework is not a description of a specific case; it is a foundation for adaptation. The challenge is how to adapt it to each case (project) and keep the basic values and features of the framework.

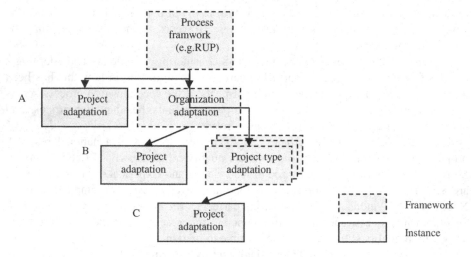

Fig. 1. Three possible approaches for adaptation

2.2 Adaptation of RUP

The process of adapting RUP can possibly take many forms. IBM Rational, the provider of RUP has defined the *Process Engineering Process (PEP)* [5]. This is a comprehensive adaptation process requiring a fairly big amount of resources (people and time). This may very well be appropriate for larger companies, but for the small ones this process may be too expensive.

Adaptation of a framework, such as RUP, can take one of (at least) three approaches; see Fig. 1. The starting point is a process framework that is general and complete with respect to tasks, roles and products. In approach A, the framework is adapted, in one step, for each project, thus representing a heavy job in each case. This can be justified for large projects where the initial adaptation process itself becomes only a small part of the total amount of work being done in the project. In approach B, the organization does an up-front adaptation producing a subset of the framework, still being a framework, but now tuned to the organizations general characteristics. This is the intentional process of PEP. In approach C, the organization first identifies and describes a set of recurring project *types*. Having knowledge of characteristics and differences of these types, an adaptation is done for each type.

No matter which approach being used; in the last step, a final adaptation is done to each case (project). The agility of this final fine tuning increases with respect to the extent of the up-front adaptation.

This is a general view of methodological adaptation or down-scaling. It applies to many types of process frameworks, including RUP. Further on, adapting RUP in practice means to decide on which process elements to keep, remove, alter or add. These decisions can be based on assumptions, experience, goals and visions. It is the quality of this underlying knowledge and experience that determines how good these decisions are.

Running an adaptation process, in general, can be seen as a knowledge management activity as experience and knowledge, both tacit and explicit, is being structured, documented and communicated trough the resulting software process description [7].

3   Research Method

Due to the cooperative nature of this research project with company external researchers acting partly as consultants and partly as researchers, we decided to adopt action research as our approach. Avison et.al. [8] describes action research as: "unique in the way it associates research and practice. ... Action research combines theory and practice through change and reflection in an immediate problematic situation within a mutually acceptable ethical framework."

Susman and Evered [9] described an approach to action research that is widely used today. We have adopted elements from this approach in our research project. The approach requires the establishment of a client-system infrastructure or research environment. In our case this was already taken care of through the researchers and company's involvement in the SPIKE research program. The approach further specifies five identifiable phases, which are iterated: *diagnosing, action planning, action taking, evaluating* and *specifying learning*. This report details some of our findings and experiences from the initial phases. Our coverage of the evaluating and learning phases are based on our own observations of the process so far. A more thorough evaluation will be carried out as the company takes the resulting process description into use in real projects.

In the diagnosing phase, we used semi structured interviews and workshops with key employees. We interviewed five employees concerning their general experience with projects in the company. This gave us the material to do a more focused interview with five other employees concerning their specific experience with RUP in the company. In addition to this, several work-meetings were held with the management of the company where the SPI approach was discussed.

In the action planning phase, the researchers made a literature survey of the field of adapting RUP. It was decided to identify possible project types run by the company. This was done during two iterations, the first one a bottom-up approach, the second one a top-down approach. The top-down approach led to definition of three project types. In order to adapt the first project type, it was decided that the researchers should facilitate a workshop where key employees were invited to define the adapted process.

The workshop was carried out as part of the action taking phase. It was carried out over two days, since it was discovered that we needed more time than originally planned. At the first day we noted that the lack of a RUP mentor slowed the process considerably due to a lot of discussion on what was actually meant by the different concepts. At the second day, one such mentor was present, and the process was much more fluent. The result from the workshop was a coarse RUP skeleton, which was given to the company for more refinement. The company has conducted two internal workshops with its employees to refine the process. In addition they have initiated a project to put this information on a Wiki web, in order to make the adapted process available to all employees.

As the project moves into the evaluation phase, the role of the scientists switches to a more observational role. We plan on following the use of the adapted process for several development projects. By taking measures along the way we hope to be able to ascertain how successful the initiative has been for the company in its current context.

4   Research Context

The company described in this case is today a Norwegian software consultancy company with 50 employees, located in two different geographic offices. During the work described in this paper the company was declared bankrupt, and then restarted with new owners. The first part of the action planning and action taking described in this paper took place before the bankruptcy. The first attempt to identify project types was done, using a bottom-up approach. Just before the bankruptcy this approach was evaluated and the company and the researchers decided that this approach did not work. The company then had about 70 employees.

When the company was restarted, the researchers continued to the work mainly together with the other office, but the focus was still the same, and the most actual people from the company did not change. The company is mainly developing software systems with heavy back-end logic and often with a web front-end, typically portals. However, they also develop lighter solutions with most emphasis on the front-end.

The company acts as an independent software supplier, though there are close relationships to the biggest customers. Of the 50 employees today, 35 are working as software developers. Java and J2EE are used as development platform. The domain of which the company develops software is mainly for the banking and finance sector, as well as for public sector. The company has run 50 development projects within the bank and finance sector the last twelve years, and about 30-40 projects within the public sector the last 15 years.

Four employees are certified RUP-mentors acting as advisors in other SW-organizations, in addition to this they run training courses in RUP and related subjects. The company utilizes their high competence in RUP and most projects are more or less inspired by RUP, however, the company's management has seen a need and a possibility to improve their use of RUP.

5 Diagnosing

The decision to initiate a project-type specific adaptation process was made by the company when SPIKE started.

The diagnosing phase was initiated by a few workshops where an internal software development process group defined the strategy in cooperation with the authors. With the past experience in mind they decided to go for a top-down approach, starting out with the complete RUP set of process elements and then customize this set to a set of defined project types. This decision was supported by the findings in two rounds of interviews in the company.

This phase of the work was conducted mainly by three different motivations:

1. The researchers needed more insight into the company, the development organization of the company, as well as the most recent software development projects conducted by the company.
2. The company needed to be more conscious about its own use of RUP; these interviews were means in that respect.
3. The use of RUP in the company needed to be documented as a basis for further work; this includes the overall use, but also strengths and weaknesses by the use, in the view of people working in projects in the company.

Interview 1: General Experiences from Project Work
5 employees having various project experiences were interviewed. The roles of these persons were developer/systems architect, project leader/manager, project leader, senior developer and developer/architect/DBA.

The intention of this group of interviews was to get a perception of common problems and challenges in development projects to establish a basis for process improvement initiatives in the company.

The interviews revealed that the customer dialogue could be better (requirements handling and project planning). The reuse of templates could be better. It is too much documentation formalism. Estimates often fail and there is a need of better change management.

Interview 2: Special Experiences with RUP
Another group of 5 employees was interviewed to get a view of their experience using RUP. The role of these persons was developer, developer/project leader, developer/project leader/test leader, project leader/requirements responsible, and customer contact.

All of the five had some knowledge and experience with RUP, some had participated on internal courses, and some had read literature. However, none had thorough knowledge and experience. About the practical use, it seemed that RUP was used just to a small extent, it depended on the type of project. The reason for this may be superficial knowledge of RUP and that some felt that RUP does not fit their needs.

These two iterations of interviews gave no clear answer, however they indicate that RUP and the use of it can be improved. The summary from the interviews was used to decide to initiate an adaptation process as described in this paper.

6 Action Planning

Projects conducted by the company varied with respect to domain, degree of experimentation, technology, contract form etc. In addition, most projects were too small to initiate a project-specific specialization (ref Figure 1, approach A). However, it seemed that this company usually ran a few similar types of projects. This lead to the idea to define a set of processes fitting each type of project. The idea is that this will reduce the need of a costly up-front specialization per project and also avoid an expensive per-project adaptation. Based on this realization the company decided to try out approach C in figure 1 in cooperation with the authors. The company would define a set of project types which covered most of their projects and define a downscaled RUP to each project type.

To define a set of project types we decided to hold a workshop to identify the company's three main project types based on a top down approach. The reason for selecting the top down approach was the company's previous failure to define project types based on a bottom up approach. The participants of the workshop consisted of people from the company with a complimentary and thorough knowledge of the company's software development projects, some of them were also RUP mentors. It was also decided that the participants should come up with a classification system to describe and distinguish the three project types.

Given the three distinct project types, the challenge was how to adapt RUP to each project type. There seemed to be wide agreement that adapting RUP was necessary, yet little information was available on how to actually carry out this adaptation process. What little information was available consisted of rather complex and expensive methods. Instead of using any of these methods we decided to go for a simpler and pragmatic approach. It was decided that the researchers should facilitate a workshop where key employees were invited to define the adapted process. The structure of the workshop was planned by the researchers based on their experience and input from the literature, and the participants were selected by the company based on their experience with different disciplines.

After this workshop the material was left to the company to refine and document with little input from the researchers.

7 Action Taking

The RUP adaptation itself was separated in four main phases:

    A. Defining the project types
    B. The definition of the mainstream project type

C. Maturing the downsized RUP
D. The initial documentation of the mainstream project activities

A: Defining the Project Types

We conducted a workshop where five participants from the company, representing a group with a complimentary and thorough knowledge of software development projects in general and RUP in special (some of them RUP mentors), were allowed to define three to four common types of projects. To be able to distinguish and describe the project types we defined a simple classification system. During a series of workshops a group representing all project roles identified a set of project capabilities to be used to describe the project types. A project capability, in this context, is a feature or a characteristic that is general to all projects but where the size or weight does vary. We identified 13 characteristics; business critically for the customer, technology knowledge, access to resources, risk, test environment, size, degree of reuse, contract form, project team, exposure, customer orientation, system integration and scope.

The three selected types of projects were Mainstream Projects, Push-button Projects and Greenfield Projects. Here presented with a few characteristics:

Mainstream projects	Push-button projects	Greenfield projects
- integration with other systems are important - the technology are well known - the size are initially unclear - the risk is moderate	- the technology is well known - low-risk project - well defined project size - often a fixed price project	- need of extensive research and innovation - the size are initially unclear - high risk project - newer fixed price

B: The Definition of the Mainstream Project Type

We selected the mainstream project type since this was the most important type for the company with respect to earning. The two other project types will be handled later.

Originally we envisaged a workshop to define a list of RUP elements necessary for the different disciplines and phases. The result from this would be a list that needed some refinement and quality assurance before it could be documented and put into use in a project. The method we ended up with was not far from this. It consisted of two days where the focus was defined by RUP elements viewed from the point of view of either the RUP phases or the RUP disciplines.

On the first day we gathered a group of employees with relevant experience from mainstream projects, meaning people that have both the theoretical and practical knowledge of RUP from projects as well as experience relevant to the defined project type. We tried to ensure that all the disciplines of RUP should be covered by the experience of the workshop participants. The process of the initial workshop was as follow:

1) The workshop facilitators (the researchers) explained the defined project type for the group and this was discussed. This was done to establish a common mindset for the rest of the work.

2) We used a whiteboard with a vertical lane for each RUP-phase (inception – elaboration – implementation – transition) to document opinions of what was especially important for each phase (based on practical experience). The workshop facilitators asked questions such as: *What is usually a challenge in this type of project? What type of methodology support do you need? What has used to work well?* All this to sharpen the focus of what is important for the project type and how a defined process can support it.

3) The workshop facilitators displayed a list of all RUP process elements using a video projector. A process element was a defined role, artifact or activity. The elements were ordered per RUP discipline. Starting at the top the group made decisions for each element whether to keep, remove or alter the element. The two previous steps was used as basis for taking decisions and was referred to during the selection process. However, this turned out to be a circumstantial process. The group and the workshop leaders agreed to only focus on *artifacts*, thus speeding up the process to a practical level. When an artifact was removed, this implicitly also indicated how roles and activities should be affected. An example of a artifact that was decided to be deselected is 'Capsule'. The RUP documentation explains that this is an artifact *"Used only for the design of real-time or reactive systems.."*, thus not relevant for the Mainstream project type described and discussed in step 1.

Step 3 was not finished by the end of the first day. One of the main reasons for this was that there was no RUP mentor present. Subsequently there was a lot of argument over what the different RUP concepts actually meant, and a lot of the time was spent searching for information. Another reason was that we initially tried to define artifacts, roles and activities; this took up a lot of time, thus it was decided to just focus on artifacts. Since the list was not finished at the end of the day, it was decided to spend a second day to finish the work. In the second day we only focused on artifacts and the company provided us with a RUP mentor. This time the process worked more fluently and we were able to finish the list of adapted RUP elements to mainstream projects.

C: Maturing the Downsized RUP

Due to the composition of the members of the workshop, some disciplines were better covered than others. This sparked some discussion in the company on how to proceed. They found it necessary to involve more people to increase the information on certain disciplines, and it was decided that to increase the usefulness of the process it was necessary to run more iterations to gather experience from all the disciplines.

Having compiled the list of process elements the company continued the process by involving more of the employees. This to incorporate more relevant experiences and, not at least, to establish a common ownership. The focus turned from selecting/deselecting process elements at a very low level to focusing on best practices, in this case meaning to focus on vital project activities. Their next step was to define critical activities for each phase of RUP. This was done in a separate internal workshop. For each phase they held a discussion on what the critical activities were. When they agreed on an activity they found a descriptive name for it and proceeded to answer two questions: 1) What is accomplished by performing this activity? And 2) What is the risk of not performing this activity, or not performing it properly?

The name of the activity and the answer to the two questions was written on a piece of paper and post-it notes and put on a large paper that covered the wall. There was one such paper for each phase.

D: The Initial Documentation of the Mainstream Project Activities

Having specialized RUP, or any other process for that matter, does not complete the job. The result must be brought out to the frontline people – the project leaders, the developers, the architects and so on. They must have the information at their fingertips in the actual situation of use in a form that makes them want to use it. There is a variety of practical ways of communication this information, from simple documents, to simple web-pages, to comprehensive hypertext documentation. Rational offers an electronic process guide that documents RUP in detail (RUP Online). This is a knowledge base with a web interface that describes roles, activities and artifacts (and templates for these – all arranged within the phases and disciplines of RUP. However, RUP online is comprehensive and may be more confusing than helpful to project members in need of specific project support. Any documentation of the process must reflect the modifications resulting from the specialization process.

Instead of using the tools from Rational, the company decided to establish a simple Wiki-web [10] with just-enough information and functionality to get the message out. This web does not resemble to the RUP-online documentation which holds a well of details. This Wiki can be seen as a common electronic whiteboard, where all users have more or less full access to the information and the rights to update it.. This Wiki Web is a company internal web-site that in simple terms describes the outcome of the workshops and the company internal process work. It explains the characteristics of the project type(s) so that the user can evaluate how well the variant suits the actual project and can also be used as a checklist to plan the project. The simple process documentation on the Wiki Web references RUP Online (web link) to lead the user to helpful descriptions and templates. A Wiki-Web also allows the users to add information thus being a dynamic process repository. One idea (not yet tested) is to store project experiences together with the process descriptions to offer later projects an insight into specific and relevant experience.

The Resulting Process Description

The resulting process documentation, presented trough the Wiki-web, is much simpler than we initially would think. It is more a guide into RUP than an independent complete process guide.

The process definition of the Mainstream type of projects is simply a list of critical activities where each activity is defined by 1) a title stating the purpose of the activity,

2) a short description, 3) the context of the activity, 4) reasons for why this is an important activity for this project type, 5) risks by omitting the activity, 6) a checklist for completion of the activity and 7) recommended problem solving approach. All these seven parts are presented on one page.

These activities are arranged with respect to the standard phases of RUP and also has some links to relevant information in RUP Online, e.g. to templates etc. This simple description is intentionally on a high level, omitting most of the details of RUP. The Wiki-web offers this information to all project members via the intranet. A separate area is created for each project where the project members document their best practices, templates used, comments to the process. In general, this is an experience reporting tool that communicates practical experiences for a given project type to others.

The case company has constituted a process group that continuously updates and refines the content of the Wiki based on real experiences being reported on the Wiki.

8 Evaluating

The company did from the beginning focus on project types. During the work described here, two different approaches were tried in order to define different types of projects. The bottom-up approach was tried first, and then the top-down approach. The bottom-up approach did not succeed as it became too complex to document a big amount of project experiences and identify a few common variants of RUP. During the workshops where this approach was tried, it was clear that the participants felt that the project types in some ways were defined already, but not given. The company had an informal definition of project types, not named ones, but with some consensus among the developers what these types were. In the workshops we tried to keep the entire focus on the characteristics of the project types, and the participants were not "allowed" to state types of projects. This approach clearly made the participants frustrated, and the approach did not bring up any defined project types based on the defined characteristics.

We did succeed with a top-down approach to defining a set of project types – starting by loosely naming typical types and then describe typical aspects trough a workshop. The participants were told to name three project types in the beginning, and this strict introduction seems to have helped the participants to reflect over what is really separating the different types of projects there were working on. The three types were relatively easy to identify and name. During the work these initial types were kept, and the belief that these were the important types grew. Even though the initial try with focus on project characteristics did not succeed, this attempt kept the focus on project characteristics during the whole work described here, and the participants were more conscious about what is a project type than the case might have been without the first try. The researchers therefore would like to recommend trying to keep focus on different aspects and characteristics of software projects.

During the work the focus has been on one type of projects only. The company did pick the type of project which was most important with respect to earnings and risk control, and the first attempt to tailor RUP was for this single type only. This focus seems to have been an important factor when it comes to the ability to tailor RUP. Having a common, well defined, mindset makes the decisions easier and the result simpler and more focused.

In this case study, a discussion of which tool to use for the documentation and deployment of the tailored RUP was postponed to a moment when the discussion about the content of the tailored RUP was in place. Adapting and documenting RUP or any other methodological framework is not done solely using a tool. The most crucial part of such a job is to involve a broad group of people having through experience with both the framework and – not at least – practical project work. The work in this case supports this presumption.

Employees in this company have knowledge of RUP above the average of what we have seen in analogous software development organizations in Norway. The work in the company shows that it is important to have a tailoring process that must be based on experience; it can be seen as a knowledge management, and documentation, process. Despite the company's knowledge of RUP, running such a process has not been easy and straight forward at all. The strategy has changed during the course of work based on new insights and achieved results (or lack of such).

9 Learning

Our motivation intentionally was to work together with the case company to adapt the RUP. We decided to try to keep it as simple and inexpensive as possible. The two authors that participated actively in the start worked with a small group from the company, thus reducing the total time spent. We also tried to use RUP as a heavy foundation by accepting the general characteristics of the method, such as the phases and the disciplines and go straight to the low-level details; the process elements. But this did not seem to be the best way. The process did become simpler and simpler as the work progressed. This helped the involved people keeping focus on what's most important; what type of process support is really needed in the projects based on experience. When starting out we intentionally did not take a standpoint with respect to *how* to document and disseminate the resulting process description. We looked into the suite of tools offered by Rational, but regardless of the rich features in those tools the company ended up with a very simple form of tool support for documentation and communication of the result, the Wiki web. In general it seems that the adaptation is best done as a simple, pragmatic process not as a heavily up-front planned and strictly managed process. It seems that the good old KISS-strategy once again have proven its superiority; Keep It Simple Stupid.

Some Specific Experiences from the Tailoring Workshops

Having good knowledge and experience is important to ensure sound decisions on how to adapt RUP. This however presupposes that such experience is available within the organization, which was the case in the project that this paper is based on. If the overall knowledge of RUP is weak the group can be strengthened by hiring a RUP-mentor. The mentor is a certified expert that will be in position to answer questions and explain details of RUP.

Having a group working through the three steps of the initial workshop should take about one working day, given that the workshop leaders have prepared the work, the focus is on artifacts from a discipline point of view, and that there is a RUP mentor present to explain any uncertainties. To ensure a good result it is vital to include people with experience from all the disciplines of RUP.

Do not try to gather too much information in one single workshop. Concentrate on one issue at a time.

It is important to be patient; the outcome of the initial workshops was nothing but an altered list of RUP process elements. This list has to be matured and quality assured before it can be documented and put into use in projects.

10 Conclusion

We have presented a simple pragmatic method for adapting the RUP to a specific project type in a company. The method involves a series of workshops in which the key success factor seems to have been focus. Focus both through a specific project type, specific process elements and through phases or disciplines. Another key success factor is that a workshop consists of persons with the proper experience with regards to the focus.

The focus on a specific project type seems to have kept the participants on track throughout the adaptation process. It seems to have eased the process since everyone had a clear concept of what should be done in that particular project type. However, the benefits from making a project type adaptation as compared to making a project- or a company specific adaptation have yet to be evaluated.

The adaptation method has been a success in that the company has come up with a simple process for their most common project type, which has been made available for all employees. Whether this process becomes a success will be determined through further studies of the actual use patterns.

Further Research

Adoption of RUP: Figure 1 shows some possible ways of tailoring RUP at different levels in a software developing organization. In this case study we have been following an organization which chose the project type adoption.

It is of interest to also follow more closely organizations selecting an organizational adoption, or a project adoption. The success and failure criteria in each case should be compared and analyzed.

Experiences from use of tailored RUP: In this case we did follow the process of tailoring and partly, documenting, a project type tailored RUP. We cannot say for sure if the tailoring has been successful until we have empirical results from the use of the tailored RUP. The next step in the research together with this company will be to collect experiences from the use of this instance of RUP.

Metrics: What kind of metrics should be applied when we are interested to measure the process of tailoring RUP in different organizations, and done in different ways? What kind of metrics should be applied when we try to evaluate the success of the use of the tailored RUP in different types of projects in different organizations? How to apply metrics when it comes to measure a software process is still an uncovered aspect of software process improvement, and we think that an association to a single process framework, like RUP, may ease the process of defining and validating metrics for software processes.

References

1. Jacobson, I., G. Booch, and J. Rumbaugh, *The Unified Software Development Process*, ed. A.W. Longman. 1999, Reading: Addison Wesley Longman. 463.
2. Krutchen, P., *The Rational Unified Process: An Introduction*. 2nd ed. 2000: Addison-Wesley. 298.
3. Bergström, S., Råberg, L., *Adopting the Rational Unified Process*. 2004, Addison-Wesley. p. 165-182.
4. Karlsson, F., P.J. Ågerfalk, and A. Hjalmarsson. *Method Configuration with Development Tracks and Generic Project Types.* in *CAiSE/IFIP8.1 International Workshop in Evaluation of Modeling Methods in Systems Analysis and Design.* 2001. Interlaken, Switzerland.
5. http://www-1.ibm.com/support/docview.wss?uid=swg21158199
6. http://www.m-w.com/dictionary.htm
7. Nonaka, I., Takeuchi, H., *The Knowledge-Creating Company*. 1995: Oxford University Press.
8. Avison, D., *Action Research*. Communications of the ACM, 1999. **42**(1): p. 94-97.
9. Susman, G., Evered, R., *An assessment of the scientific merits of action research.* Administrative Science, 1978. **23**(4): p. 582-603.
10. http://www.atlassian.com/

Acquisition of a Project-Specific Process

Olga Jaufman[1] and Jürgen Münch[2]

[1] DaimlerChrysler AG, 89081 Ulm, Germany
Olga.Jaufman@daimlerchrysler.com
[2] Fraunhofer Institute for Experimental Software Engineering (IESE),
Sauerwiesen 6, 67661 Kaiserslautern, Germany
Juergen.Muench@iese.fraunhofer.de

Abstract. Currently, proposed development processes are often considered too generic for operational use. This often leads to a misunderstanding of the project-specific processes and its refuse. One reason for non-appropriate project-specific processes is insufficient support for the tailoring of generic processes to project characteristics and context constraints. To tackle this problem, we propose a method for the acquisition of a project-specific process. This method uses a domain-specific process line for top-down process tailoring and supports bottom-up refinement of the defined generic process based on tracking process activities. The expected advantage of the method is tailoring efficiency gained by usage of a process line and higher process adherence gained by bottom-up adaptation of the process. The work described was conducted in the automotive domain. This article presents an overview of the so-called Emergent Process Acquisition method (EPAc) and sketches an initial validation study.

1 Introduction

Nowadays, automotive products are becoming more and more complex. In order to ensure the quality of safety critical products like vehicles, effective and efficient development processes are needed. As projects have different contexts and goals, tailoring methods are needed that allow adapting the generic processes to the project-specific needs. The tailoring approaches used in practice (e.g., the tailoring approach proposed by the V model [10]) usually involve checking conditions and removing objects of the base model. The V model distinguishes between tailoring at the start of a project and tailoring in the course of the project at defined points in time. One difficulty of such tailoring is the identification of the regression process modification to be performed. For example, a change of four product artifacts can result in further changes of 26 process models [12]. Further, more process tailoring often requires not only the removal of process objects, but also their replacement, or the addition of new objects. The V model tailoring method does not define how to deal with such kinds of process modifications.

To tackle the problem, different tailoring approaches are proposed in the literature. These tailoring approaches can be classified into two types [12]: component-based approaches and generator approaches. The component-based approaches try to build a

F. Bomarius and S. Komi-Sirviö (Eds.): PROFES 2005, LNCS 3547, pp. 328–342, 2005.

project-specific process based on the process parts. The generator approaches try to build a project-specific process by instantiating a typical process architecture. The advantage of component-based approaches is the ability to support reuse of process fragments (e.g., processes gained by descriptive process modeling). The main deficiency of component-based approaches is the lack of support for process adaptation and for guaranteeing consistency. The advantage of generic approaches is their ability to assure consistency and to reuse process fragments. The disadvantage of the generic approaches is the lack of support for process fragment reuse.

Our proposed solution to the problem is the Emergent Process Acquisition (EPAc) method. This method uses a domain-specific process line for top-down tailoring and refines the tailored process based on the process activities performed in a first process iteration. In this way, the initial variant of the emergent process is built. An *emergent process* is a process that needs to cope with changing goals and context characteristics, which can only be anticipated to a very limited extend before the start of the project. Therefore, the process itself needs to be highly adaptable, and support for the adaptation is necessary.

Typical reasons for the need for emergent processes are:

- Changing requirements. The requirements are not completely known at the start of the project and, in addition, the effects of new or modified requirements on the development process cannot be anticipated. Thus, the activities to be performed can only be detected in the course of the project, too.
- Changes in the project environment. One example for a business environment change is the establishment of a new business relationship (e.g., a new international collaboration). One example for a change in the development environment is a replacement of a validation technique (e.g., a project team follows a prescriptive process and recognizes that the process is not really efficient to perform module testing).

The expected advantage of our method is higher process acceptance by project teams, as the process is based on experience from past projects and feedback from actual project performance.

The paper is structured as follows: The second section describes the background information. The third section describes the EPAc method. The fourth section briefly sketches our experience gained with the usage of the EPAc method. The fifth section discusses related work and strengths of our EPAc method. Finally, Section 6 gives a short summary and an outlook on future work.

2 Background Information

A systematical state-of-the-practice analysis performed by DaimlerChrysler [6] resulted in the awareness that the software development processes are too generic for operational use. The applied tailoring approach [6] does not provide enough support to project teams. This has two reasons: First, it is difficult for process engineers (who are usually also playing a role in a development team) to identify the regression process modification if the process changes. Second process tailoring often requires not only removal of process objects, but also the replacement or addition of new objects. The applied tailoring method does not define how to deal with such kinds of process modifications. Thus, a method for acquiring a project-specific process is needed, which helps project teams to tailor their prescriptive process to their project-specific needs.

3 Acquisition Method

Our acquisition method consists of two main steps. In the first step, a domain-specific process line is used for top-down tailoring at the start of a project. The purpose of the process line is to provide domain knowledge necessary to define a suitable software development process. The approach on how the process line is built and the schema of the process line can be found in [8]. After the first development cycle, the top-down tailored process is refined based on the tracked process data. This two-step tailoring allows reducing the deficiencies of traditional tailoring methods. The next section describes the tailoring method in more details.

The acquisition method consists of four main steps (see Figure 1).

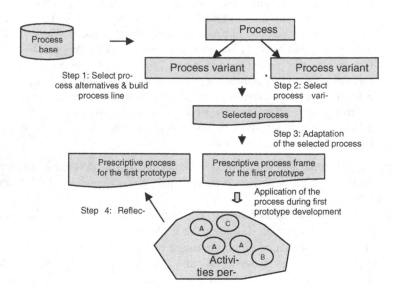

Fig. 1. Method for Acquisition of a Project-specific Process

In the first step, initial suitable process variants are selected from the process base based on the project characteristics. Second, the process line is built for the selected processes. The notion behind the process line is to capture the commonalities in reusable process building blocks and to construct the explicit process variants based on the process deviations, and by reusing the individual building blocks as applicable. In the second step, the process designer iteratively selects a process variant from the process line. Then the selected process variant is adapted to the project by removing unneeded process objects and adding the missing process objects. In this way, the prescriptive process for the development of the first prototype is built. Finally, the fourth step involves the elicitation of activities performed during development of the first prototype and refinement of the prescriptive process based on the tracked process objects. The following sections describe the four steps in more details.

3.1 Process Selection

The selection of a process variant from the process line consists of three main steps (see Figure 2). Each step is described by the attributes goal, input, activities, and output.

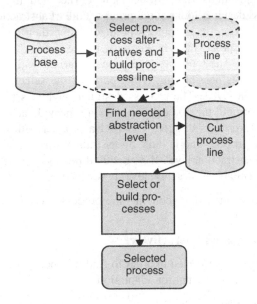

Fig. 2. Technique for Process Selection

Step 1: Select Process Alternatives and Build Process Line

Goal: The activity is performed in order to find the most suitable process variants from the process base and built the common core of the processes. In this way, the process core contains the most important process activities.

Inputs: Process base, project characteristics, the importance of the project characteristics, the number of desired process variants.

Activities:

1. Priorize the project characteristics.
2. Give number of desired process variants.
3. Select the most suitable process variants from the process base.
4. Build process line for selected process variants. The method for building the process line is described in [8].

The third and fourth activities are supported by a tool.

Output: The process line.

Step 2: Find Needed Abstraction Level

Goal: This step has to be performed in order to find the needed process description abstraction level for the project team. The idea behind this step is that the fewer experience the project team members have, the more detailed process description they need.

Input: Process line, where each process variant has an abstraction index.

Activities: Starting from the first abstraction level (i.e., with the domain-specific processes), the process designer looks at the process core of abstraction level i. If the process is too abstract from the designer's point of view, then the process designer can navigate through the process line by knowing the semantic of the abstraction index of the process variants. The tool gives the process variant with the desired abstraction index. If desired, it is possible to get the parts of the selected process variant with different abstraction levels. The process designer navigates till he finds the needed abstraction level or until the process line does not provide any more detailed process descriptions. If the process designer can find a process with the needed abstraction level, then a Cut_process_line is built by assigning variants of the process line that have the selected abstraction level. If no detailed process can be found, then the process with the most suitable abstraction level is selected.

Output: The process line, which contains the processes with the needed or most suitable abstraction level.

Step 3: Select the Process Interactively

Goal: This step can be performed in order to find the specifics of the provided process variants and to use them as input for adaptation.

Input: Cut_process_line

Activities: First, if Cut_process_line contains more than one process variant, then the supporting tool shows the variants of the cut_process_line with explicit marking of the differences between the process variants with respect to the process core. After the process designer selects one of the process variants, the tool marks the process as the selected process. If it is desired to see the difference between the selected variant and other process variants in the cut process line, the tool shows these. If the process designer would like to select another process variant, the tool provides the possibility to do this.

Output: The selected process variant.

3.2 Process Adaptation

The process adaptation can be performed in two ways (see Figure 3). If the effort for the process adaptation is lower than the effort for building a new process variant (i.e.,

ROI > 1), then the selected process should be adapted, otherwise, a new process should be built.

Step 1: Adapt Meta Model

Goal: This step is to be performed in order to tailor the process attributes to the project context.

Input: Selected process, meta model (which consists of the following process attributes: process phases, phase pre-conditions, phase post-conditions, delivery time, maturity of deliverables, activities, activity pre-conditions, activity post-conditions, priority of the activity, inputs needed to perform the activities, outputs needed to perform the activities, the interfaces to support processes, roles performing the activities).

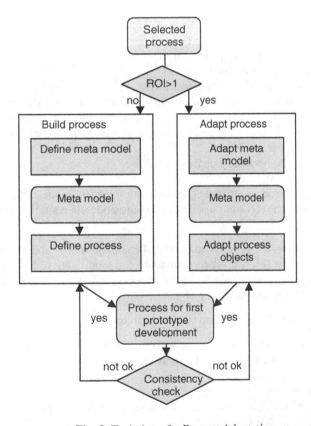

Fig. 3. Technique for Process Adaptation

Activities: The tool shows the process attributes that constitute the meta model and allows the process designer to delete unnecessary process attributes and add missing ones.

Output: The process meta model.

Step 2: Adapt Process Instance

Goal: This step has to be performed in order to tailor the process objects to the project context.

Input: meta process, selected process, if existent (1) to-do list, which describes the activities performed by project team members, (2) information about communication within the team, (3) data dependencies (e.g., between two parameters of a control device or between two control devices).

Activities: If any data (see (1)-(2)) exists, the tool shows the discrepancy between the selected process and available data. Based on this discrepancy, the process designer has the possibility to tailor the process objects by following the standard approach or the user-defined tailoring.
Standard tailoring process:

1. If the meta model contains the process attribute "milestone", then
    a) remove unnecessary milestones
    b) add missing milestones
    Output: a process with an adapted milestone
2. If the meta model contains the process attribute "phases", then the tool iteratively shows these phases for each milestone in the milestone set that are to be performed in order to achieve the milestone. Thus, for each milestone the process designer can
    a) remove unnecessary phases and
    b) add missing phases.
3. For residual process attributes (composing the meta model), the unnecessary objects are removed and missing objects are added in a similar way.

User defined process:
> The tool shows the process attributes of the meta model and allows the process designer to select a process attribute for modification. For each selected process attribute, the tool allows the process designer to remove unnecessary objects and add the necessary objects.

Output: the process for the first prototype development.

Comment: A process object cannot be removed without the approval of the project manager, if it has the priority "minimal requirement".

3.2.1 Build Process

The process construction consists of two main steps: define meta model and define process for the meta model. In the following, these steps are described in more details.

Step 1: Define Meta Model

Goal: This step has to be performed in order to define milestones.

Input: Customer requirements on the product, selected process, if existent, project plans from past similar projects.

Activities: The project manager first defines the project goals based on customer requirements. Based on the project goals and similar project plans, the project manager defines milestones. These include (1) artifacts to be delivered, (2) the time point in the project for delivering the artifacts, (3) the maturity of the delivered artifact, (4) the persons responsible for artifact delivery. The milestones are captured by the tool. Furthermore, the project manager defines the process attributes with respect to which the project-specific process should be described (e.g., tasks to be performed, priority of the task).

Output: meta model.

Step 2: Define Process

Goal: This step has to be performed in order to define the objects for the process attributes of the meta model and the relationships between the objects.

Input: milestones, meta model, if existent (1) to-do list, which describes the activities performed by project team members (e.g., log list), (2) information about persons performing the tasks in the to do list, (3) data dependencies.

Activities:
If there is a to-do list, that describes the activities performed by project team members to achieve similar milestones in past projects, the quality manager defines activities to be performed based on this list. For each activity, the quality manager creates a task. This is done by selection of the milestone (see previous step), which describes the context in which the task should be performed. Additionally, for each task the process attributes defined in the meta model are defined. For example, the priority of the task, the person responsible for the task execution, the time in which the task should be performed, can all be defined. Furthermore the tool allows its users to refine the tasks into sub-tasks, to delegate the tasks to other persons, or to inform the needed persons. The persons who need to be informed are identified by the tool based on the dependencies between the data (e.g., between two parameters of a control device or between two control devices), if such are known. If any information is missing, then the needed process attributes have to be defined based on one's own implicit experience.

Output: process for the first prototype development.

3.2.2 Check Consistency
Goal: This step has to be performed in order to prove the process stringency. This is important to ensure the required product quality.

Input: Process for the first prototype development, selected process.

Activities: The project manager checks that each process milestone and activity from the selected process with the priority "minimal requirement" is available in the process for the first prototype development. If a milestone or an activity is missing and is needed from the project manager's point of view, then the tool allows the project manager to add the missing milestones and activities.

Output: adapted process for the first prototype development.

3.3 Process Reflection

The process reflection consists of two main steps: first, elicitation and analysis of performed process objects and second, refinement and adaptation of the prescriptive process. In the following, these two steps are described in more details.

Step 1: Elicit and Analyze Performed Process

Goal: This step has to be performed in order to understand the process actually performed by project team members, and to identify the delta between prescriptive and performed process.

Input: the process for the first prototype development.

Activities: The InStep tool [4] supporting the coordination between project team members logs the status of activities performed and the time when the activities are performed. As output, the tool delivers a text log file. Our converter tool produces a xml file from the text file. This xml file is used as input for the ProM [1] and InterPol [9] tools. The ProM tool elicits a model of the performed process. The InterPol tool performs the delta analysis.

Output: performed process and the delta.

Step 2: Refine Prescriptive Process

Goal: This step has to be performed in order to update the prescriptive process based on elicited process objects.

Input: the process for the development of the first prototype (=prescriptive process), performed process, delta between performed and prescriptive process.

Activities: The tool allows the project manager to add the missing process objects to the prescriptive process and to delete the unnecessary project objects. When deleting the milestones and activities with the priority "minimal requirements", the tool asks the project manager whether he/she really wants to remove the process object with the priority "minimal requirements". When deleting a process object with the priority "minimal requirement", the tool requires justification of this deletion. Here, an algorithm described in [13] is used for on-the-fly adaptation of the prescriptive process.

Output: refined prescriptive process, which is to be understood as a project specific process.

4 Validations and Gained Experience

We validated the instantiation method in the context of a initial study. In the following, the study definition, design, and the results are briefly described.

4.1 Study Definition and Planning

In the context of the study, we compared the Emergent Process Acquisition (EPAc) method with the tailoring method proposed by the V model [10], as the V model is widely used for system development in practice. The goal of the study was to evaluate the effect of the EPAc method on the effort to develop a bus control system and on the quality of the developed system.

The hypotheses in the study were:

1. The effort for developing a system according to the V model is higher or equal to the effort for developing the system according to the emergent process designed by using the EPT method.
2. Product quality developed by following the V model is higher or equal to the product quality developed by following the emergent process designed by using EPT method.
3. The satisfaction of the project team using the EPAc method is higher than the satisfaction of the project team following the tailored V model.

4.2 Study Design and Operation

The study was designed as follows:

The factor (i.e., the independent variable) is the development process followed by students. The treatments (i.e., particular values) of the factor are (1) the process designed by tailoring the V model and (2) the process designed by using the EPT method.

The main difference between the development following the V model and the emergent process is the process stringency. The emergent process provides more flexibility at the start of a project and becomes more stringent during the course of the project. The tailored V process has the same stringency during the course of the whole project. So the groups following the emergent process are able to better reflect on their development experience than the group following the V model, as the emergent process provides more flexibility at the start of the project than the V tailored process. Following the design principle of "balancing", we balanced the number of students in the groups. Thus, each group consisted of nine students. The students were randomly assigned to the groups, fulfilling the design principle of "randomizing". Furthermore, in order to ensure tcomparability of the study results, the following independent variables had the same treatments:

- *Customer experience*: is selected as independent variable, because a customer with little experience may state system requirements that are too ambiguous. To avoid the effect of this variable, the same person stated and clarified the requirements to all three groups.
- *Complexity of developed product*: is selected as independent variable, since the more complex the product, the higher the development effort and the higher the probability for development faults. To avoid the effect of this variable, all three groups had to develop the same system for control of bus doors and lights.

- *Environment dynamism:* We simulated the same changes in the development environment (e.g., new or changed requirements, application of a new tool). This variable is considered since the frequent changes in the development environment usually cause additional development effort.
- *Tool support:* is considered since the tools can affect the development effort. Thus, all groups use the same tool chain.
- *Instrumentation:* We provided the same measurement and preparation support for all students.

The factor treatments are assigned according to the blocking design principle. We decided that two groups were to follow the emergent process and one group had to follow the V tailored process. This assignment was meant to help us interpret the study results with more significance.

Regarding our study design, we selected 28 advanced students from eights/ninth semesters, taught them the needed foundation in software engineering and tool usage, and provided them with the needed instrumentation support (e.g., the process line for the emergent groups, forms for data elicitation). After four weeks of preparation, the study started. The study duration was 14 weeks. The study consisted of three iterations. During each iteration, a prototype should be incrementally developed. Two so-called emergent groups (E1 and E2) developed the system following the emergent process and one group developed it following the tailored V model. In each emergent group, one student was selected for the role of "emergent coach". The responsibility of the emergent coach was to design a project-specific process and to manage the team. The emergent coaches designed the project-specific process by using the process line and by following the EPT method. The two emergent groups followed the project-specific process designed by their emergent coach.

Each week,

- the groups delivered the artifacts with respect to their project plan and the completed data collection forms
- they received feedback with respect to the quality of their artifacts
- a meeting between the study supervisors and the students took place. At the meeting, the students asked questions and provided feedback to the study supervisors.

The collected data was analyzed weekly. Regarding data that seemed to be unrealistic, the students were asked directly. Additionally, the summary of the collected data was reviewed by the students to avoid misunderstandings.

4.3 Results Analysis and Interpretation

In order to decide about the hypotheses, we derived metrics for *productivity*, *product quality*, and *project team satisfaction* by following the GQM method [15]. In order to evaluate productivity, we compared the effort spent per activity type (see Table 1). The first row of the table shows the activity types considered.

Table 1. Effort during the first iteration

Aktivität	10-17.11.2004			17-22.11.2004			23-30.11.2004			01-07.12.2004			Total effort		
	EG 1	EG 2	VG	EG 1	EG 2	VG	EG 1	EG 2	VG	EG 1	EG 2	VG	EG1	EG2	VG
Communication customer	0	0	0	270	300	270	0	0	0	0	0	30	270	300	300
Communication TG	0	0	600	210	120	0	90	60	60	0	0	30	300	180	600
Requirements specification	0	0	780	120	570	600	0	240	0	0	0	240	120	810	1620
Requirements review	0	0	240	0	90	450	0	0	0	0	0	0	0	90	690
Requirements adaptation	0	0	0	0	30	60	0	0	120	0	0	0	0	30	180
Architecture modeling	0	0	240	270	565	0	0	405	0	180	0	30	450	970	270
Architecture review	0	0	360	0	0	120	0	0	0	0	0	0	90	0	480
Architecture change	0	0	0	0	0	0	0	0	0	420	0	0	420	0	0
New statemate modeling	0	0	0	720	0	0	660	1080	1620	765	810	0	2145	1890	1620
Statemate review	0	0	0	0	0	240	90	180	465	0	225	0	90	315	705
Statemate change	0	0	0	0	0	0	180	500	0	15	0	1200	195	500	1200
Fault removal from statemate	0	0	0	0	0	0	135	0	120	0	0	0	135	0	120
Statemate optimization	0	0	0	0	0	0	90	0	0	0	345	60	90	345	60
Panel development	0	0	0	0	240	0	540	0	0	0	0	0	540	240	0
Panel change	0	0	0	0	0	0	0	135	0	210	0	210	210	135	210
System test	0	0	0	0	0	480	180	60	0	420	530	450	600	590	930
Integration	0	0	0	0	0	0	0	0	0	0	0	330	0	0	330
Total effort	0	0	2220	1590	1915	2220	1965	2660	2385	2010	1910	2580	5475	6485	9405

The second, third, fourth, and five rows show the effort per week per group (EG1: emergent group 1, EG2: emergent group 2, V: V group) in minutes. Finally, the sixth row shows the total (i.e., for the first iteration) effort per activity. The effort distribution for other iterations looks similar. The table 1 shows that the effort of the V group is significantly larger than the effort of the emergent groups. In order to be able to evaluate product quality, we collected both internal and external metrics (see Table 2).

Table 2. Data collected to evaluate product quality during first iteration

Metrics type	Metric	EG 1	EG 2	VG
Indirect metrics	Number of activity charts	2	4	5
	Number of state charts	8	5	3
	Number of states	56	56	59
	Number of state transitions	83	96	107
	Are the state models executable	yes	yes	yes
	Non-determinism	no	no	no
	Data Dictionary (0-5)	5	5	4, DOOR_X_OPEN undef
	Clarity (0-5)	4, as the architecture can be improved in the way that Chart EVENT CONTROL can be removed	4,5; as it would be more clear, than to remove the parallelism in charts	3, as many jumps are used
	Architecture (0-5)	4, the interfaces are well defined, but the presentation form can be improved.	5, clear separation between hardware and software, the interfaces are well defined and presented	3, the interfaces are not well defined
Direct metrics	Incorrectly implemented critical features	no	no	The bus can drive with open doors
				The bus is not driving. If a button to open the door is pressed, the control system does not open the door.
				If an accident happens, the bus does stop and does not open the doors.
	Incorrectly implemented non-critical features	The doors do not have the button to open the door by passenger.	The button showing that the door is open takes the status "off" before the door is closed.	no
		Driver light takes the status "on" before the door is completely open.	no	no
		If outside is dark and the driver light switch has the status "off", the driver light is on.	no	no

The first row in the table shows the type of the data collected. The second row shows the collected metric itself, for example, number of uncorrected implemented features. This number was defined as follows: first, we derived a standard test case set from the requirements specification. Second, we tested the delivered panels with respect to the set. Third, based on the knowledge about failed test cases, we identified features not correctly implemented. Furthermore, we separated the wrongly implemented features into critical and non-critical. In the first iteration, 18 different features should be implemented. In order to be able to focus on the critical features, we informed the groups (both emergent and V group) that in the first iteration, we would evaluate the quality only based on the critical features. Table 2 shows that the number of critical features incorrectly implemented by V group is larger than this number implemented by the emergent group. Consequently, the quality of the product implemented by the emergent group is higher that the quality of the product implemented by the V group.

We assessed project team satisfaction by asking the students participating in the study about their satisfaction. The students evaluated their satisfaction based on the scale: high (=2), ok (=1), low (=0). For each group, we built a middle value per satisfaction aspect. This middle value is shown in Figure 4. The diagram shows that the satisfaction with the work and with the task fulfillment is the same in the sub-group.

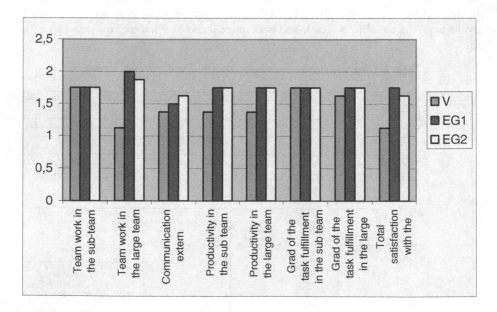

Fig. 4. Team satisfaction

All other satisfaction aspects are evaluated higher by emergent groups than by the V group. The results indicate that the EPAc method contributes to a more productive development of products, higher quality, and higher project team satisfaction.

5 Related Work

The approaches for acquisition of project-specific processes proposed in the literature can be divided into two types: top-down and bottom-up approaches. The top-down approaches can be further separated into three types: rule-based tailoring [13], constraint-based selection [16], and parameterized-based approaches. The bottom-up approaches provided in the literature can be classified in informal [2] and formal approaches [1].

The EPT method is neither an absolute bottom-up approach nor a top-down approach. It is an approach that uses top-down tailoring at the start of the project to reuse knowledge gained in past similar projects, and refines the top-down tailored process based on the performed tasks. This two-step tailoring approach allows avoiding deficiencies of the bottom-up and top-down approaches.

6 Summary and Future Work

Efficient development of qualitative systems requires suitable project-specific processes. As projects have different contexts and goals, tailoring methods are needed that allow adapting the generic processes to the project-specific needs. The tailoring approaches used in practice (e.g., the tailoring approach proposed by the V model [11]) usually involve checking conditions and removing objects of the base model. One difficulty of such tailoring is the identification of the regression process modification to be performed if an object is removed. Furthermore, process tailoring often requires not only removal of process objects, but also replacement or addition of new objects. Traditional tailoring methods do not define how to deal with such kinds of process modifications.

To tackle the problem, we provide the Emergent Process Acquisition (EPAc) method. This method uses the domain-specific process line for top-down tailoring and refines the tailored process based on the process activities performed in the first process iteration. In this way, the initial variant of the emergent process is built. This paper presented the emergent process acquisition method and the empirical experience gained with the method in the context of a study. The study shows that the emergent tailoring method significantly contributes to more efficient development of higher-quality systems.

One issue for future fwork is the validation of the EPAc method in a real context.

Acknowledgement

The authors would like to thank Alexander Raschke, Matthias Schneiderhan, Ramin Tavakoli Kolagari, and Frank Houdek for very helpful support during validation. Furthermore, our thanks go to the following people who provided valuable input in several discussions: Dieter Rombach, Kurt Schneider, Michael Stupperich. The authors would also like to thank Sonnhild Namingha from the Fraunhofer Institute for Experimental Software Engineering (IESE) for reviewing the first version of the article.

References

1. Dustdar, S., Hoffmann, T., van der Aalst, W. Mining of ad-hoc business with TeamLog, Distributed Systems Group, Technical University of Vienna, 2004.
2. Becker-Kornstaedt, U., Hamann, D., Kempkens, R., Rösch, P., Verlage, M., Webby, R., Zettel, J. The SPEARMINT Approach to Software Process Definition and Process Guidance, Workshop on Software Engineering over the Internet at ICSE'98, Kyoto, Japan, April, 1998
3. Graydon, A. ISO/IEC DTR 15504-2 Part 2: A Reference Model for Processes and Process Capability, 1998.
4. http://www.microtool.de/instep/en/prod_pm_edition.asp.
5. Humphrey, Watts S. Introduction in the TSP, Addison Wesley, 2000.
6. Jaufman, O., Dold, A., Haeberlein, T., Schlumpberger, C., Stupperich, M. Requirements for Flexible Software Development Processes within Large and Long Taking Projects, QUATIC, Porto, 2004.
7. Jaufman, O., Potznewick, S., Suitability of the State of the Art Methods for Interdisciplinary System Development in Automotive Industry, Interdisciplinary Software Engineering, 2004.
8. Jaufman, O. Process Line Framework for the Domain of Automotive System Development, SPICE 2005 Conference, 2005.
9. Kleiner, N. Verbesserungsstrategien für den Workflow-Designprozess, Dissertation, University of Ulm, 2004.
10. Droschel, W., Wiemers, H. Das V-Modell 97, Der Standard für die Entwicklung von IT-Systemen mit Anleitung für den Praxiseinsatz, Oldenbourg, 2000 (German).
11. Miers, D. The Workware Evaluation Framework, ENIX Ltd, 1996.
12. Münch, J., Schmitz, M., Verlage, M. Tailoring großer Prozessmodelle auf der Basis von MVP-L*, 4. Workshop der Fachgruppe 5.1.1 (GI): „Vorgehensmodelle – Einführung, betrieblicher Einsatz, Werkzeug-Unterstützung und Migration", Berlin, 1997.
13. Reichert, M. Dynamic Changes in Process Management Systems. Ph.D. Thesis, University of Ulm, Faculty of Computer Science, July 2000 (in German).
14. Rombach, R. Practical benefits of goal-oriented measurement. In N. Fenton and B. Littlewood, editors, Software Reliability and Metrics. Elsevier Applied Science, London, 1991.
15. Riddle, W., Schneider, H.: Coping with Process Agility. Tutorial at 2002 Software Engineering Process Group Conference (SEPG2002), Phoenix, Arizona (2002).
16. Wohlin, C., Runeson, P., Höst M., Ohlsson, M., Regnell, B., Wesslen, A. Experimentation in Software Engineering: An Introduction, Kluwer Academic Publishers, Boston, 2000.

Understanding the Importance of Roles in Architecture-Related Process Improvement - A Case Study

Per Jönsson and Claes Wohlin

School of Engineering, Blekinge Institute of Technology,
PO-Box 520, SE-372 25, Ronneby, Sweden
{per.jonsson, claes.wohlin}@bth.se

Abstract. In response to the increasingly challenging task of developing software, many companies turn to Software Process Improvement (SPI). One of many factors that SPI depends on is user (staff) involvement, which is complicated by the fact that process users may differ in viewpoints and priorities. In this paper, we present a case study in which we performed a pre-SPI examination of process users' viewpoints and priorities with respect to their roles. The study was conducted by the means of a questionnaire sent out to the process users. The analysis reveals differences among roles regarding priorities, in particular for product managers and designers, but not regarding viewpoints. This indicates that further research should investigate in which situations roles are likely to differ and in which they are likely to be similar. Moreover, since we initially expected both viewpoints and priorities to differ, it indicates that it is important to cover these aspects in SPI, and not only rely on expectations.

1 Introduction

Constraining factors such as time and budget make software development a challenging task for many organisations – a challenge that is leveraged by the fact that software plays an increasingly large role in society. In order to handle the challenge and to turn the software industry into an engineering discipline, it is necessary to put the processes in focus [27]. The goal of Software Process Improvement (SPI) is to create an infrastructure that enables effective methods and practices to be incorporated into the business [1].

The success of SPI depends on a number of factors, one of which is user (staff) involvement [21]. It has been reported that process users' attitudes often are disregarded in quality initiatives, and that putting them in the spotlight when designing SPI is an important step towards success [1, 10]. To involve process users and to regard their attitudes can be far from trivial, because process users do neither necessarily have the same viewpoints, nor the same priorities. This paper presents a case study in which we examined the viewpoints and priorities of process users at Ericsson AB, Sweden, to pinpoint differences and similarities among roles. We selected the role perspective since a number of publications report that role can be a discriminating factor when it comes to views in SPI [2, 4, 5, 6, 10, 14, 25].

F. Bomarius and S. Komi-Sirviö (Eds.): PROFES 2005, LNCS 3547, pp. 343–357, 2005.

Generic SPI frameworks, such as SEI's IDEALSM [17], Quality Improvement Paradigm (QIP) [3], and PROFES [20], all contain two important ingredients: a characterisation (or assessment, or appraisal) of the current process, and an improvement plan (or roadmap, or actions). The viewpoints of the process users are crucial in the characterisation phase, because the more diverse they are, the harder it becomes to form a baseline. Similarly, the priorities of the process users are crucial in the planning phase, because the more diverse they are, the harder it becomes to create a plan that satisfies everyone.

1.1 Background and Research Setting

Ericsson AB, Sweden, is one of the largest suppliers of mobile systems in the world, and has as customers some of the world's largest mobile operators. The study was conducted at one of Ericsson's offices (hereafter referred to as the company), which at the time had about 400 employees.

The objective of the study was to prepare improvement of the architecture documentation process at the company by examining process users' viewpoints and priorities with respect to their roles. By doing so, we were able to create an awareness of the need for and scope of SPI. With "architecture documentation process", we refer to the process of documenting the software architecture and keeping the documentation up-to-date. This is not necessarily an explicitly defined process of its own, but could, for example, be part of the development process. Our tool for examining viewpoints and priorities was a questionnaire with quantitative questions about architecture documentation.

In advance, we expected to see both diverse viewpoints and diverse priorities among process users regarding the architecture documentation process. The reason for this was mainly that architecture documentation typically has different stakeholders, such as project managers, product managers, designers and testers, most of whom have different needs and knowledge. Both needs and knowledge are factors that tend to affect how you view things and what you think is important. This is one of the reasons that software architectures should be designed and documented using multiple architectural views [5]. Since the organisational role most likely affects both needs and knowledge, we anticipated differences in both viewpoints and priorities.

We apply statistical methods to test for differences among roles. For this purpose, the following statistical hypotheses are evaluated (independently for viewpoints and priorities):

- Null hypothesis, H_0: *There are no differences among roles.*
- Alternative hypothesis, H_A: *There is a difference among roles.*

This paper is justified by two main reasons. First, it adds to existing research about similarities and non-similarities among roles, which is necessary to better understand the impact of roles in various research contexts. Second, it provides an example of empirical SPI research targeted at industry, with the focus on creating an understanding of process users' viewpoints and priorities.

1.2 Architecture-Related Process Improvement

As mentioned, we explored process users' viewpoints and opinions in order to prepare for improvement of the architecture documentation process. However, the questions posed in the questionnaire were more germane to the product (i.e., the architecture documentation) than to the process (i.e., documenting the architecture). Our reason for posing questions about the product rather than the process was that we considered the product to be more tangible to the process users than the process itself. In other words, we expected that we would get more well-founded answers by asking about the product. Furthermore, we argue that the quality of the documentation reflects the quality of the process of documenting it as much as, for example, the quality of requirements reflects the quality of the process of eliciting, formulating and managing them.

Since the software architecture of a system is a fundamental building block that has many stakeholders within the organisation, changes to architecture-related processes can have great organisational impact, including new workflows, altered mindsets and changed team structures. This further establishes the need for investigating differences in viewpoints and priorities among process users.

The paper is structured as follows. Section 2 addresses related work, while Section 3 explains the design of the study as well as how the study was carried out. The results are presented in Section 4, followed by a statistical analysis in Section 5, a general discussion in Section 6 and finally conclusions in Section 7.

2 Related Work

For an overview of the Software Process Improvement area, we recommend Zahran's book, which covers the topic from a practitioner's perspective [27]. Zahran discusses the general challenges of SPI, such as management commitment, buy-in from process users etc. There are some publications (see below) that discuss differences among roles in various contexts. In general, they show that there are differences among roles in some situations, but not in others. It all depends on what you evaluate.

Baddoo and Hall have studied de-motivators in SPI among software practitioners, in order to understand what hinders SPI success [2]. Dividing the practitioners into developers, project managers and senior managers, they find both common and unique de-motivators. They conclude that differences in de-motivators for SPI often are related to the roles that software practitioners have.

Berander and Wohlin have looked at agreement on SPI issues among traditional software development roles [4]. Their findings indicate that there is agreement among roles about communication of processes, but disagreement about, for example, importance of improvement and urgency of problems.

Conradi and Dybå have investigated how the use of formal routines for transferring knowledge and experience is perceived by developers and managers [6]. Their results show that there is a difference between the two groups; developers are more sceptical to formal routines, while managers take them for granted.

Hall and Wilson have studied views of quality among software practitioners in UK companies, with focus on two groups - managers and developers [10]. According to their findings, developers and managers differ in that they have different primary quality concerns, although the differences are not conflicting.

Karlström et al. present a method for aggregating viewpoints of process users in an organisation [14]. The essence of the method is to let process users rate factors believed to affect the SPI goal according to their viewpoints. The authors divide the process users into two groups, managers and engineers, based on their roles, and conclude that the groups differ on some factors, but not on all.

In [25], Svahnberg has studied how participants in an architecture assessment form groups when prioritising quality attributes and assessing architecture candidates. Svahnberg concludes that the role of the participant is the main influence when prioritising quality attributes, but not when assessing architecture candidates.

Questionnaires are often used as instruments in Software Process Assessment, for example the SEI Maturity Questionnaire for CMM-based assessment and the BOOTSTRAP questionnaire [27]. Klappholz et al. have developed an assessment tool, ATSE, for assessing attitude towards and knowledge of the development process [15]. While questionnaires in process assessment commonly measure the effectiveness of an improvement programme, our questionnaire was rather a part of the preparations for an upcoming improvement programme. In other words, it was not a substitute for a process assessment questionnaire.

3 Design

In this section, we outline the design of the study. We describe the contents of the questionnaire, the sampling and response rate, the technique for treating missing data, roles in the study and finally threats to the validity of the study.

3.1 Questionnaire Design

In order to assess process users' viewpoints and priorities, we designed a questionnaire consisting of six questions collecting data about the current state of the architecture documentation (the *infrastructure questions*), and one question about how to improve the architecture documentation (the *improvement question*). There was also a question asking about the process user's organisational role.

The infrastructure questions, which we believed would yield different results for different roles, were formulated as follows (words in bold are keywords used for identifying the questions later):

1. "In your opinion, to what extent does architecture documentation **exist**?"
2. "How would you, in general, describe the **form** of the architecture documentation?"
3. "How would you judge the **quality** of the documentation?"
4. "In your opinion, to what extent is architecture documentation **updated** as the system evolves?"

5. "In your opinion, how well does the architecture documentation **match** the actual architecture?"
6. "Imagine being a newly hired employee – how easy would it be to gain **insight** into the system using the current architecture documentation?"

For these questions, five point Likert scales (i.e., with five response options for each question) were used. Such scales are ordinal and are often used for collecting degrees of agreement [22]. For almost all questions, a low score indicated a negative response (little, low, seldom), while a high score indicated a positive response (much, high, often). The scale for the second question was slightly different from the others, though, in that a low score indicated text-orientation, while a high score indicated model-orientation.

The improvement question was formulated as follows: "If architecture documentation was to be improved in some way, what do you think is the most important purpose it could serve in addition to the present ones?" Five predefined purposes were given: change impact analysis, risk analysis, cost analysis, driver for development and system insight. In case these were not satisfactory, the respondent could choose "other" and suggest a new purpose as the most important one.

3.2 Sampling and Response Rate

The recipients of the questionnaire were selected using systematic sampling [22]. We obtained a list of all employees from an employee directory, and selected every second person on the list for the study. The reason for this was that another study was performed simultaneously and the employees were shared evenly between the studies.

The recipients of the questionnaire were given two weeks to fill it out and return the answers. The recipients were also allowed to reject the questionnaire if they had no time available or if they felt that it was not relevant for them. The two-week deadline seemed reasonable even for people with heavy workload. After one week, a reminder was sent to those who had not already responded or explicitly rejected the first distribution.

The population consisted of the 400 persons employed at the company. The selection of employees described above resulted in a sample of around 200 persons. While some responses were discarded because they contained invalid answers to some questions, around a third of the sample, or 65 persons, did give valid responses to the questionnaire. The other two thirds explicitly rejected the questionnaire, chose not to respond or were unable to respond before the deadline. Not all 65 respondents did answer all the questions, however. Because of that, some respondents had to be discarded, while some could be kept by imputing missing data in their answers, as described in the next section. As a result, the data presented in this paper are based on answers from 58 respondents.

In order to verify that the respondents were representative for the population, we examined the departmental distribution. We could not use the role distribution, since the roles were known only for the respondents, not the entire population. We saw that there were only minor differences in departmental distribution between the respondents and the population, and consequently considered the respondents being representative for the population. In this context, it should also be noted that the roles are in many cases closely linked to departments (i.e., testers come from the test department and so forth). While the respondent drop-out is a threat to the external validity of the study, as discussed in Section 3.5, we consider the absolute size of the sample to be satisfactory.

3.3 Treatment of Missing Data

As implied in the previous section, some of the initial respondents did not answer all the questions discussed in this paper. To be able to keep as many data points as possible, missing answers for those respondents that had answered at least five of the seven questions were imputed. The respondents that had answered only four questions or less were discarded, leaving 40 complete cases and 18 cases to impute. Only the complete cases were used as basis for the imputation.

The answers were imputed using the hot-deck k-Nearest Neighbour imputation technique, which imputes values based on the k cases most similar to the target case [7]. We have, in previous work, found this imputation technique to be suitable for Likert data [13]. The similarity metric used was the Euclidean distance calculated only for the infrastructure questions (the improvement question was disregarded because of its nominal scale). As a replacement for a missing data value, the median of the k nearest cases was used for the infrastructure questions, while the mode was used for the improvement question. Based on our previous findings, the value of k was chosen to 7, which is approximately the square root of the number of complete cases ($k = 6$, while closer, would be unsuitable when calculating the median) [13]. In the few cases when the mode was not unique at $k = 7$, k was increased to 8 instead.

3.4 Roles

The organisational roles of the respondents are rather specific for the company. Thus, in order to increase the generalisability of the results, and the replicability of the study, we have mapped the organisational roles to traditional software engineering roles. We mean that these represent the parts of software development normally discussed in software engineering literature [24]. To ensure the relevance of the resulting role list, the mapping was carried out together with a company-appointed specialist. The resulting roles, with abbreviated form and number of respondents within parentheses, are:

- *Designer* (D, 6) - creates system descriptions that the programmer can base the implementation on [19].
- *Programmer* (P, 8) - writes code that implements the requirements [19].
- *Tester* (T, 13) - catches faults that the programmer overlooks [19].
- *Functional manager* (FM, 5) - responsible for staffing, organizing, and executing project tasks within their functional areas [18].
- *Project manager* (PRJ, 8) - plans, directs and integrates the work efforts of participants to achieve project goals [18].

- *Product manager* (PRD, 4) - responsible for product related planning activities [16].
- *Architect* (A, 11) - makes decisions, coordinates, manages dependencies, negotiates requirements, recommends technology etc. [8, 11]
- *Process group member* (PGM, 3) - facilitates the definition, maintenance and improvement of the software processes used by the organisation [12].

The process group member role is derived from Humphrey's Software Engineering Process Group (SEPG) [12]. Persons who work with infrastructure, which is seen as a kind of process support, are also included in this role. The architect role stems from an organisational role with responsibility for the system as a whole and its survival in the product chain. Architecture work is a part of this role, but implementation and low-level design is not.

3.5 Validity Threats

In this section, the most important threats to the validity of the study are presented together with measures that have been taken to avoid them.

Construct Validity. Construct validity is concerned with the design of the main study instrument (i.e., the questionnaire) and that it measures what it is intended to measure [22]. A threat to construct validity is that not all respondents may have had the same perception of what architecture is. In order to avoid that, a common definition of the term "software architecture" was given in the questionnaire, and each respondent was given the opportunity to disagree and give his or her own definition.

To counter the threat that some questions would be easier to answer for persons with certain roles, the questionnaire was checked by a screening group at the company. Because several roles (product manager, project manager, architect, designer and programmer) were represented by the persons in the screening group, there should be little bias towards any particular role. The screening group also verified that the role list in the questionnaire did contain relevant organisational roles.

External Validity. External validity is concerned with the generalisability of the results [26]. The main threat to external validity is that differences (and non-differences) found among roles could be true only for the studied company. Since we are dealing with just one case, this threat cannot be ruled out. There are, however, two circumstances that we believe make our findings interesting in a wider context. First, the studied company operates, as stated, on the world market with several large, international customers. As such, it should be considered a strong industrial case. Second, by mapping the organisational roles to traditional software engineering roles, generalisability to a wider software engineering community, and greater replicability of the study, has been strived for.

Another threat to external validity is the fact that we cannot guarantee that the distribution of roles for the respondents equals the distribution of roles in the population. Since we do not know the roles of all the persons in the population, we cannot avoid this threat. We have tried to ensure that the respondents are representative of the population by looking at the departmental distribution instead.

Internal Validity. Internal validity is concerned with the relationship between the treatment (i.e., the questionnaire) and the outcome (i.e., the results collected) [26]. The imputation of data described in Section 3.3 is a threat, since it essentially is fabrication of data. However, of the incomplete cases, almost all had only one question out of seven unanswered. Only one incomplete case had two questions unanswered. Furthermore, we based the choice of imputation technique on our previous, supporting, findings.

Conclusion Validity. Conclusion validity is concerned with the statistical relationship between the treatment and the outcome [26]. A threat to conclusion validity is that we, in the data analysis, use the Kruskal-Wallis test when the number of ties in the data is large. To address this, we apply an additional Chi-Square test to validate the outcome of the Kruskal-Wallis test. It should also be noted that the Kruskal-Wallis test includes correction for ties. Thus, the effect of this threat should be minimal.

Another threat to conclusion validity is that we use the Chi-Square test when the expected frequencies in the cells are relatively small. While this may mean that the outcome is not reliable, Siegel acknowledges that for a large number of cells, the expected frequencies should be allowed to be small [23]. In our case, the number of cells is nearly 50, which Siegel hints should be enough to allow small expected frequencies. Thus, we believe that the effect of this threat should be small.

4 Results

In this section, we present the results on the questionnaire that was distributed at the company. We show the distribution of answers for the infrastructure questions as well as for the improvement question. The results are analysed statistically in Section 5.

4.1 Infrastructure Questions

Fig. 1 shows, for each of the infrastructure questions, how the answers are distributed on the response options. The exact phrasing of the questions can be found in Section 3.1. The question about to what extent documentation exists is special in the sense that the respondents made use of all five response options. As response options 3 and 4 account for 50% or more of the answers from all roles, the agreement among roles can be seen as large. Internally, architects (A) and designers (D) disagree more than the other roles, whereas on the whole, there is a consensus that documentation exists to a large extent.

For the question about documentation form, it is apparent that response option 2 dominates the answers (i.e., accounts for 50% or more) from all roles except the architects, meaning that most roles consider the documentation to be more text-oriented than model-oriented.

The answers to the question about how well the documentation matches the system indicate that all roles consider the match to be medium to good (as response options 3 and 4 dominate the answers). Again, architects have greater internal disagreement than the other roles. Also, functional managers (FM) and product managers (PRD) have a slightly more positive view than the other roles.

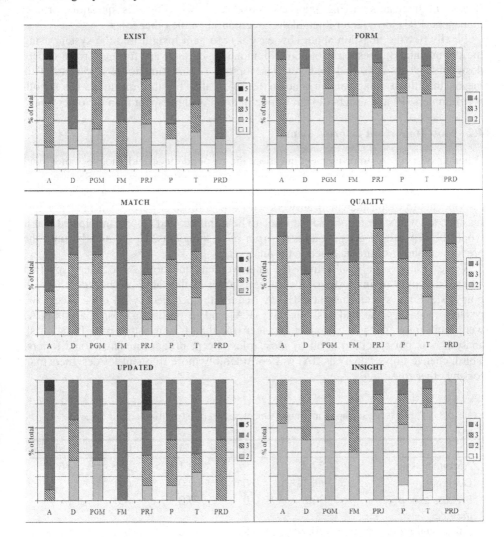

Fig. 1. Infrastructure questions; *answer distribution* (*y axis*) per *role* (*x axis*)

The question about quality of documentation has the narrowest distribution of answers of all the infrastructure questions. The respondents only made use of three of the response options in total, while most roles only made use of two, namely 3 and 4. Hence, the roles seem to agree that the documentation quality is medium or slightly above medium. The designers have a somewhat more positive view than other roles, whereas testers and programmers stand out because some of them consider the quality to be below medium.

In the answers to the question about to what extent documentation is updated, there seem to be a general consensus that the update frequency is high, with architects and functional managers having the most positive views. For this question, project managers (PRJ) have larger internal disagreement than the other roles.

Finally, for the question about how easy it is to gain insight into the system using the documentation, response option 2 dominates the answers from all roles except designers (where it is tied with response option 3) and functional managers. This means that there is agreement among the roles also for this question. Here, both programmers (P) and testers (T) have more internal disagreement than the other roles.

4.2 Most Important Improvement

When answering the improvement question, the respondents could choose "other" and add a new purpose if the predefined ones were not satisfactory (see Section 3.1). However, only one of the respondents chose to do this. We did not ask the other respondents to reconsider their answers with this additional purpose in mind for two reasons: (1) we estimated the added value to be minimal, and (2) we anticipated that it would be difficult to get new answers from all respondents. Consequently, only the predefined purposes are included in the analysis.

Table 1 shows the results from the improvement question. An ocular inspection reveals a couple of interesting differences (shown in the table as shaded cells with bold text). First, system insight (SI) was frequently specified by all roles except the product managers. Second, risk analysis (RA) and in particular cost analysis (CA) were more frequent for the product manager role than for any other role. In fact, risk analysis was not specified at all by most roles except product managers and testers. Third, change impact analysis (IA) was considerably more frequent for designers than for any other role.

Table 1. Most important improvement; answer distribution among roles

	IA	RA	CA	DD	SI
Architect	27.3	0.0	9.1	27.3	36.4
Designer	**66.7**	0.0	0.0	0.0	33.3
Process group member	33.3	0.0	0.0	0.0	66.7
Functional manager	20.0	0.0	0.0	0.0	60.0
Project manager	0.0	0.0	12.5	37.5	50.0
Programmer	25.0	0.0	0.0	25.0	50.0
Tester	0.0	7.7	15.4	0.0	76.9
Product manager	0.0	**25.0**	**50.0**	25.0	**0.0**

5 Analysis

In this section, the results from the questionnaire are analysed statistically. The null hypothesis stated in Section 1.1 is tested at significance level $\alpha = 0.05$. Two statistical tests are used, the Kruskal-Wallis test and the Chi-Square test [23]. We use these tests because we consider the data, being on ordinal and nominal scales, respectively, unsuitable for parametric tests. Both tests are applied to the infrastructure questions, whereas only Chi-Square is applied to the improvement question, because of its nominal scale.

5.1 Infrastructure Questions

The statistical significances of the results for the infrastructure questions are first calculated using the Kruskal-Wallis test. As can be seen in the second and third columns in Table 2, the results from the infrastructure questions are not significant at the selected significance level, as p exceeds 0.05 for all questions. This outcome aligns well with the results from the infrastructure questions presented in Section 4, where it can be seen that there is much agreement among the roles.

Since the Kruskal-Wallis test should be used with care when the number of ties in the data is large (as in our case) [9], we use the Chi-Square test for the infrastructure questions as well. The outcome of this test, presented in the rightmost three columns in Table 2, further confirms that there are no statistical significances in the results. This means that the null hypothesis cannot be rejected for the infrastructure questions.

Table 2. Kruskal-Wallis (left) and Chi-Square (right) outcome, all questions

	H (K-W)	p (df=7)	X^2	df	p
Exists	5.02	0.66	31.04	28	0.32
Form	4.38	0.73	12.46	14	0.57
Quality	3.62	0.82	16.41	14	0.29
Update	9.83	0.20	24.14	21	0.29
Match	5.88	0.55	17.56	21	0.68
Insight	4.12	0.77	14.91	21	0.83
Improve	N/A	N/A	47.71	28	0.046

5.2 Improvement Question

Because the data collected from the improvement question are nominal, we apply only the Chi-Square test and not the Kruskal-Wallis test. The outcome, presented in the bottom row in Table 2, shows that there is a statistically significant difference among the roles, as p is less than 0.05. Thus, the null hypothesis can be rejected in favour of the alternative hypothesis for the improvement question.

The overall Chi-Square does not pinpoint the differences. In other words, it does not identify exactly which roles that differ from others. To find the exact locations of the differences, the significances of all the partitions in the data are calculated. Each partition represents one pair of role and purpose (i.e., most important improvement), and has one degree of freedom. Simply speaking, the partition significance for a particular role-purpose pair is calculated based on the score of the pair and all scores to the left and above it. Consequently, the a priori order of the rows and columns affects the outcome of the partition significances [23]. We deal with this problem by performing an exhaustive calculation where all possible permutations of row and column order are evaluated. We argue that the pairs of role and purpose that are significant in more than 50% of the permutations can be considered significant overall. Table 3 shows the resulting pairs of role and purpose.

Table 3. Significant role-purpose pairs

Role	Purpose	Significance frequency (%)
Product manager	Risk analysis	53.5
Product manager	Cost analysis	54.7
Designer	Change impact analysis	59.1

It can be seen that product managers differ from other roles in that they more frequently chose risk analysis and cost analysis. Moreover, designers differ in that they more frequently chose change impact analysis than other roles. We see that this aligns well with some of the observations made in Section 4.2.

6 Discussion

In Section 4.1, we have seen that there seems to be much agreement among the roles regarding the infrastructure questions. This is supported by the statistical analysis in the previous section, which shows that there are no statistical differences among the roles for these questions. In other words, the respondents have fairly similar viewpoints. Our interpretation of this is that the architecture documentation process is well established at the company and that everyone has a joint understanding of how the architecture is documented and what the state of the documentation is. This is an important starting point when doing architecture-related process improvement, because it makes it easier to obtain a baseline of the current process. If the viewpoints had differed among roles, it could be difficult to find a common baseline.

Looking at individual roles, the results in Section 4.1 shows that some roles have more internal disagreement than other roles. This is true for architects and designers on the question about to what extent architecture documentation exists, and also for architects on the question about to what extent the documentation matches the system. The reason that there is disagreement within both roles may be that people with these roles work closer to the documentation and are therefore more sensitive to variations in its state. Moreover, internal disagreement is also noticeable for project managers on the question about to what extent the documentation is updated. A reason may be that project managers are more dependent on documentation update frequency when working with time and resource allocation. Finally, programmers and testers have larger internal disagreement than other roles for the question about how easy it is to gain insight into the system through the documentation. An explanation for this can be that these roles use the documentation for gaining system insight more than the other roles, and are therefore more sensitive to its ability to provide insight.

The results in Section 4.2 clearly show differences among the roles for the improvement question. System insight is the top improvement for all roles except designers and product managers. For these roles, change impact analysis and cost analysis are most important, respectively. The product manager role also stands out because it is the only role with strong focus on risk and cost analysis, and no focus at all on system insight. The reason that the product manager role differs on several accounts may be that this role has more market focus and less development focus than the other roles. The reason that the designer role differs may be that designers depend on the information in the architecture documentation more than other roles, and that this requires a strong focus on change impact analysis in order to handle ever-changing requirements.

The statistical analysis of the improvement question supports the differences among the roles outlined above. More specifically, designers' focus on change impact analysis and product managers' focus on cost and risk analysis are statistically significant. The fact that product managers do not consider system insight an important improvement is not significant, however. The existence of differences among the roles for the improvement question indicates that the priorities of respondents are different. This means that it becomes more difficult to create an improvement plan that satisfies all process users, since the plan needs to have a wider scope.

7 Conclusions

In this paper, we have presented results from a case study where we used a questionnaire for investigating process users' viewpoints and priorities regarding the architecture documentation process. The study was conducted at an office of Ericsson AB, Sweden. The objective of the study was to prepare improvement of the architecture documentation process at the company by examining process users' viewpoints and priorities with respect to their roles.

A large number of employees were asked questions about the current state of the architecture documentation and possible improvements of it. As explained in Section 1.2, we asked about the product (architecture documentation) rather than the process in order to have more tangible questions. The process users were divided into groups according to their software engineering roles. In order to analyse the results statistically, the following hypotheses were evaluated:

- H_0: *There are no differences among roles.*
- H_A: *There is a difference among roles.*

The two types of questions (current state and improvement) in the questionnaire were analysed separately. When analysing the results from the questions about the current state of the process, the null hypothesis could not be rejected. Our interpretation of this is that the company has succeeded in spreading knowledge about the process to the process users. However, some roles have larger internal disagreement compared to other roles for some of the question. This indicates that there may be underlying factors, other than role, that affect viewpoints.

When analysing the results from the improvement question, on the other hand, the null hypothesis could be rejected in favour of the alternative hypothesis. By performing a more in-depth statistical test and investigating the results from the improvement question directly, we found the following:

- System insight is not considered important to improve by the product managers. It is, however, the most important improvement for all other roles except the designers.
- Cost analysis and risk analysis are significantly more important to improve for product managers than for other roles. The reason may be a stronger market focus for this role than for the other roles.
- Change impact analysis is significantly more important to improve for designers than for other roles. The reason may be that designers use the documentation more than other roles when determining change impact.

Initially, we expected differences among roles both for viewpoints and priorities, since stakeholders of architecture documentation often are considered to have different needs and knowledge. Our expectations were however only fulfilled for priorities, as these clearly were different among the roles. It could be argued that it is "common knowledge" that priorities differ, which is why our expectations were set as they were. However, it remains difficult to foresee exactly how roles differ, which is important to know in process improvement. Furthermore, we had expected larger differences than were actually found. In any case, the fact that viewpoints, contrary to our expectations, did not differ while priorities did, leads us to conclude the following:

- It is important to cover process users' viewpoints and priorities in process improvement work, because they may not coincide with the prevalent expectations.
- Further research should investigate in which situations roles are likely to differ and in which they are likely to be similar.

Acknowledgements

This work was partly funded by The Knowledge Foundation in Sweden under a research grant for the project "Blekinge - Engineering Software Qualities (BESQ)" (http://www.bth.se/besq).

References

1. Aaen, I.: Software Process Improvement: Blueprints versus Recipes. IEEE Software 20 (2003) 86-92
2. Baddoo, N., Hall, T.: De-motivators for software process improvement: an analysis of practitioners' views. Journal of Systems and Software 66 (2003) 23-33
3. Basili, V., Green, S.: Software Process Evolution at the SEL. IEEE Software 11 (1994) 58-66

4. Berander, P., Wohlin, C.: Differences in Views between Development Roles in Software Process Improvement – A Quantitative Comparison. Proceedings of the 8th International Conference on Empirical Assessment in Software Engineering (EASE'04), Edinburgh Scotland (2004) 57-66
5. Clements, P., Bachmann, F., Bass, L., Garlan, D., Ivers, J., Little, R., Nord, R., Stafford J.: Documenting Software Architectures: Views and Beyond. Addison-Wesley (2003)
6. Conradi, R., Dybå, T.: An Empirical Study on the Utility of Formal Routines to Transfer Knowledge and Experience. ESEC/SIGSOFT FSE (2001) 268-276
7. Duda, R.O., Hart, P.E.: Pattern Classification and Scene Analysis. John Wiley & Sons (1973)
8. Fowler, M.: Who Needs an Architect? IEEE Software 20 (2003) 11-13
9. Garson, G. D.: PA 765 Statnotes: An Online Textbook. North Carolina State University, http://www2.chass.ncsu.edu/garson/pa765/statnote.htm, last checked March 3 (2005)
10. Hall, T., Wilson, D.: Views of software quality: a field report. IEE Proceedings on Software Engineering 144 (1997) 111-118
11. Hofmeister, C., Nord, R., Soni, D.: Applied Software Architecture. Addison-Wesley (2000)
12. Humphrey, W.: Managing the Software Process. Addison-Wesley (1989)
13. Jönsson, P., Wohlin, C.: An Evaluation of k-Nearest Neighbour Imputation Using Likert Data. Proceedings of the 10th International Software Metrics Symposium (METRICS'04), Chicago IL USA (2004) 108-118
14. Karlström, D., Runeson, P., Wohlin, C.: Aggregating Viewpoints for Strategic Software Process Improvement – a Method and a Case Study. IEE Proceedings on Software Engineering 149 (2002) 143-152
15. Klappholz, D., Bernstein, L., Port, D.: Assessing Attitude Towards, Knowledge of, and Ability to Apply, Software Development Process. Proceedings of the 16th Conference on Software Engineering Education and Training (CSEET'03), Madrid Spain (2003) 268-278
16. Lehmann, D.R., Winer, R.S.: Product Management. 3rd edn. McGraw-Hill (2002)
17. McFeeley, B.: IDEALSM: A User's Guide for Software Process Improvement. Handbook CMU/SEI-96-HB-001. Software Engineering Institute, Carnegie Mellon University (1996)
18. Nicholas, J.M.: Project Management for Business and Technology: Principles and Practise. 2nd edn. Prentice Hall (2001)
19. Pfleeger, S.L.: Software Engineering: Theory and Practise. Intl. edn. Prentice Hall (1998)
20. PROFES User Manual – Final Version 1999. http://www.vtt.fi/ele/profes/PUMv10.pdf, last checked March 3 (2005)
21. Rainer, A., Hall, T.: Key Success Factors for Implementing Software Process Improvement: a Maturity-Based Analysis. Journal of Systems and Software 62 (2002) 71-84
22. Robson, C.: Real World Research. 2nd edn. Blackwell Publishing (2002)
23. Siegel, S., Castellan Jr., N.J.: Nonparametric Statistics for the Behavioral Sciences. Intl. edn. McGraw-Hill (1988)
24. Sommerville, I.: Software Engineering. 6th edn. Addison-Wesley (2001)
25. Svahnberg, M.: A Study on Agreement Between Participants in an Architecture Assessment. Proceedings of the International Symposium on Empirical Software Engineering (ISESE'03), Rome Italy (2003) 61-71
26. Wohlin, C., Runeson, P., Höst, M., Ohlsson, M.C., Regnell, B., Wesslén, A.: Experimentation in Software Engineering: An Introduction. Kluwer Academic Publishers (2000)
27. Zahran, S.: Software Process Improvement: Practical Guidelines for Business Success. Addison-Wesley (1998)

Improved Control of Automotive Software Suppliers

Martin Ivarsson, Fredrik Pettersson, and Peter Öhman

Department of Computer Engineering,
Chalmers University of Technology, Gothenburg, Sweden

Abstract. There is a lack of early project control when automotive software is developed by external suppliers. This paper proposes a process improvement that targets early deliverables from suppliers as a means to improve project control. An addition to the existing automotive process employing a two-level use case approach is presented. In an example study involving Volvo 3P we show that the process improvements are applicable in real industrial development processes and that use cases are suitable for automotive requirements communication. The example also showed that use cases can be employed at the level of detail necessary to describe embedded systems.

1 Introduction

In many cases the first delivery from an automotive supplier to an OEM (Original Equipment Manufacturer) after a software product has been ordered is the first prototype. As the prototype is delivered rather late in the project there is a lack of project control, which in turn increases the risk of a misunderstanding of requirements and low software quality. The current common practice is based on traditional OEM requirement documentation (such as SRS "Software Requirement Specification"). At the supplier side, the resulting internal detailed requirements and specifications are not useful as early deliverables since most OEMs lack the competence to understand all the details in these documents. In addition, these documents might include supplier proprietary information that cannot be disclosed to the OEM.

There has been rather extensive research in quality management (e.g. [26]). Certification of software manufacturers using the CMM (Capability Maturity Model) [7, 8] or SPICE (ISO 15504) has proven useful in assessing and selecting capable suppliers. These methods do not provide any real means to check that the supplier actually follows the said process or the rate at which work is progressing. Thus they do not provide control mechanisms during development, which is the purpose of this paper.

Most research in the area of software project control (such as [27]) has focused on the actual software production process, which in the automotive domain is applicable to the processes at the suppliers. Generally (as in [28]), research has clearly pointed out the need to establish a reporting system that defines what critical data are needed and how and when they are needed. However, in the current automotive common practice process (e.g. [31]), such deliverables *between an OEM and a supplier* are missing in the time from the contractual agreement to the first delivered software prototype.

F. Bomarius and S. Komi-Sirviö (Eds.): PROFES 2005, LNCS 3547, pp. 358–369, 2005.

This paper presents a process improvement that targets early deliverables- in the requirements phase- from suppliers as an important way to improve project control. Concrete and measurable deliverables have been identified as important criteria for controlling projects according to plan [29]. In an example, we show the feasibility of using well-standardized use case models together with a proposed automotive-compliant process addition as means to obtain feedback through quantitative deliverables early in the software development process.

In order to be useable in practice, the developed process addition is cost efficient, i.e. it generates low additional resource demands for the OEM and can be used without a need of major changes to existing process activities. This is achieved by letting most of the added workload be carried out by the supplier. The existing documents and activities are not affected by the process addition, i.e. it is attachable to any iterative software development process used in the automotive industry today. As the added documents are based on and reflect the information in the existing documents, the suggested attachment is consistent with the existing process.

2 Use Case Usage

We employ use cases as early deliverables since they provide a generic solution that can be introduced into any existing development process. Use cases are useful because they give the OEM a way to describe and communicate goals to the suppliers and allow suppliers to communicate their grasp of the requirements on the system back to the OEM. This is because use cases, compared to other requirement documents, are easily understood by all stakeholders [1, 2, 3].

A well-defined use case standard is needed to enable quality control and improve communication. Today there is no common standard for what should be included in use cases. The UML has standardized the primitives of use case diagrams [18] but has not indicated exactly which topics should be included in the use cases or the manner in which they should be specified. There are a number of topics that are generally considered mandatory, which other topics that should be included depend on the context in which use cases are employed. For this study we adapt the templates presented in [4], explicitly developed for embedded systems.

The definition of use cases is often that they should specify a flow of events that the system follows in order to yield an observable value to an actor [1, 5, 6]. Fitting the needs of the automotive industry, including the possibility to describe embedded systems with use cases, our proposal expands the use case concept to enable derivation of use cases from stakeholders' needs and major functionality described in the SRS. As a result, use cases do not necessarily yield an observable value to a specific actor. This approach has previously been used in embedded system specification by Nasr et al. [16].

The proposed process additions employ use cases at two different levels of detail, similar to the strategy used by Cockburn [19]. Both levels employ Real use cases, as defined by Larman [20], as technical details and interfaces to other systems are captured. The first, *summary level* use cases, is produced by the OEM, preferably before choosing a supplier. The summary level use case model visualizes and communicates the goals of the system to the supplier and can even be made part of the contractual agreement. The other, *detailed level* use cases, is produced by the chosen supplier on the basis of the summary level use cases and the supplier's knowledge of the domain of the system. It is then delivered to the OEM in order to enable control of the progress of the work and, most importantly, to show that the supplier has a correct understanding of the requirements.

Summary level

USE CASE <number>	<use case name>
Level	
(Scope)	
Primary Actor	
Secondary Actors	
Stakeholders and Interests	
Preconditions	
Success Guarantees	
Minimal Guarantees	
Trigger	
Summary	
Special requirements	

Detailed level

USE CASE <number>		<use case name>	
Level			
Scope			
Primary Actor			
Secondary Actors			
Stakeholders and Interests			
Preconditions			
Success Guarantees			
Minimal Guarantees			
Extension Points			
Trigger			
Main Flow		Step	Action
Alternative Flows		Step	Action
Technology and Data Variation list			
Special Requirements			

Fig. 1. Detailed level and summary level use case templates

A structured way of writing use cases, including templates and guidelines, is needed (especially since two parties are involved) so that they can be used for quality assurance. To the best of our knowledge there is not a great deal of research on guidelines for writing use cases. A set of guidelines is proposed in [22] that is a collective result of the research done in the area. We have modified the style and content guidelines given in [22] to suit the automotive domain.

When new artifacts are introduced in a process, the corresponding quality assurance mechanisms must also be defined. As the literature recommends reviews to ensure the quality of requirement documents such as use cases [3, 5, 30], reviews has been chosen for the added quality assurance activities.

3   Process Addition Implementation

When requirement specifications have been delivered to the supplier, the first delivery from the supplier to the OEM is currently most often the first prototype. This creates a gap in the communication between the two parties (as illustrated in Fig. 2), hence prohibiting the OEM from controlling the supplier during the greater part of development.

Still recognizing the need to investigate and improve communication during other phases of development, we employ use cases as a deliverable to fill the gap in the requirements phase.

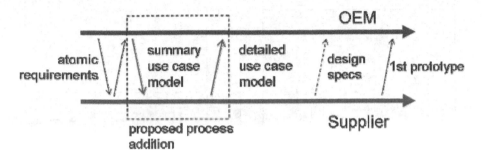

Fig. 2. Process addition scope

The remaining part of this section describes the proposed additions to the process in more detail. In order to be applicable in the automotive industry, the additions are developed to be cost effective. Furthermore, because the automotive industry is a low risk business not eager to change existing processes, the additions must be attachable to these processes, i.e. they must be able to be used without affecting existing procedures. To be attachable the process additions need to ensure consistency with other requirement documents. Hence the new documents must not introduce new requirements on the system under construction.

3.1 Process Description

This section presents the process additions that are used to introduce use cases into an organization. The existing development process that they extend is assumed to be a generic iterative development process for embedded systems.

The process description specifies a framework of activities and documents, detailing the workflow and distribution of tasks between OEM and supplier.

It is assumed that, in the existing process, the OEM specifies customer demands that are later elaborated into system requirements by the supplier [21]. In the automotive industry, customer demands most often include a partial solution to the problem. The supplier then provides a complete solution, whose details are not always understood by OEMs. The process addition provides a means to communicate the solution and assure its correctness.

Fig. 3 shows the proposed process additions together with existing adjacent activities. Each activity in the workflow in the figure requires a certain input to be carried out and subsequently produces some kind of output to be useful. The artifacts necessary for each activity to commence, denoted with "I", and the produced output, denoted with "O", are specified in Table 1.

As perspective based reading (PBR) has proven to be the most efficient review technique for finding defects in requirement documents written in natural language

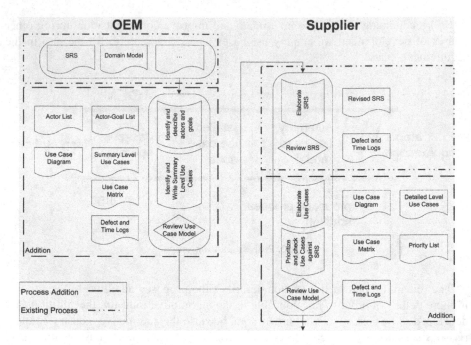

Fig. 3. Proposed process addition workflow

[9, 10], it was chosen for the added quality assurance activities (activities "Review Summary Level Use Case Model" and "Review Detailed Level Use Case Model" in Table 1). PBR has furthermore been proven to be cost effective, as more defects are found per hour as compared to any other technique used today [11]. Furthermore, as PBR provides guidance for reviewers, less experienced employees can be utilized [12]. PBR builds on the scenario-based techniques first presented by Porter et al. [11], who based their idea on the work of Parnas et al. [13].

The most salient feature of PBR is the assignment of different roles to the reviewers. The use case models are reviewed from different perspectives, guided by role-specific reading instructions and a number of checklist-like questions. On the basis of the knowledge of the automotive domain, the roles of designer, user, process expert and tester were chosen. It should be noted that the PBR technique facilitates the participation of the OEM (in the user role) in reviews of detailed level use cases at the supplier.

The resulting process is attachable to any modern iterative software development process, as documents from other parts of the process serve as input to the additional activities and not vice versa. In other words, existing documents and activities are not affected by the production of use cases. Producing SRS and Domain Model, both input to the suggested process addition, is today considered best practice and these artifacts are thus available in almost every project. Since detailed level use cases include far more detail than their summary level counterparts, most of the added workload is carried out by the supplier. In addition, most of the information included

Table 1. Input and output of the activities in the proposed process addition

	Activity (Artefact)	SRS	Domain Model	Actor List	Actor-Goal List	Use Case Names	Summary Level UC	Use Case Diagram	Use Case Matrix	Defect + Time Log	Action Plan	Contract	Detailed Level UC	Priority List
O E M	Identify Actors	I	I	O										
	Identify Goals	I	I	I	O									
	Identify Use Cases	I	I		I	O								
	Write Summary Level Use Cases	I	I	I	I	I	O	O	O					
	Review Summary Level Use Case Model	I	I	IO	IO		IO	IO	IO	O	O			
	Select Supplier	I		I	I			I	I	I		O		
S u p p l i e r	Elaborate & Review SRS	IO		I	I			I	I	I				
	Write Detailed Level Use Cases	I	I	I	I			I	IO	I			O	
	Prioritize Use Cases				I				I				I	O
	Check Use Cases against SRS	I		I	I				I	O			I	
	Review Detailed Level Use Case Model	I	I	IO	IO			IO	IO	O	O		IO	IO

in the summary level use cases should have already been elicited in an initial requirements analysis. This makes use cases cost effective in the OEM's perspective. Added workload at the supplier can of course not be neglected as a cost driver, but these activities become part of the contract negotiations and have high visibility. Hence, they will be subjected to the normal cost reduction efforts of the OEM. In reality, the amount attached to this added workload that can be billed to the OEM is not significant because of the very competitive environment of suppliers.

4 Quality Control Mechanisms

Introducing use cases as an essential delivery in the requirements phase enables a number of important control mechanisms.

Early deliveries from the supplier to the OEM make it easier to identify misunderstandings in the goals of the system and to correct them early in development. As the supplier elaborates the summary level use case model into a detailed level use case model and delivers it to the OEM, these added documents indicate whether the supplier has interpreted the requirement documents correctly. This provides a means to reach consensus between the OEM and supplier on the system under construction.

In addition, obtaining early attention from the supplier can be a problem, as many suppliers tend to give priority to the OEM with the earliest production start. The detailed use case model deliverable shows supplier progress and the delivery ensures the OEM that development has started. Later, basing the functions to be implemented in each prototype on the detailed use case model will make it possible to validate and verify a subset of the functionality of the system under construction for each prototype released. Further, the OEM can participate in setting priorities for the use cases so that the most important functionality is implemented first. Risks are minimized, as the most important parts of the system are implemented first and new parts become less important with each prototype that is released. If the schedule for a prototype is exceeded or the quality is deficient, actions can be taken before it is realized that the system is imperfect or that the project is exceeding schedule as the final release date is approaching or has even been reached.

The use case model itself is guaranteed high quality through the employment of a specialized inspection technique, PBR. Inspections disclose defects in the use case model and detect erroneous requirements in the SRS. As these inspections are carried out before proceeding to other activities, they prevent defects from propagating from the SRS to other artifacts. The delivery of inspection documents from supplier to OEM can indicate the general quality of the supplier's work and at the same time help assure that work progresses as planned.

The delivery of these artifacts forms a point in the development where the work carried out by the supplier to that time can be examined by the OEM, a so called milestone or gate. As use cases are derived from ordinary atomic requirements, measuring the quality of the use case model indicates the quality of the entire requirements phase. Depending on the type of project, different conditions, needed to be fulfilled at this point can be specified, e.g. completeness, number of defects found in review etc.

5 Example: Volvo 3P

The study involves the Embedded Software Development department (here called ESW) at Volvo 3P. Volvo 3P is a business unit in the Volvo Group that supports the three truck companies Volvo Trucks, Renault Trucks and Mack. The ESW department is responsible for the development and purchase of software used in braking systems, suspension and dashboard controls etc. This example is a part of ongoing process improvement efforts at the department and aims to show the feasibility of the proposed process additions.

To be applicable in an industrial setting, the process addition must be shown to be attachable and consistent with the existing requirements documents when applied to an actual software development process used in industry today.

The Global Development Process (GDP) [14] is a framework for project management used by Volvo companies worldwide. The GDP describes the entire development of a new vehicle, from pre-study to follow-up. The electrical engineering process is described in the GDIs shown in Fig. 4. The dashed lines represent GDP gates, and each ellipse represents a GDI. The GDIs complement the GDP and synchronize activities and deliveries around the GDP gates.

The proposed process additions are applicable to the Software Level GDI [15] as thisit describes the software development process used, including how to manage externally developed software.

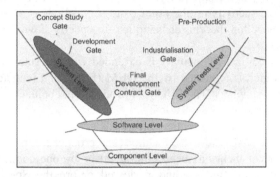

Fig. 4. Relationship between the GDIs and the GDP gateways

5.1 Docking to the Software Level GDI

This section shows how the proposed additions can be added to the process described in the Software Level GDI [15]. It should be noted that not all details of the Volvo process are disclosed in this paper. However, as the main focus of the paper is the relation between OEM (in this case ESW) and supplier, the additions to the parts of the GDI concerning externally developed software will be described. Fig. 5 summarizes the affected activities and artifacts of the GDI together with the proposed additions. An "I" denotes that the artifact serves as input to the activity, while an "O" denotes output. Even though the production of the summary and detailed level use

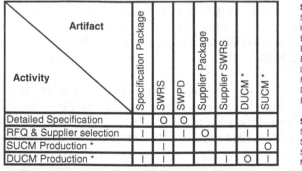

Activity \ Artifact	Specification Package	SWRS	SWPD	Supplier Package	Supplier SWRS	DUCM *	SUCM *
Detailed Specification	I	O	O				
RFQ & Supplier selection	I	I	I	O		I	I
SUCM Production *		I					O
DUCM Production *	I	I			I	O	I

* Addition

Specification Package:
Signal DB
HMI Requirements
Electrical Requirements
EE Regulation List
EE Project description
Lists of functions allocated to the node
Function specifications
Deliveries contents and scheduling
EE Architecture

Supplier Package:
SWPTP
SWDP
SWTP
MoM from SRM

Fig. 5. Summary of the relevant part of the Software Level GDI together with the process additions

case models is part of the "Detailed Specification" and "RFQ & Supplier selection" activities, respectively, these have been extracted to illustrate the inputs and outputs of the additions.

"Detailed specification" and "RFQ & Supplier selection" are the only activities of the existing process that are directly influenced. The main output of the "Detailed Specification" activity is the software requirement specification (SWRS). The "RFQ & Supplier selection" activity on the other hand serves both as a vehicle to choose a capable supplier and, for the chosen supplier, to specify how the product will be developed.

The "Detailed specification" activity is extended with the summary level use case model (SUCM), which is produced by the OEM (ESW) and is included in the RFQ sent out to potential suppliers. The SUCM is produced in conjunction with the SWRS and should reflect the goals of the SWRS.

The next activity, "RFQ & Supplier selection", is extended with the detailed level use case model (DUCM). The use case model is produced either by each potential supplier before one of them has been contracted or by one contracted supplier. In either case it should be finished and reviewed before the Specification Review Meeting (SRM), which works as a gate at the end of this activity. The DUCM constitutes one of the inputs to the Software Project Time Plan (SWPTP) and is created before this document.

5.2 Results

To be attachable, the additional activities must not affect the existing procedures. As seen in Fig. 4 above, both the SUCM and the DUCM serve as input to the "RFQ & Supplier selection" activity. However, the SUCM is only included as one of the documents delivered to the supplier as a part of the RFQ ("Request For Quotation"), not affecting the other documents involved. In addition it serves as input to the production of the DUCM, which is itself part of the addition. The DUCM serves as input to the scheduling of prototypes and helps decide what functionality should be included in these, hence affecting *when* to implement what but not *how*. Moreover, the reviews of the use case models might unveil defects in the SWRS, hence improving its quality, but do not serve as input in the production of it.

It can be concluded from the example and discussions with Volvo engineers that the process additions are attachable to the existing process at ESW, as they do not affect existing procedures.

Utilizing use cases in requirement engineering is today considered best practice but is conventionally not employed at the level of abstraction needed to support the development of embedded software at ESW. However, use cases have been employed in this type of setting before (i.e. at Rolls Royce plc (RR)) [16, 17].

As a real pilot case the proposed process additions were applied to the "Idle Adjust" function for Volvo engines. The "Idle Adjust" function constitutes an embedded system, which in the use case world means that all actors interacting with the system under construction are non-human and are either other systems or signals. The pilot study showed promising results, completely capturing the functional requirements of the atomic requirement document (SWRS), including interactions with other systems. As the use case is produced on the basis of existing requirements documents and does not add new requirements, the proposed addition is consistent with the documents in the existing process.

6 Discussion

Because the proposed solution is an addition to the existing development process, the workload in the requirements phase increase both at the OEM and at the supplier. As discussed in section 3, most of the added work is carried out by the supplier and is subjected to the normal cost reduction efforts. The effort needed for the OEM to produce summary level use cases can not however be neglected. This causes an increase in the time needed to complete this phase and subsequently makes requirement elicitation and communication more expensive. The increased costs in the early phases are however expected to be compensated by the decrease in hidden expenses later in the project. At this stage this is only an assumption and is not based on empirical knowledge. Further studies must be done to establish the return on the additional money invested. Kelly et al. [23] however concluded that more defects are found during reviews of requirement specifications than in any other documents in the software development life cycle. With respect to cost effectiveness, Doolan [24] reported that industrial experience indicates a 30-time return for every hour spent on reviewing specifications. In addition, Russell [25] reports a return of 33 hours of maintenance saved per hour of review. Use cases serve as a vehicle for uncovering defects caused by a supplier's misinterpretation of the customer's requirements, hence improving the review process during the requirements phase. This leads to fewer defects remaining late in development and consequently to lower expenses to correct them.

Another cause of extra expenses is a lack of experience in employing use cases as part of the development process. A great deal of training is needed at the OEM, and probably at the supplier as well, to enable them to utilize the solutions proposed in this paper. The money invested in training developers is however a one-off expense that in the long run should result in a much larger return. In theory this reasoning should apply to all parts of the proposed addition, although no studies have yet been done to support this.

The new artefacts can possibly replace existing requirement documents in the longer perspective. This adds the extra value of improved, standardized methods for eliciting requirements and communicating them while at the same time moving part of the expenses to the supplier.

7 Conclusion

This paper shows how to increase control over automotive software development projects by introducing new early deliverables from the suppliers. This is done by adding standards and procedures for using use case models in early phases to the existing automotive process.

In an example involving Volvo 3P we showed that the proposed process additions can be attached to an existing real life software development process. On the basis of our experiences from the example and the pilot implementation, we conclude that the process additions proposed are an important step in solving the problem of early project control when using externally developed software, which is the case at many OEMs today. Furthermore, the pilot study of a real engine control function demonstrated that the two level use case models were suitable for automotive requirement communication and showed that use cases can be employed at the level of detail necessary to describe embedded systems.

The extra workload imposed by adding activities to the existing process is mainly at the supplier side. To be cost neutral at the OEM side, the new activities must not only be added but must replace some existing activities. While this is possible, it is beyond the scope of this paper. A change in the automotive process would have taken considerable time and effort, but is a natural step after using and assessing the additions proposed in this paper.

Acknowledgments

The authors would like to thank Stéphane Verger at Volvo 3P for his valuable criticism and stimulating discussions. This research has been conducted within the project CEDES which is funded by the Swedish industry and government joint research program IVSS – Intelligent Vehicle Safety Systems.

References

1. Jacobson I., Booch G., Rumbaugh J., *The Unified Software Development Process*, Addison-Wesley (1999)
2. Jacobson I., Christerson M., Jonsson P., Övergaard G., *Object-Oriented Software Engineering – A Use Case Driven Approach*, Addison-Wesley (1992)
3. Kulak D., Guiney E., *Use Cases: Requirements in Context*, Addison-Wesley (2000)
4. Ivarsson M., Pettersson F., "A Use Case Driven Approach to Improve Quality Management of Suppliers", Technical report no 04-15, Dept of Computer Engineering, Chalmers University of Technology, Gothenburg, Sweden (2004)
5. Schneider G., Winters J.P., *Applying Use Cases, Second Edition: A Practical Guide*, Addison-Wesley (2001)
6. Cockburn A., "Structuring Use Cases with Goals", http://members.aol.com/acockburn/papers/usecases.htm (2000)
7. Humphrey W.S., *Managing the Software Process*, Addison-Wesley (1989)
8. Paulk M.C., Curtis B., Crissis M.B., Weber C.V., "Capability Maturity Model for Software, Version 1.1", CMU/SEI-93-TR-24 (1993)
9. Basili V.R., Shull F., Lanubile F., "Using Experiments to Build a Body of Knowledge", IEEE Transactions on Software Engineering, 25(4) (1998) pp. 456-474
10. Basili V., Caldiera G., Lanubile F., Shull F., "Studies on Reading Techniques", Proc. of the Twenty-First Annual Software Engineering Workshop, SEL-96-002, (1996) pp.59-65

11. Porter A., Votta L., Basili V.R., "Comparing Detection Methods for Software Requirements Inspection: A Replicated Experiment", IEEE Transactions on Softwrae Engineering, vol. 21 no. 6 (1995) pp. 563-575
12. Shull F., Rus I., Basili V., "How Perspective-Based Reading Can Improve Requirements Inspections", Computer, vol. 33 no. 7 (2000) pp. 73-79
13. Parnas D.L., Weiss D.M., "Active Design Reviews: Principles and Practices", Proc. of the Eight International Conference on Software Engineering (1985) pp. 132-136
14. Volvo 3P, "GDP Pocket Guide", Issue 4 2003-03-01 (2003)
15. Volvo 3P Trucks Standard, "SoftWare Level EEE GDI (GDI 966-88)", Volvo 3P, Issued by Andreas Nyberg and Daniel Lathuiliere
16. Nasr E., McDermid J., Bernat G., "Eliciting and Specifying Requirements with Use Cases for Embedded Systems", Proc. of the Seventh International Workshop on Object-Oriented Real-Time Dependable Systems (WORDS 2002) , San Diego, California, January 7-9 (2002)
17. Nasr E., McDermid J., Bernat G., "A Technique for Managing Complexity of Use Cases for Large Complex Embedded Systems", Proc. of the Fifth IEEE International Symposium on Object-Oriented Real-Time Distributed Computing, ISORC'02 (2002)
18. OMG 2003, "UML 2.0 Superstructure Specification", Object Management Group, http://www.omg.org/docs/ptc/03-08-02.pdf (2003)
19. Cockburn A., *Writing Effective Use Cases*, Addison-Wesley (2001)
20. Larman, C., *Applying UML and Patterns: An Introduction to Object-Oriented Analysis and Design*, Prentice Hall, Upper Saddle River, NJ (1998)
21. Weber M., Weisbrod J., "Requirements Engineering in Automotive Development: Experiences and Challenges", Software, IEEE, Vol. 20 Issue 1 (2003) pp. 16 – 24
22. Anda B., Sjöberg D., Jörgensen M. "Quality and Understandability of Use Case Models", ECOOP 2001 (2001) pp. 402-428
23. Kelly J.C., Sherif J.S., Hops J. "An Analysis of Defect Densities Found during Software Inspections", Journal of Systems Software, vol.17 (1992) pp. 111-117
24. Doolan E. P., "Experience with Fagan's Inspection Method", Software: Practices and Experiences, vol. 22 no. 2 (1992) pp. 173-182
25. Russell G. W., "Experience with Inspection in Ultra Large-Scale Development", IEEE Software, vol. 8 no. 1 (1991) pp. 25-31
26. Dunn R.H., "Software Quality Assurance: A Management Perspective", Software Engineering Project Management, Thayer and Yourdon eds., IEEE Computer Society (1997) pp. 433-440
27. Thayer R.H., "Software Engineering Project Management", Software Engineering Project Management, Thayer and Yourdon eds., IEEE Computer Society (1997) pp 72-104
28. Mackenzie R.A., "The Management Process in 3-D", Harvard Business Review Nov.-Dec. (1969) pp 80-87
29. Thamhain H.J., Wilemon D.L., "Criteria for Controlling Projects According to Plan", Software Engineering Project Management, Thayer and Yourdon eds., 1997, IEEE Computer Society (1986) pp. 426-432
30. Armour F., Miller G., *Advanced Use Case Modelling*, Addison-Wesley (2000)
31. Heumesser N., Houdek F., "Experiences in Managing an Automotive Requirements Engineering Process", Proceedings of the 12th IEEE International Requirements Engineering Conference (2004)

Enterprise-Oriented Software Development Environments to Support Software Products and Processes Quality Improvement

Mariano Montoni, Gleison Santos, Karina Villela,
Ana Regina Rocha, Guilherme H. Travassos, Sávio Figueiredo,
Sômulo Mafra, Adriano Albuquerque,
and Paula Mian

Federal University of Rio de Janeiro - COPPE Sistemas
Caixa Postal 68511 – CEP 21941-972– Rio de Janeiro, Brazil
{mmontoni, gleison, darocha, ght}@cos.ufrj.br

Abstract. Software organizations have to adapt efficiently to cope with clients needs changes and new and evolving technologies in order to guarantee business success. Moreover, organizations must continuously enhance their capability to develop software in order to increase products and processes quality. These characteristics constitute dynamic environments that require specific competences from software engineers such as knowledge related to software technologies, ability to adapt software processes concerning project characteristics, and experience on product and process quality management. This paper presents enterprise-oriented software development environments that support software engineers to execute software processes more effectively and to produce products with better quality. A main feature of these environments is the support offered to organizational knowledge management. Thus the paper also presents the main characteristics of the knowledge management infrastructure integrated to those environments. The practical experience using the environments has shown several benefits, such as an increase of product and process quality, and the preservation of organizational knowledge related to software processes and the development of software products.

1 Introduction

Software organizations have to adapt efficiently to cope with clients needs changes and new and evolving technologies in order to guarantee business success. Moreover, organizations must continuously enhance their capability to develop software in order to improve their innovation ability and increase organizational processes efficiency [1]. In order to achieve this goal, organizations must be more productive, increase the quality of software products, diminish project effort and costs, and deal with the criticality of time-to-market for commercial products [2].

These characteristics constitute dynamic environments that require specific competences from software engineers such as knowledge related to software technologies,

F. Bomarius and S. Komi-Sirviö (Eds.): PROFES 2005, LNCS 3547, pp. 370–384, 2005.

ability to adapt software processes concerning project characteristics, and experience on product and process quality management. Globalization, increasing competition, more dynamic markets and shorter cycles in product development and innovation increase the need for a better adaptation to those environmental factors. These factors establish the need for a consequent adaptation of all business processes, including software processes, to existing and future market needs [1].

Software processes are knowledge-intensive business processes, i.e., a process that relies very much on knowledge [4]. Therefore, software processes can be considered as core processes of the organization, which executions should produce or add new knowledge to the organization's knowledge repository. Moreover, software processes executions require from software engineers innovative and creative abilities [3, 4].

Since participants of software processes executions have different background knowledge and past-experiences, different domains knowledge are applied at different levels [1]. Besides that, knowledge and software processes are integrated and should be evaluated as a whole, i.e., for knowledge management to be of use in an organization, it should be effortlessly incorporated in everyday business activities. Large parts of an organization's activities, especially on the operational level, are structured around business processes [1]. Therefore, it is imperative to integrate knowledge management with software processes, which means that a computerized system that supports business processes should also support knowledge management [5, 13].

In this context, Software Development Environments (SDE) have been playing an important role to support software engineers in the execution of software processes through the application of specific procedures that combine integrated tools and techniques in accordance to particular software paradigms. Moreover, SDE are evolving to integrate knowledge management activities within software processes aiming to support developers to produce better software products based on organizational knowledge and previous experiences more effectively [6].

This paper presents **Taba Workstation** SDEs. The **Taba Workstation** was created from the perception that different domain applications have distinct characteristics that influence in the environment from which software engineers develop software [7]. It is being used to support the deployment of software processes in small and medium size Brazilian companies as part of a larger project, named QualiSoft. The objective of this project is to increase the capability of software organizations and the quality of their software products through the adequate use of software engineering techniques in their software processes.

The next section presents some basic concepts related to SDE. The **Taba Workstation** infrastructure is presented in section 3. The steps executed to support software processes deployment in small and medium size companies in the context of the QualiSoft project are presented in section 4. The section 5 presents the **Taba Workstation** Knowledge Management tools. The section 6 presents some practical results of organizations that have been using the **Taba Workstation** SDEs. Finally, section 7 presents some conclusions and points out future work.

2 Supporting Software Products and Processes Quality Improvement Through Software Development Environments and Knowledge Management

A Software Development Environment (SDE) is defined as a computational system that supports software development, maintenance and improvements. It is supposed to support individual and group activities, project management activities, enhancement of software products quality, and increase of the productivity, providing the means for the software engineers to control the project and measure the activities evolution based on information gathered across the development. SDE should also provide the infrastructure to the development and integration of tools to support the execution of software processes. Moreover, this infrastructure should maintain a repository containing software project information gathered across its life cycle.

Recent researches have demonstrated the necessity of standardization of software development methodologies in an organization aiming to increase the control and improve the quality of products produced through the execution of software development processes [8, 9]. Therefore, SDE should not only support software engineers in the execution of software processes activities, but also provide the means to execute these processes according to organizational software development standards.

The standardization of software processes can be achieved through the definition of a Standard Process, i.e., a basic process that guides the establishment of a common process across the organization [8]. This process is the base for the definition of software development processes specialized according to the software type (paradigm and technologies), and to the development characteristics (e.g., distributed or centralized development). These specialized processes can be used to define specific processes considering particularities of the software project, a.k.a., instantiated software processes. Therefore, a SDE should be developed to guide software engineers in the execution of software processes instantiated to a specific software project.

Although it is recognized the importance of standardization of software processes, software organizations must cope with many difficulties that jeopardizes the institutionalization of standard processes, for instance, the dynamism of software processes, the necessity to apply new and evolving technologies, and the people turnover. Therefore, it is imperative for the organizations to manage their members' knowledge in an efficient way in order to guarantee the improvement of their software products and processes, and to preserve organizational knowledge [10, 11].

The identification, maintenance and dissemination of different types of knowledge related to software processes from one project to another are important to increase organization competitive advantages and improve software processes and products quality [12]. Efficient management of such knowledge supports organizational learning and initiatives for software process improvement [14].

The fact that most software development organizations are process-centered provides many benefits (e.g., process-centered knowledge management systems can be designed to associate software process activities with knowledge necessary to execute it explicitly) [14]. Moreover, tacit and explicit members' knowledge related to software processes are valuable individual assets that must be captured and converted into the organizational level. The collected knowledge represents indicators of problems concerning the software process definition or the environment in which the software is being developed. This important knowledge can be used to learn about the software process and to provide the means for implementing organizational changes aiming to enhance business performance [15]. In order to acquire such knowledge efficiently, it is necessary to transform arbitrary experiences declarations in structured explicit representations through the execution of activities for knowledge acquisition, packaging, dissemination and utilization [16].

Lindvall *et al.* [17] present some benefits of a knowledge management program institutionalization: (i) efficient reuse of documented experiences; (ii) easiness to find solutions for problems within the organization; (iii) identification and storage of valuable experiences; and (iv) facility to propose measures to improve processes execution and increase software products quality. Basili *et al.* [18] and Ruhe [19] point out that by structuring and explicitly representing software process knowledge, it is possible to define efficient training programs that can increase employees' productivity and foster transference of innovative software engineering technology. Landes [20] also notes that knowledge management solutions efficiently support activities of organization members with poor experience in a specific area or domain.

Although most organizations recognize the importance of managing software process knowledge, the establishment of a knowledge management program is sometimes a laborious task. For instance, it is hard to convert tacit knowledge to explicit, and it is difficult to implement knowledge management solutions in a nonintrusive way. Weber *et al.* [21] point out problems with knowledge management systems, for instance, inadequacy of knowledge representation formats and lack of incorporation of knowledge management systems into the processes they are intended to support.

3 The Taba Workstation

The Taba Workstation was created from the perception that different domain applications have distinct characteristics that influence in the environment from which software engineers develop software [7]. During the last years, the Taba Workstation evolved to comply with the different levels of capability maturity models of software organizations and to support knowledge management activities integrated to software processes. Therefore, the main objectives of Taba Workstation are: (i) to support the configuration of process-centered software development environments for different organizations (Configured SDE); (ii) to support the automatic generation (i.e., instantiation) of software development environments for specific projects (Enterprise-Oriented SDE); (iii) to support software development using the instantiated environment; and (iv) to support the management of organizational knowledge related to software processes. Compared to similar SDEs, the fact that the Taba Workstation was developed by the research group allowed the freely distribution of the system to software development organizations.

The CASE tools integrated in the environments offer automated support to: (i) adaptation of the organization standard processes for a specific project; (ii) definition of the organizational structure [6]; (iii) acquisition, filtering, packaging and dissemination of organizational knowledge [6]; (iv) planning the organization of specific projects; (v) time, costs, risks [22], human resources planning, monitoring and control [6]; (vi) planning and execution of Configuration Management activities; (vii) identification of software product quality requirements; (viii) documentation planning; (ix) supporting the planning and monitoring of corrective actions; (x) supporting measurement and analysis activities based on the GQM method; (xi) project monitoring through the generation of periodic reports and measures; (xii) controlling of the activities executed during a specific project; (xiii) requirements management; and (xiv) post mortem analysis.

One of the greatest restrictions for knowledge sharing is the use of different concepts to describe a domain for different systems. The development of ontologies facilitates the sharing of a common terminology. The use of ontologies in the Taba Workstation infrastructure facilitates the communication between multiple users and the retrieval of knowledge stored in the environment. Considering communication, the defined ontologies reduces terminological and conceptual mismatch in a company. When retrieving knowledge items, the ontologies' supplies vocabularies whose terms are used as links among multiple knowledge/data bases contents. Moreover, when defining synonyms and acronyms for the concepts, ontologies provide linguistic equivalents, which may occur in text documents and can be used to classify and access nonformal knowledge.

The Software Engineering Ontology defines a common vocabulary to guide the registration/distribution of a company's knowledge map and software engineering knowledge in the Taba Workstation. A company's knowledge map defines for each employee its level of skills, knowledge and experiences.

The Enterprise Ontology provides concepts and attributes related to the structure, behavior and knowledge owned by companies, defining a common vocabulary to guide the description of any company. The Enterprise Ontology aims to supply a common vocabulary that can be used to represent useful knowledge for the software developers on the involved organizations in a software project. It supports the development of several CASE tools in the Taba Workstation SDEs [6].

The ontology explicit definition supported the identification of potentially useful terms and phrases, definition of ontology semantics and sub-ontologies (depicted in figure 1) that describe concepts aiming to facilitate understanding, for example:

− how the organization is perceived in its environment,
− how the organization is structured, which are their objectives and how it behaves,
− how organization's projects have been lead and how the desired and possessed abilities have been distributed into the organization,
− who are the available resources on the organization and how the distribution of authority and responsibility in the organization are accomplished.

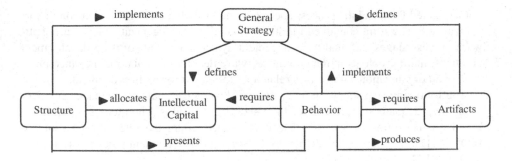

Fig. 1. Sub-ontologies of Enterprise Ontology

4   Using TABA Configured Environments to Support Software Processes Deployment in Small and Medium Size Companies

Since 2003, software engineers of several small and medium size Brazilian organizations are using the Taba Workstation in the context of the QualiSoft project to increase their capability to develop software through the adequate use of Software Engineering methods and techniques in its software processes. The QualiSoft project resulted from a contract between the RioSoft (a non-governmental organization that integrates the Softex Program - Society for the Support of Brazilian Software Production and Exportation) and the Federal University of Rio de Janeiro.

The QualiSoft project was constituted of the following activities: (i) definition of standard software development and maintenance processes adjusted for small and medium size companies; (ii) training in Software Engineering methods and techniques and in the software processes defined; (iii) adaptation of the standard process to each company; (iv) use of a Taba Configured SDE to support the use of the processes; and (iv) follow-up of the companies in the execution of pilot projects.

Since the focus of the QualiSoft project is on small and medium size organizations, we executed the project with a pool of organizations with similar characteristics aiming to decrease the overall cost and increase the project feasibility. The first phase of the project started on August 2003 and aimed to address a pool of 10 organizations. The second phase started on January 2004 and addressed a second pool of 9 organizations.

The next sections describe the following steps executed to achieve the objective of the QualiSoft project: (i) definition of software process in accordance to specific characteristics of software development and strategic goals of each organization and training using the Taba Workstation SDEs; and (ii) deployment of the defined software processes using a Taba Configured SDE.

4.1   Software Process Definition and Training Using the Taba Workstation

The first step in the execution of the QualiSoft project was to be acquainted of the individual characteristics of the organizations. In order to do so, each organization filled out a detailed form and the process specialists had to schedule regular visits on the organizations. The form contained questions related to the organizational culture, software process stages and quality management systems adopted software development practices, main problems in the current software development and maintenance processes, and organizational objectives related to software process improvement.

The following step was to define software development and maintenance standard processes adequate to small and medium size organizations. The processes defined is based on the software processes life cycle described in the international standard ISO/IEC 12207 [9] and it is adherent to the software development practices defined in the CMMI [23] Level 2 process areas.

In parallel to the processes definition activity, the members of the organizations were trained in the Software Engineering methods and techniques. During the first year, approximately 32 hours were spent on formal training. This training was performed under the form of tutorials on the following topics: Software Engineering, Software Process, Requirements Engineering, Configuration Management, Project Management and Software Products Quality. Approximately, 80 professionals were trained during this phase. After the theoretical training, project managers and software developers participated on a specific training on the standard software processes defined. Training activities during the second year included other important topics, such as Peer-review, Software Tests, Measurement and Analysis, Supplier Agreement and Knowledge Management, constituting 44 hours of formal training. During the second year of the project, more than 70 organizational members were trained.

The following step focused on the processes deployment supported by the configured environment in each organization.

4.2 Software Processes Deployment Using a Taba Configured SDE

These steps had been carried out individually in each organization considering its specific characteristics. Initially, the standard processes defined previously had been adapted by the software process specialist to each company considering the characteristics identified in the beginning of the project, such as software types developed, documents produced and software development paradigms adopted. After the approval of the adaptations by the organization, a software development environment was configured based on the adapted processes (the organization's standard process).

The configured environment was installed in each organization followed by 20 hours of hands-on training on the software tools. After this training, a pilot project was carried out. Using their configured environment each organization instantiated a specific environment for its pilot project through the execution of the AdaptPro tool.

The objective of the AdaptPro tool is to support the institutionalization of the standard processes because it facilitates the adoption of these processes in all the projects of the organization. By using the AdaptPro tool, the software engineering can execute the following activities: (i) characterize the project; (ii) plan the process that will guide the project through the adaptation of the organizational standard process considering the project characteristics; and (iii) instantiate a SDE to support the execution of the planned process. The figure 2 presents a screenshot of the AdaptPro tool. On the left side of this figure, the system presents the activities that guide the execution of the tool. On the right side of the figure, the system presents another screen to support the execution of the selected activity; in this case, it is presented the screen that supports the definition of a life cycle model to a specific project as part of the process planning activity. A list of life cycle models and the respective level of adequability to the project considering its characteristics are presented on the right side of the screen. Besides that, the user can consult the justification of the automatic identification of the adequability level and can consult the software processes defined for similar projects that used the same specialized process and life cycle model facilitating the selection of an adequate project life cycle model by the user. Moreover, the user can consult knowledge related to life cycle models directly from this screen and register knowledge related to the planning process activity, such as lessons learned. These functionalities are described in the following section.

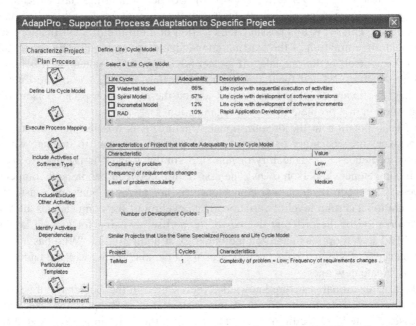

Fig. 2. AdaptPro – a tool to support process adaptation to specific projects

After planning the process, the project manager use the AdaptPro tool to instantiate the specific process to the project based on its particularities. The product of this tool is the process plan (including adaptations to support the life cycle model chosen) and a SDE to support the execution of the planned process.

The AdaptPro tool, just like the other tools of the **Taba Workstation**, is integrated to the **Taba Workstation** Knowledge Management tools. These tools are described in the following section.

5 Taba Workstation Knowledge Management Tools

The Taba Workstation is constituted of several tools integrated to Knowledge Management tools that support software engineers in the execution of software processes activities in different ways. The next sections describe the Sapiens and the ACKNOWLEDGE Knowledge Management tools.

5.1 Sapiens: A Corporate Yellow Page Tool to Support the Representation of Organizational Structure Knowledge

The analysis of corporative yellow pages has a great importance to human resources selection. Because usually most of the time the desired competence exists somewhere inside the organization, being, however, necessary to expend much time to identify, find and have access to who possesses it [18]. Sapiens is a software tool for the representation of the organizational structure with the competences required along it and is integrated to the Taba Workstation tools [6]. Besides supporting staff allocation, including the competences of each professional, it also contains search and navigation mechanisms. This way, it is possible the creation of a culture of identification, acquisition and dissemination of the existing knowledge that can be used by the organization to know itself better and take off greater advantage of its potential. It is based on the infrastructure defined for the Taba Workstation, making use of the Enterprise Ontology. Software developers can use it to find the most appropriate person to help in the solution of a problem inside the organization.

For each position in the organizational structure, it is possible to indicate which competences are necessary or relevant for its performance and to indicate which of these competences are mandatory or not. In a similar way, it is possible to indicate which competences a person owns. The association between people and competence, as well as between position and competence, is not always equal and must take in consideration a certain level of variation. This leveling of the competences allows the standardization of the different degrees of "expertise" existing for a specific ability. Predefined search options based on the ontology structure (e. g., "Who has a specific competence?", "Which are the competences for a person?") are available and the user can also create new ones.

The organizational structure knowledge represented in the Sapiens tool is used by other tools available in the environments instantiated to support the execution of processes adapted to specific projects, for instance, the RHPlan tool. The goal of the RHPlan tool is to support the human resources allocation in a software project. It also has mechanisms to help the contract order or qualification of professionals order when the necessary human resources cannot be found inside the organization. It is based on the definition of the necessary competence profiles to the accomplishment of project activities, and posterior search for organization professional that possesses similar profiles to the desired one. The project manager can search the knowledge on the existing competence inside the organization and find who possesses them. The database of professional's capabilities is provided by the Sapiens tool.

Figure 3 presents a screenshot of RHPlan tool, showing an example of human resources allocation in project activities. In the left side is possible to see all activities for the staff allocation plan creation: definition of profiles needed in the execution of each process activity, selection of professionals, request of contract or training for professionals when the available professionals in the organization do not fit the desired profile, and visualization of the human resources allocation plan.

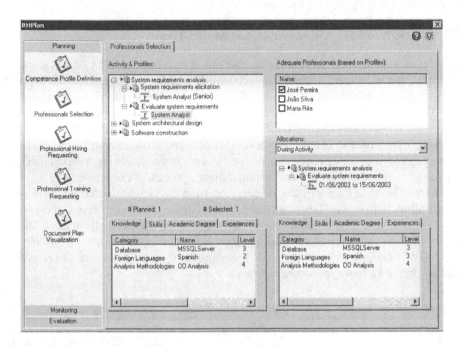

Fig. 3. Professional selection in RHPlan tool supported by organizational structure knowledge represented in the Sapiens tool

The software engineer not only can consult the knowledge competences inside the organization through the RHPlan tool, but also consult the analysis of past experiences supporting project managers in planning and controlling the human resources allocation. Project experiences are an important source of knowledge in Software Engineering and, therefore, the acquired experiences must be identified and shared [24]. Moreover, the (successful or not) lessons learned about human resources allocations in other projects are very important so previous errors can be avoided and success cases are not forgotten.

As well as Sapiens, RHPlan uses the Enterprise Ontology for its class model definition. However, while in Sapiens classes are related to staff allocation in the organizational structure, in RHPlan the allocation is carried through specific software development process activities. Both of them manipulate the same database of organization members' competences; then they are benefited by the same mapping infrastructure of ontology concepts to physical model classes. RHPlan also uses the concepts defined in the sub-ontology of Behavior to describe projects, software processes, activities, resources and distribution of necessary competences for the accomplishment of the activities.

During the knowledge acquisition, the ontology concepts can also be used to index the organizational knowledge memory. Later, during the knowledge search this same information can be used to assist the search for a specific knowledge. This functionalities are describes in the following section.

5.2 ACKNOWLEDGE: A Knowledge Acquisition Tool

In order to acquire, filter and package organization members' tacit and explicit knowledge related to software processes, an acquisition process was defined and a supporting tool named ACKNOWLEDGE was implemented and integrated into other tools in the Taba Workstation [6]. The main objective of this approach is to capture individual knowledge valuable for the organization, such as, domain knowledge (domain theory), business knowledge (best practices, knowledge about clients and new technologies), past experiences knowledge (lessons learned, common problems), and organization members' knowledge acquired during processes execution.

The ACKNOWLEDGE tool can be accessed from two icons located under the title bar of all tools from the Taba Configured SDE (figure 2 and 3). Organization members' knowledge can be acquired by clicking on the icon (🔦) and all captured knowledge can be consulted by clicking on the icon (❓). The integration of ACKNOWLEDGE to these tools avoids interruption of organization members normal routine during knowledge capture and reuse.

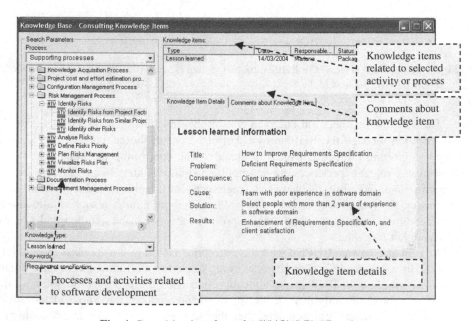

Fig. 4. Consulting interface of ACKNOWLEDGE tool

Figure 4 presents the knowledge consulting interface. In order to facilitate the search, some consulting parameters can be specified, such as, activity or process related to software development, knowledge type, and key words. The consulting interface also allows knowledge users to register comments about knowledge items. These comments are very useful during knowledge repository maintenance since they facilitate identification of knowledge items that have real value for the organization. Moreover, the comments add value to knowledge items turning them more reliable for knowledge users, and providing the means for establishment of a continuous learning cycle. During the knowledge acquisition, the ontology concepts can be used to index the organizational knowledge memory. Later, during the knowledge search this same information can be used to assist the search for a specific knowledge.

6 Success Cases of Software Processes Deployment Using Taba Workstation

The use of the Taba Workstation to support software processes deployment in small and medium size companies demonstrated several benefits in the context of the QualiSoft project described previously, such as increase of product and process quality, and preservation of organizational knowledge related to software processes. A direct benefit obtained from the use of the Taba Workstation can be exemplified by two organizations that obtained ISO 9000:2000 certification based on the software process and configured environment deployed.

The first organization to obtain the ISO certification was a software development organization that during two years was involved in software processes definition, preparation and implantation without success. After one year of the QualiSoft project, the organization obtained the ISO 9000:2000 certification. Nevertheless, the organization has obtained more practical benefits than just the ISO certification, for instance:

- decrease of rework,
- increase of software products quality,
- increase of software developers' qualification through the dissemination of software engineering knowledge,
- establishment of best practices aligned to organizational objectives,
- preservation of organizational knowledge, obtaining relative people independence during the projects. Although, the organization recognizes the importance of people, the client will not suffer from lack of quality of processes and products when people are reallocated to other projects.

The organization recognized that the Taba Configured SDEs facilitate and significantly reduce repetitive work during the definition of the specific process for a project, planning activities, project execution and monitoring. Moreover, the Taba Workstation lessons learned repository has constituted a repository of historical information to be used during other projects execution aiming to prevent the reoccurrence of common errors and problems.

The second organization to obtain the ISO certification is a software development organization that already had the ISO 9000:1994 certification and had to be compliant with the ISO 9000:2000 standards in order to renew their certificate. According to the software engineers of the organization, the Taba Configured SDE was decisive to obtain the certification renewal, because it has speeded the deployment of software processes and has facilitated the dissemination of organizational best practices.

Besides the report from these two companies, some lessons learned were identified during the regular meetings to support the process deployment in the organizations:

1. the deployment of software processes in a group of organizations in a common project and at low cost is feasible (the costs for each organization was about 40% less than a similar project conducted independently for one organization),
2. the configured environments facilitates training, deployment and institutionalization of software processes by providing case tools to assist and/or automate software development and maintenance tasks,
3. the knowledge management approach adopted in the environments is determinant for the success of the approach, because it helps the developer in executing its activities by providing useful knowledge when the developer needs it the most,
4. the knowledge acquisition approach integrated into the CASE tools enables the gradual evolution of the knowledge repository with acquisition and dissemination of lessons learned, best practices and suggestions for processes improvement,
5. the effective support of the high-level manager of each company was a critical factor to guarantee the success of the QualiSoft project.

7 Conclusions

This paper presented the Taba Workstation SDEs, enterprise-oriented software development environments that support software engineers to execute software processes more effectively and to produce products with better quality. The paper also presented the main characteristics of the knowledge management infrastructure integrated to those environments. These environments have shown to be useful for software engineers supporting the deployment and execution of software processes and the construction of software products with better quality. Therefore, the Taba Workstation SDEs guaranteed not only the increase of organizational competitive advantages, but also the enhancement of software processes and products quality.

The results of the QualiSoft project have also shown the feasibility of carrying out software process definition and deployment as a cooperative work between several companies reducing costs without diminishing the expected results. The project has also shown that it is possible to promote technology transfer between universities and software organization producing good results to all the involved parts.

The Taba Configured SDEs also support the execution of other Brazilian companies' software processes. The initial results regarding the use of these environments are promising. Three companies using Taba Configured SDEs are expected to reach CMMI Level 2 in official appraisals during 2005. A CMMI pre-evaluation was conducted successfully in one organization in January 2005, and the official appraisal is schedule to March 2005. This organization has also recently obtained the ISO 9000 certification through the support of the **Taba Workstation**.

Further information about Enterprise-Oriented Software Development Environment and its tools can be found at `http://www.cos.ufrj.br/~Taba`.

Acknowledgement

The authors wish to thank CNPq and CAPES for the financial support granted to the project Enterprise-Oriented Software Development Environments and SEBRAE for supporting these two years of QualiSoft project. We also wish to thank K. Oliveira, R. Falbo, M. Amaral and B. Diaz for their contributions to this project.

References

1. Gronau, N., Müller, C., Uslar, M.: The KDML Knowledge Management Approach: Integrating Knowledge Conversions and Business Process Modeling, Proc. of the 5th Int. Conf. of Practical Aspects of Knowledge Management, Vienna, Austria, (2004) 1–10
2. Pfleeger, S. L.: Software Engineering: theory and practice, 2nd edition, Prentice-Hall, Inc., ISBN 0-13-029049-1 (2001)
3. Eppler, M., Seifried P., Röpnack, A.: Improving knowledge intensive Processes through an Enterprise Knowledge Medium. In: PRASAD, J. (edt.): Proceedings of the 1999 Conference on Managing Organizational Knowledge for Strategic Advantage: The Key Role of Information Technology and Personnel. New Orleans (1999), In ref: [1]
4. Hamel, G., Prahalad, C.K.: The core competence of the corporation. Harvard Business Review (1990), In ref: [1]
5. Andersson, B., Bider, I., Perjons, E.: Integration of Business Process Support with Knowledge Management – A Practical Perspective, Proc. of the 5th Int. Conf. of Practical Aspects of Knowledge Management, Vienna, Austria, (2004) 227–238
6. Montoni, M., Santos, G., Villela, K., Miranda, R., Rocha, A.R., Travassos, G.H., Figueiredo, S., Mafra, S.: Knowledge Management in an Enterprise-Oriented Software Development Environment, Proc. of the 5th Int. Conf of Practical Aspects of Knowledge Management, Vienna, Austria, (2004) 117–128
7. Oliveira, K. M., Zlot, F., Rocha, A. R., Travassos, G. H., Gallota, C., Menezes, C.: Domain-oriented software development environment, Journal of Systems and Software, Vol. 172, No.2 (2004) 145 - 161
8. Eman, K. E., Drouin, J., Melo, W.: SPICE – The Theory and Practice of Software Process Improvement and Capability Determination, IEEE Computer Society Press (1998)
9. ISO/IEC 12207:2000. Information technology – software process life cycle (2000)
10. Truex, D. P., Baskerville, R., Klein, H.: Growing Systems in Emergent Organizations, Communications of the ACM, Vol. 42, No. 8, Aug. (1999) 117-123
11. Maidantchik, C., Santos, G., Montoni, M. A.: Organizational Knowledge: an XML-based Approach to Support Knowledge Management in Distributed and Heterogeneous Environments, In: Proceedings of the 16th International Conference on Software Engineering and Knowledge Engineering SEKE'04, Banff, Canada, Jun (2004) 427-430
12. Houdek, F., Bunse, C.: Transferring Experience: A Practical Approach and its Application on Software Inspections, In: Proc. of SEKE Workshop on Learning Software Organizations, Kaiserslautern, Germany, Jun, (1999) 59-68

13. Holz H., Könnecker A., Maurer F.: Task-Specific Knowledge Management in a Process-Centered SEE, K.-D Althoff, R.L. Feldmann, and W. Müller (Eds): LSO, LNCS 2176, (2001) 163-177
14. Maurer, F., Holz, H.: Process-centered Knowledge Organization for Software Engineering, In: Papers of the AAAI-99 Workshop on Exploring Synergies of Knowledge Management and Case-Based Reasoning, Orlando, Florida, Jul: AAAI Press, (1999)
15. Decker, B., Althoff, K.-D, Nick, M., Tautz, C.: Integrating Business Process Descriptions and Lessons Learned with an Experience Factory, In: Professionelles Wissensmanagement - Erfahrungen und Visionen (Beiträge der 1. Konferenz für Professionelles Wissensmanagement), eds. Hans-Peter Schnurr, Steffen Staab, Rudi Studer, Gerd Stumme, York Sure. Baden-Baden, Germany. Shaker Verlag, Aachen, Mar (2001)
16. Birk, A., Tautz, C.: Knowledge Management of Software Engineering Lessons Learned, IESE-Report 002.98/E, Jan (1998)
17. Lindvall, M., Frey, M., Costa, P., Tesoriero, R.: Lessons Learned about Structuring and Describing Experience for Three Experience Bases, K.-D Althoff, R.L. Feldmann, and W. Müller (Eds): LSO, LNCS 2176, (2001) 106-118
18. Basili, V., Lindvall, M., Costa, P.: Implementing the Experience Factory concepts as a set of Experiences Bases, In: Proceedings of the Int. Conf. on Software Engineering and Knowledge Engineering, Buenos Aires, Argentina, Jun (2001) 102-109
19. Ruhe, G.: Experience Factory-based Professional Education and Training, In: Proc. of the 12th Conference on Software Engineering Education and Training, March, New Orleans, Louisiana, USA, (1999)
20. Landes, D., Schneider, K., Houdek, F.: Organizational Learning and Experience Documentation in Industrial Software Projects, Int. J. on Human-Computer Studies, Vol. 51, (1999) 646-661
21. Weber, R., Aha, D. W., Becerra-Fernandez, I.: Intelligent Lessons Learned Systems, International Journal of Expert Systems Research and Applications 20, No. 1 Jan (2001).
22. Farias, L., Travassos, G. H., Rocha, A. R. C.: Knowledge Management of Software Risks In:. Journal of Universal Computer Science, Vol. 9, No 7 (2003), 670- 681
23. CMU/SEI, Capability Maturity Model Integration (CMMI) Version 1.1 - Staged Representation, Carnegie Mellon University, Software Engineering Institute, Pittsburgh (2002)
24. Markkula, M.: Knowledge Management in Software Engineering Projects, Software Engineering and Knowledge Engineering – SEKE, Kaiserlautern, Germany, Jun (1999)

Evaluation of Three Methods to Predict Project Success: A Case Study

Claes Wohlin[1] and Anneliese Amschler Andrews[2]

[1] Dept. of Systems and Software Engineering, School of Engineering,
Blekinge Institute of Technology, Box 520
SE-372 25 Ronneby, Sweden
claes.wohlin@bth.se
[2] School of Electrical Engineering and Computer Science,
Washington State University,
Pullman, WA 99164-2752 USA
aandrews@eecs.wsu.edu

Abstract. To increase the likelihood for software project success, it is important to be able to identify the drivers of success. This paper compares three methods to identify similar projects with the objective to predict project success. The hypothesis is that projects with similar characteristics are likely to have the same outcome in terms of success. Two of the methods are based on identifying similar projects using all available information. The first method of these aims at identifying the most similar project. The second method identifies a group of projects as most similar. Finally, the third method pinpoints some key characteristics to identify project similarity. Our measure of success for these identifications is whether project success for these projects identified as similar is the same. The comparison between methods is done in a case study with 46 projects with varying characteristics. The paper evaluates the performance of each method with regards to its ability to predict project success. The method using key drivers of project success is superior to the others in the case study. Thus, it is concluded that it is important for software developing organizations to identify its key project characteristics to improve its control over project success.

1 Introduction

There are many project characteristics that influence project success. If it is true that certain project characteristics lead to certain project outcomes, it becomes important to be able to identify similar projects, since they would likely lead to similar project outcomes. Nowadays when many software systems evolve over time and come in several releases, it becomes even more crucial to learn from past projects to increase the likelihood for success in future projects. Software organizations must understand which project characteristics are most important for them to ensure successful projects. This paper contributes with a comparison of three potential methods to use to predict project success.

F. Bomarius and S. Komi-Sirviö (Eds.): PROFES 2005, LNCS 3547, pp. 385–398, 2005.

Some examples of project characteristics include stability of requirements, knowledge of developers and management, inherent difficulty of the project, techniques and tools used (and how appropriate they are), tightness of schedule and type of application, required levels of reliability, fault tolerance, security, use of development techniques including use of object-oriented programming, design patterns, extreme programming, etc. Success indicators include timeliness of delivery, quality of software, as well as more long term properties such as maintainability and evolvability.

Some of these project characteristics can be measured objectively, while others have to be measured subjectively. The same is true for project success variables. We focus here on subjective measurement of both project characteristics and project success as also is the case in for example [1]. The focus here on subjective measures is primarily due to availability in the case study presented below.

In order to predict project success reliably, it is first necessary to find a method to identify similar projects. Projects are similar, if they show similar project characteristics and/or similar project outcomes. This paper investigates three methods to identify similar projects:

1.   Nearest neighbor. This method takes a set of projects, the base set, and computes for a new project the distance to each project in the base set. The new project is most similar to the project with the smallest distance to the new project.
2.   Friends. This approach also uses a base set of projects as well as the new project and groups them based on Principal Components Analysis (PCA) [2]. The new project is most similar to the projects with which it has been grouped.
3.   Key success driver analysis. Not all project characteristics are equally important in predicting project success. This analysis method reduces the full set of project characteristics to those that behave similarly to project success. This reduced set of project characteristics is then used to rank projects by success and failure. New projects are identified as potentially successful or not based on this classification.

We selected these three approaches, because they represent three very different approaches to similarity identification. The first method is focused on identification of the most similar project using a distance measure [3], which is a simple measure used in case-based reasoning. The second method identifies a set of similar projects using all available information. Finally, the third method is based on identification of key success drivers. Based on these key success drivers, the most similar projects are identified.

Other methods would have been possible to use as for example neural networks, clustering and so forth. However, the main objective is not to make an exhaustive comparison of methods. The objective is primarily to investigate whether is makes more sense to focus on a few key variables (in particular the key success drivers in the context of this paper) rather than all data available for different projects.

All three methods are evaluated with respect to their ability to predict project outcome (success or not). Since the impact of project characteristics on project outcomes varies over time (for example, use of the software factory concept [4] will influence the effect of project characteristics over time), we need to take this into account. Our approach is to use a sliding window of projects for the base set. This means, that the oldest projects are removed from the base set as new ones are added to it. Given the high degree of innovation and change in software development, it is not likely that the base set will ever be very large. This makes it important that methods used for prediction are able to function with small amounts of data.

The paper is organized as follows. Section 2 describes related work with respect to identifying similar projects, predicting various aspects of project success based on measurement of objective and subjective variables, and their use for various types of predictions like effort estimation, risk estimation, in addition to estimating various success factors. Section 3 describes the case study data used to illustrate the approach. Section 4 specifies the approach and illustrates the approach on the case study data. Section 5 draws conclusions and points out further work.

2 Related Work

Most prediction work has been directed towards using quantitative data, for example, measures of size, person-hours spent, number of defects and so forth. However, subjective measures have only recently been analyzed more extensively in empirical software engineering, specifically in software project assessment and evaluation. Part of the problem stems from issues related to collecting trustworthy data [5]. On the other hand, subjective measures have been used successfully for effort estimation [6, 7], and risk management [8]. Expert judgment in estimation tasks has been discussed in [9].

More recently, subjective variables have been used to map project characteristics to project success. First in [1], subjective factors were evaluated alongside objective quantitative ones to evaluate both efficiency and success of software production for projects from the NASA-SEL database [10]. The paper identifies which successful projects were also efficient and determines primary (subjective) drivers of project success. In [11], the method for analyzing subjective project characteristics and success indicators is refined and discussed in-depth, and two case studies are presented. The primary success drivers amongst the project characteristics are identified and an agreement index is established that quantifies to which degree the project characteristics that were identified as primarily connected to project success are able to predict project success. The results identified that about one third of the successful projects could be predicted accurately. We believe that this is due to the limitations of the approach, specifically that projects are classified into two categories: upper half and lower half (both based on project characteristics). The halves are denoted "good" and "bad" respectively although it is really up to each individual organization to judge where the limit between "good" projects and "bad" projects is. It is reasonable to assume that projects around the border between "good" and "bad" exhibit more uncertainty with respect to project outcome (success or failure). This could account for some of the misclassification. To circumvent this problem, an extension was proposed in [12], where a third class was introduced to try to avoid classifying projects close to the border between "good" and "bad".

However, the work so far has been focused on development of a method for identification of key success drivers in software development. Thus, the research has been focused on developing one model and then extending and improving the model. Here, the main focus is on using the developed model for prediction and to evaluate the model in comparison with two other approaches using industrial data from 46 development projects.

Prediction models in software engineering have been directed towards several different areas. Researchers have also used a large variety of statistical methods and approaches. This includes regression analysis (linear, multiple linear regression, stepwise regression) [13,14], multivariate statistics [15], machine learning [16] including neural networks [14, 17], analogies [13,18] and so forth. Some of these methods, including for example neural networks, require a substantial amount of data for model building. To address this problem, researchers have looked at methods for prediction when having few data points. This includes, for example, the use of different decision making methods such as the analytic hierarchy process [19] which is applied to effort estimation in [20]. Case-based reasoning has also been used as a means for prediction, for example, in [14, 20].

3 Case Study Data

The data comes from the NASA-SEL database [21]. Further information about NASA-SEL can be found in [10]. In total, the database available to us contains data from more than 150 projects spanning five years. Of these, we selected 46 for analysis, based on completeness of project data recorded. These 46 projects represented a variety of types of systems, languages, and approaches for software development. The actual data is not intended to play any major role. The main objective is to compare three methods for prediction purposes and in particular the importance of using key characteristics in the prediction rather than as much information as is available.

The selection criterion of projects in the database was completeness of data for 27 project characteristics. The characteristics are measured on an ordinal scale (1-5) using subjective judgment. A higher value denotes more of the quality ranked. The subjective evaluations rank the projects in terms of problem complexity, schedule constraints, nature of requirements, team ability, management performance, discipline, software quality, etc. Six success factors were measured per project. These six variables are aggregated to one variable in the evaluation here, since it does not affect the actual comparison. From an analysis point of view, it is unfortunate that the data is on an ordinal scale as seen below. However, this is the type of data that we as researchers many times face when collecting data from industrial environments. The actual variables are not crucial for the comparison of methods and hence the reader is referred to, for example, [11].

4 Analysis Method

The analysis method consists of three phases:

1. Identify a base set of projects to use in assessing new ones. This base set should describe the current spectrum of project capability of the organization. While one way is to simply take all projects finished by an organization to date, this might include old projects whose relationships between project characteristics and success indicators no longer reflects current project behavior. Reasons for changes include: changes in capability, environment, process, successful use of experience factory concepts, etc. Thus we propose to use a sliding window instead, since it is most likely that older projects no longer reflect new ones. For the case study, the first 20 projects were viewed as the initial base set, the initial experience base. This first base set was used to identify which projects in the base set were similar to which of the following 5 new projects (for the purpose of predicting project success). Then the base set was updated by removing the five oldest projects from the base set. Again, the new base set (projects 6-25) was used to identify similar projects for projects 26-30. Projects 11-30 were used to identify similar projects for projects 31-35; projects 16-35 were used to identify similar projects for projects 36-40, projects 21-40 were used to identify similar projects for projects 41-45 and finally projects 26-45 were used to identify similar projects for project 46.

2. Identification of similar projects. This paper investigates and compares three ways to identify similar projects. For each window and set of new projects identified in step one, Nearest Neighbor, Friends, and Key Success Driver are used to identify projects in the experience base that are similar to the new projects. The detailed analysis is described in the subsections below.

3. Evaluate prediction quality. New projects identified as similar (based on characteristics) with projects in the base set are assumed to show similar outcomes to those projects with respect to level of success. Since we know the level of success through the data in the database, it is possible to evaluate prediction accuracy. We use a diffusion matrix to illustrate correct predictions versus false positives and false negatives. In addition, we also use the kappa statistic as an agreement index. The agreement index is described in more detail in a software engineering context in [22] and briefly outlined below.

We selected to work with the average rather than the median, because it takes into consideration the effect of extreme or unusual values better and accentuates differences in data that the median would not show (if most project success indicators are quite similar, very little can be said about their differences). Projects are then ranked based on this average score. Similar to the original model [11], we consider a project to be successful, if it is in the top half of the projects ranked. It should be noted that all projects may be successful, but the upper half is more successful than the lower half. This is a somewhat simplistic view on success to illustrate the prediction methods. In a real case, it would be important to actually define success properly, for example the software was developed on time within budget with the correct functionality and the quality expected. Anyhow, here it is primarily a matter of relative comparison between the projects rather than distinguishing between successful project and failed projects. Projects in the top half are ranked green, in the bottom half, red. We have chosen not to use the extended model with three classes [12], since the main objective here is to compare three competing methods for prediction and the extended method tries to circumvent the prediction problem. Here, we would like to address the prediction difficulties.

New projects identified as being similar with green projects are predicted as green, while new projects identified as being similar with red projects are considered red. A diffusion matrix reports agreement between prediction using the experience base and the actual outcome (average score of success variable).

The following subsections describe the three methods for identification of similar project(s) and evaluate the ability of the methods to predict success.

4.1 Nearest Neighbor

In this method a distance measure is calculated for each new project from the projects in the experience base (the case study has 20 projects in the experience base for each iteration). The measure is a measure of dissimilarity (DS), since the most similar project in the experience base is the project with the highest value of the measure below. The measure is for ordinal data computed as:

$$ DS = \frac{1}{\sqrt{\sum_{i=1}^{n} (C_{1i} - C_{2i})^2}} $$

In the formulae, Cji is the value of variable i for project j, where only two projects are considered. One project is the new project and then it is compared with all other 20 projects one at a time. This means that the nearest neighbor is the project with the largest value of DS. More information about the measure in a software engineering context can be obtained from [3].

Table 1. Identification of Nearest Neighbour

Project	21	22	23	24	25	26	27	28	29	30	31	32	33	34
Neighbor	2	16	16	16	16	16	12	25	23	15	16	27	26	27

Project	35	36	37	38	39	40	41	42	43	44	45	46
Neighbor	20	21	35	30	26	24	30	35	35	35	26	39

The project in the experience base with the largest value for the distance measure is selected as the nearest neighbor. The nearest neighbors are listed in Table 1 for projects 21-46. The table shows that some projects end up as neighbors more often than others. Project 16 is one of those.

The outcome of the new project is predicted as the outcome of the nearest neighbor. The prediction is only concerned with whether the new project will be a success (green) or not (red). One could look more closely into the prediction of the actual value for the different success variables. However, we believe that at the stage we are making this prediction, it is sufficient to provide an indication of where the project is heading. When two or more projects have the same value for the distance measure, the newest project is selected as the nearest neighbor.

The results from using this method as a prediction method for all successive experience bases are shown in the Table 3. The method is not very accurate. Only eight projects out of 26 (about 31%) are actually predicted correctly (green-green or red-red). There are 5 false positives (19%) and 13 false negative (50%). An agreement index is also calculated, which often is referred to as kappa statistic [23]. In software engineering, the kappa statistic has been applied to inter-rater agreement of process assessments [22]. For an introduction to the kappa statistics, please refer to these references. An interpretation of the kappa statistics can be found in Table 2.

Table 2. The Altman kappa scale

Kappa statistics	< 0.20	0.21-0.40	0.41-0.60	0.61-0.80	0.81-1.00
Strength of agreement	Poor	Fair	Moderate	Good	Very good

Table 3. Diffusion matrix for Nearest Neighbour prediction

Kappa = -0.26		Outcome	
		Green	**Red**
Prediction	**Green**	27, 32, 34, 38	22, 23, 24, 25, 26, 30, 31, 35, 36, 41, 42, 43, 44
	Red	21, 28, 29, 33, 37	39, 40, 45, 46

The agreement index requires comparable scales for the two classifications, for example, as is the case when comparing the agreement between two raters using the same scale. The problem addressed here is different since we compare one prediction model with the actual outcome. This problem is inherently harder and hence the mapping in Table 2 is most likely too ambitious. Informally with respect to the scale, it is still reasonable that values below 0.20 are poor and values between 0.21-0.40 are fair. However, given that we compare predictions with outcome, we believe that 0.41-0.60 is good, 0.61-0.80 is very good and above 0.80 is utopia.

A random assignment of projects to the cells in Table 3 should on average result in an agreement index (kappa) of zero. Values below zero means that the prediction method performs worse than random assignment. This is the case for this particular method for our data set. In other words, this method fails quite dramatically in identifying an existing project to make a prediction of project success.

4.2 Friends

The second method is based on using Principal Component Analysis [2] to "package" similar projects (friends), i.e. projects whose characteristics seem to vary in the same way. The statistical package used for Principal Component Analysis (PCA) is StatView version 5.0.1. Basically, PCA tries to abstract variables (or in this case projects) that covariate into a higher level factor. The analysis method creates factors with loadings for each variable in each factor. A variable is here viewed to belong to the factor where the variable has the highest positive loading.

In the case study, all 27 project characteristics are measured on an ordinal 5 point Likert scale. While this type of analysis usually requires at least interval data, it is fairly robust with regards to using ordinal data. In addition, we only use it to identify projects that behave in a similar fashion with respect to the project characteristics. No other conclusions are drawn from the analysis.

The PCA is conducted for the 27 project characteristics to identify similar projects. Table 4 shows an example of the results of this analysis for the first experience base (projects 1-20) and one of the projects (project 21) in the first set of projects to be classified (projects 21-25). From Table 4, we see that project 21 has its highest loading in Factor 1. The other projects having this are projects 2, 3, 5, 7, 10, 12, 13 and 20. Thus, these eight projects are regarded as being the Friends of project 21.

The Friends approach extends the Nearest Neighbor approach from a single project to a set of close projects (hence the name Friends). Given that a new project is now considered to have the same level of success as its Friends, the average success value of the new project is defined as the average of the success values of its Friends.

When the Friends analysis is unable to identify any similar project, all 20 projects are used to compute the success value of the new project. Given this average success value, the projects are ranked and divided into an upper (green) and lower (red) half. This provides the prediction for the new projects in terms of either being a green or red project.

The Friends for projects 21-46 are determined as illustrated in Table 4. Comparing Friends with Nearest Neighbors, in 18 of 26 cases the Nearest Neighbor is also a Friend. In three cases there is no Friend. This method is able to identify that there are no friends, while the previous method still selects the nearest neighbor although it may not be very close.

The results for all experience bases are shown Table 5. Table 5 shows that now 11 or 42% of the project outcomes are predicted correctly. There are 3 or 12% false positives and 12 or 46% false negatives. While the correct predictions have increased, they are still no better than random, as indicated by a kappa statistic that is close to zero.

Table 4. PCA with loadings for projects 1-20 and project 21 as a new project

Orthogonal Solution

	Factor 1	Factor 2	Factor 3	Factor 4	Factor 5	Factor 6
P1	,172	,116	-,031	,300	,277	,666
P2	,845	,016	,068	,205	,233	,290
P3	,858	,273	-,014	,054	,124	,024
P4	-,156	,071	,067	,139	-,839	-,059
P5	,746	,117	-,222	,025	,249	,375
P6	,240	,925	,020	,017	,098	-,032
P7	,766	,381	,091	-,099	,024	-,168
P8	,215	,895	,033	,200	,074	,162
P9	,157	,463	,289	,100	,533	,376
P10	,936	,138	-,043	,098	-,033	-,035
P11	,001	,442	,295	-,063	,703	,069
P12	,761	-,314	,262	,210	,125	,306
P13	,849	,261	-,019	,044	,062	-,308
P14	-,079	-,165	,340	,244	,105	-,678
P15	,293	,196	-,284	,596	,464	-,194
P16	,562	,104	,607	,057	,058	-,028
P17	-,074	,085	,851	-,045	,043	-,196
P18	-,059	,058	-,056	,863	-,185	,080
P19	,484	,078	,384	,512	-,087	-,078
P20	,766	,007	,065	-,513	-,063	,076
P21	,749	-,174	,151	-,119	,279	,381

Table 5. Diffusion matrix for Friends prediction

Kappa = -0.03		Outcome	
		Green	**Red**
Prediction	**Green**	27, 32, 33, 34, 37, 38	22, 23, 25, 26, 30, 35, 36, 39, 42, 43, 44, 45
	Red	21, 28, 29	24, 31, 40, 41, 46

4.3 Key Success Drivers

The third method is based on identifying key project characteristics. These are characteristics that covariate with the success variable the most. This analysis is done using PCA with the project characteristics and the success variable.

In cases when the number of project variables exceeds the number of projects in the experience base, the original method developed in [11] has to be adapted. Otherwise the principal component analysis would lead to singularities. Our approach is to reduce the project variables to those having the highest correlations with the success variable. This can be done by setting either a threshold for the number of project variables to be included to a value n and taking the n project variables with the highest correlations, or by setting a threshold c for the correlation value.

In the case study we had 27 project variables, but only 20 projects in each experience base. We decided to set the threshold at c=0.4. The threshold is not crucial, since the main aim was to reduce the number of variables so that an analysis could be conducted. Moreover, the variables with the lowest correlation do not vary together with the success variable anyway. This resulted in different sets of variables to be investigated for the different sets of 20 projects, i.e. the experience bases obtained through the sliding window approach.

With this reduction of project variables, it was possible to perform a principal component analysis [2] and identify project characteristics grouped in the same factor as the success variable.

Initially nine characteristics are identified as being important for projects 1-20 and 6-25. This then changes to only two variables being identified as the key success drivers for the organization (projects 11-30, 16-35 and 21-40) The drivers identified are "requirements stability" and "application experience" of the development team. In the last experience base there is a change (projects 26-45). Four characteristics are included in the identified key success drivers. This shows that the success drivers may change over time, as the result of change or evolution in an organization.

Table 6. Diffusion matrix for Key Success Driver prediction

<table>
<tr><td rowspan="2">**Kappa = 0.51**</td><td colspan="2">**Outcome**</td></tr>
<tr><td>**Green**</td><td>**Red**</td></tr>
<tr><td rowspan="2">**Prediction**</td><td>**Green**</td><td>21, 27, 28, 29, 32, 33, 34, 37, 38</td><td>26, 30, 31, 36, 41, 42, 45</td></tr>
<tr><td>**Red**</td><td></td><td>22, 23, 24, 25, 35, 39, 40, 43, 44, 46</td></tr>
</table>

Given that the key success drivers have been identified, it is possible to also store the average of the identified project characteristics, and hence rank them based on the average. For new projects, the average of the key success drivers was calculated and the outcome (in terms of red or green) was predicted after comparison with the experience base. The outcome of the prediction is presented in the diffusion matrix in Table 6.

The third method is best for this data set. With this method, 19 or 73% of the projects are predicted correctly. There are no more false positives, but 7 or 27% false negatives. The kappa statistics has increased to 0.51, which in Altman's model would map to moderate agreement, see Table 2. However, we would like to regard it as fairly good given the difficulty in creating accurate prediction models in software engineering.

4.4 Discussion

Regardless of the method, this data set tends to have a relatively high number of projects classified as red, both in terms of correct classifications and terms of false negatives (red projects classified as green). This can be explained by the looking closer into the data [24], which unfortunately is impossible to fit into this paper. Anyhow, the high number of red projects among projects 21-46 can be explained when looking at the whole data set, both project characteristics and success variables. From the success variables, it is clear that in the beginning we have fairly low values and then comes a set of projects with very high scores (projects 10-20). The sliding window used in the analysis also means that the decreasing trend that we see from project 27 until project 46 results in that a majority of the new projects will turn out to be viewed as less successful (red), i.e. better projects were conducted in the past. A majority of projects is however predicted to be green since the new projects are viewed as being similar to older projects that are better and hence the level of success is overestimated. It is clear from looking closer into the data that the data behaves differently in terms of how it changes over time for project characteristics and success variables respectively. Ideally, the project characteristics and success variables should vary together as much as possible. The trends identified in the success variable are however not visible for the project characteristics, and hence we have a challenge. This challenge is partially addressed by the third method, where the project characteristics that vary together with the success variable are identified. A simple analysis of the data using descriptive statistics provides quite a lot of information that can be valuable to use in projects to come.

Due to the idiosyncrasies of this data set, it is impossible to generalize from it, except that it seems to make sense to have a method that identifies the key success drivers in terms of project characteristics. This is clearly an advantage with the third method. It provides support to identify key success drivers for organizations and use it for prediction purposes.

All three methods are independent of the actual measures defined by a specific organization. This makes them suitable for a wide variety of possible applications. Each organization can determine what they believe to be a suitable set of project characteristics to measure.

The third method also has the advantage that identifying key success drivers can help managers to plan and control success. The first two methods are aimed at prediction only. They cannot really be used for other purposes. Thus, the third method has two main advantages:

- It is the best predictor of project outcome.
- It provides management support to plan and control for success.

In addition, it should be noted that since we classify the data into two halves, some of the projects are viewed as being green although the actual average values of the success variables are decreasing. This may have been avoided if a threshold of success was set based on, for example, the first 20 projects. This is an area for future research, i.e. to look at absolute values for success rather than relative values as we have done here.

In other words, this study evaluates projects relative to other projects. When considering the data in more detail, it clearly indicates that a major improvement in terms of success was achieved after project 9. However, there is a tendency that the level of success is declining after that again and the level of success is closing in on what was seen in projects 1-9. This may be explained either with an actual decline in success or as a changed view on what is successful, i.e. our yardstick has changed.

5 Conclusions

This paper evaluated three approaches to identify similar projects. Projects are similar, if they (a) have similar project characteristics, and (b) have similar project outcomes related to levels of project success. We showed that grouping projects by key success drivers is superior to nearest neighbor and friends evaluation.

The approach also dealt with aging of projects for prediction purposes by using a sliding window of projects. An interesting question to investigate in the future is more sophisticated methods to determine the base set over time. For example, this paper assumed a sliding window of 20 projects. Is there a method to determine the "best" size for such a window of base projects? Are there ways to identify projects that should be removed from the base set (such as "atypical" projects)? How would one identify those? Essentially this is a question of the effect of both changing project environments as well as the effect of using the experience factory to determine the base set of projects that represents the key descriptors for projects (both good and bad) for a development organization.

Although the identification of key success drivers was superior to the other two methods, it is still a challenge to identify similar projects to predict success of new projects. The scales (i.e. the perception of a certain score for a variable) may change over time and hence older projects may have to be re-evaluated to ensure that we use the same scale over time. Another challenge is to understand and have methods that are able to cope with trends and to help address decreasing trends in the data (as observed here). The trends in the data may be due to changes in the context of software development. In this case it is important to be able to use information like the one in this paper or similar information to manage software organizations.

References

[1] von Mayrhauser, A., Wohlin, C., Ohlsson, M. C.: Assessing and Understanding Efficiency and Success in Software Production. Empirical Software Engineering: An International Journal, Vol. 5, No. 2, pp. 125-154, 2000.

[2] Kachigan S. K.: Statistical Analysis – An Interdisciplinary Introduction to Univariate & Multivariate Methods. Radius Press, 1986.

[3] Shepperd, M.: Case-based Reasoning in Software Engineering. In A. Aurum, R. Jeffrey, C. Wohlin and M. Handzic (eds.): Managing Software Engineering Knowledge. Springer-Verlag, Heidelberg, Germany, 2003.

[4] Basili, V. R., Caldiera, G., Rombach, H. D.: Experience Factory. In J. J. Marciniak: Encyclopedia of Software Engineering. John Wiley & Sons, Inc., Hoboken, N.J., USA, 2002.

[5] Valett J. D.: The (Mis)use of Subjective Process Measures in Software Engineering. Proc. Software Engineering Workshop, NASA/Goddard Space Flight Center, Greenbelt, Maryland, USA, pp. 161-165, 1993.

[6] Gray A. R., MacDonell S. G., Shepperd M. J.: Factors Systematically Associated with Errors in Subjective Estimates of Software Development Effort: The Stability of Expert Judgement. Proc. of the Sixth Int. Software Metrics Symposium, Boca Raton, Florida, USA, pp. 216-227, 1999.

[7] Höst M., Wohlin C.: An Experimental Study of Individual Subjective Effort Estimations and Combinations of the Estimates. Proc. IEEE Int. Conf. on Software Engineering, Kyoto, Japan, pp. 332-339, 1998.

[8] Ropponen J., Lyytinen K.: Components of Software Development Risk: How to Address Them? A Project Manager Survey. IEEE Trans. in Software Engineering, Vol. 26, No. 2: 98-112, 2000.

[9] Hughes R.: Expert Judgement as an Estimation Method. Information and Software Technology, Vol. 38, pp. 67-75, 1996.

[10] Basili V., Zelkowitz M., McGarry F., Page J., Waligora S., Pajerski R.: SEL's Software Process-Improvement Program. IEEE Software, November pp. 83-87, 1995.

[11] Wohlin, C., Amschler Andrews, A.: Assessing Project Success using Subjective Evaluation Factors. Software Quality Journal, Vol. 9, No. 1, pp. 43-70, 2000.

[12] Wohlin C., von Mayrhauser A., Höst M., Regnell B.: Subjective Evaluation as a Tool for Learning from Software Project Success. Information and Software Technology, Vol. 42, No. 14: 983-992, 2000.

[13] Myrtveit, I., Stensrud E.: A Controlled Experiment to Assess the Benefits of Estimating with Analogy and Regression Models. IEEE Transactions on Software Engineering 25(4): pp. 510-525, 1999.

[14] Shepperd, M., Kadoda, G.: Comparing Software Prediction Techniques Using Simulation. IEEE Transactions on Software Engineering", Vol. 27, No. 11, pp. 1014-1022, 2001.

[15] Ohlsson, N., Zhao, M., Helander, M.: Application of Multivariate Analysis for Software Fault Prediction. Software Quality Journal, Vol. 7, No. 1, pp. 51-66, 1998.

[16] Mair, C., Kadoda, G., Lefley, M., Phalp, K., Schofield, C., Shepperd, M., Webster, S.: An Investigation of Machine Learning Based Prediction Systems. Journal of Systems and Software, Vol. 53, No. 1, pp. 23-29, 2000.
[17] Khoshgoftaar, T.M., Szabo, R.M.: Using Neural Networks to Predict Software Faults during Testing. IEEE Transaction on Reliability, Vol. 45 No. 3, pp. 456-462, 1996.
[18] Shepperd, M.J., Schofield C.: Estimating Software Project Effort Using Analogies. IEEE Transactions on Software Engineering 23(11): pp. 736-743, 1997.
[19] Saaty, T. L., Vargas, L. G.: Models, Methods, Concepts & Applications of the Analytic Hierarchy Process. Kluwer Academic Publishers, Dordrecht, the Netherlands, 2001.
[20] Shepperd, M., Cartwright, M.: Predicting with Sparse Data. IEEE Transactions on Software Engineering, Vol. 27, No. 11, pp. 987-998, 2001.
[21] NASA-SEL: Software Engineering Laboratory Database Organization and Users Guide, Revision 2. Goddard Space Flight Center, Greenbelt, MD, USA, NASA-SEL Series, SEL-89-201, 1992.
[22] El Emam, K., Wieczorek, I.: The Repeatability of Code Defect Classifications. Proc. the Ninth International Symposium on Software Reliability Engineering, pp. 322-333, 1998.
[23] Altman D.:Practical Statistics for Medical Research. Chapman-Hall, 1991.
[24] Wohlin, C., Amschler Andrews, A.: A Case Study Approach to Evaluation of Three Methods to Predict Project Success. Technical Report, Blekinge Institute of Technology, 2004, http://www.ipd.bth.se/cwo/TR-case.pdf.

Mega Software Engineering

Katsuro Inoue[1], Pankaj K. Garg[2], Hajimu Iida[3],
Kenichi Matsumoto[3], and Koji Torii[3]

[1] Osaka University, Graduate School of Information Science and Technology,
1-3 Machikaneyama, Toyonaka, Osaka 560-8531, Japan
`inoue@ist.osaka-u.ac.jp`
[2] Zee Source, 1684 Nightingale Avenue, Suite 201, Sunnyvale, CA 94087, USA
`garg@zeesource.net`
[3] Nara Institute of Science and Technology, Nara 630-0192, Japan
`{iida, matumoto, torii}@is.naist.jp`

Abstract. In various fields of computer science, rapidly growing hardware power, such as high-speed network, high-performance CPU, huge disk capacity, and large memory space, has been fruitfully harnessed. Examples of such usage are large scale data and web mining, grid computing, and multimedia environments. We propose that such rich hardware can also catapult software engineering to the next level. Huge amounts of software engineering data can be systematically collected and organized from tens of thousands of projects inside organizations, or from outside an organization through the Internet. The collected data can be analyzed extensively to extract and correlate multi-project knowledge for improving organization-wide productivity and quality. We call such an approach for software engineering **Mega Software Engineering**. In this paper, we propose the concept of Mega Software Engineering, and demonstrate some novel data analysis characteristic of Mega Software Engineering. We describe a framework for enabling Mega Software Engineering.

1 Introduction

Over the years, sometimes borrowing from traditional engineering disciplines, software engineering has adopted several methods and tools for developing software products, or more recently, software product families. For example, from hardware engineering the concept of specifying requirements before design and implementation have been useful for software engineering. A unique feature of software products, however, is that the end product has virtually no physical manifestation. Hence, composing or taking apart a software product has virtually no cost implications. As a result, software component reuse is a common practice for code sharing among multiple projects.

We posit that "sharing" among software projects can be extended beyond code or component sharing to more and varied kinds of "knowledge" sharing. Such sharing can be achieved using what we call *mega software engineering*. Instead of narrowly engineering a product, or a product family, an organization

F. Bomarius and S. Komi-Sirviö (Eds.): PROFES 2005, LNCS 3547, pp. 399–413, 2005.

can undertake the responsibility and benefits of engineering a large number of projects simultaneously. Examples of benefits that can accrue from such a perspective are: projects that share functionality can benefit from code sharing or reuse; experts in a particular implementation aspect can contribute their expertise to all projects that can potentially use that expertise (sort of like syndicated newspaper columnist or cartoonists); historical experiences of projects can be extrapolated to similar, newer projects to eliminate repeating process mistakes; and, 'outliers,' or projects with behavior deviant from the norm can be easily distinguished for rapid problem identification and resolution.

Many existing software engineering technologies remain focused on the individual project or programmer. For instance, code browsing tools typically allow a programmer to browse through single project code bases. Similarly, a navigation system might guide a developer utilizing data from her activities alone. While organizations can utilize global knowledge, for software reuse and other process improvements, an individual programmer or manager seldom enjoys the benefits of *mega or global knowledge*. Often, in large organizations its difficult for programmers to even discover projects related or similar to their own.

Prevailing organizational software engineering technologies for individuals are locally optimized to get local benefit for the individual developers or projects at most. They do not oversee global benefit and do not optimize the technologies using knowledge and software engineering data of other developers or other projects.

In modern times, the capacity, connectivity and performance of various networks ranging from local area network to the Internet are growing rapidly. Now, we are able to collect data from not only a single project, but *all* software development activities inside an organization (or company). If the organization has close relation to other software development organizations, as sub-contractor or co-developer, we can also collect software engineering data from the other organizations. A huge collection of Open Source software now exists on the Internet, which is sometimes a crucial resource for development projects. Such information is readily available via Internet tools.

Disk capacity and CPU power of recent computer systems are also rapidly increasing. Since vast disk space is available, we can archive project data at a detailed, fine granularity. Every change of a product can be recognized as a version and stored in a version control system. Every communication made among developers can be recorded. Not only single project data, but all project data spread over distributed organizations can be easily archived.

The collected mega software engineering data includes both process and product information. Various characteristics can be extracted by analyzing the collected data. Mining a single project data would be a relatively straightforward and light task. On the other hand, mining through mega data, say tens of thousands of projects, can be computationally expensive. Since now we have enormous computational power and memory space compared to, e.g., 10 years ago, however, such analysis becomes feasible. We may want to analyze, not only the organizational software engineering data, but also software engineering data available on the Internet as Open Source projects, such as various source programs, associated documents, version control logs, mail archives, and so on.

In computer science research and practice, there are many successful uses of improved hardware capacity. For example, web data collection and mining such as Google search engine is a case in the web engineering field. In the high-performance computation field, GRID technology is an example. We think that the software engineering field should also share in advantage of the improvement of network, CPU, disk, etc. We propose to create a novel approach to software engineering field, by collecting mega software engineering data through networks, archiving the collected data for a long period, analyzing the huge data deeply, and providing knowledge for organizational improvement.

Undertaking mega engineering, however, is not straightforward. In addition to changing the programmer's mindset from engineering one product to multiple products, one has to accommodate the complexities of challenging the hierarchical socio-organizational context in which single product engineering is so deeply embedded. In this paper, we do not attempt to address such socio-organizational aspects, which have been addressed elsewhere[1]. Here we focus our efforts in describing the technology aspects of *Mega Software Engineering*: the novel analyzes enabled by performing data analysis on multiple projects, the architecture of a Mega software engineering environment, and a framework for collecting analysis data from the environment.

We depict the distinction between Mega Software Engineering and traditional software engineering in Section 2. In Section 3 we introduce some examples of core technologies of Mega Software Engineering. Section 4 outlines the framework based on Mega Software Engineering Environment. In Section 5 we compare this work to some related work, and conclude our discussion in Section 6 with a summary.

2   Overview of Mega Software Engineering

Figure 1 shows a classification of software engineering technologies based on the scale of engineering targets. The horizontal axis shows improvement feedback steps, composed of collection (measurement) step, analysis (evaluation) step, and feedback (improvement) step. The vertical axis represents the scale of the target for software engineering, which we explain in the rest of this section.

Individual Developer Software Engineering: The *first scale level* includes traditional software engineering technologies which target individual developers. Data and knowledge for each developer is collected and analyzed, then the resulting analysis is fed back to the individual developer. For instance, command history of a tool for a developer can be collected and analyzed to improve the arrangement of the tool's menu bar, or to create a command navigation feature for the developer. Many software engineering tools such as software design tools, debug support tools, or communication support tools fall in this category.

Single Project Software Engineering: The *second scale level* includes current software engineering technologies which target a single software develop-

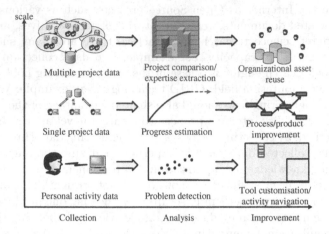

Fig. 1. Scale classification of SE

ment project, or a set of closely related development projects such as product-line development projects. The engineering data for the project is collected and analyzed to improve the project's processes and products. For example, we may collect product data such as the number of completed modules in a project, and then compare to the scheduled number. Such data can be used to monitor the project's progress and corrective action can be taken as necessary. Process engineering tools and distributed development support tools are examples of the Single Project Software Engineering scale.

Mega Software Engineering: At the *ultimate scale level*, we gather multiple project data sets from the entire organization, and compare among projects to draw meaningful conclusions. Analyzed data for project processes and products can be archived as assets of the organization. We note that there have been little software engineering research proposed and realized at this scale, since traditionally there has been limitations on network capacity, CPU power, and so on. Now those limitations have gone away; we can collect and analyze a large volume of data, and we can consider optimization strategies beyond individual or project boundaries. The results of such optimization will benefit the entire software development organization and its members, rather than benefiting simply a single developer or project.

As shown in Figure 2, we consider that Mega Software Engineering is composed of the following steps:

1. huge data collection for a large number of projects,
2. intensive data analysis beyond boundary of projects, and
3. information feedback for organizational improvement.

Technologies in Mega Software Engineering relate to one of these three steps. We will show examples of such technologies in the following section.

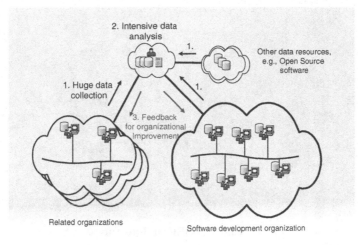

Fig. 2. Fundamental steps of Mega Software Engineering

3   Component Technologies of Mega Software Engineering

3.1   Mega Software Engineering Environment

An essential component of Mega Software Engineering is the ability to systematically collect and organize large amounts of data, from tens of thousands of software projects. This requires: (1) mechanisms for defining the data to be collected from each project, (2) systematic organization of the collected data, and (3) mechanisms for easily obtaining the data from each project.

For each of these questions, we learn from the experiences of the Open Source and Free Software communities that have demonstrated an environment for collecting and organizing vast amounts of mega data, through the pioneering efforts such as Open Source Development Network (OSDN) and the Gnu software tools. Hence, similar to the OSDN, for each project we capture complete versioned source code trees, email discussion archives, bug report and their workflow, and documents associated with the project including web pages. We use the a combination of the hierarchical file system and relational database to organize the large amounts of data.

Rather than collect such data *a posteriori*, we collect and organize such data *in situ*. A critical aspect of this is to collect data as a *side-effect* rather than as an *after-thought*. This implies the existence of a Mega Software Engineering Environment (MSEE) that can easily accommodate the development effort of tens of thousands of projects. In the following, we briefly describe the architecture of one such MSEE, SourceShare [2][3], with which we are most familiar. Other MSEE's (e.g., see [4]) have similar architecture.

Figure 3 shows the main components of SourceShare. As the figure shows, SourceShare is a web-based service. Through the web interface, SourceShare provides capabilities to:

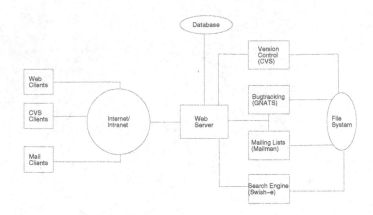

Fig. 3. MSEE architecture

- Add a new software project to the collection
- Browse through existing projects, using various sorting orders like categories, software name, contact name, or date of submission.
- Search through the software projects, either through the source code, software descriptions, mailing list archives, or issues and bug reports.

When a user adds a new software project, SourceShare requires the user to input a set of information about the software, e.g., who were the authors of the software, some keywords, a brief software description and title, etc. SourceShare stores this information in an XML file associated with the project. It also instantiates a version control repository, a mailing list, and a bug tracking system for that software project. Henceforth, users of SourceShare can start working on the project using the version control repository for their source code management. As in the case of Open Source software, SourceShare requires that all decision making and discussions about the software project be carried out using the email discussion list associated with the project. In this manner, SourceShare maintains an archive of the history of project decision making.

An MSEE provides some important features:

- Maintain and make visible tens of thousands of software projects.
- Systematically collect and organize fine-grained data on each project for source code versions, problem reports and their resolution, and project discussions.
- Provide a uniform web-based interface to all information.
- Collect data as side-effect of normal project activities.

3.2   Automatic Categorization

MSEE provides a fundamental vehicle for collecting thousands of project data sets. Within the large project data stored in archives, users frequently want to find clusters of "similar" projects. Hence, we need mechanisms to determine related projects in a large corpus of multi-projects.

Table 1. Categorization by LSA

	D1	D2	D3	E1	E2	E3	V1	V2	V3	X1	X2
D1:firebird-1.0.0.796	1	0.1	0.2	0	0	0	0.1	0.2	0	0	0
D2:mysql-3.23.49	0.1	1	0.1	0	0	0	0.1	0.2	0	0	0
D3:postgresql-7.2.1	0.2	0.1	1	0	0.1	0	0	0.5	0	0	0
E1:gnotepad+-1.3.3	0	0	0	1	1	1	0	0	0	0	0
E2:molasses-1.1.0	0	0	0.1	1	1	1	0	0.1	0	0	0
E3:peacock-0.4	0	0	0	1	1	1	0	0	0	0	0
V1:dv2jpg-1.1	0.1	0.1	0	0	0	0	1	0.8	1	0	0
V2:libcu30-1.0	0.2	0.2	0.5	0	0.1	0	0.8	1	0.8	0	0
V3:mjpgTools	0	0	0	0	0	0	1	0.8	1	0	0
X1:XTermR6.3	0	0	0	0	0	0	0	0	0	1	1
X2:XTermR6.4	0	0	0	0	0	0	0	0	0	1	1

In the Open Source and Free Software communities, categorization is carried out by human input, usually at the beginning of the project. It is unrealistic, however, to consider human categorization given the multitude of software systems that can be expected in a typical mega environment. For example, SourceForge is a huge web site for Open Source software development projects, and as of this writing it contains about 78,000 projects. Human categorization would require not only a good understanding of the individual project to be categorized, but the potential categories that can be created by upto 78,000 projects.

To this end, we are studying automatic categorization of software systems [5][6]. The first approach performs cluster analysis for the sets of source code [6]. This is based on the similarity of two sets of source code, which is defined as the ratio of the numbers of similar code lines to that of the overall lines of two software systems. The similar code lines are detected by a combination of a code-clone detection tool CCFinder [7] and a difference extraction tool *diff*.

For categorization of software systems with little shared code, we propose another approach of categorization of software systems using LSA (Latent Semantic Analysis) [8] for keywords appearing in the source code of the target systems [5]. LSA is a method for extracting and representing the contextual-usage meaning of words by statistical computations applied to a large corpus of text. It has been applied to a variety of uses ranging from understanding human cognition to data mining.

We have chosen 11 software systems from SourceForge, and software groups D1–D3, E1–E3, and V1–V3, and X1–X2 are categorized by hand in the same groups at SourceForge. Table 1 shows the similarity values which are the cosines of the column vectors of the resulting matrix by LSA. Two systems having a 1 entry implies they are very similar, and those with 0 mean no similarity in the keyword lists.

Groups E, V, and X have very high similarities inside the groups. The result shows that although there are some outliers, it would give us a good intuition of categorization of software groups. We further continue this approach to improve the categorization precision.

By adding such automated categorization tool as an analysis feature, managers and developers can easily find similar or related projects to a target project, and they can obtain useful knowledge of similar past projects.

3.3   Selecting Similar Cases by Collaborative Filtering

In the approach described above, we are able to identify cluster of software systems that are similar to each other. We cannot, however, specify which one system is the most similar to any given software system. Collaborative filtering can answer this question of finding the project most related to a given system [9]. We are studying such collaborative filtering as a means of identifying software features from activity data [10]. Here, we propose to apply the collaborative filtering technique to find a similar system (or project) from thousands of systems.

We assume that there is a list of α metrics $M = \{m_1, m_2, \ldots, m_\alpha\}$ and a list of β systems $P = \{p_1, p_2, \ldots, p_\beta\}$. Value v_{ij} can be obtained by applying metric m_i to the data set of system p_j. In similarity computation between two systems p_a and p_b, we first isolate the metrics, which had been applied to both of these systems, and then apply a similarity computation to the value of the isolated metrics. For example, two systems are thought of as two vectors in the α-dimensional metric-space. The similarity between them is measured by computing the cosine of the angle between these two vectors. Once we can isolate the set of the most similar systems based on the similarity measures, we can estimate metric value v_{ij} even when a metric m_i is not available. In such case, an estimation value, such as a weighted average of the metric values of these similar systems, is employed.

This means that collaborative filtering is robust to the defective data sets. In contrast, the conventional regression analysis requires the complete matrix of metric values, and it is unrealistic to assume complete data sets for all systems.

If a project manager finds a deviation from the scheduled project plan, she has to take corrective action to bring future performance in line with the project plan [11]. In such a situation, the project manager may want to know a viable solution for the problem. Collaborative filtering can present a set of the most similar systems to the ongoing system, so that we can explore the product and process data collected in these similar systems, and find a concrete solution. Hence, to proceed with Mega Software Engineering effectively, we need to provide not only a bird's-eye view of software systems and projects, but also concrete information useful for software developers and project managers.

3.4   Code-Clone Detection

As an example of deep analysis for the large collection of software engineering data beyond project boundaries, we will show code-clone detection tool CCFinder and its GUI Gemini for large scale of source code [7].

Code clone is a code fragment in a source file that is identical or similar to another fragment. CCFinder takes a set of source-code files as an input, and generates a list of code-clone locations as the output.

Figure 4 is an example of the display of Gemini. This is the scatterplot of detected clones between two GUI libraries Qt and GTK. These two libraries are developed independently in different organizations. Qt (version 3.2.1) is composed of 929 files and about 686K lines in total. GTK (version 2.2.4) consists of 658 files and 546K lines in total.

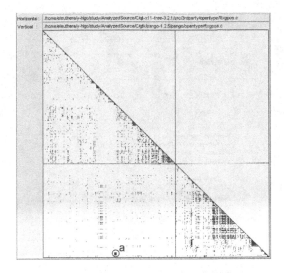

Fig. 4. Scatterplot between Qt and GTK

Each dots in the scatterplot represents existence of code clones with more than 30 tokens. Smaller tokens less than 30 tokens are eliminated here. The left-upper pane shows clones inside Qt, and the right-lower pane shows clones insider GTK. The result is symmetrical to the main diagonal line, so the right-upper half is omitted.

The left-lower pane shows clones between Qt and GTK. The overall clone density in this pane is generally lower than others, but there is one exceptional portion annotated by "a", where there are many clones, meaning that two systems share most code. This portion is the font handler for both Qt and GTK, and we know by reading README files that the font handler of Qt is imported from GTK.

Using these tools, we can quantify similarity of source codes, leading to categorization of software systems and to measurement of code reuse. Also, we can create an effective search tool for similar code portion to the huge archive of organizational software assets.

3.5   Software Component Search

Automation of reusable software component libraries is an important issue in organization. We have designed an automatic software component library that analyzes a large collection of software components, indexing them for efficient retrieval, and ranking them by the importance of components. We have proposed a novel method of ranking software components, called Component Rank, based on the analysis of actual use relations of components and also based on convergence of the significance values through the use relations [12].

Using the component rank computation as a core ranking engine, we are currently developing Software Product Archiving, analyzing, and Retrieving System for Java, called *SPARS-J*.

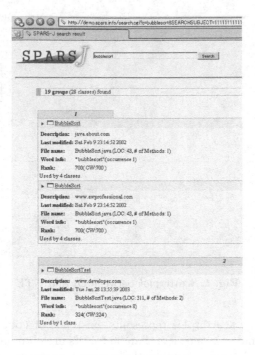

Fig. 5. SPARS-J for "bubblesort"

Figure 5 shows a display result for a query keyword "bubblesort" for SPARS-J. The result is returned almost instantly to the searcher through a web browser. There are 28 classes having the keyword. Similar or the same classes are merged into 19 groups out of 28 classes, and these 19 groups are sorted by the component ranks. The details of listed classes, which include the source code, various metric values, and various links to other classes, can be viewed simply by clicking on the web browser.

This system can become a very powerful vehicle to manage organizational mega software assets. It is easy to collect all source code created in an organization at the raw component archive. Then, the analysis for the ranking and the retrieval for the query are performed fully automatically, without using human hand. So the cost of the software asset management can reduce drastically, and developers can leverage past assets for efficient development of reliable products.

4   Mega Software Engineering Framework

To investigate various technologies in Mega Software Engineering, we are currently developing a tool collection environment called *Mega Software Engineering Framework*, as shown in Figure 6. We do not intend to build a single huge system to perform all the steps in Mega Software Engineering, but we construct a plug-

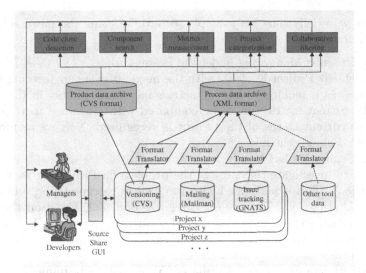

Fig. 6. Architecture of Mega Software Engineering Framework

gable framework in which individual technologies for Mega Software Engineering can easily be incorporated.

This framework is composed of following three tool collections: (1) Source-Share as a Mega Software Engineering Environment, which manages project progress and collects project data, (2) Product and Process data archives, and (3) analysis tools which extract various feedback information.

As described in Section 3.1, SourceShare employs version management tool CVS, mail management tool Mailman, and issue (bug) tracking tool Gnats [13]. SourceShare provides control and unified GUI for these tools; however, we can employ other tools for version control, mailing, or issue tracking. Note that the data collection by SourceShare is done non-intrusively. Checking into CVS repositories, sending mails, and tracking issues are performed as daily activities for software development and maintenance, not as special activities for the data collection.

As the central archives of this framework, we prepare a product data archive in the CVS format and a process data archive in an XML format. The product data archive directly reflects to the repositories of each project in the CVS format. The process data is obtained by transforming log files of CVS, Mailman, and Gnats into a standard format in XML, and it is stored into an XML database that is implemented by PostgreSQL with XML extension. This framework can easily handle process data obtained by other tools if the data is transformed into the standard format in XML.

The process data and product data in the archives are analyzed by a tool for measuring various metrics data and by the tools presented in previous sections. The analysis results are given back to the developers and managers. We are designing a unified GUI for analysis results, which would accomplish effective feedback to developers and managers.

Now we briefly show an example scenario of using the mega software engineering framework.

Step 1: Progress Monitoring under the Framework
A project, say Project X, starts with the mega software engineering framework. The progress is monitored by the metrics measurement tool in the framework, and the current metric values are compared with scheduled metrics values, so that the current status of the project is recognized. Now we assume that the project is behind schedule.

Step 2: Similar Project Search
In order to investigate the cause of the problem on Project X, we find projects similar to X. This is performed with the project categorization tool and collaborative filtering tool. The project categorization tool, based on the automatic categorization method, provides a set of similar projects to X. The collaborative filter chooses a past project Y as the most similar from the "similar" set.

Step 3: Investigation by Various Metric Views
The evolution of various metric values of Y through its beginning to end is investigated, and compared to the metrics values of X. Some outlier metric values are identified. Assume here that X's metric value for reuse rate of software components is much worse than that of Y. This can be detected by measuring amount of code clones between Project X and past projects including Y.

Step 4: Improvement
Since we know that the reuse in Project X is not as actively done as Project Y, we try to promote the reuse actively in X by using the software component search tool. The developers start to browse the product data archive and to search useful legacy software components in Y or similar projects. The reuse rate of X increases to the similar level of Y, and the schedule delay is recovered.

5   Related Work

- Global Software Development
  Due to the rapidly increasing network capacity and speed, and differentiated cost structures, Global Software Development is an active area of software engineering research and practice [14]. Although analysis shows deficiency of global software development, compared to same site work [15], the importance of Global Software Development will continue to increase and strong support tools to ease site distance barrier are required. For example, Herbsleb and Mockus have proposed an "expertise browser" to help locate far flung experts and contributors of software modules [16]. The Mega Software Engineering framework provides a fundamental environment of code sharing and message exchanging for Global Software Development. Also, our approach provides directly needed knowledge or asset to developers or managers, rather than a point solution of e.g., providing assistance in finding expertise.
- Knowledge Sharing
  There are several researchers investigating light-weight knowledge extraction and sharing among developers. For example, Curanic *et al.* analyze link information

to provide related knowledge [17], while Ye and Fischer describe a system for automatically providing source-code components that is not well identified or understood by a developer [18]. The light weight approach focuses on a single developer or a single project. Our approach explores knowledge or information which is based on deeper analyses of multiple projects, and a huge collection of software engineering data.

- Measuring and Analyzing Open Source Project Data
  German and Mockus have proposed a measurement tool collection for CVS and mail data [19]. They generate various statistical values for Open Source development projects. Similarly, Draheim and Pekacki use CVS data to determine several process metric values [20]. Finally, Mockus and Votta use CVS data to classify the causes of changes made to software products [21]. These approaches are also considered to be examples of analysis techniques in Mega Software Engineering. However, their systems are more specific to getting the objective statistical values or classification. We are trying to build a more flexible framework for a large collection of projects, in which we can extract both inter-project knowledge of process and product for various objectives. Thus, we employ an exchangeable standard format in XML for process data, and use a standard database to archive it. Once the data is in the form of a standard database, we can apply various techniques for data mining for traditional data.

- Measurement-Based Improvement Framework
  There is a large body of research and practical implementation of measurement and improvement frameworks. Goal Question Metrics paradigm is an example in which suitable metrics are derived from measurement objectives [22]. The frameworks of software process improvement such as CMM and SPICE are also cases that aim measurement-based improvement for organization, and Personal Software Process targets improvement for personal capability [23]. We might consider that Mega Software Engineering would be an improvement framework similar to those. However, Mega Software Engineering is different in the sense that it assumes organizational-wide huge data collection of many projects and software systems, rather than a single person or single project. Also, the analyses made by Mega Software Engineering are more intensive and deeper ones compared to per-project metric values made by earlier frameworks.
  Also, Mega Software Engineering can be considered as a framework in the context of software process improvement such as CMMI or ISO-9001. Applicability and effectiveness of Mega Software Engineering in such context have to be explored further in various industrial environments.

- Experience Factory
  Vic Basili's group has developed and successfully applied the concept of an "Experience Factory," where organizations systematically collect and reuse past experiences [24]. Indeed, Neto et al. propose a "knowledge management" framework for storing such experience base for organizations [25]. Dingsoyr et al. report practical experiences and recommendations for "knowledge reuse" [26]. We believe that Mega Software Engineering is an evolution of the Experience Factory concept, enriched from the "communal" aspects of Open Source software development. Hence, instead of requiring a separate organizational element that

captures and packages relevant "experience elements," we propose to directly capture the contents of software engineering activities, and make "experience" available through deep analysis of this raw data.

6   Summary

We have proposed a novel concept of Mega Software Engineering, and presented several of its core technologies. We described a framework that allows for pluggable technologies for mega software engineering. Previous work in software engineering research has given limited attention to data collection and analysis of tens of thousands of projects. Rapid advances in hardware and communication technologies allow the application of various technologies to huge data collection and intensive analysis. Therefore, we believe that we are at the best starting point to utilize the benefits of Mega Software Engineering.

This work is supported by Ministry of Education, Culture, Sports, Science and Technology of Japan, the Comprehensive Development of e-Society Foundation Software program.

References

1. Melian, C., Ammirati, C., Garg, P.K., Sevon, G.:   Collaboration and Openness in Large Corporate Software Devlopment. In: Presented at the European Academy of Management Conferenec, Stockholm, Sweden (2002) Available from http://www.zeesource.net/kc.shtml.
2. Dinkelacker, J., Garg, P., Nelson, D., Miller, R.: Progressive Open Source. In: ICSE, Orlando, Florida (2002)
3. ZeeSource: (SourceShare) http://www.zeesource.net.
4. Halloran, T.J., Scherlis, W.L., Erenkrantz, J.R.: Beyond Code: Content Management and the Open Source Development Portal. In: 3rd WS Open Source SE, Portland, OR, USA (2003)
5. Kawaguchi, S., Garg, P.K., Matsushita, M., Inoue, K.: Automatic Categorization for Evolvable Software Archive. In: Int. WS Principles of Software Evolution, Helsinki, Finland (2003) 195–200
6. Yamamoto, T., Matsusita, M., Kamiya, T., Inoue, K.: Measuring Similarity of Large Software Systems Based on Source Code Correspondence. In: PROFES 2005, Oulu Finland (2005)
7. Kamiya, T., Kusumoto, S., Inoue, K.: CCFinder: A Multi-Linguistic Token-based Code Clone Detection System for Large Scale Source Code. IEEE TSE **28** (2002) 654–670
8. Landauer, T.K., Foltz, P.W., Laham, D.: Introduction to latent semantic analysis. Discourse Processes **25** (1998) 259–284
9. Sarwar, B., Karypis, G., Konstan, J., Riedl, J.: Item-based Collaborative Filtering Recommendation Algorithms. In: Int. World Wide Web Conf. (WWW10), Hong Kong (2001) 285–295
10. Ohsugi, N., Monden, A., Morisaki, S.: Collaborative Filtering Approach for Software Function Discovery. In: Int. Symp. Empirical SE (ISESE), vol.2, Nara, Japan (2002) 45–46

11. : Project Management Institute, A Guide to the Project Management Body of Knowledge 2000 Edition (2000)
12. Inoue, K., Yokomori, R., Fujiwara, H., Yamamoto, T., Matsushita, M., Kusumoto, S.: Component Rank: Relative Significance Rank for Software Component Search. In: ICSE, Portland, OR (2003) 14–24
13. Gnu: (Gnats Project) http://www.gnu.org/software/gnats.
14. Herbsleb, J.D., Moitra, D.: Global Software Development. IEEE Software **18** (2001) 16–20
15. Herbsleb, J.D., Moitra, D.: An Empirical Study of Speed and Communication in Globally Distributed Software Development. IEEE TSE **29** (2003) 481–494
16. Mockus, A., Herbsleb, J.D.: Expertise Brower: A Quantitative Approach to Identifying Expertise. In: ICSE, Orlando, FL (2002) 503–512
17. Cubranic, D., Holmes, R., Ying, A., Murphy, G.C.: Tool for Light-weight Knowledge Sharing in Open-source Software Development. In: 3rd WS Open Source SE, Portland, OR, USA (2003) 25–30
18. Ye, Y., Fischer, G.: Supporting Reuse by Delivering Task-Relevant and Personalized Information. In: ICSE, Orlando, FL (2002) 513–523
19. German, D., Mockus, A.: Automating the Measurement of Open Source Projects. In: 3rd WS Open Source SE, Portland, OR (2003) 63–68
20. Draheim, D., Pekacki, L.: Process-Centric Analytical Processing of Version Control Data. In: Int. WS Principles of Software Evolution, Helsinki, Finland (2003) 131–136
21. Mockus, A., Votta, L.G.: Identifying Reasons for Software Changes Using Historic Database. In: ICSM, San Jose, CA (2000) 120–130
22. Basili, V.R. In: Goal Question Metrics Paradigm, in Encyclopedia of Software Engineering (J. Marciniak ed.). John Weily and Sons (1994) 528–532
23. Humphrey, W.S.: Introduction to the Personal Software Process. Addison-Wesley (1996)
24. Basili, V.R., Caldiera, G.: Improve Software Quality by Reusing Knowledge and Experience. Sloan Management Review **Fall** (1995) 55–64
25. Neto, M.G.M., Seaman, C.B., Basili, V., Kim, Y.: A Prototype Experience Management System for a Software Consulting Organization. In: SEKE 2001, Buenos Aires, Argentina (2001)
26. Conradi, R., Dingsoyr, T.: Software Experience Bases: A Consolidated Evaluation and Status Report. In: 2nd PROFES 2000, Oulu, Finland (2000) 391–406

Software Development and Experimentation in an Academic Environment: The Gaudi Experience

Ralph-Johan Back, Luka Milovanov, and Ivan Porres

Turku Centre for Computer Science,
Åbo Akademi University, Department of Computer Science,
Lemminkäisenkatu 14 A, FIN-20520 Turku, Finland
{backrj, lmilovan, iporres}@abo.fi

Abstract. In this article, we describe an approach to empirical software engineering based on a combined software factory and software laboratory. The software factory develops software required by an external customer while the software laboratory monitors and improves the processes and methods used in the factory. We have used this approach during a period of four years to define and evaluate a software process that combines practices from Extreme Programming with architectural design and documentation practices in order to find a balance between agility, maintainability and reliability.

1 Introduction

One of the main problems that hinders the research and improvement of various software construction techniques is the difficulty to perform significant experiments. Many processes and methods in software development have been conceived in the context of large industrial projects. However, in most cases, it is almost impossible to perform controlled experiments in an industrial setting due to resource constraints.

However, university researchers also meet with difficulties when experimenting with new software development ideas in practice. Performing an experiment in collaboration with the industry using newly untested software development methods can be risky for the industrial partner but also for the researcher, since the project can fail due to factors that cannot be controlled by the researcher. The obvious alternative is to perform software engineering experiments inside a research center in a controlled environment. Still, this approach has at least three important shortcomings.

First, it is possible that a synthetic development project arranged by a researcher does not reflect the conditions and constraints found in an actual software development project. This happens specially if there is no actual need for the software to be developed. Also, university experiments are quite often performed by students. Students are not necessarily less capable than employed software developers, but they must be trained and their programming experience and motivation in a project may vary. Finally, although there is no market pressure, a researcher often has very limited resources and therefore it is not always possible to execute large experiments.

F. Bomarius and S. Komi-Sirviö (Eds.): PROFES 2005, LNCS 3547, pp. 414–428, 2005.

These shortcomings disappear if the software built in an experiment is an actual software product that is needed by one or more customers that will define the product requirements and will carry the cost of the development of the product. In our case, we found such customer in our own environment: other researchers that need software to be built to demonstrate and validate their research work. This scientific software does not necessarily need to be related to our work in software engineering.

In this paper we describe our experiences following this approach: how we created Gaudi, our own laboratory for experimental software engineering, and how we studied software development in practice while building software in Gaudi for other researchers. This experience is based on experiments conducted during the last four years. The objective of these experiments was to find and document software best practices in a software process that focus on product quality and project agility.

As we proposed in [1], we chose Extreme Programming [2] (XP) as the framework process for these experiments. Extreme Programming is an agile software methodology that was introduced by Beck in 2000. It is characterized by a short iteration cycle, integration of the design and implementation phases, continuous refactoring supported by extensive unit testing, onsite customer, promoting team communication and pair programming. XP has become quite popular these days, but it has also been criticized for lack of concrete evidences of success [3].

This paper is structured as follows: in Section 2 we describe the Gaudi Software Factory as a university unit for building software in the form of controlled experiments. Section 3 present the typical settings of such experiments and portrays their technical aspects. Section 4 discusses the practices of the software process, while Section 5 summarizes our observations from our experience in Gaudi. Due to space limitations, this article focuses on presenting the qualitative evaluation of these experiments. The reader can find more detailed information about the actual experiments in [5].

2 Gaudi and Its Working Principles

Gaudi is a research project that aims at developing and testing new software development methods in a realistic setting. We are interested in the time, cost, quality, and quantitative aspects of developing software, and study these issues in a series of controlled experiments. We focus on lightweight or agile software processes. Gaudi is divided into a software factory and a software laboratory.

2.1 Software Factory

The goal of the *Gaudi software factory* is to produce software for the needs of various research projects in our university. Software is built in the factory according to the requirements given by the project stakeholders. These stakeholders also provided the required resources to carry out the project. A characteristic of the factory is that the developers are students. However, programming in Gaudi is not a part of their studies, and the students get no credits for participating in Gaudi – they are employed and paid a normal salary according to the university regulations.

Gaudi factory was started as a pilot experiment in the summer of 2001 [4] with a group of six programmers working on a single product (an outlining editor). The following summer we introduced two other products and six more programmers. The work continued with half-time employments during the following fall and spring. In the fourth cycle, in the summer of 2003, there were five parallel experiments with five different products, each with a different focus but with approximately the same settings. Altogether, we have carried out 18 software construction experiments in Gaudi to this day. The application areas of the software built in Gaudi are quite varied: an editor for mathematical derivations, software construction and modeling tools, 3D model animation, a personal financial planner, financial benchmarking of organizations, a mobile ad-hoc network router, digital TV middleware, and so on.

2.2 Software Laboratory

The goal of the *Gaudi software laboratory* is to investigate, evaluate and improve the software development process used in the factory. The factory is in charge of the software product, while the laboratory is in charge of the software process. The laboratory supplies the factory with tasks, resources and new methods, while the factory provides the laboratory with the feedback in the form of software and experience results. The laboratory staff is composed of researchers and doctoral students working in the area of software engineering.

The kinds of projects carried on by the factory are quite varied and the application area, technology, and project stakeholders changed from project to project. However, there were also common challenges in all the projects to be addressed in the laboratory: product requirements were quite often underspecified and highly volatile and the developer turnaround was big.

Research software is often built to validate and demonstrate promising but immature ideas. Once it is functional, the software creates a feedback loop for the researchers. If the researchers make good use of this feedback, they will improve and refine their research work and therefore, they will need to update the software to include their improved ideas. In this context, the better a piece of research software fulfills its goal, more changes will be required in it. High developer turnaround is a risk that needs to be minimized in any software development company and the impacts of this have to be mitigated. In a university environment, this is part of normal life. We employ students as programmers during their studies. But, eventually, they will graduate and leave the programming team. A few students may continue as Ph.D. students or as part of a more permanent programming staff, but this is more the exception than the norm.

Our approach to these challenges was to use agile methods, in particular on Extreme Programming, and to split a large development project into a number of successive smaller projects. A smaller project will typically represent a total effort of one to two person years. This also is the usual size of project that a single researcher can find financing for in a university setting per year. A project size of one person year is also a good base for a controlled experiment. It is large enough to yield significant results while it can be carried out in the relatively short period of three calendar months using a group of four students.

3   Experiments in the Gaudi Factory

The Gaudi laboratory uses the Gaudi factory as a sandbox for software process improvement and development. Software projects in the factory are run as a series of monitored and controlled experiments. The settings of those experiments are defined a priori by the laboratory. After an experiment is completed, the settings are reviewed and our project standards are updated. In this section we describe the project settings and arrangements for Gaudi.

3.1   Schedule and Resources

A Gaudi experiment has a tight schedule, usually comprising three months. Most of the experiments are performed during summer, when students can work full-time (40 hours a week). In practice, this means that the developers start their work the first day of June and the final release of the software product is the last day of August. In projects carried out during the terms, students work half time (25-30 hours a week).

All the participants in an experiment are employed by the university, including the students working as developers, using standard employment contracts. All members of the same development team sit in the same room, arranged according to the advice given by Beck in [2].

3.2   Training

We should provide proper training to the developers in a project before it starts. However, the projects are short so we can not spend much time on the training. We chose to give the developers short (1-4 hours) tutorials on the essentials of the technologies that they are going to use. The purpose of these tutorials is not to teach a full programming language or a method, but to give a general overview of the topic and provide references to the necessary literature. We consider these tutorials as an introduction to standard *software best practices*, which are then employed throughout the Gaudi factory. Besides general tutorials that all developers take, we also provide tutorials on specific topics that may be needed in only one project, and which are taken only by the developers concerned. An example of the complete set of tutorials can be found in [5].

3.3   Experiment Supervision, Metrics Collection and Evaluation

We have established an experimental supervision and metric collection framework in order to measure the impact of different development practices in a project.

The complete description of our measurement framework is an issue for a separate paper, but in this section we outline its main principles. Our choice is the Goal Question Metric (GQM) approach [6]. GQM is based upon the assumption that for an organization to measure in a meaningful way it must first specify the goals for itself and its projects, then it must trace those goals to the data that are intended to define those goals operationally, and finally provide a framework for interpreting the data with respect to the stated goals [6]. The current list of goals for the Gaudi factory as we see them can be found in [5] and its metric framework in [7].

4   Software Practices in Gaudi

In this section we describe the main practices in our process and our observations after applying them in several projects. We started our first pilot project [4] with just a few basic XP practices, evaluating them and gradually including more and more XP practices into the Gaudi process. After trying out a new practice in Gaudi we evaluate it and then, depending on the results of the evaluation, it either becomes a standard part of the Gaudi process, is abandoned, or is left for later re-implementation and re-evaluation. In this section, we discuss our experience with the agile practices which have been tried out in our projects. Some of the practices are adopted into our process and became a standard part of it, while some are still under evaluation.

The list of all these practices can be found in [5]. The technical report also includes percentages of activities performed by developers.

We now proceed as following: first we give a general overview of a practice, then we present our experience and results achieved with this practice. Finally we discuss possible ways to improve these practices in Gaudi environment. For the reader's convenience we split the practices into four categories: requirement management, planning, engineering and asset management.

4.1   Requirement Management Practices

Requirement management in XP is performed by the person carrying out the customer role. The requirements are presented in the form of user stories.

Customer Model
The role of the customer in XP is to write and prioritize user stories as defined in the next practice. The customer should also explain and clarify the stories to the development team and define and run acceptance tests to verify the correct functionality of the implemented stories. One of the most distinctive features of XP is that the customer should work onsite, as a member of the team, in the same room with the team and be 100% available for the team's questions.

As could have been guessed directly, it is hard to implement the onsite customer model in practice [8, 9]. Our experience confirms this. Among the 18 Gaudi projects, there was a real onsite customer only in one project – FiPla [7]. Before this the customer's involvement was minimal and it was in the Feature Driven Development [10] style: the offsite customer wrote requirements for the application, then the coach transformed these requirements into product requirements. Then the coach compiled the list of features based on the product requirements, and the features were given to the developers as programming tasks.

Studying the advantages of an onsite customer was one of the main objectives of the FiPla project. In this project the customer was available for questions or discussions whenever the development team felt this was necessary. However, the customer did not work in the same room with the development team. This was originally recommended by XP practices [11], but it was considered to be unnecessary because the customer's office situated in the same building with the development team's premises – this was considered to be "sharing enough".

Apparently, being an onsite customer does not increase the customer's work load very much [7]. One might even wonder whether an onsite presence is really necessary based on these figures. However, the feedback from the development team shows that an onsite customer is very helpful even though the customer's input was rather seldom needed. The developers' suggestion about involving the customer more in the team's work could also be implemented by seating the customer in the same room with the programmers. The feeling was that there could have been more spontaneous questions and comments between the developers and the customer if she had been in the same room.

Since summer 2004 we started using a customer representative or so called *customer proxy* model in Gaudi. The difference between these two customer models were that the customer representative does not commit himself to be always available to the team and in order to make decisions he had to consult the actual customer who was basically offsite. In both cases all customer-team communications were face-to-face, without e-mail neither phone discussions.

It is essential to have an active customer or customer's representative in an experimental project when the customer model itself is not a subject for the experiment. This allows us to keep the developers focused on the product, not the experiment and not be disturbed by the experimental nature of project.

User Stories

Customer requirements in XP projects are presented in the form of user stories [2]. User stories are written by the customer and they describe the required functionality from a user's point of view, in about three sentences of text in the customer's terminology.

We have used both paper stories and stories written into a web-based task management system. An advantage of paper stories is their simplicity. On the other hand, the task management system allows its users to modify the contents of stories, add comments, track the effort, attach files (i.e. tests or design documents) etc. It is also more suitable when we have a remote or offsite customer. Currently we are only using the task management system and do not have any paper stories at all.

In many projects, product or component requirements are represented in the form of tasks written by programmers. Tasks contain a lot of technical details, and often also describe what classes and methods are required to implement a concrete story. A story normally produces 3-4 tasks. When a story is split into tasks, the tasks are linked as *dependencies* of the story, and the story becomes *dependent* on tasks. When we used paper stories, we just attached the tasks to their stories. This is done in order to ensure the bidirectional traceability of requirements. Moreover, it is possible to trace each story or task to the source code implementing it. This is discussed in the Configuration Management practice. It is essential that each story makes sense for the developers (see Section 4.2) and it is estimable (we talk about the estimations in the Section 4.2).

4.2 Planning Practices

The most fundamental issues in XP project planning are to decide what functionality should be implemented and when it should be implemented. In order to deal with these issues we need the planning game and a good mechanism for time estimations.

Planning Game and Small Iterations

The *planning game* is the XP planning process [2]: business gets to specify what the system needs to do, while development specifies how much each feature costs and what budget is available per day, week or month. XP talks about two types of planning: by scope and by time. Planning by time is to choose the stories to be implemented, rather than taking all of them and negotiating about a release date and resources to be used (planning by scope).

The team estimates all the stories for the project and writes their estimations directly for the stories (we will discuss the estimation process in more details in the Section 4.2). These estimations are not very precise, the error is 20% on average [5], but can be smaller. E.g., in the FiPla [7] project the estimation error for the whole effort was 10% (approximately 30 hours). The estimations create an overall project plan and immediately tell us whenever some stories should be postponed to the next project or whether there is time to add more stories.

The task managements and bug tracking system allows us to submit tasks and bugs, and to keep track of them. Currently, we use the JIRA task management to keep track of task estimations. These kinds of systems are easy to use and provide an overall view of which tasks and bugs are currently under correction, which are fixed and which are open. This is especially important when the customer cannot act as an onsite customer (see Section 4.1).

In our experience, the planning game, the small releases and time estimations are very hard to implement without well-defined customer stories and technical tasks, and hence, without an active customer or customer representative.

Time Estimations

The essence of the XP release planning meeting is for the development team to estimate each user story in terms of ideal programming weeks [2]. An ideal week is how long a programmer imagines it would take to implement a story if he or she had absolutely nothing else to do. No dependencies, no extra work, but the time does include tests.

We have two estimation phases in the Gaudi process. The first phase is when the team estimated all of the stories in ideal programming days and weeks. These estimations are not very precise and they are improved in the second estimation phase when the team splits stories into tasks. When programmers split stories into technical tasks they make use of their previous programming experience and try to think of the stories in terms of the programs they have already written. This makes sense for the programmers and makes the estimating process easier for them.

The estimated time for a task is the number of hours it will take one programmer to write the code and the unit tests for it. These estimations are done by the same programmers that are signed up for the tasks, i.e., the person who estimates the task will later implement it. This improves the precision of the estimations. The sum is doubled to allocate time for refactoring and debugging. This is the estimation of a story for solo programming. In case of pair programming we need to take the Nosek's [12] principle into consideration: *two programmers will implement two tasks in pair 60 percent slower then two programmers implementing the same task separately with solo programming.* This means that a pair will implement a single task 20% faster then a single programmer. Similarly, to get the estimation for an iteration we have to sum the estimations of all stories the iteration consists of. Project estimation will be the sum of all its iteration estimations.

Estimating tasks turns out to be rather easy even for inexperienced programmers. The accuracy of the estimations depends, of course, on the experience of the developer. Experience in the particular programming language turns out to be more important than experience in estimation. Examples of the estimation accuracy in Gaudi can be found in [5].

XP-style project estimation is useful to plan the next one or two iterations in the project, but they can seldom be used to estimate the calendar length or resources needed in a project.

4.3 Engineering Practices

Engineering practices include the day-to-day practices employed by the programmers in order to implement the user stories into the final working system.

Design by Contract

Design by Contract [14] (DBC) is a systematic method for making software reliable (correct and robust). A system is structured as a collection of cooperating software elements. The cooperation of the elements is restricted by *contracts*, explicit definitions of obligations and guarantees. The contracts are *pre-* and *postconditions* of methods and *class invariants*. These conditions are written in the programming language itself and can be checked at runtime, when the method is called. If a method call does not satisfy the contract, an error is raised. Some reports [15, 16] show that XP and design by contract fit well together, and unit tests and contracts compliment each other.

Our first experiment with Eiffel and DBC showed very good results. First of all, the use of this method was one of the reasons for the low defect rate in the project [7]. As the development team commented out: *"All the tests written (to a complete code) always pass and the tests that don't pass have a bug in the test itself"*. Most of the bugs were caught with the help of preconditions, when a routine with a bug was called during unit testing. Most of the unit tests were written before the actual code, but the contracts were specified after it because the programmers did not get any instructions from their coach on when the contracts should be written. Example data for the post-release defect rate of the software developed with DBC is reported in [7].

Stepwise Feature Introduction

Stepwise Feature Introduction (SFI) is a software development methodology introduced by Back [17] based on the incremental extension of the object-oriented software system one feature at a time. This methodology has much in common with the original *stepwise refinement* method. The main difference to stepwise refinement is the bottom-up software construction approach and object orientation. Stepwise Feature Introduction is an experimental methodology and is currently under development.

We are using this approach in our projects in order to get practical experience with the method and suggestions for further improvements. Extreme Programming does not say anything about the software architecture of the system. Stepwise Feature Introduction provides a simple architecture that goes well with the XP approach of constructing software in short iteration cycles. So far we have had positive feedback from using SFI with a dynamically typed object-oriented language like Python. An experiment with SFI and Eiffel, a statically typed object-oriented language showed us some aspects of the methodology which need improvement. The explanation of these findings requires a more thorough explanation of SFI than what is motivated in this paper, so we decided to discuss this in a separate paper. Developers found SFI methods relatively easy to learn and use. The main complain was the lack of tool support. When building a software system using SFI, programmers need to take care of a number of routines which are time consuming but which could be automated. The most positive feedback about SFI concerned the layered structure: it clarifies the system architecture and it also helps in debugging, since it is relatively easy to determine the layer in which the bug is introduced.

Pair Programming

Pair programming is a programming technique in which two programmers work together at one computer on the same task [18]. Pair programming has many significant benefits for the design and code quality, communication, education etc [19, 20, 21, 22, 23]. Programmers learn from each other while working in pairs. This is especially interesting in our context since in the same project we can have students with very different programming experience.

In our first experiments we were enforcing developers to always work in pairs, later on when we had some experienced developers in the projects, we gave the developers the right to choose when to work in pair and when to work solo. In the 2003 projects pair programming was not enforced, but recommended, while in summer 2004 two months were pair programming and one month solo. We leave it up to the programmer whether to work in pairs while debugging or refactoring. The percentage of the solo-pair work for the five projects of 2003-2004 is reported in [5].

All of the developers agree that the code written in pairs is easier to read and contains less bugs. They also commented that refactoring is much easier to do in pairs. However there are different opinions and experiences on debugging. In some projects developers said that it was almost impossible to debug in pair because *"everyone has his own theory about where the bug is"* and *"while you want to scroll up, your pair want to scroll down, this disturbs concentration during debugging"*. In other projects programmers preferred pair debugging because they found it easier to catch bugs together. We think that working in pairs should be enforced for writing all productive code, including tests, while it should be up to the developers, whenever debug or refactor in pairs or solo. It would be interesting to know which part of the code is actually pair programmed and which solo. A possible solution to distinguish between pair and solo code is to use specific annotations in the code [24], as used in Energi [25] projects, where the origin (pair or solo) of the code is described by comments.

Unit Testing
Unit testing is defined as testing of individual hardware or software units or groups of related units [26]. In XP, unit testing refers to tests written by the same developer as the production code. According to XP, all code must have unit tests and the tests should be written before the actual code. The tests must use a unit test framework to be able to create automated unit test suites.

Learning to write tests was relatively easy for most developers. The most difficult practice to adopt was the "write test first" approach. Our experience shows that if the coach spends time together with the programmers, writing tests himself and writing the tests before the code, the programming team continues this testing practice also without the coach. Some supervision is, however, required, especially during the first weeks of work. The tutorial about unit testing focused at the test driven development before the project is also essential. The implementation of the testing practice also depends on the nature of the programming task. Our experience showed that the "write test first" approach worked only in the situation where the first programming tasks had no GUI involved because GUI code is hard to test automatically.

In many projects the goal is to achieve 100% unit test coverage for non-GUI components. A program that calculates test coverage automatically provides an invaluable help to achieve this goal to both programmers and coaches.

Continuous Refactoring and Collective Code Ownership
Refactoring is the process of changing a software system in such a way that it does not alter the external behavior of the code, yet improves its internal structure [27]. XP promotes refactoring throughout the entire project life cycle to save time and increase quality [28]. This practice together with pair programming also promotes collective code ownership, where no one person owns the code and may become a bottleneck for changes. Instead, every team member is encouraged to contribute to all parts of the project.

Pair programming, continuous refactoring, collective code ownership, and the layered architecture make the code produced in the Gaudi factory simpler and easier to read, and hence more maintainable. As mentioned before, larger products are developed in a series of three-month projects and not necessarily by the same developers. To ensure that a new team that takes over the project gets to understand the code quickly, we usually compose the team with one or two developers who have experience with the product from a previous project, the rest of the team being new to the product. In this way new developers can take over the old code and start contributing to the different parts of the product faster. When the team is completely new, the coach will help the developers to take over the old code.

4.4 Asset Management

Any nontrivial software project will create many artifacts which will evolve during the project. In XP those artifacts are added in the central repository and updated as soon as possible. Each team member is not only allowed, but encouraged to change any artifact in the repository.

Configuration Management and Continuous Integration

All code produced in the Gaudi Software Factory, as well as all tests (see Section 4.3), are developed under a version control system. We started in 2001 using CVS but now most projects have migrated to Subversion, which is now the standard version control system in Gaudi. The source code repository is also an important source of data for analyzing the progress of the project, since all revisions are stored there together with a record of the responsible person and date and time for check-in. The metrics issues were discussed in the Section 3.3.

Due to the small size (four to six programmers) of the development teams in Gaudi, we do not use a special computer for integration, neither do we make use of integration tokens. When a pair needs to integrate its code, the programmers from this pair simply inform their colleagues and ask them to wait with their integration until the first pair checks in the integrated code. The number of daily check-ins varies, but there is at least one check-in every day. In many cases integration is just a matter of few seconds.

It is important to be able to trace every check-in to concrete tasks and user stories [29]. For this purpose programmers add the identification of the relevant task or story to the CVS or Subversion log. The identification is the unique ID of the story or task in the task management system (SourceForge or JIRA). The exception is when the programmers refactor or debug existing code, it is then very hard (or impossible) to trace this activity to a concrete task or story. Therefore check-ins after refactoring or debugging are linked to the "General Refactoring and Debugging" task (see Section 4.1).

Agile Documentation

When a story is implemented, the pair or single programmer who implemented it should also write the user documentation for the story. The documentation is written directly on the story or in a text file located in the project's repository. This file is divided into sections, where each section corresponds to an implemented story. If the stories are on a web-base task management system, the documentation is written directly in the stories – this simplifies the bidirectional traceability for stories and their documentation. Later on the complete user documentation will be compiled from the stories' documentation. Documenting a user story is basically rephrasing it, and it takes an average of 30 minutes to do it.

This approach allows us to embed the user documentation into the development process. Bidirectional traceability of the stories and user documentation makes it easy to update the corresponding documentation whenever the functionality changes. The documentation examples from one of the Gaudi projects can be found in [5].

5   Conclusions and Related Work

In this paper we have presented Gaudi, our approach to empirical research in software engineering based on the development of small software products in a controlled environment. This approach requires a large amount of resources and effort but provides a unique opportunity to monitor and study software development in practice.

The software process used in Gaudi is based on agile methods, especially on Extreme Programming. In this, paper we have discussed the adoption and performance of 12 different agile practices. We believe that our collected data represents a significant sample of actual software development due to its size and diversity, and lends support for many of the claims made by the advocates of Extreme Programming.

There have been several efforts to study and validate how agile methods are used in the industry, such as the survey performed i.e. in [30, 31]. An industrial survey can help us to determine the performance of a completely defined process such as XP, but it cannot be used to study the effects of different development practices quantitatively, since the researchers cannot monitor the project in full details. Instead, the survey has to be based on the qualitative and subjective assessments of project managers of the success of the different development practices used in their projects. Abrahamsson follows a research approach that is similar to ours, combining software research with software development in *Energi* [25]. The main focus of his research is to evaluate agile methods proposed by other researchers in the field. In contrast, our intention is to perform empirical experiments not only to evaluate existing practices but also to propose new practices that we think will improve the overall software process.

The Gaudi framework project started in 2001 and have completed 18 projects during a period for 4 years representing an effort of 30 person years in total. This work has been measured and the results of these measurements are being used to create the so called Gaudi process. Once this process is completely defined it will be tested again in empirical experiments. It is possible to argue that this approach will result in a software process that is optimized for building software only in a university setting. Although this criticism is valid, it is also true that most of the challenges found in our environment such as scarce resources, undefined and volatile requirements and high programmer turn around are also present in many industrial projects.

In the previous section, we have evaluated each practice in detail. However, we would like to discuss some of the overall experiences obtained from the framework project.

Agile Methods Work in Practice: As overall conclusions of our experiences is that agile methods provide good results when used in small projects with undefined and volatile requirements. Agile methods have many known limitations such as difficulties to scale up to large teams, reliance on oral communication and a focus on functional requirements that dismisses the importance of reliability and safety aspects. However, when projects are of relatively small size and are not safety critical, agile methods will enable us to reliably obtain results in a short time.

The fact that agile methods worked for us does not mean that is not possible to improve existing agile practices. Our first recommendation is that architectural design should be an established practice. We have never observed a good architecture to "emerge" from a project. The architecture has been either designed a priory at the beginning of a project or a posteriori, when the design was so difficult to understand that a complete rethinking was needed.

Also, we established project and product documentation as an important task. XP reliance on oral communication should not be used in environments with high developer turnaround. Artifacts describing the software architecture, design and product manual are as important as the source code and should be created and maintained during the whole life of the project.

Project Management and Flying Hats: Another observation is that in many cases the actual roles and tasks performed by the different people involved in a project did not correspond to the roles and tasks assigned to them before the project started. This was due to the fact that the motivation and interest in a given project varied greatly from person to person. In some cases, the official customer for a project lost interest in the project before it was completed, e.g. in less than three months. In these cases, another person took the role of a customer just because that person was still interested in the product or because a strong commitment to the project made this person to take different roles simultaneously even if that was not his or her duty.

Our conclusion is that standard management tasks such project staffing, project supervision and ensuring a high motivation and commitment from the project staff and different stakeholders are as relevant in agile process in a university setting as in any other kind of project.

Tension Between Product and Experiment: Finally, we want to note that during these four years we have observed a certain tension between the development of software and the experimentation with methods. We have had projects that produced good products to customer satisfaction but were considered bad experiments since it was not possible to collect all the desired data in a reliable way. Also, there have been successful experiments that produced software that has never been used by its customer.

To detect and avoid these situations a well-defined measurement framework should be in place during the development phase of a project but also after the project has been completed to monitor how the products are being used by their customers.

References

1. Back, R.J., Milovanov, L., Porres, I., Preoteasa, V.: XP as a Framework for Practical Software Engineering Experiments. In: Proceedings of the Third International Conference on eXtreme Programming and Agile Processes in Software Engineering – XP2002 (2002)
2. Beck, K.: Extreme Programming Explained: Embrace Change. Addison-Wesley (1999)
3. Abrahamsson, P.: Extreme Programming: First Results from a Controlled Study. In: Proceedings of the 29th EUROMICRO Conference "NewWaves in System Architecture", IEEE (2003)
4. Back, R.J., Milovanov, L., Porres, I., Preoteasa, V.: An Experiment on Extreme Programming and Stepwise Feature Introduction. Technical Report 451, TUCS (2002)
5. Back, R.J., Milovanov, L., Porres, I.: Software Development and Experimentation in an Academic Environment: The Gaudi Experience. Technical Report 641, TUCS (2004)
6. Basili, V., Caldiera, G., Rombach, D.: The Goal Question Metric Approach. Encyclopedia of Software Engineering. John Wiley and Sons (1994)

7. Back, R.J., Hirkman, P., Milovanov, L.: Evaluating the XP Customer Model and Design by Contract. In: Proceedings of the 30th EUROMICRO Conference, IEEE Computer Society (2004)
8. Korkala, M.: Extreme Programming: Introducing a Requirements Management Process for an Offsite Customer. Department of Information Processing Science research papers series A, University of Oulu (2004)
9. Korkala, M., Abrahamsson, P.: Extreme Programming: Reassessing the Requirements Management Process for an Offsite Customer. In: Proceedings of the European Software Process Improvement Conference EUROSPI 2004, Springer Verlag LNCS Series (2004)
10. Palmer, S.R., Felsing, J.M.: A Practicel Guide to Feature-Driven Development. The Coad Series. Prentice Hall PTR (2002)
11. Beck, K.: Embracing Change with Extreme Programming. Computer 32 (1999) 70–73
12. Nosek, J.: The Case for Collaborative Programming. Communications of the ACM 41 (1998) 105–108
13. Meyer, B.: Eiffel: The Language. second edition edn. Prentice Hall (1992)
14. Meyer, B.: Object-Oriented Software Construction. second edition edn. Prentice Hall (1997)
15. Feldman, Y.A.: Extreme Design by Contract. In: Proceedings of the 4th International Conference on Extreme Programming and Agile Processes in Software Engineering, Springer (2003)
16. Heinecke, H., Noack, C. In: Integrating Extreme Programming and Contracts. Addison-Wesley Professional (2002)
17. Back, R.J.: Software Construction by Stepwise Feature Introduction. In: Proceedings of the ZB2001 – Second International Z and B Conference, Springer Verlag LNCS Series (2002)
18. Williams, L., Kessler, R.: Pair Programming Illuminated. Addison-Wesley Longman Publishing Co., Inc. (2002)
19. Cockburn, A., Williams, L.: The Costs and Benefits of Pair Programming. In: Proceedings of eXtreme Programming and Flexible Processes in Software Engineering XP2000. (2000)
20. Constantine, L.L.: Constantine on Peopleware. Englewood Cliffs: Prentice Hall (1995)
21. Johnson, D.H., Caristi, J.: Extreme Programming and the Software Design Course. In: Proceedings of XP Universe. (2001)
22. Müller, M.M., Tichy, W.F.: Case study: Extreme programming in a university environment. In: Proceedings of the 23rd Conference on Software Engineering, IEEE Computer Society (2001)
23. Williams, L.A., Kessler, R.R.: Experimenting with Industry's Pair-Programming Model in the Computer Science Classroom. Journal on Software Engineering Education (2000)
24. Hulkko, H.: Pair programming and its impact on software quality. Master's thesis, Electrical and Information Engineering department, University of Oulu (2004)
25. Salo, O., Abrahamsson, P.: Evaluation of Agile Software Development: The Controlled Case Study approach. In: Proceedings of the 5th International Conference on Product Focused Software Process Improvement PROFES 2004, Springer Verlag LNCS Series (2004)
26. Institute of Electrical and Electronics Engineers: IEEE Standard Computer Dictionary: A Compilation of IEEE Standard Computer Glossaries. New York (1990)
27. Fowler, M.: Refactoring: Improving the Design of Existing Code. Object Technology Series. Addison-Wesley (1999)

28. Roberts, D.B.: Practical Analysis of Refactorings. PhD thesis, University of Illinois at Urbana-Champaign (1999)
29. Asklund, U., Bendix, L., Ekman, T.: Software Configuration Management Practices for eXtreme Programming Teams. In: Proceedings of the 11th Nordic Workshop on Programming and Software Development Tools and Techniques NWPER'2004. (2004)
30. Ilieva, S., Ivanov, P., Stefanova, E.: Analyses of an Agile Methodology Implementation. In: Proceedings of the 30th EUROMICRO Conference, IEEE Computer Society (2004)
31. Rumpe, B., Schröder, A.: Quantitative survey on extreme programming projects. In: Third International Conference on Extreme Programming and Flexible Processes in Software Engineering, XP2002, May 26-30, Alghero, Italy (2002) 95–100

Issues in Software Inspection Practices

Sami Kollanus

Department of Computer Science and Information Systems,
P.O.Box 35 (Agora), FI-40014 University of Jyväskylä, Finland
sami.kollanus@jyu.fi

Abstract. The motivation for this research comes from a need to improve
software inspection practices in software organizations. Even if inspections are
well defined and regularly used in an organization, there may be some problems
which can greatly reduce inspection effectiveness. The paper presents a list of
inspection related problems which are known in the literature. It also relates
some experiences from two case organizations. In addition, this paper provides
an approach which helps identifying problems of this kind and directing limited
improvement resources effectively.

1 Introduction

Since Michael Fagan published his software inspection method [2] almost 30 years
ago, it has inspired several researchers who work with inspections. Existing research
is strongly concentrated on different inspection methods and on different factors in
inspection effectiveness. For example, Laitenberg and DeBaud [12] have introduced
these research areas in their survey. There is very little systematic research conducted
about inspection adoption and improvement in an organization.

Research which would describe how software industry is really practicing
inspections is still lacking. However, some references are available. Johnson [7]
reported about an informal survey, which indicated that 80% of the 90 respondents
practised inspection irregularly or not at all. Also, CMM [18] assessment results may
be a useful indicator about the use of inspections. A recent report of the Software
Engineering Institute [19] shows that about 55% of the assessed organizations
between the years 1999-2003 are still below the third level where some kinds of
formal reviews are required. These statistics obviously emphasize organizations
which take their process improvement seriously. It can only be guessed how small the
fraction of the whole software industry that would reach the third CMM level is, and
how well this indicates the use of inspections. Regardless of the missing facts about
the inspection use in industry, there is certainly need for inspection improvement. The
major motivation for this paper comes from that need.

There is already some support for inspection improvement in the form of maturity
models (see [10] and [21]). Those models describe what kinds of elements an
organization should have in their inspection practices, and can assess the current level
of inspection practices in an organization. The assessment may also give some

F. Bomarius and S. Komi-Sirviö (Eds.): PROFES 2005, LNCS 3547, pp. 429–442, 2005.

suggestions about where the improvement actions should be directed to. However, even if inspections are formally defined and regularly used in an organization, there may be some problems which make inspections ineffective or in the worst case may totally prevent the inspection practice. This paper introduces a problem based approach to inspection improvement. This approach is created to help an organization to identify possible problems in their inspection practices. It may also help the organization to target its improvement actions effectively.

The major focus of this research was on the field of problems related to software inspections. There is no existing systematic research about inspection problems, although there are problems known in several areas. Therefore, the first thing in this research was to list the known problems in the literature. The second task was to collect empirical experiences from two case organizations. These experiences were used to evaluate the original problems listed to get some ideas for inspection improvement. An additional goal was to find some new problems from the case organizations.

The following section will give some background knowledge about the case studies. Section 3 will present a list of known inspection problems and possible solutions. It also includes some case experiences about the problems listed. Section 4 discusses more fully the case experiences, and Section 5 will introduce a problem based approach for inspection improvement.

2 Case Studies

The case studies in this research had the following goals:

- to evaluate the validity of the inspection related problems found in the literature
- to find some new problems
- to find out how the case organizations are practicing inspections or more informal reviews

The case experiences were collected from two organizations, the selection being based on their size. Both of these organizations (> 250 employees) have a quite well defined software development process. These organizations are referred to as the organization A and the organization B in this paper. It was a conscious decision to choose organizations which already had some experience about inspections. This naturally means that problems emphasized here may differ from those of a small organization which does not use inspections regularly.

2.1 How Were the Case Studies Conducted?

The case studies included three interviews in each of the two organizations. The organizations were asked to find interviewees from different levels in the organization. The recommended roles were *quality manager*, *project manager* and *software developer*. The case organizations had no difficulties in finding relevant interviewees.

The first part of an interview focused on evaluating current inspection practices in the organization. This evaluation was made based on the Inspection Capability Maturity Model (ICMM) [10]. It is quite similar to the internationally well known CMMI [18] model, but assesses only the maturity of inspection practices instead of the whole software development process. In addition, participants were asked whether they partake regularly in more informal reviews. The next subsection will briefly introduce the summary of these results as background knowledge about the case organizations. The primary focus of this paper is on the other part of the interviews.

In the other part of the interviews, problems which may occur in inspection practices were discussed. First, the participants were asked to evaluate the current inspection practices in their organization without any further explanation given to them. They had to give a grade for their organization with scale from 1 to 5 (5 being the best). Then the interviewees were asked to freely talk about the most important inspection related problems in their organization. Finally, the participants went through a list of inspection problems, which have been mentioned in the literature. The problems in this list are described in the next section of this paper. They had to comment on how familiar the suggested problem seemed in their own organization. They were asked to rate the frequency of the problem occurrence in their work, using a scale from 1 to 5: one meaning never and five that it happened all the time. Those numerical results are not presented in this paper, as they were collected from only six interviews - these averages would not tell anything useful.

2.2 How Are the Case Organizations Practicing Inspections?

Both of the case organizations have included reviews in their defined software development process. In addition, the defined form of the reviews is quite similar to inspection, although not as formal as the traditional inspection process [2]. However, based on the interviews, the real practice is still on the initial ICMM level in both of the case organizations.

There was a clear difference between the case organizations in everyday inspection activity. The second level in ICMM requires inspecting requirements and some design documents in every project. The organization A satisfied this requirement pretty well, but the organization B appeared to have still quite a bit of work to do with it. Another requirement of the second ICMM level is to arrange inspection training at least for the inspection leaders. Neither organization had any kind of inspection training. The organization A, which had a better inspection performance, would have satisfied even most of the ICMM third level requirements if it had had inspection training for all the relevant stakeholders. The organization B still had some more work to do with the second level.

3 Problems in Inspection Practices

This section will introduce a list of problems which may occur in inspection practices. The issues in the list are primarily derived from the literature. The following subsections give a detailed description about each of the problems. Each problem description includes possible symptoms, solutions and experiences from the case organizations. These problems are not categorized here and neither are they in any specific order. Case experiences are presented here very briefly. Section 4 includes some more discussion about the case results.

3.1 Meeting Scheduling May Cause Delay

It may be hard to find a common inspection meeting time for all the participants. Typically, inspection scheduling is made later than scheduling for most of the other tasks. Votta [2] suggests that up to 20% of the requirements and design development interval is spent just waiting for reviewers to meet. In his research, typical waiting time in bigger projects is two weeks.

In the conclusion of his research, Votta [2] casts doubts on the effectiveness of inspection meetings. According to Gilb and Graham [5] in an optimal situation 80% of the defects could be found during preparation and 20% in the inspection meeting. Votta [22] noticed in his research that the gain of inspection meetings was only 4% in defects when compared with inspections without meeting. However, he doesn't suggest totally rejecting inspection meetings.   He suggests the replacement of a traditional meeting with *Deposition*, a meeting in which the participants would include only the author, the reviewer and maybe a distinct moderator.

Later several researchers (for example [6][8][13]) have suggested virtual inspection as a solution to scheduling problems. By virtual inspection we refer here to tool-supported inspection process, involving no physical meeting. Some researches have found virtual inspections just as effective as the traditional inspection and cheaper to arrange [8][13]. Among other results, Stein et al. [20] found virtual inspection a feasible method for their case study, but they still did not suggest eliminating meetings. Their study shows that some of the defects may be hard to find without meetings.

Solution: A solution for scheduling problem may be found in a kind of alternative meeting arrangement. One should be able to plan the schedule beforehand and allocate it to work plans. In an optimal situation inspection, the schedule would be part of the project planning and resources would be allocated from the beginning of each project.

Experiences: This was seen as a problem, but not as a very important one. In the organization B, the chances of not inspecting a document at all were greater when the schedule appeared to be busy. In the organization A, the problems experienced were related to their customers, who sometimes had difficulties in finding time for inspections.

3.2 Meetings Consume Resources with Few Gains in Finding New Defects

The previous subsection already referred to this problem. Votta [22] found, in his research, that synergy was very low in inspection meetings. Later Porter and Votta [15] supported this by their research. It should be noticed that this is a quite limited aspect in an inspection meeting. Votta [22] also found meetings useful in finding false positives. A meeting can also be a good learning situation.

There may also be other reasons, such as poor preparation, creating the same effect. If the participants are not well prepared, usually very few major defects are found [5]. In the studies mentioned ([15], [22]), data was collected in an environment in which inspections are practiced extremely well. The conclusion in these studies was that a traditional inspection meeting is not effective and should be replaced with some alternative method. Laitenberg and DeBaud [12] suggest that an organization should start with a traditional meeting-based inspection and maybe later go on to some alternative meeting arrangements.

Solution: First, the reasons for this problem should be identified. If there is some obvious reason, like poor preparation, it should be dealt with first. If there are no other problems, some alternative meeting arrangements could be entertained. However, the other aspects relating to the purpose of the meeting should be considered carefully before any rearrangements. For example, in some organizations a meeting can be the element which maintains discipline in the whole inspection process.

Experiences: The organization B arranged meetings infrequently, and the interviewees there were quite unfamiliar with them. In the organization A, only one participant experienced this as a problem.

3.3 Poor Inspection Support Material

There may be insufficient support material for inspectors. The material can be poorly designed, and often there is no material at all. This may cause noticeable inefficiency in the inspection process. Typically, individual defect finding is based on checklists or is of ad-hoc type [12]. Laitenberg et al. [11] criticize the fact that checklists are usually too general. Checklists tell what kind of defects could be found, but do not show how to find them. Porter and Votta [15] found that inspection material increase defect finding rate even among experienced professionals.

Solution: Laitenberg et al. [11] suggest perspective-based reading (PBR) as a solution to this problem. PBR is based on scenarios, which give more specific guidelines for the reader than typical checklists. Rifkin and Daimel [16] found that training which focused on document reading skills improved defect finding rate remarkably. In their training, the participants made their own checklists and learned how to use them. The conclusion is that good inspection support material which guides in defect finding can remarkably improve the defect finding rate in inspection.

Experiences: Both of the organizations had at least some checklists, but neither of them used these. However, only one of the interviewees experienced this as an outstanding problem.

3.4 Participants Don't Understand Inspection Process

It may be that the participants do not understand their own role in the inspection process. They may not know which of their own documents should be inspected, when it should be done, and how the inspection should be conducted. In his work in which Karl Wiegers [23] writes generally about software reviews, he states that lack of common understanding can lead to inconsistencies in review objectives, review team size and composition, forms used, recordkeeping, and meeting approaches. Wiegers also writes that it may not be clear who is running a review meeting, and that meetings may lose their focus, drifting from finding defects to solving problems or challenging the author's programming style. As a conclusion, he states that these kinds of problems affect inspection effectiveness and in the worst case the inspection may not take place at all.

Solution: Wiegers suggests that training is the best way to ensure common understanding about review process between the participants. Also Fagan [3] emphasizes the importance of training. He even warns about starting inspections in an organization if not based on proper training. Fagan writes that some companies having started inspections without proper training had not succeeded that well.

Experiences: This was seen as a relatively small problem. Most of the problems experienced were related to uncertainty about which documents should be inspected.

3.5 Criticism May Be Directed at Author

Wiegers [23] claims that initial attempts to hold reviews sometimes lead to personal assaults on the skills and style of the author. If authors feel personally attacked, they may not be willing to allow their future documents to be reviewed. In the worst case they may seek for revenge.

Solution: Wiegers [23] emphasizes the role of the inspections leader, who should control the meeting. Having capable and well trained inspection leaders can be a solution.

Experiences: This was not experienced as a problem in the case organizations.

3.6 Poor Inspection Planning

According to Wiegers [23], in many projects inspections are seen as milestones in the project plan. If the inspection is arranged as a milestone, there is no time for rework. This may cause the project to slip in its schedule. Gilb [4] recommends inspecting documents not only just before the milestone, but several times during the working process.

Solution: The solution is naturally to plan and arrange inspections in time. However, this may not be so simple. Project managers must first understand inspection advantages and processes. Proper training for the managers is, therefore, also needed.

Experiences: The organization A found these kinds of problems very rare. The organization B experienced some delays, especially with requirement documents. However, this was not seen as an important problem. Moreover, poor planning may not have been the major reason for the delay.

3.7 Meeting Straying to Irrelevant Issues

Already Fagan [2] emphasized the purpose of defect-finding and warned about discussions in inspection meetings. Also Gilb and Graham [5] comment on this. If discussion and problem solving is allowed, it can easily take the whole time. This is a widely agreed viewpoint, which Johnson [7] has, however, criticized. He claims that the most important benefit of a meeting is learning and that collective problem solving is an important factor in learning. In the same article [7] Johnson suggests a kind of asynchronous tool-supported defect-logging instead of a physical meeting. In any case it is obvious that discussion and logging cannot be effectively arranged in the same meeting. It is good if there is support for the author in problem solving, but this should not take place in a meeting, which should be focused on logging and finding defects.

Solution: Training is again seen as the solution for this. Inspection leaders are the key players in meetings and they should be well trained. Also, training for all the participants may help. If the purpose of the meeting is clear for everybody, there will be less temptation to drift into problem solving.

Experiences: This was a well-known problem in both of the organizations. The problem comes up occasionally, but not for all the time. However one of the interviewees in the organization B thought this as a considerable problem, often seen in the organization.

3.8 Poor Preparation

According to Gilb and Graham [5], preparation is the most critical part in the inspection process. They claim that without preparation, the result is a group review, which probably finds only 10 % of all the defects that could have been found in a more rigorous inspection. There may be different reasons for this. Managers may have a temptation to save resources or single participants may feel too busy to prepare carefully.

Solution: Wiegers [23] suggests that the preparing time of the participants should be recorded. However, this may not be enough to guarantee a good preparation if there is no control over the collected information. Someone on the management level should have the responsibility for the inspection practices and for motivating the participants. The organization should also have standards about proper preparation time in different kinds of inspections.

Experiences: This was experienced as the most important problem in both of the organizations, and was seen very often. One of the interviewees commented that it was rare to have a meeting where all the participants would have been well prepared.

3.9 Wrong People Participate

Wiegers [23] suggests that there may be participants who do not have the appropriate skills or knowledge to find defects. Overall, the level of expertise of individual participants is the most important factor in inspection effectiveness [17].

Solution: In the worst case this can be a complicated managerial issue. It is hard to find obvious solutions apart from training. Rifkin and Deimel [16] got good results when they arranged inspection training which focused on defect-finding skills instead of regular inspection processes.

Experiences: The organization A very rarely experienced any of these problems. The problems, which the organization B faced occasionally, were usually related to customers, who sometimes did not have the proper expertise to review the documents.

3.10 Roles May Be Missing

Defining different roles for the participants has been one of the key ideas in inspection from the beginning [2]. Porter et al. [14] claim that in practice participants use ad-hoc or checklist based defect-detection techniques to discharge identical general responsibilities. This causes considerable overlap in their work and makes defect-finding ineffective.

Solution: This is an organizational issue. Porter et al. [14] suggest that the participants should not only have different roles, but also different tasks in inspection. This means there should be customized material (checklists, scenarios etc.) for different roles. In their research Porter et al. [14] found that totally distinct responsibilities with scenario tasks produced the best result. As a method it was remarkably more effective than the one based on a checklist, which had more vague responsibilities.

Experiences: Neither organization used different roles in inspections. The organization A experienced it as a small problem and the organization B did not regard it as a problem at all.

3.11 Poor Quality Documents Waste Time

Kelly & Shepard [9] refer to this problem in their article. They concentrated on code reviews in their research and noticed the importance of clean and well documented code in inspection. Poor documentation wastes the participants' time. According to Gilb and Graham [5], a poor quality work product should not be inspected at all. Their support for preconditions in inspection is meant, in particular, to avoid unnecessary work.

Solution: Good standards help authors to make good quality documents. Good checklists may also help authors in their work. Gilb & Graham [5] suggest creating preconditions for inspections. The inspection leader should check these preconditions before starting the inspection process.

Experiences: This problem occurred quite rarely in the organization A and was not experienced as any problem in the organization B. In B, incomplete documents were unlikely to be inspected at all.

3.12 Bad Attitude

An author may not be willing to bring his or her documents to inspection if it is not compulsory. The question is about attitude. Many organizations regard inspections in their processes as obligatory. However, if inspections remain just mandatory unpleasant tasks, the participants will be less likely to do their work well. So, these kinds of attitude problems may significantly influence inspection effectiveness.

Solution: The solution is again in training. The participants should understand the benefits of inspections. In the best case the participants may regard inspections as an opportunity to get help and aid others in their work. The managers should also clearly understand this, because they have a big role in creating a proper atmosphere in an organization.

Experiences: This was not a problem in the organization A and only occasionally was seen as such in the organization B. In both of the organizations the interviewees saw more attitude problems in the willingness to read others' work documents. It appears to be a challenge to motivate all the participants to prepare carefully for the inspection meetings.

3.13 Too Much Material in Inspection

Gilb and Graham [5] warn about reduced inspection effectiveness if there is too much material in any one inspection. They suggest that in preparing a phase, a typical optimum rate is one page per participant per hour. According to Gilb and Graham this time is needed to find defects which would not be found in more informal reviews.

Solution: There is often a question about the attitude towards inspections. There is no trick which could resolve these attitudinal problems. It needs time and a lot of work to build up an organizational culture which would respect inspections on every level of the organization. It may not be appropriate in every situation to try and inspect every piece of documentation. With large documents, Gilb and Graham [5] advice estimating the product quality by inspecting only selected parts of the documents.

Experiences: Both of the organizations rated this as a minor problem. However, there was some variance in the answers. One of the interviewees complained about excessive amount of material in inspections.

3.14 No Resources Allocated for Inspections

In many projects inspections are included within some other tasks, for example within requirements engineering, and there are no resources allocated specifically for inspections. In these cases employees are often too busy to use their time for inspections. This typically results in a poor preparation and a significant loss in inspection effectiveness.

Solution: This is a management level issue. Resource allocation is one of the basic signs of management commitment. In this case project managers should have proper training about inspection benefits. There should also be an organizational project planning standard, which takes inspections into account.

Experiences: The organization A had no problems with this, because they had explicitly allocated resources for inspections. The organization B was in a quite opposite situation. They did not have separate resources allocated for inspections and they were having problems with this. However, one interviewee did not experience this as a problem.

4 Discussion About the Case Studies

This section discusses the case results. It should be noted that strong conclusions cannot be made based on six interviews in two case organizations. However, some interesting aspects can be found there.

It is not easy to draw conclusions from the interviews, because the answers varied considerably. However, two problems clearly came up in both the organizations:

– Poor preparation
– Straying to irrelevant issues

In addition, one of the case organizations experienced it as a real problem that there were no clearly allocated resources for inspections. There was nothing unexpected in these results. By contrast, it was somewhat surprising that none of the interviewees had faced any criticism directed at the author in inspection meeting. There were also quite a few problems experienced in the authors' attitudes to bring work products for inspection. It became evident that the interviewees had experienced a variety of problems in willingness to read others' work products. Employees basically want to get comments about their own work, but are lazy to read others' documents themselves.

It became obvious that the state of the whole organization was not easy to discover with those few interviews. Many interview questions yielded very different answers, even in the same organization. This may indicate that different project groups work in different ways. Another possible reason is that the interviewees simply interpreted the questions differently. In any case, it would have required more information to find out the real state of the whole organization in each case. For any future work at least the questions should be clarified. Maybe a general questionnaire could be designed and added to the interviews.

The interviews appeared to provide quite a limited amount of information of the real problems in the organizations. Some of the problems in the question list would have required more background knowledge than the interviewees had. For example, neither organization used clearly differentiated roles in their inspections. However, the missing roles were not experienced as a noteworthy problem, because the interviewees had not been thought the meaning of roles before. Neither organization used any kind of support material, but this was not experienced as a problem.

There appeared to be some problematic issues which didn't exist, because there were some other urgent problems in the inspection practices. For example, in one of the case organizations it was usual not to arrange an inspection if the schedule was busy. That organization, of course, did not appear to have many problems with delayed inspection meetings or poor quality documents in inspection. Any such problems are unlikely to surface if inspections are not arranged at all.

Some possible problems, found in the literature, are very hard to identify in interviews. For example, Basili [1] found in his experiments that due to attitude problems, participants found very few defects in code inspections. They put more trust in testing and did not show motivation for inspections if they knew that the code was to be tested later. Identifying these kinds of symptoms would require systematically collected statistics about inspection effectiveness. Secondly, a lack of inspection metrics can be a problem itself. Gilb and Graham [5] state that there is no sense in inspection improvements without using some metrics to verify the improvement.

The major conclusion from the case studies was that just a few interviews do not provide enough information to identify all the real problems in inspection practices. At least some more interviews would be needed in the case organizations to understand their practices better. In addition, the experiences collected in the interviews did not appear to reveal all the problems in the organizations. Therefore, a more careful analysis and interpretation of the results is required to create well reasoned improvement suggestions.

5 A Problem Based Approach to Inspection Improvement

The motivation for writing this paper was improvement of inspection practices in software organizations. This section makes a suggestion about how to use problem analysis in inspection improvement. First, it is recommended to use some inspection maturity model (see [10] and [21]) as a tool to asses the current state in an organization and to identify the possible improvement areas. This problem-based approach is not suggested to replace other improvement actions, but to complete them. Even well defined regularly used inspection practices may have some problems which have a dramatic effect on inspection effectiveness. A problem analysis presented here can help an organization to identify problems of this kind and direct their improvement actions effectively.

The problem analysis suggested here includes the following five tasks:

1. **Assess inspection practices:** The current state of inspection practices should be assessed based on some inspection maturity model [10][21]. If this has not been done before, it can be undertaken at the same time with the problem analysis. The assessment may reveal some problems which would be hard to detect otherwise.
2. **Collect experiences:** The second task is to collect experiences about possible problems with interviews or questionnaires. The list presented in this article can be used as a basis for this. The task is to find out how regularly the different problems are experienced.
3. **Identify real problems:** The next task is to identify the most regular and serious problems based on an assessment and on collected experiences. It was found in the

case studies that collected experiences probably do not reveal all the significant issues. This identification of the real problems should, therefore, include a more careful analysis by an expert with sufficient knowledge about inspections. The focus in this task is to analyze the degree of effect that the identified problems have on inspection effectiveness in the organization. Finally, the importance of each identified problem is estimated in scale from 1 to 5.

4. **Estimate required effort:** This task estimates the effort required to correct the problems. The required improvement effort to handle a problem is estimated in scale from 1 to 3. One in this scale means the problems which take a lot of time to be dealt with. These are usually problems which require change in the whole organizational culture. Three in this scale means issues which are pretty easy to fix with small changes in inspection practices.

5. **Prioritize problems:** The final task is to prioritize the improvement actions to handle the identified problems. The estimated values from the tasks 3 and 4 are multiplied. The problems which get the highest result values are recommended to be handled first.

6 Conclusions

This paper has discussed problems which may occur in inspection practices. The paper presents a list of known problems in the literature. Secondly, it includes experiences from two case organizations. Finally, it introduces a problem-based approach to inspection improvement, which was the major motivation for writing this paper. The approach helps an organization to identify the problems which are causing loss in inspection effectiveness. It may also help in prioritizing inspection improvement actions effectively.

Probably the inspection of the problems in inspection practices varies in different kinds of organizations. However, the two case studies in this research cannot provide any explanation for this variation. The studies should have included many different kinds of organizations in order to allow finding of any convincing trends in their experiences. This is a challenge for the future work. However, this research brought up some factors which may have some bearing on inspection problems. These possible factors might include inspection maturity, organization size and average project size.

It should be noted that the literature includes also references to some problems which may cause difficulties in inspection improvement. These kinds of issues were excluded from this paper, but would be an interesting research area for any future studies. Inspections are obviously practiced effectively in very few organizations. It would be worth of a deeper study to find out what the real obstacles to inspection improvement are.

Acknowledgements

I am grateful to the case organizations for their co-operation in this research. I want to thank the anonymous reviewers for their comments. Finally, I want to give my thanks to Jussi Koskinen and Markku Sakkinen for supporting my work.

References

1. Basili, V.R.: Evolving and Packaging Reading Technologies. J. Systems Software, Vol. 38, 1 (1997) 3-12
2. Fagan, M.E.: Design and Code Inspection to Reduce Errors in Program Development. IBM Systems Journal, Vol. 15, 3 (1976) 182-211
3. Fagan, M.E.: Advances in Software Inspections, IEEE Transactions on Software Engineering, Vol. 12, 7 (1986) 744-751
4. Gilb, T.: Planning to Get the Most out of Inspections. Software Quality Professional, Vol. 2, 2 (2000)
5. Gilb, T., Graham, D.: Software Inspection. McGraw-Hill: New York (1993)
6. Harjumaa, L., Hedberg, H., Tervonen, I: A Path to Virtual Software Inspection. Proc. of Asia-Pacific Conference on Quality Software, Hong Kong (2001)
7. Johnson, P.M.: Reengineering Inspection. Communications of the ACM, Vol. 41, 2 (1998) 49-52
8. Johnson, P. M., Tjahjono, D: Does Every Inspection Really Need a Meeting? Empirical Software Engineering, Vol. 3, 1 (1998) 9-35
9. Kelly, D, Shepard, T.: Qualitative Observations from Software Code Inspection Experiments. Proceedings of the 2002 Conference of the Centre for Advanced Studies on Collaborative research, Toronto, Canada (2002)
10. Kollanus, S.: ICMM – Inspection Capability Maturity Model. The IASTED International Conference on Software Engineering, Innsbruck, Austria (2005)
11. Laitenberg, O., Atkinson, C, Schlich, M., El-Emam, K.: An Experimental Comparison of Reading Techniques for Defect Detection in UML-Documents. Technical Report NRC 43614, National Research Council of Canada (1999)
12. Laitenberg, O., DeBaud, J.-M.: An Encompassing Life-Cycle Centric Survey of Software Inspection. J. Systems and Software, Vol. 50, 1 (2000) 5-31
13. Perpich, J. M., Perry, D. E., Porter, A. A., Votta, L. G., Wade, M. W.: Anywhere, Anytime Code Inspections: Using the Web to Remove Inspection Bottlenecks in Large-Scale Software Development. Proceedings of the 19th International Conference on Software Engineering. Boston, Massachusetts, United States (1997) 14-21
14. Porter, A., Votta, L., Basili, V.R..: Comparing Detection Methods for Software Requirements Inspections: A Replicated Experiment. IEEE Transactions on Software Engineering, Vol. 21, 6 (1995) 563-575
15. Porter, A., Votta, L.: Comparing Detection Methods for Software Requirements Inspections: A Replication Using Professional Subjects. Empirical software engineering, Vol. 3, 4 (1998) 355-379
16. Rifkin, S., Deimel, L.: Applying Program Comprehension Techniques to Improve Software Inspections. Presented at the 19th Annual NASA Software Engineering Laboratory Workshop, Greenbelt, MD, USA (1994)
17. Sauer, C., Ross, J, Land, L., Yetton, P.: The Effectiveness of Software Development Technical Reviews: A Behaviorally Motivated Program of Research. IEEE Transactions on Software Engineering, Vol. 26, 1 (2000) 1-14
18. SEI: Capability Maturity Model Integration version 1.1. Software Engineering Institute (2002) <URL: http://www.sei.cmu.edu/cmmi/>
19. SEI: March 2004 release of the SW-CMM Maturity Profile. Software Engineering Institute (2004) <URL: http://www.sei.cmu.edu/sema/pdf/SW-CMM/2004marSwCMM.pdf>

20. Stein, M., Riedl, J., Harner, S.J., Mashayekhi, V.: A Case Study of Distributed, Asynchronous Software Inspection. Proceedings of the 19th International Conference on Software Engineering. Boston, Massachusetts, United States (1997) 107-117
21. Tervonen, I., Iisakka, J., Harjumaa, L.: Looking for Inspection Improvements through the Base Practices. Proc. Workshop on Inspection in Software Engineering, Paris, France (2001) 145-152
22. Votta, L.: Does Every Inspection Need a Meeting? Proceedings of the 1st ACM SIGSOFT Symposium on Foundations of Software Engineering, Los Angeles, CA, USA (1993) 107-114
23. Wiegers, K. 1998. Seven Deadly Sins of Software Reviews. Software Development, Vol. 6, 3 (1998)

Risk-Based Trade-Off Between Verification and Validation – An Industry-Motivated Study

Kennet Henningsson and Claes Wohlin

Blekinge Institute of Technology, PO BOX 520, 37225 Ronneby, Sweden
{Kennet.Henningsson, Claes.Wohlin}@bth.se

Abstract. Within industry the demand for short lead-time and reduced effort consumption is in focus. For an associated industry partner the lead-time and effort focus has meant turning the interest towards the Verification and Validation (V&V) process. The industry cooperation motivating this study aims at providing a tailored and applicable V&V process, where the order of verification and validation may be changed as well as the amount of V&V activities conducted. Through the industry cooperation as well as industrial and academic experience, a method has been formulated that address how to select a suitable V&V process depending on the functionality being developed. The method describes how a suitable process is created and selected, where the appropriate process is identified based on functionality and coupling between the system entities being developed. It is concluded that the method provides support, structure and clarification to address the possibilities to a trade-off between verification and validation.

1 Introduction

Software process models have evolved over the years starting with the waterfall model [1] into agile processes [2] In-between several process models have been proposed and used, including the spiral model [3], incremental and evolutionary development [4, 5] among others. The introduction of new models is a response to the constant need of improvement in software development. Companies are constantly making trade-offs between cost, delivery time, quality, and delivered functionality. The software community also recognizes that not all types of software need the same treatment. Different processes, methods, techniques, and tools are used depending on the type of software [6] [7, 8]. Safety-critical software has different requirements than computer games, and hence the development process has to be adapted accordingly.

It is clear that different types of software need different processes. If taking this one-step further, different functionality needs different processes. However, this requires processes that are possible to tailor [9, 10]. In other words, the software process needs to be flexible. Process tailoring is discussed in the context of the Capability Maturity Model (CMM) in [9]. In a joint project with an industrial partner, in this case UIQ Technology (a subsidiary of Symbian), it was decided that an attempt should be made to tailor their verification and validation (V&V) activities [11] based

F. Bomarius and S. Komi-Sirviö (Eds.): PROFES 2005, LNCS 3547, pp. 443–457, 2005.

on the types of functionality being developed. Verification is concerned with whether the software is developed correctly and validation is focused on whether the correct software is developed. The company works in an environment where some functionality is fairly standard or similar to other functionality that has been developed previously and other functionality is leading edge services that have not been developed before. The company wants to work with flexible processes to ensure as short lead times as possible for their software.

These different types of functionality require different approaches to V&V, or at least open up for an opportunity to run the V&V activities differently. For example, standard functionality is straightforward to develop from a user point of view; the company is confident of what functionality the user desires. On the other hand, the user has high expectations when it comes to the quality of service for this type of functionality. Thus, in this case a possible scenario is that there is rather little need for validation, but a high need for verification. At the other end of the spectrum, there are completely new functions that are not currently available on the market. To ensure that these services meet the needs on the market, it is important to validate their usefulness with users or representatives for the markets in some sense. Normally, the expectations on correctness are less for new functionality and hence it may be discussed how much verification is needed. In this case, the validation is probably more critical than the verification, the situation can occur when it is necessary to negotiate quality, or functionality, of the delivered product [6]. This reasoning implies that different ways of handling V&V can be applied for different types of functionality within the same project.

The functionality characteristic indicates the uncertainty whether the correct functionality is implemented or not, i.e. likelihood for changes and, to some extent, faults. However, this does not provide the true picture of the risk (risk meaning exceeded budgets, too low quality, and increased project lead-time). There is a need for determining the risk impact as well. A system entity's coupling, i.e. connections to other system entities indicate the magnitude of the risk. The magnitude shows the number of dependencies each entity has, and how large the ripple effect would be by a late change or fault. It is likely that for a system entity with a high number of connections, the impact would be larger than for a low-coupled entity. By determining the functionality characteristic for the system entity as well as the coupling, sufficient information is available for risk assessment.

Bottom-line is that the company wanted a risk-based approach to their V&V activities, providing the possibility to determine which risks to take in terms of how much verification, and how much validation that should be performed for different types of functionality.

This paper presents a method for selecting a suitable V&V process based on being flexible regarding both the amount (in relative terms) of V&V needed and the order of the activities. The method is motivated by industry needs, and it is developed from an industrial case using an exploratory approach. The method is presented in a number of steps that can be adapted to different situations depending on the functionality being developed. This method is partly illustrated using input from the industrial partner where the need for this type of approach was identified.

The contribution of this paper is the formulation of a method for tailoring the V&V process, involving changing order and extent of the V&V process. Moreover, the method is illustrated using input from an industrial interview study. The suggested method is presented in Section 2, where the method is presented in generic terms. Section 3 presents a partial application of the method in the company context. In Section 4, the paper is concluded.

2 Verification and Validation Process Tailoring Method

The method presented supports the verification and validation (V&V) trade-off by addressing the traditional order and scope (or amount) of V&V activities. Adaptation of the V&V process adheres to a system entity's functional characteristics. The term system entity is used as the part of the product that provides specified functionality to the overall product or user of the product. The system entity relates to a coherent collection of requirements, defining the functionality. The V&V trade-off within the proposed method is implemented by process selection among a set of pre-developed and described process alternatives. A prerequisite for this method is a flexible and adjustable process for V&V being present in the company applying this method. The method does not suggest or exclude any specific V&V activities. The objective is to provide decision support for choosing how to apply the existing V&V activities.

Fig. 1 presents the addition to the standard process typically present for handling verification and validation.

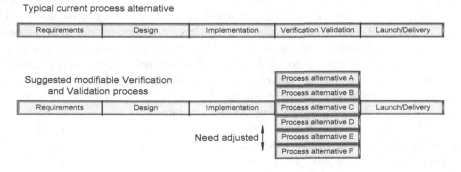

Fig. 1. The replacement of the traditional V&V process with a selection of alternatives corresponding to the varying functionality demands and risk impact assessment

The core of the method is the adaptation of the V&V processes. The adaptation is guided by the product needs, the essential attributes, and risk reduction. Risk is assessed by determining the coupling for a system entity. The list below outlines the steps of the method.

1. Functionality classification – Classifying the functionality according to the validation complexity and scope required to assure a valid product.

2. Coupling classification – A subjective evaluation in early stages regarding the level of coupling for the system entity at hand.
3. Process alternatives – Developing a set of process alternatives defining order and scope for the V&V processes.
4. Attributes affected by the process alternatives – Identifying the core attributes involved in determining the success of the project.
5. Process recommendation – Based on the system entity at hand, i.e. the type of functionality and coupling of the entity and the alternative processes, recommendations of a suitable process or processes are provided.
6. Establish impact on the attributes per process alternative – Based on the alternative processes, what is the likely impact on the monitored core attributes.
7. Analyzing attribute impact – From the process recommendation it is possible to see whether that process fulfils the project goals with sufficient probability. It may be decided whether to take a specific alternative process or not, depending on the risk associated with the choice.
8. Feedback and re-evaluation of the process selection – Improving the process selection and monitoring the process impact on a continuous basis improves the method and builds trust, and hence it is an important part of the method.

Sections 2.1 through 2.8 present the steps of the method in more detail, and Section 2.9 discusses possible future extensions of the method.

2.1 Functionality Classification

For adapting the processes according to the system entity, it is required to examine each system entity. Each system entity has a set of properties; one property is the functionality. A system entity's characteristics, i.e. functionality, govern, along with the coupling classification (Section 0), the recommendation of what process alternative or alternatives to use. Given that the functionality drives the choice of V&V activities, it is suitable for classification. The apparent alternative is to classify requirements, but the vast amount of requirements would make it impossible to base the recommendation on single requirements. Functionality classification focuses on a group of requirements associated with a specific system entity.

The functionality classification scheme depends on the company's domain and prior history. The classification scheme shown in Table 1 is an illustration and exemplification. The number of classification alternatives also needs to be decided in each specific application of the method. The functionality classification accounts for if the validation is internal (performed within the company) or external (performed or involving external parties). Further, the classification considers if the verification and validation is particularly challenging for any reason. Each classification is assigned a classification on a nominal scale. The classification represents the difficulty and potential risk of changes and faults connected to each entity.

It is important to differentiate between internal and external validation. Internal validation takes place within the organization and is associated with less lead-time consumption, based on easier transition between development and testing and that the developing organization still has the control over the V&V activities.

External validation involves external resources, being customer, users, user reference groups, legislators, assessors, or other. This process consumes additional lead-time and is not under the developing organization's control. However, the accuracy of the V&V might improve in comparison to internal V&V.

Table 1. Suggested generic functionality classification

Value	Classification Name	Validation opportunities	Exemplification
1	Well-known functionality	Internal – based on experience	Functionality typically developed by the organization prior to this specific project, historically the organization is experienced and capable with the domain and the required functionality.
2	Standard functionality	Internal – with aid of standards External – if standard interpretation is required	Functionality related to complying with a standard, for example communication protocol, language specification, storage facility, encryption, or other standard.
3	Familiar functionality	External, possible internal – based on the level of experience	Functionality not previously developed by the organization, but partial experience within the general functionality and domain exists.
4	New experience functionality	External – based on the knowledge possessed concerning the requirements	Functionality where the organization lacks previous experience and domain knowledge. This is typically related to breaking new ground for the organization in question, but experience is present in the community.
5	Exploratory functionality	None – not possible to determine what is the correct functionality	Functionality that is typically breaking new ground also within the community, implying that the domain knowledge and experience does not exist.

The classification needs to reflect the nuances of the functionality affecting the V&V process. Concerns are directed towards that a too detailed classification might render it impossible to separate classifications without extensive education effort. The recommendation is to use common sense when creating the classifications. The classification is essential for the process recommendations later in the method, and for that reason, needs special attention. The functionality classification needs to represent the functionality categories present in the product and related to the verification and validation in full, at the same time, it must be feasible to separate the classes clearly.

The next section discusses the coupling classification, illustrating dependencies and connections for a system entity.

2.2 Coupling Classification

By classifying the functionality, it is possible to assess the probability for a change occurring in the system entity dealt with. However, it is also necessary to discuss the impact of the potential change for providing a complete risk assessment.

The impact of interest in this paper is to handle the time-consuming changes and faults to stay in control of, and try to minimize, lead-time and effort. The lead-time and effort consumption of a change or fault is influenced by the number of dependencies an entity has. It seems reasonable to believe that an alteration made to a central, highly coupled entity consumes more lead-time and effort, than a similar alteration to an entity with low coupling.

The coupling is subjectively assessed on an ordinal scale from 1-5, 1 lowest, and 5 highest coupling. The experience of the person assigning the coupling determines the value. Though this method is blunt, subjective, and not always repeatable, it is possible to perform early, and provides sufficient support for further evaluation of the risk.

The next section, Section 2.3, addresses the creation of, and describes the process alternatives.

2.3 Process Alternatives

The recommendation is to create the processes alternatives in advance, for two reasons: 1) Not limiting the process alternatives to the problems faced and 2) The upcoming project can facilitate the process alternatives directly, i.e. the process alternatives are in place from the start.

When handling verification and validation, there are two tailoring alternatives. One is the order, and the other is the scope of the V&V activity. Order and scope are labeled modification variables in this paper. When creating the process alternative all combinations of the modification variables is documented and investigated.

Dealing with the order of V&V, there are two natural alternatives, verification first or validation first. The characteristics of the system entity's functionality are typically more or less suitable for one or the other of these alternatives. Section 2.5 describes this further.

In addition to rearrange the order of V&V, the scope (or amount) is also subject for modification. In our model the scope of V&V activities are separated into two groups, high and low, shown in Table 3. The implication of high and low is not determined by the method, and it is up to the organization applying the method to make that definition. The characteristics of the system entity's functionality as well as change impact (moderated by coupling) motivate the variance in scope. An example is that well-known functionality might not require extensive external validation; instead could be directly submitted for verification to more rapidly reach a final state for the system entity. The process alternatives and the scope generate eight possible alternatives; these alternatives are listed along with the affected attributes in Table 3. Section 2.4 discusses the affected attributes further.

2.4 Attributes Affected by the Process Alternatives

Depending on the requirements on the V&V process, a generic set of important attributes is presented, namely number of changes, number of defects, project effort, and project lead-time. These attributes are often mentioned or indicated in literature, for example in [12, 13], and are judged as important for many companies. Though these attributes are generic, an adaptation is possible to suit the needs of an organization for selecting an appropriate process.

Conflicts between attributes are probable, meaning that maximization of two attributes may be contradictory, and in the example, there is, for example, a contradiction between low numbers of faults and minimum project effort [1, 14, 15]. The rationale being that in many cases a low number of faults typically requires extensive testing, which consumes effort. Table 3 lists the attributes along with the process alternatives. Section 2.5 continues by describing the process recommendation task.

2.5 Process Recommendation

The goal of decreasing effort and shorten project lead-time is vital. However, to shorten project lead-time it is necessary to reduce the scope of for example verification and validation. But simply decreasing the scope of these activities increases the risk for overrun of both time and budget, due to a high number of changes and faults. To handle this risk and focus the resources on the crucial parts of the system, the functionality and coupling classification is used to recommend a suitable process.

The process recommendation combines the classification of functionality and coupling by building a process selection key for each system entity. The characteristics of the functionality and coupling reflect in this two-parted key. The structure of the key is: [funct.class.value : coupl.rank]. The functional value is obtained from Table 1 (nominal scale) and the coupling is a rank (1-5) on an ordinal scale. By producing a key for each component, it is possible to use the key to recommend a process.

The mapping between a system entity's characteristics and process alternatives is the basis for process recommendation. The suitability of the recommendations is essential, and it is a task for the organization to establish. One or more processes, as described in Table 2, are matching the keys produced by the classification process.

At this stage, the focus is on recommending an appropriate process based on the key generated by the classifications, without reflecting on the impact on the attributes.

The founding idea behind the recommended processes is that if the functional characteristic of an entity represents uncertainty, it is wise to start the validation process early, to avoid a high number of changes due to un-validated requirements late in the process. On the other hand, if the functional characteristic represents familiarity and stability, it is possible to decrease the effort of validation in favor of early and thorough verification. This is based on the assumption of few changes in the requirements and minimal uncertainty and misunderstanding. Late changes are unwanted for many reasons, promoting sufficient validation activities preventing the risk for additional and unnecessary changes, possibly avoided by the selection of an appropriate process.

Additionally, the process selection reflects the potential impact of late changes and faults, from the aspect of system entity coupling. A change to high coupling component is likely to consume more effort and project lead-time, and hence posing a greater risk if not properly handled.

Table 2. Functionality classification and process recommendation

Key range	Processes	Motivation
[1-2 : 1-3]	P4, P3, P2, P8	Key representing easy internal validation, with low coupling, possibility to go for low V&V, or focusing on finalizing the product through high verification.
[1-2 : 3-5]	P1, P2	Key representing easy internal validation, with high coupling, high verification is recommended.
[3-4 : 1-2]	P6, P3	Key representing challenging validation, with low coupling, high validation early is recommended, possible lower verification
[3-4 : 2-4]	P6, P3, P5	Key representing challenging validation, with intermediate coupling, early and high validation recommended, but also high verification.
[4-5 : 4-5]	P5	Key indicating tough validation and high coupling, early and high validation is recommended.

The processes alternatives are assigned an identification number, as in Table 3. The identification number is used to connect suitable processes to each key or key range. The keys produce links to one or more process alternatives. Table 2 states the generated keys, and recommended processes, as well as a motivation for the process recommendations. In Table 2 a key range is used, comprising a range of classification also some values occur more than once, i.e. there is an overlap. The main motivation being that there are borderline cases in the classification of functionality due to the subjective judgment of the classification.

The next section analyzes the impact on the attributes based on the selected processes.

2.6 Establish Impact on the Attributes per Process Alternative

The selection of appropriate process alternatives requires that the likely impact on the attributes presented in Table 3 is established.

Based on the keys created, a set of alternative and suitable processes are determined. For each of the keys and the suitable processes the predicted impact on the attributes is established. The impacts presented in Table 4 are used as an illustration. Actual impacts have to be determined in each specific case. The effects of the impact on the attributes are limited to two, i.e. increase, or decrease. A horizontal arrow indicates no impact. In Table 3, arrows indicate the expected impact. It is important to stress that the impacts need to be established within each organization and representing the best knowledge of the organization. Section 3.1 discusses the company cooperation. However, the recommendation is to use surveys to capture the knowledge within the organization. This includes using existing documentation from past projects, available literature, and the tacit experience of the personnel.

The assumption is that the selection is done in a sensible way. In other words, the selection is done so that the best possible outcome is expected. For example, a process with extensive validation is not chosen for well-known functionality.

As described, the order of verification and validation change when creating the process alternatives. By starting with verification and ending with validation, it is assumed that the number of faults found late in the process decreases, but postpones the validation. This means that there is a risk that the number of changes late in the process increases. This alternative is used when a small number of changes are expected.

Starting with validation is expected to decrease the number or change requests, but might increase the number of faults at late stages in the process. The reason is that early validation will prevent misunderstandings and varying interpretations, but may delay the fault identification. This alternative is used when a high number of changes are expected if no proper action is taken.

When discussing the amount of V&V, two alternative levels are used, i.e. high and low. The actual meaning of these levels is not defined here, and is up to each company applying the method. High verification is likely to decrease the number of faults, but will consume more effort and also increase project lead-time. Low verification is likely to increase the number of faults. However, a beneficial influence on effort and probably also project lead-time, with certain reservations for that high number of faults is likely to prolong the project. This alternative should be used when a low number of changes are expected, thus fully using the verification effort. It is also important to acknowledge the system entity's coupling, and the impact of potential changes and defects. Changes to highly coupled entities might cause ripple effects, generating faults or changes in other entities, or require extensive re-verification.

High validation decreases the number of change requests, but is likely to increase project effort and lead-time. Low validation is likely to increase the number of change requests, and possible the number of faults, but project effort and lead-time is likely to decrease, given that the cost for correcting the changes and faults surpasses the gain of decreased validation. This alternative should be used when a high number of changes are expected and not continuing with major verification efforts based on invalid functionality specifications.

When the impact on all attributes is established for each key and process alternative, the table is completed and a suggestion is presented as in Table 3. Table 3 is an exemplification based on the authors' experience though company cooperation.

The next section, Section 2.7, addresses the analysis of the attribute impact.

Table 3. Table presenting process alternatives, attributes, and expected impact

Process ID	Order	Verification	Validation	#Change requests	#Fault	Project Effort	Project Lead-time
P1	Effort	High	High	↓	↓	↑	↑
P2		High	Low	↑	↓	↑	↑
P3		Low	High	↓	↑	↓	↓
P4		Low	Low	↑	↑	↓	↓
	Order	Validation	Verification				
P5	Effort	High	High	↓	↓	↑	↑
P6		High	Low	↓	↑	↓	↓
P7		Low	High	↑	↓	↑	↑
P8		Low	Low	↑	↑	↓	↓

2.7 Analyzing Attribute Impact

This step compares the recommended processes and the expected outcome for the monitored variables to the prioritized attributes for the project at hand. The goal is to find the most appropriate process based on the functionalities' characteristics for the specific system entity, providing the desired impact on the monitored attributes.

The recommended process(es) presents an expected impact on the attributes, as presented in Table 3. This needs to be compared to the outcome of the project. If the project goal is to decrease project lead-time, process alternatives with the likely impact of decreased project lead-time is a suitable choice. However, based on the functionality characteristics, the recommended processes might not provide the desired impact on the important attributes from an overall project perspective.

The analysis is influenced by risk assessment, asking if the recommended process is likely to cause overrun of the limited resources, typically effort and project lead-time. Further, the quality is also an important factor to evaluate, if an increase in faults and changes is likely, then the risk for lower quality can be too high.

The main usage of Table 3 is to see how the attributes are affected based on the selected process. However, it is possible to exclude or include processes alternatives based on the attribute viewpoint as well. If there are specific demands for a system entity, for example, the number of fault must be low, when addressing the number of faults column in Table 3, it is possible to exclude process alternatives that is likely to increase the number of faults.

The exclusion or inclusion of processes from the column viewpoint is also a desirable alternative when dealing with prioritized or fixed attributes.

Besides excluding processes, the alternative is to modify the input, i.e. the functionality characteristics or coupling for the system entity developed. In this case, an adaptation would alter the product to suit the desired process. For example, this can be done to meet highly prioritized lead-time demands.

A final alternative is to accept the potential mismatch between the recommended process and the predicted outcome, and be informed of the potential risks, and address these risks as they appear. This is still an improvement over being surprised when the risks turn into problems. The final handling is still up to the organization implementing this method for verification and validation trade-off.

2.8   Feedback and Re-evaluation of the Process Selection

Despite testing and evaluation, no process is without openings for improvement. The approach suggested in this paper is by itself a process improvement approach targeting lead-time and effort optimization. However, the method described, including this section, does not stand above improvements.

To assure that the best possible method is used for tailoring the company's process, evaluation and improvement are required. Within this method, there are three central areas for improving the accuracy and correctness of the method: 1) Functionality and coupling classification, 2) Process recommendation, and 3) Variable outcome.

The feedback and re-evaluation of the process selection aims at assuring the correctness of these three areas. If they are not performing according to expectations, i.e. supplying correct recommendations, the outcome of the process selection is likely to fail.

To address the evaluation of the three central areas, a three-phased approach is suggested. The approach is described briefly, and should be implemented according to suitability within the organization implementing this tailoring process.

The reason for presenting a three alternative approach is to cover the majority of situations, from when little historical data is available to when the historical database is sufficient for deducting statistics. The three alternatives are: 1) Value-based evaluation, 2) General statistic evaluation, and 3) Specific statistic evaluation.

Value-based evaluation: This is carried out by surveying project personnel, typically project managers and stakeholders interested in the core attributes. The focus is on the compliance and correctness related to the functionality classification and interconnections. Also, the prediction reliability of the core attributes is subject for evaluation, it should be determined if the right processes were recommended.

General statistic evaluation: This is done by comparing the outcome of the project by any previously completed project regarding the level on the core attributes. This would indicate if the process tailoring was beneficial or not.

Specific statistic evaluation: This is done by comparing the outcome with a prior project representing the same categories in terms of classification.

2.9 Method Extension

There are possible extensions of the process described in Sections 2.1 through 2.7. The described process is though sufficient for supplying value for the organization adopting the approach to verification and validation trade-off. Four possible extensions are identified:

- Additional events of V&V.
- Finer grained scope for V&V, i.e. not only low and high.
- Increased set of attributes, i.e. more than four attributes.
- Magnitude of impact on the variables, i.e. more different levels.

Additional events of V&V are to add a third or fourth, and so on, activity of V&V, creating a process of verification then validation, followed by another event of verification activities.

Increasing the granularity of the scope of V&V is also a possible extension. The scope could be divided into more levels for example, high, medium, low or any other division.

The proposed method handles a set of basic attributes these attributes are not final. Thus, it is possible to extend the model with more attributes.

The magnitude of impact on the attributes is also a possible extension. In the current proposal the impact is indicated as an increase, a decrease or not affected. It would be desirable to have a magnitude on these increases or decreases as well. This would, for example, make it possible to prioritize a small increase in project lead-time in favor of a large decrease in the number of changes.

3 Investigation at the Company

The method presented in Section 2 is a result of a close cooperation between researchers at the university and UIQ Technology. The focus is on improving their V&V processes by tailoring the process based on characteristics of the different system entities in the software products. This section provides some first reactions and experiences when introducing the concept of adaptable V&V processes.

3.1 Company Cooperation

The cooperation between the company and the researcher is a long-term activity. The researcher has been present in the company's facilities and also through related studies, introduced and familiarized with challenges and goals of the company, becoming familiar with the company, its personnel and the products.

The development of method for V&V trade-off originates from the environment and knowledge of challenges and desires from the company.

Through close interaction and frequent discussion with a company representative having long experience and a good understanding of the goals of the company the method has emerged. The main contribution by the researcher is to formulate and structure the model based on industry input. In addition, the objective has been to make the method generally applicable and focusing on the few but prominent and important issues. The key contact person and main point for cooperation is operating as a line manager with extensive experience and insight within the company. The line manager is head of the development department, being responsible for several parallel projects. Additional responsibilities include providing sufficient support and knowledge in the form of process support to the developers. The line manager is also in involved in customer negotiations addressing contracting issues such as delivery dates and product content and quality.

Thus, the line manager is interested in process improvements that could help the company to deliver higher quality products in a shorter time with less effort.

3.2 Company Challenge

The main challenge for the company is to deliver high quality in as short time as possible. The demands typically force the company to deliver their products with increased functionality, extended features, higher quality and in less time. This challenge requires a new perspective on the commonly used processes within the company. An adapted way of handling the processes has been seen as one way of meeting the challenges ahead. The alternative process (including selection of a suitable V&V process) requires handling the system or system parts differently based on the characteristics of them. To gain effort and lead-time, adaptable processes are considered, but changing processes imply risk. To handle the risk it is necessary to trade-off verification and validation in such a way that the overall project lead-time and effort does not suffer, typically by finding a large number of faults or changes late in the process. On the other hand, too much lead-time may be consumed if both verification and validation is operated to a full extent, when not called for.

The proposed method addresses the verification and validation trade-off by dealing with the order and scope of these two activities. Both verification and validation is quality assuring activities, focusing typically on providing answers to whether the right functionality is being developed and if it is operating as intended.

3.3 Company Result

The company study, at this stage, is performed through discussions. In addition, a structured interview took place, which discussed the handling of the creation of alternative processes and the process selection at the company.

The interview focused on three parts: important project success attributes for the company, the feasibility and applicability of the suggested method, and finally the creation and difference between the alternative processes.

This section describes the result from the interview. The most important attributes for the company is the ones described in Section 2.4: lead-time, effort, number of defects, and number of changes. The success of the project relates to the timeliness of the delivery as well as the quality of the product. During the interview, the applicability of the method was discussed. The method is apprehended as applicable and suitable in the requirements management, and project planning phase of a typical project within the company.

The issues of creating the process alternatives and determining the likely outcome resulted in that four classes of functionality were found suitable and hence to be used. However, this adaptation is natural since the method has been formulated from a balance between a generally applicable method and the wishes from UIQ Technology. As the method suggests that each key is accompanied with a set of suggested processes and likely impacts. Thus, the suitable processes were decided upon for each key and the outcome variables were determined.

The result shows that it is clear that different keys generate different selections of processes. However, it is also clear that some process alternatives are most desired and highly prioritized, and some process alternatives are not selected at all. It is clear that the preferred processes are initiated with validation, which to some extent contradicts the typical process starting with verification and ending with validation.

4 Conclusions

The main contribution of this paper is how to deal with adaptability and in particular how classification and the creation of tangible keys can be used to select a suitable process alternative. The proposed method deals with the creation of keys focused on tangible characteristics for the functionality and component under development, providing guidance on selecting a suitable process alternative.

The verification and validation trade-off, discussed in this paper, deals with the necessity of finding the right balance between these two important activities without extending the resource consumption or lower quality in any case. In the case of the studied company there are two challenges. The first is to avoid a too safe route, and hence not fulfilling the timeliness of the product. The second is to avoid a too risky route, and risking a vast amount of faults and changes in the later stages of development, and as a result pushing the delivery date and increasing the cost.

There is also a clear connection between the success in reaching the timeliness and fulfilling market demand, and the success of the company. This strengthens the necessity of tailored processes that delivers as good results as possible. To tailor processes, it is required to monitor the circumstances under which the process shall operate, motivating the attribute and characteristics monitoring described in this paper. However, it is easy to understand that these characteristics and attributes are not the only ones of importance. Further work could be directed towards investigating other characteristics and attributes and their influence on the verification and validation process, and hence the process selection. However, it is impossible to cover all possible characteristics, and hence simplifications are required. It is argued in this paper that the method described in Section 2 is a sufficient and working starting point for the discussion of an adaptable approach to verification and validation trade-off, based on functional and coupling characteristics.

In summary, it is concluded that this approach should be feasible to obtain processes that are better tailored for the needs of different types of functionality.

Acknowledgement

Special thanks are addressed to UIQ Technology participating in this study. This work was partly funded by The Knowledge Foundation in Sweden under a research grant for the project "Blekinge - Engineering Software Qualities (BESQ)" (http://www.ipd.bth.se/besq).

References

[1] W. Scacchi, "Process Models in Software Engineering", in J. J. Marciniak (ed.), Encyclopedia of Software Engineering, Wiley, New York, 2003.

[2] K. Beck, Extreme Programming Explained: Embrace Change, Addison-Wesley, Publishing Company, Reading, 2000.

[3] B. Boehm, "A Spiral Model of Software Development and Enhancement", Computer, vol. 21, pp. 61-72, 1988.

[4] W. Royce, "Trw's Ada Process Model for Incremental Development of Large Software Systems," presented at 12th International Conference on Software Engineering, 1990.

[5] T. Gilb and S. Finzi, Principles of Software Engineering Management, Addison-Wesley Publishing Company, Wokingham 1988.

[6] B. Ramesh, J. Pries-Heje, and R. Baskerville, "Internet Software Engineering: A Different Class of Processes", Annals of Software Engineering, vol. 14, pp. 169-195, 2002.

[7] F. Keenan, "Agile Process Tailoring and Problem Analysis (APTLY)", presented at 26th International Conference on Software Engineering, Edinburgh, Scotland, UK, 2004.

[8] P. Xu, "Knowledge Support in Software Process Tailoring", presented at 38th Hawaii International Conference on System Sciences, Hawaii, 2005.

[9] M. P. Ginsberg and L. H. Quinn, "Process Tailoring and the Software Capability Maturity Model", Software Engineering Institute, Carnegie Mellon University, Pittsburgh, Technical report, ESC-TR-94-024, November 1995.

[10] P. Donzelli, "Tailoring the Software Maintenance Process to Better Support Complex Systems Evolution Projects", Journal of Software Maintenance and Evolution: Research and Practice, vol. 15, pp. 27-40, 2003.

[11] J. Radatz, "IEEE Standard Glossary of Software Engineering Terminology," IEEE Standards Board, New York, Standard IEEE std. 610.12-1990, 1990.

[12] R. T. Futrell, D. F. Shafer, and L. I. Shafer, Quality Software Project Management, Prentice Hall, Upper Saddle River, 2002.

[13] G. Succi and M. Marchesi, Extreme Programming Examined, Addison-Wesley Publishing Company, Boston, 2001.

[14] L. Chung, B. A. Nixon, E. Yu, and J. Mylopoulos, Non-Functional Requirements in Software Engineering, Kluwer Academic, Boston, 2000.

[15] B. Boehm and H. In, "Identifying Quality-Requirement Conflicts", IEEE Software, vol. 13, pp. 25-35, 1996.

Investigating the Impact of Active Guidance on Design Inspection

Dietmar Winkler, Stefan Biffl, and Bettina Thurnher

Vienna University of Technology, Institut of Software Technology,
Karlsplatz 13, A-1040 Vienna, Austria
{Dietmar.Winkler, Stefan.Biffl,
Bettina.Thurnher}@qse.ifs.tuwien.ac.at

Abstract. Software inspection helps to improve the quality of software products early in the development process. For design inspection recent research showed that usage-based reading of documents is more effective and efficient than traditional checklists. Usage-based reading guides actively the inspector with pre-sorted use cases, while traditional checklists let the inspector figure out how best to proceed. This paper investigates the impact of active guidance on an inspection process: We introduced checklists that give the inspector a process to follow, which should be as flexible as traditional checklists but more efficient. We compared the performance of this approach in a controlled experiment in an academic environment with traditional checklist and usage-based reading. Main results of the investigation are (a) checklists with active guidance are significantly more efficient than traditional checklists for finding major defects and (b) usage-based reading is more effective and efficient than both types of checklists. These results suggest that active guidance improves the efficiency of inspectors while the upfront investment into usage-based reading pays off during inspection.

Keywords: inspection process improvement, reading techniques, software product improvement, empirical software engineering, active guidance.

1 Introduction

Software inspection is a current approach for quality improvement of software products in industrial environment, since Fagan introduced it in 1976 [5]. Inspection is a defect detection technique to reduce defects in software artifacts and to improve software product quality [4][17]. The inspection method is classified as a static verification and validation technique, which doesn't need executable software. Therefore, inspection approaches are applicable to written text documents, e.g. design documents, as well.

Inspection in our context concentrates on defect detection in early stages of software development, i.e. in design documents. The early elimination of defects leads to a higher level of product quality, due to a lower number of remaining defects and, as a consequence, to a reduction of required resources (e.g. budget, time, etc.). Therefore, inspection is one important approach for software product improvement.

F. Bomarius and S. Komi-Sirviö (Eds.): PROFES 2005, LNCS 3547, pp. 458–473, 2005.

In order to find defects, inspectors have to traverse the document under inspection. Reading is a key activity in defect detection processes to (1) understand the document under inspection and (2) compare the inspection artifact to a set of expectations regarding content, structure and product quality. This comparison and recognition helps to spot defects. Because of this key activity, several reading techniques (RTs) have been developed to improve inspection process quality.

In general, inspectors have to learn reading and to analyze the software artifacts applying reading techniques. Systematic reading techniques consist of series of steps that help inspectors to understand particular aspects of a document with active reading work and to use this information for defect detection. Important characteristics of RTs are [13]: usability (simplicity to follow predefined guidelines) [16], applicability to different document notation and application domains, repeatability of inspection results, document coverage, and target defects.

Therefore, a well-designed RT must achieve those requirements and uses available knowledge on the structure of a document to provide guidance through the most important parts of the document. RTs support readers while inspecting the document in an active or passive way. Readers using a passive approach inspect the artifact regarding a number of steps sequentially (e.g. given checklist items). Active guidance includes a detailed inspection process (*how to perform an inspection*) and a separation of perception (*what to inspect*) [3][14].

Empirical studies in academic environment use checklists (CBR), scenarios (SBR), use cases (UBR), or perspectives (PBR) [1] [12] to focus on different types of defects, e.g. defect severity classes, document locations, impact of individual defects, etc. to investigate the benefits of the individual RT approaches. Examples for empirical studies are: checklist-based RT (CBR) [15][27] and usage-based RT (UBR) [23][24][25][26][27]. Gilb et al. presents an overview and comparison of CBR and SBR [7]. Families of empirical studies must be performed to provide generalization of empirical findings, e.g. [6][11][18][19][21][29].

Checklist-based reading (CBR) approaches use sequentially predefined items, which lead the inspector through the document under inspection. Inspectors have to traverse the document several times for a complete coverage of the specification document and the checklist. The new checklist-based RT variant (CBR-tc) uses a tailored checklist to provide an active guidance to the inspector. Inspectors have to analyze requirements and system function and prioritize them according to their knowledge of the application domain. This proceeding is included in the inspection process. Usage-based approaches (UBR) use expert prioritized use cases and scenarios for defect detection. Inspectors follow them and traverse the document in order to find defects. The main advantage of UBR is the application of expert prioritized use cases to find the most important defects and the support of active guidance.

This paper presents the results of a large-scale experiment in academic environment at Vienna University of Technology [28]. The empirical study cover a checklist-based reading technique (CBR-gc) using a generic checklist, and a usage-based reading technique approach (UBR) with use cases and a new CBR variant, a tailored checklist (CBR-tc). The aim of this paper is the investigation of the impact of active guidance on the number of defects found at different severity classes (crucial and major defects).

The remainder of this paper is structured as follows. Section 2 presents the reading techniques compared in our experiment. Section 3 describes research questions and Section 4 outlines the empirical study. Section 5 presents the study results. Section 6 discusses the results. Section 7 concludes and outlines directions for future research.

2   Checklists and Usage-Based Reading Techniques

A well-design reading technique is a structured approach to support inspectors in defect detection processes. We cover two classes of RTs, (a) the checklist-based (CBR-gc) approach using a generic checklist and (b) the usage-based RT (UBR) approach. Furthermore, we introduce a new checklist-based RT variant (CBR-tc). This new variant includes tailored checklist items, which support the reader by active guidance through the specification document.

A *checklist-based RT (CBR-gc)* is a method, which typically consists of a set of questions for general purposes, usually independent from a specific notation [7]. Inspectors traverse the document according to every checklist item several times sequentially and report defects found during inspection. CBR-gc offers little guidance on defect detection processes. Therefore, the results depend strongly on the individual inspectors and suffer from variability according to inspector capability.

RTs including active guidance aim to support inspectors during reading processes and improve disadvantages of CBR-gc. Active guidance helps inspectors to traverse the document under inspection, providing guidelines, how to perform inspection and what to inspect, e.g. according to defect types, etc. [14]. We use two different approaches, a tailored checklist (CBR-tc) and usage-based RT approach (UBR).

CBR-tc is a modified checklist providing active guidance to the inspector. A more application specific checklist lead the inspector through the inspection process, performing the following major steps:

1. Analysis of requirements and system function within the requirements document.
2. Investigation and prioritization of correlations between requirements and system functions according to the experience of the inspector.
3. Tracking of requirements and functions according to their importance through the document under inspection.
4. Report differences and defects.
5. Select the next most important requirement and proceed until the time is up or the inspector has covered all requirements and system functions.

CBR-tc leads the inspector through the specification document in an active way regarding application domain and focus on important defects, due to a prioritization task at the beginning of individual inspection. Nevertheless, it depends on the knowledge of the inspector to perform a correct ranking.

Usage-based reading (UBR) focuses on prioritized use cases and support active guidance, due to given guidelines and scenario representations [24]. Use cases represent the user view and spot defects, which are normally hard to find. Inspectors read prioritized use cases sequentially, apply them to the design specification and report defects. Because of this focus, UBR improve the understanding of inspectors and support them in finding more severe defects.

Most experiments focus on defect detection for individual inspectors and teams, concerning time variables and performance measures [2][23]. But there is very little concern for the effort of inspection preparation, i.e. the time interval before inspection within the inspection environment. Because inspection managers prefer using existing inspection material, there is a very low hurdle applying a checklist-based reading technique for individual inspection. More sophisticated reading techniques such as UBR and SBR need to be tailored upfront to the document under inspection.

Thus, there are several criteria that need to be considered when deploying a defect detection technique in practice: Effort for individual inspectors, effectiveness and efficiency of defect detection when applying a reading technique and upfront investment due to tailoring of documents.

Concerning CBR-gc the preparation phase requires very low effort because of the usage of a generic checklist, i.e. very less or no additional effort to adapt checklists to different application domains.

Experts almost need more effort to the preparation of CBR-tc reading technique approaches, because there is a context to the application domain. Experts also have to pay attention to the requirements document to provide active guidance to inspectors. Additional effort is necessary during individual inspection for analysis and prioritization of requirements and system functions.

Obviously, UBR reading technique approaches require most pre-work of experts depending on given artifacts according to their notation. Textual requirements notation requires the translation of requirements into use cases and a prioritization of use cases afterwards. In case of given use cases, i.e. the notation of requirements contains scenarios and use cases, experts have to prioritize them according to their expert knowledge.

This paper represents the empirical results of our investigations of active guidance according to effectiveness, efficiency, and effort, also regarding defect severity classes and reading technique approaches.

3   Research Questions

The main focus of this paper is the investigation of the impact of active guidance on design inspections with respect to time variables and performance measures. We use the results of an external replication of the UBR experiment as described in [27] and [28]. In addition to CBR and UBR inspection we introduce a slightly adjusted version of CBR, namely CBR-tc (CBR using tailoring approaches to prioritize requirements and corresponding system functions).

The UBR reading technique approach uses guidelines how to proceed during inspection and a predefined prioritized list of use cases [20]. The ranking of use cases is important to focus on crucial defects and to guide the inspector through the design specification. Nevertheless, this ranking requires additional effort by expert before inspection started. Further information on the importance of use-case ranking was discussed in a previous paper [28].

CBR-gc inspectors apply a generic checklist for multiple purposes to find defects in the software artifact. Inspectors have to traverse the document several times according to every checklist item to achieve full document coverage. They do not apply any use cases or scenarios at all.

In this paper we introduce a slightly adjusted checklist to provide active guidance for checklist based reading. The initial checklist consists of a strict proceeding to identify requirements, system functions and their correlation. Additionally, the inspectors have to prioritize the requirements according to their subjective importance according to their own knowledge of the application domain. Therefore, inspectors need additional effort for this task during inspection proceeding. The inspectors use this prioritized requirements to traverse the specification document. This approach enables a deeper understanding of the specification document and the system requirements as well as system functions.

The application of an individual reading technique approach requires a different amount of effort for experiment preparation concerning RT specific tasks:

- *CBR-gc* uses checklists [15], which were developed before the experiment for generic purposes. The application of CBR-gc does not require any additional effort.
- *CBR-tc* also uses checklists, but leave the tailoring process to the inspection (as a part of the inspection process) according to the individual knowledge of the inspectors. Inspectors have to identify, classify and prioritize requirements, system functions and their dependability.
- *UBR* provide use cases and scenarios [26], which are unique to the application domain and the software document. Experts find use cases, and prioritize them according to the application domain to guide the inspector active through the inspection process.

The purpose of this paper is the investigation of *inspection effort*, *effectiveness* and *efficiency* of defect detection regarding the influence of active guidance. Inspection effort is importance in industrial environment for acceptability and applicability of inspections in general regarding deadlines and cost. Inspection effectiveness is the number of found defects in relation to all defects within the software document. One of the major goals of software inspection is the reduction of defects in software products to improve software quality [4][18]. Because different RTs focus on different defect classes (e.g. defect severity), it is interesting to point out the best applicable RT. Efficiency joins effort and effectiveness and depicts the number of found defects in a defined time interval (i.e. defects per hour).

3.1 Variables

The experiment setup contains two different types of variables [27] [28], (a) independent and (b) dependent variables. We use the reading technique used as *independent* variable, i.e. *CBR-gc*, *CBR-tc*, and *UBR*. CBR-gc applies a generic checklist for general purposes (predefined within the experiment environment). CBR-tc provides a checklist including the procedure how to proceed during inspection, i.e. finding and prioritizing requirements, classifying system functions and locating associations, etc.). UBR implies a predefined order of use cases (including expert know how) for inspection. We controlled the influence of inspector experience by randomly assigning reading techniques to inspectors.

We use *dependent variables* to capture the performance of the individual inspection procedures regarding different reading technique approaches. Following standard practice in empirical studies we focus on time variables and performance measures. Therefore, we capture *inspection time* in minutes (preparation and inspection time) and the *number of defects* found during inspection. Regarding performance measures we investigate the influence of active guidance to *inspection effectiveness* and *efficiency* (the number of defects per hour) according to the reading techniques applied. Furthermore, we pay special attention to defect severity classes. Experts ranked the defects according to three defect severity classes: critical defects *class A)*, major defects *(class B)*, and minor defects *(class C)*. For evaluation purposes, we focus on finding important defects in the classes A or A+B (including class A or class B defects).

3.2 Hypotheses

In the experiment we observe the performance of inspectors who apply one of three reading techniques: CBR-gc, CBR-tc, or UBR. As main goal of this paper we investigate research hypothesis regarding inspection effort, effectiveness and efficiency according to the reading technique approach used and the influence of active guidance. In more detail we evaluate the following hypotheses:

Inspection Effort: Inspection effort includes inspection preparation and inspection duration as part of the individual inspection process. We do not cover effort of experts as part of the overall inspection preparation, i.e. ranking of use cases, generation of guidelines, checklists, etc.

CBR-gc inspectors have to traverse the document several times according to every checklist item to achieve full document coverage. Therefore, we expect the highest overall inspection effort. CBR-tc inspectors use active guidance but have to perform an additional tailoring session to analyze requirements and system function including prioritization. This additional session increase preparation time.

H1: Effort (CBR-tc) < Effort (CBR-gc): In summary we expect a lower effort through active guidance (CBR-tc), because the inspectors benefit from better understanding of the application domain and document under inspection.

Effectiveness: In this paper we consider effectiveness as the number of defects found at three different severity classes (critical, major, and minor) regarding the overall number of seeded defects of every severity class.

H21: Effectiveness (UBR) > Effectiveness (CBR-gc): UBR inspectors benefit from active guidance using prioritized use cases and scenario. Therefore, we expect a higher effectiveness in relation to CBR-gc inspectors, who have to read the document several times sequentially. Additionally, UBR readers focus on important defects due to an expert ranked approach of prioritization. Experts are familiar with the design specification including background knowledge of seeded defects.

H22: Effectiveness (UBR) > Effectiveness (CBR-tc): The argument is similar to H21 for UBR inspectors. CBR-tc inspectors perform tailoring and prioritization of requirements and system functions without background knowledge. We expect an advantage of expert ranking effects for important defects according to inspection effectiveness regarding UBR approaches.

H23: Effectiveness (CBR-tc) > Effectiveness (CBR-gc): The argument is similar to H22 under the assumption that the analysis of requirements and system functions during the preparation phase improve defect detection and effectiveness. CBR-gc inspectors traverse the design specification several times using a generic checklist without special attention on the application domain.

Efficiency: Efficiency combines effort and effectiveness and is defined as the number of detected defects per time interval, i.e. per hour. To investigate efficiency we summarize overall inspection effort (including preparation and inspection time) and total number of matched (seeded) defects.

H31: Efficiency (UBR) > Efficiency (CBR-gc): We expect a higher efficiency for UBR inspectors because of active guidance of inspectors using use cases and scenarios. CBR-gc inspectors traverse the specification document several times without active support by the reading technique. Therefore, UBR inspectors will find more defects and need less effort.

H32: Efficiency (UBR) > Efficiency (CBR-tc): The argument is similar to H31. Additionally CBR-tc is classified as a method with active guidance with focus on prioritized requirements and system functions. Because of an additional effort for this analysis and prioritization task, inspection effort will increase. Obviously, efficiency will decrease.

H33: Efficiency (CBR-tc) > Efficiency (CBR-gc): Active guidance and prioritized requirements and system functions improve efficiency of CBR-tc in contrast to CBR-gc, where the inspectors have to traverse the document under inspection several times sequentially. The expected additional effort for prioritization compensates CBR-gc approaches.

4   Experiment Description

The experiment was conducted at Vienna University of Technology in academic environment in December 2003. This study is a replicated experiment as described in [27] and [23] involving 127 inspection participants. We leave the details to the original developers of UBR and the experiment environment. In this section we will briefly describe key aspects of the experiment and point out the basic experiment proceeding, used artifacts, and involved subjects.

4.1   Experiment Proceeding

The empirical study consists of three major phases, a preparation phase, the inspection execution, and the evaluation phase:

Experiment preparation: Experts had to prepare inspection artifacts, e.g. require-ments document, design specification, guidelines for reading techniques, and questionnaires. Using 3 different RT approaches, corresponding tasks had to be performed by experts before conducting the inspection within the experiment environment. We do not cover organizational aspects in this paper.

Additional to the preparation of guidelines and questionnaires, this preparation phase included:

- Conductance and prioritization of use cases by experts for UBR.
- Preparation of checklist items for tailoring tasks to support inspectors for CBR-tc. Inspectors have to perform analysis and prioritization of requirements and system functions during the inspection process using those guidelines.
- Preparation of a generic checklist for CBR-gc. This approach did not require much additional effort because of the generic structure of the checklist (re-use of this checklist).

Inspection execution: The experiment execution included three steps: a *training and preparation* session, *individual inspection*, and *data submission*. Inspectors got an overview of the inspections process and learned basics about inspection and different reading technique approaches during a short training session. Individual inspection included (a) the inspection preparation, i.e. reading the document under inspection, analysis and prioritization of requirements and system functions (CBR-tc) etc., (b) the defect detection and reporting process, and (c) data submission. During data submission step, all inspectors had to log their candidate defects electronically for quality assurance purposes. This data submission task also included questionnaire results and time stamps for processes and defects findings.

Data evaluation: After individual inspection, experts mapped candidate defects, i.e. defects noted by individual inspectors, to reference defects, i.e. real defects seeded by experts. The data, derived from the database were checked for consistency and correctness. We excluded the data from subjects, who delivered inconsistent data or did not follow the experiment process properly.

Also note, that candidate defects that refer to one true seeded defects were counted only once at the first clock time of defect detection.

For statistical evaluation we use the Mann-Whitney test to investigate *effort* and *efficiency* and a chi square test to test *effectiveness*. The significance level of rejecting the hypotheses is set to 0.05 for all tests.

4.2 Software Artifacts

The artifacts describe a taxi management system and include (a) a textual requirements definition, (b) a design document, (c) use case documents, (d) several guidelines for reading technique approaches, and (d) questionnaires for capturing experience and feedback information.

- The *textual requirements document* was used as a reference document and was assumed to be accurate.
- The *design document* describes an overview of the software modules and their individual context. The document includes the internal representation (between two or more modules) as well as the external representation (between the user and the taxi management system). The design document consists of 9 pages, including 2500 words, 2 sequence charts, and 39 known defects, i.e. seeded defects.

- Defect reports were linked to 39 *seeded defects* at different severity classes (13 crucial (class A), 15 major (class B), and 11 minor (class C) defects) spread all over the document, which were seeded before inspection by experts during experiment preparation. *Class A* means a heavy adverse affect on functionality which will appear very often (highest risk). *Class B* contains important rarely used defects or unimportant often used defects (medium risk). *Class C* defects are neither crucial nor very important (low risk).
- The *use case document* contained 24 use cases from user view-point in task notation. Experts prioritized those use cases according to their importance for the usage-based reading technique application.
- RT specific *guidelines* support the individual inspectors and lead them through the inspection process while applying the assigned reading technique.
- We use two types of questionnaires to achieve (a) background information of the individual inspectors (experience questionnaire) at the beginning, and (b) feedback on the RT applied (feedback questionnaire) at the end of inspection.

4.3 Subjects

127 software engineering students were taking part in the experiment using CBR-gc, CBR-tc, or UBR reading technique approaches. The experiment was fully integrated into the course as a practical part to practice software inspection and learn key aspects of software product improvement in early stages of software development. We controlled the influence of inspection capability by randomly assigning reading techniques to inspectors.

To our knowledge this is the largest empirical study comparing UBR and CBR RT approaches. Similar experiments involved a total number 12 [3], 23 [27], 62 [23], and 42 participants [14].

Table 1. Number of inspectors by RT

RT	Number of Insp.	Percentage
CBR-gc	24	19%
CBR-tc	48	38%
UBR	55	43%
Total	127	100%

Table 1 displays the distribution of inspectors with respect to reading technique roles. We used the CBR-gc reading technique as control group involving 19% of inspectors.

5 Experiment Results

In this section we present the empirical results of the study. We pay attention to inspection effort, effectiveness (number of defects found), and efficiency (defects found per hour).

5.1 Effort

Inspection effort includes preparation time and inspection duration. The inspectors logged the clock time for each individual task; reading the specification and design document, tailoring and prioritizing of requirements – summarized in preparation time and inspection time. Table 2 displays the mean and standard deviation for the three reading techniques.

Table 2. Individual preparation and inspection time in minutes

		CBR-gc	CBR-tc	UBR
Mean	Preparation	43.3	46.0	42.8
	Inspection	120.3	110.0	117.7
	Total	163.5	155.9	160.6
Std.Dev	Preparation	15.7	19.0	22.5
	Inspection	27.9	30.8	28.1
	Total	25.1	34.6	29.5

All three RTs have a similar total effort on average. Concerning preparation time, CBR-tc inspectors need somewhat longer because of an additional tailoring and prioritization task in contrast to CBR-gc and UBR inspectors, but the subsequent inspection duration is shorter. In summary, CBR-tc inspectors need somewhat less effort for overall inspection.

Concerning our research hypothesis we observe that there is no significant difference of inspection effort between all three RT approaches.

5.2 Effectiveness

In the context of this paper we define effectiveness as the number of seeded defects found by an individual inspector in relation to the overall number of seeded defects within the design document. The experiment setup contains 39 seeded defects, summarized by 13 crucial, 15 major and 11 minor defects. To figure out the benefits of the individual RTs we investigate crucial defects (class A), important defects (class A and class B), and all defects found by inspectors.

Table 3 summarized mean values and standard deviations of effectiveness according to defect classes and reading techniques.

Table 3. Effectiveness by defect class and reading technique

	Defect	CBR-gc	CBR-tc	UBR
Mean	Class A	24.4	29,2	35.8
	Class A+B	26.3	28,1	33.1
	All defects	24.9	25,2	29.8
Std.Dev	Class A	19.2	13,5	14.4
	Class A+B	14.4	10,0	11.0
	All defects	10.9	8,8	11.9

On average there is a notable difference between the effectiveness of CBR-gc, CBR-tc, and UBR, that is consistent for all classes of defects investigated. UBR inspectors found more defects than CBR-tc and CBR-gc inspectors for every defect class. Also CBR-tc dominates CBR-gc for every subset of defects. The performance advantage of UBR is greatest for defects belonging to class A. Note the smallest standard deviation at CBR-tc with respect to all defects.

Fig. 1 depicts effectiveness of three reading technique with respect to defect severity classes.

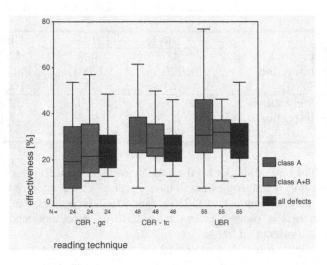

Fig. 1. Effectiveness of three reading techniques

Table 4 shows the results of our investigation according to significance values. There is a notable difference concerning all defect severity classes and all couples of reading techniques investigated.

Table 4. p-values for effectiveness according to defect classes and RT

	Class A	Class A+B	All Defects
CBR-gc / UBR	<0,001(S)	0,021(S)	0,018 (S)
CBR-tc / UBR	<0,001(S)	<0,001(S)	0,029(S)
CBR-gc / CBR-tc	<0,001(S)	0,022(S)	0,043(S)

Therefore, we can actually confirm our research hypotheses: UBR with expert ranking significantly outperforms all other reading techniques, due to active guidance including the prioritized use cases applied. Thus, the performance advantage of UBR is greatest for all defects. CBR-tc also dominates CBR-gc for every subset of defect severity classes, because of the impact of active guidance for CBR-tc inspection.

Additionally we investigated the ratio of *false positives*, i.e. the ratio of candidate defects that do not match to true defects regarding all defects found be individual inspectors. Because the inspectors did not know the number of real defects, they reported all possible defects, which were matched to real defects by experts. We did not recognize significant differences concerning false positives at noted defects and false positives. We did register significant differences with respect to non reference defects. CBR-gc inspectors received the highest number of wrong defects because of a non-active guidance through the inspection process using a generic checklist.

5.3 Efficiency

We combine the measures of effort and effectiveness to investigate inspection efficiency, i.e. defect detection rate per hour. Effort is concerned as the total amount of preparation and inspection time in minutes. We also use the total number of matched defects to derive efficiency.

Table 5. Inspection efficiency (number of defects found per hour)

	Defect	CBR-gc	CBR-tc	UBR
Mean	Class A	1.1	1,5	1.8
	Class A+B	2.7	3,1	3.6
	All defects	3.6	3,9	4.5
Std.Dev	Class A	0.8	0,7	0.8
	Class A+B	1.4	1,2	1.3
	All defects	1.5	1,4	1.7

Table 5 displays mean values and standard deviations for three defect classes with respect to the reading technique approaches. The results show that UBR inspectors achieve the highest efficiency according to all defect severity classes. We measured the lowest efficiency for CBR-gc inspectors, and somewhat between for CBR-tc inspectors.

Table 6. P-values for efficiency according to defect severity and reading techniques

	Class A	Class A+B	All defects
CBR-gc / UBR	0,002(S)	0,023 (S)	0,053(-)
CBR-tc / UBR	0,059(-)	0,098(-)	0,079(-)
CBR-gc / CBR-tc	0,039(S)	0,166(-)	0,400(-)

Table 6 shows a summary of p-values, derived by the Mann-Whitney test, for defect classes and all three reading techniques used. We notice significant differences for crucial defects (class A) by comparing RTs using active guidance (UBR and CBR-tc) with respect to CBR-gc. Furthermore, we recognize significant differences for important (class A or class B defects) defects concerning CBR-gc and UBR but not for all defects.

One interesting finding is that there is no significant difference at efficiency at CBR-tc and UBR (both RTs with active guidance). This implies that active guidance focus the inspectors efficiently on the more important defect classes.

6 Discussion

In this section we summarize the empirical results from our experiment concerning the comparison of CBR-gc, CBR-tc, and UBR. Analyzing our empirical results we derive the following implications for this comparison:

Effort of inspection duration: Inspectors from all reading techniques required a similar overall amount of time for inspection. Although CBR-tc inspectors needed longer for preparation due to their additional classification and prioritization phase of requirements and system functions, but they used also less time for the subsequent inspection phase. They benefit from better understanding of the application domain and the document under inspection.

We used the Mann-Whitney test for statistical evaluation, but we do not register any significant differences. One possible reason might be some kind of group effect, because we did not specify any upper limit for overall inspection duration.

Effectiveness: The analysis of the results supports all hypotheses (*H21-H23*) nominally for reading technique approaches. We found significantly differences according to all defect severity classes, i.e. crucial, major, and minor defects.

The impact of active guidance due to expert ranking of use cases influences effectiveness at any class of defects. The reasons might be (a) a well performed prioritization process by experts during inspection preparation phase, (b) the active guidance of use cases and scenarios during inspection, and (c) a well-formed presentation of the application domain due to use-case notation. Therefore UBR outperforms all CBR RT approaches. One disadvantage of this approach is the effort, spent by experts during the prioritization phase, because these activities were executed in the before the inspection process started at all.

The comparison of CBR-tc and CBR-gc also shows significant differences according to inspection effectiveness for all defect severity classes. Inspection effectiveness also benefits from the additional task of analysis and prioritization of requirements and system functions, using the CBR-tc approach, due to a better understanding and structuring of the application domain and the active guidance through the inspection process.

Efficiency: Our hypotheses are confirmed as well. UBR is most efficient and CBR-gc is less efficient. Concerning all defects, there is no significant difference at any comparison of RTs.

The results also show significant differences at RTs using active guidance in comparison to CBR-gc (which does not use active guidance) according to crucial defects (class A). We assume the influence of use cases and scenarios as the main reason for those findings. Nevertheless, active guidance improves inspection efficiency in comparison to generic checklist approaches. Tailoring of requirements (CBR-tc) improve efficiency due a structured approach and a deeper understanding of the document under inspection in comparison to a generic checklist approach. Nevertheless, use cases and scenarios approaches exceed efficiency of CBR-tc.

Analyzing the data from our experiment we conclude that UBR with expert ranking shows highest effectiveness and efficiency and therefore best overall performance.

The comparison to CBR-tc implies that the analysis, classification and prioritization of requirements and system functions have some influence on the performance of inspection. Active guidance, as provided by CBR-tc and UBR improve efficiency due to a reduction of overall inspection effort. Concerning effectiveness, the UBR reading technique approach, outperforms the tailored checklist approach and the generic checklist approach. The usage of use cases and scenarios lead to a deeper understanding of the application domain and improve effectiveness.

7 Conclusion and Further Work

Inspection is an important approach to reduce defects in software engineering artifacts. Reading techniques such as UBR can focus inspector attention on specific types of defects, i.e. crucial defects. Active guidance lead to a better understanding and a more structured approach of inspection proceeding and, therefore, improves inspection effectiveness and efficiency.

This paper presented a large-scale external experiment replication in the UBR family of experiments [2] in an academic environment. In addition to previous empirical studies, we introduced a new reading technique variant, a tailored checklist approach (CBR-tc) to investigate the impact of active guidance on inspection performance.

Main results of the study were: (a) active guidance improves inspection effectiveness and efficiency, (b) UBR expert know-how has significant effects of on defect detection rates; (c) the application of use cases and scenarios improve document understanding and inspection performance, and (d) both RTs with active guidance perform significantly better than CBR-gc.

Further work is to investigate the impact of inspector capability on defect detection: The empirical studies in this family of experiments have investigated defect detection according to different UBR and CBR approaches without regarding inspector capability in detail. Whereas we aware that inspector capability is an important factor to achieve well-performed inspection results.

References

1. Basili V.R., S. Green, O. Laitenberger, F. Lanubile, F. Shull, S. Soerumgaard, and M. Zelkowitz, "The Empirical Investigation of Perspective-Based Reading", *Empirical Software Engineering Journal*, vol. 1, no. 2, pp. 133-164, 1996.
2. Basili V.R., F. Shull, and F. Lanubile, "Building Knowledge through Families of Experiments," *IEEE Trans. Software Eng.*, vol. 25, no. 4, pp. 456-473, July/Aug. 1999.
3. Denger C., Ciolkowsky M., Lanubile F. *Investigation the Active Guidance Factor in Reading Techniques for Defect Detection*. ISESE 2004.
4. Ebenau R.G. and S.H. Strauss, *Software Inspection Process*. McGraw-Hill, 1994.

5. Fagan M., "Design and Code Inspections To Reduce Errors In Program Development", *IBM Systems J.*, vol. 15, no. 3, 1976, pp. 182-211.
6. Fusaro P., F. Lanubile, and G. Visaggio, "A Replicated Experiment to Assess Requirements Inspection Techniques," *Empirical Software Eng.: An Int'l J.,* vol. 2, no. 1, pp. 39-57, 1997.
7. Gilb T., Graham D., *Software Inspection*, Addison-Wesley, 1993.
8. ITU-T Z.100, Specification and Description Language, SDL, ITU-T Recommendation Z.100, 1993.
9. ITU-T Z.120, Message Sequence Charts, MSC, ITU-T Recommendation Z.120, 1996.
10. Jeffery, R.; Scott, L.; Has twenty-five years of empirical software engineering made a difference? *Software Engineering Conference, 2002. Ninth Asia-Pacific , 4-6 Dec.* 2002 pp. 539 -546
11. Juristo N. and A.M. Moreno, *Basics of Software Engineering Experimentation.* Kluwer Academic, 2001.
12. Laitenberger O., Atkinson C. "Generalizing Perspective-based Inspection to handle Object-Oriented Development Artifacts", *Proc. of the Int. Conf. on Software Engineering*, 1999.
13. Laitenberger O., DeBaud J.-M., "An encompassing life cycle centric survey of software inspection", *Journal of Systems and Software*, vol. 50, no. 1, 2000, pp. 5-31.
14. Lanubile F., Mallardo T., Calefato F., Denger C., Ciolkowksi M. *Assessing the Impact of Active Guidance for Defect Detection: A Replicated Experiment.* METRICS 2004.
15. Miller J., M. Wood, and M. Roper; "Further experiences with scenarios and checklists", *Empirical Software Engineering Journal,* vol. 3, no. 1, pp. 37-64, 1998.
16. Nielson, J.; "*Usability Engineering*", San Diego: Academic Press, 1993.
17. Parnas D., Lawford M., "The role of inspection in software quality assurance", *IEEE Trans. on SE, vol. 29(8), August 2003*, pp. 674-676.
18. Porter A., L. Votta, "Comparing Detection Methods for Software Requirements Inspections: a Replicated Experiment using professional subjects", *Empirical Software Engineering Journal,* vol. 3, no. 4, 1998, pp. 355-379.
19. Porter A., L. Votta, and V. Basili, "Comparing Detection Methods for Software Requirements Inspections: a Replicated Experiment", *IEEE Transactions on Software Engineering vol. 21, no. 6*, pp. 563-575, June 1995.
20. Saaty T.L., Vargas L.G.; "*Models, Methods, Concepts & Applications of the Analytic Hierarchy Process*"; Kluver Academic, 2001.
21. Sandahl K., Blomkvist O., Karlsson J., Krysander C., Lindvall M., Ohlsson N.: *An Extended Replication of an Experiment for Assessing Methods for Software Requirements Inspections*, Kluwer Academic Publishers, 1998
22. Shull F.J., "*Developing Techniques for using Software Documents: A Series of Empirical Studies*", PhD thesis, University of Maryland, College Park, www.cs.umd.edu/~fshull/pubs, 1998.
23. Thelin T., C. Andersson, P. Runeson, N. Dzamashvili-Fogelström "A Replicated Experiment of Usage-Based and Checklist-Based Reading", *Metrics 2004.*
24. Thelin T., P. Runeson, and B. Regnell, "Usage-Based Reading—An Experiment to Guide Reviewers with Use Cases," *Information and Software Technology*, vol. 43, no. 15, pp. 925-938, 2001.
25. Thelin T., P. Runeson, C. Wohlin, T. Olsson, and C. Andersson, "How Much Information Is Needed for Usage-Based Reading? —A Series of Experiments," *Proc. First Int'l Symp. Empirical Software Eng.*, pp. 127-138, 2002.

26. Thelin T., Runeson P., Wohlin C., "Prioritized Use Cases as a Vehicle for Software Inspections", *IEEE Software*, vol. 20(4), July/August 2003, pp. 30-33.
27. Thelin T., Runeson P., Wohlin C., "An experimental comparison of usage-based and checklist-based reading", *IEEE Trans. on SE*, vol. 29(8), August 2003, pp. 687-704.
28. Winkler D., Halling M., Biffl St. "*Investigating the Effect of Expert Ranking of Use Cases for Design Inspections*", Euromicro 2004.
29. Wohlin C., P. Runeson, M. Höst, M.C. Ohlsson, B. Regnell, and A. Wesslén, *Experimentation in Software Engineering - An Introduction*, The Kluwer International Series in Software Engineering, Kluwer Academic Publishers, 2000.

An XP Experiment with Students – Setup and Problems

Thomas Flohr and Thorsten Schneider

Software Engineering Group, University of Hannover,
Welfengarten 1, 30167 Hannover, Germany
{Thomas.Flohr, Thorsten.Schneider}@Inf.Uni-Hannover.de

Abstract. Designing experiments to be carried out with students as subjects in an XP setup is a difficult task: Students lack experiences with XP, there are limited resources, the experiment might not be taken seriously and other effects interfere. This paper presents an experiment using student subjects examining test-first in comparison to classical-testing. We proved several hypotheses about test coverage, number of test-cases, contacts with customer, acceptance for test-first, development speed and not required features. While designing the experiment we noticed that it is useful to include some additional XP techniques on top of test first, because of our special setup and the demands we had. Despite careful planning and conduction of the experiment we still faced a number of problems. In this paper we also discuss the problems with our experimental setup.

1 Introduction

Extreme Programming (XP) by Kent Beck [1] is the best-known agile Method. XP is a collection of several practices to be obeyed during software development projects.

The effectiveness of most XP practices is only weakly confirmed by empirical data gained through experiments. A single XP technique can either be examined in isolation, in a complete XP setup, or in a mixed setup in which some other XP techniques are applied as well. In winter semester of 2004/05 the Software Engineering Group of the University of Hannover conducted an experiment and for practical reasons (e.g. limited hardware resources and realistic setup) we decided to choose the last alternative, in which some other XP techniques are applied at the same time. Objects of investigation were test-first and classical-testing. For the automatic tests we used the JUnit framework.

We designed two experimental setups: a test-first setup including test-first and some other XP techniques (pair programming, on-site customer and user stories) and a classical-testing setup including the same XP techniques, but test-first was replaced by a classical-testing approach.

– Students should implement a useful program (e.g. not a small and abstract programing task) because students do not take synthetic tasks seriously.

F. Bomarius and S. Komi-Sirviö (Eds.): PROFES 2005, LNCS 3547, pp. 474–486, 2005.

- As in real life the requirements on the program are sometimes vague.
- The experiment should take place at the same location and time for all participants to create equal conditions for everyone and also because of our limited resources.
- Implementation during the experiment is restricted to our computer lab. Homework is not allowed in order to maintain comparability and control.

To meet these criteria we carefully designed a setup. Nevertheless we faced problems while designing and conducting the experiment. The focus of this paper lies on a description of the experiment's setup, the problems we faced and how we avoided some of them. This paper does not include the results of the experiment, because the experimental run is not completely finished.

1.1 Related Work

So far most techniques of XP were studied in isolation in controlled experiments. Case studies often observed more complex XP settings with multiple XP techniques.

Müller and Hagner observed 19 graduate students with some experience in XP [2]. In their experiment test-first was compared to traditional development separately. The students were divided in two groups to apply one of the approaches each. Each group had to implement the main class of a graph library which only contains declarations of methods. The experiment included unit and acceptance tests. Objects of investigation was programming speed, reliability of the final code and program understanding (reuse of code). The authors conclude that test-first for a traditional developer is not necessarily faster than traditional development.

In a further case study Müller and Tichy report about experiences, when realizing an XP course with students [3]. The study focused on pair programming, iteration planning, test-first, refactoring and the question of the best size of a team for an XP-project. One result was that pair programming is no problem for students, but test-first is hard to learn in the beginning.

Noll and Atkinson [4] report about a case study dealing with a comparison between XP and traditional development at a university. A class was divided into 4 teams; each consisted of 6 to 8 students and each team had to develop a web-based room reservation system. Two teams followed XP and two teams followed the traditional approach. One result was that the teams following the traditional approach delivered less robust code, but their solutions had more features. The test-first teams delivered more robust code with less features, but the user interface was sloppy and difficult to use. It was also observed that requirements were interpreted by the teams to their favor, despite an always available customer. The authors advise to prefer a strong customer (e.g. professor) and to outline the differences between XP and traditional development better.

Lindvall et al. [5] report about an eWorkshop about different empirical findings in agile Methods. Objects under discussion were team size, personnel, reliability, training requirements, refactoring and documentation in agile projects. The authors conclude that 10% of qualified personnel in an agile project with pair programming might be enough. Furthermore, they concluded that the requirements are addressed earlier (because the customer steadily gives input) and less formal training is required, because the developers train each other.

1.2 Outline

This paper is structured as follows: section two gives a detailed definition of our understandings of test-first and classical-testing and contains a list of partly proved statements about test-first gained from literature. Section three summarizes the hypotheses of test-first and classical-testing we verified. It also contains information on how to measure the experimental data. Section four describes the prerequisites, setup, and conduction of the experiment. Section five contains a discussion about the setup, what problems we faced and how we avoided some of them. Finally the conclusion gives suggestions what to avoid in experiments with students as subjects.

2   Test-First and Classical-Testing

Before we show a detailed description of test-first and classical-testing we give a list of definitions we use throughout this paper. We are not completely satisfied with the terms used in JUnit, because they collide with the terms we used in our lectures and they are not always intuitive. Table 1 shows our definitions:

Table 1. Comparison of our definitions and respective terms in the JUnit-Framework

Our terms	Terms in JUnit-Framework
Test-case: Verification whether the return value of one method matches the specified value or not.	assert-statement
Test: Verification whether a method or functionality fulfills the specification. A test includes at least one test-case.	TestMethod
Test-set: A collection of tests belonging together, because they test the same class or functionality.	TestCase
Test-suite: A collection of Test-sets belonging to one package or application.	TestSuite

Test-first with unit tests (*test-first* for short) is one of the core techniques of XP. The basic cycle in the test-first approach is to write one single test-case gained from the program specification, make it run with the easiest implementation and then continue with the next test-case. The Test-first approach can be specified in more detail in the following way:

1. Write one single test-case.
2. Run this test-case. If it fails continue with step 3. If the test-case succeeds, continue with step 1.
3. Implement the minimal code to make the test-case run.
4. Run the test-case again. If it fails again, continue with step 3. If the test-case succeeds, continue with step 5.
5. Refactor the implementation to achieve the simplest design possible.
6. Run the test-case again, to verify that the refactored implementation still succeeds the test-case. If it fails, continue with step 5. If the test-case succeeds, continue with step 1, if there are still requirements left in the specification.

The classical-testing approach is less specified. In general test-cases in the classical-testing approach are written after some code is implemented, but there is no specific rule when to write test-cases. One can summarize classical-testing as follows:

1. Read the specification.
2. Design the program
3. Write a few lines of code, some method(s), class(es), package(s) or the whole application.
4. Write some (new) or no test-suites, tests-sets, tests or test-cases gained from the specification.
5. Run the tests. If they succeed, continue with step 1, 2, 3 or 4. If the tests fail, continue with step 6. If there are no more further requirements and the code is tested enough (perspective of the developer), exit the classical-testing cycle.
6. Remove the errors in the implementation and continue with step 5.

Partly (statistically) proved statements about test-first are known from literature [1] and our experiences:

– Developers write more test-cases, because they start to test earlier and more systematically.
– Development is driven by tests, so test-coverage should be 100% percent.
– Developers do not implement not-required features and therefore also increase their development speed.
– Developers are more likely to discuss requirements with the customer earlier, because they are forced to think of requirements earlier.
– Developers trust their program code more.

3 Our Hypotheses

We derived several hypotheses from the above statements. This section gives a short overview of these hypotheses. For each hypothesis we also give methods or metrics on how to gain the data. We obtained the metrics by applying the GQM paradigm [6, 7]. This paper does not center on this process, so we only give a very short summary: for each hypothesis, which can be categorized as a goal, we obtained a set of questions. Several metrics were refined from the questions.

Our hypotheses centered on:

3.1 Number of Test-Cases

Our assumption is that the test-first approach produces more test-cases than the classical-testing approach, because the creation of test-cases starts earlier and development is driven by tests. We gain data by counting the test-cases and compare the ratio between the source code of the application and the number of test-cases.

3.2 Test-Coverage

Since development is driven by tests, test-first should produce 100% test-coverage (method-coverage, statement-coverage and conditional-coverage). Due to the fact, that most participants of the experiment are not quite familiar with test-first and JUnit we intuitively suppose that the test-coverage will be around 90% and classical-testing should result in 70% test-coverage, because trivial methods and some branches are not tested and all test-cases are written after coding. To determine the test-coverage the Eclipse plug-in Clover (version 1.1.4) is used.

3.3 Development Speed

The project's requirements are written on story-cards. We define the development speed as the time needed to meet the requirements of a story-card (also including the time for writing and executing the test-cases). Our assumption is that classical-testing will be faster than test-first, because less time is spent on testing. The measurement result is the time needed to meet the story-card's requirements.

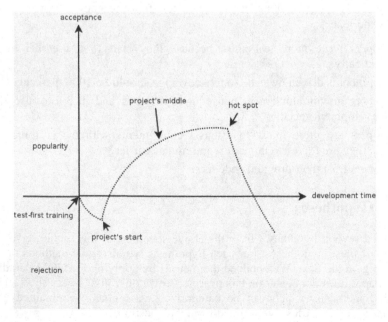

Fig. 1. Acceptance curve

3.4 Acceptance

We assume that students' acceptance for test-first can be mapped to the curve shown in Figure 1. After a test-first training students have a slight rejection towards test-first, because they suppose that it will slow down the development process. Shortly after, they change their opinion, because they realize that test-first can guide through the development process. Afterwards the acceptance steadily increases until the hot spot (final hours of development) is reached. After the hot spot the acceptance decreases rapidly, because time is short and will not be "wasted" for testing. The acceptance is gathered from questionnaires handed out to the students throughout the experimental run to verify or discard the assumed curve.

3.5 Not Required Features

Test-first is based on implementing the minimal functionality and new code is only written when a test fails, so the application should not contain any additional features. We assume that the classical-testing approach contains more not required features than the test-first approach. Automatically gathering data for this hypothesis is quite difficult, so we can only gain some tendencies by examining the application and the source code.

3.6 Contact with Customer

We assume that students using test-first will think of requirements earlier, so they will also ask the customer more early and often. With classical-testing the development process is not primary focused on requirements, therefore students will ask later. Data regarding the customer contacts is gained by measuring the contact times and frequency.

4 Experimental Setup

We started our experiment with 19 graduate students in the middle of October 2004. The students knew that they were part of an experiment and were asked to fill out questionnaires, so we got an impression of their abilities and experiences.

4.1 Results of the Survey

All students had attended a software engineering course and 12 of them had prior knowledge of test-first. 16 students had knowledge of JUnit and understood how to use it. One student even used it in a professional way.

14 students had average or above average knowledge in Java, the remaining 5 students had at least some basic knowledge in Java. Only 3 students never used Eclipse. 7 participants only had experiences with software projects in university, 7 had an industrial project before (6 months maximum) and 5 designed software in a

professional way in the industry for many years. 12 students attended at least one meeting with a real customer before.

4.2 Groups and Schedule

We divided the group of 19 students into two smaller groups, 11 in the test-first group and 8 in the classical-testing group. Each group was again divided in teams of two people each, so we had 5 teams and a one-person team in the test-first group and 4 teams in the classical-testing group. All pairs were randomly composed.

Chronologically, the experiment was limited to the length of the winter semester. We had a total of 13 weeks and in each week the experiment session lasted 4 consecutive hours. The experiment took place in our computer lab (some sessions were dropped because of Christmas and New Year) and each student could get 6 credit points (ECTS) for participation.

The experiment itself was divided into 3 phases and the phases are described in the next subsections. Figure 2 shows the phases and the schedule of the experiment.

20.10.2004	27.10.2004 (I)	27.10.2004 (II)	27.10.2004 (III)	3.11.2004 - 26.1.2005	26.1.2005	2.2.2005
Introduction: Eclipse (all students)	Introduction: Test-first (11 students)	Introduction: FLOW (all students)	Introduction: Practical trail (all students)	10 weeks for development	Release of final version	Annoucement of empirical data
Testing with JUnit (all students)	Classical-testing (8 students)					
General Trail	Special Trail	Prog. Task Trail	Practical Trail			
Training phase				Development phase		Analysis phase

Fig. 2. Experiment's phases and schedule

4.3 Training Phase

The experiment started with a training phase being subdivided into four trails and which lasted two weeks:

General Trail (two hours): Every student attended the general trail. We started to show how to write a small "Hello World!" application using Eclipse. Later we presented how to the implement a stack in Java. At the same time we also showed some handy features of Eclipse. After we finished the implementation of the stack, we introduced the JUnit framework. First we gave some small general information about JUnit and then we showed how to write unit tests to test our implementation of the stack.

Special Trails (for each group one hour): In the special trails the two groups received a special training. Precisely, we showed both groups how to implement a small application converting decimal numbers to roman numbers (we took the idea from [8]). This was taught in the way they had to develop the programming task later. Therefore, the test-first group only got an introduction, how to develop this application using test-first. For the classical-testing group we first implemented the application and then wrote several use cases to test it.

Programming Task Trail (45 minutes): After the general trail and the special trails, we presented the programming task. All students attended this trail. The students should implement a library for FLOW in Java. FLOW is a research project in our department. The core idea of FLOW is to model flows of communication within projects which can be direct as well as indirect via documents.

Practical Trail (45 minutes): Before we started the real development phase, every team should make some practical programming experiences learned from the special trail. So we prepared a small programming task (implementation of an "isPrimeNumber-method") for every team.

4.4 Development Phase

The development phase has lasted 10 weeks in which the students should implement the FLOW library from scratch. In each session each team worked separately and implemented an own version of the library. Every session lasted 4 consecutive hours and after two hours we had a break of 15 minutes, so the students were "forced" to relax.

For each session we had basic rules to control the experiment and create an equal environment for everyone:

- Every team could only program in the four hours of every session, so conditions were equal for everyone.
- Students could not transfer any of the source code to another computer (e.g. via internet, disk or CD). This rule prevented, that some diligent students got an advantage over lazy students by programming at home. For the same reason we collected every story card, questionnaire and sketch drawn by the teams after each session. In the next session we handed the material out again.
- During the sessions every team had access to a library containing the documentation of the Java API, two online books about Java, one tutorial about Eclipse and JUnit, an introduction to the FLOW concepts and all documents and source codes from the different trails of the training phase. Besides, we restricted the access to the Internet, so students did not use their time for searching solutions for their programming problems on the Internet (and some students are very good in doing this).
- We asked the students not to talk about anything regarding the experiment with other participants of the experiment (except the team mate), because discussion about the experiment could influence the results. Of course this is very hard to control, because there is no way to avoid it. Therefore we only appeal to the student's honour.
- We avoided mentioning any results we observed in the experiment, because it could influence the students. We also avoided mentioning any opinions we had about the different test approaches. None of the participants knew any of our hypotheses.

– To avoid any competition between the teams students did not get a mark for the participation. Each student could earn the certificate and the credit points quite easily.

We included several XP techniques in our experimental setup as well, whereas they were not objects of investigations:

Pair Programming: Every team consisted of two students programming as a pair on a single workstation.

On-site Customer: We simulated an on-site customer who was available for question regarding the requirements of the FLOW library at any time during the experiment. Besides, we also offered an advisor being able to answer technical question, whereas the technical advisor could not answer any question regarding the customer requirements.

User Stories: Requirements were written on story cards by the on-site customer. Developers estimated the time they need to implement the functionality. Story cards were given in a fixed order, and the customer handed the story cards out in this order, so it was only necessary to estimate the time for implementation. Every story card contained at least one functionality. Our basic cycle for each story card was:

1. Hand out the next story card to a team.
2. The team started to implement the new functionality and asked the customer for an acceptance test if they thought that they tested enough (internally by unit tests) and implemented all the necessary features.
3. If the customer was satisfied with the functionality, we checked in the current state of the code in our CVS system and continued with step 1. If the customer was not satisfied the students had to continue with step 2.

4.5 Analysis Phase

In the analysis phase we present the empirical results of the experiment to the students. Since the experiment is not finished, the analysis phase has not been conducted so far.

4.6 Geometrical and Technical Setup

Due to the geometrical restrictions of our computer lab and the fact that all 19 students have to program at the same time we arranged our computer lab as shown in Figure 3.

Our lab was equipped with 10 workstations, each with a TFT screen. The operating system was Linux and an Eclipse platform (version 3.0) was installed on each workstation. For the experiment the computer lab was divided in 3 zones. On the left side the 6 test-first groups were placed. On the right side the classical-testing groups were placed. Discussions with the customer take place in the back of the computer lab or on the team's workplace.

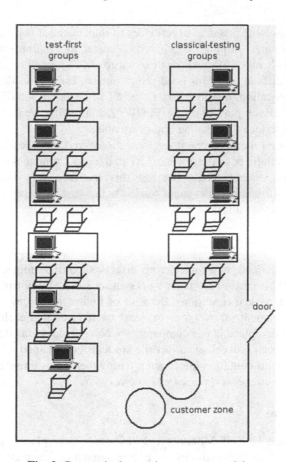

Fig. 3. Geometrical setup in our computer lab

5 Discussion

We designed the experiment in a way to avoid a number of mistakes we had in mind. Nevertheless we faced some problems while conducting the experiment.

5.1 The Programming Task

In the beginning we looked for one appropriate programming task. It should be testable, interesting for students and the result should be useful for our department at the same time. Our first thought was to avoid graphical user interface, because it is hard to test and will distract students into paying attention to a beautiful appearance of their application. We had the idea to develop a code metric plug-in for the Eclipse platform and formulate the unit tests with PDE JUnit which is an extension to the JUnit framework. Eclipse offers a lot of extensions-points reducing the effort to implement a graphical user interface to a minimum, so this task seemed to be appropriate.

After we made some practical experiences in implementing a plug-in, we cancelled this idea. Development of plug-ins is based on searching familiar solutions ("Monkey See/Monkey Do" rule [9]) and reading large API's, so that access to plug-in development is difficult even for good programmers. Finally we decided to turn to a normal Java application, due to the fact that all students are familiar with Java. The new idea was to develop a library for FLOW. Additionally, we demanded a minimal command line interface to make the library useable.

When we started the experiment we soon discovered that the idea of the minimal interface was a failure, because students invested a lot of time to design this interface. Furthermore, the students could not test this interface very well, so they were immediately confronted with some code being not testable in the way we demonstrated it in the trails.

5.2 Geometrical Setup

In a good experimental setup interfering effects should be minimized as much as possible. So in best case every team works in an isolated environment at the same time and under the same conditions. Because of limited resources we could not offer an isolated environment for everyone. At least we realized that each team could work at the same time and place in our computer lab. Nevertheless, this does not avoid, that students disturb each other (and in fact the students complained a little bit about the noise). Worse, teams could get information from other teams unintentionally, because the distance between the workplaces was not very far.

5.3 Workstations

In the first session all TFT-Monitors and keyboards were placed on one side of the table. We realized that this setup makes pair programming difficult, because only one student of a team could really develop. The other student's distance to TFT and keyboard was too far. We encouraged the students to change the seats after some time (they could decide this time), but this was difficult to control. Therefore, we put TFT and keyboard for the next sessions in middle of the table. After this both students equally participated on the development process and no further problems with pair programming occurred.

5.4 Students' Experiences with XP and Missing Seriousness

Lack of a serious background makes it difficult to conduct good experiments and software projects at universities. Students do not take practical courses in university seriously or often do not possess appropriate knowledge of agile or traditional development processes (and do not know the pains linked to this processes [10]). Therefore they often do not follow all the principles they learned in software engineering courses. To eliminate the missing knowledge our experiment included an introduction to testing, JUnit, test-first and traditional testing. Additionally, we offered unlimited aid regarding technical and software engineering problems. Nevertheless, we observed that students had difficulties to follow the test-first approach. Some teams integrated functionality in their application without writing the test-cases before. Because of the experimental setup we tried to interfere as little as possible in the development process. We only asked, why they write source code without writing the test-cases before. At least after some sessions all test-first teams followed the test-first approach quite well.

6 Conclusions

This paper presented an experimental setup to compare test-first to classical-testing. We observed how difficult it is to conduct a good experiment with students, mainly because of a lack of students' experiences with XP. From our point of view and our experiences we suggest:

- Start the experiment with a programming task being testable, especially when the students are inexperienced with XP. Avoid any (graphical) user interface in the beginning. We believe a library is a suitable programming task.
- Choose a serious and useful programming task, otherwise students will not take it seriously and the customer will not play their role seriously.
- When applying pair programming on one workstation make sure that both students can attend the development process (equally). For example by putting monitor, keyboard and mouse in the middle of the table or by changing the seats.
- Be aware that most students are not familiar with XP and do not know the drawbacks of traditional development processes. Therefore an extensive practical XP course before an experiment's start is an adequate possibility to avoid this. Maybe a complete change of mindset is necessary to perform XP techniques in an effective way?

Despite the problems we faced during design and conduction of the experiment, we presented a carefully designed experimental setup. We encourage computer scientist to think of other setups.

References

1. Beck, K.: *Extreme Programming Explained*. 2000: Addison-Wesley
2. Müller, M.M., Hagner, O.: *Experiment about Test-first programming*. IEEE Proceedings Software, 2002. **149**(5)
3. Müller, M.M., Tichy, W.F.: *Case Study: Extreme Programming in a University Environment*. in *International Conference on Software Engineering*. 2001. Toronto, Ontario, Canada: IEEE Computer Society
4. Noll, J., Atkinson, D.C.: *Comparing Extreme Programming to Traditional Development for Student Projects: A Case Study*. in *XP 2003*. 2003. Genova, Italy
5. Lindvall, M., et al.: *Empirical Findings in Agile Methods*. in *Extreme Programming and Agile Methods - XP/Agile Universe 2002*. 2002: Springer-Verlag
6. Basili, V., Caldiera, G., Rombach, H.: *Goal question metric paradigm*, in *Encyclopedia of Software Engineering*, J.J. Marciniak, Editor. 1994, John Wiley & Sons: New York. p. 528-532

7. Basili, V.R., Selby, R., Hutchens, D.: *Experimentation in Software Engineering*. IEEE Transactions on Software Engineering, 1986
8. Lipscombe,   R.:   Test   First: Roman   Numeral   Conversion, http://www.differentpla.net/node/view/58, 2004
9. Gamma, E., Beck, K.: *Contributing to eclipse Principles, Patterns and Plug-Ins*. the eclipse series, ed. E. Gamma, L. Nackman,J. Wiegand. 2004
10. Lappo, P.: *No Pain, No XP - Observations on Teaching and Mentoring Extreme Programming to University Students*. In *Conference on eXtreme Programming and Agile Proceses in Software Engineering*. 2002. Alghero Sardinia

Views from an Organization on How Agile Development Affects Its Collaboration with a Software Development Team

Harald Svensson[1] and Martin Höst[2]

[1] The Royal Institute of Technology, Forum 100,
SE-164 40 Kista, Sweden
[2] Lund University, Box 118, SE-221 00 Lund, Sweden

Abstract. The purpose of this study is to investigate how agile development affects collaboration in an organization. Agile processes have received interest from the software development community during the last years as they address changes, such as new customer requirements or re-prioritization of development tasks, which is important to manage in software development. Most of the research published about agile processes are based on opinions from teams applying these processes. However, since software development is an activity where many parties often collaborate, it is interesting to investigate from an organizational point of view, how agile development affects collaboration between these teams and their organizations. An agile process based on extreme programming, XP, was applied by a team during eight months. The team interacted with its surrounding organization regularly. People from the organization which the team collaborated with were interviewed to understand how the use of the process affected their collaboration with the team. The results show that the interviewed people perceived an improvement of their collaboration with the team, as the team started develop software in an agile way.

1 Introduction

Successful software development projects are characterized by project teams that collectively take responsibility of their engineering processes. Further, a team should recognize the team members' viewpoints on how team performance can be improved, as stated in [4]. This is also true when developing software, as confirmed in [7]. Software development projects of today are often large and involve a lot of people with different abilities. It is important to recognize their viewpoints on how collaboration can improve, in order to deliver fault free software on time. The study addresses this issue, by recognizing how an organization perceives its collaboration with a software development team.

Agile methods have received interest from the software development community during the last years, perhaps mainly due to the fact that they address changes which is important in software development. Agile methods emphasize

F. Bomarius and S. Komi-Sirviö (Eds.): PROFES 2005, LNCS 3547, pp. 487–501, 2005.

simple and direct communication as a means for improving software development results. Communication is facilitated as people sit close to each other, daily meetings are performed and charts on team performance are made visible. These aspects and more enable a simple and direct communication, which help manage changes in software development. Further, collaboration is based on communication as mentioned in [6]. Thus, the use of an agile process ought to improve collaboration in an organization, as agile methods facilitate communication. The purpose of the study is to investigate whether this is the case.

In the study, an agile process was introduced to a large organization with a complex software development environment, which included both support and maintenance of several systems. In these kinds of environments changes occur frequently such as new versions of requirements and re-prioritization of tasks. A team applied the agile process during eight months. The team wanted to improve its software development process by using this kind of process, as iterative development and an improved ability to handle changes were appealing to the team. The process was based on XP [1], but not identical to it since some parts of the process were not introduced and others were adapted to fit the team's development environment. The team collaborated with its surrounding organization to develop software.

This paper investigates how collaboration between a team and its surrounding organization was affected, from an organizational point of view, during introduction of an agile process. Most of the research published about agile processes are based on viewpoints from teams applying these processes, but this study provides input on how an organization considers use of an agile process. Hence, interviews were conducted with the organization on how it perceived its collaboration with the team before, during and after the process was introduced. The results of the study may help understand how agile development affects collaboration in organizations, seen from an organizational perspective. The study presented in this paper is part of a case study where the purpose was to investigate the effects of introducing an agile process based on XP to a large organization with a complex software development environment. The results presented in this paper concern how the surrounding organization perceived that their collaboration with the software development team changed as the agile process was introduced to the team. The results presented in [11] address the team's performance by analyzing quantitative data before and after the agile process was introduced. Finally, the results presented in [12] concern how the team perceived their use and adaptation of the agile process.

Section 2 contains related work and Section 3 presents the research methodology. In Section 4, the study context is described. Section 5 details the introduction of the agile process. Section 6 presents the research results. Section 7 summarizes the main conclusions from the study and Section 8 includes discussion of the results and future research.

2   Related Works

Most of the research concerning introduction and use of agile processes are based on opinions from the teams applying these processes, such as [6, 14, 8, 9]. However, as stated in [7] it is important to recognize viewpoints on improvement issues from different perspectives when developing software.

[10] reports on an Italian company who introduced XP in two projects. The company had recognized the fact that introducing an agile process into an organization affects more people than just the software engineers. The output from the study were experiences of introducing XP from a non-programmer's perspective. Three different perspectives were presented including viewpoints from project managers, customers and an quality assurance team. Two observations were made from the customer's point of view. First, customers tend not to accept requirements which are not written down. The customers representatives felt that it would be difficult getting contracts signed without formally specifying the requirements. The second observation was that people representing the customer did not own the customer's requirements. This meant that they sometimes lacked the authority or knowledge to resolve issues. Often, they had to contact the real customer and ask for advice. Further, this detachment of a real customer in the team reduced the emotional commitment from the customer. The project managers observed that XP allowed software engineers to maintain and enhance their programming abilities. That is, through practices such as *Pair Programming*, *Collective Code Ownership* and *Coding Standard* were the engineers supported to improve their skills in software development. The company was ISO 9001-certified, and the quality team observed that using XP improved the company's quality system by providing guidelines for project management. Further, the quality team noticed that XP focuses on a few key process aspects which allowed the software engineers freedom to customize the rest of their work processes. Therefore, the quality team concluded that XP can be adapted to fit the ISO 9001 framework.

To summarize, the non-programmer's perspective on using XP was that XP supports a software development team to improve its development skills. Further, XP is not a hinder for an organization pursuing a quality management system based on ISO 9001, as its contents can be adapted to the framework. However, it is important to have a real customer in a team to handle business issues when developing a system.

3   Research Methodology

This section presents the research method used when drawing conclusions on how the organization perceived the agile process' effect on its collaboration with the team. Further, the validity of the study is discussed. The study is conducted at a Swedish software development company, described in Section 4.

As stated earlier, collaboration is based on communication as confirmed in [6]. Further, agile methods facilitate communication in various aspects. For instance, new requirements are addressed through frequent and informal contacts with customers. Another example is the practices pair programming and planning game which are used as means for intensifying communication in software development teams. Based on this argument, we claim that agile development improves collaboration in an organization as agile methods facilitate communication. Thus, the research question is:

> *Hoe does use of an agile process affect collaboration in a software development organization?*

The term collaboration can mean different things to different people. Therefore, it is motivated to define what the term means in the study. As stated in [13] the concept of collaboration is often defined as communicative interaction, where trust is considered a critical success factor for improving collaboration. Trust is gained when mutual goals are achieved and when involved parties can rely on each other that joint activities will be performed as agreed. An increased trust is usually a sign of improved collaboration. In the study, the term collaboration is defined as working together where several parties may achieve something beyond what either would have achieved separately. This concept also involves trust. Thus, an improved collaboration is based on whether the organization perceived that it increased its trust to the team and that they performed better together than they did prior to the introduction of the agile process.

Further, how collaboration is affected due to the introduction of a software development process may be investigated in a number of ways. The approach that was chosen in the study was to interview people from the organization before, during and after the introduction of the process and perform an analysis of the recorded interviews, as described below. This approach had several advantages. First, since we had limited experience of how the team and its surrounding organization collaborated, it was difficult to know where on a more detailed level the research should be performed. For instance the collaboration efforts could be modelled in some sort of a communication path, but such approaches are based on an extensive knowledge how the team collaborates with its surrounding organization. Further, since there is little research performed on this issue there is a risk of missing important information if a more detailed research approach is chosen. The interview approach used in the study addresses this issue, since the interviewees provide information from different angles, based on their experiences. Hence, the risk of missing important information was reduced by performing interviews on the organization.

Customer representatives, which collaborated with the team, acted as intermediaries of the organization's viewpoint on how the agile process affected the organization's collaboration with the team. Although the results of the study are based on interviews with customer representatives, it is the organization's viewpoint that is gathered. The customer representatives had other work tasks than those that were customer related. Thus, they were part of the organization and should not be considered as customers. More information on the study participants is provided in Section 4.

The customer representatives were interviewed before, during and after the agile process was introduced. The number of customer representatives was three which is many in terms of number of customers in XP projects. Therefore, considering the nature of the study which concerns organizational input based on customer representatives involved in agile development projects, the number of study participants is adequate. Qualitative analyses were conducted on the interview results, and conclusions were drawn based on the analyses. The conclusions drawn before introducing the agile process, were compared with conclusions drawn during and after the process was introduced. Thus, any effects the agile process had on the collaboration between the customer representatives and the software development team was investigated.

A flexible qualitative design approach [2] was used for the research. Flexible means an evolving design which starts with a single idea or problem that the researcher seeks to understand. The study was explorative in character since it investigated how agile development may affect the collaboration between a software development team and its surrounding organization, which we had limited experience of. The procedure of drawing conclusions from the interviews followed the steps in the model [5] shown in Figure 1.

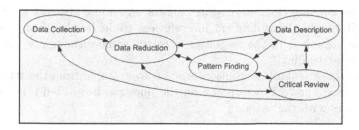

Fig. 1. A general model of qualitative studies

Below, the steps mentioned in Figure 1 are described in a detailed manner in order for the reader to better understand how the procedure for drawing conclusions from the interviews was conducted.

Data Collection. Data was collected through interviews. Three participants were interviewed. Each participant was interviewed three times, one time before the agile process was introduced, one time during introduction of the process and finally one time after the process was introduced. The length of the interviews ranged from approximately 10 to 30 minutes. The interviews were of the type open-guided interviews described in [5]. Open-guided interviews means a research question being enlightened by in advance planned question areas, where the interviewees can respond with open answers. Audio software was used to record the interviews. One person at a time was interviewed. Thus, personal opinions were not biased by other's opinions.

Data Reduction. To easier perform the analysis, the amount of data to be analyzed was reduced. The data reduction procedure was to remove sentences that did not address the research question. The recorded interviews were transcribed and reviewed.

To illustrate the data reduction process an example is provided from the study. The following text was recorded from an interview with one of the study participants. The text shown is a response on the question how the study participant communicates with the team.

> *Often I communicate with the team rather informally. It can be at a lunch or if I meet a team member in the corridor. Personally, I like that approach, formal meetings require preparation and take a lot of time.*

Here, the ambition is to recognize what parts of the text that refer to the research question. For instance, the fact that communication is of an informal nature is relevant to the question, thus that sentence is kept. However, the sentence where the respondent states his preference for informal communication does not address the question. Thus, that sentence is not kept.

Data Description. This step prepares data for analysis where possible conclusions may be drawn. By coding the data without loosing its meaning, a better overview of the data is provided. Each response's content is interpreted to a certain question, and characterized its content on a more abstract level in forms of codes. Responses from different interviewees could be classified to the same code, if the meanings of the responses were the same although not necessarily with the same wording.

To illustrate the data description process an example from the study is provided. The text shown is a response on the question how often the respondent communicates with the team.

> *Well, I communicate with the team a few times a week if I would make some kind of average guess. It is not every day at least.*

The response was replaced by the code *"Communication occurs a couple of times a week on average."* Thus, the text is described in a manner that better answers the research question.

Pattern Finding. The purpose of this step is to structure gathered data, in forms of codes, thus enabling reflection on how the codes correlate to each other and the research question. By seeking patterns in the data, conclusions may be drawn that answer the research question.

To illustrate how data can be ordered when seeking patterns an example is provided from the study. Table 1 presents two aspects of the research question. These aspects divide the research question into subparts which may help draw valid conclusions. The aspects were identified when interviewing the study participants. Each row in the table corresponds to codes from one study participant on experiences how his collaboration with the team changed, as the agile process was introduced. By viewing codes ordered in some form, patterns can be found which may provide a deeper understanding of the phenomenon studied.

Table 1. Experiences made by the organization when collaborating with the team

Team influence on collaboration	Organizational influence on collaboration
"The team provides better time estimates after the introduction of the agile process." "The team answers questions faster after the introduction of the agile process."	"Internal projects require much attention, which reduces available time to communicate with the team." "The organization does not understand terms used in the agile process, which makes communication with the team more difficult."

Critical Review. The last step of the qualitative data analysis process presented in Figure 1, is a critical review of the drawn conclusions. The purpose is to investigate if alternative interpretations and conclusions can be drawn. Thus, the validity of the conclusions is tried. The conclusions were reviewed subjectively by us, in an attempt to validate them.

3.1 Validity

A number of threats to flexible design studies that applied to the study, are mentioned in [2]. Description and respondent biases are threats that may affect the validity of results gained. Description refers to the risk of providing invalid descriptions of what you have seen or heard, based on inaccuracy or incompleteness of data. To counter this, audit trail was used. That is, the interviews were recorded with audio software, transcribed and stored electronically. Further, daily notations were written down to maintain a research log. Respondent bias refers to how respondents interact with the researcher, for instance providing answers they judge the researcher wants. To counter this, it was made clear to the study participants that our researcher role was neutral to whether the introduced process had any positive effects on the collaboration or not, thus they did not have to feel any pressure for liking or disliking the process. The countermeasures were subjectively considered to have a positive impact on the validity of the results.

4   The Study Context

This section includes presentations of the case company and the study participants.

4.1   The Company

The study was conducted at a Swedish software development company. About 1500 people are employed by the company. Out of these 1500 approximately 250 work as software developers. The case company develops and maintains more than 30 software systems, with several code tracks. In addition to this, a number of software releases are delivered to customers each year. Apart from developing new functionality the company also corrects, adapts and modifies software systems. Thus, the case company has an evolutionary and maintenance software development environment.

4.2   The Study Participants

The target population for the research was people in the organization that collaborated with the software development team. Three persons, acting as customer representatives, were chosen to participate in the study. To ensure that the study participants were representative of the target population, they were subjectively assessed through interviews before participating in the study. Two persons worked as project leaders, and the third as an interface to external customers by receiving requirement specifications, support issues and so forth. The project leaders worked with several software development teams, and they represented several customers. The third person who interacted regularly with external customers had daily meetings with teams to discuss development issues. The study participants had worked at the case company for about four years and they were all around 35 years old. Each participant was interviewed three times, to gain input on their views on the collaboration with the software development team before, during and after the agile process was introduced. Thus, there was in total nine interviews.

5   Introducing the Agile Process

This section provides an understanding on what was introduced and how it differed from the standard XP. This is important information when analyzing how the organization's attitude varied as the agile process was introduced to the team. The comparison between the introduced agile process and the standard XP is provided in Section 5.1. Further, changes in collaboration between the team and its surrounding organization as a result of introducing the agile process are identified. These changes are presented in Section 5.2.

The agile process was based on XP, but not identical to it. Not all of XP was introduced and some parts of XP were adapted to fit the team's development environment. Further, a large part of XP did not affect how the team developed software. Thus, efforts were spent on introducing the parts of XP that generated changes in the team's software development process.

The text in this section is structured as follows. First, the section contains a comparison between the introduced process and XP to clarify how the processes differ in content. Finally, changes in the organization's way to collaborate with the software development team are identified, as a result of introducing the agile process.

5.1   Comparing the Introduced Process to XP

Table 2 presents differences regarding the introduced agile process which the team applied versus the standard version of XP. The table contains the practices that were implemented differently than XP advocates.

Table 2. Differences regarding the agile process versus XP

Planning game does not include user stories. No customer is present during planning game.	Planning game includes user stories. Customer is present during planning game.
Pair programming is adapted. Software tasks are solved individually, but pairs meet regularly to discuss results.	Software is developed in pairs. Two persons shift places periodically, one writes and the other thinks strategically.
Coding standards are used for different systems.	One coding standard is used for all software development.
Simple designs may include needs for future integration of new functionality.	A simple design include what is needed for the moment.
Continuous testing covers only part of a system.	Continuous testing covers a whole system.
On-site customer is an internal customer representative, and is not part of the team and not available all the time.	On-site customer is a real customer and is part of the team and available all the time.
Continuous integration of a system occurs at least once a week.	Continuous integration of a system occurs at least once a day.

5.2   Changes in Collaboration Due to the Introduced Process

The introduced process changed how the team and its surrounding organization collaborated. Below, a summary of the practices that had most impact on how the team and its surrounding organization collaborated is presented. These practices were identified by interviewing people in the organization that collaborated with the software development team.

Planning Game. The planning aspect mentioned in the practice *Planning Game* was important for the team when collaborating with its surrounding organization. The organization's current and future needs were included in the team's planned software development releases. The practice *Planning Game* had a positive effect on the collaboration since it provided the organization with a better insight of the team's software development progress.

Small Releases. The team delivered new software releases to the organization, as covered by the practice *Small Releases*. To continuously release new versions of software was important in the collaboration between the team and its surrounding organization, since the organization was able to continuously review a system while it was being developed.

On-site Customer. The practice *On-site customer* addresses an important aspect that affected the collaboration between the team and its surrounding organization, and that is the role of the customer. The team discussed development issues with the customer representatives. These meetings acted as a communication channel between the team and the organization. The practice *On-site customer* had a positive effect on the collaboration between the team and its surrounding organization since it provided the organization and the team with means for discussing software development issues on a more detailed level.

The practice *40-hour week* addresses an important issue in software development projects, and that is time. The standard version of XP does not recommend working overtime more than a couple of weeks in a row. The team applied the practice whenever possible, but if something urgent needed to be solved the team worked overtime if necessary. Thus, the collaboration was not affected negatively seen from an organizational perspective, since the team was always available if necessary. However, if the practice would have been applied as advocated by the standard XP it is likely that the organization would had regarded this as negative due to the team's refusal of working overtime.

6   Results

The interview answers underwent qualitative analyses, according to the steps described in Section 3. The customer representatives were interviewed before, during and after the agile process was introduced. Based on these analyses a number of conclusions were drawn concerning collaboration issues between the team and its surrounding organization. Thus, the study investigated how agile development affected the collaboration between the team and its surrounding organization. The results are based on interviews with the customer representatives. That is, from an organizational point of view.

6.1   Conclusions Drawn Before Introducing the Agile Process

Below, conclusions are listed concerning collaboration issues between the team and its customer representatives before introducing the agile process.

1. The customer representatives feel that there is sufficient communication with the software development team.
2. The customer representatives do not trust that the software development team will deliver software when it has promised to.
3. The customer representatives feel that the software development team does not inform them about recent changes in work issues. The team should provide feedback more often to the customer representatives.
4. The customer representatives feel they provide the software development team with enough information so that the team can perform well with their issues.
5. There does not exist any formal way of communicating with the team. For instance, it varies which person in the team is contacted, how often and in which way.

6.2   Conclusions Drawn During Introduction of the Agile Process

Below, conclusions are listed concerning collaboration issues between the team and its customer representatives during introduction of the agile process.

1. The customer representatives feel that there is sufficient communication with the software development team.
2. Two of three customer representatives feel that the software development team has improved its ability of keeping delivery dates.
3. Two of three customer representatives feel that the software development team reduced the elapsed time before providing the customer representatives with answers.
4. The customer representatives feel that the software development team does not inform them about recent changes in work issues. The team should provide feedback more often to the customer representatives.
5. There does not exist any formal way of communicating with the team. For instance, it varies which person in the team is contacted, how often and in which way.

6.3   Conclusions Drawn After Introducing the Agile Process

Below, conclusions are listed concerning collaboration issues between the team and its customer representatives after introducing the agile process.

1. The customer representatives feel that there is sufficient communication with the software development team.
2. Two of three customer representatives feel that the software development team has improved its ability of keeping delivery dates.
3. Two of three customer representatives feel that the software development team reduced the elapsed time before providing them with answers.
4. Two of three customer representatives feel that the software development team informs them about recent changes in work issues.
5. The customer representatives feel that the software development team has improved its competence level and spread it throughout the team.
6. There does not exist any formal way of communicating with the team. For instance, it varies which person in the team is contacted, how often and in which way.

6.4   Trends Regarding the Collaboration Between the Team and Its Surrounding Organization

The text in this section presents trends regarding the organization's perception of how its collaboration with the team changed, as the team was introduced to the agile process. The trends regarding the organization's viewpoints are based on a subjective analysis of the drawn conclusions before, during and after the introduction of the agile process. The trends are shown in Table 3.

As shown in Table 3, the subjective analysis concluded that the organization perceived the introduction of the agile process positively. The team was considered more service-minded as it more often informed its surrounding organization with software development issues and answered more quickly on questions generated from the organization.

Table 3. Trends regarding collaboration issues between the team and its surrounding organization

There is sufficient communication between the team and its surrounding organization.	The introduction of the agile process did not affect how often the team and its surrounding organization communicated, according to the organization.
There does not exist any formal way of communication between the team and its surrounding organization.	The introduction of the agile process did not affect how the team and its surrounding organization communicated, according to the organization.
The organization feels that the team has improved its ability of keeping delivery dates.	The introduction of the agile process had an improvement of the team's ability to deliver software at agreed dates, according to the organization.
The organization feels that the team provides more feedback regarding software development issues.	The introduction of the agile process meant that the team more often informed the organization about software development issues, according to the organization.
The organization feels that the team has reduced the elapsed time before providing it with answers.	The introduction of the agile process meant that the team more quickly provided its surrounding organization with answers, according to the organization.

These positive aspects may be a result of the introduced changes in how the team developed software. As the team started to plan their work in detail they may have gained a better insight in how their work progressed and could therefore more easily inform the organization on software development issues. Further, the focus on the customer role may have made the team more service-minded and as the team started to discuss software development issues in pairs, knowledge was spread which made the team as a whole more competent.

7   Main Conclusions

Below, the main conclusions from the study are listed. They are subjectively derived and concern how agile development affects the collaboration between a software development team and its surrounding organization seen from an organizational point of view. The main conclusions are based on conclusions derived from interviews with customer representatives before, during and after the introduction of the agile process.

1. The introduction of the agile process did not affect the way or how often the customer representatives communicated with the software development team.
2. After introducing the agile process, the customer representatives perceived that the software development team responded to them with answers more quickly.

3. After introducing the agile process, the customer representatives increased their trust to the software development team.
4. After introducing the agile process, the customer representatives perceived that anyone in the team could more likely provide them with requested information when asked for.

The empirical data presented in this paper is based on subjective opinions of those interviewed. However, to better understand the effects of introducing the agile process, the quantitative data presented in [11] could be considered. An analysis of the data shows an improvement of productivity during the intro- duction of the agile process. Hence, we can argue that the introduction of the agile process had a positive effect, when referring to the analysis of the quantita- tive data. This conclusion supports the views of the customer representatives, as they argued that the team responded more quickly on questions and started to deliver software releases at agreed dates, when the agile process was introduced. Further, the customer representatives perceived that the team improved its level of knowledge, which surely affects the team's productivity in a positive way.

The effects from introducing the agile process presented in [12] is based on the team's viewpoint. As stated in [10] it is important to recognize different perspectives when introducing software development processes in organizations. The team's opinion was that the introduction of the agile process did not alter the way or how the team communicated with its surrounding organization. The team discussed software development issues with its customer representatives. The team perceived that the practice *Planning Game* improved its understanding how it should plan its work. However, contrary to what is advocated by the standard XP, the customer representatives did not participate in the planning game since they were busy and occupied with other work tasks. As stated in [1], the planning game is an important tool for communication between customer and software engineers. Thus, it is possible that the collaboration between the team and its surrounding organization would have been even better if the customer representatives would have participated in the planning game.

8   Discussion and Future Research

The results show that the introduction of the agile process had a positive affect on the collaboration between the software development team and its surrounding organization. A stated in the main conclusions, the organization did not perceive that it changed the way or how often it communicated with the team. Thus, the improved collaboration is a reaction of how the team changed its software de- velopment process. Earlier research mentioned in [13] has identified trust as a critical success factor in collaboration issues, which this research also supports. The organization increased its trust to the team as the team started deliver soft- ware at agreed dates and more frequently informed the organization regarding software development issues.

However, it is important to try to understand the underlying causes of why use of the agile process improved the collaboration between the team and its surrounding organization. A better understanding of this issue may help organizations realize how to introduce and adapt agile methods in order to maximize results from collaboration efforts. First of all, the fact that the team members were placed closer to each other probably played an important part, since this facilitated the team's communication. Another factor was the introduction of the pair programming concept, where pairs helped themselves solve software issues. In our opinion, this contributed to an increased transfer of knowledge within the team. The planning game resulted in better time estimations from the engineers which may have contributed to the increased level of trust to the team from the organization. These activities and many more resulted in an improved performance by the team which was recognized by the organization, as it received the benefits of how the team developed software.

The results indicate that this informal approach to communication between the customer representatives and the team facilitated use of the agile process. Informal communication [3] is characterized as casual, spontaneous and can for instance appear in the form of ad-hoc conversations or memos. The credibility of the contents may be low, but the speed when communicating is high. Formal communication on the other hand is characterized as deliberate and impersonal with a high credibility of contents, but with a low speed when communicating. The style is in form of reports, briefings, tables or diagrams and so forth. Further, formal communication can easily be reviewed and referenced to since its contents is under configuration control. Future research may investigate if agile methods perform best in environments where informal communication channels are used, or if software development results can improve as a result of introducing agile methods in environments where formal communication channels is the norm.

The overall conclusion from the case study is that the organization perceived that use of the agile process had a positive affect on its collaboration with the software development team. Although there is no ambition to generalize the results from the case study, they indicate that agile development facilitates collaboration between software development teams and their surrounding organizations. Hopefully, these results may inspire others to conduct research to further explore how agile development affects collaboration in organizations.

Acknowledgements

Many thanks to the study participants at the case company who were willing to share their experience regarding collaboration issues with a team using an agile software development process.

References

1. Beck, K.: Exreme Programming Explained - Embrace Change. Addison-Wesley. (2000)
2. Robson, C.: Real World Research - Second Edition. Blackwell Publishing Ltd. (2002)

3. Müller, R.: Communication of Information Technology Project Sponsors and Managers in Buyer-Seller Relationships. Henley Management College, Brunel University. (2003)
4. Katzenbach, J. R. and Smith, D. K.: The Wisdom of Teams - Creating the High-Performance Organization. Harperbusiness Essentials. (1993)
5. Lantz, A.: Intervjumetodik - Den professionellt genomförda intervjun (in Swedish). Studentlitteratur. (1993)
6. Abrahamsen, P.: Samarbete, samverkan, samvaro (in Swedish). SVENSKA FÖRLAGET liv & ledarskap ab. (2003)
7. Reifer, D.: How Good Are Agile Methods?. IEEE Software, Volume 19, Issue 4, 16–18, July-August (2002)
8. Grenning, J.: Launching Extreme Programming at a Process-Intensive Company. IEEE Software, Volume 18, Issue 6, 27–33, November-December (2001)
9. Schuh, P.: Recovery, Redemption, and Extreme Programming. IEEE Software, Volume 18, Issue 6, 34–41, November-December (2001)
10. Murro, O. and Roberto, D. and Giampiero, M.: Assessing XP at a European Internet Company. IEEE Software, Volume 20, Issue 3, 37–43, May-June (2003)
11. Svensson, H.: A Case Study on Introducing an Agile Process to the Industry. The International Conference on Empirical Assessment of Software Engineering (EASE'04), Edinburgh, Scotland. (2004)
12. Svensson, H. and Höst, M.: Introducing an Agile Process in a Software Maintenance and Evolution Organization. 9th IEEE European Conference on Software Maintenance and Reengineering, Manchester, UK. (2005)
13. Blomqvist, K. and Hurmelinna, P. and Seppnen, R.: Playing the collaboration game right - balancing trust and contracting. Technovation, Volume 25, Issue 5, 497–504, May (2004)
14. Rising, L. and Janoff, N. S.: The Scrum Software Development Process for Small Teams. IEEE Software, Volume 17, Issue 4, 26–32, July-August (2000)

Adapting PROFES for Use in an Agile Process: An Industry Experience Report

Andreas Jedlitschka[1], Dirk Hamann[1], Thomas Göhlert[2], and Astrid Schröder[2]

[1] Fraunhofer Institute for Experimental Software Engineering,
Sauerwiesen 6, 67661 Kaiserslautern Germany
{jedl, hamann}@iese.fraunhofer.de
[2] BMW Car IT GmbH,
Petuelring 116, 80809 München, Germany
Thomas.Goehlert@bmw-carit.de
Astrid.Schroeder@bmw.de

Abstract. Background: Agile methods are starting to get established not only in new business organizations, but also in organizations dealing with innovation and early product development in more traditional branches like automotive industry. Customers of those organizations demand a specified quality of the delivered products.
Objective: Adapt the PROFES Improvement Methodology for use in an industrial, agile process context, to ensure more predictable product quality.
Method: An explorative case study at BMW Car IT, which included several structured interviews with stakeholders such as customers and developers.
Result: Adapted PROFES methodology with regard to agility and initial product-process dependencies, which partially confirm some of the original PROFES findings.
Conclusion: The cost-value ratio of applying PROFES as an improvement methodology in an agile environment has to be carefully considered.

1 Introduction

Agile methods have a reputation for being faster, more customer-related, and more flexible in the case of unknown or changing requirements. As a result, agile methods are being established not only in new business organizations, but also in organizations dealing with innovation and early product development in more traditional branches, like automotive industry. Nevertheless, customers of those organizations demand a specified quality of the delivered product. It is here that software process improvement (SPI) promises to contribute to an organization's process maturity and, therefore, to obtaining stable and predictable product quality. Today, it is widely accepted that SPI, similarly to software development, has to be performed in a systematic and managed way. The PROFES (ESPRIT project no. 23239: "PROduct Focused improvement of Embedded Software processes") improvement methodology [1] provides a framework of methods and tools that supports industries in their product-driven process improvement. In contrast to traditional process-driven improvement

F. Bomarius and S. Komi-Sirviö (Eds.): PROFES 2005, LNCS 3547, pp. 502–516, 2005.
© Springer-Verlag Berlin Heidelberg 2005

approaches that are mostly based on process capability and maturity models (e.g., [2]), PROFES starts with the product and especially with product quality to identify improvement potential. The quality attributes are preferably defined by the customer and used to drive improvement activities. This does not mean that, for example, process assessments are not used, but they are not the only source for improvement initiatives. Another important aspect of the PROFES approach, and especially of the idea of systematically managing experience with technology application, is to base decisions on a comprehensible and documented basis, or, in other words, on empirical evidence [3], [4], [5].

On the other hand, agile software development approaches have also become more and more important today (e.g., [6]). Two of the main characteristics of agile development approaches are short cycle times and less documentation in usually small teams. Nevertheless, certain development activities including necessary documents are explicitly demanded and set up.

So far, not much experience exists in improving agile software development processes and maturity. Basically, two scenarios are possible for coming up with a software process improvement (SPI) approach for agile software development: a) define an agile-specific SPI approach from scratch, or b) use an existing SPI approach and adapt it to the specific needs of an agile approach.

For this work we have chosen the second scenario, since the aim of the company, BMW Car IT, was to get a pragmatic solution with early results. The main reason to do so was the expectation to come up with initial results in a shorter period of time. Therefore, an existing software process improvement approach was chosen as the starting point, namely PROFES, since it is especially designed for and used in the embedded domain (due to the automotive background of the company). Before PROFES could be used for an existing agile development process, PROFES had to be adapted.

Research question: Is PROFES, although developed as an improvement method for more traditional software development processes, transferable (after the typical, organization-specific adaptations) to an agile process environment?

To answer this question, we started with the identification of major quality issues and product-process dependencies across eight projects. With regard to the quality issues, we documented the shortcomings mentioned by the customers and provided related Goal-Question-Metric-based quality models. To identify product-process-dependencies (PPD), we performed structured interviews. The findings from the quality models and the PPD interviews were combined with information we were able to obtain from a previous CMMi assessment. This led us to the areas with major improvement potential. Finally, we extended the agile process framework with the necessary concepts to keep the PROFES continuous improvement cycle running.

The research question can be answered positively. In addition, we were able to confirm that PPDs found in traditional processes are also valid in agile processes.

The remainder of the paper is structured as follows. First, in chapter two, we give the necessary background to understand the case, a brief insight into the company, the development process at hand, and a sketch of the PROFES methodology. Chapter three gives a summary of related work. The methods used during the study are described in chapter four. The steps performed to adapt PROFES to the agile environment are shown in chapter five. In chapter six we summarize the main findings and present some lessons learned. The paper is concluded in chapter seven.

2 Background

Software has become a fast-growing element in the modern automotive industry (c.f., Fig. 1). During the next few years, the effort for research and development (R&D) of software-based functions will surpass the one for pure electronic R&D. Searching for a better position to meet the challenges of the next decades, the BMW Group founded BMW Car IT in 2002 as a competence center for automotive-specific IT know-how. The task of BMW Car IT is to identify, evaluate, and integrate software-based technologies and methods for and in the BMW Group development process. Therefore, three subgroups are concentrating on different aspects of information technology in the automobile. The Man-Machine-Interface (MMI) group is researching methods and processes enabling the efficient development of MMIs. The second group works on integrated data management to support abstract communication and interaction of car functions. The research on concepts to modify or upgrade software after the cars have left the manufacturing base is done in the software transfer group. Important aspects are coordinated authorized access in different areas of security as well as the guarantee for consistency after changes take place. These fields of research at BMW Car IT are the prerequisite to enable software as a product in the automotive industry.

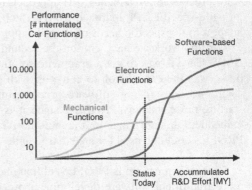

Fig. 1. Potential of Software Technologies

2.1 The Process Context

Influenced by traditional software process improvement teaching, the need for stable and predictable processes was identified. The mission for innovation and the vagueness of customer requirements were accepted as main influencing factors for the targeted development process. To establish such a process, a separate project was started to identify possibilities and assess them for the specific demands. Therefore, and to support the business process, different approaches

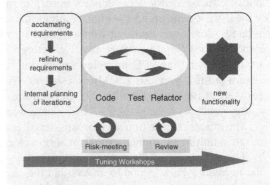

Fig. 2. The agile process at BMW CarIT

ranging from agile methods like "XP" to traditional approaches like the "V-Model" were taken into account. It was found that due to the need for flexibility with regard to customer requirements, fast delivery of first product versions, and involvement of the customer, an agile model will fit the needs best. Nevertheless, it was not the aim to instantiate the Agile Manifesto [7] as is, but a combination of techniques from different agile approaches (mainly XP, but also FDD and Scrum) is needed. The process, as depicted in Fig. 2, uses iterative development with preparation similar to the planning game, selective pair programming, unit tests, refactoring, and acceptance tests.

2.2 The SPI Context: PROFES Methodology in a Nutshell

After having applied the process for half a year, a CMMi assessment found some improvement potential. The company's goal to achieve higher quality complies with the target to fulfill CMMi requirements, but the question was how to find an integrated and proper approach for this company to apply, monitor, and assess the improvement actions. Therefore, a flexible but comprehensive improvement approach was needed. The decision for an existing approach was made between the IDEAL (Initiating, Diagnosing, Establishing, Acting, Learning) approach [8], and the PROFES approach [1]. Since the IDEAL approach was not explicitly defined for the embedded domain and defines SPI activities mainly based on the results of a CMM-based software process assessment, the PROFES approach was chosen as the basis for the agile SPI approach.

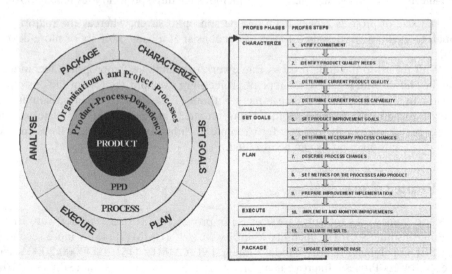

Fig. 3. The PROFES Improvement Methodology

The PROFES improvement methodology [1], [9], [10] uses a modified version of the Quality Improvement Paradigm (QIP) [11]. To illustrate and emphasize the importance of the product as a driver for process improvement, it is placed into the center of the PROFES improvement circle (see Fig.3). The product is the starting point for any improvement activities, starting with the identification of the product quality needs and the determination of the preliminary product quality goals. Product-Process-Dependencies (PPD) [12], [13] form the linking element between the product and the product development processes. PPD models are used to find and determine the required process changes such that stated product quality improvement goals are achieved. The PROFES improvement methodology consists of six phases, which are further refined into twelve steps. The phases are depicted in Fig. 3. A detailed description can be found in [1].

2.3 Project Context

Projects at BMW Car IT deliver mainly textual documents, containing concepts, feasibility studies, and proof of concept. The evidence is shown by developing (throwaway) prototypes that will, as such, not be used in production. To better understand the context, we give a brief categorization of the projects. In contrast to pure software development, the customer of BMW Cat IT is mainly interested in the transfer of knowledge, which is typical for R&D organizations. Four different types of projects occur:

- *Feasibility study*, which is an evaluation of solutions regarding realizability
- *Specification*, e.g., of software to be delivered from externals
- *Prototype*, which is a proof of concept of the previous deliverables
- *Concept*, which is a detailed description of a solution for a given problem with alternatives and evaluation. Concept includes the three project types listed above.

The size of projects ranges from one person up to seven, whereas the majority is small to medium-sized; only a few projects consist of a number of six or more developers.

With regard to the agile process framework of techniques, appropriate techniques can be chosen with regard to the type of project. For example, the role of the customer varies. In projects initiated by customers without IT background, many assumptions must be made without the customer being on-site. This changes if the customer directly participates in the project, for example with his own developers. Thus, in the first case a customer proxy can be installed.

3 Related Work

Generic frameworks for Software Process Improvement (SPI) are the Software Engineering Institute's (SEI) Capability Maturity Model® (CMM)[1] [14], or more recently, the SEI Capability Maturity Model® Integrated (CMMI)[2] [15], ISO9000:2000[3], and the Software Process Improvement and Capability Determination (SPICE)[4] [16]. These frameworks are standards for assessing organizational and software process maturity. They can be used for benchmarking against an ideal set of requirements. But they do not propose concrete SE techniques to be used in specific project situations.

---

[1] http://www.sei.cmu.edu/cmm/cmm.html
[2] http://www.sei.cmu.edu/cmmi/
[3] http://www.iso.ch/iso/en/iso9000-14000/iso9000/iso9000index.html
[4] http://www.sqi.gu.edu.au/spice/

Traditional SPI approaches are thought of as being related to plan-driven development processes.

The most prominent continuous SPI approaches are SEI's IDEAL Model [17] and the QIP, which can be seen as the software engineering equivalent of Total Quality Management [18]. The aim for continuity is reflected through the cyclic nature of the above mentioned improvement approaches. The relation between PROFES and QIP was mentioned before.

Recently, "revolutionary" approaches are coming up, especially in the area of the Internet. They tackle what they call the "bureaucracy" by moving the human factor (communication) into the main focus. To facilitate reading, we summarize all those approaches under the name "agile methods". A recent survey is given in [19]. Nevertheless, according to Boehm [6] a liberal interpretation of CMMI includes agile methods.

Traditional as well as agile methods have to overcome issues like short time to market, frequently changing requirements, low budgets, and high quality demands. Addressing desires such as speeding up software development (more software parts with fewer staff in shorter time) and dealing with vague requirements (late changes) Manhart & Schneider [20] added single agile practices (e.g., test first) to their QIP-based process improvement toolbox.

In addition, there is a lot of research going on to replace ore enrich traditional techniques with those compatible with agile development. Especially in the area of measurements [21], [22], [23], [24] and [25] have given much attention to retrospective-like practices.

The main difference between Manhard & Schneider's work and the work presented here is the starting point. They started with the traditional software development process, including process improvement, and brought agile aspects into that framework to improve the development process. Our work started from a given agile process framework and the task was to show how a "traditional" process improvement method (PROFES) can support higher product quality and learning from experience.

4 Research Method

The research approach can be summarized as follows. First, we performed a survey among eight experts on the customer site of BMW Car IT (*customer interviews*). Each expert is a customer's representative responsible for one project at the customer site. These experts are the most important stakeholders and have the broadest quality overview regarding requirements and issues. Out of the eight customer projects, six had already finished the starting phase. One project had just been started, whereas another one was just finished. The aim of this survey was to identify relevant product qualities and related characteristics from a customer perspective. The interviews were structured as follows: After some initial questions, we asked for the expected deliverables. For each deliverable, we asked for positive as well as negative experience related to quality. We concluded with questions related to the customer's quality requirements.

For the purpose of finding initial PPDs we used goal-oriented interviews based on the well-known Goal-Question-Metric (GQM) method [26] (*PPD interviews*). We interviewed four senior employees of BMW Car IT (two project leaders, one technical coordinator, and one developer). For each goal we interviewed each person; additionally, we interviewed two persons each for the project types *prototype* and *concept*.

To find further details and to evaluate the initial findings, we conducted five additional interviews. The interviews were comparable to retrospectives. We confronted the project members with the quality requirements and issues of the customer (our findings from the *customer interviews*). Thus, we asked, e.g., how did you achieve customer satisfaction, or how will you avoid this problem in the future. This led to concrete techniques and more detailed PPDs. Table 1 gives an overview of the sequence of the interviews.

Table 1. Sequence of interviews

Step	# Interviews	Interviewees	Purpose of the Interview
1	8	Experts on customer site	Identify product qualities and related characteristics
2	4+4	Senior employees	Identify initial PPDs
3	5	Project members	Evaluate the initial findings

With regard to the acquisition and evaluation of the PPDs, a more quantitative analysis of the projects was not possible, since a measurement program was not in place before.

5   Adapting PROFES for Use in an Agile Environment

Before describing what has been done, we give some restrictions. Some are due to practical reasons, whereas others are due to time restrictions. The first step was to decide whether PROFES should be applied in a specific project (bottom-up) or whether it should be applied across projects (top-down) right from the beginning. Taking into account the inhomogeneity of the projects in that company, yielding transferability issues, it was decided to start top-down. Due to time restrictions we skipped phases four (execute) and five (analyze). In phase three, we suggested how to adapt the development process to support PROFES in future.

5.1   Product Quality Criteria

For the analysis of the first series of the *customer interviews*, we distinguish between the *concept* and *prototype* project types and categorized the quality criteria accordingly. We found that some requirements and issues are valid for both types of projects, so they were assigned to the category *generic*. Since the company is working in the area of software, we used ISO 9126 as a starting point and extended the given criteria with company-specific criteria like "development time" and "cooperation". The first one was already addressed in PROFES, whereas the latter one is a new but very important one in this context. Both of them are valid across the company's products (projects). Other criteria, like functionality and usability, are more specifically related to the type of project.

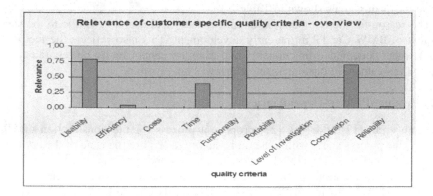

Fig. 4. Overview - distribution of the quality criteria relevance

Fig.4 gives a summary of the analysis of the customer survey. The x-axis depicts the extended list of quality criteria and the y-axis shows the relevance. The relevance is the standardization of the weighted customer statements consisting of number and kind (fulfilled, unfulfilled, wished, and unimportant).

In contrast to the original PROFES approach, where for each project the quality attributes have to be acquired in advance, in the context of R&D, quality and project goals are a matter of evolution, and thus difficult to obtain in advance. In addition, because of the innovative character of R&D projects, the knowledge about what will happen might have a lower level than in more traditional software development.

Table 2. Quality characteristics chosen for further investigation and number of related PPDs found during the interviews

Quality characteristic	Operational problem area	# PPDs
Collaboration	Communication	8
	Infrastructure	
	Controlling	
	Risk management	
Time	Time divergences	9
	Customer overview	
Functionality & Usability	Innovation / Feasibility	7
	Suitability / Understandability	

Within this work, we did not explicitly perform a process assessment as described in PROFES step 4 to identify further process improvement potential. Instead, we used information from a CMMi assessment that was performed during the year before our work started. The identified weaknesses in addition to the findings from the customer interviews were used as a basis for the definition of the improvement goals.

Based on the customer interviews and the results from the CMMi assessment, we chose the quality goals shown in Table 2.

The reason for the combination of functionality and usability is due to the special context of BMW Car IT in the early development. This also reflects the fact that in requirement documents, functionality and usability cannot really be separated, so an explicit assignment of customer statements was not possible.

5.2 Product-Process-Dependencies

Hamann et al. [12] and Birk [27] propose a process for the construction of PPDs. Ideally, the process starts with a literature survey to acquire the state of the art and the state of the practice. In parallel, expert interviews and analysis of existing data are used to get organization-specific information. The theoretical and practical information is combined into initial PPD models. During its life cycle, the PPD is continuously evolved and evaluated (if applied).

For the purpose of this project, we used the analysis of the *PPD interviews*, which yielded initial quality models and more concrete insights with regard to problems. We found eight PPDs for *collaboration*, nine PPDs for *time*, and seven PPDs for *functionality & usability*. These PPDs are already in use and have shown their applicability in different projects (up to four) (c.f. Table 2). Additionally, we found detailed information with regard to metrics.

Further on, we analyzed the PPDs found during the PROFES project with respect to their transferability into this organization. We found four PPDs (candidates), from which two have already been successfully applied, among them a PPD related to development time, which is positively influenced (shortened) by having project and iteration planning installed.

Further investigation of the PPDs provided by the PROFES project yielded few operational results; in most cases, the context was not provided in a way that would have allowed a goal-oriented selection. A comparison with the PPDs developed from the interviews showed that they can be seen as operationalization of the abstract PROFES PPDs that were candidates for this environment. For those PPDs that could not be operationalized, detailed investigation will be done in future projects. In the case of design and requirements PPDs, work has already started. That was the reason for separating the relevant PPDs into two groups: those that are applicable directly, and those that have to be detailed further.

5.2.1 The Influence of Context Factors on PPD Evolution

Many authors have already discussed the need of context factors. Birk describes a two-layer model with different abstraction levels based on taxonomies, e.g., for processes [27]. In many cases, information about the company, like domain, size, etc. as well as project and team characteristics are used to describe the context in which a certain technology has been applied in.

Since this work was performed in a project organization, we started with the characterization of the projects. On this level the more general context factors describe the kind of project, (1) the definition of work, (2) the number of team members, (3) the number of stakeholders, (4) the responsible group, and (5) the proximity to production. The context factor definition of work is a four-dimensional vector, whose axes are related to the proportions of conceptual work, coding, theoretical investigation, and demonstration. Each axis has four possible values: none, low, medium, and high. These factors were provided by the interviewees for their specific project. Later on, the more technology-specific factors were acquired, for example, what Jedlitschka et al. [4] call pre-condition for the application of the technology.

The interviews with experts, such as project managers and leading developers, yielded context factors, technology experience, and best practices. Due to the clarity of the process, the relationship between PPD and process area was implicit.

PPDs found in this company differ from the PROFES PPDs [1], especially in the handling of context factors. To allow us to also learn from negative experience, we extended the status of context factors. A context factor can also be "negatively validated". Additionally, we do not only have a single context model for one PPD, but a separate context model for each single application. This gives us the opportunity to provide "historic" information and assures that we do not loose information through the process of aggregation. Nevertheless, we provide aggregated context information to the user, thus not overloading him with unnecessary information. Additionally, we do have descriptions of the contexts in which a PPD has been applied, and so we are able to validate them on different levels.

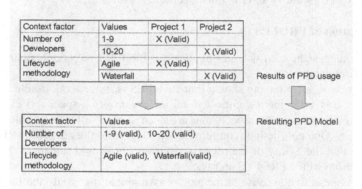

Fig. 5. Resulting problems of simple context aggregation

The example given in Fig.5 depicts the problem that would arise with "simple" aggregation of context factors. Assume we would have applied a certain technique in two different projects, *Project 1* and *Project 2*. The technique was applied successfully in *Project 1* using an agile life cycle method and eight developers. The same technique was also successfully applied in a waterfall-driven project with 19 developers. "Simple" aggregation would lead to the assumption that the technique is also applicable in a project within an agile environment and with a team consisting of 18 persons, or vice-versa. Although validated in their specific combination, the new combination is only a hypothesis and not validated yet. By taking the "history" into account, we help the decision maker not to be trapped by misleading assumptions.

The downside of this approach is that we have to explicitly deal with contradictory findings. One reason, especially for contradictions over a longer time-span, might lay in the evolution of the organization. If there are contradictions, the reason is in the application itself or within the relationships of the context factors; the discriminating one is missing. In this case we suggest a careful investigation of the context factors, e.g., through technology reviews, followed by aggregation supported by the technology experts. Returning to the given example, the PPD could be separated considering the lifecycle as a separating context factor. The conclusion is that only those PPDs can be aggregated (automatically) that vary in the instances for only one context factor. Additionally, we need to differentiate between the levels of validity; a PPD that has been applied successfully, e.g., eight times, has a greater validity than one that has only been applied once.

5.2.2 PPD Repository
In contrast to the original PROFES approach where the PPDs are stored in a database-driven repository, the PPDs are stored in a *Wiki*[5]. This allows distributed "content (PPD) management", since everyone is allowed to provide information. In general, the process team hosts the *Wiki* and supports people with their PPD-related work. Especially in case of contradictions, the process team acts as "mediator", thus is responsible for resolving the contradiction as mentioned above. This very open solution might only fit an organization with smoothly cooperating developers where security is not a big issue. We are well aware that for bigger organizations and those with more separated projects, security and PPD management are an issue.

5.3 Adaptation of PROFES

Finally, we suggest how to use and evolve the PROFES methodology in the agile process environment.

The main issue, after having shown that PROFES is, in general, usable in an agile environment, and after having collected initial organization-specific PPDs, was to extend the agile process with aspects that are necessary in order to be able to benefit from PROFES. One conflicting requirement with regard to the adaptation of the agile process was that the agility of the process environment should remain. This required some adaptations of the PROFES approach.

The first issue is that because of the agile environment, the goals and therefore the quality attributes are not fixed from the beginning. The goals are to be defined during the project itself. The original PROFES approach requires the goals right from the beginning, since they are used to perform the goal-oriented tailoring, that is, selection of the right technology taking the quality goals into account.

The second issue is that the iterations are very short, i.e., on average six weeks, which makes it very hard to fulfill all PROFES steps. Nevertheless, we found that many projects have a rough plan that spans more than one iteration, especially if the project has already been running for some time.

---

[5] *Wiki* is in Ward's original description: The simplest online database that could possibly work. *Wiki* is a piece of server software that allows users to freely create and edit Web page content using any Web browser. *Wiki* supports hyperlinks and has a simple text syntax for creating new pages and cross links between internal pages on the fly [from http://wiki.org/wiki.cgi?WhatIsWiki].

The third issue is that the projects do not have the resources to deal with formal PPD construction. In some cases, when, for instance, a new technique was applied, PPD construction is implicitly done, but the formal description has to be supported by the organization, i.e., the process team.

Fig.6 depicts the extension of PROFES with regard to the agile environment. Whereas the standard PROFES methods can be applied on the organizational level and on the project level, we found that on iteration or group level, some more "light-weighted" methods are to be used.

Based on these circumstances, we suggest to adapt PROFES as follows:

- In the phase *start of project* after the initial requirements elicitation, the initial goals for the project are available. Based on these goals, it is possible to apply PROFES. In this phase we propose to use "heavy-weighted" activities like assessments, but also the preparation and enactment of a measurement plan.
- In the subsequent iterations, the application of PROFES is useful if important aspects have been changed, e.g., quality goals. In the beginning of the projects, this occurs quite often, so the suggestion is to use only "light-weighted" PROFES aspects, like interviews with customers and usage of an online PPD repository. For now, the company has decided to use regular requirements meetings and resulting lists of requirements and issues to track product quality from a customer perspective. These lists are also used to select appropriate techniques. After having applied the technique, the application experience has to be stored in the *Wiki*.

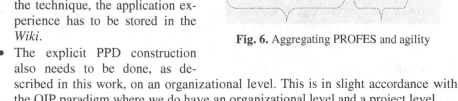

Fig. 6. Aggregating PROFES and agility

- The explicit PPD construction also needs to be done, as described in this work, on an organizational level. This is in slight accordance with the QIP paradigm where we do have an organizational level and a project level.

6 Main Achievements and Lessons Learned

Based on the work presented here, we present results for four perspectives.

For the PROFES perspective, we have provided evidence that PROFES is highly adaptable because of its flexibility in using the underlying methods and technologies. A more comprehensive guideline with references to known alternatives would be helpful, but could not replace an introduction-/adaptation phase of PROFES in a new organization. Ideally, the target process is also adapted to improve the integration of PROFES. This includes, for instance, a higher documentation effort for the developer, or the extension of the project cycle by an additional iteration cycle.

For improving PROFES, we suggest to

- consider negative experience as valuable for being stored in the PPDs
- extend the customer-oriented view of PROFES beyond the product quality horizon with aspects like quality of cooperation if there is an influence on the product quality

For the agile perspective, we found that the proposed approach supports learning. Traditionally, agile environments heavily depend on interpersonal communication (socialization [28]) to transfer knowledge. The approach proposed here extends this kind of communication by active knowledge elicitation, i.e., by using interviews, and the publication of this knowledge within PPDs. In cases where "light-weight" is not the key issue, continuous assessments [29], in comparison to traditional assessments, reduce the effort (time and resources) needed for assessments [30] and thus contribute to the agile idea.

For the organization perspective, we found that:

- the primary benefit is the exploration of the customer quality requirements, and the integrated way of achieving their fulfillment.
- PROFES assists in the development of a learning organization, which is a critical success factor for the evolution of an organization, especially in R&D.
- the need for achieving higher capability or maturity levels in a process becomes a more sophisticated aspect. This helps to invest available resources in product quality-related processes in a goal-oriented manner with respect to the organizational needs.

From a customer perspective, we found that:

- the integration of the customer in product quality improvement gives him the chance to articulate his quality requirements explicitly, but he also assumes the risk of failure if he does not do so.
- through the methodological assistance, it becomes easier to formulate product quality requirements that are easier to understand and realize by developers.

7 Summary

With this work we have shown that PROFES as an improvement method can be applied in an agile environment. The adaptation of PROFES to the organization-specific requirements did not exceed the expected effort. Besides this finding and the acquisition of the initial PPDs, some of the original PROFES PPDs were revalidated. So we have at least initial indicators that techniques are transferable between traditional and agile environments.

Adaptations with regard to the agile process framework were necessary in the area of measurement and documentation. We did not start a dedicated measurement program (although measurement is also a topic in agile environments); instead, we proposed retrospectives using the quality models to track progress and quality, and to discuss the usability of PPDs. To overcome the issue of documentation in agile environments, we proposed a *Wiki*-based PPD infrastructure.

The experience we made at BMW Car IT show that combining PROFES with an agile approach is possible and useful, although, it requires some effort, in particular, when the issue is to keep the resulting process possible as "light-weighted" as possible. At BMW Car IT, we use process review meetings at the end of each iteration to reflect upon and document the context factors under which certain best practices did or did not work. In summary, the cost-value ratio of applying PROFES in an agile environment has to be carefully considered.

Acknowledgements

We would like to thank all interviewees at the customer site who have contributed to the success of this work by providing their expert knowledge. Without their support, this work would not have been possible. We would also like to thank Dietmar Pfahl for fruitful discussions and the anonymous reviewers for giving valuable feedback, thus helping to improve the paper. Furthermore, we are grateful to Sonnhild Namingha from the Fraunhofer Institute for Experimental Software Engineering for reviewing a previous version of this paper.

References

[1] The PROFES Consortium. The PROFES User Manual. Fraunhofer IRB Verlag, Stuttgart, Germany, 1999.
[2] CMMI Product Team. Capability Maturity Model Integration CMMI, Version 1.1 CMMI for Systems Engineering and Software Engineering (CMMI-SE/SW, V1.1) Staged Representation. Technical Report CMU/SEI-2002-TR-002, Software Engineering Institute, Carnegie Mellon University, Pittsburgh, Pennsylvania 15213, December 2001.
[3] Kitchenham, B.A.; Dybå, T.; Jørgensen, M.; "Evidence-based Software Engineering", in Proc. Intern. Conf. on Software Engineering, May 2004 Edinburgh, Scotland, UK, pp. 273-281
[4] A. Jedlitschka; D. Pfahl, and F. Bomarius: "A Framework for Comprehensive Experience-based Decision Support for Software Engineering Technology Selection"; In Proc. of Intern. Conf. SEKE 2004. Banff, Canada, 2004, pp. 342-345
[5] A. Jedlitschka; M. Ciolkowski: Towards Evidence in Software Engineering; In Proc. of ACM/IEEE ISESE 2004, Redondo Beach, California, August 2004, IEEE CS, 2004
[6] B.Boehm; Get Ready For Agile Methods With Care; Computer, Vol. 35, 2002, pp.64-69,
[7] Agile Alliance. Manifesto for Agile Software Development, http://www.agilemanifesto. org, 2001
[8] B. McFeeley. IDEAL: A User's Guide for Software Process Improvement. Handbook CMU/SEI-96-HB-001, Software Engineering Institute, Carnegie Mellon University, Pittsburgh, Pennsylvania 15213, February 1996.
[9] A. Birk, J. Järvinen, S. Komi-Sirviö, P. Kuvaja, M. Oivo, and D. Pfahl. PROFES – A Product Driven Process Improvement Methodology. In Proceedings of the Fourth European Conference on Software Process Improvement (SPI '98), Monte Carlo, Monaco, Dec 1998.
[10] M. Oivo, A. Birk, S. Komi-Sirviö, P. Kuvaja, and R. v. Solingen. Establishing Product Process Dependencies in SPI. In Proceedings of the European Software Engineering Process Group Conference 1999 – European SEPG99, Amsterdam, The Netherlands, June 1999.

[11] V.R. Basili, G. Caldiera, and H.D. Rombach: Experience Factory; in: Marciniak JJ (ed.), Encyclopedia of Software Engineering, Vol. 1, pp. 511-519, John Wiley & Sons, 2001.

[12] D. Hamann, J. Järvinen, A. Birk, and D. Pfahl. A Product–Process Dependency Definition Method. In Proceedings of the 24th EUROMICRO Conference: Workshop on Software Process and Product Improvement, Volume II, pages 898–904, Västerås, Sweden, August 1998. IEEE Computer Society Press.

[13] D. Hamann, J. Järvinen, M. Oivo, and D. Pfahl. Experience with explicit modelling of relationships between process and product quality. In Proceedings of the Fourth European Conference on Software Process Improvement (SPI '98), Monte Carlo, Monaco, Dec.1998.

[14] Jalote, P.; "CMM in Practice. Processes for Executing Software Projects at Infosys" Addison-Wesley, Reading; 1999.

[15] Chrissis, M. B.; Konrad, M.; Shrum, S.; "CMMI. Guidelines for Process Integration and Product Improvement"; Addison-Wesley, Boston; 2003,

[16] El Emam,K.; Drouin,J.-N.; Melo,W. (Eds.); "SPICE. The Theory and Practice of Software Process Improvement and Capability Determination"; IEEE CS, Los Alamitos, 1998.

[17] Gremba, J.; Myers, C.: "The IDEALSM Model: A Practical Guide for Improvement" in Software Engineering Institute (SEI) publication, Bridge, issue three, 1997.

[18] S.K.M. Ho; TQM – An integrated approach; School of Business, Hongkong Baptist University; 1999

[19] P. Abrahamsson, O. Salo, J. Ronkainen, and J. Warsta. Agile Software Development Methods. Review and Analysis. VTT publications 478, VTT Electronics, Espoo, Finland, 2002.

[20] P. Manhart, K. Schneider: Breaking the Ice for Agile Development of Embedded Software: An Industry Experience Report; IN Proc. Of the 26th Intern. Conf. on Software Engineering (ICSE'04), Mai 2004, Edinburgh, Scotland, pp 378-386

[21] M. Visconti and C. R. Cook. An Ideal Process Model for Agile Methods. PROFES 2004, pages 431–441.

[22] A. Birk, T. Dingsoyr, T. Stalhane; Postmortem: never leave a project without it; IEEE Software, Vol. 19 , Issue: 3 , May-June 2002, pp. 43 - 45

[23] J. Kerievsky. Continuous Learning, Proc XP. 2001.

[24] C. T. Collins and R. W. Miller. Adaption: Xp style, Proc XP. 2001.

[25] T. Dingsøyr and G. K. Hanssen, Extending Agile Methods: Postmortem Reviews as Extended Feedback, Learning Software Organizations Workshop, Chicago, Illinois, USA, 2002

[26] V.R. Basili, G. Caldiera, and H.D. Rombach: Goal Question Metric Paradigm; in: Marciniak JJ (ed.), Encyclopedia of Software Engineering, Vol. 1, pp. 528–532, John Wiley & Sons, 2001.

[27] A. Birk: A Knowledge Management Infrastructure for Systematic Improvement in Software Engineering; Ph. D. diss., Dept. of Computer Science, University of Kaiserslautern, Germany; Stuttgart: Fraunhofer IRB Verlag; 2000.

[28] I. Nonaka, H. Takeuchi. The Knowledge-Creating Company: How Japanese Companies Create the Dynamics of Innovation. Oxford University Press, New York 1995.

[29] J. Järvinen. Measurement based continuous assessment for software engineering processes. PhD thesis, VTT Publications, Technical Research Centre of Finland, 2000.

[30] J. Järvinen and R. v. Solingen. Establishing continuous assessment using measurements, in Proc. of the 1st International Conference on Product Focused Software Process Improvement 8PROFES'99), Oulu, Finland, June 22-24. 1999, pp. 49-67

Agile Hour: Teaching XP Skills to Students and IT Professionals

Daniel Lübke and Kurt Schneider

University Hannover
{daniel.luebke, kurt.schneider}@inf.uni-hannover.de

Abstract. Agile Methods, like Extreme Programming, have increasingly become a viable alternative for conducting software projects, especially for projects with a very short time-to-market or uncertain customer-requirements. Using a technique called Agile Hours it is possible to convey many feelings associated with an Extreme Programming project. Within 70 minutes, a project is performed in which a product is built with Lego bricks. We applied this approach to (1) students and (2) IT professionals. By comparing the two groups, we found that both behaved comparable: we observed a number of interesting differences, although of minor importance. Both groups seemed to benefit from the Agile (Lego) Hours.

1 Introduction

In opposition to the established process-oriented software-methodologies, agile methods have increasingly become common for conducting software projects during the last years. These methods are built around very light-weight techniques [1] aimed at producing high-quality software in projects with very short time-to-market, with uncertain or even unknown customer requirements [2].

All agile methods share common values which are described in the Agile Manifesto [3]. The Agile Manifesto's authors "have come to value...

- ...Individuals and interactions over processes and tools,
- ...Working software over comprehensive documentation,
- ...Customer collaboration over contract negotiation,
- ...Responding to change over following a plan."

These values have proven to be useful in scenarios where requirements are rapidly changing and huge efforts to plan upfront waste resources [4-7].

The best-known agile method is Extreme Programming (XP) [1, 8] originally introduced by Kent Beck. XP consists of 12 practices, which support each other. These practices are project guidelines prescribing how to deal with requirements, how to manage code etc.

We started using the Extreme Hour when we were teaching agile methods in a software engineering lecture. The Extreme Hour was originally developed by Merel [9]. It is a very short simulation of an XP project. In this simulation, no software is

F. Bomarius and S. Komi-Sirviö (Eds.): PROFES 2005, LNCS 3547, pp. 517–529, 2005.

being developed but instead products are constructed by being drawn on paper. Later on, we modified the Extreme Hour and called the generalization "Agile Hours". For example, we developed it further by using Lego bricks instead of drawing. We called this particular variant the "Agile Lego Hour". In our terminology, Agile Hour is a more general term than Extreme Hour (drawing) and Agile Lego Hour (building).

We not only used the Agile Hours to introduce XP to (1) computer science students but had also the opportunity to teach XP to (2) IT professionals in an industrial Java User Group. In this paper we compare the behaviour of the two groups during the Agile Hours. On this empirical basis, we infer a number of lessons learned about the Agile Hour, and Agile *Lego* Hours in particular. We explored the options and potentials of Agile Hour variants. We present our observations from this exploration. Obviously, those observations need further confirmation through (controlled) experiments; we hope our findings will help to guide this continuing empirical work.

In the next section of this paper, typical problems of teaching XP in general are discussed. Afterwards, the Agile Hour is presented as our approach to deal with those problems. In the forth section, we discuss the differences between the Agile Hour and actual XP projects. Afterwards, we share common experiences of six Agile Hours we conducted. In the last two sections the differences between the students' and IT professionals' reaction to the Agile Hour and XP are analyzed.

2   Problem of Conveyance

2.1   Conveying XP Experience

XP favours and utilizes many social capabilities of the project's participants. Therefore, it is difficult to teach XP without practicing it. Because many things need to be experienced in order to fully understand them and realize their consequences, it simply is not sufficient to know what practices XP comprises, what they are called and what to do. XP, like other agile methods, needs to be experienced! In this case, we mean by experience (1) an observation combined with (2) associated feelings and (3) derived reasoning and conclusions. Experiences are stronger than (theoretical) knowledge, as they are more memorable and the reasoning can be used in future situations. Agile methods (like XP) evolved from programmers' *experiences* in the first place and can only be fully understood when combined with own experiences concerning their practices. Furthermore, many of the practices' dependencies can hardly be inferred in theory. However, they become obvious when the method is applied to a problem.

Moreover, XP practices are completely different from other established process models, like the waterfall-model [10] or the V-model used by the German government [11, 12]. Therefore, it is even more challenging to introduce XP to IT professionals who have used and got used to the above-mentioned traditional processes and their underlying assumptions. They often do not believe that some software projects could be run this way. Some have even learned to *resent* this option.

Besides the "softness" of this topic, time-constraints are further complicating the teaching of agile methods. In university, a lecturer often faces about 100 students in a software engineering lecture, all of whom are supposed to understand agile methods within two or three weeks. In the best case, this requires an opportunity for about 100 students to somehow gain the necessary *experience*. In industry agile method courses, one does not have such a high number of participants, but their time is more expensive and, thus, even more limited. Employees are rarely assigned for a longer time just to see whether a new methodology is good or not. Neither a large number of students nor highly expensive IT professionals can conduct real XP projects for learning only.

2.2 From the Extreme Hour to the Agile Lego Hour

The first time we had to teach XP was in an introductory level Software Engineering lecture, which includes a chapter about Agile Methods. Because of the above-mentioned problems, we decided to organize the corresponding exercises as Extreme Hours. An Extreme Hour lasts 70 minutes. Because of this, Extreme Hours are an easy and time-effective way to convey the most important aspects. Extreme Hours have been successfully used in different variations (e.g. [13]). With our own minor variations, we called them "Agile Hours" to indicate the more general approach.

During the above-mentioned lecture we organized five Agile Hours. However, we encountered some disadvantages: Students could easily cheat with drawing because drawing a computer or some kind of controller is very easy and can solve arbitrary tasks. Furthermore, we found drawing is dissimilar from programming in important aspects:

- Programming is a more constructive task than drawing,
- With computers, operations like moving, deleting and reorganizing source code is much easier than to alter a drawn picture,
- Parts of drawings cannot be easily organized in hierarchical structures like packages, modules etc.
- Programming nowadays often uses components and frameworks for solving reoccurring tasks; programmers have to search for such solutions to their problems in libraries.

Finally, the quality assurance (QA) role was a very ungrateful role to play: The students doing the QA job did not participate at the planning game and development, and therefore could not participate in the most important activities.

To eliminate this effect, we decided to modify the Agile Hour more drastically. We replaced drawing by the use of Lego bricks and removed the QA role completely. The usage of Lego bricks addresses the outlined problems with drawings:

- Lego bricks are assembled in a constructive manner,
- Lego bricks can be easily removed or shifted around in a model,
- Lego bricks can be assembled to modules,
- Lego bricks are predefined components of which limited types are available.

We call this new variant "Agile Lego Hour", as it uses Lego bricks. We conducted two Agile Lego Hours in different environments: One with 6 students, the other with 11 IT professionals during a Java User Group meeting. In the remainder of this paper we focus on comparing Agile Lego Hours in the two different environments.

3 Description of an Agile Lego Hour

For helping participants to understand agile methods, we introduced agile methods with a strong focus on XP before starting with the Agile Hour. The lecture provided the students with necessary theory.

For the IT Professionals we did a 30-minute introduction explaining the basics of XP and the origin of agile methods.

Afterwards, the participants chose their roles: For Agile Hours, two customers are needed; the rest of the participants work as developers. We acted as trackers and coaches who supervised the project and answered questions concerning the method. After the roles had been assigned, the project goal was given to the whole team. These project goals should be mechanical items buildable with elementary Lego bricks and should offer enough freedom for the customers to shape the project according to their ideas. We found "Mosquito Hunter" and "Family Spaceship" appropriate project goals because they represent general ideas, everyone has a general understanding of their functionality, and they call for mechanical (e.g. Lego) implementation.

The following main part of the Agile Lego Hour is divided into 7 phases of exactly ten minutes (and zero seconds!) each. In each phase the remaining time is projected onto a wall and as such is visible to all participants. The phases are:

1. **Story Cards & Spike:** In the first ten minutes, the customers write down their story cards for the given project idea. This is done on a flipchart, while reserving some space to the left, which is needed later on in the planning game (see figure 1). Story cards correspond to 1-2 lines on the flipchart each. In the meantime the developers are pairing, i.e. grouping to a team of 2 developers. Each team builds a prototype independently to get ideas for the project and to get accustomed to the Lego bricks available. During this phase the trackers supervise the story card creation process.

2. **Estimation of Priorities and Effort:** In the second phase the developers present their prototypes which are destroyed afterwards. Then, the customers have to explain the story cards to the developers and to prioritize them. Three levels are available: "A" for very important/cannot ship without, "B" for important and "C" for nice to have but not necessary. The priority is written next to the story cards. After this presentation, the developers have to estimate the needed effort in points. The Agile Hour (like XP) uses an abstract effort unit, e.g. "points". Those points are calibrated using the prototypes (coaches simply "assign" them a number of points). All further estimations are carried out *in relation* to that number. If, for example, a prototype was assigned eight points, then a story card of four points should cause half the effort.

3. **Iteration I planning:** In the next phase the customers decide which story cards they want to have implemented next. They can "buy" story cards as long as their total points do not exceed the points achieved in the prototype phase. This rule implies that developers will be able to build the same number of points again during the next iteration (constant efficiency). Customers have to select next tasks based on this assumption. Developers may be faster or slower, but the initial guess is they will work at the same

speed. Afterwards, the developers organize themselves in new pairs and plan how to develop the chosen story cards in the next iteration.

4. **Iteration I:** While the customers add new story cards to the flipchart, the developers are implementing the chosen story cards. Pair programming with Lego bricks means that one developer of a pair may search for specific Lego bricks while the other one assembles the bricks to the pair's model. Typically, at the end the whole iteration product is assembled from the pairs' models.

5. **Product Presentation & Estimation of Priorities and Effort:** In the beginning of this phase, the developers present the so far developed product and the customers are judging if it fulfils their requirements. The judgement has to be based on the selected story cards. Features are only completed if they are visibly built – no hand waving and talking about how it might work is allowed. Any missing features or other shortcomings are added as story cards to the flipchart. The points of all successfully completed story cards are summed up and can be used to "buy" story cards for the second iteration. Afterwards, the customers present the new story cards and prioritize them as in phase 2. Likewise, the developers estimate the effort of the new story cards and eventually update the points of story cards already existing. This phase is normally the one, in which time easily runs out and the trackers need to speed up the process causing stress in the development process.

6. **Iteration II planning:** Customers choose story cards to complete in the second iteration. Again, the estimated effort (points) of these story cards must not exceed the points completed in the first iteration. Developers arrange in new pairs and plan how to implement the chosen story cards.

7. **Iteration II:** The second iteration is carried out like the first one, except the customers do not need to create new story cards. Instead, they are able to look at how the development is done and are able to get an impression of pairing.

After the second iteration the developers again present their product and the customers must decide whether to accept or to reject it. In all cases, the customers could accept the developed product although some small issues remained which would need to be fixed in a future iteration.

Finally, participants discussed their experiences and *reflected* on what had happened during the agile hour. We helped them to emphasize the parallels to XP projects. Reflection is very important, as it reaps the benefits of experiences: during reflection, the above-mentioned "reasoning and conclusions" are derived that help participants in future (real) projects. Emerging discussions answer questions and clarify misunderstandings and unclear aspects. For example, having only one stick per pair was mentioned as awkward. Students found it hard during integration of their results to be unable to "contribute" by drawing themselves. This phenomenon can be traced back to a real development situation in which there is only one computer per pair. In another example, customers complained about the short story card format they were forced to use. During reflection, they realized that real story cards are almost as short as our lines on the flipcharts, so the short format – and the restrictions associated with it – stays the same. Third, quality requirements caused problems: they were treated like normal story cards, but were highly orthogonal in nature. Reflection made obvious that this effect was again not a fault of the agile hour but a phenomenon waiting in real projects, too.Figure 1 shows a part of a prioritized story card flipchart, and the final result of an "automated mosquito hunter".

Fig. 1. (a) Story cards with priorities and estimated effort (b) Mosquito Hunter built with Lego

4   Agile Hour as a Model of XP Projects

Agile Hours (in particular Agile Lego Hours) are models of XP projects. Because of this, it is necessary to question (a) for whom this model is informative, (b) what the relevant attributes are, and (c) what model attributes do not match reality. Relevant attributes of the model (the Agile Hour) correspond to relevant attributes of reality (XP projects), and observations in the model will be mapped back to reality. Both model and reality have several attributes that are not relevant. Those attributes must not be mapped back, as there is no reasonable mapping. For example, building with Lego can be mapped back to writing Java code (relevant), but the weight of a Lego brick may have no (relevant) correspondence in an XP project.

- Agile Hours are designed to convey relevant properties of XP projects to people, who do not have any experiences in agile, especially XP, projects.
- The model focuses on the process, and not on the programming tasks. Because of this, relevant activities are e.g. *pair programming*, *onsite customer*, *story cards*, *planning game*, and *time pressure*. All of them except the last one are XP practices [1].
- Other practices are not included in the Agile Hour, like *test first*, *coding standards*, and *40 hour week*, because it is not possible to simulate them in the given time-frame or they are specific to programming.
- A summary of the Agile Lego Hour's attributes is given in table 1. Before conducting the Agile Lego Hours, we expected the *planning game*, *pair programming*, and the *onsite customer* to be the dominant attributes which the participants would recognize.

Table 1. Relevant and non-relevant attributes of the Agile (Lego) Hour

Attribute	Type	Relevant	Explanation
Acceptance Tests	XP Practice	Yes	Customers decide after each iteration if the features are working as expected or problems arise out of the implementation.
Onsite Customer	XP Practice	Yes	Customers are available for questions all the time
Pair Programming	XP Practice	Yes	Developers are grouped in pairs and have different tasks in that pair. Pairs are changing between iterations and prototype.
Planning Game	XP Practice	Yes	Efforts are estimated using a relative metric which is refined during the process. Customers pick the most business-critical stories and prioritize requirements.
Short Releases	XP Practice	Yes	Iterations only last exactly 10 minutes allowing immediate customer feedback.
Spike/ Prototype	XP Practice	Yes	A prototype is built upfront in order to explore the problem domain.
Story Cards	XP Practice	Yes	Requirements are collected story card-like at a flipchart.
Time Pressure	Project Constraint	Yes	Time pressure is always applied by the minimal time window of 10 minutes and the projection of the remaining time.
Uncertain Requirements	Project Constraint	Yes	Customers do not know the exact requirements before project start.
Continuous Builds	XP Practice	Partly	Lego Models are integrated in a short period of time but due to the time-constraint mostly at the end of the iteration like in normal projects.
Embrace Change	Agile Value	Partly	During iterations the customers are allowed to introduce new story cards contrary to existing requirements. However, only two iterations are carried out.
Refactoring	XP Practice	No	Refactoring in XP Projects is done during the test-first cycle while "refactoring" in Agile Hours is only done to integrate further components.
Test-First	XP Practice	No	Lego constructions cannot be automatically tested; therefore, test-first development is not possible.
Coding Standards	XP Practice	No	No Coding Standards can be applied for building Lego objects.
40 Hour Week	XP Practice	No	The Agile Lego Hour is too short to simulate a 40 Hour Week.

Because agile methods and XP in particular are very useful for time-limited projects and unsure customers, two relevant attributes are the *time pressure* and *uncertain requirements*.

5 Experiences with Agile Hours

While conducting Agile Hours (and by comparing *Extreme* Hours with Agile *Lego* Hours, in particular), we recognized some pitfalls in both and some decisive differences between them.

- The first problem is the **QA role** in the Extreme Hour. If there is an odd number of participants, introducing a QA role for it, looks nice at first glance. However, the role is unsatisfying from a learning perspective, since QA people do not participate in important parts, like the Planning Game. Therefore, the learning effect is worse than with participants being developers or customers. Because of this, we came to avoid the QA role in later Agile Hours and had fewer problems with this setup.
- Another set of problems comes with **pair programming**: Participants do not like to switch pairs (relevant effect: occurs in XP projects, too) or are sometimes even falling back to teamwork with 10 people building one big team. This is an irrelevant effect of the model only: In real XP projects, it is impossible to program with 10 persons at a computer, however building with Lego bricks or drawing on a sheet of paper is. In this case, the trackers have to try to encourage pairing. Furthermore, the room should be set up to hinder full-team work. For example, Lego bricks should not be put on one table but instead be left in distributed boxes for pairs.
- Concerning **story cards**, trackers should take care, that story cards really define *functional* requirements. If there are too many quality story cards, like "machine must not hurt children", it is very difficult to realize these. This is especially true for Agile Lego Hours, because it is nearly impossible to model quality properties, which is a slight disadvantage compared to Extreme Hours with mere drawings.

However, there are many **advantages** for Agile Lego Hours outweighing the disadvantages:

- For using Lego bricks we assume team-sizes may be smaller: we conducted the best Extreme Hours using drawing with 4 to 5 developer pairs, while the same level could be accomplished in an Agile Lego Hour with 3 pairs using Lego bricks.
- If one reduces special-purpose Lego bricks (e.g., looking like computers or antennas), developers cannot cheat by claiming powerful components. In Extreme Hours developers often drew computers, chips, sensors and controllers which, as they said, could literally do everything during the acceptance tests. This drives the approach to the absurd. With limited Lego bricks pretending unlimited features is less tempting.

- It is as hard to destroy prototypes as in real life (relevant effect): Whereas prototype *drawings* were put aside easily, destroying Lego prototypes in front of the participants really hurts. Like in real projects there is a big temptation to stick with prototypes despite their declared mission: being thrown away.

Finally, we found Agile Lego Hours to be more fun than Extreme Hours. While this observation may be very subjective, it was confirmed by comparing 24 questionnaires from Extreme Hours with 17 questionnaires from Agile Lego Hours. Lego bricks seem to stimulate a certain play instinct and are better received.

The essential reflection phase ties participants´ experiences from "playing with Lego" back to the serious world of software development. We consider it an advantage to provide a fun learning environment – given participants recognize its implications for their (serious) studies and work.

6 Differences Between Students and IT Professionals

While doing experiments, workshops or alike with students, often the question is raised to which extend these results are transferable to the professional area. This question is justified because both groups are different. Very different is their *background*: IT Professionals have more experience and have normally better knowledge about tools, programming languages and project management – it has been their business for several years if not decades. In contrast, students are more used to learning, are more willing to adopt new practices, and are even better at some new methods. Both groups have in common an interest for IT and related subjects.

Furthermore, IT professionals are normally older than students. Because of this, it is not necessarily sure, that playful methods being successful with students really work with IT professionals as well.

We had the opportunity to conduct an Agile Lego Hour with IT Professionals participating in an industrial Java User Group. While the Agile Lego Hour took place in the same way like the students' ones, at some points the IT Professionals behaved differently and had other problems, which are certainly related to their experiences:

- The main difference was that IT Professionals were stuck much more to an opposition of the roles of developer against customer. This contradicts XP practices in which developers are required to communicate and collaborate with the customer. However, IT Professionals wanted crystal-clear contracts in their story cards.
- Especially the story-cards and the relative effort estimation seemed to be a major annoyance. The problem with story cards was that they are too sketchy and not every detail is written down. For people who are only used to binding, detailed contracts it is difficult to get used to such a way of defining requirements ("that's not written here, so we don't have to do that", although the customer obviously meant it that way).
- Problems also arose with effort estimation in XP. It is based on relative estimation of points assigned to story cards. This makes cost- and time-estimations for comprehensive functionality upfront impossible. The ability

to estimate cost and time has been considered very important by the IT
professionals.

- Team organization between students and IT Professionals was different, too.
  Students normally organize in groups for learning and know each other quite
  well. Because of this, pairing was easy and the teams were focused on their
  tasks. Contrary, the group of IT professionals spent most of the time
  discussing solutions and organizational questions which probably is related
  to the "Big Design Upfront"-approach normally taken. This was inherently
  apparent during the prototype phase, in which an IT professional pair sorted
  bricks according to their size to be better prepared for the project, instead of
  exploring the problem domain. The reason given for this behaviour was that
  unless "I really know what the customer wants I benefit the team most by
  preparation". In the second iteration, IT Professionals reverted from pair
  programming to team work which ended in a group meeting inefficiently
  discussing implementation problems.

All in all, students seemed to be more pragmatic which seems to be a beneficial
attitude during Agile Hours and XP projects. Consequently, students realized more
customer requirements during the two iterations, although the team compromised
fewer developer pairs.

However, the IT Professional group reflected better about their Agile Lego Hour
and about XP: During the reflection participants were aware that the second iteration
went wrong and was inefficient. Furthermore, better questions and better realization
what XP would change compared to their existing processes created a better
discussion with them than with the students.

7 Analysis of the Questionnaires

After each Extreme and each Agile (Lego) Hour we handed out questionnaires asking
the participants about what XP practices they think they recognized and what they
feel about the Agile Hour. For comparing students to IT professionals only
questionnaires of Agile *Lego* Hours are considered in order to have a comparable
setup (see figure 2 and 3).

Most of the XP practices were rated similarly by the students and by the IT
Professionals. However, there are some slight differences: The *onsite customer* and
the *planning game* have been recognized by more IT Professionals than by students.
We suppose this is influenced by the different backgrounds the two groups have. For
IT Professionals it is not ordinary that the customer is always reachable to ask
questions while the students are used to intensive support by their lecturers.

Because the second iteration of the IT Professionals was more team work than pair
programming, the answers to *pair programming* and *collective ownership* seem
reasonable.

Interestingly, some practices were recognized by participants, which we thought
they would not. For example, *simple design* and *40 hour week* were recognized by
some IT professionals and *continuous integration* has been identified by both students
and IT professionals. The *40 hour week* probably can be traced back to an additional

comment on the same questionnaire which states that the time pressure is very intense and thus is very exhausting.

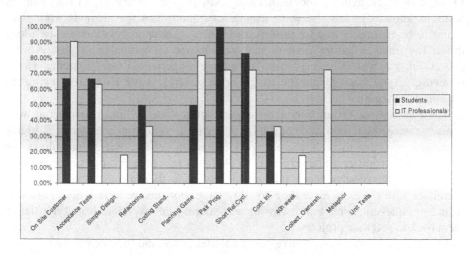

Fig. 2. Answers of the participants which XP practices they recognized

All in all, the questionnaires results confirm our expectations of the Agile Hour's most relevant attributes: Besides *short release cycles*, the *onsite customer*, *planning game*, and *acceptance tests* were recognized by most participants.

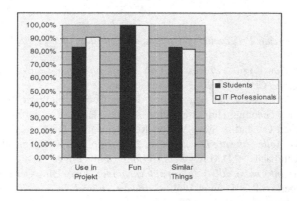

Fig. 3. Results of the Agile Hours

What both groups share is the enthusiasm about the Agile Lego Hour our as a way to learn XP: All of the participants said that they had fun attending the Agile Lego Hour and over 80% would like to attend to similar "classes" for other topics. Moreover, the Agile Lego Hour seems to be a good way to promote XP or at least agile methods: Over 80% of the students would like to use XP in some projects and even more - over 90% - of the IT Professionals answered that they would do so, too.

8 Conclusions and Outlook

In order to teach agile methods, including XP, it is necessary to not only convey textbook knowledge but also some experiences about how the methods work. This seems to be especially true for professionals using classic process models for a long time. They had a harder time to get used to the new methodologies. A very successful way of allowing these necessary experiences are Extreme Hours (drawing), Agile Lego Hours (building), or in general: Agile Hours (following the 70-minute scheme).

These *models of XP projects* allow experiencing those XP practices dealing with project management and communications. However, reflection afterwards is highly necessary in order to realize a significant learning effect. Reflection allows the participants to transfer all the experienced elements to software projects, the possible advantages and disadvantages this might have for their projects, and how this correlates with the experience they possibly have. For this, reflection does not mean filling out questionnaires but discussing and sharing the experiences and translating them back to software projects.

Encouraged by the very positive participant feedback and the interest we received, we will continue to use Agile Hours with students and with other IT professionals in the future, polishing the approach of Agile (Lego) Hours further.

Through this paper, we want to encourage others to try Agile Hours with both professionals and in student education. We hope to provide a good start by offering our insights and describing our newest variant, the Agile Lego Hour.

References

1. Beck, K., *Extreme Programming Explained: Embrace Change*. 1999: Addison-Wesley Pub Co. 224.
2. Goetz, R. *How Agile Processes Can Help in Time-Constrained Requirements Engineering*. in *TCRE 2002*. 2002. Essen, Germany.
3. Kent Beck, M.B., Arie van Bennekum, Alistair Cockburn, Ward Cunningham, Martin Fowler, James Grenning, Jim Highsmith, Andrew Hunt, Ron Jeffries, Jon Kern, Brian Marick, Robert C. Martin, Steve Mellor, Ken Schwaber, Jeff Sutherland, Dave Thomas, *Manifesto for Agile Software Development*, 2001, http://www.agilemanifesto.org/.
4. Dietmar Rohrbach, P.D.M.A. *Realisierung und Pflege von vier Versicherungs produkten*. in *Informatik 2004 - Informatik verbindet*. 2004. Ulm, Germany.
5. Martin Lippert, S.R., Henning Wolf, *Software entwickeln mit eXtreme Programming*. 2002, Heidelberg: dpunkt.verlag. 282.
6. Wright, K., *XP success story: CodeFab develops for Noggin*, 2002, http://builder.com.com/5100-6374_14-1046489-1-1.html.
7. Object Mentor, *Success Story: How Scrum + XP changed Primavera*, 2004, http://www.objectmentor.com/resources/articles/Primavera.
8. Ron Jeffries, A.A., Chet Hendrickson, Ronald E. Jeffries, *Extreme Programming Installed*. 2000: Addison-Wesley Professional. 288.
9. Merel, P., *Extreme Hour*, 2004, http://c2.com/cgi/wiki?ExtremeHour.

10. Royce, W. *Managing the Development of Large Software Systems*. in *IEEE WESCON*. 1970.
11. Versteegen, G., *Das V-Modell 97 in der Praxis*. 1999: dpunkt.verlag. 442.
12. IABG, *Das V-Modell*. 2004.
13. Silicon Valley Patterns Group, *Silicon Valley Extreme Hour*, 2005, http://c2.com/cgi/wiki?SiliconValleyExtremeHour.

Measuring Similarity of Large Software Systems Based on Source Code Correspondence

Tetsuo Yamamoto[1], Makoto Matsushita[2], Toshihiro Kamiya[3], and Katsuro Inoue[2]

[1] College of Information Science and Engineering, Ritsumeikan University,
Kusatsu, Shiga 525-8577, Japan
Phone: +81-77-561-5265, Fax:+81-77-561-5265
tetsuo@cs.ritsumei.ac.jp
[2] Graduate School of Information Science and Technology, Osaka University,
Toyonaka, Osaka 560-8531, Japan
Phone: +81-6-6850-6571, Fax:+81-6-6850-6574
[3] Presto,Japan Science and Technology Agency,
Current Address:Graduate School of Information Science and Technology, Osaka University,
Toyonaka, Osaka 560-8531, Japan
Phone: +81-6-6850-6571, Fax:+81-6-6850-6574
{matusita, inoue, kamiya}@ist.osaka-u.ac.jp

Abstract. It is an important and intriguing issue to know the quantitative similarity of large software systems. In this paper, a similarity metric between two sets of source code files based on the correspondence of overall source code lines is proposed. A Software similarity MeAsurement Tool SMAT was developed and applied to various versions of an operating system(BSD UNIX). The resulting similarity valuations clearly revealed the evolutionary history characteristics of the BSD UNIX Operating System.

1 Introduction

Long-lived software systems evolve through multiple modifications. Many different versions are created and delivered. The evolution is not simple and straightforward. It is common that one original system creates several distinct successor branches during evolution. Several distinct versions may be unified later and merged into another version. To manage the many versions correctly and efficiently, it is very important to know objectively their relationships. There has been various kinds of research on software evolution[1, 2, 3, 4], most of which focused on changes of metric values for size, quality, delivery time or process, etc.

Closely related software systems usually are identified as product lines, so development and management of product lines are actively discussed[5]. Knowing development relations and architectural similarity among such systems is a key to efficient development of new systems and to well-organized maintenance of existing systems[6].

We have been interested in measuring the similarity between two large software systems.This was motivated by our scientific curiosity such as what is the quantitative similarity of two software systems. We would like to quantify the similarity with a solid

F. Bomarius and S. Komi-Sirviö (Eds.): PROFES 2005, LNCS 3547, pp. 530–544, 2005.

and objective measure.The quantitative measure for similarity is an important vehicle to observe the evolution of software systems, as is done in the Bioinformatics field. In Bioinformatics, distance metrics are based on the alignment of DNA sequences. Phylogenetic trees using this distance are built to illustrate relations among species[7]. There are huge numbers of software systems already developed in the world and it should be possible to identify the evolution history of software assets in a manner like that done in Bioinformatics.

Various research on finding software similarities has been performed, most of which focused on detecting program plagiarism[8, 9, 10]. The usual approach extracts several metric values (or attributes) characterizing the target programs and then compares those values.

There also has been some research on identifying similarity in large collections of plain-text or HTML documents[11, 12]. These works use sampled information such as keyword sequences or"fingerprints". Similarity is determined by comparing the sampled information.

We have been interested in comparing all the files. It is important that the software similarity metric is not based on sampled information as the attribute value (or fingerprint), but rather reflect the overall system characteristics. We are afraid that using sampled information may lose some important information. A collection of all source code files used to build a system contains all the essential information of the system. Thus, we analyze and compare overall source code files of the system. This approach requires more computation power and memory space than using sampled information, but the current computing hardware environment allows this overall source code comparison approach.

In this paper, a similarity metric called S_{line}, is used, which is defined as the ratio of shared source code lines to the total source code lines of two software systems being evaluated.

S_{line} requires computing matches between source code lines in the two systems, beyond the boundaries of files and directories. A naive approach for this would be to compare all source file pairs in both systems, with a file matching program such as diff[13], but the comparison of all file pairs does not scale so that it would be impractical to apply to large systems with thousands of files.

Instead, an approach is proposed that improves efficiency and precision. First, a fast, code clone (duplicated code portion) detection algorithm is applied to all files in the two systems and then diff is applied to the file pairs where code clones are found.

Using this concept, a similarity metric evaluation tool called SMAT(Software similarity MeAsurement Tool) was developed and applied to various software system targets. We have evaluated the similarity between various versions of BSD UNIX, and have performed cluster analysis of the similarity values to create a dendrogram that correctly shows evolution history of BSD UNIX.

Section 2 presents a formal definition of similarity and its metric S_{line}. Section 3 describes a practical method for computing S_{line} and shows the implementation tool SMAT. Section 4 shows applications of SMAT to versions of BSD UNIX. Results of our work and comparison with related research are given in Section 5. Concluding remarks are given in Section 6.

2   Similarity of Software Systems

2.1   Definitions

First we will give a general definition of software system similarity and then a concrete similarity metric.

A software system P is composed of elements $p_1, p_2, \cdots, p_m$, and P is represented as a set $\{p_1, p_2, \cdots, p_m\}$. In the same way, another software system Q is denoted by $\{q_1, q_2, \cdots, q_n\}$. We will choose the type of elements, such as files and lines, based on the definitions of the similarity metrics described later.

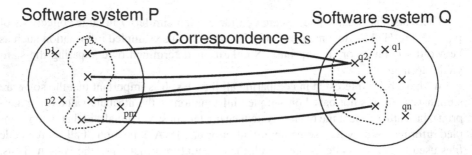

Fig. 1. Correspondence of elements Rs

Suppose that we are able to determine matching between p_i and q_j ($1 \leq i \leq m, 1 \leq j \leq n$), and we call *Correspondence* R_s the set of matched pair (p_i, q_j), where $R_s \subseteq P \times Q$(See Figure 1). *Similarity* S of P and Q with respect to R_s is defined as follows.

$$S(P, Q) \equiv \frac{|\{p_i | (p_i, q_j) \in R_s\}| + |\{q_j | (p_i, q_j) \in R_s\}|}{|P| + |Q|}$$

This definition means that the similarity is the ratio of the total number of p's and q's elements composing R_s to the total number of elements of P and Q. The numerator is the total number of p_i and q_i possibly related to R_s, and the denominator is the total number of p_i and q_i. If R_s becomes smaller, S will decrease, and if $R_s = \phi$ then $S = 0$. Moreover, when P and Q are exactly the same systems, $\forall i (p_i, q_i) \in R_s$ and then $S = 1$.

2.2   Similarity Metrics

The above definition of the similarity leaves room for implementing different concrete similarity metrics by choosing the element types or correspondences. Here, we show a concrete operational similarity metric S_{line} using equivalent line matching.

Each element of a software system is a single line of each source file composing the system. For example, if a software system X consists of source code files $x_1, x_2, \cdots$ and each source code file x_i is made up of lines $x_{i1}, x_{i2}, \cdots$. Pair (x_{ij}, y_{mn}) of two lines x_{ij} and y_{mn} between system X and system Y is in correspondence when x_{ij} and y_{mn} match as equivalent lines. The equivalency is determined by the duplicated code detection method and file comparison method that will be discussed in detail later in this paper. Two lines with minor distinction such as space/comment modification and identifier rename are recognized as equivalent.

S_{line} is not affected by file renaming or path changes. Modification of a small part in a large file does not give great impact to the resulting value. On the other hand, finding equivalent lines generally would be a time consuming process. A practical approach for this is given in Section 3.

It is possible to consider other definitions of similarity and its metrics. A comparison to other such approaches is presented in Section 5.

3   Measuring S_{line}

3.1   Approach

A key problem of S_{line} is computation of the correspondence. A straightforward approach we might consider is that first we construct appended files $x_1; x_2; \cdots$ and $y_1; y_2; \cdots$ which are concatenation of all source files $x_1, x_2, \cdots$ and $y_1, y_2, \cdots$ for systems X and Y, respectively. Then we extract the longest common subsequence (LCS) between $x_1; x_2; \cdots$ and $y_1; y_2; \cdots$ by some tool, say $diff$[13], which implements an LCS-finding algorithm[14, 15, 16]. The extracted LCS is used as the correspondence.

However, this method is fragile due to the change of file concatenation order caused by internal reshuffling of files, since $diff$ cannot follow line block movement to different positions in the files. For example, for two systems $X = a; b; c; d; e$ and $Y = d; e; a; b; c$, the LCS found by $diff$ is $a; b; c$. In this case, a subsequence $d; e$ cannot be detected as a common sequence.

Another approach is that we try to greedily apply $diff$ to all combination of files between two systems. This approach might work, but the scalability would be an issue. The performance applied to huge systems with thousands of files would be doubtful.

Here, an approach is proposed that effectively uses both $diff$ and a clone detection tool named $CCFinder$[17].

$CCFinder$ is a tool used to detect duplicated code blocks (called $clones$) in source code written in C, C++, Java, and COBOL. It effectively performs lexical analysis, transformation of tokens, computing duplicated token sequences by a suffix tree algorithm[18], and then reports the results. The clone detection is made along with normalization and parameterization, that is, the location of white spaces and lines breaks are ignored, comments are removed, and the distinction of identifier names is disregarded. By the normalization and parameterization, code blocks with minor modification are effectively detected as clones.

Applying $CCFinder$ to two sets of files $\{x_1, x_2, \cdots\}$ and $\{y_1, y_2, \cdots\}$ finds all possible clone pairs (b_x, b_y), where b_x is a code block in x_1, or $x_2, \cdots$. and b_y is that of y_1, or $y_2, \cdots$, and b_x and b_y are identical without considering difference of line breaks, white spaces, comments, user-defined identifiers, constant values, and so on. This process is performed by simply specifying two sets of file names or directory names containing $\{x_1, x_2, \cdots\}$ and $\{y_1, y_2, \cdots\}$. $CCFinder$ reports all clone pairs among the files. Those clone pairs found are members of the correspondence.

Code clones are only non-gapped ones. Closely similar code blocks with a gap block(unmatching to them) such as l_1l_2 and $l_1l_xl_2$ are not detected as a larger clone $l_1 * l_2$ but identified as two smaller clones l_1 and l_2. When the lengths of l_1 and l_2 are less than threshold of *CCFinder*(usually 20 tokens[1]), then *CCFinder* reports no clones at all. To reclaim such small similar blocks and similar directives undetected by *CCFinder*, *diff* is applied to all pairs of the two files x_i and y_j, where *CCFinder* detects a clone pair (b_x, b_y) and b_x is in x_i and b_y is in y_j, respectively. The result of *diff* is the longest common subsequences, which also are considered members of the correspondence. The combined results of *CCFinder* and *diff* is to increase S_{line} by about 10%, compared to using only *CCFinder*.

3.2   Example of Measurement

A simple example of computing S_{line} with *CCFinder* and *diff* is given here. Consider a software system X and its extended system Y as shown in Figure 2. X is composed of two source code files A and B, while Y is composed of four files A', A'', B, and C. Here, A' and A'' are evolved versions of A, and C is a newly created file.

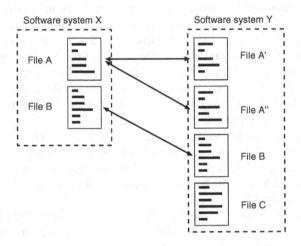

Fig. 2. How to find a correspondence

At first, *CCFinder* is applied to detect clones between two file sets $\{A, B\}$ and $\{A', A'', B, C\}$. This finds clones between A and A', A and A'', and B and B. Assume that no clones are detected between other combination of files. Each line in the clones found across files is put into the correspondence.

Next, *diff* is applied to the file pairs A and A', A and A'', and B and B. Then, the lines in the resulting common subsequences by *diff* are added to the correspondence

---

[1] The threshold 20 used here is determined by our experiences of CCFinder[17]. Based on the analyses of our experiences, a practical threshold is 20 to 30. If we set a further lower number, say 5, a lot of accidentally similar substrings (e.g., a=b+c is a clone of x=y+z) are detected as clones, and the precision of the resulting similarity value is degraded.

obtained by the clone detection. The correspondence finally we obtain includes all the clones found by *CCFinder* and all the common subsequences found by *diff*.

This approach has benefits in both computation complexity and precision of the results. We do not need to perform *diff* on all the file pair combinations. Also, we can chase movement of lines inside or outside the files, which cannot be detected by *diff* alone.

3.3   SMAT

Based on this approach, we have developed a similarity evaluation tool *SMAT* which effectively computes S_{line} for two systems. The following is the detailed process of the system. An overview is illustrated in Figure 3.

INPUTS: File paths of two systems X and Y, each of which represents the subdirectory containing all source code.

OUTPUTS: S_{line} of X and Y $(0 \leq S_{line} \leq 1)$.

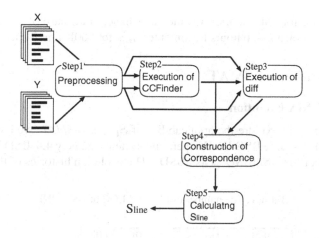

Fig. 3. Similarity measuring process

Step 1 Preprocessing:

All comments, white spaces, and empty lines are removed, which do not affect the execution of the programs. This step helps to improve the precision of the following steps, especially Step 3.

Step 2 Execution of *CCFinder*:

We execute *CCFinder* between two file sets X and Y. *CCFinder* has an option for the minimum number of tokens of clones to be detected, and whose default is set to 20.

Step 3 Execution of *diff*:

Execute *diff* on any file pair x_i and y_j in X and Y respectively, where at least one clone is detected between x_i and y_j.

Step 4 Construction of Correspondence:

The lines appearing in the clones detected by Step 2 and in the common subsequences found in Step 3 are merged to determine the correspondence between X and Y.

Step 5 Calculating S_{line}:

S_{line} is calculated using its definition; *i.e.*, the ratio of lines in the correspondence to those in whole systems. Note that the number of lines after Step 1 is used hereafter, where all comments and white spaces are removed.

SMAT works for the source code files written in C, C++, Java, and COBOL.

For given two systems, each of which has m files of n lines, the worst case time complexity is as follows: *CCFinder* requires $O(mn \log(mn))$[17]. *diff* requires $O(n^2 \log n)$ [13] for a single file pair and we have to perform $O(m^2)$ execution of *diff* for all file pairs. So in total, $O(m^2 n^2 \log n)$ is the worst case time complexity.

However, in practice, the execution of *diff* is not performed for all file pairs. In many cases, code clones are not detected between all file pairs, but only a few file pairs.

Practically, the execution performance of *SMAT* is fairly efficient, since it grows super-linearly. For example, it took 329 seconds to compute S_{line} of about 500K line C source code files in total on a Pentium III 1GHz CPU system with 2G Bytes memory, and 980 seconds for 1M line files. On the other hand, in the case of using only *diff* for all file pairs, it took about 6 hours to compute S_{line} for 500K line files.

4   Applications of SMAT

4.1   BSD UNIX Evolution

Target systems. To explore the applicability of S_{line} and *SMAT*, we have used many versions of open-source BSD UNIX operating systems, namely 4.4-BSD Lite, 4.4-BSD Lite2[19], FreeBSD[2], NetBSD[3], OpenBSD[4]. The evolution histories of these versions

Table 1. The number of files and LOC of BSD UNIX

FreeBSD

Version	2.0	2.0.5	2.1	2.2	3.0	4.0
No. of files	891	1018	1062	1196	2142	2569
LOC	228868	275016	297208	369256	636005	878590

NetBSD

Version	1.0	1.1	1.2	1.3	1.4	1.5
No. of files	2317	3091	4082	5386	7002	7394
LOC	453026	605790	822312	1029147	1378274	1518371

OpenBSD

Version	2.0	2.1	2.2	2.3	2.4	2.5	2.6	2.7	2.8
No. of files	4200	4987	5245	5314	5507	5815	6074	6298	6414
LOC	898942	1007525	1066355	1079163	1129371	1232858	1329293	1438496	1478035

4.4BSD

Version	Lite	Lite2
No. of files	1676	1931
LOC	317594	411373

[2] http://www.freebsd.org/
[3] http://www.netbsd.org/
[4] http://www.openbsd.org/

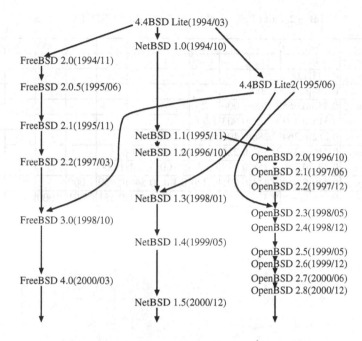

Fig. 4. BSD UNIX evolutional history

are shown in Figure 4[5]. As shown in this figure, 4.4-BSD Lite is the origination of
the other versions. New versions of FreeBSD, NetBSD, and OpenBSD are currently
being developed in open source development style. 23 major-release versions, as listed
in Figure 4, were chosen for computing S_{line} of all pair combinations. The evaluation
was performed only on source code files related to the OS kernels written in C(i.e., *.c
or *.h files).

Results. Table 1 shows the number of files and total source code lines of each version after the preprocessing of Step 1. Table 2 shows part of the resulting values S_{line}
for pairs of each version. Note that Table 2 is symmetric, and the values on the main
diagonal line are always 1 by the nature of our similarity.

As a general tendency, S_{line} values between a version and its immediate ances-
tor/descendant version are higher than the values for non-immediate ancestor/descendant
versions. Figure 5 shows S_{line} evolution between FreeBSD 2.2 and other FreeBSD versions. The values monotonically decline with increasing version distance. This indicates
that the similarity metric S_{line} properly captures ordinary characteristics of software
systems evolution.

Figure 6 shows S_{line} between each version of FreeBSD and some of NetBSD. These
two version streams have the same origin, 4.4-BSD Lite, and it is naturally assumed
that older versions between the two streams have higher S_{line} values, since younger
versions have a lot of independently added codes. This assumption is true for FreeBSD

---

[5] http://www.tribug.org/img/bsd-family-tree.gif

Table 2. Part of S_{line} values between BSD UNIX kernel files

	F 2.0	F 2.0.5	F 2.1	F 2.2	F 3.0	F 4.0	Lite	Lite2	N 1.0	N 1.1	N 1.2	N 1.3
FreeBSD 2.0	1.000											
FreeBSD 2.0.5	0.833	1.000										
FreeBSD 2.1	0.794	0.943	1.000									
FreeBSD 2.2	0.550	0.665	0.706	1.000								
FreeBSD 3.0	0.315	0.392	0.421	0.603	1.000							
FreeBSD 4.0	0.212	0.264	0.286	0.405	0.639	1.000						
4.4BSD-Lite	0.419	0.377	0.362	0.226	0.138	0.101	1.000					
4.4BSD-Lite2	0.290	0.266	0.258	0.179	0.133	0.100	0.651	1.000				
NetBSD 1.0	0.440	0.429	0.411	0.291	0.220	0.140	0.540	0.450	1.000			
NetBSD 1.1	0.334	0.348	0.336	0.254	0.193	0.152	0.421	0.431	0.691	1.000		
NetBSD 1.2	0.255	0.269	0.265	0.225	0.190	0.158	0.331	0.436	0.553	0.783	1.000	
NetBSD 1.3	0.205	0.227	0.225	0.201	0.208	0.179	0.259	0.366	0.445	0.622	0.769	1.000

F 2.0 means FreeBSD 2.0, Lite means 4.4BSD-Lite, N 1.0 means NetBSD 1.0.

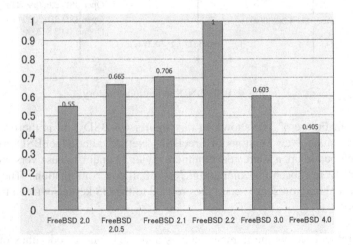

Fig. 5. S_{line} of FreeBSD 2.2 and other versions

2.0 through 2.2. However, for FreeBSD 3.0 and 4.0, the youngest version NetBSD 1.3 has higher values than other NetBSD versions (Figure 6 A and B). This is because both FreeBSD 3.0 and NetBSD 1.3 imported a lot of code base from 4.4-BSD Lite2 as shown Figure 4. *SMAT* clearly spotted such an irregular nature of the evolution.

Cluster Analysis. Classifications were made of OS versions using a cluster analysis technique[20] with respect to S_{line} values shown above. For the cluster analysis, we need to define the distance of two OS versions. We defined it by $1 - S_{line}$. A cluster is a non-empty collection of OS versions, and the distance of two clusters are the average of the pairwise distances of the numbers of each cluster. To construct a dendrogram, we start with clusters having exactly one version, and merge the nearest two clusters into one cluster. The merging process is repeated until we get only one cluster. The den-

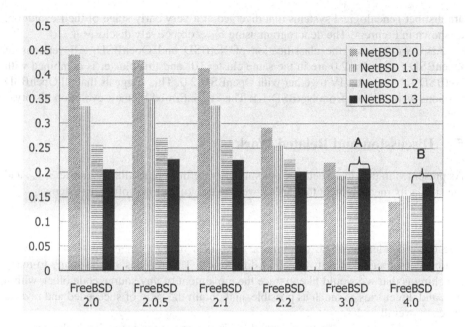

Fig. 6. S_{line} between FreeBSD and NetBSD

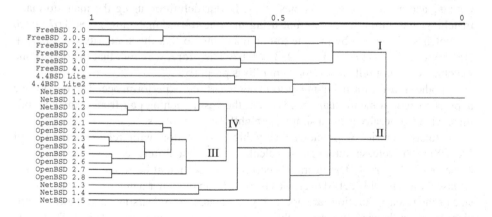

Fig. 7. Dendrogram of BSD UNIX

drogram from this cluster analysis is shown in Figure 7. The horizontal axis represents the distance. OS versions categorized on the left-hand side are closer ones with high similarity values to each other.

This dendrogram reflects very well the evolution history of BSD UNIX versions depicted previously by Figure 4. Further, as shown in Figure 7, all FreeBSD versions are contained in Cluster I and all OpenBSD are in Cluster II. FreeBSD and OpenBSD are distinct genealogical systems that diverged at a very early stage of their evolution, as shown in Figure 4. The dendrogram using S_{line} objectively discloses it.

Also, we can see the classification of NetBSD and OpenBSD. All versions of OpenBSD except for 2.0 are in the same cluster III, and this cluster is combined with NetBSD 1.1 in cluster IV together with OpenBSD 2.0. This suggests that all OpenBSD versions were derived from NetBSD 1.1. This is confirmed by their evolution history.

5   Discussion and Related Work

As presented in previous sections, our similarity definition, similarity metric S_{line}, and the similarity measurement tool *SMAT* worked fine to various software systems.

5.1   Metric S_{line}

The correspondence which determines S_{line} is a many-to-many matching between source lines located within files and directories. The reasons of the many-to-many matching is that we would like to trace the movement of any source code block within files and directories as much as possible, and obtain the ratio of succeeded and revised codes to overall codes.

It is possible to use one-to-one matching in the correspondence, but it characterizes the similarity metric too naively to duplicated source code. Assume that a system X is composed of a file x_1, and a new system X' is composed of two files x_1' and x_2' where both x_1' and x_2' are the same copies of x_1. In our definition using the many-to-many matching, the similarity is 1.0, but using the one-to-one matching gives 0.67, since x_1 matches x_1' (or x_2') by the one-to-one matching so that the similarity is $(|\{x_1\}| + |\{x_1'\}|)/(|\{x_1\}| + |\{x_1', x_2'\}|) = 2/3 \cong 0.67$. Therefore, we think that the one-to-one matching does not reflect development efforts properly.

Another reason for using many-to-many matching is performance. The one-to-one approach needs some mechanism to choose the best matching pair from many possibilities, which generally is not a simple, straightforward process.

Actually, metric S_{line} showed very high correlation with release durations of FreeBSD. The release durations are calculated from the difference of OS release dates presented in Figure 4. The Pearson's correlation coefficient between S_{line} values and release durations of FreeBSD versions is -0.973. On the other hand, the increases of the size or the release durations are not highly correlated. The Pearson's correlation coefficient between the size increases(Table 1) and the release durations is 0.528. Therefore, we think that S_{line} is a reasonable measures of release durations in this case.

5.2   SMAT

SMAT worked very efficiently for large software systems. To compute S_{line}, execution of *diff* for all possible file pairs would have been a simple approach. However, the execution speed would have become unacceptably slow as mentioned in 3.3. Combining *CCFinder* and *diff* boosted the performance of *SMAT*. Also, as mentioned before, the movement and modification of source code lines can be traced better by *CCFinder*, which effectively detects clones with different white spaces, comments, identifier names, and so on. The matching computation using only *diff* cannot chase those changes.

There are a lot of researches on clone detection and many tools have been developed [21, 22, 23, 24, 25, 26, 27].We could have used those tools instead of *CCFinder*.

5.3   Related Work

There has been a lot of work on finding plagiarism in programs. Ottenstein used Halstead metric valuations[28] of target program files for comparison[29]. There are other approaches which use a set of metric values to characterize source programs[30, 31, 32]. Also, structural information has been employed to increase precision of comparison[33, 34]. In order to improve both precision and efficiency, abstracted text sequences (token sequences) can be employed for comparison[8, 9, 10, 35]. Source code texts are translated into token sequences representing programs structures, and the longest common subsequence algorithm is applied to obtain matching.

These systems are aimed mainly at finding similar software code in the education environment. The similarity metric values computed by comparison of metrics values do not show the ratio of similar codes to non-similar codes. Also, scalability of those evaluation methods to large software system such as BSD UNIX is not known.

In reverse engineering field, there has been research on measuring similarity of components and restructuring modules in a software system, to improve its maintainability and understandability[36, 37, 38]. Such similarity measures are based on several metric values such as shared identifier names and function invocation relations. Although these approaches involve important views of similarity, their objectives are to identify components and modules inside a single system, and cannot be applied directly to inter-system similarity measurement.

There are many literatures for detection of code clones and patterns[17, 21, 22, 23, 24, 25, 26, 27]. Some of those proposed metrics for the clones; however they have not been extended to the similarity of two large software systems.

A study on the similarity between documents is presented by Broder[11]. In this approach, a set of fixed-length token sequences are extracted from documents. Then two sets X and Y are obtained for each document to compute their intersection. The similarity is defined as $(|X| \cap |Y|)/(|X| \cup |Y|)$.

This approach is very suitable for efficiently computing the resemblance of a large collection of documents such as world-wide web documents. However, choosing token sequences greatly affects the resulting values. Tokens with minor modification would not be detected. Therefore, this is probably an inappropriate approach for computing subjective similarity metric for source code files.

Manber[12] developed a tool to identify similar files in large systems. This tool uses a set of keywords and extracts subsequences starting with those keywords as fingerprints. A fingerprint set X of a target file is encoded and compared to a fingerprint set Y of a query file. The similarity is defined as $|X \cap Y|/|X|$.

This approach works very efficiently for both source program files and document files and would fit exploration of similar files in a large system. However, it is fragile to the selection of keywords. Also, it would be too sensitive to minor modifications of source program files such as identifier changes and comment insertions.

Broder and Manber methods are all quite different from those developed and presented herein, since they do not perform comparison on raw and overall text sequences, but rather on sampled text sequences. Sampling approaches would get high performance, but the resulting similarity values would be less significant than our whole text comparison approach.

6   Conclusion

A proposed definition of similarity between two software systems with respect to correspondence of source code lines was formulated as a similarity metric called S_{line}. An S_{line}-based evaluation tool *SMAT* was developed and applied to various software systems. The results showed that S_{line} and *SMAT* are very useful for identifying the origin of the systems and to characterize their evolution.

Further applications of *SMAT* to various software systems and product lines will be made to investigate their evolution. From a macro level analysis viewpoint, categorization and taxonomy of software systems analogous to molecular phylogeny should be an intriguing issue to pursue. From a micro level analysis view point, chasing specific code blocks through system evolution will be interesting to perform.

References

1. Antoniol, G., Villano, U., Merlo, E., Penta, M.D.: Analyzing cloning evolution in the linux kernel. Information and Software Technology 44 (2002) 755–765
2. Basili, V.R., Briand, L.C., Condon, S.E., Kim, Y.M., Melo, W.L., Valett, J.D.: Understanding and predicting the process of software maintenance release. In: 18th International Conference on Software Engineering, Berlin (1996) 464–474
3. Cook, S., Ji, H., Harrison, R.: Dynamic and static views of software evolution. In: the IEEE International Conference On Software Maintenance (ICSM 2001), Florence, Italy (2001) 592–601
4. Kemerer, C.F., Slaughter, S.: An empirical approach to studying software evolution. IEEE Transactions on Software Engineering 25 (1999) 493–509
5. The First Software Product Line Conference (SPLC1): The First Software Product Line Conference (SPLC1), http://www.sei.cmu.edu/plp/conf/SPLC.html (2000) Denver, Colorado (2000)
6. Clements, P., Northrop, L.: Software Product Lines: Practices and Patterns. Addison Wesley (2001)
7. Baxevanis, A., Ouellette, F., eds. In: Bioinformatics 2nd edition. John Wiley and Sons, Ltd., England (2001) 323–358
8. Schleimer, S., Wilkerson, D., Aiken, A.: Winnowing: Local algorithms for document fingerprinting. In: Proceedings of the ACM SIGMOD International Conference on Management of Data. (2003) 76–85
9. Prechelt, L., Malpohl, G., Philippsen, M.: Jplag: Finding plagiarisms among a set of programs. Technical Report 2000-1, Fakultat fur Informatik, Universitat Karlsruhe, Germany (2000)
10. Wise, M.J.: YAP3: Improved detection of similarities in computer program and other texts. SIGCSEB: SIGCSE Bulletin (ACM Special Interest Group on Computer Science Education) 28 (1996)

11. Broder, A.Z.: On the resemblance and containment of documents. In: Proceedings of Compression and Complexity of Sequences. (1998) 21–29
12. Manber, U.: Finding similar files in a large file system. In: Proceedings of the USENIX Winter 1994 Technical Conference, San Fransisco, CA, USA (1994) 1–10
13. Hunt, J.W., McIlroy, M.D.: An algorithm for differential file comparison. Technical Report 41, Computing Science, Bell Laboratories, Murray Hill, New Jersey (1976)
14. Miller, W., Myers, E.W.: A file comparison program. Software- Practice and Experience 15 (1985) 1025–1040
15. Myers, E.W.: An $O(ND)$ difference algorithm and its variations. Algorithmica 1 (1986) 251–256
16. Ukkonen, E.: Algorithms for approximate string matching. INFCTRL: Information and Computation (formerly Information and Control) 64 (1985) 100–118
17. Kamiya, T., Kusumoto, S., Inoue, K.: CCFinder: A multilinguistic token-based code clone detection system for large scale source code. IEEE Transactions on Software Engineering 28 (2002) 654–670
18. Gusfield, D.: Algorithms on strings, trees, and sequences. Computer Science and Computational Biology. Cambridge University Press (1997)
19. McKusick, M., Bostic, K., karels, M., Quarterman, J.: The Design and Implementation of the 4.4BSD UNIX Operating System. Addison-Wesley (1996)
20. Everitt, B.S.: Cluster Analysis. Edward Arnold, 3rd edition, London (1993)
21. Baker, B.S.: On finding duplication and near-duplication in large software systems. In: Second Working Conference on Reverse Engineering, Toronto, Canada (1995) 86–95
22. Baxter, I.D., Yahin, A., Moura, L., Sant'Anna, M., Bier, L.: Clone detection using abstract syntax trees. In: Proceedings of the International Conference on Software Maintenance, Bethesda, Maryland (1998) 368–378
23. Ducasse, S., Rieger, M., Demeyer, S.: A language independent approach for detecting duplicated code. In: Proceedings of the International Conference on Software Maintenance, Oxford, England, UK (1999) 109–119
24. Johnson, J.H.: Identifying redundancy in source code using fingerprints. In: Proceedings of CASCON '93, Toronto, Ontario (1993) 171–183
25. Johnson, J.H.: Substring matching for clone detection and change tracking. In: Proceedings of the International Conference on Software Maintenance, Victoria, British Columbia (1994) 120–126
26. Kontogiannis, K.: Evaluation experiments on the detection of programming patterns using software metrics. In: Proceedings of Fourth Working Conference on Reverse Engineering, Amsterdam, Netherlands (1997) 44–54
27. Mayrand, J., Leblanc, C., Merlo, E.: Experiment on the automatic detection of function clones in a software system using metrics. In: Proceedings of the International Conference on Software Maintenance, Monterey, California (1996) 244–253
28. Halstead, M.H.: Elements of Software Science. Elsevier, New York (1977)
29. Ottenstein, K.J.: An algorithmic approach to the detection and prevention of plagiarism. ACM SIGCSE Bulletin 8 (1976) 30–41
30. Berghel, H.L., Sallach, D.L.: Measurements of program similarity in identical task environments. ACM SIGPLAN Notices 19 (1984) 65–76
31. Donaldson, J.L., Lancaster, A.M., Sposato, P.H.: A plagiarism detection system. ACM SIGCSE Bulletin(Proc. of 12th SIGSCE Technical Symp.) 13 (1981) 21–25
32. Grier, S.: A tool that detects plagiarism in pascal programs. ACM SIGCSE Bulletin(Proc. of 12th SIGSCE Technical Symp.) 13 (1981) 15–20
33. Jankowitz, H.T.: Detecting plagiarism in student Pascal programs. The Computer Journal 31 (1988) 1–8

34. Verco, K.L., Wise, M.J.: Software for detecting suspected plagiarism: Comparing structure and attribute-counting systems. In Rosenberg, J., ed.: Proc. of 1st Ausutralian Conference on Computer Science Education, Sydney, Australia (1996) 86–95
35. Whale, G.: Identification of program similarity in large populations. The Computer Journal 33 (1990) 140–146
36. Choi, S.C., Scacchi, W.: Extracting and restructuring the design of large systems. IEEE Software 7 (1990) 66–71
37. Schwanke, R.W.: An intelligent for re-engineering software modularity. In: Proceedings of theThirteenthInternational Conference on Software Engineering, Austin, Texas, USA (1991) 83–92
38. Schwanke, R.W., Platoff, M.A.: Cross references are features. In: Proceedings of the 2nd International Workshop on Software Configuration Management. (1989) 86–95

Tool Support for Personal Software Process

Jouni Lappalainen

Department of Information Processing Science, University of Oulu,
P.O.Box 3000, FIN-90014 OULU, Finland
Jouni.Lappalainen@oulu.fi

Abstract. Improving the software development process is something that many organizations aim for. Many methods have been devised to reach this goal, one of which focuses on the personal level of software development, namely the Personal Software Process[SM1] (PSP[SM]). There is a dire need for automated tool support for PSP, since the method is laborious if used manually. During four university-level courses several tools were studied and later evaluated using feature analysis. As one result, a requirements set for an ideal PSP tool was devised. The results of the evaluation showed that none of the evaluated tools fulfilled the acceptance threshold set for a tool, though one of them can be modified so that it could be used within the setting of an academic PSP course.

1 Introduction

Structured and disciplined development process is commonly found to be helpful in software quality improvement efforts. Methods and models such as SW-CMM or CMMI have traditionally been more focused towards an organizational approach of software engineering. In the end, the work is done by individuals, and their capabilities to address the requirements of organizational software engineering models have been at least varied if not limited. As a personal level software development and quality process, Watts S. Humphrey developed the Personal Software Process[SM] in the mid-1990s. If the PSP is used as described in [1] and followed faithfully, it is very laborious due to the constant measuring of own work. The "tools" provided in [1] are essentially document templates and statistical formulae, and these have been found inadequate to at least classroom usage during several courses in University of Oulu [2] [3] and Copenhagen Business School [4]. The practical need in teaching has prompted the question: how can the Personal Software Process be supported with software tools? In order to find the answer to this an analysis of what kinds of tools exist and ideal tool requirements is conducted.

The problem is approached qualitatively, by studying the feedback given by students in PSP courses. This feedback, combined with personal experiences from the same courses as well as a comprehensive literature study, is used as the material while evaluating the software tools. To select the appropriate way to evaluate software tools, methodology identified during the DESMET-project is used [5]. The tools for

---

[SM1] Personal Software Process and PSP are service marks of Carnegie Mellon University.

F. Bomarius and S. Komi-Sirviö (Eds.): PROFES 2005, LNCS 3547, pp. 545–559, 2005.

the analysis cover some of those used in classroom setting as well as those not used during the courses. This is to give more validity to the results of the study, if not the analysis itself. The selection is also to be more of a descriptive set of the types of tools, rather than a comprehensive set of tools available.

Rest of the paper has been organized as follows. The following sections give a short overview of PSP method as well as tools used to support it. This is followed by the description of the evaluation method and evaluation context, after which a section summarizing some of the features of an ideal PSP tool is presented. Results of the evaluations of the tools are outlined and briefly discussed in section 6. Finally, section 7 provides some concluding remarks.

2   Overview of the PSP Method

The PSP aims to enable an individual software engineer to improve the quality of the product by improving the quality of the process she uses to develop the product. This is achieved by introducing elements to the process that help the user of the PSP to plan, track and analyze both the product and the process, as well as manage the development project on a personal level. The PSP is often taught as a course, where these elements to the process are gradually introduced into the initial, or the baseline process, as is suggested by [1]. After augmenting the baseline process with product and process measurements, standard reporting features and the general process structure, the process elements introduced deal with personal project management issues. This PSP1-level adds test reporting as well as size and effort estimating into the process elements. The following PSP2-level gives the user tools for software quality management on a personal level, code and design reviews to name a few. Finally, the PSP3-level introduces cyclical development concepts to the process in order to scale the PSP for larger projects.

According to Humphrey [6], the PSP "is based in part on the quality management principles of W. Edwards Deming and Joseph M. Juran. In a more general sense, these methods follow principles that Frederick Winslow Taylor introduced over 100 years ago." Some founding principles behind the PSP can be seen to be process tracking, project planning, product and process measurement, analyzing of that data, and process improvement based on the analysis. Here only a cursory overview of the PSP is given, and for example many of the methods, process elements and statistical formulas that the PSP uses cannot be discussed. For more information about the PSP, the reader is encouraged to refer to [1].

As so many other software engineering issues, the PSP is by no means a single solution to all possible problems, or "the silver bullet" if wished. Considerably crucial points for critique have been found over the years, one of which is the already mentioned amount of work the PSP demands from the user [7]. Disney and Johnson have also studied the problems in collecting the PSP data [8], and found that the data collected doesn't always properly and accurately reflect the reality. This is partly due to the sometimes overwhelming amount of data that needs to be collected, and partly to the fact that when recording some data from the process, the software engineer needs to switch her context of thought from solving the problem (design, coding, etc.) to the recording of data. This interleaving of two different tasks can cause inaccuracies in the data and hinders the motivation to collect the data. In addition to the problems in collecting data, there are also many different ways of defining productivity, which is one of the key metrics of the PSP. The straightforward approach to counting lines of code that is adopted in the PSP – setting aside the excoriating in the measurement literature – can cause considerable fluctuations in productivity when taking into account such issues like code reuse, commenting, and the amount of base code. Assumed linearity between the amount of work and the size of the product can cause problems as well, which is often highlighted when using historical data as the basis of resource estimations.

3 PSP Tools

Following the "no silver bullet" –principle, software tools can help the user of the PSP, but they will not solve all the problems (which is just as with processes). Such standard tools as word processors, spreadsheets and statistical packages will provide a starting point. In the end, though, in addition to those basic tools, CASE-environments or similar programs that are specifically developed for the purpose of supporting the PSP are needed.

For the purposes of this text it is considered that a PSP tool is such a tool that can assist in executing at least some portion of the PSP. Even though the definition allows tools that are something else than pieces of software, and Humphrey's fundamentally manual way of conducting the PSP is analyzed as one tool in this text, the study here concentrates on software tools. The concept of a software tool is rather common, but a more thorough analysis and evolutionary view can be found in [9]. The PSP on the other hand is defined in almost excruciating detail in [1].

Therefore, the requirements for a PSP tool are stated by the PSP. The Software Engineering Institute has issued a specification for a PSP tool [10] (which has then been removed from distribution). Although the specification assumes heavy usage of spreadsheets and/or document forms, some points in it are applicable to a more general variety of tools:

- customization
- privacy of data
- free selection of the current process phase
- phase and time tracking
- project planning and estimating support
- issue logging
- software design must be produced
- phases of a software development process

These points can be elaborated into detailed requirements. With the more general tool evaluation and selection criteria [11] that takes into account such issues as reliability, usability, efficiency and maintainability, a basis for a requirements set can be com-

548   J. Lappalainen

bined. This set was modified, mostly by adding requirements that were deemed necessary by experiences from the PSP courses, a set consisting of 110 distinct
requirements can be defined. Some of those requirements are implicitly described
later in this text while discussing some of the features of an ideal PSP tool.

For the purposes of managing the different kinds of tools and putting them into
perspective, a classification of PSP tools can be devised. Figure 1 shows the classification hierarchy according to the experiences from the tools used in the PSP courses.
All PSP tools can be divided into manual and automated tools, as well as into being
either "custom-built" for PSP or not. Generic tools are either mental models (such as a
mathematical formula) or common tools designed assist in various work tasks (e.g.
word processors). PSP-specific tools can support the whole process or just a part of it.
At the same time, the tools designed for PSP may either need direct attention from the
user during the enactment of the process, resulting into a switching of mental context
by the user, or function completely unobtrusively to the user.

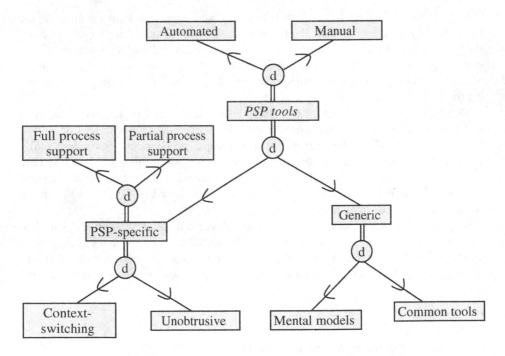

Fig. 1. Classification hierarchy for PSP tools using EER-type notation

It is interesting to note that in his book [1] Humphrey states that it would be good
to have a completely automated PSP tool, but that such a tool is nearly impossible
because of the human judgment required in several parts of the process. The set of
manual tools that he gives leaves many things to be improved, and even if the completely automated PSP tool would be impossible to realize (in the near future at least),
automated tool support can ease the overhead of data collection and analysis, as well

as improve the quality of both collected and analyzed data. Depending on the point of view, the set of tools given in [1] can be interpreted to consist from 1 (document templates) to over 50 or even as much as nearly 100 different tools (each metric, form, statistical formula, etc. calculated separately). In this study the "1"-option is adopted.

4 Tool Evaluation Using DESMET Feature Analysis

For all purposes relevant here, the DESMET methodology [5] can be viewed as a set of nine related evaluation methods that have a higher-level rationale for selecting between them. This high-level method enables the organization conducting a tool or method evaluation and selection to select the most appropriate evaluation method, given the context of the organization. The DESMET method is not particularly adamant whether the target being evaluated is a method or a tool (or a combination of the two), and thus in the context of a PSP tool evaluation can be viewed to apply to tools as such. It should be noted that the DESMET evaluations assume that the target of evaluation is always comparative between several candidate tools (or methods).

4.1 Selecting the Appropriate Evaluation Method

The different evaluation methods can be classified into quantitative, qualitative and hybrid methods, as well as by the organization of the evaluation. Both quantitative and qualitative methods can be organized as formal experiments, case studies or surveys. In addition to these, qualitative methods have a feature analysis method that allows the screening of candidate tools with little resources. Hybrid methods include the qualitative effects analysis (subjective – qualitative – opinion on how much effect the evaluation target has) and benchmarking (quantitative results of standard tests are evaluated qualitatively).

Main limitations concerning the DESMET method include two issues. Firstly, a combination of several different tools or methods cannot be evaluated very well. This is not a problem in the context of this study, since a single tool that could support the user of the PSP is searched for. Secondly, the organization conducting the evaluation should have a controlled production process, so that the changes caused by the tool in evaluation can be observed with some reliability. If a PSP course is taken as the organization, it has a rather stable process, and PSP itself is very strictly defined, so this shouldn't cause many problems either considering the reliability of the results of the evaluation. Final note about the limitations of the DESMET method that should be addressed here is that the method is aimed more for industrial than academic organizations. The four different types of contexts for industrial evaluation that have been identified in [5] differ somewhat from that of the academic evaluation. In the PSP courses held in the University of Oulu, the students require support from the tool in learning the PSP-method. This is close to the industrial context described by Kitchenham, where a tool is selected to a single project.

In addition to the evaluation context, the other criteria defined [5] for selecting the appropriate evaluation method (nature of the impact of the tool, nature of the tool itself, the scope of impact and the maturity of the tool, the learning curve associated with the tool and the measurement capability of the organization) point towards the selection of the feature analysis screening as the evaluation method. Other, more practical issues also favor this choice, such as the time and resources available. This has the adverse effect that the results of the evaluation may not be as reliable as with formal experiment for example. Some of the effects regarding reliability by subjectivity involved in feature analysis screening are attempted to minimize by including representatives of potential user groups (students, teachers) into the evaluation process. Alternative DESMET-approaches for tool evaluation within this context can be identified, which each have their own advantages and drawbacks. According to [5], qualitative evaluation methods are more suited for analyzing the appropriateness of a tool than quantitative evaluations. Qualitative case study can be used for establishing more profound understanding of the features and appropriateness of a tool, as has been the case for some of the tools of this study. Though this alternative may yield more reliable results than feature analysis screening, it is not so applicable to a situation where a tool or a set of tools is needed to be selected from a larger set, for example to be candidate tools for a further evaluation, with limited time and resources.

4.2 Feature Analysis on PSP Tools

The feature analysis screening executed on the PSP tools is discussed here shortly, by describing the set of candidate tools selected for evaluation, the features and their scoring scheme used in the evaluation, and the analysis principles of the evaluation results. Other issues concerning the evaluation planning, execution and analysis are recognized [5] and attended to, but not discussed here.

This study is mainly concerned with evaluating the tools used in the four PSP courses held in the University of Oulu and Copenhagen business school (in 2001). Some other tools that were identified while preparing for these courses have also been taken into the evaluation to improve the possibilities of finding acceptable tool support for future courses. The most applicable tool is the one that meets the require

Table 1. The list of tools used in the PSP courses studied

Course	Tool	Description
Oulu 2000	PPLogControl	Automated time-tracking tool
	EvalPPLog	Parser for the log file of PPLogControl
	Document templates	Electronic version of manual forms of [1]
	Student-authored tools	Small helper tools that the students created as assignments during the course
CBS 2001	OpenStat	Generic statistics program
Oulu 2002	Logfile parsers	Student-authored parsers for PPLogControl log files
Oulu 2003	LEAP	Tool to help in a PSP-style process, by CSDL in University of Hawaii
	Hackystat	Next generation process support software from the developers of LEAP

ments of an ideal tool to an acceptable degree. The set of tools (previously not used in course settings) for each of the firs four courses studied is listed in table 1. In addition to these, two tools outside these courses are included into the evaluated set, PSP Studio and Process Dashboard. In addition to the feature analysis, the analysis findings of the latter tool are compared against the feedback and experiences of the PSP course arranged in 2004 in the University of Oulu.

As mentioned above, the feature set that is used to evaluate a PSP tool is devised by modifying the IEEE set of CASE tool selection criteria [11], and reviewing it with the representatives of potential user groups of the tool. User participation was also solicited while determining priorities for the features, as well as the level of accepted support for each feature. The prioritizing and scoring schemes follow the proposition of Kitchenham [5]. Every feature has a distinct description for each grade (between 0 and 5), making the scoring of the features more explicit. Each feature has as well an acceptance level for each user group to determine if the tool can be acceptable from the part of the current feature in classroom use.

A tool can be accepted only, if both user groups accept that every mandatory feature has acceptable level of support from the tool. While analyzing the evaluation results, this is visible in that the main emphasis is put on the mandatory features. The rest of the features are analyzed if all mandatory features achieve the acceptance treshold. Since the feature analysis allows the features to form hierarchies, 24 of the 110 features are compositions of lower features (e.g. "reliability" consist of issues like "data integrity", "robustness", etc.). The remaining, atomic features can be used as a metric describing the overall suitability of the tool. Even if in {5} single numeric metrics for overall results are discouraged, for the sake of simplicity in *reporting* here the results of the study, a metric of mandatory atomic features that achieve the acceptance treshold is used. This is because during the evaluation process this metric was found to be most descriptive from the set of several metrics used.

5 Requirements of an Ideal PSP Tool

The requirements for a tool that supports the PSP ideally can be derived from the scoring scheme of the feature analysis. Because each feature has a written description for each grade it can have, the ideal situation would be the one described by the highest score of every feature. Only some of the requirements, namely those that have most influence over the issues regarding the PSP, are outlined here. It should be noted, that the requirements are "client requirements", or general descriptions of what the tool should be able to do and how, not exact specifications.

5.1 Non-functional Requirements

Some issues concerning reliability, usability and efficiency are discussed here. Requirements for maintainability, transferability and other general requirements, as well as many other than those outlined here from the previous categories can be identified.

The tool should inhibit the unauthorized use of the tool, as well as unauthorized viewing of the data collected by the tool. In the case of centralized data storages, other than personal data of the user cannot be accessed. Other, common information security related issues are also valid to an ideal PSP tool. Technical solutions can be used to some extent, but at least equally important can be considered to be the security awareness of the users.

The tool should support the reliable storing and retrieval of data. The integrity of the data should be ascertained by internal solutions and data cannot be distorted while storage or retrieval [12]. In practice this can be difficult to achieve, but techniques such as checksums and noting potential data storage problems can minimize the effects that reduce the integrity of data to some extent.

The tool should be so robust and stable that it will not stop its execution without an explicit instruction from the user. Should such an unlikely event occur despite all precautions, the effort required to restore correct state of execution should be minimal. More accurate limits (in terms such as mean time between failures) could be specified, but for purposes of this study this is not done.

Regarding efficiency, the tool has two directions for requirements. As far as hardware is concerned, no unreasonable resources should be needed [13]. From the user viewpoint, all the required functions are initiated and executed automatically, and keystrokes or mouse movements are needed rarely if at all. With the PSP, the increase in overhead caused by measuring one's work should be minimized close to zero with the help of the tool [14].

The usability of the tool must be good. This requires that the tool must be easy to use for both beginner and advanced users. For example, during the user interface design both instructive texts and shortcuts for common tasks should be available [15]. Since the users are students in a PSP course, the learning curve associated with the tool must be initially low. Intuition and basic knowledge of the PSP should be enough for a user to be able to use the tool without additional time and work [16].

The nonexistence of the need to switch the context of thought by the user is essential to an ideal PSP tool. The use of the tool may not interfere with the thought process in the middle of software development. The trouble with removing the need for this context-switching is the quality, granularity and accuracy of the data required by the PSP [8]. For example, if the time tracking during the design phase of the process were automated to that extent that no context-switching is necessary, the tool should be able to read the very thoughts of the user and determine when those thoughts are related to the design effort and when not. Other, possibly a bit more realistic problems can be found in [1].

5.2 Functional Requirements

The tool should cover all phases of software development process (at least those that are applicable to the personal level) [9]. In addition, every phase must be internally comprehensive, so that all PSP functions can be executed with the tool. Disregarding every other requirement, this should be well within bounds to be implementable. The transitions between phases should be unnoticeable by the user and her actions or the tools she uses tell the tool what is the current phase of the process [14].

To function, the tool should not require any specific software. Taking into account the most common operating systems and platforms, independence from all other programs should be enforced. In reality, this can be approximated e.g. through the use of virtual machines, or by developing mutually compatible versions of the tool for different platforms.

The process that the tool supports should be customizable, and the tool should be able to reflect these changes. User should be able to add, edit and remove process phases as necessary and different process approaches (iterative, prototyping, etc.) must be supported. Task management must be flexible and for example reordering the tasks must be uncomplicated [17]. The process model must be built into the tool, but it may not restrict the user to use just that kind of a process.

The tool should automate the defect management. This includes that the defects are classified (one example classification is given in [1], but others must be possible too) automatically, without user intervention, and logged for historical data analysis [8]. Logging requires information about the injection and removal phases of the defect, duration of defect removal, etc. as specified in [1]. Even though the defects are logged automatically, a manual interface to insert and edit the defect entries should be provided. While defect logging could be automated at least to a certain extent, the classification of defects is rather difficult, since it requires perception of contexts in a way that is not typical for computers and programs [17].

Product size measurement should be automated, and at least logical lines of codes should be used as a metric, while other options can be provided too. In this context the programming language used and possible standards that the code should adhere to must be identified. All line of code —measures should be logged with the tool, and categorized to facilitate LOC-accounting as defined in [1].

All required data should be collected automatically, and the tool should remove the need for user to collect the PSP process data [8]. In many cases the PSP presumes the data to be of such nature that it is automatically collectable. Also manual data entry should be provided for management reasons. For time data the requirement for automated data collection poses some challenges, since the tool must be able to detect the difference between productive working time and times of other activities. This requirement is closely related with the ability of the tool to detect transitions between process phases.

All the calculations on the data collected required by the PSP should be automated by the tool. The user shouldn't need to calculate anything by herself. This applies to estimating and planning phases, as well as data collection and analysis phases of the process [19]. Especially with resource management and estimating the calculations must be automated. As far as estimation methods are concerned, at least the PROBE method defined in [1] should be supported, but other popular estimation methods could be implemented as options.

From other concepts of the PSP, the tool should provide automated support for planned value management and earned value tracking, process improvement feedback in some form (the PSP provides process improvement proposal forms for this), and checklists used in reviews. The checklists - or at least their outlines – should be generated automatically from the results of the data analysis of previous projects. Tool should also enforce the use of checklists somehow.

6 Tools and Their Evaluation Results

The basis for the feature analysis was the feedback from students together with the first-hand experiences from using the tools in question. To give some perspective on the results and the discussion of them, a short description of the student profiles and assignments used in the courses is provided first.

6.1 Scenario and Student Feedback

Most of the tools evaluated here have been used in the context of an academic PSP course. Each course has featured at least slightly differing sets of tools, and a mixture of users and programming assignments. While the first two courses utilized the exercise sets given in [1], the latter three have used customized assignment specifications, mainly to do with devising small helper tools to augment the functionality in other tools used in the course. A typical profile of a student given by a student enrolling a course in this study included an indication of a study year of 2 or higher, mediocre or better programming skills with several thousand lines of codes written prior to the course, little or no knowledge of statistics, and a position in an industrial software organization (although this was more common with students of more study years than 2 or 3). A summary of the background information about the courses and the data collected is presented in table 2.

Table 2. Course details

	Oulu 2000	CBS 2001	Oulu 2002	Oulu 2003	Oulu 2004
Course length (weeks)	10	14	10	11	10
PSP level achieved	2	3	3	3	3
Number of participants	31	22	32	13	23
Pass %	65%	77%	53%	31%	48%
Study year	3-4	4-5	3-5	2- n	2- n
Amount of tool-related feedback comments	33	36	100	60	87

The discrepancy between passed amount of students and number of comments about the tools is noticeable between the last two courses and those that preceded them. This is partly explained by the fact that the last courses introduced explicit solicitations for tool commentary in the form of a distinct question in feedback questionnaire that the students were able to submit after each assignment. Although, with every course, all tool-related comments were taken into account despite the form or document they were delivered in.

Initially students were either requesting better tools rather explicitly, or were dismayed by the amount of documents needed.

- *"Tools needed for paperwork"*
- *"Far too many forms/templates. Writing data to zillion forms takes too much time"*
- *"don't you have any program that can automate all the calculations for PSP?"*

With the course tool selection maturing and course staff gaining experience, the quality of tools as well as their deployment to the students improved. Still many problems persisted.

- *"Practically every program I used in development failed at least once, including JBuilder and PPLogControl"*
- *"Working parser would help time tracking a lot."*
- *"Actually using PSP would require a tool that is quite 'invisible', e.g. actual development time, sizes and defect data should be calculated automatically."*
- *"You actually can live with LEAP after you learn (the hard way) what it can/ cannot do."*

6.2 Tool Scoring and the Results of the Feature Analysis

The feedback data is used to score each feature for each tool. By analyzing the scores in respect with the acceptance levels for each feature, the tools can be measured for their suitability for the classroom use in given context. For this analysis, a listing (unordered one) of all mandatory atomic feature names is given in table 3.

Table 3. Listing of those atomic features that were determined to be of mandatory priority

Feature name	Feature name	Feature name
Data integrity	Required software	Size measurement
Security	Supported software	LOC-accounting
Robustness	Hardware support/-need	Statistical estimation
Learning curve	Method support	Planned value
Knowledge requirements	Language support	Earned value
Ease of use	Process modelling	Automatic calculation
Response times	Checklists	Improvement feedback
Ease of installation	Data collection	Tool implementation cost
Context-switching	Time data	Organizational effects
Workload efficiency	Process coverage	Defect classification
Resource optimization	Phase transitions	Defect logging

With this feature set and the predetermined acceptance levels, each tool is scored and analyzed. Results of that analysis are shown in table 4. It should be noted that there are two different acceptance percentages shown per tool. The first one is from the analysis against the acceptance levels set by the representative of teaching staff, while the second results from the acceptance levels of students. A short, written comment about the applicability of the tool is also included.

It can be determined from the results in table 4 that generic tools are not good for supporting the PSP, but rather a tool designed specifically for the PSP support is needed. Even though none of the tools that were selected for the evaluation provided explicitly acceptable level of support for the PSP, the Process Dashboard tool did come close to the acceptance threshold. Because the tool that the results showed to be the most suitable for the course context was one that wasn't used in any of the courses, it was selected to be the candidate for further studying.

The next PSP course organized in the University of Oulu that was arranged during the fall of 2004 utilized Process Dashboard in order to gather student feedback and experiences such as those from the previous courses. The aim was to validate the findings of the feature analysis conducted in this study, and compare the anticipated student feedback on the tools used (based on the feature scores from the analysis) to the actual response. Experiences for basing opinions on continued use of the tool in PSP courses were also gained.

Table 4. Acceptance percentages for mandatory atomic features for each tool

Tool	Acceptance %	Comment
Document templates	39 % (teacher) / 39 % (student)	Good coverage, but completely manual
Student-authored tools	36 % / 30 %	Good in the very narrow field that they apply to
PPLogControl	61 % / 58 %	Coverage is narrow
EvalPPLog	42 % / 36 %	Batch-style program, applicable only to the analysis phase of the process
OpenStat	39 % / 39 %	Supports the statistics needed in the PSP, but no other process support
Logfile parsers	39 % / 36 %	Batch-style programs, same as EvalPPLog, operational problems
LEAP	76 % / 58 %	Full process support, but problems in usability and stability
Hackystat	64 % / 55 %	Unnoticeable, no context-switching, but support isn't exactly for the PSP
PSPStudio	73 % / 67 %	Wide process coverage, but a lot of context-switching required
Process Dashboard	97 % / 91 %	Some context-switching required, but otherwise very nearly acceptable

6.3 Discussion of the Result Validation Case

The overall result of Process Dashboard being the most suitable from the evaluated tools was validated during the Oulu 2004 course. In addition to the personal experiences of the teaching staff, the feedbacks from the students enforce this view. One student, who happened to have experience from both the Leap and Dashboard tools, commented

- *"Tool is great. Much better than the "Leap". The data is gathered in a good way."*

It could be derived from the feature analysis results that the most critical issues with the Process Dashboard tool in the classroom setting have to do with context-switching, learning curve associated with the tool, and workload efficiency. This is only partly visible from the student feedback, though. Majority of the comments regarding tools and their usage were positive, acknowledging the assistance the tool provided. While the support for learning curve and workload efficiency -features is visible from, even though not dominant in the student feedback, context-switching is not so evident. This may be partly due to the lack of constant reference point, such as the Hackystat tool, being available for the course participants, even though issue of context-switching was discussed during the lectures.

- *"I want "always on top" –property to dashboard tool bar."*
- *"Scheduler was a pain before the logic sank in."*

Some unexpected issues were found also from the tool usage, namely cross-platform support and usability issues. Although quite severe, at least considering the classroom usage of the tool, these issues are technically solvable. Therefore it is possible to develop the Dashboard tool so that it can be viewed to achieve the minimum acceptance level for a PSP course tool. The feature analysis framework developed in this study can be used to evaluate new versions of the tool, as well as completely new tools for course usage. Reuse of the existing evaluation framework is also encouraged by the experience on the time required evaluating, possibly several tools, against over one hundred features.

7 Summary

Ten different tools were analyzed in order to determine their support for the PSP. A feature analysis was conducted for the tools, which required identifying certain features that the tool should implement, as well as a construction of a scoring scheme for the tools based on those features. Over one hundred features were identified. Some of the most crucial ones were described in their ideal state of support, thus outlining a requirements set for an ideal PSP tool. These requirements may be impossible to implement with current technology, but they serve as a reference point for future PSP tool evaluations. The thought about the realism of the requirements [17] should be remembered, though, when creating requirements that are to be implemented, but in this text the ideal case was set as the goal of the study.

From the tools analyzed, none were found to be acceptable as such for use in a PSP course. This was determined from the acceptance levels user group representatives stated for each feature in preparation for the feature analysis. The best suited tool was selected as a candidate for further research, which validated some of the results of the feature analysis, and highlighted some new points of development before the tool could be considered acceptable for continuous use in classroom setting.

References

1. Humphrey, W.S.: A Discipline for Software Engineering. Addison-Wesley, Reading, Mass. (1995)
2. Abrahamsson, P. and Kautz, K.: Personal Software Process: Classroom Experiences from Finland. In: Kontio, J., Conradi, R. (eds.): Software Quality – Proceedings of the 7th European Conference on Software Quality. Lecture Notes in Computer Science, Vol. 2349. Springer-Verlag, Heidelberg (2002) 175-185
3. Abrahamsson, P., Kautz, K., Sieppi, H. and Lappalainen, J.: Improving Software Developer's Competence: Is the Personal Software Process Working? In: Bunse, J., Jedlitschka, A. (eds.): Empirical Studies in Software Engineering – Proceedings of the First International Workshop, WSESE 2002 Rovaniemi, Finland. Workshop Series on Empirical Software Engineering, Vol. 1. Fraunhofer-Institut für Experimentelles Software Engineering IESE, Kaiserslautern (2003)
4. Abrahamsson, P. and Kautz, K. Personal Software Process: Experiences from Denmark. In: Fernandez, M. (ed.): Proceedings of the 28th Euromicro Conference September 4-6, 2002 Dortmund, Germany. IEEE Computer Society. Los Alamitos, CA. (2002) 367-374
5. Kitchenham, B.: DESMET: A Method for Evaluating Software Engineering Methods and Tools. Technical Report TR96-09. Dept. of Computer Science, University of Keele, U.K. (1996)
6. Humphrey, W.: The Personal Software Process: Status and Trends. IEEE Software, Vol. 17, no. 6 (2000)
7. Johnson, P. and Disney, A.: The Personal Software Process: A Cautionary Case Study. IEEE Software, Vol. 15, no. 6 (1998) 85-88
8. Disney, A. and Johnson, P.; Investigating Data Quality Problems in the PSP. In: Osterweil, L., Scherlis, W (eds.): Proceedings of the 6th ACM SIGSOFT International Symposium on Foundations of Software Engineering, Lake Buena Vista, Fl. ACM Press, New York (1998) 143 – 152
9. Harrison, W., Ossher, H. and Tarr, P.: Software Engineering Tools and Environments: A Roadmap. In: Proceedings of the Conference on the Future of Software Engineering. Limerick, Ireland. ACM Press, New York (2000) 261 – 277
10. Software Engineering Institute: A Specification for Automated Support for the PSP. Carnegie Mellon University, Pittsburgh, PA (1996)
11. IEEE Computer Society: IEEE Recommended Practice for the Evaluation and Selection of CASE Tools. IEEE Std 1209-1992. The Institute of Electrical and Electronics Engineers, New York (1993)
12. Parker, D.: Computer Security Management. Prentice-Hall, Reston (1981)
13. Moore, C.: Lessons Learned from Teaching Reflective Software Engineering Using the Leap Toolkit. In: Proceedings of the 22nd International Conference on Software Engineering. Limerick, Ireland (2000) 672 – 675
14. Johnson, P., Kou, H., Agustin, J., Zhang, Q., Kagawa, A. and Yamashita, T.: Practical Automated Process and Product Metric Collection and Analysis in a Classroom Setting: Lessons Learned from Hackystat-UH. In: Proceedings of the 2004 International Symposium on Empirical Software Engineering. Los Angeles, CA (2004)
15. Molich, R. and Nielsen, J.: Improving a Human-Computer Dialogue. In: Communications of the ACM, Vol. 33, No. 3 (1990) 338 – 348
16. Kemerer, C.: How the Learning Curve Affects CASE Tool Adoption. In: IEEE Software, Vol. 9, no. 3 (1992) 23 – 28

17. Fugetta, A.: Software Process: A Roadmap. In: Proceedings of the Conference on the Future of Software Engineering. Limerick, Ireland (2000) 25 – 34
18. Morrell, L. and Middleton, D.: The Software Engineering Learning Facility. In: Proceedings of the Seventh Annual Consortium for Computing in Small Colleges Central Plains Conference on the Journal of Computing in Small Colleges. Branson, MO (2001) 299 – 307
19. Morisio, M.: Applying the PSP in Industry. In: IEEE Software, Vol. 17, no. 6 (2000) 90 – 95

An Experience Factory to Improve Software Development Effort Estimates

Ricardo Kosloski and Káthia Marçal de Oliveira

Universidade Católica de Brasília,
SGAN 916 - Módulo B - Pós Graduação - Campus II,
Brasília - DF – Brasil, CEP: 70790-060
rikoslos@brturbo.com, kathia@ucb.br

Abstract. It is well known that effort estimate is an important issue for software project management. Software development effort can be obtained from the size of the software and the productivity of its development process. Nowadays the Function Point Analysis stands out as an approach largely used for software size estimate, while productivity values are extracted from international historical databases. Some databases show the median value of various productivity projects while others present all data according to some specific characterization of the projects. We argue that defining a framework of characteristics that impact on software project productivity can improve comparison between finished projects and the new ones that need an effort estimate. This article presents an approach to effort estimate with continuous improvement of the estimates using some characterization of the projects. Continuous improvement is based on the use of an experience factory.

1 Introduction

Planning and controlling software development projects demand a lot of attention from the managers. Appropriate effort estimate is an important part of this task. It is particularly important to the organizations, because too high an estimate may result in loosing a contract to a competitor, whereas too low an estimate could result in a loss for the organization [2].

One way of defining effort estimates consists in relating the software size, to the effort required to produce it, by means of a value of productivity [18] (i.e., effort = productivity x software size). The effort is defined in man/hours and is the quantity of work required to realize the software development project [9]. The software size can be defined by its functional content using methods such as the well estabilished Function Point Analysis [17, 18]. The productivity can be computed as the relationship between the effort required for the software construction and the functional size of this software [18].

Productivity values can be found, organized according to some characteristics, in historical databases [13, 19]. However, each organization should set up its own historical productivity database, so as to better reflect its own relationship with its customers in software development [8]. The similarity of old projects with new ones

F. Bomarius and S. Komi-Sirviö (Eds.): PROFES 2005, LNCS 3547, pp. 560–573, 2005.

could thus result in better productivity value itself resulting in better effort estimate of the future projects. Another important part of this work is the definition of appropriate characteristics to compare the similarity of projects.

This article presents an approach to effort estimate based on appropriate characterization of the projects. The characterization of the projects is continuously improved so as to reach a better productivity definition for each new project based on past projects with similar characterization. Continuous improvement approaches for software organizations have been defended by different authors [2,14,20]. In this context, Basili *et al.* proposed the concept of experience factory to institutionalize the collective learning of the organization that is at the root of continual improvement and competitive advantage. Since the main idea of experience factory is to use past experiences and since we believe that the effort estimate of old projects can help in a more accurate definition of new estimates, we decided to base our approach on the experience factory.

In the following sections we present a brief review of the use of productivity for effort estimates (section 2) and experience factory (section 3). Next, we present the definition (section 4) and use (section 5) of the experience factory for software development effort estimate. Section 6 presents our conclusions and ongoing work.

2 Using Productivities in Software Effort Estimates

The productivity can be defined as the ratio between the quantity of work required to develop a software and the size of this software [9,21]. In this case, the effort is accounted in man/hours while the size can be measured by different kinds of metrics (e.g., Function Point Analysis–FPA [12], NESMA [22] and COSMIC [6]). Benchmarking studies concluded that the productivity obtained by sizing the software in function points is more consistent and allow better comparisons [17,18]. Also FPA is a functional software size metric that can have its elements extracted from the requirements of the system, available early in the developing process [7], and FPA is independent of the technology used for implementation [12] and can be used to determine whether a tool, an environment, a language or a process is more productive than an other within an organization or among organizations [2,10].

We found different factors, in the relevant literature, which can impact the software development productivity. Some authors [5,8,21] show that the experience of the software development team in the technology used or in the system's business area, is an important factor for the correct definition of productivity. Others defend that schedule restrictions imposed to the software development [2,23] and software complexity [19,23] impact the productivity. Software size is also a relevant factor in effort estimate and impacts the productivity [2,5,17,21,23]. Maxwell [19] say that the use of CASE tools in software development projects can improve the productivity. Finally, productivity increases with reuse because consumers of reusable work products do less work in the software construction [15].

Two main historical databases for software productivity are proposed by the Software Productivity Research (SPR) group [29] and the Institute of Software

Benchmarking Standards Group (ISBSG) [13]. SPR presents an average of productivity values characterized by the programming language used in the projects and ISBSG has more than two thousand projects registered according to a specific taxonomy for characterization. However, both SPR and ISBSG miss some important characteristics found in the literature as relevant for software development productivity (for instance, experience of the development team and schedule restrictions are not considered). Another problem is that the ISBSG historical database only shows the realized projects productivity, without supplementary information about the accuracy of the early projects' estimates. These problems make it difficult for a company to use the productivity proposed by these groups and apply it to its own projects.

Also, registered productivity is not enough to improve the accuracy of the effort estimate [19]. In this paper, the authors report an analysis on software projects characteristics to understand their influence on the productivity. For them, identifying the characteristics or combination of characteristics, that help to understand the values registered in the historical database of productivities, can be useful to find new software projects productivity by comparison with similar past projects.

3 Experience Factory

Since 1939 when Schewart or Deming proposed the PDCA (Plan-Do-Check-Act) cycle for process continuous improvement, the idea of an evolutionay improvement in an organization has been applied in different contexts [14]. The PDCA has four steps. It begins with the planning and the definition of improvement objectives. Next, the planning is executed (Do) and then evaluated (Check) to see if the initial objectives are achieved. Actions are taken based on what was learnt in the check step. If the changes are successful, they will be incorporated as new practices in the process. If not, it is necessary to go through the cycle again with modifications in the original plans.

In 1994, Basili et al [3] defined the concept of experience factory aimed at capitalization and reuse of life cycle experience and products. The experience factory is a logical and physical organization supported by two major concepts: a concept of evolution - the Quality Improvement Paradigm (QIP), and a concept of measurement and control - the Goal-Question-Metric approach.

QIP is based on the PDCA, it emphasizes the continuous improvement by learning from experience, both at the level of projects and at the level of organizations. It builds on experimentation and application of measurement [28]. The model consists of the following six steps:

- Characterize: Understand the environment based on available models, data, etc.
- Set Goals: On the basis of the initial characterization set quantifiable goals for success and improvement;
- Choose Process: On the basis of the characterization and of the goals, choose the appropriate process to improve;

- Execute: Execute the process constructing the products and providing project feedback based upon the data on goal achievement that are being collected;
- Analyze: At the end of each specific project, analyze the data and the information gathered to evaluate the current practices, identify problems, record findings, and make recommendations for future projects improvement;
- Package: Consolidate the experience gained in the form of new, or updated and refined, models and other forms of structured knowledge gained from this and prior projects, and store it in an experience base so it is available for future projects.

An appropriate and unambiguous characterization of the environment is a prerequisite to a correct application of the paradigm [3]. This characterization requires that we classify the current project with respect to a variety of characteristics. It allows to isolate a class of projects with characteristics similar to the project being developed. Characterization provides a context for reuse of experience and products, process selection, evaluation and comparison, and prediction.

The Goal-Question-Metric approach (GQM) [4] is the mechanism used by the QIP for defining and evaluating a set of operational goals using measurement. The main idea of the GQM is that measurement should be goal-oriented [4,28]. It is a top-down methodology starting with the definition of an explicit measurement goal that is refined in several questions that break down the goal into its major components. Then, each question is refined into metrics that, when measured, will provide information to answer the questions. By answering the questions we will be able to analyze if the goal has been attained. As a result of this process we have a model in three levels [4]: the conceptual level, where a goal is defined for an object (product, process or resource) from various points of view; an operational level, where questions are defined for the goal and characterize the object of measurement with respect to a selected quality issue from the selected point of view; and, the quantitative level, representing a set of data associated with each question in order to answer it in a quantitative way.

4 Continuous Improvement for Software Development Effort Estimates

With the need of providing better estimates for each new software development project and inspired by the idea of continuous improvement based on prior, we decided to define and build an experience factory for software effort estimate. To define this experience factory we had to attend each one of the steps of the QIP. The following sections will present the characterization (Section 4.1), the improvement goals definition (section 4.2) and the estimate process defined (section 4.3). The three other steps (execute, analyze and package) should be executed for each new project that need effort estimate.

4.1 Characterization

To address this step we had to define how we will characterize each project that need effort estimate. Considering that effort is the product of a software size and the productivity of the team, and that software size is already established by Function Point Analysis approach, we decided to look for the factors that have influence on the productivity of personnel in the software development.

In order to define these factors, we looked carefully in the literature and interviewed two specialists (with more than five years of experience) in the effort estimate area. Table 1 shows those factors with the references that relate them to software productivity. It also describes the possible values for each factor. The factors were grouped in different categories: **(C1) software project**, with 4 general characteristics about the software to be developed; **(C2) software project development**, with 15 factors about the software development itself; **(C3) software size**, with 4 factors about the size and its measurement method; **(C4) work effort**, with 4 factors related to the work needed to the software construction; and, **(C5) team experience**, with 6 factors related to the human aspects.

We consider that the software size will be estimated with FPA [12] or NESMA [22]. Both methods produce the size in function points, but the measurement obtained by NESMA (called estimated count) is more generic, based on media values, whereas the measurement obtain with FPA (called detailed count) is more detailed.

Thus, at the beginning of each software development project, we need to charaterize the software project according to these factors. From this characterization, we can select, in the experience database, the projects with similar characteristics. The recorded productivity of these projects will support the project manager in estimating the effort for his-her project. The search for similar projects is done by a simple query in the project database using the characteristics selected by the project manager.

Table 1. Software development project characterization

Impact Factors [authors]	Possible values
C1.1–Precedentedness [5]	Very low, high or extra high as defined by [5] analyzing the software project according with the organizational understanding of product objectives, the experience in working with related software systems, the concurrent development of associated new hardware and operational procedures and the need for innovative data processing architectures algorithms
C1.2-Application type [15,16]	Transaction and production systems, management information systems, etc
C1.3-Software complexity[5, 19]	The functional complexity as defined by FPA [12] method in simple, media or complex functions
C1.4-Business area type [13,19]	Accounting, banking, legal, health, etc
C2.1-Development Type [13]	New development, maintenance–enhancement or corrections of bugs
C2.2-Development platform[13]	PC, Mainframe or mixed;
C2.3-Development paradigm[13]	Object oriented or structured
C2.4-Primary programming language[13,29];	The main programming language used
C2.5-Development techniques [13]	1-Data modeling; 2-Prototyping; 3-Project management; 4-Metrics; 5-Tests; 6-JAD; 7-

	Requirement management
C2.6-Use of CASE Tools Levels [5;9]	As defined by [9]: 0-Tools not used at all 1-Tools used only as an aid to less than 20% of documentation 2-Tools used for documenting at least 50% of the high-level design 3-Tools used for documenting at least 50% of the high-level and detailed design 4-Tools used for design and automatic code generation of at least 50% of the system 5-Tools used for design and automatic code generation of at least 90% of the system
C2.7-Reuse Level [5,15]	0 – there is no part of the software ready to be to reused 1 – there is less than 20% of the software ready to be to reused 2 - there is between 20 and 50% of the software ready to be to reused 3 - there is between 50 and 80% of the software ready to be to reused 4 - there is more then 80% of the software ready to be to reused
C2.8-Development schedule restrictions [2,23]	The schedule restrictions imposed in the software development by the client.
C2.9-Effort estimate schedule restrictions [2]	The time spent to do the effort estimate
C2.10-Software development process maturity level [5,25]	As defined by CMMI [11]: levels 1, 2,3, 4 or 5, The company level while developing the software project.
C2.11-Max team size [2,5,16]	The maximum size of the team during the devlopment
C2.12-Size team variation tax [13];	the relationship between the maximum and minimum team size
C2.13-Registration data method	As defined by [13]: Method A: Staff Hours recorded in their daily activties Method B: Derived from time records that indicate, for example, the assignment of people to the project. Method C: Productive time only spent by each person on the project.
C2.14-Project Scope[13]	The software development phases (planning, design, specify, build, test and/o implementation) that were considered in the effort estimate
C2.15-Project elapsed time [13];	The time in months to develop the software project estimated at the beginning and collected at the end of the software development.
C3.1-Count approach [13, 17,18,22]	FPA-IFPUG or NESMA
C3.2-Function size metric used [13]	IFPUG-3.0,IFPUG-4.0
C3.3-Software size [2,7,10,12,13,16,17,18,21,23];	The value obtained by the application of FPA method at the beginning and end of the software

	development
C3.4-Function point adjustment factor [12,13];	From the FPA/NESMA count at the beginning and end of the software development
C4.1-Total work effort [2,16,19,21]	Effort for the whole software development estimated at the beginning and collected at the end of the software development.
C4.2-Work effort by activity in the development life cycle [13]	Effort for each activity (planning, design, specify, build, test, implementation) estimated at the beginning and collected at the end of the software development.
C4.3-Efficiency of the use of the project time [8,27];	Percentage of the project time, lost with team health problems, vacations, training, meetings and general absences
C4.4-Rework [11]	Total work effort recorded by each person for the rework tasks
C5.1-Size measurement technical experience [7,10,17] C5.2-Size measurement experience in the application business area [7,10,17]; C5.3-Software development technical experience [2,21] C5.4-Software development experience in the application business area) [2,21] C5.5-Requirements development technical experience [9] C5.6-Requirements development experience in the application business area [7]	Mean of the team evaluation, defined using [5]: 0-No previous experience at all 1-Familiarity (through course or book) but no working experience 2-Working experience on one previous project or up to 20 worked hours of use 3-Working experience on several previous projects or between 21 and 100 worked hours of use 4-Thoroughly experienced

4.2 Goals Definition

According to the frame proposed by [28] we defined the following goal:

Analyze: The effort estimates
For the purpose of: Understanding
With respect to: The accuracy of the estimate
From the viewpoint of: The project management

As previously defined effort = size x productivity. Therefore, the questions and metrics of the GQM were defined to evaluate both size and productivity (Table 2). We focus on the absolute and relative errors in the measurements and on understanding their respective causing factors. The absolute error is the difference between the values of a variable, measured at the beginning and at the end of a software project development. The relative error is the ratio between these two values in percentage.

Table 2. Questions and metrics to analyze the effor estimate

Questions	Metrics
1-What is the error in the size estimate?	**M 1.1-**Size estimate absolute error **M 1.2-**Size estimate relative error
2-What were the schedule constraints imposed to the initial count of the software development project?	**M 2.1-**Fastness of the count (number of function points counted by day and by each counter); **M 2.2-**Percentage of additional hours used in the count (by "additional hours" we mean that hours beyond the normal work day journey)
3-What is the effort estimate error?	**M 3.1-**Absolute error between estimated and real work effort; **M 3.2-**Relative error between estimated and real work effort **M 3.3–**Initial productivity (estimated) **M 3.4–**Final productivity (measured) **M 3.5-**Productivity absolute error **M 3.6-**Productivity relative error
4-What is the elapsed time estimate error?	**M 4.1-**Absolute error between estimated and real elapsed time **M 4.2-**Relative error between estimated and real elapsed time
5-What were the schedules constraints imposed to the software development project?	**M 5.1-**Percentage of additional work hours with respect to the total work effort of the software development project. Additional hours means hours beyond the normal day of work.

Table 3. Effort Estimate Process

Activity	Description
Choose an estimate approach	Evaluate the level of detail of the system development to choose between the software size estimate method to be used in the beginning of the project (detailed – IFPUG or estimated – NESMA)
Plan the estimate	Plan the steps of the estimate, that is, who will do it, when and what effort will be required.
Approve the plan	Obtain acceptance and commitment from the managers for the plan defined.
Obtain the system documentation	Get the system documents needed for the estimate
Execute the software size estimate / measurements	Use the FPA/NESMA to measure (estimate) the software size
Execute the effort estimate	Select the characteristics of the framework to search similiar projects, then choose a productivity value and compute the effort estimates
Approval of the estimate	Present the results and approve them with the management

568   R. Kosloski and K.M. de Oliveira

4.3 Choose Process

Since the improvement expected is the accuracy of the effort estimate, the process choosen for the experience factory is the software effort estimate process. We found two proposals in the literature: the Personal Software Measurement process (PSM) [24], and the process described by Agarwal [2]. The PSM process consists in the following steps: select estimate approaches, map analogies, compute and evaluate estimates. We notice that some activities are too generic and would require some more detail (for example: "compute estimates" depends on the method used). Also the activity applied after the estimate (evaluate estimates) is not part of the effort estimate that interest us. Agarwal proposal also deals with this process in a generic way, but adds the importance of an historical database as a source of useful information to calibrate the estimates.

We are focused in the effort estimated obtained by the use of the software size and the development productivity values. We defined, therefore, a specific process based on those proposals. The resulting process is presented in table 3.

5 Applying the Approach

We are applying this approach in a large company in Brazil. This company has been working with effort estimate for more than five years and is continually worried about getting better estimates in its projects. Currently, it uses historical databases from SPR and ISBSG to get productivity values. To apply this approach we followed some steps:

i)   extended the company's tool to register the 33 characteristics defined;
ii) populate the database with prior projects to have a starting point;
iii) simulate some effort estimate by similarity considering the prior projects; and,
iv) doing effort estimate for new software projects.

To do the first step (i) we just made an evolutive maintenance in the tool already used in the company. This tool already supported the function point count of projects. We extended the data model and included three new facilities: one to characterize a software project using the 33 characteristics defined, another to allow searching similar projects in the database, and one to support the collection of the results of the metrics defined by the GQM approach.

In [26] the authors report that a difficulty with the experience factory is to have the first experiences registered in the database with lessons learned to motivate its use. They suggest populating it with information from the literature and from prior experience done before the use of the experience factory. Therefore, to populate the database with prior projects (step (ii)) we analyzed the documentation of 30 projects that had the effort estimated during the last 5 years in the company. Unfortunatelly since we have 33 characteristics it was difficult to find projects well documented to get all the characteristics. We got 27 of the 33 characteristic defined for 7 projects (it was not possible to find out information about C2.8, C2.9, C4.2, C4.3, e C4.4). For the other projects we did not have the information, neither in the documentation, nor by interviewing the managers (some of them were not working in the company anymore).

Table 4 shows the characterization of the 7 projects. Table 5 shows the projects with similar characteristics. Table 6 shows the metrics' results. We see that we had effort error more than 100% (S1, S2, S5 and S7) and elapsed time error more than 50% for three systems (S1, S4 and S5).

Table 4. System Characteristics

Char.	S1	S2	S3	S4	S5	S6	S7
C 1.1	Very low	Very low	High	Very low	Very low	Extra high	Very low
C 1.2	MIS	MIS	MIS	MIS	MIS	MIS	MIS
C 1.3	simple=71 media=12 complex=17	simple =67 media =18 complex =15	simple =51 media =23 complex =26	simple =61 media =18 complex =21	simple =79 media =13 complex =8	simple =62 media =14 complex =24	simple =89 media =0 complex =11
C 1.4	banking legal	banking pensions	banking legal	banking Administration	banking Administration	banking Legal	Health
C 2.1	develop.	develop.	develop.	develop.	develop.	develop.	develop.
C 2.2	PC, mainframe	PC, mid-range	PC, mid-range	PC,mid-range	PC,mid-range	PC,mid-range	PC,mid-range
C 2.3	structured	structured	object oriented	object oriented	object oriented	structured	object oriented
C 2.4	Natural	Natural	Java	Java	Java	Cold Fusion	Java
C 2.5	1,2	1,2,3,4,5	1,2,3,4,5,7	1,2,3,4,5,6	1,2,3,4,5	1,2,3,4,5,7	1,2,3,4,5
C 2.6	1	2	3	2	2	3	2
C2.7	0	1	1	1	1	2	0
C2.10	1	1	1	1	1	1	1
C 2.11	22	18	14	14	6	14	9
C 2.12	> 250%	80%	63%	55%	100%	50%	80%
C 2.13	C	C	B	B	B	A	B

C2.14	all phases	all phases	all phases	all phases	all phases	all phases	all phases
C2.15i	12	12	16	7	5	11	6
C2.15f	27	17	21	11	8	13	9
C 3.1/ C3.2 i	NESMA	IFPUG4.1	NESMA	NESMA	NESMA	IFPUG4.1	NESMA
C 3.1 / C3.2 f	IFPUG4.1	IFPUG4.1	IFPUG4.1	IFPUG4.1	IFPUG4.1	IFPUG4.1	IFPUG4.1
C.3.3i (FP)	2324	1967	1710	698	277	2008	224
C3.3f (FP)	3023	3446	2421	1124	625	2183	395
C3.4i	1.12	1.12	1.05	1.01	0.94	1.22	0.97
C3.4f	1.12	1.12	1.05	1.01	0.94	1.22	0.97
4.1i (hour)	22032	18647	19152	7818	3103	19678	3164
4.1f (hour)	49010	43091	32617	13903	8106	21705	7194
C5.1	1.0	2.30	2.5	2.0	3.0	2.5	1.7
C5.2	0.50	1.0	1.5	1.0	1.0	3.8	0.3
C5.3	2.4	3.4	2.6	2.25	1.0	3.0	2.0
C5.4	1.6	2.3	1.8	1.5	0.5	3.0	1.0
C5.5	3.5	2.10	2.3	2.6	2.5	2.7	1.3
C5.6	0.75	1.30	2.7	1.2	1.0	3.7	0.0

Legend: i=Initial of the software development / f = final/end of the software development
FP=function point

Table 5. Analogous systems (same magnitude when needed)

System	Analogies
1 and 2	C1.1, C2.8, C1.2, C2.1, C2.3, C2.4, C 3.1, C3.2, C2.13, C2.11, C3.3 (difference in initial size less than 20%), C3.4, C1.3
3 and 5	C1.4, C2.1, C2.3, C2.4, C3.1, C3.2, C2.13, C2.5 (only one different technique used)
3 and 1	C1.2, C2.1, C2,8, C3,1, C3.2, C3.3, M2.1, C1.3
4 and 5	C2.8, C3.1, C3.2, C3.3, C2.1, C2.3, C2.4, C2.13, C2.5 (only one different technique used)

With this information we could start the QIP cycle for each new project. The complete evaluation of this approach will take some years since we need to estimate the effort at the beginning of a software development project, wait for its completion and then analyze the metrics. Thus, to have an idea about the pontential improvement we could get, we decide to do some simulations (step (iii)) with the 7 projects already

Table 6. Metrics Results

Metrics	S1	S2	S3	S4	S5	S6	S7
M 1.1 (FP)	699	1479	711	426	348	175	171
M 1.2 (%)	30.1	75	42	61	126	8.7	76
M 2.1 (FP/day)	186	65,2	57	- X -	92,3	29,8	75
M 3.1 (hours)	26978	24444	13465	6085	5003	2027	4030
M 3.2 (%)	123	131	70	78	161	10.3	127
M 3.3 (1) (hour/FP)	9.48 (SPR)	9.48 (SPR)	11.20 (SPR)	11.20 (SPR)	11.20 (SPR)	9.8 (*)	12.9 (*)
M 3.4 (2) (hour/FP)	16.2	12,50	13.40	12.40	13.00	9.94	18.2
M 3.5 (hour/FP)	6.70	3.02	2.20	1.20	1.20	0.14	5.3
M 3.6 (%)	71	32	20	11	16	1.5	40.5
M 41 (months)	15	5	5	4	3	2.3	3
M 4.2 (%)	136	42	31	57	60	21	50

Legend:FP=function point ; * - ISBSG

Table 7. Precisions of Effort Estimate

System	Using SPR			Using our approach		Final Effort (hour)	Precisions Errors (%)		
	Initial Size (FP)	SPR Product ivity (h/FP)	Effort (h)	Hist. Productivity (h/FP)	Effort (h)		SPR	Our appr oach	Improve ment
2	1967	9.48	18648	From System 1 (16,2 h/FP)	31865	4309 1	131	35	73
3	1710	11.20	19152	From system 5 (13.0 h/FP)	22230	3261 7	70	46	35
3	1710	11.20	19152	From System 1 (16,2 h/FP)	27702	3261 7	70	18	74
4	698	11.20	7818	From system 5 (13.0 h/FP)	9074	1390 3	78	53	32

characterized. The idea was to look for two similar projects, define the effort estimate of one based on the productivity of the other and check if it would be better than the effort actually estimated for this project. Table 6 shows the absolute estimate error with the SPR database (used in the company for those projects) and our approach. Project 1 and 5 were used as reference in evaluation of estimates of the other projects. We can see that just with this small simulation we can have improvement in the effort estimate (two projects around of 30% and two around of 70% of improvement).

The step (iv) is in progress.

6 Conclusion and Ongoing Work

Effort estimate is a fundamental input for software development project management. The continuous improvement of the effort estimate accuracy would lead an organization to improve its capacity to carry out its commitments, delivering its software products on time and, therefore, bring competitive advantage.

This article presents an approach for continuous effort estimate improvement by using the experience factory concept. We are applying this approach in a company in Brazil that use measurement process for more than five years. We expect that, at each new project, we will reach better accuracy of the effort estimates by using more realistic productivity values obtained from past similar projects, registered in an historical database. We already populated the experience database with 7 projects and did some simulation to evaluate our approach. Our next step will be to use this initial database for estimating software effort in new software projects. We are also studying new ways of computing the similarity of a new project to old ones in the database. We plan to experiment using Case Based Reasoning [1].

Acknowledgments

This work is part of the "Knowledge Management in Software Engineering" project, which is supported by the CNPq, an institution of the Brazilian government for scientific and technological development.

References

1. AAMODT, Agnar; PLAZA, Enric; CASE-BASED Reasoning: Foundational Issues, Methodological Variations and Systems Approaches, AI Communications, IOS Press, Vol. 7:1, pp. 39-59, 1991.
2. AGARWAL, Manish, Kumar; YOGESH, S. Mallick; BRARADWAJ, R. M., et all, Estimating Software projects, ACM SIGSOFT, p.60, 2001
3. BASILI,V.;CALDIERA,Gianluigi;ROMBACH,H.Dieter "The Experience Factory", Encyclopedia of Software Engineering, John Wiley & Sons, 1994, V.1 pp. 476-496
4. BASILI,V.,Rombach, H.Goal Question Metric Paradigm; Encyclopedia of Software Engineering – 2, 1994
5. BOEHM, Barry et al,Software Cost Estimate With COCOMO II, Prentice Hall PTR, 2000
6. COSMIC, Measurement Manual, The COSMIC Implementation Guide for ISO/IEC 19761:2003, Version 2.2, 2003
7. DEKKERS, Carol; AGUIAR, Mauricio; Using Function Points Analysis (FPA) do Check the Completeness (Fullness) of Functional User Requirements, Quality Plus, 2000
8. FARLEY,Dick. Making Accurate Estimates, IEEE, 2002
9. FENTON, N., PFLEEGER, S. Software Metrics A Rigorous & Practical Approach, 2nd. Ed., PWS Publishing Company, 1997.
10. FUREY, Sean, Why we should use Function Points, IEEE, 1997
11. JOHNSON, Donna I.; BRODMAN, Judith G.; "Realities and Rewards of Software Process Improvement", IEEE 1996

12. IFPUG, CPM – Counting Practices Manual, release 4.1.1; IFPUG – International Function Point Users Group; 2000
13. ISBSG. International Software Benchmarking Standards Group. The Benchmarking, Release 8, ISBSG; 2003.
14. JOHNSON, Corine N., The Benefits of PDCA, Quality Progress, pp.120, 2002
15. LIM, Wayne C., Effects of Resue on quality, Productivity, and Economics, IEEE, 1994
16. LOKAN, Chris; TERRY, Wright; HILL, Peter R.; STRINGER, Michael; "Organizacional Benchmarking Using the ISBSG Data Repository", IEEE, 2001
17. LOW,Graham C., ROSS, D.Jeferry, "Function Points in the Estimate and Evaluation of the Software Process, IEEE, 1990
18. Martin, Arnold; PEDROSS, Peter; Software Size Measurement and Productivity Rating in Large Scale Softwre Development Department, IEEEE, 1998
19. MAXWELL, Katrina, FORSELIUS, Pekka, Benchmarking Software Development Productivity, IEEE, 2000
20. MCFEELEY, Bob, IDEAL: A User´s Guide for Software Process Improvement, SEI,1996
21. MORASCA,GIULIANO, ,Sandro, GIULIANO, Russo. An Empirical Study of Software Productivity, IEEE, 2002
22. NESMA, Estimate Counting, Netherlands Software Metrics Users Association, 2003
23. POTOK,VOUK, Tom; VOUK, Mladen. Development productivity for comercial SW Using OO Methods; ACM, 1995
24. PSM, Pratical Software Measurement, Adison Wesley, 2002
25. RUBIN, Howard A ., Software Process Maturity: Measuring its Impact on Productivity and Quality, IEEE, 1993
26. RUS,Ioana, LINDVALL, Mikael, SEAMAN, Carolyn, BASILI, Victor, Packaging and Disseminating Lessons Learned from COTS-Based Software Development, IEEE, 2003
27. SHEPPERD, Martin; CARTWRIGHT, Michele; Predicting with Sparse Data; IEEE, 2000
28. SOLINGEN, R., BERGHOUT, Egon, The Goal / Qestion / Metric Method: A practical Guide for Quality Improvemnet of Software Development. London: McGraw-Hill. 1999. 195 p.
29. SPR, "The Programming Language Table", Software Productivity Research, 2001

An Instrument for Measuring the Maturity of Requirements Engineering Process

Mahmood Niazi

National ICT Australia, Sydney, NSW 1430, Australia
Mahmood.niazi@nicta.com.au

Abstract. Requirements problems are widely acknowledged to have impact on the effectiveness of the software development process. In order to improve the requirements engineering (RE) process and to reduce requirements problems, Sommerville et al. [1] have developed a requirements maturity model. Literature shows that the measurement process, designed in this model, is very confused and can lead organizations to incorrect results. This is because the measurement process is ambiguous and no strategic and systematic approach is used to decide different scores for various RE practices.

The objective of this paper is to propose a measurement instrument for Sommerville et al.'s model to effectively measure the maturity of the RE process. The main purpose of proposing this measurement instrument is to develop better ways to assist practitioners in effectively measuring the maturity of the RE process. This instrument provides a very practical structure with which to measure the maturity of the RE process. I have tested this instrument in one case study where only one category of RE process, i.e. 'requirements elicitation' was used as an exemplar. The case study results show that the measurement instrument has potential to assist practitioners in effectively measuring the maturity of 'requirements elicitation' category of the RE process. Thus, I recommend organizations trial this instrument for other categories of RE process in order to further evaluate its effectiveness in the domain of RE process.

1 Introduction

Requirements problems are widely acknowledged to have impact on the effectiveness of the software development process [2; 3]. Many software projects have failed because they contained a poor set of requirements [4]. No software process can keep delivery times, costs and product quality under control if the requirements are poorly defined and managed [5]. In order to produce software that closely matches the needs of an organisation and the stakeholders, great attention needs to be paid to improvement of the RE process [5; 6].

In order to improve the RE process and to reduce requirements problems, some researchers have published their work [1; 5]. Sommerville et al.'s model is derived from existing standards and has three levels of maturity: Level 1-Initial, Level 2-repeatable and Level 3-Defined. The model can be used to assess the current RE

F. Bomarius and S. Komi-Sirviö (Eds.): PROFES 2005, LNCS 3547, pp. 574–585, 2005.

process and it provides a template for requirements engineering practice assessment. It is based upon 66 good requirements practices which are classified into Basic, Intermediate and Advanced. Against each practice, four types of assessments are made: 3 points are scored for standardized practice, 2 for normal use, 1 for discretionary use and 0 for practices that are never used. This model classifies organizations with less than 55 points in the basic guidelines as Level 1-Initial, organizations with above 55 points in the basic guidelines and less than 40 points in the intermediate and the advanced guidelines as Level 2-Repeatable and organizations with more than 85 points in the basic guidelines and more than 40 points in the intermediate and advanced guidelines as Level 3-Defined.

In earlier work, in order to use the Sommerville et al. maturity model, the author has conducted an empirical study with Australian practitioners [7]. This study was a two-fold process; firstly, requirements process maturity was assessed using the requirements maturity model developed by Sommerville et al. and secondly, the types and number of problems faced by different practitioners during their software project was documented. In this study the interviews were conducted with twenty-two Australian practitioners. During interviews the practitioners had the opinion that although all the practices, in Sommerville et al. maturity model, are very well defined, the measurement process designed for these practices was very confused and could lead organizations to incorrect results. This is because the measurement process is ambiguous and no strategic and systematic approach is used to decide different scores for various practices. The practitioners in this study were very happy with the list of practices for RE process but they wanted more formal and structured measurement instrument in order to assess the maturity of the RE process. Somerville et al. have also indicated this: "this assessment scheme is not a precise instrument and is not intended for formal accreditation" [1:p29].

I have developed an instrument in order to effectively measure the maturity of the RE process. The objective of this paper is to describe this measurement instrument and to test this instrument in one case study.

To focus this study, I investigated the following research question:
RQ. Does the proposed measurement instrument help practitioners measure the maturity of their RE processes?

The main reason for addressing this research question is to develop better ways in order to assist practitioners in effectively measuring the maturity of the RE process.

This paper is organised as follows. Section 2 provides background. Section 3 describes the development process of an assessment instrument. In Section 4 the assessment instrument is described. In Section 5 a case study is presented. Finally the paper presents a summary of conclusions and recommendations for practitioners as concluding remarks.

2 Background

RE is often considered an important process of the software life-cycle. This is because software industry and research communities have realised the difficulties of producing high quality requirements [8]. It has been observed through RE literature that one can achieve better quality requirements if the RE process is properly defined

[4; 5]. Despite the importance of RE processes, little research has been conducted to reduce the requirements problems and to improve requirements quality.

Several studies have been conducted to identify the problems with RE process [3; 4; 9-13]. To highlight few of these:

- El Emam and Madhavji [4] described a field study that indicated that there are seven key issues that must be addressed in a successful RE process improvement effort: package consideration, managing the level of detail of functional process models, examining the current system, user participation, managing uncertainty, benefits of case tools and project management capability.
- Hall et al. [3] discussed the requirements process problems in twelve software companies. Their main findings show that the requirements process is a major source of problems in the software development process.
- Nikula et al. [10] analysed the requirements engineering practices in a survey with twelve small and medium enterprises in order to understand current requirements engineering practices and the desire to improve them. Their results show that the problem is not in the practitioners' lack of desire for improvement, but in management not knowing that many requirements engineering issues can be solved with standard practices that are well documented in the literature.
- Finally, Siddiqi and Chandra [12] mentioned a gap between current research and practice and in order to reduce this gap they suggested a continuous discussion between researchers and practitioners.

Only identification of requirements problems is not sufficient but a holistic approach is required in order to reduce these problems and to achieve quality requirements [6; 7]. A very limited work has been done in developing ways to reduce requirements problems by improving the requirements process. One of these is the REAIMS (Requirements Engineering Adaptation and IMprovement for Safety and dependability) project, partially funded by the European Commission, started at the University Of Lancaster UK [1]. The objective of REAIMS was to provide a framework for improving the RE process for dependable and safety-related systems and to assess this in a real industrial context [1]. In this project a requirements maturity model was developed that was derived from the Capability Maturity Model [14]. A set of guidelines was proposed for a requirements maturity model.

The aim of the present study is to design a measurement instrument to measure the effectiveness of each practice designed in Sommerville et al. requirements maturity model [1]. This measurement instrument should provide requirement practitioners with some insight into designing appropriate RE processes in order to achieve better results.

3 A Requirements Process Maturity Assessment Instrument Development Process

An examination of the RE literature, together with the previously conducted empirical study [7], highlights the need to develop an instrument to effectively measure the maturity of RE process. The requirements process maturity assessment instrument (RPMAI) development was initiated by creating its success criteria. Objectives are set to clarify the purpose of the instrument and outline what the instrument is expected to describe. These criteria guide development and are later used to help evaluate the instrument.

The RPMAI building activities involved abstracting characteristics from three sources:

- RE literature data [3; 15-18]
- Interviews data [7]
- Sommerville etc al Maturity Model [1; 5; 19]

Figure 1 outlines the stages involved in creating the RPMAI.

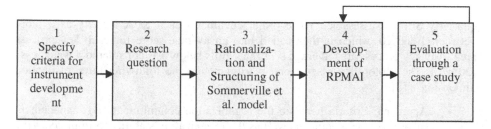

Fig. 1. Activities involved in building the requirements process maturity assessment instrument

The first stage in RPMAI development is to set the criteria for its success. The motivation for building these criteria for RPMAI development comes from empirical research with eleven Australian software development companies [7]. In order to design the RPMAI the following criteria have been decided.

- Consistency

The RPMAI features need to be consistent and complete. Language between different components of the RPMAI will be consistent. The RPMAI will include all the information, which is necessary, and there will be no conflicts between different parts of the instrument. The structures of different components of the RPMAI will have consistent granularity.

- User satisfaction

The end users need to be satisfied with the results of the measurement instrument. The end users will be able to use the measurement instrument and will achieve specified goals according to their needs and expectations without any confusion and ambiguity.

- Ease of use

The complex models and standards are unlikely to be adopted by the organizations as they require lot of resources, training and efforts. The RPMAI will have different levels of decomposition starting with the highest level in order to gradually lead the user through from a descriptive framework towards a more prescriptive solution. The structure of the RPMAI will be flexible and easy to follow.

In order to address these criteria, a research question (see Section 1) was developed in stage 2. The stage 3 is the stage where the author undertook a rationalisation and structuring of Sommerville et al. [1] model. The stage 4 is the stage where RPMAI was developed. The final stage is where an evaluation of the RPMAI was performed using a case study.

4   A Requirements Process Maturity Assessment Instrument

At Motorola an instrument has been developed in order to assess the organization's current status relative to software process improvement and to identify weak areas that need attention and improvement [18]. Diaz and Sligo [20] describe the use of this instrument: "at Motorola Government Electronics Divisions, each project performs a quarterly SEI self-assessment. The project evaluates each KPA activity as a score between 1 and 10, which is then rolled into an average score for each key process area. Any key process area average score that falls below 7 is considered a weakness" [20:p76]. The Motorola's assessment instrument has the following three evaluation dimensions [18]

- Approach: Criteria here are the organization commitment and management support for the practice as well as the organization's ability to implement the practice.
- Deployment: The breadth and consistency of practice implementation across project areas are the key criteria here.
- Results: Criteria here are the breadth and consistency of positive results over time and across project areas.

Motorola's instrument successfully assisted in producing high quality software, reducing cost and time, and increasing productivity [20].

In this paper, I have adapted Motorola's instrument [18] and based on the work of Sommerville et al. [1] and Niazi et al. [16] developed an instrument in order to effectively measure the maturity of the RE process. There are many compelling reasons for adapting Motorola's instrument:

- it is a normative instrument designed to be adapted;
- it has been successfully tried and tested at Motorola; and
- it has a limited set of activities.

In order to be used effectively in the domain of RE, I have tailored the Motorola instrument and made some minor changes in different evaluation activities of three dimensions using literature and the empirical study (as shown in Appendix A). The structure of the RPMAI is shown in Figure 2.

The 66 best practices designed by Sommerville et al. can be divided into 8 categories: requirements documents, requirements elicitation, requirements analysis and negotiation, describing requirements, system modelling, requirements validation, requirements management and requirements for critical systems. These categories are shown as 'requirements process category' in Figure 2. Figure 2 shows that requirements process category maturity indicates requirements process maturity [5]. These requirements process categories contain different best practices designed for RE process [5]. For each best practice an instrument has been developed, in this paper, in order to effectively measure its maturity.

In order to effectively measure the maturity of RE process, the following steps have been adapted in RPMAI [15; 16; 18] (One example is provided in Table 1):

- Step 1: For each practice, a key participant who is involved in the RE process assessment calculates the 3-dimensional scores of the assessment instrument.
- Step 2: The 3-dimensional scores for each practice are added together and divided by 3 and rounded up. A score for each practice is ticked in the evaluation sheet.
- Step 3: Repeat this procedure for each practice. Add together the score of each practice and average it to gain an overall score for each requirements process category.
- Step 4: A score of 7 or higher for each requirements process category will indicate that specific category maturity has been successfully achieved [16; 18]. Any category maturity with an average score that falls below 7 is considered a weakness [16; 18].
- Step 5: It is possible that some practices may not be appropriate for an organization and need never be implemented. For such practices 'Not applicable' (NA) option is selected. This NA practice should not be used in calculating the average score of requirements process category.

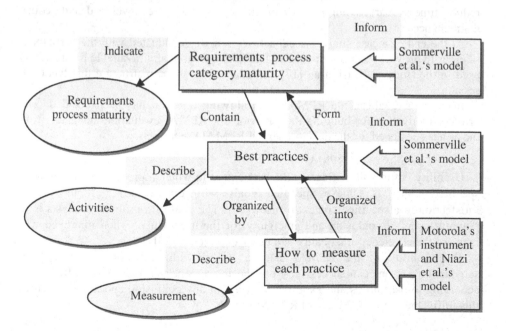

Fig. 2. The structure of RPMAI [1; 5; 16; 19]

At the end of this measurement process it will be very clear to companies to know which requirements process categories are weak and needs further consideration.

5 The Case Study

The case study method was used because this method is said to be powerful for evaluation and can provide sufficient information in the real software industry environment [21]. The case study also provides valuable insights for problem solving, evaluation and strategy [22]. Since the RPMAI is more applicable to a real software industry environment, the case study research method is believed to be a more appropriate method for this situation. Real life case study was necessary because it:

- Showed that the RPMAI is suitable or will fit in the real world environment.
- Highlighted areas where the RPMAI needs improvements.
- Showed the practicality of the RPMAI in use.

In the case study, a participant from Company A has used RPMAI and measured the RE process maturity of his/her company independently without any suggestion or help from the researcher. Company A is a multinational company that provides software services, employing (101-500) professionals worldwide and less than 10 in Australia. The main purpose of the company is to develop warehouse management system, manufacturing executive systems and ERP integration. The process improvement programme was initiated 3-5 years ago in Company A. This improvement programme was initiated to: shorten software development cycle times, reduce time-to-market, improve the quality of the software developed and reduce maintenance.

At the end of a case study, a feedback session was conducted with the participant in order to provide feedback about RPMAI. The questionnaire (available from author) used in the study of Niazi et al. [17] was adapted in order to structure this feedback session.

In order to evaluate the RPMAI the following criterion has been decided. The primary motivation for building this criterion for RPMAI evaluation emanates from the criteria designed for the development of RPMAI (Section 3).

- Usability of the RPMAI

Usability is formally defined as the "the extent to which a product can be used by specified users to achieve specified goals with effectiveness, efficiency and satisfaction in a specified context of use" [23]. The goal of a usability analysis is to pinpoint areas of confusion and ambiguity for the user which, when improved will increase the efficiency and quality of a users' experience [23].

The usability of the RPMAI can be linked with 'ease of use' and 'user satisfaction'. If one can successfully use the instrument and achieve specified goals according to user needs and expectations without any confusion and ambiguity then this fulfils the usability criteria of RPMAI [23].

5.1 Implementation of RPMAI

In this case study, in order to evaluate the RPMAI, the requirements elicitation category is used as an exemplar. A participant of Company A has carried out requirements elicitation category assessment using RPMAI (Section 4). I have summarised the assessment results in Table 1.

The key points of this assessment are as follows:

- It is clear from Table 1 that requirements elicitation process of Company A is weak (i.e., score is < 7).
- In order to achieve matured requirements elicitation process, the Company A needs to improve all those individual practices with less than seven score as shown in Table 1.
- Table 1 shows that Company A is not developing prototypes for poor understood requirements.
- In Company A, stakeholders are not identified and consulted.
- Requirements rationale are not recorded

Table 1. Practice evaluation sheet for Requirements Elicitation category (6+6+4+8+6+6+6+4+ 6+2+10+8+6=44/No of practices) -> 78/13=6, Average core=6

Requirements Elicitation	0	1	2	3	4	5	6	7	8	9	10	NA
Assess System Feasibility							X					
Be sensitive to organizational and political consideration							X					
Identify and consult system stakeholders					X							
Record requirements sources									X			
Define the system's operating environment							X					
Use business concern to drive requirements elicitation							X					
Look for domain constraints							X					
Record requirements rationale					X							
Collect requirements from multiple viewpoints							X					
Prototype poorly understood requirements			X									
Use scenarios to elicit requirements											X	
Define operational processes									X			
Reuse requirements							X					

- Scenarios are strongly used to elicit requirements
- Requirements sources are recorded
- Operational processes are well defined

Out of thirteen requirements elicitation practices, ten are identified as weak practices. The results suggest that Company A should focus on these weak practices in order to improve its requirements elicitation process and to reduce problems associated with requirements elicitation. Only three practices of requirements elicitation are well defined in Company A. The weak requirements elicitation practices, identified by RPMAI, can be improved using the guidelines provided by Sommerville et al. [19].

5.2 The Case Study Lessons Learned

The case study was conducted in order to test and evaluate the RPMAI in the real world environment. The lessons learned from this case study are summarised as follows:

- A participant agreed that the RPMAI is clear and easy to use.
- A participant was able to successfully use the RPMAI without any confusion and ambiguity in order to measure the RE process maturity.
- A participant agreed that RPMAI is general enough and can be applied to most companies.
- The RPMAI provides an entry point through which the participant can effectively judge the effectiveness of different requirements elicitation practices.
- A participant who used the RPMAI was fully agreed and satisfied with the assessment results
- A participant was agreed that the use of RPMAI would improve the RE process maturity.
- All the components of the RPMAI are self explanatory and require no further explanation to be used effectively.
- The RPMAI is capable of determining the current state of the 'requirements elicitation' category of the RE process.

In summary, the participant was very satisfied with the use of RPMAI. The participant was also very satisfied with the structure of the RPMAI. The participant suggested to extend the RPMAI to include all phases of the RE process. He also suggested providing some guidelines about who should do this assessment in a company.

6 Conclusion and Future Work

This research has met its objectives and aim with respect to providing an instrument in order to assist practitioners in measuring the maturity of the RE process. The main purpose of proposing this measurement instrument was to develop better ways in order to assist practitioners in effectively measuring the maturity of the RE process. In order to design this instrument some criteria were decided for its success. The research question was that: Does the proposed measurement instrument help practitioners measure the maturity of their RE processes? The results of the case study are very positive. However, only one category 'Requirements Elicitation' was used as an exemplar in the case study. Thus, I recommend organizations trial this instrument for other categories of RE process in order to further evaluate its effectiveness in the domain of RE process. Further large case studies using other RE categories will further evaluate the effectiveness of the RPMAI.

In particular, one aspect that the participant considered important is to provide some guidelines about who should be using the RPMAI in a company. This comment is very positive and a valuable suggestion. RPMAI is a dynamic instrument that will be extended and evolved based on feedback and input from software industry. This suggestion will be considered in future work by developing some guidelines for its use. It is hope that I will be able to continue further evaluation of RPMAI through multiple case studies in order to improve it and to make it more complete.

Acknowledgements

I am thankful to Professor Ross Jeffery (Program leader, Empirical Software Engineering NICTA) and Dr. Mark Staples (Researcher at NICTA) for their comments to complete this paper.

References

1. Sommerville, I., Sawyer, P. and Viller, S.: Requirements Process Improvement Through the Phased Introduction of Good Practice, Software Process-Improvement and Practice (3). (1997) 19-34.
2. Sommerville, I.: *Software Engineering Fifth Edition.* Addison-Wesley.(1996).
3. Hall, T., Beecham, S. and Rainer, A.: Requirements Problems in Twelve Software Companies: An Empirical Analysis, IEE Proceedings - Software (August). (2002) 153-160.
4. El Emam, K. and Madhavji, H. N.: A Field Study of Requirements Engineering Practices in Information Systems Development. Second International Symposium on Requirements Engineering. (1995) 68-80.
5. Sommerville, I., Sawyer, P. and Viller, S.: Improving the Requirements Process. Fourth International Workshop on Requirements Engineering: Foundation of Software Quality. (1998) 71-84.
6. Niazi, M.: Improving the Requirements Engineering Process: A Process Oriented Approach. Thirteenth Australasian Conference on Information Systems (ACIS02). (2002) 885-898.
7. Niazi, M. and Shastry, S.: Role of Requirements Engineering in Software development Process: An empirical study. IEEE International Multi-Topic Conference (INMIC03). (2003) 402-407.
8. Lamsweerde, A., van: Requirements Engineering in the year 00: A research perspective. 22nd International Conference on Software Engineering (ICSE). (2000) 5-19.
9. Kamsties, E., Hormann, K. and Schlich, M.: Requirements Engineering in Small and Medium Enterprises, Requirements Engineering 3 (2). (1998) 84-90.

10. Nikula, U., Fajaniemi, J. and Kalviainen, H.: Management View on Current Requirements Engineering Practices in Small and Medium Enterprises. Fifth Australian Workshop on Requirements Engineering. (2000) 81-89.
11. Nuseibeh, B. and Easterbrook, S.: Requirements Engineering: a roadmap. 22nd International Conference on Software Engineering. (2000) 35-46.
12. Siddiqi, J. and Chandra, S.: Requirements Engineering: The Emerging Wisdom, IEEE Software 13 (2). (1996) 15-19.
13. Niazi, M. and Shastry, S.: Critical success factors for the improvement of requirements engineering process. International conference on software engineering research and practice. (2003) 433-439.
14. Paulk, M., Weber, C., Curtis, B. and Chrissis, M.: *A high maturity example: Space shuttle onboard software, in the Capability Maturity Model: Guidelines for improving software process.* Addison-wesley.(1994).
15. Beecham, S., Hall, T. and Rainer, A.: Building a requirements process improvement model. Department of Computer Science, University of Hertfordshire, Technical report No: 378 (2003).
16. Niazi, M., Wilson, D. and Zowghi, D.: A Maturity Model for the Implementation of Software Process Improvement: An empirical study, Journal of Systems and Software 74 (2). (2005) 155-172.
17. Niazi, M., Wilson, D. and Zowghi, D.: A Framework for Assisting the Design of Effective Software Process Improvement Implementation Strategies, Accepted for publication: Journal of Systems and Software (2005)
18. Daskalantonakis, M. K.: Achieving higher SEI levels, IEEE Software 11 (4). (1994) 17-24.
19. Sommerville, I. and Sawyer, P.: *Requirements Engineering - A good Practice Guide.* Wiley.(1997).
20. Diaz, M. and Sligo, J.: How Software Process Improvement helped Motorola, , IEEE software 14 (5). (1997) 75-81.
21. Yin, R. K.: *Applications of Case Study Research.* Sage Publications.(1993).
22. Cooper, D. and Schindler, P.: *Business research methods, seventh edition.* McGraw-Hill.(2001).
23. ISO/DIS-9241-11: International Standards Organization, ISO DIS 9241-11: Guidance on Usability. (1994).

24. Appendix A

Measurement Insptrument [18]

Score	Key Activity evaluation dimensions		
	Approach	Deployment	Results
Poor (0)	No management recognition of need No organizational ability No organizational commitment Practice not evident Higher management is not aware of investment required and long term benefits of this practice	No part of the organization uses the practice No part of the organization shows interest	Ineffective

Weak (2)	Management begins to recognize need Support items for the practice start to be created A few parts of organization are able to implement the practice Management begins to aware of investment required and long term benefits of this practice	Fragmented use Inconsistent use Deployed in some parts of the organization Limited to monitoring/verification of use	Spotty results Inconsistent results Some evidence of effectiveness for some parts of the organization
Fair (4)	Wide but not complete commitment by management Road map for practice implementation defined Several supporting items for the practice in place Management has some awareness of investment required and long term benefits of this practice	Less fragmented use Some consistency in use Deployed in some major parts of the organization Monitoring/verification of use for several parts of the organization No mechanism to distribute the lessons learned to the relevant staff members	Consistent and positive results for several parts of the organization Inconsistent results for other parts of the organization
Marginally qualified (6)	Some management commitment; some management becomes proactive Practice implementation well under way across parts of the organization Supporting items in place Management has wide but not complete awareness of investment required and long term benefits of this practice	Deployed in some parts of the organization Mostly consistent use across many parts of the organization Monitoring/verification of use for many parts of the organization A mechanism has been established, and used in some parts of the organization, to distribute the lessons learned to the relevant staff members	Positive measurable results in most parts of the organization Consistently positive results over time across many parts of the organization
Qualified (8)	Total management commitment Majority of management is proactive Practice established as an integral part of the process Supporting items encourage and facilitate the use of practice A mechanism has been established to use and monitor this practice on continuing basis Management has wide and complete awareness of investment required and long term benefits of this practice	Deployed in almost all parts of the organization Consistent use across almost all parts of the organization Monitoring/verification of use for almost all parts of the organization A mechanism has been established, and used in all parts of the organization, to distribute the lessons learned to the relevant staff members	Positive measurable results in almost all parts of the organization Consistently positive results over time across almost all parts of the organization
Outstanding (10)	Management provides zealous leadership and commitment Organizational excellence in the practice recognized even outside the company	Pervasive and consistent deployed across all parts of the organization Consistent use over time across all parts of the organization Monitoring/verification for all parts of the organization	Requirements exceeded Consistently world-class results Counsel sought by others

Author Index

Lecture Notes in Computer Science

For information about Vols. 1–3448

please contact your bookseller or Springer